CAMBRIDGE SOl

THE TRANSITION IN BENGAL, 1756–1775

A STUDY OF SAIYID MUHAMMAD REZA KHAN

CAMBRIDGE SOUTH ASIAN STUDIES

These monographs are published by the Syndics of the Cambridge University Press in association with the Cambridge University Centre for South Asian Studies. The following books have been published in this series:

MUHAMMAD REZA KHAN

THE TRANSITION IN
BENGAL, 1756-1775

A STUDY OF
SAIYID MUHAMMAD REZA KHAN

ABDUL MAJED KHAN

CAMBRIDGE
AT THE UNIVERSITY PRESS
1969

CAMBRIDGE UNIVERSITY PRESS
Cambridge, New York, Melbourne, Madrid, Cape Town, Singapore, São Paulo

Cambridge University Press
The Edinburgh Building, Cambridge CB2 8RU, UK

Published in the United States of America by Cambridge University Press, New York

www.cambridge.org
Information on this title: www.cambridge.org/9780521071246

© Cambridge University Press 1969

First published 1969
This digitally printed version 2008

A catalogue record for this publication is available from the British Library

Library of Congress Catalogue Card Number: 68–29329

ISBN 978-0-521-07124-6 hardback
ISBN 978-0-521-04982-5 paperback

CONTENTS

ILLUSTRATIONS

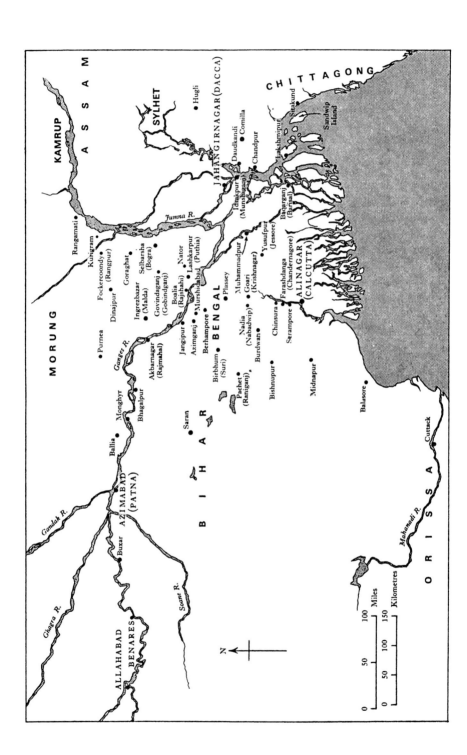

PREFACE

This study is not the first to be made of Reza Khan in recent years. As early as 1925 Imtiaz Muhammad Khan wrote two articles for the *Calcutta Review*, published by the University of Calcutta.[1] These sketched the whole career of the Khan, but concentrated particularly upon his trial, in the author's view the 'dominant feature of his life'.[2] His study necessarily suffered from the limitations of space within which it was published, and contains some errors, but above all it suffered from not being broadly set against the political background of the period. The trial, however minutely described, cannot be understood except as part of a political campaign. Imtiaz Muhammad Khan's articles were soon followed by two other articles on Reza Khan and the Chitpur family, of which he was the founder, by Ameer Ali Midhut Jang, most probably of the Khan's family. These were published in Calcutta's Muslim Institute journal, the *Muslim Review*.[3] Though less ably presented, Midhut Jang's articles have their merits too. Besides giving a genealogical table, beginning with Reza Khan and brought down to 1927, the author brought to light a portrait of the Khan, a photographic copy of an eighteenth-century original painting.

Dr N. Majumdar in her *Justice and Police in Bengal, 1765–1793 —a study of the nizamat in decline*, published in 1960, also dealt with Reza Khan in a broader fashion. However, her interest was primarily in judicial and police administration, and particularly in the changes which took place after 1772. Her work does explain Reza Khan's role in the development of the judicial administration, but mainly in the post-trial period, when the Khan had been restored to the office of Naib Nazim. Her main emphasis thus falls on the period after 1775, the year at which this study ends. Another thesis, written earlier but published as a book in 1961, *The Judicial Administration of the East India Company in Bengal, 1765–1782* by Dr B. B. Misra also has an extensive notice of Reza

[1] 'Reza Khan and his trial', by I. M. Khan, *The Calcutta Review*, Dec. 1925, Feb. 1926.
[2] See *Calcutta Review*, Feb. 1926, p. 269.
[3] 'An Account of Muhammad Reza Khan', by A. A. M. Jang, the *Muslim Review*, vol. II, no. 1, vol. III, no. 4 (1927, 1929).

Preface

Khan, but Dr Misra's emphasis has been more on the evolution of the new judicial institutions than on Reza Khan.

Apart from these studies there are no other modern works which have Reza Khan as their main subject.[1] Of course no general work on the period fails to make some mention of the Khan, but the whole weight of interest in the period after Plassey has been upon the military and political activities of the Company, upon the careers of such figures as Clive, Verelst, Hastings, Francis, Shore and Cornwallis and even of Charles Grant or Jonathan Duncan, or more recently upon the European sources of their ideas. But to neglect the Indian side of the story in this way, to fail to examine the activities, personages and ideas of Mughal Bengal, though natural, is distorting. Monographs, it is true, have been written on Mir Qasim and Mir Jafar of the post-Plassey period and there has also been a more recent study of the conflict between Siraj-ud-daulah and the East India Company. Most of them, though excellent studies in themselves, fail to take any adequate notice of the great transition through which Bengal was then passing. The conflict of the age intensified in the career of Reza Khan, a Mughal representing an old system and yet serving the English who were soon to introduce a new one, one result of which was his personal tragedy. As Shore remarked in 1782, 'he has often...been blamed, where his hands were tied up'.[2]

English contemporaries of Reza Khan had little doubt of the Khan's importance and stature. In England Dow thought it worth while to include a violent propagandist attack upon the Khan in his popular *History of Hindostan*.[3] James Grant in his *Analysis of the Finances of Bengal* cast him as 'the great defaulter', the wholesale plunderer.[4] Colonel Caillaud thought it necessary to pass on to Hastings the warning he had received 'from a man who

---

[1] There is, however, an article on 'Some Records re Reza Khan's trial' by Nani Gopal Choudhury in the *Proceedings of the Indian Historical Records Commission*, 1946.
[2] Quoted by N. Majumdar, *Justice and Police in Bengal, 1765–1793*, p. 196.
[3] See below, chapter 11.
[4] Grant based his comment on the basis of twenty volumes Persian accounts 'procured through the influence of a light and private purse' which in the end failed him 'to provide an adequate basis on which practical proposals could be based'. Grant, however, did not know the Khan personally but from what he had learnt from report, 'in Hindostan, a Mussulman could not be found characterized by greater reputed virtues of honour, sagacity and moderation locally understood' (Firminger, *Fifth Report*, II, xix–xx, 167–8).

Preface

sees far into things with much judgement and penetration'—'To Beware of Mahomed Reza Cawn!' Warren Hastings's Council, while the Khan was still a prisoner under trial, on the other hand could write 'Although Mahomed [Reza Khan] can no longer benefit by our good opinion of him, yet we cannot omit to express our thorough conviction that he ever served the Company with a fidelity, integrity and ability which they can hardly expect to experience in any future officer of government whom they may chuse from the same class of people'.[1] If Reza Khan loomed so large in the eyes of Englishmen of his day, it would seem that a revaluation of the man and his career would not be out of place. By reworking a limited but most important period in Reza Khan's career, in considerable detail, it is hoped that the balance may in part be redressed.[2]

The sources used for this study have been relevant official documents, supplemented by contemporary private papers and private accounts, mostly in English and some in Persian. While basic facts have been sought from official records preserved in the India Office Library and in the British Museum, and in one case also from the records in the National Archives of India, private records and accounts have been helpful in understanding them. In life Reza Khan and Warren Hastings clashed, but Warren Hastings's papers on the career of Reza Khan in the British Museum have been most illuminating. Indeed no study of eighteenth century Bengal is possible without Hastings's papers. When Hastings was absent from Bengal, Richard Barwell was there, and Barwell's letters which are already published in *Bengal Past and Present* offer an insight into men and events of the period which cannot perhaps be obtained anywhere else. Philip Francis arrived in Bengal about the time when this study of Reza Khan closes and yet Francis's own papers and collections, now in the India Office Library, fill up some of the most vital gaps. The Committee of Secrecy's letter of 28 August 1771 ordering the arrest of the Khan

---

[1] For Caillaud's letter to Hastings, 27 March 1772, see Add. MSS. 19133 f. 89, and for Calcutta Council's letter to Court, 10 November 1773, see M. E. Monckton-Jones, *Warren Hastings in Bengal, 1772–1774*, p. 199.

[2] Reza Khan was acquitted and reinstated as Naib Nazim, but the fact that he had been tried at all permanently damaged his reputation. Its recovery was made difficult by Grant's *Analysis* and almost impossible by Hindu nationalist writings in Bengali in the late nineteenth century, seeking to glorify Nandkumar as a martyr. Bankim Chandra Chattopadhyaya's *Ananda Math* (see Bibliography, p. 361) also seemed to depict him almost as a villain.

Preface

could only be found in Francis's collection. For Reza Khan's conception of Alivardian Bengal again we are indebted primarily to him.[1] Where these three have failed, three Persian histories have been most helpful. Of these three Persian histories, two, the *Seir* and the *Muzaffarnamah* are available in English translation,[2] though a major part of the latter has yet to be translated from its Persian text;[3] the third, the *Tarihk-i-Muzaffari*, is available in the Persian original in the British Museum.[4] The authors of these Persian histories, Saiyid Ghulam Husain Khan Tabatabai, Karam Ali and Muhammad Ali were no impartial observers; while Ghulam Husain was a critic of the Khan, the other two were admirers—they both named their works after Muzaffar Jang, that is Reza Khan. The same lack of impartiality can, of course, be traced in all contemporary accounts of men and events. Caution had therefore to be exercised while using all private accounts, whether in English or in Persian. While an attempt has been made to leave out no relevant official records, no claim is made to have exhausted all sources of information.[5] The object has been to present a connected account of the Khan's career in the hope that it will make some contribution to our knowledge of the man and provide a fresh review of the circumstances in which he lived and worked.

The book grew out of a Ph.D. thesis submitted to London University in 1966. I was introduced to historical research by Professor A. B. M. Habibullah of Dacca University when he was my teacher in Calcutta University. He later suggested the subject of this study, and Professor C. H. Philips recommended me for direct Ph.D. registration. The work took a long time to complete. That I could complete it, is largely due to the encouragement of these two gentleman, and to the ungrudging personal and professional help that I received from Mr J. B. Harrison, Reader in South Asian History at the School of Oriental and African Studies of the University of London. My wife Roquaiya could not have done more to relieve me of all my obligations and duties except to my work.

[1] Some papers are available also in the private collection of Lord North, Francis's patron, at the P.R.O. in London.
[2] For part of the *Muzaffarnamah* see *BengalNawabs* by Sir J. N. Sarkar.
[3] Only the I.O. copy of the manuscript has been used for this study.
[4] The British Museum Persian Manuscript No. OR 466.
[5] By 'Official records' only the English East India Company records are meant. No notice has been taken of the records of other European nations which also had their trade connections with Bengal. For detail, the Select Bibliography may be seen.

Preface

Yet I owe much to the kindness and assistance of many others, though I could not possibly name them all. Dr P. Hardy bore the brunt of my early trials and tribulations. Professor A. L. Basham (now of A.N.U.), Professor Riaz ul Islam (now of Karachi University) and Dr B. N. Pandey spent hours of their valuable time with me. Colleagues at Dacca University and some of my former pupils, particularly Dr M. R. Tarafdar, Dr A. B. M. Husain and Mr Matiur Rahman helped me in various ways. In this context I wish to remember Dr A. F. Salahuddin Ahmad and Dr Mukhlesur Rahman of Rajshahi University and Sj. Santosh Basu of Viswabharati University, with gratitude. I am particularly indebted to two successive Vice-Chancellors of Dacca University, Dr Mahmud Husain (who is now in Karachi) and Dr Muhammad Osman Ghani. Another former Vice-Chancellor, the late Dr W. A. Jenkins, helped me with a travel grant to consult old and rare books in Calcutta. At different stages I received financial support from the Government of East Pakistan and the British Council.

National Archives of India, the Asiatic Society of Pakistan and the Dacca Consulate of the Federal Republic of Germany made records available to me. I am equally obliged to the Librarians and staff of the India Office Library, the SOAS Library, British Museum and Calcutta National Library and of the Libraries of the Universities of Dacca and London.

I would also like to thank Dr T. G. P. Spear and Professor C. R. Boxer who suggested publication of this work; the Syndics of the Cambridge University Press and their staff; and Cambridge University Centre for South Asian Studies which honoured me by including this book in its series of Cambridge South Asian Studies.

In making this book ready for publication I have received help in many ways from my present colleagues in Victoria University of Wellington: Professor F. L. W. Wood, Professor J. C. Beaglehole, Professor P. Munz, Dr T. H. Beaglehole and Miss D. F. Crozier are only some of them. Miss G. Grellier, secretary in the Department of History, has also been of much help to me.

A.M.K.

Department of History
Victoria University of Wellington
New Zealand

xi

COMPANY SERVANTS

A LIST OF SOME COMPANY SERVANTS WITH THEIR MUGHAL TITLES BY WHICH THEY WERE GENERALLY KNOWN TO THE INDIANS

Name	Title	Meaning of the Title
1 Admiral Watson (of H.M. Navy)	Dilir Jang	The Courageous in Battle[1]
2 Lord Clive	Saif Jang	The Sword in War
	Sabit (or Sabut) Jang	The Firm in War
	Amir ul Mamalik	The Grandee of the Empire
	Muin-ud-daulah	The Eminent in the State
	Zubdat ul Mulk	The Select of the Kingdom
3 Major Killpatrick	Dilawar (or Dilir) Jang	Courageous in War
4 Colonel Forde	Shitab Jang	The Brisk in War
5 Colonel Coote	Saif Jang	The Sword in War
	Nasir Jang	The Succourer in War
6 General Carnac	Maham-ud-daulah	The Affairs of the State
	Basalat Jang	The Valorous in War
7 Major Adams	Muzaffar ul Mulk	The Triumphant of the Empire
	Saif-ud-daulah	The Sword of the State
	Ghalib Jang	The Subduer in War
8 Major Fletcher	Musta id Jang	Ready in War
9 Captain Knox	Dilawar Jang	The Courageous in War
10 H. Vansittart	Munir ul Mulk	The Illuminer of the Empire
	Ali Jah	High in Rank
	Shams-ud-daulah	The Sun of the State
	Nasir ul Mulk	The Succourer of the Empire
11 J. Spencer	Munawwir ul Mulk	The Illuminator of the Empire
	Maham-ud-daulah	The Affairs of the State

[1] Admiral Watson was not a Company servant but he came to fight a war in Bengal that was declared by (rather on behalf of) the Company in 1756.

Company Servants

		Babar Jang	The Lion in War
12	H. Verelst	Fakhr-ud-daulah	The Pride of the State
		Saif Jang	The Sword in War
13	F. Sykes	Intizam-ud-daulah	The Administration of the State
14	R. Becher	Izzat-ud-daulah	The Dignity of the State
15	S. Middleton	Mushir ul Mulk	The Counsellor of the Empire
		Murad-ud-daulah	The Desire of the State
		Ikhtiar Jang	Supremacy in War
16	W. McGwire	Jasarat Jang	Intrepidity in War
17	R. Marriot	Sarfaraz-ud-daulah	The Exalted of the State
18	J. Johnstone	Iftikhar-ud-daulah	The Distinguished of the State
19	J. Graham	Babar Jang	The Lion in War
20	G. Vansittart	Hoshyar Jang	Wary in War
21	W. Hastings	Jaladat Jang	Daring in War
		Umdat ul Mulk	The Support of the Kingdom[1]

[1] The list is taken mainly from *CPC*, I, 467–8. For other names see *Seir*, II, 225; *CPC*, III, 372; W. Hastings Papers, Add. MSS. 29096, ff. 215–16; *H.M.S.*, 193; 65: *PP* Fourth Report, 1773, p. 542 (Motiram's letter to John Johnstone).

ABBREVIATIONS

Add. MSS.	Additional Manuscripts, British Museum
App.	Appendix
Bengal Army	History of the Rise and Progress of Bengal Army. By Captain A. Broome
Bengal Nawabs	Bengal Nawabs by Sir J. N. Sarkar (containing translated extracts from three eighteenth-century Persian works on Bengal's history, works of Azad al Husaini, Karam Ali and Yusuf Ali and published from Calcutta in 1952)
BPC	Bengal Public Consultations (Reference by date)
BPP	Bengal Past and Present. Calcutta
BRP	Board of Revenue Proceedings or Bengal Revenue Proceedings (distinguished by I.O. records range and vol nos)
BSC	Bengal Secret and Military Consultations (Reference by date)
CDR	Chittagong District Records (a Bengal Government publication)
Considerations	Considerations on Indian Affairs. By W. Bolts
Court's letter	Despatches to Bengal
CPC	Calendar of Persian Correspondence (usually followed by vol. no. and entry no.)
Dacca Cons.	Dacca Factory Records
DUHB	History of Bengal, published by Dacca University, vol. II
Famine Papers	Extracts from Records in the India Office relating to Famines in India, 1769–1788, compiled by George Campbell, to which is appended Remarks by W. W. Hunter
Fifth Report	The Fifth Report from the Select Committee of the House of Commons on the Affairs of the East India Company, 28 July 1812 as edited by W. K. Firminger and published in 3 volumes in 1917
Forrest, Clive	Life of Lord Clive. By G. W. Forrest
Francis MSS	Private papers and collections of Sir Philip Francis in the I.O. Library
FWIHC	Fort William–India House Correspondence, a publication of the National Archives of India
Gleig, Hastings or Warren Hastings	Memoirs of the Life of Right Hon. Warren Hastings by G. R. Gleig

Abbreviations

Grant, *Analysis*	*Historical and Comparative Account of the Finances of Bengal*, By James Grant, 1786. (Available in *Fifth Report*, vol. II)
H.M.S.	*Home Miscellaneous Series*, India Office
India Tract 378	India Office tract no. 378, containing Luke Scrafton's *Observation on Vansittart's Narrative* and J. Z. Holwell's *Address to Luke Scrafton in reply to his Observation on Vansittart's Narrative*
I.O.	India Office Library.
I.O.R.	India Office Records
JASB	*The Journal of the Asiatic Society of Bengal*, Calcutta
JBORS	*The Journal of the Bihar and Orissa Research Society*, Patna
Khulasat	*Khulasat ut Tawarikh*, by Kalyan Singh. (Translated in *JBORS*, vols. V, VI)
LCB	*Letter Copy-Book of the Resident at the Durbar at Murshidabad* (2 vols. in one. Published, Calcutta, 1919)
Letter to Court	Letters received by the Directors from Bengal
Malcolm, *Clive*	*The Life of Robert, Lord Clive*. By J. Malcolm
Mir Jafar or *Mir Jafar Khan*	*The Career of Mir Jafar Khan, 1757–1765 A.D.* By Atul Chandra Roy
MN	*Muzaffarnamah* by Karam Ali (unless referred to *Bengal Nawabs*, the reference is to I.O. copy of the MSS.)
MP or *Murshidabad Proceedings*	*The Proceedings of the Controlling Council of Revenue, Murshidabad* (Reference by date)
Orme MSS.	Robert Orme's collections (O.V. and India volumes) at the India Office Library
PCC	*The Proceedings of the Committee of Circuit*
PP	Parliamentary Papers of *the India Office Records, Parliamentary Branch Nos. 6 and 7*
recd.	Recorded date of receipt of a letter
Reflections	*Reflections on the Government of Indostan* by Luke Scrafton
Secret Cons.	Consultations of the Fort William Council in their secret session (commencing in 1768 and different from BSC)
Seir	*Seir Mutaqherin* by S. Ghulam Hussain Khan. (The references are to the English version)
TM	*Tarikh-i-Muzaffari*. By Saiyid Muhammad Ali
Transactions in Bengal	*A Narrative of the Transactions in Bengal during the Soobahdaries of Azeem us Shan Jaffer Khan, Shuja Khan Sirafraz Khan and Alyvirdy Khan* by F. Gladwin, being an English translation of Salimullah Munshi's *Tawarikh-i-Bangala*

Abbreviations

TP   *Trial Papers.* Proceedings of the Fort William
            Council especially held for the trial of Reza
            Khan during 1772–1774. Typed copies procured
            from India are indicated as Miscellaneous
            Proceedings Vol. 39A and 39B in India Office
            Library. These are referred to as *TP* I, *TP* II

View   *A View of the Rise, Progress and Present State of*
            the English Government in Bengal. By H. Verelst

CHAPTER I

INTRODUCTION:
THE TWILIGHT OF MUGHAL BENGAL

In a public letter of 25 November 1791 the government of Lord Cornwallis reported from Calcutta to the Directors of the East India Company in London,

We are much concerned to advise you of the decease of the Nabob Mahomed Reza Khan...
His honourable character, his regard to the English for a long period of time, and the services he had rendered in Bengal are testified upon the records of this Government and well known to the Company in England. His public and private worth equally made him an object of esteem, and they entitle his memory to respect.[1]

Such was the obituary notice of a man who had been a vital part of Bengal's history for over thirty years and witness to its history for nearly half a century. He had observed the irremediable decline of two empires, that of the Safavids in the land of his birth, Iran, and that of the Mughals in India, the land of his adoption. He had participated in the events which led to the eclipse of the Nawabs and to the rise of the English East India Company in Bengal. He had been the agent of the Company, the defender of the Nizamat, and had been a leading figure throughout what may be called the Anglo-Mughal phase in Bengal's history. That phase was brought to an end on 1 January 1791 with Cornwallis's abolition of the office of Naib Nazim and the final transfer of the Sadar Nizamat Adalat. Nine months later, having worked almost to the end upon cases which had been awaiting his decision before Cornwallis's regulations were passed, Reza Khan died. It is the purpose of this book to study afresh the important, formative period of Reza Khan's career, down to the year 1775, and to reconsider his part in the events which shaped the pattern of British rule in Bengal.

To understand Reza Khan's career, and indeed to understand events in Bengal between 1756 and 1775 it is necessary, in the first

---

[1] India Office Records (or I.O.R.), Bengal Letters Received, volume 30, pages 481–2.

The transition in Bengal, 1756–1775

place, to forgo the benefits of hindsight. To Reza Khan, as to every Indian of his day, this period was not that in which the British Indian Empire was founded, it was a phase in the long history of the Timurid empire. The overriding reality was that Bengal was Mughal. The reigning prince was named on the coin and in the Khutba and thus enjoyed the two prerogatives of sovereignty. He might be a tool in the hands of a minister, his mandates might be evaded or disregarded, nevertheless he was deemed 'the sole fountainhead of honour', and 'every outward mark of respect, every profession of allegiance, continued to be paid to the person who filled the throne of the house of Timour'.[1] Moreover no usurper, however daring, felt able to outrage the general feeling by treating the emperor's name with disrespect: Nadir Shah sacked Delhi, but acknowledged Muhammad Shah as emperor; the Abdali invaded India repeatedly, but did not subvert Timurid sovereignty. Bolts may have been right in thinking in 1772 that 'if the youngest writer in the service had been sent with the authority of the Company to our Shah Allum, it was certain that his Majesty would have granted away the remainder of his empire...',[2] but it was also true that the Mughal grant was necessary, however obtained. Reza Khan had lived in Mughal Delhi as a boy and in Mughal Bengal under the still vigorous and effective rule of Alivardi Khan as a young man. On the issue of Timurid sovereignty he remained unyielding to his dying day, and no account of his relationship with Warren Hastings and the Company is intelligible if this is forgotten.

It is also necessary to consider what the nature of the Anglo-Mughal relationship was when Reza Khan came to Bengal, and the character it took after Plassey, if the Khan's behaviour is to be understood correctly. Before 1756, as Ghulam Husain noted, the English were known in Bengal 'only as merchants'.[3] The Mughal rulers and nobles were not unaware of the military abilities of the Europeans; mercenary Portuguese, Dutch, French and English had long served in the imperial armies, especially in the artillery. During the Maratha invasion of 1742 Alivardi had sought the co-operation of the three European nations in Bengal, the Dutch,

---

[1] J. Malcolm, *The Life of Robert, Lord Clive*, I, 402–3.
[2] W. Bolts, *Considerations on Indian Affairs*, p. 31.
[3] Ghulam Husain Khan Tabatabai, *Seir Mutaqherin* (or *Seir*) (English tr.), II, 220.

2

The twilight of Mughal Bengal

French and English,[1] and in 1744 he again asked the English for the loan of the services of thirty or forty Europeans to command his troops as 'his people were not trained up to the use of fire-arms' as the Europeans were.[2] Again from Drake's narrative it appears that the Nawab Siraj-ud-daulah's army, when it captured Calcutta in June 1756, contained several Europeans and Indo-Portuguese.[3] The latter may have been connected with the contingent which Murshid Quli Khan had recruited through the Portuguese padre at Bandel.[4] It is also known that the Bengal Nawabs continued to maintain Christian troops, most probably Portuguese, at Chittagong right down to 1760–1 when the district was handed over to the English.[5]

The fact remains that for a century the English appeared in Mughal Bengal as traders and that contact with them had been mostly indirect. In their negotiations for the acquisition of the three villages of Kalikata, Sutanuti and Govindapur in 1698 from Azim us Shan, in those for the acquisition of further privileges from Farukh siyar in 1717 and in the political conspiracies of 1757 and 1760, the negotiators most extensively used had been Armenians, Christian by religion and Persian in culture.[6] In more normal times the Company had been represented in the Bengal Subahdar's court by native vakils or agents, usually Hindu, and these would treat with the Nawab's Mutasaddis, secretaries or clerks, also usually Hindus. Only on very rare and important occasions did the Nawab himself grant interviews to the Vakils, whose highest level of access was normally to the Rai-Rayan (a Hindu minister heading the revenue department) or to the Naib or deputy.[7]

This was only natural, for the military aristocrats of the imperial or provincial courts did not hold merchants in any high regard: they were useful subjects to be protected but not to be cultivated on the social level. Merchants did upgrade themselves by turning soldier or administrator. Mir Jumla for example, a merchant in

---

[1] Bengal Public Consultations (or BPC), 29 July 1742. The English did not participate then as it was thought 'not for the Company's interest' to do so.
[2] BPC, 16 Nov. 1744. The request did not receive any better response.
[3] See S. C. Hill, *Bengal in 1756–1757*, vol. I, appendix 66. Attempts were made through priests to detach them from fighting for the 'Moors'.
[4] See Orme MSS. (I.O.), *India*, IX, 2166 ff.
[5] W. K. Firminger, *Chittagong District Records* (or *CDR*), I, 150.
[6] Such as Khojah Sarhad, Khojah Petruse and Khojah Gregory.
[7] The Naib (usually a near relation of the Nawab) headed the administration.

3   1-2

The transition in Bengal, 1756–1775

origin, ended as one of the greatest Mughal generals, the conqueror of Assam.[1] But the reverse process did not take place, though a prince or noble might engage in commercial transactions as an extension of political power.[2] The Nawabs long maintained a virtual monopoly, exercised through selected favourites, of the trade in salt, betelnut, opium and saltpetre, or of the trade to Assam by way of Rangamati, while the Faujdars of Sylhet and Chittagong, by virtue of their office, enjoyed certain exclusive trade privileges within their respective jurisdictions.[3] The presence of an English merchant company in Bengal, however considerable its trade, could not disturb the picture of Bengal as a Mughal Subah.

Moreover the pattern was not, in its essentials, broken even when the English returned to Calcutta in January 1757 at the head of forces from Madras. Admiral Watson of His Britannic Majesty's navy, and Colonel Clive, commander of the Company's forces were military leaders who could be recognised by and admitted to a Mughal society of military aristocrats. Their attack upon Hugli bandar or port on 9 January 1757 and their plundering of the merchants of that city[4] called forth a protest from Siraj-ud-daulah that the English were acting 'not like merchants', but simultaneously the Nawab declared to Clive, 'I know you are a soldier and as such I should chuse to be your friend'.[5] Clive had struck the right note, both by his victories and by bringing a letter of commendation from the Nawab of Arcot and demanding in another to be regarded as an officer of the King of England who, as he told Jagat Seth, was not 'inferior in power to the Padsha [or Mughal Emperor] himself'.[6] And with an intuitive understanding of the Indian attitudes he had appealed directly to the Nawab Siraj-ud-

[1] Mir Jumla was a seventeenth-century example (*DUHB*, II, 339–50). One more recent example was Mir Habib, 'for sometime a peddling broker at Hooghly' (F. Gladwin, *Transactions in Bengal*, p. 141).

[2] Instances being the viceroys Shaista Khan and Azim us Shan (*DUHB*, II, 373–5).

[3] J. Reed's letter, 17 Dec. 1770 (*see Proceedings of the Murshidabad Council of Revenue*, or *MP*, 20 Dec. 1770).

[4] This attack was undertaken according to a resolution of a Council of War dated 30 Sept. 1756 'to attack Hughley or any other Moors town or to take reprizals in the river on any other Moors vessels' (*see Home Miscellaneous Series* (I.O.) (or *H.M.S.*, 95; 85), the hardest hit among the merchants being Khwaja Wajid, called the Fakhr ut tujar (*H.M.S.*, 193; 14, 20).

[5] Siraj-ud-daulah to Clive, 1 Feb. 1757. *H.M.S.*, 193; 27.

[6] Clive to Jagat Seth, 21 Jan. 1757. *H.M.S.*, 193; 17.

4

The twilight of Mughal Bengal

daulah, declaring 'I esteem your excellency in the place of my father and mother, and myself as your son, and should think myself happy to lay down my life for the preservation of yours'.[1]

Colonel Clive, Admiral Watson and Major Killpatrick, known to the Indians then by their Mughal titles respectively as Sabut Jang (Firm in War), Dilir Jang (Courageous in War) and Dilawar Jang (Courageous in War)[2] were acceptable as soldiers, men of rank. They had also a claim to acceptance because they were Christians. The Nawab, in his letters to Clive, could appeal for his due regard to the treaty relationship between them on this ground: 'After having made peace to begin war again no religion can justify. The Marattas have no Books of God, yet are just to their contracts. You have the Book of God, if you are not just to your contracts it will be astonishing and unaccountable'.[3] The fact that Clive and his fellow countrymen were people of the Book in itself gave them a status superior to that of the heathen natives.[4] However it was Clive's soldierly virtues and his professions of filial attachment which made him a particular object of regard. To the Nawab, and his nobles, Clive was one of their sort, a soldier and a nobleman, who would appreciate the gift of two leopards 'extremely good at catching deer', because he doubtless shared their own taste for hunting.[5] By 30 March 1757, Clive could report with satisfaction to the Nawab of Arcot that 'the Nawab in this country respects us'.[6] The respect was paid to the soldier, not to the merchants of the Company. 'Tell Roger Drake' not to 'disturb our affairs', Siraj-ud-daulah wrote to Clive on 10 March 1757, in a tone which showed scant respect to one who was constitutionally Clive's superior in Bengal.[7] In the same letter, again, Siraj-ud-daulah had asked Clive to 'send Dilher Jung (the Major) that I may speak my

[1] Clive to Siraj-ud-daulah, 3 Feb. 1757. *H.M.S.*, 193; 30.
[2] Clive was known in India as Sabut Jang (correctly Sabit Jang), a title which was conferred on him by the Nawab of Arcot (Malcolm, *Clive*, I, 400–1). Ghulam Husain referred to Watson as Admiral Dilir Jang Bahadur (*Seir*, II, 225) while the Major is referred to as 'Dilher Jung' in the Nawab's letter to Clive dated 10 March 1757 (*H.M.S.*, 193; 65). A list giving the Mughal names and titles of some of the early English officials of the Company in Bengal is given on pp. xii–xiii.
[3] Siraj-ud-daulah to Clive, 19 Feb. 1757. *H.M.S.*, 193; 56.
[4] Hafiz ullah Khan, eldest son of Sarfaraz Khan appealed to Clive for protection 'for the prophet Jesus's sake' (recd. 19 July 1757. *H.M.S.*, 193; 80).
[5] Siraj-ud-daulah to Clive, 24 March 1757. *H.M.S.*, 193; 88.
[6] *H.M.S.*, 193; 80.
[7] *H.M.S.*, 193; 64–65.

mind to him and send him back to you'.[1] The Nawab was greatly annoyed at Drake's correspondence with Manikchand—he was Siraj-ud-daulah's governor of Calcutta during occupation in 1756—and complained 'I have delivered to Mr Watts the three Lack of rupees and I will finish the rest of the business in ten or twelve days, then why should Roger Drake write these letters privately'.[2] Even William Watts enjoyed a better status in the eyes of the Nawab. The reason was not merely the Nawab's disgust with Drake for causing trouble, but also the fact that irrespective of his official position (as Second of the Calcutta Council holding the chiefship of Kasimbazar) he was the accredited agent of Clive at Murshidabad. Watts was all the more welcome because he had brought with him a contingent of artillery troops, one officer, one sergeant, one corporal and fifteen privates,[3] for which the Nawab had sent an urgent request to Clive. 'I desire that when you dispatch Mr Watts to Muxadabad', the Nawab had written to Clive on 14 February 1757, 'you will send 25 artillerymen with him for my service'.[4] Clive had readily complied with the Nawab's request, offering politely to pay for the troops himself. Watts could have no better way of creating a favourable impression at the city. While Clive and the Nawab corresponded direct or through Watts, Company business at the Durbar continued as before through a Vakil.

The development of this new relationship between the Nawab and the English commanders was cut short, of course, by the development of a conspiracy at Murshidabad against Siraj-ud-daulah. As a new element introduced through Watts into the political life of Murshidabad, the English also became, for the first time, involved in it. The Anglo-Mughal relationship entered a new stage of development.

The newness was not in the origin of the conspiracy, but lay in the direction of its development. Soon after his accession to the masnad in 1756 the Nawab had faced a conspiracy at Murshidabad and a revolt at Purnea. Mir Jafar then urged Shaukat Jang to fight

[1] Siraj-ud-daulah to Clive, 10 March 1757. *H.M.S.*, 193; 64–5. Major Killpatrick was meant.
[2] *Ibid.* Drake had written to Manikchand urging the early return of goods plundered in Calcutta by the Burdwan mutasaddis and servants, adding 'Don't look on this as a trifling thing below your notice'. (*H.M.S.*, 193; 65).
[3] Clive to Siraj-ud-daulah, 16 Feb. 1757. *H.M.S.*, 193; 57.
[4] Siraj-ud-daulah to Clive, 14 Feb. 1757. *H.M.S.*, 193; 57.

The twilight of Mughal Bengal

the Nawab, assuring him that several commanders and grandees at Murshidabad, including himself, looked upon Shaukat Jang 'as their only resource against the growing and daily cruelties of Seradj-ed-doulah's',[1] almost in the same way as a conspiracy headed by Haji Ahmad, grandfather-in-law of Reza Khan, had invited Alivardi to rise against Sarfaraz Khan on the latter's accession in 1739.[2] Siraj-ud-daulah had better success in 1756 against Shaukat Jang than Sarfaraz had against Alivardi in 1740. One reason for Siraj-ud-daulah's success had been his tighter grip over his capital, for all thoughts of getting rid of the Nawab, says William Watts in his memoirs, 'availed little, since the attempt was equally difficult and dangerous; and failing in it sure to be attended with sudden and certain destruction'.[3] In the conspiracy of 1757, however, there was, for the conspirators, 'one way to move, or rather to lessen the risk; and this also was easily discovered. It was procuring the countenance and assistance of the English'.[4] The English were no longer merely merchants of Kasimbazar, cut off from the social and political life of Murshidabad, as they had been only the previous year; they were now in Murshidabad, enjoying the friendship of the Nawab and, what is more, being courted by the latter for military assistance against the threatened invasion of the Abdali. The recapture of Calcutta by Sabut Jang and Dilir Jang,[5] and the forcing of the treaty of Alinagar[6] in February did not, to the Murshidabad nobles, mean anything more than emergence of powerful rivals of Siraj-ud-daulah, and to be courted against the latter.[7] The presence of Watts at Murshidabad was an additional advantage, and to make use of this, one of the enemies of the Nawab, Khuda Yar Khan, took the first move and 'sent several messages to Mr. Watts'.[8] By 26 April 1757 Watts had reported a message also from Mir Jafar two days earlier saying that if the English were 'content' Rahim Khan, Rai Durlabh and Bahadur Ali Khan and others 'are ready and willing to join their force, seize the Nabob and set up another

[1] *Seir*, II, 196.   [2] Gladwin, *Transactions in Bengal*, 154–5.
[3] W. Watts, *Memoirs of the Revolution in Bengal*, 76.   [4] *Ibid.*
[5] That is, Clive and Watson.
[6] This was the name given to Calcutta.
[7] There was no sense of alarm. Similar was the reaction of the Mughals in Oudh, after Plassey. Omar Quli Khan, Mir Jafar's agent, wrote: 'your reputation is lost by the Frengees [Christians] having beat you; therefore they all cry out they are no soldiers in Bengal!' (*H.M.S.*, 193; 201–2).
[8] Watts, *Memoirs*, 76.

person that may be approv'd of'.[1] A revolution began but it was not yet clear who was to replace Siraj-ud-daulah. The determination of this matter came ultimately to lie in the hands of the English. The Fort St George Council had already advised the Fort William Council on 13 October 1756 'to effect a junction with any powers in the provinces of Bengal that may be dissatisfied with the violences of the Nawab's government, or that may have pretensions to the nawabship...'[2] On 23 April 1757, the Calcutta Council directed Clive to sound out the 'great people' at the Durbar and 'learn how they stand affected with respect to a revolution'.[3] By 1 May the Select Committee had received information of a conspiracy at Murshidabad and they spoke of themselves as allies, for they thought that with a revolution 'it would be a great error in politics to remain idle and unconcerned spectators of an event, wherein by engaging as allies to the person designed to be set up we may benefit our employers and the community very considerably...'[4] But a further consultation on 12 May shows that they were quite ready to act as principals, for they then seriously considered whether the Marathas should be supported before finally deciding upon the 'project of establishing Mier Jaffier in the Subaship if it can by any means be effected'.[5] Even later, when the determination of Mir Jafar seemed in doubt only a week before the battle of Plassey, Clive was putting up for consideration the notion of bringing in the Birbhum Raja, the Marathas or even Ghazi ud din Khan, after the rains.[6]

The conspirators at Murshidabad, before Plassey, scarcely appreciated the nature of the English power which they were calling to their assistance. Mir Jafar, an immigrant into Bengal during Shuja Khan's time, was an almost uneducated soldier,[7] accepted into the ruling aristocracy because of his noble birth—he was a Najafi Arab Saiyid—and then because he had married Shah Khanum, Alivardi's half-sister. He was no politician[8] and unlike

[1] Watts's letter, 26 April. BSC, 1 May 1757.
[2] S. C. Hill, *Bengal in 1756–1757*, I, 239–40.
[3] Consultations and proceedings of the Bengal Select Committee, 23 April 1757.
[4] BSC, 1 May 1757.   [5] BSC, 12 May 1757.
[6] BSC, 23 June 1757.
[7] A. C. Roy, *The Career of Mir Jafar Khan (1757–1765)*, p. 2.
[8] It is interesting to note Umichand's assessment of Mir Jafar. He told Robert Gregory on 15 Feb. 1758 that 'the present Nabob Meir Mohamed Jaffier would not keep the Government long that he was a soldier and not fit to govern' (Gregory's letter, 16 Feb. BSC, 18 Feb. 1758). He proved correct.

The twilight of Mughal Bengal

Alivardi whose name, Mahabat Jang, he later took for himself, Mir Jafar was never able to act as principal. (He had twice before been involved in conspiracies, one led by Ataullah Khan, Reza Khan's father-in-law in 1747, and the other when Shaukat Jang had revolted in Purnea in 1756.[1]) Even now he does not seem at first to have aimed personally at the masnad. In settling terms with the English he depended entirely on Rai Durlabh—Ghulam Husain states positively that the agreement was concluded in Mir Jafar's name by Raja Durlabhram[2]—and Scrafton reported on 30 November 1758 that 'the Nabob had only a cypher treaty and even that is lost'.[3] The pivotal figure in the conspiracy appears to have been Rai Durlabh, eldest son of Raja Janaki Ram, brought up and ushered into the military aristocracy by assignment of an army command and, on his failure as deputy governor of Orissa, made the Nizamat Diwan,[4] the job of a mutasaddi, which fitted him. Rai Durlabh had been warned that 'if we [the English] were once permitted to march this way we should not quit Muxadabad these 3 years',[5] and it was he who objected to the lavish monetary promises in the treaty drafted at Calcutta, saying 'where shall he and Meer Jaffier be able to raise such a sum as two crores and a half in a month's time . . . '[6] However, he was silenced by the promise of five per cent for all that he could get for the English. Mir Jafar was made to sign an obligation without the least idea of its implications, and the manoeuvre was an achievement of Watts, for he knew that Mir Jafar was a 'tool in the hands of Roydulub'.[7] When, at last, on 24 June 1757, the day following Clive's victory at Plassey, Mir Jafar received a message of congratulation from the real victor, expressing a 'hope to have the honor of proclaiming you Nabob'[8] the new Nawab could only recognise Clive as the maker of his fortune.

It was only natural, for Mir Jafar had been used to serving the

[1] *Seir*, II, 24–25, 196.   [2] *Seir*, II, 237–8.
[3] Luke Scrafton to Hastings, 30 Nov. 1758 (Add. MSS. 29132, f. 52). Walsh and Scrafton had been introduced to Siraj-ud-daulah by Clive as 'a relation of mine and another person' on 3 Feb. 1757 (*H.M.S.*, 193; 30). Though Scrafton belonged to Dacca establishment, at Clive's request the Select Committee had posted him to Murshidabad to assist Watts (BSC, 28 April 1757).
[4] *Seir*, II, 2–6, 117–18. He was opposed to Siraj-ud-daulah because the latter had raised a Kashmiri Hindu, Rai Mohan Lal, to the post he once held.
[5] Watts's letter to Clive, 6 June. BSC, 11 June 1757.
[6] Watts to Clive, 3 June 1757. *H.M.S.*, 808; 57.
[7] *Ibid.*   [8] *H.M.S.*, 193; 165.

9

masnad for nearly thirty years, never even dreaming, perhaps, of ascending to it himself. He was very grateful to Clive personally and gratefulness soon developed into fondness for the brave young soldier. Clive, for his part, addressed Mir Jafar in terms of personal devotion: 'Whenever I write to your excellency it is the same as if I was writing to my father. Such regard and friendship as a son has for his father such have I for your excellency, and whenever I have any favour to request it is for your excellency's advantage.'[1] It is important not to lose sight of the nature of the Anglo-Mughal relationship immediately after the battle of Plassey. Clive was serving the interests of the Company, even of Britain, but to Mir Jafar government meant personal government, and his approach to Clive was also personal. The Nawab did not know the Company and felt no obligation to it: it was Clive to whom he felt and expressed his gratitude. This was understood, moreover, by the Company's servants in Bengal, and that was why, when Drake departed in June 1758 Watts, Manningham and Becher who had been appointed governors by rotation in a joint minute resigned their post, which was unanimously offered to Clive.[2]

The Nawab did know a few Englishmen besides Clive, some of them quite well, but even these, Watts, Amyatt and Manningham, were seen rather as agents of Clive than of the Company. Again Hastings gained the Nawab's confidence as Clive's man and at Clive's commendation. On 18 August 1759 Hastings acknowledged this in a letter to Clive. He wrote saying that the Nawab 'knew no body amongst the English but yourself to whom he had every obligation and that nothing but his friendship for you restrained him from retaliating the many insults which he pretended to have received from the English'.[3] He went on, 'I am much obliged to you for the desire you are pleased to express to maintain my influence at the Durbar, which (though not on this occasion) I fear will shortly fall very low indeed. It is (I own with great concern I learn) that your resolution is fixed to return this season to Europe'.[4] Curious though it may appear, the Nawab does not appear to have understood that the Company was not an individual but an impersonal and corporate body of merchants. When Clive

---

[1] Clive to Mir Jafar, 15 July 1757. *H.M.S.*, 193; 180.
[2] Joint minute of Watts, Charles Manningham and Richard Becher. BPC, 26 June 1758.
[3] Warren Hastings, Resident at Murshidabad to Clive, 18 Aug. 1759. (Add. MSS. 29096, f. 169).   [4] *Ibid.*

The twilight of Mughal Bengal

was about to go home, early in 1760, Mir Jafar sent with him seven packets of curiosities for his ally, Clive's master in London, and with them a letter addressed as though to some individual chief or ruler. The letter in Warren Hastings's translation, reads:

After particulars of my earnest desire to see you w[hich] w[oul]d prove of ye [the] greatest advantage to me: which exceeds anything yt [that] could be written or spoke, I proceed to address myself to your heart ye repository of friendship.

The lights of my eyes, dearer yn [than] my life, the Nabob Zobdut ool Mulk Mayenodowla Sabut Jang Bahadr [Clive] is departing for his own country. But his continuance in Bengal was in every respect satisfactory. It is my perpetual wish that the return of the [...?] light of my eyes above mentioned may happen very speedily; because I call him my son though I esteem him more yn a son. A separation from him is most afflicting to me. If you dispatch him speedily, to these parts and grant me ye happiness of seeing him again, it will be a real obligation.[1]

The wording of the Nawab's letter also serves as a reminder that to Mir Jafar and to his contemporary Indians (except perhaps a few merchants of Calcutta, Madras or Bombay) Clive was no Englishman as we might understand the term, but Nawab Sabut Jang Bahadur. Clive had been inducted into the Mughal system under this title by the Nawab of Arcot,[2] as the Armenian Khojah Gregory had been transformed into Gurghin Khan by the Nawab of Bengal. Before he left Bengal in 1760 Clive was a full-blown mansabdar with the rank of six thousand *zat* and five thousand horse,[3] and the title of Zubdat ul Mulk conferred by the Mughal Emperor. The title, particularly that of Nawab, indicated that he was placed at par with the Mughal nobility, and above that of nobles of non-Mughal and Indian origin who, irrespective of whether they were Hindus or Muslims, bore the title of Raja.[4] After Clive, all the governors of Fort William (except Holwell) and principal officers of the Company's army and civil service were similarly granted Mughal titles, and so included within the imperial system.[5] Of the months immediately preceding Plassey, Watts commented in his Memoirs that the nobles at Murshidabad 'were

[1] See Warren Hastings Papers. Add. MSS. 29096, ff. 215–16.
[2] Malcolm, *Clive*, I, 400–1.
[3] *Ibid.* p. 405. Malcolm makes a mistake. *Zat* means rank.
[4] Two current examples were Raja Asad uz Zaman Khan of Birbhum and his kinsman, Raja Kamgar Khan, of Narhat Semai in south Bihar.
[5] A list mentioning some of them is given on pp. xii–xiii.

persuaded they could merit very much from the Company's servants, by laying open his [the Nawab's] secrets, and thereby shewing them, what these people thought they did not least suspect, the danger to which they stood exposed', after Plassey the acceptance of Englishmen into the Mughal system became even more complete. By January 1759 Clive had also been offered the Diwani of Bengal from Delhi.[1] Room had been found in the past for all nationalities in the imperial service; there was no reason why the English should not be found a place.

Clive, though more considerate towards Mir Jafar than many of his countrymen, could yet urge William Pitt, on 7 January 1759, to consider the possibility of establishing a British dominion in Bengal, arguing that 'Mussulmans are so little influenced by gratitude' that the Nawab would doubtless 'break with us' whenever his interest would require it.[2] The Mughal attitude however was that a working partnership was perfectly possible. This is perhaps best illustrated by the conditions which a number of Mughal chiefs proposed to Major Munro in 1764 as the basis of agreement to be signed by the English in the name of Jesus and Mary.[3] The first article of the proposed agreement ran, 'The Company should in every respect regard as its own the honour and reputation of the Moghals who are strangers in this country and make them its confederates in every business'. Other articles laid down that 'whatever Moghals whether Iranis or Turanis come to offer their services should be received on the aforesaid terms' and that 'should anyone be desirous of returning to his own country... he should be discharged in peace'.[4] This was the political climate of Bengal when Reza Khan first came to prominence, and, sharing with the Nawabs and other Mughal leaders an absolute ignorance of English attitudes and objectives, the Khan, like the Nawabs, seems to have aimed at a sort of Anglo-Mughal rule within the framework of Timurid sovereignty.

Reza Khan, coming into Timurid India from outside, was accepted into the ruling community, was granted office and jagir,[5]

---

[1] Clive to William Pitt, 7 Jan. 1759. Quoted: G. W. Forrest, *The Life of Lord Clive*, II, 412. [2] *Ibid.*

[3] *Calendar of Persian Correspondence* (or *CPC*), vol. I, nos. 2416, 2418.

[4] *CPC*, I, 2423.

[5] It may be interesting to observe that, though it would have been none too difficult for him to acquire a zemindari, the Khan could never think of acquiring one, due perhaps to his inability to shake off his sense of identity with the

The twilight of Mughal Bengal

and in return accepted the Mughal pattern of government as right and proper. Alivardi provided the example of what a Nawab should be. Haji Ahmad, Alivardi's brother and Reza Khan's grandfather-in-law, and Nawazish Muhammad Khan who headed the civil administration of Bengal under the Nawabs Shuja Khan and Alivardi Khan, provided him with his yardstick or ideal as an administrator.[1] As Naib at Marshidabad,[2] Reza Khan was to work in conjunction with the English towards the model which these men had provided. What the Alivardian traditions in Bengal were, Reza Khan has set out in his own words.

The ryots [cultivators] tho not rich, were content. The Zemindars and Talookdars were father and friend of the people. They maintained a proper police and were accountable for every branch of it. Complaints were readily heard and justice administered. The lands were well cultivated and the Zemindars and Talookdars found their interest in encouraging it and promoting an increase of inhabitants. If either fell off, a supervisor was sent to assist the Zemindar and relieve the people.

Rents were proportioned to the value of produce of land and newcomers were assisted with utensils...[3]

As for revenue,

in former times there was none determined, the landlords gave a present or tribute to the sovereign. In the reign of King Akbar the revenues were settled and increased under his successors, but still the general interest was considered. The people were not oppressed. The Zemindars and Talookdars being men of property paid their rents duly and were honoured and encouraged. If they failed Amils were sent, not to dispossess them, but to inquire into the causes of their default and to relieve them.[4]

ruling community. A zemindar, however powerful, was after all a subject of the Mughals whose invariable maxim, Ghulam Husain says, was to 'keep them low' (*Seir*, III, 181). India, Reza Khan maintained, was a Dar ul Harb (Reza Khan's note, Francis MSS. (I.O.) Eur. E 13, p. 417). He obviously shared the current notion of the Muslim rulers in India, to whom it was not strictly a Dar ul Islam—a Muslim homeland. Muslims living in Hindustan (that is, North India) did so, according to the same notion, as rulers or as sojourners only. A jagir, however insecure, like an office under government, conferred a more dignified status.
[1] The Naib, assisted by the Hindu chief of the Khalsa, the Rai-Rayan and the Jagat Seth, acting as government banker, administered the country since Shuja Khan's time. This model was adopted by Clive.
[2] Reza Khan's designation underwent several changes.
[3] Reza Khan's note, Feb. 1775 (Francis MSS. (I.O.) Eur. E 28, pp. 345–56).
[4] *Ibid.*

13

The transition in Bengal, 1756–1775

For collection of revenue

the Kistbund[y] or rent was settled yearly, viz. upon the first of April [the Bengali month of Baisakh which begins in April].

The Zemindars and Talookdars received rent for inhabited places monthly and for corn grounds at the time of harvest.

They made their own payments 6/16 at the end of the first half year and 10/16 at that of the latter. But a monthly examination was made by the officers of government, respecting the state of farms, probable prospects of collecting rents or reasonable grounds for raising them.

As a result, the Khan declared, in Alivardi's Bengal

ballances were formerly very uncommon; whenever they arose, inquiry was made into their causes. If they appeared reasonable the rent was lowered and the deficiency was remitted. If not, it was charged to and recovered from the Zemindars.

Reza Khan also describes the traditional government policy towards trade and manufacture. He says

the workmen made [goods] of their own accord, and sold to whomsoever they pleased. Merchants of all nations bought and sold without hindrance. The trading people were rich and consumption immense. There was then a great export of the produce of the country and a vast influx of specie. The governing power never interfered in trade, but encouraged the merchants and redressed every grievance;

and bankers then

were a numerous and useful body. The people trusted their property readily in their hands and in return their assistance enabled the landholder to make good his engagement to government and rendered remittance easy and promoted cultivation.

He likewise sets out the pattern of judicial administration, recording that

in this country justice has been administered to the people agreeable to the ancient established laws. There are books in which laws are clearly expressed and set forth.[1]

Two courts were appointed–viz. the Adawlut Alia or King's court for criminal matters etc. The sentence of this court was presented to the Nabob who examined the proceedings, consulted the judges, and

---

[1] By 'books' the Khan was obviously referring to the Quran and the Sunna or traditions of Islam, as also to the *Fiqh* literature, particularly of the Hanafi school.

confirmed or rejected it. The Khalsa decided all disputes relating to property, land, debts etc. But an appeal lay to the Sudder or city where cause was ultimately determined. These Khalsa courts were held essential towards a due collection of the revenue. [And] they were established in the several districts of Dacca, Poorania [Purnea], Silhet [Sylhet], Rajemahal, Rangpur, Boglepore [Bhagalpur] and Hougley [Hugli].[1]

Reza Khan also had a clear picture of the nature of landed property in Bengal and of the reciprocal duties of the ruler and the ruled which appears to be based on the traditions to which he was heir. He states,

The Zemindars and Talookdars are masters of their own lands. The Prince may punish them but cannot dispossess them. Their rights are hereditary. Princes have no immediate property in lands. They even purchased ground to erect mosques and buryal places.

The Prince is to receive the revenues of the state, to make such laws and regulations only as are consistent with justice; to study the general good of the country, and to cherish all his subjects.

The Zemindars and Talookdars are to protect, encourage and comfort the ryots and others under them and it is the duty of them all to pay their rents faithfully and to give obedience to the laws.

Finally he sums up the whole tradition by describing what he believed to be the essence of the ruler's duty. It was

To issue such orders and regulations only as are consistent with the customs and manners of the country;

To enforce obedience thereto in the officers of the state as well as in the people;

To protect and encourage manufacturers, merchants, bankers and all ranks of people;

To hear and decide all complaints impartially and without delay;

To pay attention to the local customs of the several Mahals or districts in settling their Bundobust and mode of collection;

To obtain a constant communication of all events and observation of consequence in every part of the province.[2]

Reza Khan's whole career as Naib at Murshidabad can be seen as an attempt to hold as far as possible to his traditional ideal of

[1] Reza Khan's note, Feb. 1775 (Francis MSS. (I.O.) Eur. E 28, pp. 345–56).
[2] *Ibid.*

15

government, to protect the old Mughal ordering of society against the changes and encroachments which the English sought to impose. Or, to put it another way, his constant aim, especially in the period which forms the subject of this study, was to persuade his English masters to accept Mughal ideals and practices as their own.

CHAPTER 2

THE EARLY LIFE OF REZA KHAN AND HIS FIRST PUBLIC OFFICE IN 1756

About the early life and career of Reza Khan little is recorded. We know that he was born in a Shia family of Shiraz in Iran (or Persia),[1] probably in 1717,[2] the third of the four sons of Saiyid Hadi Ali Khan, the physician. Muhammad Husain Khan, the eldest son, was his full brother; Muhammad Ali Khan, the second, and Muhammad Ismail Khan, the youngest son, were his half brothers, born of a different mother.[3]

When the Khan was about ten years old his father migrated with his four sons to India.[4] India under the Timurids had always attracted men of talent and fortune seekers from Iran (which also included the Persianised and Shia dominated Iraq) and from Turan or Central Asia.[5] The break-up of the Shia empire of the Safavids begun by the revolt of the Sunni or orthodox Ghilzai Afghans in 1709, and accelerated by ten years of full scale war thereafter,[6] made the Mughal courts even more attractive to the fugitive noblemen from Iran. The Saiyid first took his family to Delhi, where his brother Naqi Ali Khan was a court physician and favourite of the Emperor Muhammad Shah (1717–48). Then, much later, they moved to Bengal where the Saiyid secured the post of Hakim or physician at Murshidabad, the capital of the province, thanks to the good offices of another Delhi court physician, 'the complement of doctors, the reservoir of the physical and philosophical learning, the Galen of his time', Alavi Khan.[7] The move was made during the nizamat or governorship of Alivardi Khan (1740–56),[8] probably not long after the invasion of Nadir Shah (1739) had destroyed and impoverished the city of Delhi. The Saiyid became the physician and courtier of Alivardi Khan,[9] the Bihari historian Ghulam Husain calling him 'the honourable, the

---

[1] *Tarikh-i-Muzaffari* or *TM*, 473; *Seir*, III, 4.
[2] *TM*, 473; *Seir*, III, 150.   [3] *TM*, 473.   [4] *TM*, 474.
[5] The term Mughal in Timurid India meant the Muslim immigrants from Iran and Turan. While Turan generally meant the region north of Iran, Iran meant the vast area from the Tigris in the west to the Attock or Indus in the east. *Seir*, I, 51 fn.   [6] L. Lockhart, *The Fall of the Safavi Dynasty*, 86–7, 109.
[7] *Seir*, II, 107.   [8] *TM*, 474.   [9] *Seir*, II, 158–9.

illustrious and respectable'.[1] Alivardi awarded him an annual salary of Rs. 14,000.[2] On the death of Hadi Ali, Alivardi Khan gave the post to his eldest son Muhammad Husain Khan, who was said to be 'a learned man and an able physician'.[3]

Nothing is known of the life and education of the young Reza Khan in Delhi and Murshidabad, except by inference. Doubtless he received the usual upper class training, learning to read and write Arabic and Persian, to behave with gravity and circumspection, curbing every emotion and impatience, and to handle arms and a horse.[4] By tradition his family belonged to one of the learned professions and there is some suggestion that he had learnt something of medicine.[5] In later life he was certainly regarded as a patron of the Murshidabad physicians, who were said to belong to his 'cabal'[6] and in 1767, when the English were busy cutting salaries and officers in Dacca, the one item to stand intact was the Rs. 1518-10-0 which used to be spent on medicine and a 'black' doctor.[7] Reza Khan also seems to have been fascinated by history.[8] Ghulam Husain says that the Khan made nothing 'of talking much, and in relating during whole hours together stories which he has picked up in ancient times and books, without once minding the ignorance and unadequateness of his audience'.[9] (The sarcastic tone of the quotation may be due to Reza Khan's refusal to look after Ghulam Husain's property when he was on pilgrimage, and to liaise between him and his bankers.)[10] Reza Khan's passion for the past may, perhaps, have been of use to him when, under the English, he was seeking to preserve the old society; it certainly seems to have made him more bound by tradition and backward looking than was desirable. He was also very particular about diction and form in letter writing, then considered a great art. Ghulam Husain also tells us, in his un-

---

[1] *Seir*, II, 107. [2] *TM*, 474.
[3] *Seir*, III, 150. The amount of his cash salary is not known but one Muhammad Husain was paid a salary of Rs. 76,871 from Dacca revenues during 21 months of Reza Khan's administration at Dacca though under head of military charges (Dacca Factory Records, or Dacca Cons., no. 6, f. 31). In addition he also had some jagir land in Dacca which was later exchanged for some other land near Murshidabad (*H.M.S.*, 584; 184–5, 691). After his death five years before that of Reza Khan his son succeeded to his post (*TM*, 474).
[4] L. Scrafton, *Reflections on the Government of Indostan* (or *Reflections*), 19.
[5] *Seir*, III, 101–2.
[6] *Seir*, III, 13, fn. 9. [7] F. Sykes report. BSC, 18 Apr. 1767.
TM, 474. [9] *Seir*, III, 148. [10] *Seir*, III, 70–1.

The early life of Reza Khan

favourable way, that the Khan enjoyed cards and dice,[1] and was
fond of society, though he would not allow others to behave in-
formally in his presence, or even to smoke his hookah.[2] He
obviously had his share of the Mughal aristocratic pride and
looked down on the Hindustanis, the earlier, now naturalised,
Muslim immigrants.[3] Haji Mustafa[4] describes Reza Khan more
kindly as a man of great sense, 'when he pleases', and a fine figure
even at the age of seventy: '...his chest is so broad, his body so
erect, his tone of voice so loud, and his eyes so very full of fire...',
that he seemed likely to live to be a hundred.[5]

Apart from Reza Khan's father and his eldest brother both being
court physicians of Alivardi Khan, a further rise in the family
fortune occurred when the Nawab chose Reza Khan to be husband
of a daughter of his niece Rabia Begum.[6] Reza Khan entered the
ruling family, by this marriage, linking his fate with their fortunes.
There is still no record of his occupying any government post,
but he was provided for by the grant from the revenues of a growing market as marriage dowry[7] and presumably with a suitable cash
allowance.[8] Besides the Nawab himself, there were certainly many
possible patrons for the Khan: his mother-in-law Rabia Begum,
daughter of Haji Ahmad, was married to one of the leading elder
nobles, Ataullah Khan Sabut Jang, who held the Faujdari of
Rajmahal and Bhagalpur, and her brothers, the sons-in-law of
Alivardi, Nawazish Muhammad Khan, Shahmat Jang; Saiyid
Ahmad Khan, Saulat Jang and Zainuddin Muhammad Khan,
Haibat Jang, were the governors of Dacca, Purnea and Patna.
Another daughter of Rabia Begum was betrothed to Siraj-ud-
daulah, Alivardi's grandson, but died before the marriage, and yet
another married Ikram-ud-daulah, Siraj-ud-daulah's younger

[1] *Seir*, III, 148.   [2] *Seir*, III, 150.   [3] *Seir*, III, 83.
[4] 'Hajee Mustapha' was the name of a French Creole, M. Raymond, who
published the translation of Ghulam Husain's *Seir* under the pseudonym of
Nota Manus in 1789 in 3 volumes and dedicated it to Hastings (*Seir*, I, Preface
dated 1 March 1902). Perhaps it was this 'Mustepha' who corresponded with
Hastings in English and was made the Superintendent of Murshidabad
Pilkhana in 1772 by Hastings in order to reduce the influence of the Khan's
favourite Niamat (Add. MSS. 29133, f. 298). Mustepha was interested in
'elephant buying in Sylhet' (*ibid.*, f. 313) and he remitted Rs. 3000 to Constantinople in 1772 (*ibid.*, f. 309).   [5] *Seir*, III, 150, fn. 110.
[6] He married possibly in the early 1740's while in his early twenties.
[7] Bahramganj, granted under the seal of the Diwan Nawazish Muhammad Khan,
was resumed in 1796 (I owe this to Dr K. M. Mohsin).
[8] Mir Qasim on his marriage received Rs. 200 p.m. (*JBORS*, v, 344).

brother. Reza Khan was linked through his mother-in-law with Amina Begum, the mother of the Nawab Siraj-ud-daulah (1756–57). It is as Siraj-ud-daulah's Faujdar of Katwa that we first find Reza Khan in public office, in 1756.

His appearance on the public stage was short-lived and not very glorious. Alivardi Khan had died on 10 April 1756 and within two months his successor Siraj-ud-daulah had started his punitive action against the English at Calcutta. Karam Ali[1] relates that Reza Khan, as Faujdar of Katwa, was ordered to march 'with a dasta (regiment) of troops by way of Hugli to the sea for the purpose that in case the English tried to escape in ships he would prevent them from going out of the country'.[2] The Khan failed in his mission, for despite his title of Muzaffar Jang, the Victorious in War, he was no soldier.[3] Karam Ali explains that his failure was due to 'lack of materials', but the removal of the Khan from his post by Siraj-ud-daulah soon after the capture of Calcutta in June 1756 suggests that the Nawab thought him unfit to command so important a position in the defence of Murshidabad.[4] The personal set-back of Reza Khan was swallowed up, however, in the general overthrow at Plassey in June 1757. From that upheaval the Khan did not re-appear politically for nearly three and a half years.

Whatever the wider results of Plassey, it made existence very precarious for the family of Alivardi. True, Mir Jafar, by his marriage to Shah Khanum, Alivardi's half-sister, had also been linked with the family, and it was this relationship which gave him a better claim than other rivals of Siraj-ud-daulah. Nevertheless, once he was raised to the masnad (throne) in June 1757 all members of the old ruling family became suspect.

The first victim of the revolution was the Nawab Siraj-ud-daulah himself. Mir Jafar might not have exerted himself much in the pursuit of the fugitive from Plassey and then Murshidabad, but the English insisted. Clive wrote on 24 June to Khuda Yar Khan, Khwaja Abdul Hadi and Rai Durlabh not to let their enemy escape,[5] while his agents, Watts and Walsh, pressed Mir

---

[1] The author of *Muzaffarnamah* dedicated his work to Reza Khan. The work narrates Bengal's history up to Reza Khan's arrest in 1772. Karam Ali, who belonged to Alivardi's family, was a protege of Reza Khan.
[2] *MN* (see extracts in J. N. Sarkar, *Bengal Nawabs*, pp. 63–4).
[3] The title meant formal incorporation in the Mughal military aristocracy.
[4] The Khan's successor proved no more successful (Forrest, *Clive*, I, 439–41).
[5] *H.M.S.*, 193; 165. All the three were Alivardian officers who had joined Mir Jafar against the Nawab Siraj-ud-daulah.

The early life of Reza Khan

Jafar to 'use all possible means of apprehending Surajah Dowlat who would otherwise create him much trouble in future'.[1] When the fugitive was brought to Murshidabad Mir Jafar put him into the custody of his son Miran, and made it clear that his life was not to be endangered.[2] Nevertheless Siraj-ud-daulah was murdered, apparently on Miran's orders; a death which, as Scrafton commented, 'fix'd'[3] the revolution. After that all the members of Alivardi's family felt threatened.

The family's troubles were only increased by the loyalty shown to them from the country which they had governed for nearly thirty years including an 'independent' rule for seventeen of them.[4] At least two movements seem to have been formed in favour of Siraj-ud-daulah's younger brother Mirza Mahdi. Holwell reports that Rajballabh[5] supported his candidature, and even proposed it to Clive,[6] while Mir Jafar and his son blamed the same plot on Rai Durlabh, who boasted to Scrafton, early in October, 'in ten days you may expect to see Bengal in a flame'.[7] Fears of conspiracy in favour of the ousted family were certainly in the air, for Hastings warned Sumner on 12 November that the new government was in confusion and that there was 'no saying what party may be forming'.[8] Whether Mirza Mahdi was actively concerned or not, before the month of November was out he was dead, crushed to death between two planks.[9] Miran justified the act: 'killing the snake and keeping its young is not the act of a wise man'.[10]

The savage execution of a boy of fifteen marked the degree of suspicion and enmity which Mir Jafar had come to feel towards Rai Durlabh, his late partner in the conspiracy against Siraj-ud-daulah. It was not only that Rai Durlabh's name had been linked

[1] Watts and Walsh to Clive, 26 June 1757. *H.M.S.*, 808; 60–1.
[2] W. Watts, *Memoirs*, 115.
[3] Scrafton to Roger Drake, 3 July 1757. *H.M.S.*, 808; 65.
[4] Alivardi's family held high offices also under Shuja Khan (1727–39).
[5] Rajballabh, not to be confused with Rai Durlabh's son of that name, was like his father Krishnadev a Majmuader (an officer in Qanungo's office) and served under Saiyid Razi Khan (Sarfaraz Khan's son-in-law) before Alivardi seized the masnad from the Nawab Sarfaraz Khan (1739–40). Under the new regime he served under Gokulchand, Shahmat Jang's Diwan, and rose to be the latter's deputy at Dacca. His son Krishnadas took shelter in Calcutta, which aggravated the Nawab's rupture with the English in 1756 (W. Hastings to H. Vansittart in 1760. Add. MSS. 29132, f. 103).
[6] J. Z. Helwell, *Address to Luke Scrafton* (or *India Tract*) 378; 39.
[7] Scrafton to Clive, 8 Oct. 1757. *H.M.S.*, 808; 92.
[8] Add. MSS. 29096, f. 2.   [9] *Seir*, II, 251.   [10] *MN*, f. 100.

with a movement in favour of the young prince, but that after the revolution Mir Jafar and Rai Durlabh were opposed in their relations with the English. Mir Jafar, when he was chosen to supplant Siraj-ud-daulah, had dreamt of establishing a regime on the Alivardian model. He had taken Alivardi's title of Mahabat Jang for himself and conferred on his son Miran the title of Shahmat Jang once worn by Nawazish Muhammad Khan.[1] Rai Durlabh was concerned not with the old regime but with the five per cent which he was to receive on all he secured for the Company, and with the profits which he, his son Rajballabh, and his brothers Kunjabehari, Rasbehari and Brindaban could secure for themselves from the revenue administration of the country.

Mir Jafar also felt personally deceived by Rai Durlabh, on whom he had relied in the final negotiation with the English. The new Nawab found himself indebted to the extent of over two crores of rupees to the English and pressed for payment even at his very first meeting with Watts and Walsh.[2] Rai Durlabh must have known that the sum demanded by the terms of the treaty—of which Mir Jafar had not even bothered to keep a copy[3]—were excessive, but the five per cent commission had closed his mouth.[4] The Nawab is said to have told Hastings in 1758, when the sanad for the twenty-four parganas was being claimed, that 'he only promised the Company a tract of land the revenues of which amount to a lack of rupees, and that if it was otherwise worded in the treaty it was owing to the knavery of Roydoolub who had deceived him'.[5] Rai Durlabh appeared both disloyal and deceitful.

The Nawab's anger was further roused by Rai Durlabh's later actions. Scrafton, immediately after Plassey had reported to Drake, 'The Gentoos [Hindus] stand in awe of us. Flatter promise and use every method to get into favour. Roydullub even seems now attached to us'.[6] Rai Durlabh showed his attachment by assisting Scrafton to buy up a large tract of land at Berhampore,

---

[1] *Seir*, II, 238.
[2] Watts to Clive, 3 June; Watts and Walsh to Clive, 26 June 1757. *H.M.S.*, 808; 57, 60. The total amounted to Rs. 2,29,00,000 (A. C. Roy, *Mir Jafar Khan*, p. 293).
[3] 'There is one lucky circumstance. The Nabob had only a cypher treaty and even that is lost' (Scrafton to Hastings 30 Nov. 1758. Add. MSS. 29132, f. 52).
[4] Watts to Clive, 3 June 1757. *H.M.S.*, 808; 57.
[5] Hastings to Clive, 1 Dec. 1758. Add. MSS. 29096, f. 65.
[6] Scrafton to Drake, 3 July 1757. *H.M.S.*, 808; 65.

The early life of Reza Khan

despite the Nawab's 'disgust',[1] and by indulging Scrafton, Clive's
agent at Murshidabad, in revenue farming under the fictitious
names of 'Mittinjay' (Mrityunjay) and 'Mittoochund' (Mitthu
Chand),[2] where he used his new wealth in lending to the zemindars at exorbitant rates.[3] All such currying of English favour was
done at the Nawab's expense.

While Clive was writing to the Nawab blaming his ministers for
the delay in paying off the promised sum,[4] Scrafton at Murshidabad was busy setting up a party in opposition to the Nawab,
designed 'to be a continual check on him'.[5] Of this party, Rai
Durlabh was most probably the central figure. The Rai Durlabh–
Scrafton entente was necessarily obnoxious to the Nawab with
whom Scrafton, early in November 1757, came almost to a breaking point.[6] Clive intervened to restore working relations between
the Nawab and Rai Durlabh on the one hand and possibly between
Scrafton and the Nawab on the other but that was a patchwork
which collapsed by the middle of 1758.

A major reason for the breakdown was that by January 1758 the
Nawab had been forced, to his great dismay, to assign the revenues
of Nadia, Burdwan, Hugli, Hijli and certain Dacca estates to the
English as a means of redeeming his debts.[7] In the Dacca estates
this led to a joint administration continued until January 1759,[8]
and eventually in the major districts to direct English administration. The traditional image of the Nawab's government was
seriously injured by this measure, for not only was Mir Jafar
prevented from exercising his legitimate authority in the assigned
districts,[9] but also the English, particularly at Dacca, used their
power to extend their trade privileges at the cost of the Nawab's

[1] BPC, 15 May 1758; Hastings to Drake, 20 June 1758. Add. MSS. 29096, f. 13.
[2] Scrafton to Hastings, 25 Aug. 1758. Add. MSS. 29132, f. 6. Not until 14 Dec.
1759 did the Calcutta Council officially appoint any Resident at Murshidabad.
Until then both Scrafton and Hastings held the post unofficially and on private
nomination by Clive and Watts. For first official appointment of Hastings
in December 1759, Add. MSS. 29132, f. 101.
[3] In one case a loan of Rs. 50,000 rose in one year to Rs. 88,000 (see Scrafton to
Hastings, 28 Nov. 1758. Add. MSS. 29132, f. 48).
[4] Clive to Mir Jafar, 7 July 1757. H.M.S., 193; 177.
[5] Scrafton, *Reflections*, 99.
[6] Scrafton to Clive, 30 Nov. 1757. H.M.S., 808; 100.
[7] BSC, 8 Dec. 1757 and 21 Jan. 1758.
[8] Hastings to Clive, Jan. 1759. Add. MSS. 29096, f. 105.
[9] Hastings to Clive, Nov. 1758 and 19 Jan. 1760. Add. MSS. 29096, ff. 59–60, 201.

own revenues.[1] Moreover the loss of these rich districts was imposed upon the Nawab at a time when his soldiery were starving and when his own life was repeatedly threatened by troops demanding their arrears of pay.[2]

The injury was the more unbearable because the joint administration further strengthened the links between Scrafton and Rai Durlabh. So close had their relationship become that the decline in Rai Durlabh's power, which became noticeable in July 1758, was described by Hastings as the decline of 'much of our power and influence at the Durbar'.[3] Clive in May 1758 attempted to take some of the sting out of the situation by transferring the administration of the revenues of the assigned districts to Nandkumar, and in August Scrafton's position at Murshidabad was taken over by Hastings, the Second at Kasimbazar factory.[4] Since Nandkumar had been Rai Durlabh's paid agent in Clive's camp,[5] the Nawab cannot have been much mollified. In August, therefore, Clive moved the seat of Nandkumar's administration from Murshidabad to Hugli, where he concurrently held the double appointment of Company's Tahsildar (collector) and Diwan of the Faujdar Amir Beg Khan.[6]

One of the declared objects of the move was 'to avoid giving the Nabob and the great men about him umbrage in seeing such large sums coming into the public treasury and sent out again for the use of the English'.[7] The move did little to heal the breach between Mir Jafar and Rai Durlabh, for all that it made plain was that the latter's agent had now become the 'idol' of Watts, who had become Clive's 'vizir'[8] in administrative matters, and had won the support of Clive.

[1] Hastings to W. B. Sumner (Dacca chief), 30 Jan. 1759; to Governor Holwell, 19 Feb. 1760. Add. MSS. 29096, ff. 111–12, 223–5.
[2] Hastings to Clive, 15 Sept. 1758, C. Manningham, 30 March 1759, and to Holwell, 19 Feb. 1760. Add. MSS. 29096, ff. 28, 135, 225.
[3] Hastings to Clive, 24 July 1758. Add. MSS. 29096, f. 20.
[4] Watts, the Chief, had never resided at Kasimbazar since Plassey. Hastings the Second and Sykes the Third managed all affairs at Kasimbazar. Hastings, in addition, assisted Scrafton at the Durbar until he became the successor.
[5] The task of Nandkumar, then known in Bengal as the 'black' colonel, was to 'cement' and 'increase' the friendship between Rai Durlabh and Clive (Richard Barwell's note on Nandkumar, no date, BPP, XIII, 104).
[6] BPC, 19 Aug. 1758 and Scrafton to Hastings, 31 Aug. Add. MSS. 29132, f. 14.
[7] Clive to Hastings, 10 Sept. 1758. Quoted by G. R. Gleig, *Warren Hastings*, I, 64.
[8] Scrafton to Hastings, 27 Aug. and 31 Aug. 1758. Add. MSS. 29132, ff. 13–14.

The early life of Reza Khan

When Scrafton left Murshidabad in August, Rai Durlabh felt so insecure that he sought and obtained the protection of English troops for his family during their move from Murshidabad to Calcutta early in September. Earlier he had arranged through the English support his own escape to Calcutta as a member of the Nawab's entourage when the latter visited Calcutta as the first Bengal Nawab ever to do so with a large party of officers and zemindars, the visit being especially arranged as a demonstration of the new status of the English in Bengal, particularly for the rival European nations to take note of it.[1] On the Nawab's return from Calcutta, Rai Durlabh had stayed back much to the Nawab's relief. But he reacted sharply to Rai Durlabh's canard that the Nawab had set troops upon his house at Murshidabad and characterised the report as motivated to create differences between him and Clive. Hastings admitted that the Nawab was right. Miran had placed spies upon Rai Durlabh's relations and effects so as to oblige them to render satisfactory accounts to Rai Umid Ram, the Rai-Rayan. But this had occurred while Mir Jafar was in Calcutta, and, Hastings said, he knew of 'no such thing being attempted' since Mir Jafar's return.[2] The Nawab, however, had his own charges of conspiracy to make against Rai Durlabh. Immediately after Rai Durlabh's family had left on 11 September for Calcutta, escorted by Ensign MacDowall, a plot to murder the Nawab was discovered on 13 September. The plan was to surround the Nawab as though demanding pay, and to cut him down when he visited the Imambara during the Muharram celebrations. The plot, Hastings reported, was 'rendered ineffectual, the Nabob having received timely notice of it'.[3]

A letter allegedly from Rai Durlabh to Khwaja Abdul Hadi was discovered, saying that a certain Mir Ali had been directed to defray the expenses of the conspiracy. Harun Khan, formerly of Rai Durlabh's risala or cavalry, stated that the money was sent by Rai Durlabh in the form of a bill for two lakhs of rupees.[4] The incriminatory letter also stated that Mir Kazem[5] had only 'half

[1] Malcolm, *Clive*, I, 375. 'The Nabob, thank God, leaves tomorrow' (Scrafton to Hastings 24 Aug. 1758. Add. MSS. 29132, f. 6).
[2] Hastings to Clive, 24 Aug. 7 and 9 Sept. 1758. Add. MSS. 29096, ff. 22–5.
[3] Hastings to Clive, 15 Sept. 1758. Add. MSS. 29096, f. 28.
[4] Hastings to Clive, 18(?) Sept. 1758. Add. MSS. 29096, ff. 28–9.
[5] An Arab Saiyid and an old Alivardian officer, then Paymaster of Mir Jafar's troops (*Seir*, II, 272, 280.)

25

engaged his consent' to the scheme, for which Rai Durlabh had obtained Clive's approval through Watts and Scrafton.[1] A report of the plot, together with the supposed letter from Rai Durlabh, was sent to Clive by Mir Jafar as evidence of Rai Durlabh's treachery. But though Hastings had treated the matter seriously at Murshidabad, as Scrafton told him, in Calcutta it was given little importance.[2] Clive, who regarded the story as an instance of the 'dark design of these Mussulmen', argued that while Rai Durlabh's life and fortune were in his hands he would not have dared to attack a man so well regarded by Clive as Mir Jafar.[3] The story was believed at Murshidabad. Khwaja Abdul Hadi, when confronted, could not deny the allegation[4] and, against Mir Kazem's oath on the Quran denying the allegations, there was the seal of that gentleman affixed to a secret agreement detailing the plot.[5] Also, the role of the alleged plotters fitted in all too well with their known attitudes. It was well known that Scrafton was hostile to the Nawab: to him Mir Jafar was 'an animal', a man compounded of 'folly', 'obstinacy and treachery', a rascal who needed to be 'bullyed' and ruled with a 'rod of iron'.[6] In September 1758 he had expressed to Hastings his hope that on Clive's departure 'all personal connection' with Mir Jafar would stop, and that when 'we have any thing of a force we shall not be long without a second rupture with the government'.[7] Scrafton's intimates at Murshidabad included Rai Durlabh and Mir Kazem and perhaps Khwaja Abdul Hadi, together with Ghulam Shah and Mirza Kazem,[8] who was a close relation of Alivardi Khan's Begum.[9] The only part of the plot to which Mir Jafar would not give credence was that relating to Clive, to whom he sent the letter as proof of Rai Durlabh's mischiefs.

In Calcutta a jury presided over by Nankumar declared the

---

[1] The letter is quoted in Malcolm, *Clive*, I, 382–3.
[2] Scrafton to Hastings, 28 Nov. 1758. Add. MSS. 29132, f. 48.
[3] Clive to Hastings, 6 Oct. 1758. Quoted in Malcolm, *Clive*, I, 381.
[4] *Seir*, II, 272, 274.
[5] *Seir*, II, 272–4. The seal was affixed by one of the Mir's intimates who is said to have had access to it. The document contained a pledge by the disaffected army leaders to 'stand by each other'.
[6] In different letters of Scrafton. See *H.M.S.*, 808; 92 and, Add. MSS. 29132, ff. 52, 71.
[7] Scrafton to Hastings, 2 Sept. 1758. Add. MSS. 29132, f. 18.
[8] Scrafton to Hastings, 27 Dec. 1758. Add. MSS. 29132, f. 62. Ghulam Shah later defected to Shah Alam (Major Carnac's letter, BSC, 21 Feb. 1761).
[9] *Seir*, I, 357.

26

The early life of Reza Khan

letter a forgery,[1] though the verdict did not satisfy Amir Beg Khan, the Faujdar of Hugli and Mir Jafar's principal channel of contact with Clive and the English. Amir Beg went away 'greatly disgusted', particularly against Watts, Nandkumar's patron.[2] In Murshidabad, however, Khwaja Hadi and Mir Kazem were immediately dismissed and subsequently killed,[3] while Miran took the wealth of Mirza Kazem.[4] The murder of Khwaja Hadi on his way to banishment from Bengal deprived Mir Jafar of an able officer while Rai Durlabh, Nandkumar and Rajaram (the head of espionage under Alivardi and Siraj-ud-daulah) came closer together in Calcutta.[5] It also seemed to Calcutta to have finally weakened the English position at Murshidabad. Scrafton commented that he knew of no one in the city who would be found attached to the English should a rupture occur.[6] To the members of Alivardi's family it threatened grave disaster.

Mir Jafar and Miran were naturally led to suspect all those closely connected with the old order, and in particular Alivardi's Begum and her two daughters, Ghaseti and Amina. Accordingly, after the three ladies had been 'kept confined in the most indecent manner', Miran sent them all as prisoners to Dacca, with Lutfunnessa, Siraj-ud-daulah's widow, and her four-year-old daughter.[7] Rabia Begum probably also went with them accompanied by her son-in-law Reza Khan.

The reason for their sharing the prisoners' circle in Dacca is not given anywhere. Rabia Begum and Amina Begum were known to be much attached to one another and after both were widowed by the Afghans had been much together. The Khan may well have felt personally safer away from Murshidabad. But it was certainly to the advantage of both to keep Rabia Begum's large personal fortune away from the covetous eyes of the Nawab and his son. The ladies of Mirza Kazem's household were plundered of a crore

1 Scrafton to Hastings, 28 Nov. 1758. Add. MSS. 29132, f. 48.
2 Scrafton to Hastings, 28 Nov. and 23 Dec. 1758. Add. MSS. 29132, ff. 48, 60.
3 Khwaja Hadi was murdered by the Afghans in November near Teliagarhi and Mir Kazem was murdered by the Rohillas in the following month (Dec. 1758) at Murshidabad (*Seir*, II, 275; *MN*, ff. 102–3), but in both these cases Miran was suspected to have had a secret hand (*India Tract* 378; 45).
4 *Seir*, I, 357.
5 *BPP*, XIII, 105.
6 Scrafton to Hastings, 27 Dec. 1758. Add. MSS. 29132, f. 62.
7 *Seir*, II, 281.

27

of rupees.[1] Rabia Begum may have been almost as rich,[2] her son-in-law was considered to have a 'family claim to Subahship',[3] they were on every count safer away from the Durbar.

For about a year Reza Khan and his mother-in-law were left in peace at Dacca. Indeed Mir Jafar did not seem to regard Reza Khan as any political threat, for he had readily confirmed the Khan's elder brother as court physician. But by the end of 1759 Mir Jafar's financial straits had driven him to contemplate a move against Rabia Begum.

The Nawab's debts to the Company had not been paid off. The revenues of the assigned districts of Nadia and Burdwan had been so mismanaged by Nandkumar, despite the Nawab's warnings against his method of collection,[4] that they were retained beyond the stipulated period, and put under direct English management.[5] The increase in the privileged trade of the Company's servants and their gumashtahs and Banians had also begun to eat into the revenue yields from customs dues.[6] As a result the Nawab was driven to so starve his troops that Hastings could report 'their horses are mere skeletons, and the riders little better. Even the Jamatdars are many of them clothed with rags.'[7] By January 1760 the Nawab had been able to pay only three out of thirteen months arrears of pay,[8] even though he had cut down the number of his forces,[9] had borrowed heavily from the merchant-bankers of Murshidabad and Kasim-bazar—fifty lakhs from Jagat Seth alone—and had anticipated revenues from the zemindars.[10] When, in 1759, Prince Ali Gauhar, son of the Emperor Alamgir II (1754–59), threatened the province, supported by many chiefs of northern India and also of Mir Jafar's dominions, and Mir Jafar was forced to raise troops to

[1] *Seir*, II, 357.
[2] While leaving Bengal on banishment in 1747 Ataullah Khan carried with him a vast sum of 60 lakhs of rupees, 70 elephants besides other precious stuff and gold (*Seir*, II, 69). Rabia returned to Alivardi 'with all her fortune' (*Seir*, II, 114).
[3] Hastings to Vansittart, 15 May 1762. Add. MSS. 29097, p. 57.
[4] Hastings to Clive, Nov. 1758. Add. MSS. 29096, ff. 59–60.
[5] In Feb. 1760 we find Hugh Watts in Burdwan and Howitt in Nadia (BPC, 21 Feb. 1760).
[6] Hastings to Sumner, Jan. 1759, and to Holwell, 19 Feb. 1760. Add. MSS. 29096, ff. 111 and 224.
[7] Hastings to Holwell, 19 Feb. 1760. Add. MSS. 29096, f. 225.
[8] Hastings to Caillaud, 31 Jan. 1760. Add. MSS. 29096, f. 214.
[9] Hastings to Clive, 14 Sept. 1759. Add. MSS. 29096, f. 184.
[10] Hastings to Clive, 9 Aug. 1759. Add. MSS. 29096, ff. 164–5.

resist him, the financial position became desperate. The Nawab was 'advised' to appropriate funds from Rabia Begum.[1]

Reza Khan bowed before the storm and saved his family, but to do so he had to secure the powerful patronage of the English. From an account given later by Hastings it seems that Mir Qasim had initiated the approach to the Nawab through Hastings and possibly Clive and Caillaud too,[2] who were in Murshidabad in December 1759 and January 1760. Clive was there to take his leave of the Nawab before setting out for England and Caillaud was there to get introduced at Murshidabad before taking the command of the troops against the second invasion of Ali Gauhar (now Shah Alam).

Mir Qasim's part in the saving of Rabia's wealth and in introducing Reza Khan to the English is not clear. But we know that relations between Mir Qasim and Reza Khan were bitter, and from Muhammad Ali[3] that Reza Khan paid 25,000 gold ashrafis, say four lakhs of rupees, to Mir Qasim.[4] Would it be too much to suggest that it was Mir Qasim who gave Mir Jafar the advice to appropriate Rabia Begum's wealth and that the 25,000 ashrafis were a bribe to win him over to the Khan's side? Certainly there is no other explanation available for the payment of so large a sum. This could well have been the occasion, of which Mir Qasim spoke later to Hastings, when Reza Khan was compelled to submit 'to a necessity against which he had no remedy', and when the Khan 'knew very well the dangerous situation in which his mother-in-law...stood...on account of her great wealth'.[5]

It may be perhaps this unscrupulous conduct of Mir Qasim—paralleled by his plundering of Lutfunnessa, the Begum of Siraj-ud-daulah[6]—which made Reza Khan his sworn enemy, and swung the Khan to the support of Mir Jafar and Miran. Mir Jafar was ready for a reconciliation, for he was surrounded by disaffection. From Calcutta, Rai Durlabh was continuously in correspondence with the Marathas and with the Prince, now the Emperor Shah

[1] Hastings to Vansittart, 14 June 1762. Add. MSS. 29098, p. 57.
[2] *Ibid.*
[3] Muhammad Ali was an officer under Reza Khan. He was also the author of the *Tarikh-i-Muzaffari*, an historical work dedicated to Reza Khan.
[4] *TM*, 475, p. 894. An ashrafi, a gold coin, was worth between Rs 13 and Rs 16 (*Seir*, I, 30, fn.)
[5] Hastings to Vansittart, 15 May 1762. Add. MSS. 29096, pp. 58–9.
[6] The event was in 1757 when the fugitive Nawab was captured with his wife. Mir Qasim took a casket valued at lakhs of rupees from her (*Seir*, II, 329–40).

The transition in Bengal, 1756–1775

Alam, and busy welding together the anti-Mir Jafar elements in Calcutta, notably Nandkumar and Rajaram, who at one time were respectively soliciting from the Emperor the posts of Diwan, Naib Diwan, and Head of the Intelligence service.[1] Moreover, since Prince Ali Gauhar had become emperor many chiefs and Zemindars of Bengal had declared their loyalty to him. Among them were Asad uz Zaman Khan, the Raja of Birbhum and his kinsman Kamgar Khan, the Raja of Narhat-Samai.[2] Two of Mir Jafar's principal army commanders, Rahim Khan and Ghulam Shah also seized the earliest opportunity of going over to the Emperor.[3] Ghulam Husain records that there was a most dangerous expression of regret for Siraj-ud-daulah's overthrow, 'whether amongst the knowing one or amongst the simple, whether in public or in private'.[4] In such a situation there was mutual advantage for both the Nawab and Reza Khan in coming together. The Khan had, besides, a hatred for Mir Qasim, in common with Miran, who had begun looking with suspicion on Mir Qasim's growing friendship with the English.[5]

The moves which Reza Khan had taken to save the family fortunes had also been of great importance to his future in that he was thereby brought into contact with the English. What form that contact took in the early months of 1760 is not clear. But there is some evidence that the Khan was in touch with the governor (probably Holwell), early in February 1760, on a matter seemingly of great political importance.[6] Holwell succeeded Clive as governor on 9 February 1760, and Reza Khan may have been involved in Holwell's plans for linking tgoether the Alivardians, men such as Mirza Muhammad Ali, Siraj-ud-daulah's Faujdar of Hugli,[7] in opposition to Mir Jafar, Clive's protégé. Holwell had many grievances against Clive, and also against Mir Jafar, who did not pay to him the regard paid to Clive or honour him with a title

[1] Barwell's account of Nandkumar (*BPP*, XIII, 105).
[2] *Seir*, II, 332.
[3] *Seir*, II, 339–41, 244.
[4] *Seir*, II, 283.
[5] See chapter 3.
[6] Reza Khan's letter, received (or recd:) 7 Feb. 1760 (*CPC*, I, 269).
[7] In reply to Holwell's request for support for Muhammad Ali's candidature, Hastings replied on 30 Jan. 1760 that it was too late to do it now. He knew nothing of Sulaiman Beg's appointment 'till I saw him clothed in the Kelleat [Khilat]'. Sulaiman succeeded Amir Beg who left for Basra. (For Hastings's letter, Add. MSS. 29096, f. 211).

despite solicitations for it.[1] He had, therefore, concerted a plan for the removal of Mir Jafar by a direct settlement with Shah Alam, negotiated through Rai Durlabh and Kamgar Khan and supported by Caillaud and Sumner. Whatever was Reza Khan's position in the matter, this much is known, that in mid 1760 he was already recognised by the English as a very important person in Bengal. When Henry Vansittart succeeded Holwell on 27 July, the change was notified to the Nawab, to the Nawab's son, to the Raja of Nadia and to Reza Khan.[2]

[1] 'I entirely agree with you that a title with other suitable honours either conferred on you by the Nabob or . . . from the Court will add much to your dignity . . .' Hastings to Holwell, 30 Jan. 1760. Add. MSS. 29206, f. 211.
[2] Letters dated 24 July and 10 Aug. 1760. *CPC*, I, 280–2, 325.

CHAPTER 3

THE INVOLVEMENT IN POLITICS, 1760–1763

Reza Khan's appointment as Faujdar of Islamabad committed him to politics: only success in politics could ensure his survival. Yet the appointment was an ambiguous one. Reza Khan himself described it as a favour done by Mir Jafar on account of his relationship with the Nawab Alivardi Khan. But the invasion of the Emperor Shah Alam and the concurrent swing in public opinion in favour of the ousted family were to lead the Nawab and Miran to eliminate many Alivardians on suspicion of disloyalty. Between January and June 1760 three favourites of the former regime, Shah Abdul Wahab Khan, Yar Muhammad Khan and Agha Sadiq, son of Agha Baqar, a Dacca zemindar, were all executed.[1] As the alarm of Miran and his father grew, the imprisoned aunt and mother of Siraj-ud-daulah were also killed near Dacca.[2] Ghulam Hussain says that Miran had another 300 suspects on his list for physical elimination after his return from Bihar.[3] Why then was Reza Khan appointed?

One answer may be that Reza Khan's known enmity towards Mir Qasim had made him more acceptable, for Mir Qasim was already a suspect by the beginning of 1760, though not yet an open rival of Miran. While Miran was striving to make himself independent of the English, recruiting European deserters,[4] creating a large body of Rohilla-Afghans,[5] sending missions to the Deccan

[1] They were officers of Siraj-ud-daulah. Agha Sadiq or Sadaqat Muhammad Khan was engaged by Siraj-ud-daulah to murder Husain uddin Khan who ruled at Dacca for and on behalf of his uncle, Husain Quli Khan, who again was deputy of the nominal Naib Nazim, Nawazish Muhammad Khan. After the murder, Agha Sadiq fled to Murshidabad, but the infuriated supporters of Husain uddin murdered his father Agha Baqar and brother Mirzai. Mirzai's Taluq Lakshmipur was given to the English in 1757, while Agha Sadiq's estate in Bakarganj came under Hastings' administration in 1758. Agha Sadiq, like Shah Abdul Wahab, was blown off from the mouth of a gun (*Seir*, II, 123, 332; Hastings Papers, Add. MSS. 29096, ff. 21, 38; *India Tract* 378; 44).
[2] *Seir*, II, 368–71; *India Tract* 378; 54.   [3] *Seir*, II, 367.
[4] Hastings to Clive, 3 Oct. 1758. Add. MSS. 29096, f. 45.
[5] *Seir*, II, 279.

to recruit there and make contact with the French,[1] Mir Qasim was cultivating Hastings's friendship. Again while Miran was seeking to eliminate Rai Durlabh's influence in internal administration, and to substitute that of Keneram, Munilal and Rajballabh, whose well-established influence in Dacca was a barrier to the growth of English power in the area, the English were seeking to push Mir Qasim into the Patna post, by persuading Ram Narain to move to Murshidabad as Rai Rayan.[2] The attempt to advance Mir Qasim only increased Miran's hostility. Hastings wrote to Caillaud in July 1760, Mir Qasim 'has been recommended, strongly recommended to the Nabob by the Colonel [Clive], Mr Holwell and yourself, the consequence of which has been that both the Nabob and his son became his enemies and plotted his destruction'.[3]

Reza Khan's appointment may also be viewed as a banishment. The death of Miran on 3 July 1760 by lightning—or by machinations of Mir Qasim or the English as rumour had it[4]—brought Mir Qasim to power. On Miran's death the Nawab's starving soldiery, throwing aside restraint, insulted the Nawab's mutasaddis (secretaries) in the streets, and surrounded the Nawab's palace. It was Mir Qasim who restored order, by advancing three lakhs of rupees to the troops and standing surety for payment of the rest of their arrears of pay.[5] Though Miran's minor son Mir Saidu was officially invested in his father's offices,[6] it was Mir Qasim who became *de facto* Diwan. With Mir Qasim at the head of Murshidabad administration there was clearly no place for Reza Khan near the person of Mir Jafar at the capital. Banishment to Dacca was the common fate of those out of favour, appointment to the more remote, politically inconsequential and economically unrewarding Faujdari of Chittagong, was even more effective.

But, it might be asked, why give any post to him when he was out of office? While part of the answer lies in the fact that until the revolution in October 1760 Mir Jafar and not Mir Qasim had the final say in all matters and that the Nawab was already thinking of putting Mirza Daud, the Safavid prince who was betrothed to

---

[1] Hastings to Clive, July 1758. Add. MSS. 29096, ff. 17–20.
[2] Hastings to Holwell, no date, April or May ?? 1760. Add. MSS. 29096, ff. 233–4. The scheme failed, it is not known why. Perhaps Ram Narain declined.
[3] Hastings to Caillaud, July 1760. Add. MSS. 29096, f. 267.
[4] *Seir*, II, 370 fn., 194.
[5] Hastings to Fort William, 18 July. BSC, 28 July 1760.
[6] Mir Jafar to Governor, recd. 8 July 1760. *CPC*, I, 272.

33

The transition in Bengal, 1756–1775

Miran's daughter, at the head of administration,[1] the main reason of the arrangement may have been the persistent demand of the English for the removal of Agha Nizam from Chittagong; also, links had been recently established between the Khan and the English. The previous Thanadar, Agha Nizam,[2] who succeeded the Diwan Mahasingh in 1165 B.S. (1758–9) and was confirmed in 1166 (1759–60)[3] had fallen foul of the English. They had been very anxious to open a factory at Chittagong, but when in October 1758 Samuel Middleton was sent there from Lakshmipur by the Calcutta Council, Agha Nizam had refused him permission, because his parwana from Mir Jafar was addressed to Mahasingh and not to him.[4] In November, Verelst and his Council at Lakshmipur wrote angrily that Agha Nizam was throwing every impediment on their way, and that the Thanadar and his durbar 'had determined not to permit the English to purchase cloth in his country'.[5] Agha Nizam also proved a stickler for legality over the concurrent question of the grant of Taluqdari rights of the Company in Lakshmipur.[6] With the accession of Hastings's influence at Murshidabad upon the rise of Mir Qasim's power in government, the opportunity had arisen of removing Agha Nizam and of replacing him by Reza Khan. Some time before October 1760, therefore, Reza Khan became the Faujdar of Chittagong.[7]

Reza Khan's Chittagong appointment did not last long. The Company had long had its eye on Chittagong.[8] Rebuffed in 1758 by the Nawab, Scrafton had commented that Chittagong 'will require a season when we can command instead of requesting'.[9]

---

[1] In October 1760, being asked by Vansittart to name the person whom he considered the most proper to head the administration, the Nawab named Mirza Daud first and then a few others including Mir Qasim (Hastings's note on the Transactions at Muradbagh. Add. MSS. 29198, f. 7).

[2] The name is also given as Nazim. The designation varied with its holder.

[3] *CDR*, I, 170.   [4] BPC, 26 Oct. and 27 Nov. 1758.

[5] BPC, 27 Nov. 1758   [6] BPC, 28 June 1759.

[7] In Feb. 1760 Reza Khan was in the Nawab's camp at Suri (*CPC*, I, 269) and on 10 Aug. Vansittart wrote to him for supply of boats at Dacca (*CPC*, I, 326) when obviously the Khan was at Dacca, perhaps on his way to the new post. Jasarat Khan, and not Reza Khan, was the ruler in Dacca during 1757–60.

[8] The Company's earliest recorded interest may be dated from Dec. 1683 (Forrest, *Clive*, I, 281), which was renewed by Heath's attempt to capture it in 1688 (*ibid.*, I, 288). After Plassey, the Directors showed their interest again in their letter to Bengal, dated 3 March 1758.

[9] Scrafton to Hastings, 23 Dec. 1758. Add. MSS. 29132, f. 60.

34

The involvement in politics, 1760–1763

Holwell, when he was governor, had again applied for Chittagong, but Mir Qasim replied that 'Islamabad was not in the gift of the Diwan', being a jagir of Mir Falouri, Mir Jafar's second son.[1] When Vansittart took charge, he re-opened the matter in August 1760 when the Rai Rayan, Umid Rai, was in Calcutta, negotiating a settlement of the Nawab's outstanding debts and the reversion of the assigned districts of Nadia and Burdwan to the Nawab. Umid Rai, perhaps a large sharer of the lavish bribes distributed by Kasinath,[2] offered to use his influence to secure for the Company both a factory and the grant of Chittagong and Sylhet as their Faujdari.[3] On a further approach to the Nawab there was again a refusal.[4] Meanwhile, with Miran's death, Hastings became busy securing confirmation of the headship of the administration in Mir Qasim's hands in opposition to Rajballabh, who was now seeking confirmation as Mir Saidu's Diwan[5] and his eventual succession to the masnad in supersession of Mir Saidu's claims. As he put it, the choice was between two men, 'the Nabob Cossim Allee Cawn [Mir Qasim] and Maharaja Rajebullub, for it can hardly with propriety be asserted that the dispute any ways regards the infant [Mir Saidu] who has been nominated to that honour'.[6] Caillaud backed Rajballabh, urging that a 'Gentoo' was more to be trusted than a Muslim.[7] Hastings recognised the force of the argument and of its practice under Alivardi's rule, but nevertheless backed Mir Qasim. It was sound policy never 'to leave the Nabob without a subject for his jealousy to feed on and inculcate in him a due sense of dependence on the English alliance', and Mir Qasim was such a subject.[8] He reinforced the case for Mir Qasim by pointing out that he could secure Chittagong for the Company, and indeed privately 'declared himself ready to use all his influence to that effect'.[9] Secret discussions with Mir Qasim followed, by which he was assured of English support on Mir Jafar's death,[10] and the post of Naib Subahdar at once, and

[1] Hastings to Governor, no date (July ??) 1760. Add. MSS. 29132, f. 110.
[2] He negotiated for the Company to secure the Zemindari sanad for 24 parganas and spent Rs. 67,067 for his expenses at the Durbar (Add. MSS. 29096, f. 110).
[3] BSC, 1 Sept. 1760.
[4] Vansittart to Mir Jafar, 18 Sept. CPC, I, 458.
[5] Hastings to Caillaud, July 1760. Add. MSS. 29096, f. 267.
[6] Hastings to Governor, no date. Add. MSS. 29132, f. 103.
[7] Hastings to Caillaud, July 1760. Add. MSS. 29096, f. 267.   [8] *Ibid.*
[9] Hastings to Governor, no date. Add. MSS. 29132, f. 110.
[10] Vansittart's evidence in 1767. Add. MSS. 18469, f. 5.

35

he in turn promised to grant to the Company the Chittagong, Midnapur and Burdwan districts for the maintenance of their troops, in aid of the Nawab. Implementation of the secret treaty was enforced in October by a demonstration of English troops. Mir Qasim was installed as Naib Subahdar, with all powers of the Nizamat,[1] and Mir Jafar left for Calcutta in self exile, where he abdicated a few months later.[2] Mir Jafar to the end had resisted the grant of Chittagong,[3] which was nevertheless duly handed over by Mir Qasim to the Company in jagir.

The revolution of 20 October undermined Reza Khan's new position as Faujdar of Chittagong. Soon after the changes at Murshidabad, Vansittart had written to Reza Khan to continue collecting the revenues, though now for the Company.[4] But his continuance in office was now temporary, for a Council, consisting of Verelst, Randolph Marriot and Thomas Rumbold, with Walter Wilkins as assistant, was created,[5] and a force, consisting of two companies from Calcutta and another from Dacca, was prepared in late November, ready to take over the charge of the district.[6] The Fort William Council were not at all sure how the Khan would react to his deposition. In Midnapur and Burdwan, the other two new Company districts, there was opposition to the change. The Raja of Burdwan and the Faujdar of Midnapur, summoned to Calcutta, failed to come. Two requests to Mir Qasim by 15 November to compel them to obey had produced no effect, and ultimately military action was necessary in both districts.[7] The creation of a military force for Chittagong reflected the Company's fear that Reza Khan, too, would resist the change.

[1] See secret treaty. BSC, 27 Sept. 1760 and BPC, 10 Nov. 1760.
[2] Vansittart to Mir Qasim, 20 Dec. 1760. *CPC*, I, 717.
[3] Hastings's note on transactions at Muradbagh. Add. MSS. 29198, f. 4.
[4] Vansittart to Reza Khan, 19 Nov. 1760. *CPC*, I, 588.
[5] BPC, 8 Nov. 1760.
[6] BPC, 17 Nov. 1760.
[7] Not only did Tilokchand, the Raja of Burdwan, not pay any heed to the orders of the Governor but it was also reported that he had fled with his family to the jungles (BPC, 17 Nov. 1760). The Raja was afraid of losing his estate since in 24 parganas the English had dispossessed the former owners (Holwell's evidence in 1767. Add. MSS. 18469, f. 19). Misri Khan apparently gave a quiet possession to Johnstone when he was sent to Midnapur, but he soon joined Tilokchand in Burdwan. Capt. White engaged them, killing 500 of the 'enemy' in Dec. 1760 (BSC, 5 Jan. 1761). For Johnstone, trouble was created by Rajaram, whom Clive once protected against Mir Jafar (BSC, 9 Feb. 1761).

The involvement in politics, 1760–1763

As the Council said, they felt 'uncertain as to the disposition of the Nabob of Chittagong in respect to the delivering up the possession of that country'.[1] The fears proved groundless, for the Khan replied to Vansittart's letter of instruction with professions of obedience and of great attachment to the Company.[2] When in December Vansittart wrote again, asking him to wait on Verelst at Chittagong,[3] Reza Khan was in Tipperah engaged in a punitive expedition, but Verelst, on his arrival at Lakshmipur on 21 December, found another submissive letter from the Khan which induced a confidence in him to enter Chittagong 'in perfect peace'.[4] The Khan left the expedition in Tipperah to his Diwan, Ram Mohan, and joined Verelst at Sitakund, 24 miles from Chittagong, on 1 January 1761, entering the city with him four days later.[5] The English had occupied the district 'without molestation',[6] and by the middle of February 1761 the Khan had already rendered a full and satisfactory account of his stewardship for the Company.[7] He then left for Calcutta, Karam Ali reports, for discussion, apparently with Vansittart.[8]

In his six weeks with Verelst in Chittagong, the Khan had established a very close friendship with Verelst. He had also contrived to cause a dispute between the English and Mir Qasim—over the expenses of the Tipperah expedition—which lasted throughout Mir Qasim's period as Nawab (1760–63).[9] Mir Qasim complained that Reza Khan had endeavoured to obtain a post, the Faujdari of Tipperah, by force, or the appearance of it—a view Hastings put to Vansittart;[10] the Khan would have argued that he was driven by Mir Qasim's action in granting his district to the English without providing for him elsewhere. It might have been argued that the grant of jagir of the district to the Company did not *ipso facto* terminate the Khan's Faujdari authority in the district[11]—

[1] BPC, 17 Nov. 1760. [2] Reza Khan to Vansittart, recd. 16 Dec. CPC, I, 700.
[3] Vansittart to Reza Khan, 28 Dec. 1760. CPC, I, 738.
[4] Verelst's letter, 22 Dec. BPC, 29 Dec. 1760. [5] CDR, I, 143–4.
[6] Letter to Court, 5 June 1761. [7] CDR, I, 156. [8] MN, f. 127.
[9] This was one of the 11 items of demand handed to Mir Qasim by Messrs Amyatt and Hay just before the declaration of war (CPC, I, 1778 A).
[10] Hastings to Vansittart, 16 June 1762. Add. MSS. 29098, f. 58, p. 113.
[11] Verelst did not take up Faujdari authority of criminal justice until after he was directed to do so by the Fort William authorities. He applied to Calcutta on 6 June 1760 (CDR, I, 178) and was asked in reply dated 24 June to 'exercise the same authority in your cutcherries as we do in ours' (CDR, I, 20). In Calcutta the Mughal subject did not come under English criminal jurisdiction until Aug. 1758 (BPC, 3 Aug. 1758).

37

but the English practice in Calcutta, the twenty-four parganas, and more recently in Midnapur suggested very clearly that the English would take over the political authority as well. It might equally be argued that Mir Qasim had not intended any personal hostility to Reza Khan—but his action in depriving the Khan's elder brother of his post of Hakim strongly suggested that he was at enmity with the family.[1]

What is certain is that it was after he had been told of the transfer of Chittagong to the English that Reza Khan, late in 1760, had invaded Tipperah, and that he had imposed a two anna cess on Chittagong revenues to defray the cost of the operation.[2]

Krishna Manikya,[3] the Raja of Tipperah against whom the expedition was undertaken, had been in charge of the administration only for the previous two years,[4] and he seems to have used the confusion caused by the revolution at Murshidabad to withhold payment of the revenues. He had engaged to pay Rs 1,00,001 for the year 1167 (1760–61) and it is clear from Marriot's report of 5 April 1761—virtually the close of the revenue year—that even by that date he had paid nothing.[5] Reza Khan had good cause for despatching his Diwan to Tipperah, and for marching himself when the Raja refused to surrender.[6]

But he acted without Mir Qasim's authority. It is not certain that any prior sanction was needed for mobilising his troops, for even according to the then current notion of the Faujdar's function, it was his special business to keep the zemindars in check 'but in case he attempted to resist...to attack him immediately' so as to oblige him 'to wear in his ears the ring of obedience, as well as to carry on his shoulder the trappings of submission'.[7] Imposition of a cess to meet the needs of a specific purpose was also a time honoured practice. In any event it was deemed by him no less legal than the general increase that he effected in the revenue

---

[1] Mir Qasim had deprived Muhammad Husain Khan of his Hakim's post, ostensibly to reward Saiyid ul Mulk Asad ullah Khan who had cured his son, but on the Saiyid's refusal gave it to one Mukarram Ali (*TM*, 474).

[2] Verelst's letter, 3 Jan. 1761. *CDR*, I, 143.

[3] About June 1761 he sought to create further complications in the Anglo-Nawab relation by offering to the governor the lease of the district. Vansittart was not totally opposed to the idea (*CPC*, I, 1203 and 1212).

[4] Previous to that the district was under Shamshir, a Faujdar (*CDR*, I, 13).

[5] Marriot to Chittagong Council, 5 April 1761. *CDR*, I, 13.

[6] Vansittart to Mir Qasim, 10 March 1761. *CPC*, I, 1008.

[7] *Seir*, III, 176–7.

38

demands in the district. Since 1713–14 about four rupees had been added to the original demand of one rupee by previous Thanadars and Diwans.[1]

What caused the dispute was the English interpretation of their right under the jagirdari sanad to all the revenues of the assigned land as though the district were ceded territory.[2] The role of the English as jagirdar was quite new and Reza Khan can scarcely have foreseen the quarrel his action would cause. All the same it served his purposes very well.

It did so, too, because on 3 January 1761, Verelst wrote to the Fort William authorities suggesting that the conquest of Tipperah initiated by Reza Khan would be a valuable acquisition for the Company.[3] Calcutta, now keen to acquire further territory, responded very favourably,[4] and on 24 February Verelst ordered Lieutenant Mathews to reduce the Raja 'to a state of obedience to the government of Islamabad'.[5] Marriot was sent from the Chittagong Council on 15 March to settle and receive the Tipperah revenues,[6] and by the 26th he had reached Nunagarh, the Raja's residence near Comilla, and forced the Raja to submit.[7] The Raja was made to sign two agreements: in one he agreed to pay the original revenue of Rs 1,00,001, together with Rs 45,463 to pay for the charges of the troops, and in the other to pay a Salami or Nazarana of Rs 1,11,191-6-3, both in thirteen monthly instalments.[8]

Meanwhile Reza Khan had gone to Calcutta to present his case to Vansittart, supported by Verelst's recommendation. The outcome had been that on 10 March Vansittart had written to Mir Qasim asking him to appoint Reza Khan as Faujdar of Tipperah and promising that the Khan would pay, through Verelst, the revenues contracted for by the Raja.[9] The Nawab did

---

[1] The land which paid R. 1 in Mir Hadi's time paid Rs. 5-5-10½ in Reza Khan's time. Reza Khan's contribution in this increase was 6 annas 4¾ gandas. The two anna cess was a further addition (*CDR*, I, 155, 169–80). 20 gandas make an anna and 16 annas a rupee.

[2] The Company had a different interpretation when they paid Clive a fixed sum for his jagir of 24 parganas.

[3] *CDR*, I, 143. The operations in Tipperah were by then placed under orders of the Chittagong Council.   [4] Fort William letter, 20 Jan. 1761. *CDR*, I, 3.

[5] *CDR*, I, 158.   [6] *CDR*, I, 159.

[7] Marriot's letter 26 March 1761. *CDR*, I, 9.

[8] The second agreement was made out for fear of incurring the Nawab's displeasure (*CDR*, I, 9). It is not known why 'displeasure'.

[9] Vansittart to Mir Qasim, 10 March 1761. *CPC*, I, 1008.

not receive this with a good grace, rather he replied asking Van-sittart to direct Verelst to re-instate the Raja, despite his 'mis-conduct'. He followed this up with instructions that Verelst should instruct the Raja to wait on Jawan Mard Ali Khan, one of the old, non-political servants of the government, as the new Faujdar of Tipperah.[1]

The appointment of Jawan Mard Ali Khan annoyed Vansittart. He characterised the Faujdar-designate as 'capable of nothing but creating disturbances',[2] he repeated his plea for Reza Khan, and he asked for the transfer of Tipperah to the English. These suggestions were turned down by the Nawab, and, though the dispute lingered on until July, the Nawab made it clear that he could not transfer the district to the English without grave dis-credit.[3] Since Vansittart was the person most keen to establish the influence and credit of Mir Qasim, whom he had helped to instal as Nawab, he could not persist further in his demands. On 5 July, therefore, he ordered the Chittagong Council to hand over Tipperah to the Nawab's people.[4] By 10 August the orders had reached Marriot at Comilla.[5]

The dispute about payment for the military expenses incurred continued, however, and this, political rather than economic, formed one of the eleven final demands made upon Mir Qasim before the outbreak of war between the Nawab and the English in 1763. The English position was unreasonable—their military action could properly have been thought of as part of their obliga-tion as jagirdar of the three districts including Chittagong,[6] and in any case they had demanded payment of the expenses from the Raja and had received at least one instalment of Rs. 10,000.[7]

[1] Mir Qasim to Vansittart, recd. 2 April 1761. *CPC*, I, 1067, and 1069. Jawan Mard appears to have been a Nawabi officer in another Tipperah campaign of 1729 (*Bengal Nawabs*, pp. 5–7).
[2] Vansittart to Mir Qasim, 23 June 1761. *CPC*, I, 1230; to Rai-Rayan 14 July. *CPC*, I, 1258.
[3] Mir Qasim to Vansittart, recd. 18 July 1761. *CPC*, I, 1263. Vansittart, on 20 July, while concurring with the Nawab, asked him to reconsider the matter (*CPC*, I, 1266). On 24 July he wrote again asking the Nawab to honour the Khan with 'a post worthy of him' (*ibid.*, I, 1268), but in a reply received on 3 Aug. he was informed that the Nawab had appointed another man as Faujdar of Islamabad (*CPC*, I, 1282). Reza Khan was formally dismissed.
[4] *CDR*, I, 21. [5] *CDR*, I, 23.
[6] Mir Qasim referred to this condition in a letter recd. 7 July 1763 (*CPC*, I, 1813).
[7] By 5 April Rs. 10,000 was received by Marriot (*CDR*, I, 13). Unless the Raja had defaulted by July 1761 a sum of Rs. 46,003 should have been collected from him according to agreement (see *CDR*, I, 9).

The involvement in politics, 1760–1763

Reza Khan had been at the root of all the disputes which had arisen between the Nawab and the English over the district of Tipperah. Intentionally or not he had caused Mir Qasim a great deal of trouble, and as a result the Nawab's enmity was confirmed. But the Khan won the admiration of those Englishmen with whom he came in contact, and this was to prove of the greatest value to him.

Reza Khan was particularly fortunate in having had Verelst to deal with, as first chief of Chittagong, rather than Ellis or Sumner, who had both refused the post.[1] Verelst was a critic on principle of the revolution which had brought Mir Qasim to power. He had opposed Vansittart's action as a breach of 'a treaty executed in the most solemn manner'[2] with Mir Jafar. He had done so before he became, like the overwhelming majority of the Company's servants in Bengal, a personal critic of Vansittart. Since he had disliked the manner of Mir Qasim's elevation, he already had common ground with Reza Khan. The Khan's 'prudent and polite behaviour',[3] and the quality of his administration of Chittagong further won Verelst's regard. Verelst even advised the governor and the newly formed Committee of New Lands to seek the Khan's advice in matters of land grants and other allied subjects.[4] Reza Khan's full co-operation in making Verelst master of the detail and history of the revenue administration of the district,[5] a six week task, laid the foundations of a very stable personal friendship between the two. It was with Verelst's commendation and an excellent reputation, therefore, that Reza Khan went to meet Vansittart at Calcutta.[6] He too became a friend of the Khan, his protector and his strongest advocate.

Vansittart's first efforts to secure a post worthy of Reza Khan failed when Mir Qasim refused to appoint him Faujdar of Tipperah. It ended ultimately in his formal dismissal from the nominal appointment which he held till July 1761 as Faujdar of

[1] BPC, 8 Nov. 1760.   [2] *Ibid.*
[3] Hastings to Vansittart, 15 May 1762. Add. MSS. 29097, p. 58.
[4] *CDR*, I, 180.
[5] H. Verelst wrote a short account of revenue history of Chittagong in 1761. (*CDR*, 169–80). He much appreciated the usefulness of these and when the scheme of supervisorship was introduced in 1769 his instruction to the young officers was to collect information on history of the districts.
[6] Mir Qasim complained later that the Khan went to Calcutta without his knowledge or permission (Hastings to Vansittart, 16 June 1762. Add. MSS. 29098, f. 58).

The transition in Bengal, 1756–1775

Chittagong.[1] But the Khan's action in securing payment by the Nawab of Rs. 65,000 which he had collected at Chittagong and paid into the Nawab's treasury, before he had heard of the district's transfer to the English, encouraged Vansittart to further effort. Mir Qasim, in the beginning, had denounced the Khan's 'false accounts'[2] and urged the governor not to 'listen to his lies',[3] but the Khan was able to prove his point in the presence of Batson, the chief of Kasimbazar factory and Umid Rai, the Rai-Rayan, so that the Nawab had to admit the authenticity of the Khan's accounts.[4] He did so grudgingly and was very slow in paying what the English held to be their due.[5] By contrast Reza Khan, indebted for a sum of Rs. 10,591 when he left Chittagong, paid the amount as soon as it was asked for.[6] The result of these incidents was further to establish the Khan's standing. They also opened a way to good relations with Batson, one of the severest English critics of Mir Qasim. Of course they also put an end to hope of receiving preferment for Reza Khan, who passed his days at Murshidabad, with occasional visits to, and correspondence with, Calcutta.[7]

That Reza Khan had no part in Mir Qasim's administration became increasingly an asset, however, for the revolution of October 1760 steadily became the focus for the discontent which had its origin in Vansittart's coming from Madras to head the government at Fort William. The Company's servants in Bengal, headed by their most senior member, P. Amyatt, looked upon Vansittart's arrival as a blow to their interests. Their dislike of Vansittart came to be extended to Mir Qasim who was looked upon as Vansittart's creature. A suspicion that Vansittart had privately gained by the revolution only sharpened the ill feeling. Mir Qasim attempted to isolate the two issues and to win Amyatt's support by sending Ghulam Husain, the author of the *Seir*, to Calcutta.[8] Ghulam Husain had been very friendly with Amyatt

[1] Mir Qasim to Vansittart, recd. 3 Aug. 1761. *CPC*, I, 1282.
[2] Vansittart to Mir Qasim, 5 March 1761. *CPC*, I, 992. Reza Khan to Vansittart, recd. 16 Dec. 1760. *CPC*, I, 700. Mir Qasim to governor, recd. 16 April 1761. *CPC*, I, 1091.
[3] Vansittart to Mir Qasim, 22 April 1761. *CPC*, I, 1104.
[4] Vansittart to Reza Khan, 27 May, to Rai-Rayan, 23 June 1761. *CPC*, I, 1188, 1231.
[5] Mir Qasim to Vansittart, 18 July 1761. *CPC*, I, 1263.
[6] The Khan was asked to pay S. Batson (*CPC*, I, 1054) and so he did (*CPC*, I, 1188).
[7] *CPC*, I, 1188, 1629.   [8] *Seir*, II, 412.

at Patna, but in the end he was told that since Vansittart had elevated Mir Qasim to the masnad and declared himself his protector, Amyatt could only side with Mir Jafar and Ram Narain.[1]

Two issues particularly roused antagonism against Mir Qasim and Vansittart: the fate of Ram Narain and the duty free trade of the Company's servants. Clive had steadily protected Ram Narain against Mir Jafar, and Vansittart, initially, had continued that policy, ordering Carnac, in February 1761, to remember Clive's promise to protect Ram Narain's 'person, fortune and honour',[2] and Coote, in April,[3] to secure him in his government. By 20 June however, English protection was withdrawn,[4] after Mir Qasim had put his accounts under examination by Rajballabh,[5] who eventually succeeded Ram Narain in the Naibat,[6] in August. By September Ram Narain had given a bond for fifty lakhs of rupees which had been adjudged due from him.[7] Vansittart supported the Nawab because the treaty obliged him not to protect any of the Nawab's subjects against his master and because it was very essential to enable the Nawab to fulfil his financial obligations, but to the critics it was an act of betrayal—the abandonment of one who had served the Company well and had been assured of its protection. This was even more resented because, by the end of 1761, it became apparent that the Nawab's growing strength was detrimental to the interests of the private trade of the Company's servants and their native dependents and servants. Ever since 1752, when the Company's purchases had been taken from the hands of the established coterie of dadni merchants (merchant contractors) and entrusted to the English servants of the Company, acting through their gumashtahs, the problem of trade had been growing. The gumashtahs, mainly Bengali Hindus, had increased the privileged trade of the English, particularly the private trade of the

[1] *Seir*, II, 416–17. [2] BSC, 9 Feb. 1761.
[3] BSC, 21 April 1761. [4] *CPC*, I, 1229.
[5] Mir Qasim to Vansittart, recd. 8 and 16 June, 1761. *CPC*, I, 1208, 1220. From examination of accounts it became necessary to dismiss Ram Narain, for otherwise accounts or appearance of collectors could not be enforced (Mir Qasim to Vansittart, recd. 16 and 18 June, 1761. *CPC*, I, 1220, 1227).
[6] Rajballabh, charged by Hastings in 1762, as the 'chief author' of disputes between the Nawab and the English (letter to Vansittart, 27 May) was replaced on 25 June 1762 by Nobit Roy (Add. MSS. 29097, pp. 77–8; 29098, pp. 135–6, 141, 152–3).
[7] Vansittart approved it in a letter to Mir Qasim, 21 Sept. 1761. *CPC*, I, 1331.

Company's servants; with consequent loss to government revenues and to those merchants who did not enjoy the protection of the English. This was one cause of the clash with Siraj-ud-daulah, and though Mir Jafar had declared the gumashtahs of the English entitled to all the privileges granted in their imperial sanads,[1] the invasion of the internal trade of the province by the Company's servants and their agents soon became a cause of conflict with him too. While Clive was in Bengal some check was placed upon this new extension of privilege,[2] but on his departure English pressure increased. Hastings bluntly complained to Holwell, in February 1760, 'we have been at the expence of so much blood and treasure to little purpose, if we are to be bound by the precedents drawn from the abject state in which we remained before the battle of Plassey'.[3]

Vansittart's policy of strengthening Mir Qasim called, however, for a reversal in such attitudes. By mid 1762 Hastings, as Resident at Mir Qasim's durbar was speaking of a grievance 'which calls loudly for redress', but meaning this time 'the oppressions committed under the sanction of the English name' which 'bode no good to the Nabob's revenues, to the quiet of the country or honour of our nation'.[4] Criticism of Vansittart's policy here enlisted the strongest personal interests of the Company's servants. By October 1762 the Dacca factory was already preparing for war, on the ground of the 'general insolence of the natives, with interruptions put upon the trade in general'.[5]

A further threat to the private trader of the English was also seen in the power and influence of certain Armenians in Mir Qasim's government, notably the brothers Gregore and Petruse. Petruse had been a key figure in the revolution of 1757, as the link between Watts and Mir Jafar; Gregore[6] was equally important in the revolu-

---

[1] Mir Jafar's sanad dated 27 July 1757. BPC, I.O., Range 1, vol. 30, pp. 9–10.
[2] 'We have not ... any right to trade in salt and betel nut ... I myself know that none of the Comp's servants, not even the Col. [Clive] himself has ever engaged in it without the Nabob's perwanah' (Hastings to Sumner, no date, but about Jan. 1759. Add. MSS. 29096, f. 112). While Mir Jafar favoured Hastings and Sykes and Nandkumar as Hugli Diwan favoured a few others with passes for sending up salt to Patna (Add. MSS. 29096, ff. 45, 46, 58) the activities of the servants of Dacca factory caused too many complaints (Hastings to Sumner, 8 Dec. 1758. Add. MSS. 29096, f. 80).
[3] Hastings to Holwell, 19 Feb. 1760. Add. MSS. 29096, f. 224.
[4] Hastings to governor, 25 April 1762. Gleig, *Hastings*, I, 107–8.
[5] Dacca Cons., 7 Oct. 1762.
[6] In India he was known as Gurghin Khan and not as Gregore.

tion of 1760.[1] Hastings argued that Gregore was a useful instrument who, 'whether considered as a creature of the Nabob or a dependent of the English, must see that his interests and safety depended upon the Nabob's welfare and a good understanding between him and the English'.[2] Hastings, however, had long had a trade connection with Petruse to whom he was heavily indebted even as late as 1770.[3] Others, notably W. Ellis, had found the Armenians, merchants and officers, a source of serious rivalry and opposition to their private trade, especially in Bihar opium. They saw their power at court in a far from favourable light.[4]

The Armenians were equally the subject of general hatred by many of the old officers of government, for the fall of many Nawabi officials after the revolution of 1760 was attributed to their influence. As Scrafton put it, 'the power of the Armenians is one of the coffee-house arguments made use of to raise the mob against the revolution in favour of the present Nabob'[5] Mir Qasim.

There was not, perhaps, a single group of old ruling class and aristocracy which had not suffered from the revolution: the three principal mutasaddis, Keneram, Munilal and Chikan, who were imprisoned on charges of embezzlement and made to disgorge their wealth;[6] Ghulam Husain Khan, long Darogha of the Nawab's Hall of Audience[7] and a revenue farmer;[8] the principal Jamadars or army leaders in Bihar, many of them in service since Shuja Khan's time; Umid Rai, the Rai-Rayan; Ram Narain, the Naib of Patna; Rajballabh of Dacca; Raja Sitaram;[9] and indeed most of the old

---

[1] Hastings' note on Transactions at Muradbaug. Add. MSS. 29198.
[2] Hastings to Vansittart, 23 May 1762. Add. MSS. 29098, p. 58.
[3] Hastings to Petruse, 4 July 1770. Add. MSS. 29125, f. 41.
[4] For example Verelst wrote to Clive on 19 Dec. 1764 (after Mir Qasim was driven out from Bengal and Bihar) thus: For Mir Qasim's attempts to shake off his dependence on the English 'we are not a little indebted to that public spy, Coja Petruse, and in some degree to his brother Coja Gregory . . .' Quoted in Forrest, *Clive*, II, 269.
[5] As quoted by Vansittart, 30 May 1762. Add. MSS. 29132, f. 195.
[6] These three anti-English Mutasaddis were the first to suffer (Vansittart's letter 20 Oct. BSC, 24 Oct. 1760; Kalyan Singh's *Khulasat*, *JBORS*, v, 352).
[7] He was a relation of Alivardi who made him the Darogha (*Seir*, II, 393).
[8] It appears that his relations with the English, particularly Scrafton and also possibly Hastings, were not good (Scrafton to Hastings, 28 Nov. 1758. Add. MSS. 29132, ff. 48–50).
[9] The first three were ultimately killed at the outbreak of war with the English (*CPC*, I, 1973) but Sitaram, one of the principal Diwans of the Nawab, was tried and found guilty of treason and executed in 1762 (Add. MSS. 29097, p. 54).

aristocracy of Bengal and Bihar, who were dispossessed of their jagirs, altamghas and other grants in Bihar.[1] The army Jamadars saw themselves directly replaced by Gregore, who was given the principal charge of the Nawab's new modelled army, and whose troops garrisoned the Bihar frontier posts.[2] But, as Hastings observed, 'whatever act of the Nabob's displeases any individual, how many soever will be attributed to Gregore's influence'.[3]

Vansittart agreed with Hastings that any one placed in Gregore's position would have incurred a similar general hostility, and he had no personal objection to the power given to Gregore and Petruse. But he saw the folly of Mir Qasim's behaviour by which 'he exposes his favourites to universal jealousy and disgust by sacrificing all those who us'd to hold the chief places in the country'.[4] Such behaviour weakened the Nawab, for every complaint that the Nawab made against the Company's people could be represented 'as an indirect attempt of the Armenians to get all trade and all powers in their own hands'.[5]

The remedy for Mir Qasim was to 'endeavour to make himself a succession of friends', by giving his favour to a wider circle, including the members of the old privileged class. Vansittart put Reza Khan forward as the sort of person who should be appointed.[6] In 1762, when Sulaiman Beg, Faujdar of Hugli died, Vansittart suggested Reza Khan as a suitable successor, and news that Gregore was 'pushing' for the position only made Vansittart more urgent in pressing the Khan's claims.[7] Mir Qasim's reply was that the Khan's appointment would create jealousies between him and the governor, and that he had chosen Mirza Saleh[8] for the post.

---

[1] The Nawab had 'called in all the Sunnuds most of which he destroyed' (Rumbold's letter, 6 July. BSC, 21 July 1767).
[2] Hastings to Coote, 14 May 1762 (Add. MSS. 29097, p. 52), to Vansittart, 23 May 1762 (Add. MSS. 29098, p. 55).
[3] Hastings to Vansittart, 10 June, 1762. Add. MSS. 29098, p. 102.
[4] Vansittart to Hastings, 2 May 1762. Add. MSS. 29132, ff. 172–3.
[5] *Ibid.*   [6] Vansittart to Hastings, 12 April 1762. Add. MSS. 29132, f. 143.
[7] Vansittart to Hastings, 2 May 1762. Add. MSS. 29132, ff. 172–3.
[8] Mirza Saleh, not to be confused with his namesake who was governor of Orissa, was a merchant who suffered owing to English 'reprizals against the Moors' in 1756–57 (BPC, 3 April 1758). Both Clive and Watts agreed to Mir Jafar's request that the Mirza should not be disturbed from his hereditary lands south of Calcutta when the district was made over to the English, but the Council disagreed (BSC, 4 Jan. 1758). The dispossessed Mirza was then given a share in Jessore Zemindari by Mir Jafar and put in possession by Clive (Add. MSS. 29132, ff. 48–50). This later became the endowed estate of Muhammad Moshin.

The involvement in politics, 1760–1763

Vansittart refused to accept the argument, and he was suspicious that Mirza Saleh was only a cover for Petruse or Gregore.[1] Hastings pressed Reza Khan's claims again, on 14 May 1762. The Nawab refused to consider them, declaring that the Khan, who had a family claim to Subahdari, was disaffected and would be continually engaged in plots against him, 'without appearing openly in them'. To appoint him at Hugli, in the neighbourhood of Calcutta, would be 'to nourish a snake in his bosom'.[2] Mir Qasim thus closed the question. In the process he succeeded in winning Hastings to his own view of Reza Khan, so that Hastings wrote to Calcutta upholding Mir Qasim's attitude and condemning the Khan.[3] It may be that the hostility which Hastings displayed against Reza Khan after his return to Bengal as governor in 1772 had its origin in this episode.

Mir Qasim may have been right in his judgement of Reza Khan's loyalty, but his rejection for office was one more step in the process of isolating himself from the old holders of power and making himself, much to Vansittart's regret, dependent on 'one or two new men of a different nation and religion'. Before the final rupture with the English in 1763 he went to destroy the military potential of the powerful zemindars of Bengal and Bihar, notably Raja Asad uz zaman Khan of Birbhum and his kinsman Kamgar Khan, with English help; to drive Mirza Daud, the Safavid prince, to take refuge with Batson at Kasimbazar;[4] to stiffen the confinement of the sons of Sarfaraz Khan at Dacca;[5] and to raise the banker Bulaqidas as a counterpoise to the house of Jagat Seth.[6]

[1] Vansittart to Hastings, 7 May 1762. Add. MSS. 29132, ff. 177–8, 195–6.
[2] Hastings to Vansittart, 15 May 1762. Add. MSS. 29097, pp. 57–60.
[3] Hastings to Vansittart, 23 May and 16 June 1762. Add. MSS. 29098, pp. 52, 53, 113.
[4] This led to Batson's dismissal (Court's letters, 8 Feb. and 1 June 1764).
[5] Skukr ullah Khan particularly was 'extremely suspected' by Mir Qasim (*Seir*, II, 439). Mir Qasim was evidently alarmed by the moves of Shuja-ud-daulah of Oudh to replace him by Mir Jafar, sons of Sarfaraz Khan or a person 'from the presence'. Whatever might have been the truth behind the story, the Nawab was evidently alarmed by a report to this effect from the Nawab Salar Jang (Salar Jang's letter to Mir Qasim, 1762. Add. MSS. 29099, ff. 43–4).
[6] At the commencement of his war with the English the Nawab had both Jagat Seth Mahtab Chand and his brother Maharaja Swarup Chand murdered. Twelve years later Mir Qasim, in a letter to Hastings from his exile, wrote in justification that 'fate led me to despatch to the hells these two wretches, who had destroyed a world and whose cunning manoeuvre and intrigues caused the death of so many Subahdars'. In the same letter he also justified the des-

47

The transition in Bengal, 1756–1775

The field was thus steadily cleared for Reza Khan. When Mir Qasim was defeated and driven into exile, and Mir Jafar restored in July, 1763, Reza Khan stood out as an obvious candidate for high office, uncompromised by his past actions either with the old nobility or the English.[1]

truction of the leading Mutasaddis, 'so many traitorous usurpers and fomenters of strife'. (Mir Qasim's letter. *BPP*, LVII, 19).
[1] Rai Durlabh and Nandkumar had fallen in February 1761. The plotting against the Nawab Mir Jafar, a virtue in Holwell's day, had become a crime when Hastings and Vansittart decided to strengthen Mir Qasim in that office. Hastings's long standing dislike of Nandkumar, dating perhaps from 1758, led to Nandkumar being the main sufferer then and in 1762. Nandkumar became also a cause of dispute between Coote and Vansittart. Carnac, a critic of Vansittart, became Nandkumar's main support after Coote had left. For special proceedings against Nandkumar in 1761 and 1762 India Office records, Range 168, vol. 16 (31 Jan.–19 Feb. 1761) and vol. 17 (31 July–4 Oct. 1762), may be seen.

CHAPTER 4

THE NAIBAT AT DACCA, 1763-1765

The restoration of Mir Jafar to the Subahdari of Bengal in 1763 opened the prospect of a new career for Reza Khan. Mir Jafar was proclaimed Subahdar at Calcutta on 7 July[1] and a declaration of war was made against Mir Qasim for alleged open acts of hostility to the English.[2] The declaration invited 'all manner of persons' to the standard of Mir Jafar and to assist him in defeating the designs of Mir Qasim. By 15 August Reza Khan had reached Dacca to take up his new appointment as Naib Nazim or Deputy governor.[3]

Though the Dacca appointment was a very high distinction Reza Khan was not initially very enthusiastic about it. Two main reasons made it unwelcome to him: the fear of the machinations of Nandkumar against him, and the disorders and confusion at Dacca.

Nandkumar had become the principal minister of Mir Jafar immediately on the latter's restoration. Despite a very strong personal dislike of Hastings and Vansittart for Nandkumar the English had to agree to the Nawab's demand for his appointment.[4] Mir Jafar was insistent, possibly, because Nandkumar, besides being a fellow sufferer since Vansittart's arrival in 1760, and his secret agent working against Mir Qasim's nizamat,[5] was, to him, an expert on the English in Bengal. With a war in hand against Mir Qasim the English had to oblige Mir Jafar, particularly because the number of alternatives had also been reduced by Mir Qasim. Mir Qasim, 'the best Mutseddee in his own court' had taken away with him to Bihar 'every Mutseddee and every officer in whom he

[1] The declaration of war, 7 July 1763. *CPC*, I, 1814.
[2] *Ibid*. The declaration of war followed the death of Amyatt, who was alleged to have been treacherously murdered by Mir Qasim. Haji Mustapha who made an enquiry on the matter gives a different story. Muhammad Taqi Khan had arranged a party in Amyatt's honour and had sent two envoys inviting Amyatt to the shore, but Amyatt refused to accept the General's invitation. After this Amyatt's boatmen were ordered to bring the boats to the river bank. This order was answered 'by two musket-balls, and then by a volley'. Boats were boarded and slaughter followed (*Seir*, II, 476, fn. 251). Before this incident Ellis made a surprise attack on Patna fort in June (*Seir*, II, 471-4).
[3] *TP*, I, 190.   [4] BSC, 7 July 1763.   [5] *BPP*, XIII, 105.

The transition in Bengal, 1756–1775

could repose the least confidence'[1] and he trusted none. With the turn of events going against him he had had them all physically eliminated. The mutasaddis so removed were Ram Narain of Patna, Rajballabh of Dacca, Rajballabh's son,[2] and the Rai Rayan Umid Rai. In the circumstances the English tolerated Nandkumar as the Nawab's minister but sought to minimise the evil by forcing Rai Durlabh into the Nawab's camp. Nabakrishna[3] was also with the Nawab, as he left Calcutta, a further check on Nandkumar. Nabakrishna joined the camp, apparently, as Major Adam's munshi or Persian secretary. But though the English had started interfering in the selection of the Nawab's officials, they did not seem as yet to have done more than recommend Reza Khan in general terms to the Nawab. The lack of interest on the part of Vansittart; the Khan's strongest supporter so far, was inevitable. The disputes with the Council's majority over relations with Mir Qasim's government had added to his frequent nervous complaints the fatigues 'which have been and are the severer upon me' as he complained in his letter of 18 April 1763 to the Directors, asking to be permitted to return home the next season.[4] By early July his spirits had revived by private reports that 'the Compy. have resolved to support the authority of the governor—and that they will write in a manner to give me satisfaction. But alas! all is too late; the news concerning Mr. Amyatt's party...is too shocking to write'.[5] The declaration of war against Mir Qasim spelled the ultimate frustration of his mission in Bengal. Vansittart certainly was in no mood to commend Reza Khan to the Nawab with any enthusiasm.

Reza Khan, lacking any definite English protection, was reluctant to accept office while his enemy Nandkumar held sway over the Nawab, and seems to have viewed the Dacca post almost as a trap. Reza Khan later claimed to have been a partyman of Mir Jafar, as witness the advice of his elevation to the Subahdari which

---

[1] Hastings to Vansittart, 23 May 1762. Add. MSS. 29098, pp. 57–8.
[2] He was Krishnadas, who contributed to the rupture between Siraj-ud-daulah and the English in 1756. He appears to have been in charge of Dacca revenues in Mir Qasim's time where by July 1762 the deficiency had risen to over 20 lakhs, about 5 lakhs being attributed to the exactions of the English (Hastings to Vansittart, 23 May, 10 July 1762. Add. MSS. 29098, pp. 56, 153–4).
[3] N. N. Ghose, *Maharaja Nubkissen Bahadur*, p. 25. He founded the Sovabazar Raj family.
[4] Vansittart to Court. 18 April 1763.
[5] Vansittart to Hastings. Add. MSS. 29132, f. 245.

The Naibat at Dacca, 1763–1765

Mir Jafar took care to send him.[1] But the Nawab initially intended the Dacca post for Muhammad Ali Beg, to whom a Khilat had been given by Vansittart by 10 July at the Nawab's desire.[2] It was only after Mir Jafar reached Murshidabad on 24 July that the arrangement about Dacca was reversed and the Khan was chosen for the post.[3] Reza Khan later explained the change as due to Nandkumar's jealousy of the good relations between Mir Jafar and Reza Khan, established when they met at Murshidabad.[4] When Dacca was offered, the Khan, therefore, at first declined the post, telling the Nawab that he preferred to accompany him.[5]

The Nawab insisted, however, that the Khan should go to Dacca, bring the zemindars of that extensive province to obedience 'by mildness and good management' and collect revenues in order to help the war efforts against Mir Qasim. Reza Khan, aware that Nandkumar's 'chief object was to place me at the greatest distance possible from the Nawab's person', persisted in his refusal. He made the fact that the affairs at Dacca were in a state of utmost confusion, and that four months of the revenue year had already elapsed, the grounds for a refusal really based on the danger of becoming 'a subject for calumniators to work upon'. The Nawab thereupon used English mediation, and Major Adams on behalf of the Nawab pleaded with Reza Khan, assuring him that he did not foresee any 'grounds of variance between him [Mir Jafar] and me'. At the next meeting with the Nawab the Khan 'was obliged to acquiesce', but even then he did not readily depart for Dacca. The army which was moving up against Mir Qasim left Murshidabad on 28 July and the Khan accompanied the Nawab up to Sooty despite the Nawab's directions to proceed immediately to Dacca. The Khan's purpose was to secure a written agreement from the Nawab to protect him from any future disputes which might arise because of Nandkumar's presence in the Nawab's camp. During a prolonged halt at Sooty lasting until 2 August, forced on Mir Jafar and Major Adams by the opposition of Mir Qasim's army,[6]

---

[1] Reza Khan's memorial, *TP*, I, 190.
[2] Vansittart's letter, 10 July. *CPC*, I, 1817.
[3] The date given by Reza Khan is 10 Muharram (*TP*, I, 190) but the letter to court dated 23 Sept. 1763 puts Mir Jafar's entry in Murshidabad on 24 July.
[4] In response to the Nawab's appeal for help, Reza Khan had offered 'all the money, effects, camels and elephants which I possessed' (*TP*, I, 190).
[5] The account of Reza Khan's appointment is taken from *TP*, I, 190–4.
[6] It was called 'obstinate' and 'uncommon'. Letter to Court, 23 Sept. 1763.

4-2

The transition in Bengal, 1756-1775

Reza Khan secured his written document. On Mir Jafar's again asking him to leave for Dacca the Khan presented his written memorial for the Nawab's concurrence. Nandkumar sought to prevent the Nawab from signing the document and asked the Khan to leave this with his vakil at the Durbar for more thought on it. At this point, however, Mir Jafar intervened, rebuked Nandkumar for causing an unnecessary altercation and finally signed the memorial after writing down the answers to the Khan's demands in his own hands.[1]

The document, which eventually helped the Khan's acquittal in his trial in 1772-4, embodied four demands from the Khan. In the first article the Khan covered himself by limiting his financial obligations, irrespective of the formal agreement for a stipulated sum, to the amount of the actual collections, 'until the disturbances are at an end'. By the second article, the Khan had the former establishment of the Dacca force of 'horse and foot' confirmed. By the third article the Nawab was bound not to entertain any application for any Dacca post, and by the last article the Nawab agreed to allow the usual expenses of servants wages (Sihbundy), collection charges (Seranjamy) and contingencies (Lawazimat) agreeably to the accounts.[2]

Having thus secured himself against any possible harassment or interference, and having received permission to restore the Dacca establishment to its former strength the Khan returned to Murshidabad and on 11 August set out for Dacca, where he arrived four days later.[3]

The Khan's fear of intrigue behind his back at the durbar was not the only reason for his demand for a free hand in Dacca. His complaint that the administration was in disorder and confusion really was an understatement. In fact there was no government at all in Dacca by 1763.

The attention of the Murshidabad government had long been concentrated on North Indian developments. Later the developments in and around the European trading centres along the Bhagirathi also attracted notice. But very little attention was paid to the eastern province of Dacca. The result was that immediately after the revolution of 1757 the Dacca Faujdar, Jasarat Khan, for

[1] Reza Khan's memorial. *TP*, I, 193.　　　[2] *Ibid.* I, 202-4.
[3] After return from Sooty the Khan was at Murshidabad for 4 or 5 days (*TP*, I, 194).

52

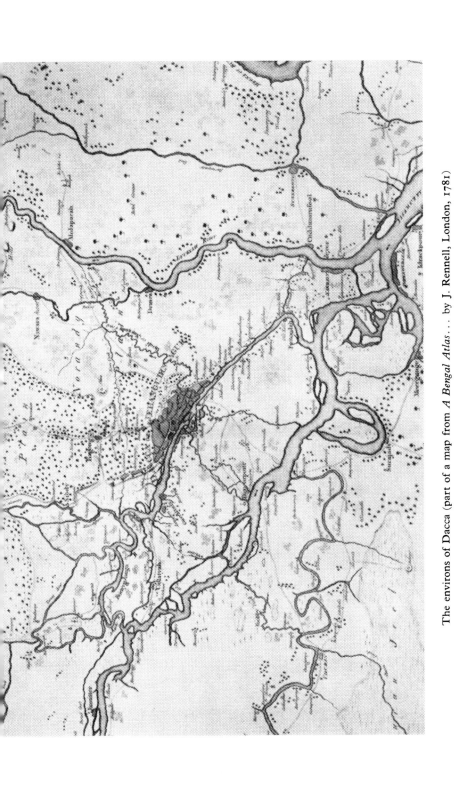

The environs of Dacca (part of a map from *A Bengal Atlas* . . . by J. Rennell, London, 1781)

The Naibat at Dacca, 1763–1765

want of adequate troops and credit was obliged to ask for and obtain the support of a company of English sepoys from Calcutta in order to guard against any attempt by Amani Khan, one of the sons of Sarfaraz Khan, to seize the Dacca fort.[1] The Dacca administration lost further prestige in 1758 when a sort of a joint administration was set up, besides the grant of Lakshmipur, within its territorial jurisdiction, to the English as a Taluq. The joint administration ended early in 1759, but by then instances of successful and often violent defiance to governmental authority by the Company's servants and their dependents had become so common that the government had ceased to enjoy much respect. Its diminished prestige was further reduced by the grant of Chittagong to the English in 1760 and by the prolonged English interference in Tipperah in 1761. By April 1763, more than two months before the formal declaration of war upon Mir Qasim, his Naib in Dacca, Muhammad Ali Beg, together with Agha Nizam, Saiyid Badal Khan, Qamar Ali and the Faujdar of Rangamati[2] had been imprisoned by the English. The managers of the administrative machine were thus swept away in April, and the machine itself was largely destroyed by the English occupation of Dacca city. (The Company's factory had been abandoned on 7 July and a panic flight to Lakshmipur had followed, but with the arrival of troops the Dacca Council had decided to take Dacca.)[3] On their return to the city on 17 July the Council decided to try to run the government 'in the name of our honourable masters'. But when the sons of Sarfaraz Khan, the Shahr Amin who maintained order in the city, and several other principal Mughals, had all been taken prisoner, the Council soon found that they could not manage the administration of so large a district by any English agency. *Ad hoc* local assistance had to be sought. The Hindu mutasaddis, or chief officers, of the late Diwan and Shahr Amin and one Agha Saleh were found to be willing to accept the task of governing. A person had also been appointed on behalf of the Company, a sort of a Resident to sit at the cutcheri and ensure that the new officers were not negligent in the discharge of their duties. Guards were also provided to protect the native officers from insults.[4] Scarcely

[1] BSC, 20 Oct. 1757. The English feared French attack from the sea.
[2] Letter to Court, 18 April 1763; Mir Qasim to Vansittart, recd. 30 April 1763. *CPC*, I, 1756.
[3] Dacca Cons., 11 July 1763.   [4] *Ibid.* 20 July 1763.

53

had this makeshift organisation been brought into existence, when on 23 July Mir Jafar's restoration as Subahdar was proclaimed. Agha Saleh, the governor for the Company, took the occasion to secure the release, upon his own surety, of the imprisoned Mughal nobles, but they were confined to their houses, while two companies of Barqandazes or matchlockmen occupied the city for the Company.[1] Outside the capital the control of the province was shared by Mir Qasim's officers and the English. Verelst from Chittagong had taken the Mughal administrative divisions of Tipperah and Sandwip into his hands besides establishing his grip over the Shiqdaris of Homnabad and Patira (Pattikera ?), both in the modern Comilla district, which continued until the end of 1763 or early 1764.[2] On the other hand Abid Ali Khan, Mir Qasim's Faujdar at Rangpur, held out until four companies were sent against him in November 1763 and the Zemindar of Babupur remained defiant until his reduction in February 1764.[3]

This was the situation when Reza Khan reached Dacca in mid-August 1763, a situation, as he said, 'even worse than it had been before reported'. All the officers of revenue had absconded. Also the accounts and records were not to be found in their proper repository.[4] Immediately after Muhammad Ali's arrest and transfer to Calcutta in April some of the zemindars had run away and others were evading payment.[5] The Khan, in 1773, explained the disorders with an economy of truth by putting the blame on the 'disturbances of the Sonnasies' (Sanyasis) and unstated 'other causes'.

At least one of the 'other causes' was certainly the commotion created by Thomas French, a servant of the Company at Dacca. A week before Reza Khan's arrival, the Dacca Council took note of various complaints against French 'who in opposition to our majority voices, asserts his right of sending for any man whom he suspects to have stolen his effects'. The matter was all the more serious because French was exercising his assumed rights principally on higher officers of the government. A. W. Senior, then chief of the Dacca factory, failed to secure the release of Gorachand, a

[1] Dacca Cons., 23 July 1763.
[2] Mir Jafar's letters, recd. Oct. 1763 and Jan. 1764 (*CPC*, I, 1899; BSC, 21 Jan. 64) also Dacca letter. BSC, 16 Jan. 1764.
[3] Dacca Cons., 9 Nov. 1763; BSC 10 Jan., 16 Jan., 8 Feb. 1764.
[4] *TP*, I, 194.
[5] Muhammad Saleh to Muhammad Ali (April 1763). *CPC*, I, 1755.

The Naibat at Dacca, 1763–1765

Naib of the Shahr Amin. Consternation became general after French had put three principal officers of the Subahdari into confinement under some pretext or other, obliging the Diwan to ask Senior for a special guard for his 'head Moorey' or head clerk and driving Senior and Ralph Leycester to resolve on giving protection to all officers of the government.[1] French, justifying his conduct, denounced the majority for showing 'extra-ordinary lenity and respect...to the very people who had taken up arms against us and some of them too inveterate enemies to the English' and declared 'it has always been customary here...for any member of the factory to secure any person who he suspected had rob'd or defrauded him'.[2] The dispute had not ended when the Khan arrived at Dacca to find his office totally deserted and the records untraceable.

A yet bigger problem was to secure the retransfer of the districts under the occupation of the English, particularly of Verelst. It seemed too delicate a matter to demand them directly from Verelst and the Khan therefore asked the governor Vansittart for letters to the gentlemen of Dacca, and Lakshmipur and also to Verelst directing them to assist him. Vansittart complied with the Khan's request and sent the letters for use when necessary.[3] The Khan's extreme cautiousness in dealing with the English may also be traced in his care to secure from Major Adams a letter to the chief of the Dacca factory, on 3 August, asking the latter to deliver up to the Khan 'all the state prisoners and effects of the country government'.[4] The Khan thus had the support of Calcutta, and Vansittart certainly welcomed the Khan's posting to Dacca.[5] French was reproved for his actions, and with John Cartier's arrival as chief at Dacca in November 1763, Reza Khan's problems must have been eased locally.

But while Verelst continued in occupation of many districts of the Dacca Naibat until early in 1764, Reza Khan's position re-

---

[1] Dacca Cons., 8 Aug. 1763.
[2] French's minute, Dacca Cons., 12 Aug. 1763.
[3] Vansittart to Reza Khan, 6 Sept. 1763. *CPC*, I, 1862.
[4] Major Adams to Fort William, 10 Aug. 1763. *BPP*, VI, 248.
[5] It appears that Vansittart was more interested in appointments near Calcutta (*CPC*, I, 1846) and had even appointed one Ahsanullah Khan at Jessore (*CPC*, I, 1842). About Dacca he had no say (*CPC*, I, 1830) but welcomed the Khan's appointment (*CPC*, I, 1838). Spencer's Council, however, claimed that the Khan's posting to Dacca was obtained through English solicitations 'tho with the Nabob's also' (letter to Middleton, BSC, 13 Dec. 1764).

mained very delicate. It seems that one move proposed by or through the Khan to secure the early return of the districts was for Sandwip to be given to the Company.[1] The Khan also sought the English favour by paying money to them at Dacca without waiting for the Nawab's orders. Such moves, however, exposed the Khan to the 'insinuation of some designing person', for the Nawab wrote rather warmly to Vansittart, about the districts retained by Verelst and about the money paid to the English without his orders, both in October and again in December.[2] At the same time two letters written by Reza Khan to Mir Jafar reporting the English failure to restore the occupied districts were forwarded to Vansittart, perhaps with the intention of sowing discord between the Khan and the English.[3] If this was the intention, the scheme failed, for Vansittart, very correctly, refused the suggested offer of Sandwip and so disarmed the possible criticism in Mir Jafar's court and also assured the Khan that his enemies could not do him any harm.[4] If the Khan had feared that Nandkumar had been seeking to discredit him with the English, he must have been still further reassured by Vansittart's action in complaining of the appointment of Lahori Mal as Diwan of Hugli and the continuance of Jagat Chand as the Nawab's agent at Calcutta, for both were associates of Nandkumar: the complaints against them were therefore complaints against his enemy, Nandkumar.[5]

Any worries which the Khan may have experienced about his standing with the Nawab or with Vansittart did not prevent him from setting vigorously about his task of restoring the Dacca administration. His first task was to organise his secretariat, and by all possible methods of persuasion, mild or severe, to set his writers and public officers to work. Records had to be built up by collecting all the loose papers available and by connecting and methodising them. The mufassal officers were encouraged by circular letters assuring encouragement and protection.[6] Once the machine was functioning he set out to collect as much money as possible for the prosecution of the war. This was no easy task while

---

[1] *CPC*, I, 1893.   [2] *CPC*, I, 1899, 1903, 1956.
[3] The letters were reports rather than complaints (*CPC*, I, 1957 and 1958). The Khan alleged that he received 'thro the intrigues of Raja Nundcomar orders for the confiscation of goods and imprisonment of several individuals, . . . dependents of the factory . . .' (*TP*, I, 195).
[4] Governor's letters, 5 Oct., 24 Nov. 1763. *CPC*, I, 1893, 1950.
[5] Governor to Mir Jafar, 29 Oct. 1763. *CPC*, I, 1919.   [6] *TP*, I, 194.

The Naibat at Dacca, 1763–1765

the issue of the war was still undecided, for 'no one paid his revenue with alacrity or yielded due obedience',[1] and when the full amount urgently required could not be collected he did not hesitate to borrow money from the bankers and shroffs on his own responsibility.[2]

His efforts in the beginning were mainly directed to collecting money. But when the war against Mir Qasim developed into war against his allies, the Emperor and Shuja-ud-daulah, his service extended to other fields. The increased dimensions of the war rendered the existing strength of the English troops upcountry inadequate to meet the challenge.[3] All available troops had to be rushed to the front, with the result that Chittagong, where three battalions of 600 sepoys each were maintained for the defence of both Dacca and Chittagong,[4] was ordered in March 1764 to forward two thirds of its strength, keeping only eight companies of 60 men each at Chittagong and two at Dacca.[5] The move created an immediate problem for the Khan, for he had to arrange transport.[6] But the large-scale denuding of East Bengal of troops was also fraught with danger, for a 'few idle reports' might create disturbances in the neighbourhood of Dacca.[7] The Khan, prompted by Vansittart but without orders from the Nawab, set about the raising of a large defence force, working in close liaison with Cartier.[8] This effort only ceased when the battle of Buxar on 23 October made it no longer necessary. The bungling of Nandkumar also added to the Khan's war work at Dacca. Supplying provisions for the army in Bihar was Nandkumar's responsibility, but he failed in his task, though to a large extent this was due to much of Bihar having lain uncultivated during the prolonged war. The result was that troop movements were restricted by lack of supplies and Carnac was obliged to return to the Soane river in the Spring of 1764.[9] Vansittart turned again to Dacca for assistance. The Khan

---

[1] *Ibid.*
[2] One lakh so borrowed (*CPC*, I, 1892) from Bulaqidas remained long unadjusted.
[3] Total English strength on 30 Dec. 1763 was 1080 Europeans, 5600 sepoys (BSC, 30 Dec. 1763). Mir Jafar's troops in July 1764 numbered 33,000 men.
[4] BSC, 13 Jan. 1764.   [5] BSC, 29 March 1764.
[6] Vansittart to Reza Khan, 28 March 1764. *CPC*, I, 2128 A.
[7] Vansittart to Mir Jafar, 25 April 1764. *CPC*, I, 2186.
[8] Reza Khan to Vansittart, 24 April 1764 (recd.); Vansittart to Reza Khan, 25 April and 10 May 1764 (*CPC*, I, 2175, 2185, 2223).
[9] Letter to Mir Jafar. BSC, 16 April 1764.

assisted in grain procurement and in the continuous despatch of supplies to Patna from May 1764 until September, when the operation was stopped 'on account of the price being greatly enhanced and the distance rendering it very tedious to be transported...'[1]

By April 1764 the stock of the Khan had risen very high with the English, perhaps by way of contrast with the sharp decline from tolerance to hostility in their attitude towards Nandkumar. Nandkumar had been accepted as Mir Jafar's principal minister in the hour of crisis, but had never been trusted. As the war progressed he was to seem less and less desirable.

The English would have very much wished Rai Durlabh to replace Nandkumar, and that is why he was made a member of the Nawab's camp, almost against the Nawab's wishes. He was left without any employment until December, and was then given the Diwani of the Nizamat, a position of little power while the entire revenue administration conducted through the Khalsa remained under Nandkumar's control. The appointment must be seen as the Nawab's way of expressing his annoyance at Nandkumar's failure to collect more than a fraction of the revenues, rather than any serious wish to favour Rai Durlabh.[2]

Mir Jafar was pressing Nandkumar about the revenue collections because the emperor had agreed to grant a sanad for Bengal as soon as the Nawab paid fifty per cent of the annual tribute of twenty-eight lakhs with an additional five lakhs as Nazarana. The news of this agreement, sent by Rai Durlabh, reached Vansittart on 10 January 1764.[3] Nandkumar may have been implicated in the negotiations for the agreement. He secured his title of Maharaja from the Emperor about this time.[4] Earlier in December Vansittart had been apprised of Shuja-ud-daulah commending Nandkumar to Mir Jafar both on his own behalf and that of the Emperor urging him to make the Raja 'the sole manager of all the affairs of the three provinces'.[5] On hearing the news of the agreement, the Council became even more anxious to establish their control at the Durbar. They had their own claims on Mir Jafar, for the un-

---

[1] Vansittart to Reza Khan, 7 May 1764 (*CPC*, I, 2211) and also BSC, 7 June, 8 Aug. and 17 Sept. 1764.
[2] Rai Durlabh to Vansittart, recd. 10 Jan. 1764. *CPC*, I, 2014; also BSC, 16 Jan. 1764.   [3] *Ibid.*
[4] Hasan Ali Beg to Adams, recd. 7 Dec. 1763. *CPC*, I, 1966.
[5] Shuja to Mir Jafar, recd. 7 Dec. 1763. *CPC*, I, 1970.

The Naibat at Dacca, 1763–1765

defined losses to private trade caused by Mir Qasim's abolition of inland duties on trade, and by the war, and for the cost of the war against Mir Qasim, though this had been declared by the Company and not by Mir Jafar. While these claims were not met they had no wish to see any money go to the emperor, and on 19 January they directed Major Knox to prevent any remittance to the emperor.[1]

The extension of the war, when Shuja-ud-daulah gave protection to Mir Qasim, after he had been driven from Bihar, added fear to the English dislike of Nandkumar. On 3 April 1764 the Calcutta Council advised Carnac to bring about the dismissal of Nandkumar.[2] They recalled the past experience of the man's intriguing dispositions, pointed out his shameful neglect in collecting grain for the army, and voiced their apprehensions that he had 'many connections at so critical a juncture as this, against our government'[3]. This last was the real trouble, for they knew Nandkumar had wide contacts with the North Indian chiefs and with the Emperor. The English were afraid of Nandkumar, and afraid of exciting him 'to form worse designs'. Carnac was directed to have him dismissed, if it could be done immediately; otherwise he was not to divulge the Council's suspicions, which would antagonise both the Nawab and Nandkumar.[4]

On the same day as the Council were sending their directions to Carnac regarding Nandkumar, Carnac at Patna was discussing his suspicions about Nandkumar with the Nawab.[5] Carnac's suspicions were roused by Mir Ashraf who accused the Raja of being engaged in anti-English activities.[6] The Council, on hearing from Carnac, decided that now that public notice of their suspicions had already been taken, Carnac was to press the Nawab for the dismissal of the Raja. As it has always been his custom, they said, 'to endeavour to make himself of consequence with all parties', they became far more apprehensive now that the Raja would take 'every measure for strengthening his interest with our enemies in order to secure for himself an asylum'. In the circumstances the Council decided that they would abandon Rai Durlabh, for whom

[1] BSC, 16 and 19 Jan. 1764.   [2] BSC, 16 April 1764.
[3] BSC, 3 April 1764.   [4] *Ibid.*
[5] Carnac's letter 17 April. BSC, 26 April 1764.
[6] Mir Ashraf's complaint was that Nandkumar was in secret consultation with Mir Qasim, and also that he was secretly advising Balwant Singh of Benares not 'to revolt from his master' Shuja, while it was the policy of the English to detach him to the side of Mir Jafar and the English (BSC, 11 Oct. 1764).

59

they had so long pleaded, if Nandkumar could be dismissed. Carnac was told to accept the sending back to Calcutta of Rai Durlabh if this would induce Mir Jafar to send Nandkumar too.[1] Carnac found the task impossible, without using force and he would not use force 'at this critical juncture'. The Nawab was 'put so much out of temper by this affair', that it had made him incapable of entering into any public business for a number of days.[2] Carnac also came to change his tone about him after Captain Swinton and Dr Fullerton had failed to make the Raja's principal accuser Haji Abdullah produce any proof of treachery.[3] The Council contented themselves, therefore, with installing Batson[4] as Resident at the Durbar, with specific instructions to watch all correspondence and to tell the Nawab that the English would not accede to any treaty he might make unless it met their conditions of the surrender of Mir Qasim, Sombre and the deserters into the English hands.[5]

It was in this atmosphere of bitterness about Nandkumar that the Council thought of Reza Khan for a new service. Bengal was exposed to an enemy thrust across Sarkar Saran, Ballia, Purnea and Rangpur and the Council decided that Reza Khan was the only man they knew who could be trusted to act in conjunction with the English troops north of the Ganges.[6] Their choice was testimony of their appreciation of the Khan's activities as Naib of Dacca. Private and individual regard for the Khan's merit received the official recognition of the entire Council. They hesitated to recommend him to the Nawab, however, 'lest it should increase his jealousy and uneasiness from what has already pass'd concerning Nundcomar'.[7]

Their doubts were well founded for, as will be seen, the Nawab was already at odds with Reza Khan. A certain amount of misunderstanding was inevitable in the circumstances in which both the

[1] BSC, 16 April 1764.
[2] BSC, 26 April 1764.
[3] Carnac's letter 22 April, 16 May 1764. BSC, 7, 10 and 24 May 1764. Haji Abdullah, source of Mir Ashraf's information, was in Mir Qasim's service before joining service under Nandkumar.
[4] The Nawab had particularly complained against Batson in Jan. and Feb. 1764 (*CPC*, I, 2032, 2041, 2058, 2061).
[5] BSC, 29 May 1764. The English demand led to continued hostility with Shuja, who suffered himself to be driven out of his country than to give up Mir Qasim, who was, however, rendered otherwise ineffective.
[6] BSC, 16 April 1764 (letter to Carnac).   [7] *Ibid.*

The Naibat at Dacca, 1763–1765

Nawab and Reza Khan were placed. The Nawab needed money, and more money which the Khan found it difficult to supply, though, as he says, he did not 'slacken in my assiduity but remitted whatever I was able to realize'.[1] On his appointment at Dacca the Khan had found everything in disorder, and since then the economy of the region had received a further blow in January 1764 from excessive floods, particularly in the areas around Lakshmipur, which evidently destroyed the standing crops besides preventing further cultivation. Nandkumar, the Khan later alleged, set out to widen the misunderstanding and estrange the Nawab's affections from him. The orders which the Khan was receiving from the Nawab for confiscating goods and properties of individuals, though designed by Nandkumar to embitter the Khan's relations with the English, resulted actually in further desertions at a time when he was busy in allaying the 'consternation of the zemindars and the people of the town'. The Khan made strong representations to the Nawab against these proceedings, urging the impropriety of the practice. Thereupon Nandkumar maliciously propagated the idea that the Khan was disregarding the Nawab's commands in order to ingratiate himself with the English with a view 'even to the niza-mat', for which the Khan was further alleged to have applied to the Council.[2] The insinuation worked on the Nawab's mind partly because Nandkumar was supposed to know the English, since he had lived and worked with them for a long time[3] and had his son-in-law, Jagat Chand, continuously posted at Calcutta, partly because the attitude of the English towards the Nawab was still unintelligible to him.[4]

Reza Khan was well informed of the developments in the Nawab's camp, possibly through his agent Riza Quli Khan. When, in April or May, he received an order from the Nawab to repair to Murshidabad with all his officers and accounts, not even leaving a deputy at Dacca,[5] he was naturally alarmed. The Khan sought

---

[1] *TP*, I, 194.   [2] *TP*, I, 195.
[3] The Raja's connection with Calcutta may be dated from the time of Alivardi Khan when he took asylum there (*BPP*, XIII, 102).
[4] Mir Jafar's uncertainty about English intentions is seen in a letter which Vansittart received on 17 Jan. 1764 (summary in *CPC*, I, 2025). He complained that the servants of the Company '. . . do everything that is conducive to the ruin of his affairs . . .' He adds 'Mir Qasim was an enemy of the English and yet they conciliated him; while His Excellency who is a true friend of the Company is treated in this manner'.
[5] *TP*, I, 195.

61

Vansittart's advice, but was told not to fail to wait on the Nawab at Murshidabad.[1]

The Khan was to have moved as soon as he heard that Mir Jafar had set out from Patna, but when the latter reached Murshidabad on 24 August 1764 Reza Khan was not there. He had been delayed, he said, 'by the violence of the weather'. But his absence was interpreted by Nandkumar as a proof of his thesis that Reza Khan 'had projects in his head'. The Maharaja's comments, made in the presence of Riza Quli, reached the Khan, who hurried to Murshidabad and almost immediately saw the Nawab. The Nawab received him with the sarcastic remark that he had imagined the interview would take place at Calcutta, but Nandkumar commented that the Khan must surely have brought fifteen or twenty lakhs of rupees with him for the Nawab. The Khan was silent in the face of the Nawab's remarks, but he protested against the taunting demand of the Raja, and offered to place the accounts under scrutiny. Nothing further of importance happened, however, during the Nawab's brief stay at Murshidabad, and on the third day after their meeting the Nawab asked the Khan to wait at Murshidabad until his return, and left for Calcutta. The Khan accompanied the Nawab to Mankura, the first stage of the Nawab's journey down to Calcutta.[2]

The Nawab's departure for Calcutta without settling anything with him worried Reza Khan and his anxiety was increased by the Nawab's inordinate delay there. By October anxiety had developed into real panic. He had not left any responsible deputy at Dacca, for he had neither had instructions to do so nor had he anticipated the delay that was occurring. There were a few persons to look after the fort during his absence, but no one to take charge of revenue administration. The season for collection was passing, and he was apprehensive that the further delay would cause irreparable loss in revenue for which he would be held responsible. The Khan therefore wrote to Vansittart asking to be called to Calcutta to settle his business with the Nawab, or for some other way out of his difficulties to be suggested.[3] The Khan did not write to the Nawab, perhaps because he feared that he was too much under the influence of the hostile Nandkumar.

Reza Khan's letter to Vansittart secured the Nawab's permission

---

[1] *CPC*, I, 2369, 2372.   [2] *TP*, I, 195–7.
[3] Reza Khan to Vansittart, recd. 17 Oct. 1764. *CPC*, I, 2439.

for the despatch of his officers to Dacca, but none for the Khan to go either to Calcutta or to Dacca, though he was assured that the Nawab was well disposed towards him.[1] Reza Khan accordingly arranged to send Ismail Khan[2] and Ram Sankar Roy, the Khan's Diwan, to Dacca to start the work of collection. But by the time they had got away October was almost over, and the Khan repeated his request to be called to Calcutta.[3] There was now an additional reason for a visit; he wished to bid farewell to Vansittart; and to be personally introduced by him to John Spencer who had come from Bombay to succeed him.[4]

The request was refused, possibly because neither Vansittart nor Spencer wanted further to complicate matters between themselves and Mir Jafar. The Nawab, who had always entertained a fear of Vansittart, deferred meeting him to settle financial terms as long as he could, though Spencer, through Nabakrishna, had assured him that everything would be settled to his satisfaction.[5] The Nawab on his arrival at Calcutta on 3 September, however, found himself in a situation he had perhaps never anticipated. He was presented with a heavy demand for money, forty lakhs for the gratuity to the Company and twenty-five lakhs for the troops of the Company and the British King.[6] The Nawab had first been asked for ten lakhs as restitution money for the sufferers, but two or three days after his arrival in Calcutta the demand was enhanced to forty lakhs. At times the Nawab even wondered whether Vansittart was planning to take the government out of his hands, for it was made clear to him that he could not go back to Murshidabad until he had agreed to the English demand. Nandkumar was also used to put pressure on the Nawab, being promised a five per cent commission for persuading the Nawab to agree. Further insults were added to injury by the English, for when the Nawab

---

[1] Vansittart to Reza Khan, 18 Oct. 1764. *CPC*, I, 2440.
[2] We do not know, but maybe this Ismail was Reza Khan's youngest brother.
[3] See Governor's letters to Reza Khan, 6 and 9 Nov. 1764 (*CPC*, I, 2449, 2454).
[4] Spencer joined as Second in Calcutta Council on 24 May (letter to Court 27 Sept. 1764), succeeded Vansittart in November 1764, and was replaced by Clive on the latter's arrival in May 1765.
[5] Nabakrishna's evidence. BSC, 26 Aug. 1766. Quoted in Ghose, *Maharaja Nubkissen Bahadur*, pp. 33–4.
[6] Evidence of Nabakrishna and Nandkumar. BSC, 19, 26, 27, 28, 29 Aug. 1766; Mir Jafar's letter (summary in *CPC*, I, 2455, recd. 10 Nov. 1764); A. C. Roy, *Mir Jafar*, pp. 276–92. Nandkumar later complained that he did not receive his five per cent commission (BSC, 26 Aug. 1766).

agreed to pay forty lakhs for the 'sufferers', another eight lakhs was promptly demanded, this time by Spencer. Vansittart also persisted in protecting his own creature Ahsan ullah Khan, the Amil of Jessore whom Mir Jafar accused of misappropriating Rs. 1,80,000.

In the circumstances Reza Khan's arrival was deemed undesirable. The Khan was assured that the friendship between them was not so weakly founded as to need a personal interview, and that the Nawab would shortly send him back to Dacca.[1] However, the Nawab's return from Calcutta was further delayed as reports of Clive's reposting to Bengal had reached Calcutta and the Nawab anxiously waited for him. Mir Jafar at last returned to Murshidabad sometime in December 1764.

His return brought no comfort for Reza Khan. On arrival at Murshidabad, Mir Jafar formally installed Nandkumar as head of the administration of the country and its revenues. (Rai Durlabh had stayed in Calcutta.) And if Mir Jafar had formerly been insistent in his demands for money, he was even more so now that he owed vast sums to the English. Reza Khan was asked to pay the revenues according to Nandkumar's calculations,[2] which were evidently based on Mir Qasim's exceptional agreement with Muhammad Ali for 1170 B.S. (1763–4) from Dacca, which was for Rs.38,86,242. Of this sum Rs. 29,63,181 had already been accounted for, presumably including the collections before and after the Khan's appointment in 1170 which ended in April 1764.[3] Reza Khan denied responsibility for the remainder as he had not entered into an agreement for any stipulated sum. For the current year of 1171 (1764–5) of which he had already spent several months idly and against his wish at Murshidabad he did not agree to pay more than Rs. 26,19,178, which was nearly thirteen lakhs less than Mir Qasim's demand. Nandkumar was trying to impose the same sum as current demand from Dacca. The Khan only tendered Rs. 3,82,105 as proceeds of the collection for the current year, an obviously inadequate sum.

A few days later the Khan found himself a prisoner. A Chubdar summoned the Khan to see the Nawab and on his arrival at the Durbar, Muzaffar Ali Khan, the Darogha or superintendent of the

[1] Governor to Reza Khan, 9 Nov. 1764. *CPC*, I, 2454.
[2] *TP*, I, 197.
[3] Mir Jafar to Spencer, recd. 30 Dec. 1764. *CPC*, I, 2522.

The Naïbat at Dacca, 1763–1765

Diwan Khana asked the Khan to wait in his office when he apparently went to inform the Nawab. As soon as Muzaffar Ali left, the Khan found himself surrounded by three companies of sepoys under the command of Qaim Beg, the commandant of the Nawab's troops. While the Khan was thus surrounded, the Nawab sent for the Khan's vakil, Riza Quli, and through him sent a draft paper for the Khan to sign. The draft declared that the Khan admitted his indebtedness for a sum of sixteen lakhs of rupees and sought permission to resign his appointment at Dacca on the ground of his proved inability to discharge his duties. The Khan refused to sign and protested that the post was not of his seeking and that he had not contracted for any fixed sum. The Nawab when he heard of the Khan's objection is said to have exclaimed that he did not understand books and accounts: all that he needed was money. The situation of the Khan seemed so desperate that his vakil advised him not to make any further reply. Muzaffar Ali then came from the Nawab's presence and communicated the Nawab's orders, that the Khan was to stay where he was until the matter was settled and that he must be unattended except by an Abyssinian slave and by Riza Quli. The Khan's servants were all sent away and he was forced to pass the night at the Diwan Khana, while guards were placed around the Khan's house in the city. Next day Muzaffar Ali was sent to the Khan with an agreement for a further sum of twenty-two lakhs for the current year for the Khan's signature and sealing. The Khan refused to sign it, but he sent his seal to Nandkumar through Riza Quli for the Maharaja to seal the document if he so liked. Nandkumar refused to seal the document, demanding that this should be done in the Khan's house. The Khan thereupon went personally to Nandkumar and the document was sealed and kept by the Maharaja.[1]

The transactions were no happy experience for the Khan who at one time was even apprehensive for his life. That the matter did

---

[1] *TP*, I, 197–9.

From Reza Khan's own accounts, as verified at the enquiry held at Dacca early in 1774, the Khan had, during the period of 21 months from 11 Bhadra 1170 (August 1763) to the end of Chaitra 1171 (April 1765) collected a total sum of Rs. 35,19,520-11-4-2 and had in addition received a cash sum of Rs. 18,722-15-0 from his predecessor, Agha Saleh, who administered for and on behalf of the Company. The collections and expenditures were both made under two heads, Huzury or King's estates and departments and Nizamat or the Nazim's estates and departments.

65

The transition in Bengal, 1756–1775

HUZURI MAHAL (King's Estates) Total Collection   Rs. 27,91,753- 7- 7-3
Expenses:

Irsala or cavalry of Husain Ali Khan	Rs. 2,18,235- 4-0
Muhammad Husain Khan	76,871- 0-0
Malbous Khas (supplies for royal wardrobe and also for the	
Nawab's wardrobe)	48,505-14-0
Salary of Reza Khan at 7,500 p.m.	1,57,000- 0-0
Cutcheri servants	53,163-12-5
Nawara (boats)	1,360-11-0
Topkhana (artillery)	21,259- 8-0
Contingent charges (paper, oil, etc.)	4,453- 8-17
Belghaur Khana (alms to the poor)	5,700- 0-0
Darul Shafa (hospital)	3,037- 4-0
Rozinadaran (alms to objects of charity)	891- 0-0
Nazar (presents) at Punyah (at Murshidabad?)	9,614- 8-0
Resum (customary payments) to officers of the Khalsa	
(at Murshidabad?)	6,124- 5-5
Hundian (or premium on remittance)	32,013- 0-0
Khilats at Punyah of 1171 (at Dacca?)	41,579-12-3
Allowance to sepoys (of Capt. Grant) for suppressing	
Rajendra, zemindar of Babupur	25,719- 0-0
Allowance to Nazir of cutcherries	3,591- 4-0
Loss of batta (discount) on Arcot rupees	5,859- 3-15
Charges making a road to Tesgong (Tejgaon)	2,580- 4-0

NIZAMAT MAHAL (Nazim's Estates) Total Collection   Rs. 7,27,767- 3-16-3
Expenses:

State Prisoners (Families of Sarfaraz Khan, Alivardi Khan,	
Shaukat Jang, etc.)	65,054- 4-15-0
Writers of the Cutcheri	42,739- 1- 9-1
Jawan Ali Khan, Mushrif or Accountant of the Emarat or	
Building dept.	708- 0- 0-0
Officers of Topkhana (Artillery)	40,396-10- 6-2
Officers of Nawara (Flotilla)	113,654- 9- 8-0
Materials for ornamenting boats	26,380- 2-12-2
Allowances to boatmen posted at Rangamati	6,239-12- 9-2
Dost Muhammad and boatmen of 'Kaus Baur'	1,319- 0- 0-0
Repairs to Rangamati fort	4,800- 0- 0-0
Repairs to Dacca fort	7,511- 2-15-0
Pilkhana (elephants)	61,482-14- 0-2
Magazine of Arms and ammunition	5,038- 9- 0-0
Making charges for guns	40- 1- 0-0
Raja Jugal Kishore, Accountant of the Nawara	5,566- 6-10-0
Contingency charges (paper, oil etc.)	10,691- 0-18-3
Nazar at Punyah (perhaps at Murshidabad)	738- 1-10-0
Boat hire	5,061- 3- 5-1
Cost of cheese sent to Murshidabad	2,432- 0- 3-2
Batta (discount) on Arcot rupees	931- 1-11-1
Langhar Khana (charity kitchen), Rozinadar (daily charity)	
Husaini Dalan, Muharram expenses	8,858- 4-15-0
Paid to Shukur ullah, Jamadar at the English factory	3,043- 9- 0-0
Allowances to Kanuram Harkara (spy)	1,946- 9-15-0
Allowances to Nil Chand and his officers	360- 0- 0-0

not go so far was due, Reza Khan told Governor Spencer, to the arrival of Samuel Middleton as the Company's new Resident at the Nawab's Durbar.[1] In his official instructions for guidance as Resident, Middleton had been directed by the Council to regard it as his duty to protect Reza Khan, since the Council believed that some person or persons about the Nawab were endeavouring to bring about his ruin. The instructions ran: '...you will if necessary remind His Excellency of this our interposition in his behalf, confirming it in the strongest terms...'[2] Middleton had intervened according to his instructions. One day he called both Nandkumar and Reza Khan to the Residency at Muradbagh and it was agreed in his presence that Reza Khan would pay Rs. 26,86,000 as the current year's revenue and another Rs. 1,30,000 for the past year. Nandkumar assured Middleton that he would speak to the Nawab on the matter and draw up papers accordingly.[3]

Since Middleton's arrival the Khan felt secure even if Nandkumar were to play a further game by preventing the Khan's departure for Dacca although a major part of the current year was already over. The Khan was in a difficult position again. Nandkumar did nothing to revise the agreement reached in the presence of Middleton. Perhaps his intention was to cause such arrears in the Dacca collections as would eventually discredit him with his protectors, the English, whose interest, like the Nawab's, was in the maximisation of revenue.[4] The Nawab, at Nandkumar's prompting or from irritation at his ill usage in Calcutta, was sometimes 'urgent' with the Khan, but he evidently had no wish seriously to persecute the Khan, 'an old friend' of his.[5] Reza Khan for his part bided his time, for he understood the Nawab's character. In mid-January 1765 he took the opportunity of the Nawab being in a jovial mood after returning from a hunting expedition to Plassey— the Nawab's last—to secure permission to leave for Dacca with his wife and children. He also obtained a favourable endorsement of his application for a reduction in the rigour of the agreement

During the period of these 21 months remittances to Murshidabad amounted to Rs. 22,34,648-6-5.
Credit balance in Reza Khan's hands stood at Rs. 1,812-12-8-3.
(Based on Dacca Factory Records. India Office, vol. 6, ff. 31–2.)

[1] Reza Khan to Spencer, recd. 10 Jan. 1765. *CPC*, I, 2534.
[2] BSC, 13 Dec. 1764.
[3] Reza Khan to Spencer, recd. 10 Jan. 1765. *CPC*, I, 2534.
[4] Spencer to Reza Khan, 12 Jan. 1765. *CPC*, I, 2538.
[5] Mir Jafar to Spencer, recd. 10 Jan. 1765, *CPC*, I, 2536.

5-2

forced from him by Nandkumar. On the Khan's narration of the circumstances of the Tahood (or agreement) the Nawab wrote in his own hand, 'exert your best endeavours and set your mind at ease'.[1] Thus relieved, Reza Khan left Murshidabad on 24 January 1765 and reached Dacca six days later. The Khan felt such great relief at returning to Dacca that he sent a second remittance of Rs. 20,000 as a token of his gratitude to Spencer, the first remittance of a similar amount having been sent earlier from Murshidabad.[2] The Khan's stay at Dacca was, however, destined to be short. In less than three weeks, on the death of Mir Jafar, he received a call to return to Murshidabad, this time for a higher position.

[1] *TP*, I, 200, 204.
[2] Reza Khan's statement of presents given to Englishmen by him (BSC, 6 June 1765). Senior, chief of Kasimbazar, also claimed that he had protected the Khan (*PP* Third Report, 1772, p. 309).

CHAPTER 5

THE NAIBAT SUBAHDARI
AT MURSHIDABAD, 1765

On Mir Jafar's death Reza Khan became a part of the new political
settlement between the Company in Bengal and the new Nawab.
He was drawn also into the internal politics of rival factions among
the Company's servants. This involvement was ultimately to
prove dangerous, but in 1765 one party was to raise him to power,
another to confirm him in what Hastings later called 'the
sovereignty of this province'.[1]

Mir Jafar died at about noon on Tuesday, 5 February 1765, but
he had already, on 29 January, seated Najm-ud-daulah, his eldest
surviving son, on the masnad with all due ceremony.[2] Shortly
before his death, on the morning of 5 February, the old Nawab
committed his son Najm-ud-daulah, the rest of the family and
Nandkumar to the protection of the governor and Council in a
letter to Spencer. In a postscript, perhaps added after Mir Jafar's
death, Nandkumar, 'your servant' professed his attachment and
obedience to the Company and asked for such kindness from them
as he had received from the late Nawab.[3] The Nawab had also
sent for Middleton, but before the Resident was ready to go to the
killah or fort the Nawab was reported dead and he then, accompanied by George Gray, Captain Stables and S. Droze, went
to attend the installation ceremony of the new Nawab. There, as
the Company's representative, he offered nazr to the Nawab as did
the Jagat Seth[4] and other leading citizens of Murshidabad.

Najm-ud-daulah commenced his rule by publicly assuring the
Resident that 'whatever engagements his father had entered into
...he would strictly adhere to...', and by publicly expressing
the hope that the Company would favour him as they had his

---

[1] Hastings to Court's Secret Committee, 1 Sept. 1772. Add. MSS. 29125, f. 134.
[2] Middleton's letters, 29 Jan., 5 Feb. 1765. BSC, 4 and 8 Feb. 1765.
[3] Mir Jafar and Nandkumar to Spencer, recd. 7 Feb. 1765. CPC, I, 2549.
[4] The Jagat Seth was a hereditary title of the most senior member of the house,
and Maharaja, of the next senior member. After the murder of Mahtab
Chand and Swarup Chand by Mir Qasim the titles came to be held by Khoshal
Chand and Udai Chand respectively.

father. His inaugural speech also contained an expression of appreciation of the attachment and services of Nandkumar whose confirmation in the office he had held under Mir Jafar was also announced. After the Durbar ceremony the Nawab was proclaimed through the city and orders and notices were sent to different parts of the country.[1] To Middleton everything seemed to be in perfect tranquillity,[2] but the authorities in Calcutta had a different view.

Middleton's letter of 29 January reporting Mir Jafar's illness reached Calcutta on 31 January. Spencer's comment was that 'prevention at all times is better than remedy', and, apparently to forestall any possible disturbances or attempt by Shuja-ud-daulah to exploit the situation, he took various measures. Capt. Grant was ordered to stay with Middleton and to take command of the Company's sepoys; other officers were sent to Murshidabad on the pretence of sending them to Monghyr; four companies of troops and a subaltern were ordered from Burdwan to Murshidabad, and Middleton was authorised to detain any officer or detachment of troops that should pass through Murshidabad, if he so desired. The Resident was to keep the governor constantly informed of developments in Murshidabad and to await instructions should the Nawab die. Middleton was also urged to take these measures discreetly, however, so as to cause no umbrage should Mir Jafar recover.[3]

On hearing of the Nawab's death and Najm-ud-daulah's accession Spencer and his Council became more active, and John Johnstone[4] was recalled from Burdwan to help in their deliberations. The Council, on 8 February, reiterated its decision of 31 January to support 'as yet' Mir Jafar's family. They had not decided what the new relations with the Nawab should be, but they were determined on big changes, and believed it was of great consequence to reseat Najm-ud-daulah on the masnad 'in a proper and public manner [so] that he as well as the whole country may see that he receives his government from the Company'. Middleton was therefore directed 'to discourage to the utmost any

---

[1] Najm-ud-daulah also asked his brothers, Saif-ud-daulah or Najabat Ali Khan and Murbarak-ud-daulah, the nominal Nazims of Bihar and Orissa to look upon him as they did upon their father, but it does not appear that he had any message for Mir Saidu, his nephew and son of Miran.

[2] Middleton's letter, 5 Feb. BSC, 8 Feb. 1765.

[3] Spencer's letter, 31 Jan. and 1 Feb. BSC, 8 Feb. 1765.

[4] Chief of Burdwan, member of Council, and later a severe critic of Clive.

The Naibat Subahdari at Murshidabad, 1765

application for Sunnuds for the provinces from any quarter' for though sanads without the Company's backing were not effective 'yet they might in improper hands be sufficiently so to embarrass our affairs'. If any sanad was necessary it should be 'procured thro our influence alone'.[1] This was, of course, no real problem since Shah Alam was already in an English camp living under English protection.

Exactly a week after Najm-ud-daulah had started functioning as Nawab Nazim at Murshidabad, the Council at Calcutta, reinforced by the arrival of Johnstone from Burdwan and Major Hector Munro from up country, took up the succession question. The majority decided to 'permit and confirm' Mir Jafar's nomination of Najm-ud-daulah, despite John Burdett's plea for the succession of Mir Saidu, Miran's minor son. The majority agreed that Mir Saidu had a prior right according to the 'order of succession in Europe'. But Najm-ud-daulah, though born of a slave girl,[2] had been recognised as Chhota Nawab during Mir Jafar's lifetime and as Nawab after Mir Jafar's death. As matters stood, any alteration in favour of Mir Saidu would 'run the hazard of fresh convulsions and parties in the country' while the English were still engaged in a distant war against Shuja-ud-daulah. Another reason against Mir Saidu's succession was the long period of minority rule that would ensue.[3]

Burdett was not reconciled to the majority view. It would seem that in pleading for Miran's son he was pushing the private views of Rai Durlabh, who was desirous of controlling the Murshidabad government, from which he had been successfully excluded by Nandkumar. He therefore characterised the new arrangement at Murshidibad as 'entirely plann'd and executed by Nundcomar, a man so much disaffected to us' and he countered the argument of Saidu's minority by suggesting the remedy, 'our appointing proper ministers to manage the affairs of the government under our inspection'.[4] Whether, in thus suggesting a change of ministers as

---

[1] BSC, 8 February 1765.
[2] Burdett even sought to deny legitimacy of Najm-ud-daulah by describing him as a son of a concubine. The majority called him Mir Jafar's son 'tho not by his married wife'. Najm-ud-daulah's mother, Munni Begum, was a slave girl owned by Mubarak-ud-daulah's grandmother who made a gift of her to Mir Jafar. Unlike a free woman, a slave did not need a formal marriage to bear a child of her master. As soon as she gave birth to a son, she ceased to be a slave, and became an 'ummul walad'. A son so born was as much a legitimate heir as one born of a free woman.   [3] BSC, 12 Feb. 1765.   [4] *Ibid.*

71

well as of Nawabs, he was merely a spokesman for Rai Durlabh is not clear, but we do know that Rai Durlabh had given a note promising money to Burdett.[1] Burdett failed to undo Najm-ud-daulah's accession, but his denunciation of Nandkumar could not be so easily set aside. After Hastings's departure from Bengal the opposition to Nandkumar had weakened, and Spencer and some of the members of the Council seemed prepared to overlook the widely voiced objections to the Maharaja, provided he could recommend himself to them by paying the stipulated money to the Company regularly. The Resident had therefore been ordered, on 31 January, to support the ministers of Mir Jafar in case anything happened to the Nawab.[2] The neutral attitude of tolerating Nandkumar in his present position became almost impossible after Burdett had denounced him in a public document, the more so as the Directors had already declared that 'Nundcomar is a person improper to be trusted with his liberty...', and had made a request to the Calcutta authorities to keep a watch over all his actions.[3]

The adjourned council, when it met again on 14 February, took up the question of new ministers who should be, as Burdett had put it, 'under our inspection'. The Council now resolved to appoint Reza Khan as Naib Subah 'who shall have immediately under the Nabob the chief management of all affairs'. Under him the revenue administration shall be divided between Rai Durlabh and Nandkumar, so that 'their power as near as possible shall be equal'. Two other measures to extend the Company's authority over the Nawab's government were also decided upon: it was resolved to vest the Company's government with power to veto the appointment of any public servant of the Nawab's government and it was decided that the Nawab should have no military force of his own. The Nawab was, however, to be allowed to keep only such troops as were 'immediately requisite for the dignity of his person and the business of his collections'. For the maintenance of the Company's army, as the only defence force of Bengal, the Nawab was to continue to pay five lakhs a month as a permanent assignment which, it was agreed with Mir Jafar only four months before, was to be a temporary measure for the duration of the emergency

[1] Rai Durlabh's note to W. B. Sumner, recd. 5 Sept. BPC, 16 Sept. 1765.
[2] Spencer's letter to Middleton 31 Jan. reiterated by Council, 1 Feb. BSC, 8 Feb. 1765. [3] Court's letter 22 Feb. 1764.

of the war against Shuja-ud-daulah.[1] The idea of the other two measures was not new, either. Vansittart had tried them both with Mir Jafar. As far back as July 1763 Vansittart had asked the Nawab to inform him whenever the Nawab sent any officer into the country so that 'knowing who are His Excellency's friends and who his enemies' the governor could take measures accordingly.[2] Though the then circumstances did not allow the assertion of the principle as a matter of right, there was at least one instance when Vansittart had appointed an amil and sent his appointment for subsequent approval by the Nawab.[3] Mir Jafar had reacted more sharply when, in June 1764, Vansittart had asked him to discharge his troops and rely on the Company's forces or to place his select troops under Carnac's[4] command and again in July to place them under Munro's command[5] and had asserted his independence in matters of Bakshigari, or paymastership and command.[6] The plea used by Vansittart had been the saving of money then spent on useless troops and diverting it to the maintenance of the more effective troops of the Company. The Nawab had answered the governor by awkwardly raising a question about the revenues earned by the Company from the Jagiri districts which were meant to pay for the troops employed in his service.[7] Spencer and his Council were determined not to allow any such freedom to Najm-ud-daulah.[8]

The choice of Reza Khan as Naib Subahdar was an obvious one, given that the Council's intention was to break the power of Nandkumar and to impose upon the Nawab some one more amenable to English control, for the mutual hostility of the Khan and the Maharaja was well known. The move was also necessary to protect Reza Khan. He had repeatedly appealed for protection

[1] BSC, 14 Feb.; Spencer to Court, 14 March 1765.
[2] Vansittart to Mir Jafar, 27 July 1763. *CPC*, I, 1833.
[3] Vansittart to Mir Jafar, 12 Aug. 1763. *CPC*, I, 1842. Mir Jafar confirmed the appointment of Ahsanullah Khan, but not as Amil of Nadia. Mir Jafar posted him to Jessore (Vansittart to Mir Jafar, 22 Aug. 1763. *CPC*, I, 1846).
[4] Vansittart to Mir Jafar, 12 June 1764. *CPC*, I, 2300.
[5] Vansittart requests Mir Jafar to look upon the Mughal cavalry raised by Munro 'as his servants', to pay their wages through Munro, and to dismiss some of his own cavalry (Vansittart's letter, 3 July 1764. *CPC*, I, 2321).
[6] Mir Jafar's letter, recd. 10 Nov. 1764. *CPC*, I, 2455.
[7] Vansittart did not deny the validity of the Nawab's claims. The Jagiri districts, he said, produced about fifty lakhs, but 'the Company's expenses have been doubled in this war' (Vansittart's letter, 25 July 1764. *CPC*, I, 2353).
[8] The majority's minute. BSC, 20 Feb. 1765.

against Nandkumar, who was determined 'to retain his power and crush this man'.[1] The Khan's need for protection was definitely greater after Mir Jafar's death, for despite Nandkumar's enmity Reza Khan could settle his affairs with Mir Jafar, as he did twice, to his own advantage.[2] With the greater influence of Nandkumar on the young Nawab, Reza Khan was in greater danger. Ensuring his security was also a responsibility of the Council, though Spencer may well have been influenced in his favour for private reasons.[3]

Having selected Reza Khan, Spencer had to make sure that the Khan's joining his new post as Naib Subahdar did not prove a risky gamble. Reza Khan later asserted to Johnstone,[4] one of the architects of his new fortune, that he had never wished for the new post, and there is no evidence that any move came from him, and in view of the reports already circulating that Clive was due at any moment,[5] he might well have preferred his safe Dacca post. In order, therefore, to secure Reza Khan against any eventuality it was also resolved by the Council that the Nawab was to stipulate in his treaty with the Company that the Khan could not be removed from his Naib Subahdari without the acquiescence of the Council and that, should it become necessary later to agree to Reza Khan's removal from Murshidabad, he was to be reposted to Dacca, a post which should be guaranteed for him. The consequential arrangement that the Council agreed on was that the Khan should continue to hold his Dacca appointment and that any officer sent there should be told that he held it for the Khan who would have the reversion.[6]

Some such guarantee was necessary, for despite the Council's resolution strenuous efforts were still being made to retain Nandkumar and the existing arrangement. The alarm had been raised at Murshidabad by Spencer's failure to reply to Najm-ud-daulah's letter of 6 February, and by the absence even of any letter of condolence.[7] Nandkumar sent his son-in-law Jagat Chand to

---

[1] The majority's minute. BSC, 20 Feb. 1765.   [2] See chapter 4.
[3] The Khan had paid Rs. 20,000 to Spencer in 1764 when he was called to Murshidabad by the Nawab and another Rs. 20,000 after his safe return to Dacca in Jan. 1765 (Reza Khan's statement. BSC, 6 June 1765). These payments were tokens of gratefulness for Spencer's protection.
[4] Reza Khan to Johnstone, the third letter recd. May 1765. *PP*, 4th Report, 1773, p. 542.
[5] Clive had sailed from Portsmouth in June 1764.
[6] BSC, 14 Feb. 1765.
[7] Najm-ud-daulah to Spencer recd. 16 Feb. BSC, 16 Feb. 1765.

Calcutta to get the existing arrangement approved by the English. The envoy, who held the post of the Nawab's agent at Calcutta, offered eleven lakhs to Spencer for his support for the maintenance of the *status quo* and money was also offered to Leycester and other members of the Council.[1] The offers proved ineffective. However, when George Gray arrived from Malda to take his seat in the Council,[2] Nandkumar proved to have a supporter. Gray dissented from the Council's resolution of 14 February 'from my heart',[3] or, if Clive's later allegation that Gray had received Rs. 25,000 from Nandkumar when he attended Najm-ud-daulah's installation was true,[4] from his pocket. Gray maintained that the Nawab Najm-ud-daulah 'has as little occasion for Mahomed Reza Cawn to help him on account of his youth, as his father had for Meer Cossim on account of his age'.[5] To him Reza Khan was a man of 'aspiring temper' and 'is by no means of a sufficient rank to hold a post which commands such distinguished Mutseddies as the Roy Royon and the Nizamat Duan'.[6] Gray also feared that the Khan would turn out 'all the old officers' put in by Nandkumar whom he designated as Rai-Rayan; and also that he would retaliate on the Nawab for the wrongs he had suffered at the hands of Mir Jafar. Gray was equally opposed to the division of power between Nandkumar and Rai Durlabh as decided by the Council on the ground that it could not be done without altering the form of government.[7]

Gray's opposition only delayed the execution of the Council's proposed measures. The majority asked Gray for an alternative to Reza Khan's appointment, and when he could suggest nothing better than Nandkumar's continuance under the existing arrangement, they brushed his objections aside.[8] The Council then drew up the new treaty, signed it in two copies and despatched a delegation to impose it. This consisted of John Johnstone and Ralph Leycester from the Council, to be joined by Samuel Middleton, the Resident at the Durbar, and A. W. Senior, the chief of Kasimbazar on their arrival at Murshidabad. Johnstone

---

[1] Leycester's minute in Council as given in the appendices to the BSC, 1765 I.O. records, Range A, vol. 6.
[2] Gray was succeeded by Richard Barwell at Malda. He joined Council on 16 Feb. 1765
[3] BSC, 19 Feb. 1765.   [4] BPC, 26 Jan. 1766.
[5] BSC, 19 Feb. 1765.   [6] *Ibid.*
[7] *Ibid.*   [8] BSC, 19 and 20 Feb. 1765.

being named leader of the delegation, the controlling power over the army at Murshidabad was also given to him.[1]

With the arrival of Johnstone and Leycester at Murshidabad on the evening of 23 February the scene of activity shifted from Calcutta to Murshidabad. The Durbar had been much agitated by Spencer's letter of condolence of 11 February which spoke of measures being decided in Calcutta.[2] Agitation became real fear when Spencer's letter of 14 February arrived, with instructions to the Nawab to forward a letter from the governor to Reza Khan and send along with it one from his own summoning the Khan to Murshidabad 'against the arrival of our deputies'.[3] The Nawab's reply was to send Spencer's letter to Reza Khan back to Calcutta with a protest. The argument used was that the revenue year was nearly at an end and that if Reza Khan was called to the capital he would use this as an excuse to evade due discharge of his commitments. Since Reza Khan had so far only paid six lakhs, he should not be called to Murshidabad till the year's end, in two months' time.[4] The Nawab at the same time wrote to Reza Khan directing him not 'to stir from Dacca'.[5] The young Nawab feared that Reza Khan was being brought to Murshidabad to be raised to the masnad; he therefore played for time, in the hope that Clive would soon arrive. It was certainly difficult for him to understand the Council's actions, for he had done all he could to please them by publicly and in writing binding himself to honour all obligations accepted by his father. With the precedent of Mir Jafar's supersession by Mir Qasim before him, and his fears doubtless excited by Nandkumar, his alarm was very understandable.

The delegation met the Nawab on 25 February in a private audience, gave him the governor's message and explained to him the new draft treaty. The young boy of 16 or 17 calmly read the terms, compared them with those which were executed by his father, and signed both the copies. The Nawab had no alternative but to follow the line of least resistance and hope time would bring a change. When the delegation proposed to defer the ceremony of

[1] Instructions to the Delegation. BSC, 20 Feb. 1765.
[2] This was in reply to the Nawab's letter of 6 Feb. which was received by Spencer on 7 Feb. (BSC, 8 Feb. 1765). Spencer wrote on 11 Feb. (*CPC*, 1, 2554).
[3] Governor and Council to Najm-ud-daulah. BSC, 14 Feb. 1765.
[4] Najm-ud-daulah to Spencer, recd. 20 Feb. 1765. *CPC*, 1, 2566.
[5] Delegation's letter 25 Feb. BSC, 28 Feb. 1765. For summary of the Nawab's letter to Reza Khan, *CPC*, 1, 2567.

re-installation of the Nawab until the arrival of Reza Khan, the Nawab readily concurred.[1]

The delay was welcome to all, to each for his own purpose. The Nawab and Nandkumar were fighting to delay a decision until the arrival of Clive and also that of the imperial Sanad, which was to them most essential to give sanction to Najm-ud-daulah's accession. Nandkumar had a private object, for he had to attend the marriage ceremony of his son with Raja Krishna Chandra's daughter,[2] but he also used the time to try Leycester again with money if 'he would but endeavour to keep things in the state they were',[3] and to tempt Senior with five lakhs of rupees' to withhold his favours from Mahomed Reza Cawn'.[4] The English delegation's official reason for delay was that Reza Khan had still to arrive. But they also wished to find out more about the revenues of the province and the 'people most worthy and capable of being entrusted with the management of those branches'.[5] Though Gray's opposition to Reza Khan, and Burdett's preference for Rai Durlabh (who had followed the delegation to Murshidabad), had been overruled, the delegation were in fact still looking for possible alternatives to Reza Khan. Before and after their meeting with the Nawab they were busy reporting to Calcutta on possible candidates: Mirza Eraj Khan, an old Mughal noble, father-in-law of Siraj-ud-daulah, and Mir Jafar's deputy at Murshidabad from 1763; Ismail Ali Khan, another relative, and guardian of one of Mir Jafar's sons;[6] Asad ullah Khan, a Mughal chief of Shuja's army and brought to Bengal by Major Munro.[7] All were dismissed as 'creatures dependent on Nundcomar' and 'from age and weakness utterly unfit for undertaking and conducting so weighty a charge as that of Naib Subah'.[8] Finally even Reza Khan delayed. Spencer had written directly to him to proceed to Murshidabad as well as writing to him by way of the Nawab.[9] But he had also had orders from Najm-ud-daulah not to stir. He took eight days on the way from Dacca to Murshidabad, a length of time which suggests

---

[1] Delegation's letter, 25 Feb. BSC, 28 Feb. 1765.
[2] Delegation's letter, 3 March. BSC, 6 March 1765.
[3] Leycester's minute, BSC. Appendices, I.O. Records, Range A, vol. 6.
[4] Senior's evidence. *PP*, Third Report, 1773, p. 309.
[5] Delegation's letter, 25 Feb. BSC, 28 Feb. 1765.
[6] This least known son of Mir Jafar was Mir Jan.
[7] *CPC*, I, 2544, 2432, 2426.
[8] Delegation's letter, 25 Feb. BSC, 28 Feb. 1765.   [9] BSC, 14 Feb. 1765.

The transition in Bengal, 1756–1775

that his delay was purposeful. He could not disoblige Spencer, he could not disobey the Nawab, and he would not enter Murshidabad until at the delegation's request, Najm-ud-daulah wrote, on 25 February, asking him to hurry to the city. He reached the capital on the 28th.

Even then the installation of the Nawab was delayed for another three days. When it took place on 3 March 1765 it made very plain the power of the Company. Gray had already protested in Calcutta against the ceremony being held up for Reza Khan's coming as a measure which carried 'the appearance of too much respect and consideration for him to the diminution of the Nabob's authority'.[1] Now the authority of the emperor was also publicly lowered.[2] Najm-ud-daulah had applied for the emperor's sanction to his succession, and this had been sent through Shitab Rai and under the emperor's private seal. Nandkumar therefore came to the delegates' headquarters at Motijhil to ask 'whether a tent shou'd as usual on such occasions, be erected without the city, where the Nawab might publickly and with due reverence receive the Perwanna of the King'. Since the delegates had come to make the Nawab take his government from the Company and not from the emperor, they naturally resented the 'impropriety of such a measure' and hurried to the palace to prevent it. As they reported, the Nawab was 'easily convinced' and he 'readily acquiesced in receiving the government only from the Company'.[3] Such slighting of the emperor's parwana must have created abhorrence in the Nawab and among the nobility at Murshidabad, including the Khan. It also created an uproar among the English as well. Carnac refused to obey directions to proclaim Najm-ud-daulah in the camp in the circumstances which he regarded as 'the greatest indignity that could be offered to His Majesty, being directly [opposed] to the constitution of the empire'.[4]

Whatever the private feelings of Najm-ud-daulah or Reza Khan might have been, the Nawab was publicly reinvested as the

[1] BSC, 28 Feb. 1765.
[2] At the same time the English secured sanad for five Northern Sarkars around Muslipatam. The English interest in being kind to the emperor was to prevent M. Law from securing any advantage from him. The French were returning to Bengal after the Treaty of Paris, 1763 (Spencer's letter to Court, 14 March 1765).
[3] Delegation's letter, 3 March. BSC, 6 March 1765.
[4] Carnac's letter, 21 March. BSC, 9 April 1765. For Gray's protest, BSC, 6 March 1765.

The Naibat Subahdari at Murshidabad, 1765

Subahdar of Bengal, Bihar and Orissa on Sunday the 10th Ramzan corresponding to 3 March 1765. On the same day Reza Khan was formally installed in his office as Naib Subahdar.[1] The Nawab conferred, Karam Ali says, the titles of Mubariz ul Mulk (the Foremost in the Kingdom), Muin-ud-daulah (the Eminent in the State), Muzaffar Jang (the Victorious or Triumphant in War) on Reza Khan together with a Khilat of five pieces, a jewelled aigrette, a scimitar, a sword and a male elephant. Titles and similar gifts were bestowed on the Nawab's brothers and friends.[2] Copies of the treaty between the Nawab and the English as drawn up by the Council on 20 February were formally exchanged.[3]

Under Clause Two of the new treaty the Nawab undertook as essential 'for myself, for the welfare of the country and for the Company's business' to have a person 'fixed with me with the advice of the Governor and Council in the station of Naib Subah who shall accordingly have immediately under me the chief management of all affairs'. And 'as Mahomed Reza Cawn the Naib of Dacca', the Clause further read, 'has in every respect my approbation and that of the Governor and Council I do further agree that the trust shall be conferr'd on him and I will not displace him without the acquiescence of those gentlemen'. The Clause further provided that in case of the Khan's removal he would 'be reinstated in the Naibship of Dacca with the same authority as heretofore' provided, of course, that the Khan had 'acquitted himself in his administration'.[4] By Clause Three it was further provided that 'the business of the collection of the revenues shall be under the Naib Subah' and that the English should have the right to object to any mutasaddi or officer and that the Nawab should pay due regard to their objection.[5] Limitations were thus imposed on the power of the Nawab, but Reza Khan had, through the same process, been raised to the highest position short of the Nizamat itself. The Khan acknowledged his gratefulness to Spencer together with a remittance of Rs. 50,000 two days later, on 5 March 1765.[6]

---

[1] Delegation's letter, 3 March. BSC, 6 March 1765.
[2] *MN*, f. 151. Karam Ali appears slightly incorrect. The first of the three titles was a subsequent acquisition, perhaps through Clive and from the emperor (the Nawab's letter, 6 March. *CPC*, I, 2599 and *Seir*, III, 4).
[3] Delegation's letter, 3 March. BSC, 6 March 1765.
[4] BSC, 20 Feb. 1765.   [5] *Ibid.*
[6] Reza Khan's statement. BSC, 6 June 1765.

The transition in Bengal, 1756–1775

The formal exchange of the copies or the treaty, however, did not automatically transfer the control of the administration to Reza Khan. In Gray's language, the delegates seemed 'to find no difficulty in persuading the Nabob to agree to their proposals';[1] trouble arose about actual vesting of authority in the Khan's hands. It became necessary for the delegates again to intervene since neither Nandkumar nor the zemindars and other officers of the Cutcheri who worked under Nandkumar 'made the usual acknowledgements of the Naib Subah'. The Nawab did not consult the Khan and as Nandkumar still appeared as the Nawab's principal adviser the delegates found it again necessary to intervene, and this time in the presence of the Nawab, to make both Nandkumar and the Munshi or secretary understand the limits of Nandkumar's authority.[2]

Parallel to the opposition to Reza Khan went resistance to the delegates' attempts to find out the details of the revenue administration. This was essential if there was to be an equal division of powers and functions between Nandkumar and Rai Durlabh as planned, but, though Johnstone was an acknowledged expert on revenue,[3] they could make no progress. First the Nawab was hostile to the enquiries, 'this slighting treatment',[4] until he was made to see that Johnstone was 'promoting His Excellency's interests'.[5] After Reza Khan had been installed as Naib Subah, Nandkumar and his followers began to throw obstacles in their way. The delegation found there were no proper accounts since the commencement of the war against Mir Qasim in 1763, and when Nandkumar was asked for information they got none. Thus when he was asked about the Bihar revenues he replied that he did not know what was settled and what was collected, and he declared that there were no Bihar papers with him at Murshidabad. The Maharaja shelved his own responsibility and directed them to Raja Dhiraj Narain,[6] who managed the Bihar revenues at Patna. Nor could they get any information on the Rajshahi zemindari which

[1] BSC, 6 March 1765.
[2] Delegation's letter, 7 March. BSC, 16 March 1765.
[3] Johnstone's first experience in revenue matters was gathered in Midnapur. He was posted there in 1760 because of his knowledge of the 'Moors' language (BPC, 8 Nov. 1760). He was later posted to Burdwan another 'ceded' area.
[4] The Nawab's letter, recd. 5 March. *CPC*, I, 2596.
[5] The Nawab's letter to Spencer, recd. 19 March 1765. *CPC*, I, 2608.
[6] Ram Narain's brother rewarded by Mir Jafar (*Seir*, II, 556).

was being supervised by Nandkumar's brother. The central office of the zemindari which was situated at Murshidabad was set on fire on 20 March and all the records were destroyed.[1] The delegates, with Reza Khan's help, were able to make a rough survey, but obstruction caused such delay that they had not completed the division of revenue work between Nandkumar and Rai Durlabh, when a sudden new development threw the whole plan out of gear.

The development was the production by George Vansittart of damaging proof of Nandkumar's enmity towards the English. It will be recalled that there had been two earlier enquiries about Nandkumar in 1764, once early in the year when he was exonerated by Carnac,[2] and again in October when the Council decided that any public enquiry would foment distrust and jealousy in Mir Jafar which, as Leycester pointed out, 'in our dependence on his government for supplies of money to carry on the war, at this juncture may be productive of very dangerous consequences'.[3] The Council did then order private reports from Carnac, Batson, Swinton, Stables and Fullerton on the matter, and another look at Carnac's earlier enquiry. Henry Vansittart, before he left Bengal in November, tried to persuade Mir Jafar again to dismiss Nandkumar, but when Mir Jafar refused the matter was dropped. Now George Vansittart, returning from up country, following his chief Major Munro's relinquishing the command to Carnac,[4] brought new and telling evidence of the Maharaja's questionable conduct during the war.

The issue had been re-opened by Mir Ashraf, an English protégé in Bihar, who had been the original complainant against the Maharaja. The Mir had requested George Vansittart to enquire again into his allegation that the Maharaja had been secretly thwarting the English attempt to detach Balwant Singh from the side of Shuja-ud-daulah and the Emperor, then, with Mir Qasin, at war with the English and Mir Jafar. Mir Ashraf had also alleged that Carnac was prejudiced in favour of the Maharaja.[5]

---

[1] Delegation's letter, 22 March. BSC, 25 March 1765.
[2] 'That Nundcomar's later behaviour has been such as to remove almost entirely the suspicion of his being engaged in treachery, however faulty he may have been in other particulars' (Carnac's letter, 16 May. BSC, 24 May 1764).
[3] BSC, 11 Oct. 1764.   [4] G. Vansittart was Persian Secretary to Munro.
[5] G. Vansittart's report. BSC, 16 March 1765. The enquiry was revived in Oct. 1764 also by Mir Ashraf and at that time through W. Billers. The Mir then had alleged that Carnac had even forced a paper from him stating that Nandkumar was guiltless (BSC, 11 Oct. 1764).

Vansittart accordingly enquired further and learnt from Balwant Singh that Nandkumar had written to him two or three times, and to Shuja some fifty times. This was confirmed by Randolph Marriot on 25 February. Their testimony made more credible an alleged letter from Nandkumar to Balwant Singh, furnished by Mir Ashraf, which read:

'I have had the pleasure to receive your letter by hands of Deendyaul Missir. A treaty is now sent from hence under the care of the said Missir. I who am sincerely your well wisher and look upon your prosperity as my own, write you out of friendship that your revolting from your master and forgetting your duty is contrary to the rules of honour and justice. Here, these gentlemen are every minute changing their counsels and pursue nothing with steadfastness, you should not place any confidence in their writings and agreements.'[1]

This evidence was given to the delegation at Murshidabad by George Vansittart on his way to Calcutta. They decided that the facts 'as attested must for the present destroy all confidences between us and Nundcomar', and they postponed the allocation of revenue duties between the Maharaja and Rai Durlabh pending further advice from Calcutta. There the Council reacted sharply to Vansittart's report, supported by new documents, and on 16 March they directed the delegation to deprive Nandkumar and his agents of any share in the collections and to send him to Calcutta for an enquiry. Spencer wrote to the Nawab also, conveying these wishes of the Council.[2]

The Council's directions brought about a small-scale revolution at Murshidabad. On the morning of 20 March, when the delegates were preparing to carry Spencer's letter to the Nawab, Nandkumar called on them. He was promptly detained in the Residency in the custody of Captain Stables, who had orders to keep him engaged in conversation till their return. At the fort the Nawab opposed the delegate's proposal to detain the Maharaja, and insisted on his release while he wrote to Spencer on the matter. They considered the Nawab was merely wasting time, and they left the fort determined to hold the Maharaja until Spencer's reply should arrive.

---

[1] This letter was not new. It was already on the Company's record by 11 Oct. 1764 (BSC, 11 Oct. 1764), but the Mir would not show it to Carnac, as he thought he was prejudiced in the Raja's favour. Mir Ashraf was, however, willing to show it to Carnac in the presence of Batson and Billers, but Carnac would not agree to sit on an enquiry on this in concert with them (Vansittart's report. BSC, 16 March 1765).   [2] BSC, 16 March 1765.

At the Residency they had had three apartments cleared for the detenue.[1]

The Nawab regarded the action as an affront to his prestige and dignity and sent Reza Khan in the evening to urge the Raja's release and his despatch to the palace. The Khan returned unsuccessful but carrying a letter for the Nawab wherein the delegates promised to see the Nawab the next day, 21 March. Before the delegates were ready to move, however, the Nawab was himself at the Residency insisting on the immediate release of the Maharaja. As the delegates reported, 'he scarce kept within the bounds of decency'. Not knowing how to act in the circumstances, and being without orders to use force, the delegates were obliged to allow Nandkumar to leave the residency with the Nawab. In this the delegates were to a large extent influenced by the fact that Nandkumar had much influence not only over the Nawab, but also over 'all the sepoys and their commandant' Qaim Beg.[2]

Najm-ud-daulah's insistence upon the release of Nandkumar was to a large extent influenced by his desire to maintain the prestige of the Nizamat in his own city, for he gave an undertaking to the delegates that he would send Nandkumar to Calcutta if the governor insisted.[3] The Nawab possibly had some hopes that Spencer would not further drag the public image of the Nizamat through the mire, for he looked upon the whole affair as originating from the enmity of Mir Ashraf, an old 'liar and child of selfishness'. The Mir's enmity he believed to have sprung from Nandkumar's refusal to grant a jagir to his sister Bibi Raushan and that of Balwant Singh from a dispute over certain territories which Nandkumar had claimed for the Bengal government—a matter which formed the subject of a recent memorial to Carnac. The Nawab could not understand how else a matter which had been enquired into during Mir Jafar's last visit to Calcutta and finally settled by Governor Vansittart could be revived.[4] With these explanations

[1] Delegation's letter, 21 March. BSC, 25 March 1765.
[2] *Ibid.* There appears some discrepancy regarding the identity of the envoy. The Nawab's letter mentions Muzaffar Ali, not Muzaffar Jang, as his envoy to the delegation (*CPC*, I, 2616 dated 21 March).
[3] *Ibid.*
[4] Though unknown to the Nawab, the reason why the case was dropped then was that 'the hopes that Major Carnac's seeming conviction of his innocence had removed also the Board's suspicions ... might be some inducement to forward the supplies [of money] which depend so much upon him' (BSC, 11 Oct. 1764. Leycester's minute).

the Nawab asked Spencer to drop the whole matter, declaring that if Nandkumar were sent to Calcutta he himself, with his household and servants, would go there too. He complained bitterly against the conduct of the delegation, which had brought his government to contempt, imprisoned the Maharaja 'regardless of his rank and station', and obliged him to beg and entreat 'in the most suppliant manner'.[1]

The case against Nandkumar may well have had very little merit—Clive was later to ignore it—but it was mixed up with the internal dispute between Carnac and Vansittart, now extended to the latter's successor, Spencer. Vansittart had secured the dismissal of Carnac,[2] and Spencer's government refused to let slip the occasion for a further blow against his policies. They therefore paid little heed to the Nawab's plea and by a letter of 25 March asked for Nandkumar to be sent down to Calcutta in order to 'increase the friendship between him and the English'. Spencer, however, made this concession that the Maharaja was to be escorted both by the Company's troops and those of the Nizamat. At the same time the delegates were directed to use all means short of force to secure the Maharaja.[3]

The Nawab felt humiliated but submitted to the necessity. On 29 March the delegates met the Nawab and the latter gave his leave to Nandkumar. However, as a concession to the Nawab's prestige, it was arranged that the Nawab's sepoys would escort the Maharaja from Murshidabad to Calcutta, joined on the way by the English troops from Kasimbazar.[4] Nandkumar reached Calcutta on 4 April, the guards were taken off, and the governor personally met the Maharaja and advised him not to pay or receive visits from anyone or otherwise correspond with anyone without his prior consent. Measures were taken to ensure that Nandkumar complied.[5]

Nandkumar's exit, even if it damaged all Mughal government in Bengal, immediately freed Reza Khan from apprehended obstructions from the Maharaja. Events were developing simultaneously

---

[1] Najm-ud-daulah to Spencer, 21 March 1765. *CPC*, I, 2616.
[2] Like Coote, Carnac was also a critic of Vansittart and Mir Qasim. Vansittart had secured Carnac's dismissal (Court's letter 8 Feb. 1764) along with that of his other critics, Amyatt, Ellis, Hay and Johnstone. Events in England, however, resulted in Carnac's reinstatement by Court in April 1764 (Court's letter, 10 April 1764).
[3] BSC, 25 March 1765; *CPC*, I, 2617.
[4] Delegation's letter. BSC, 1 April 1765.   [5] BSC, 4 April 1765.

to free him from Rai Durlabh also. Rai Durlabh had come to Murshidabad with high hopes of being put in power on terms of equality with Nandkumar. Since December 1763 he had held the Diwani of the Nizamat, with the management of estates producing a revenue of six lakhs a year.[1] Mir Jafar did not dismiss him, but in December 1764, when Mir Jafar returned to Murshidabad, the Raja had stayed behind, much to the Nawab's annoyance. Mir Jafar had asked Spencer to send Rai Durlabh to Murshidabad but the Raja sent his brother Brindaban with other servants to manage Rai Durlabh's office at Murshidabad in January 1765.[2] As the delegates understood, Rai Durlabh was to be given a share in the Khalsa daftar in addition to what he already possessed as Nizamat Diwan. But when the trouble with Nandkumar began the delegates had warned Calcutta that 'if Nundcomar be totally laid aside, the Nabob should be strenuous in his objection' to Rai Durlabh,[3] and so it now turned out. The Nawab had inherited his father's hatred for Rai Durlabh[4] and, if correspondence with the enemy powers was a crime for Nandkumar, the Nawab accused Rai Durlabh also of a similar crime.[5] The delegates, who had a clearer idea of the extent of the Nawab's compliance at Murshidabad, had recommended that Rai Durlabh ought not to be forced on him.[6] Maybe they were sufficiently influenced by the gifts of the Nawab and Reza Khan not to be too insistent on this particular point, which must in any case have appeared as a minor concession to the Nawab, who had already been forced to yield on issues of greater importance. The authorities at Calcutta had a different view and they insisted upon rewarding the man who had been 'one of the most forward in showing an attachment to us' and had earlier received 'particular promises of being well rewarded',[7] perhaps from Spencer and Burdett, his main supporters in Calcutta. The Nawab was not opposed to Rai Durlabh's continuing in the share of the administration which he held under Mir Jafar, but he was

[1] Delegation's letter, 22 March. BSC, 25 March 1765.
[2] Mir Jafar's letter to Spencer, recd. 26 Dec. 1764 (*CPC*, I, 2510); Spencer to Mir Jafar, 12 Jan. 1765 (*CPC*, I, 2539).
[3] Delegation's letter, 22 March. BSC, 25 March 1765.   [4] *CPC*, I, 2625.
[5] The Nawab complained that he had a letter from Shuja to Rai Durlabh (letter of 5 April. BSC, 9 April 1765) and then handed it to Johnstone (*CPC*, I, 2625). Delegates suggested an enquiry 'for our credit' (letter 19 April. BSC, 22 April 1765). Council rejected Rai Durlabh's criminality (*ibid.*).
[6] Delegation's letter, 22 March. BSC, 25 March 1765.
[7] BSC, 26 March 1765.

not prepared to grant any additional power to him. The Nawab's attitude had hardened after what had happened to Nandkumar. At Murshidabad, the delegates, their number now reduced by departure of Leycester for Calcutta late in March, declined 'urging further a subject that seemed disagreeable',[1] and the governor also ultimately agreed not to insist further in the matter, though not before he had made a last effort to persuade the Nawab through Reza Khan.[2]

While these disputes were going on over Nandkumar and Rai Durlabh, the reorganisation of the Murshidabad secretariat had continued as a joint effort by Reza Khan and the delegates. The entire Khalsa daftar[3] was divided up so that each part might be given to a separate mutasaddi. The division effected, it was claimed, without causing any inconvenience or confusion, was deemed the safest system since it was designed to make it impossible for any superintendent to acquire any improper influence in the country. Another advantage claimed was that at need any mutasaddi could be displaced without disturbance to the whole, which would be impossible if the whole department were under one or two men. (It was also possible, under this scheme, to accommodate Nandkumar should he be cleared of the charges against him.) A central office called the Ektay Sharifah was created to co-ordinate the work of these different mutasaddis and one Ramnarain Mustaufi, an experienced man and a former assistant of the Qanungo, was placed at its head. The reorganisation in many ways followed the administrative plans of Mir Qasim who had abolished the exorbitant powers of the Rai-Rayan and had placed land revenue in the hands of a number of officers, each responsible for territories paying from five to forty lakhs per annum. The methods of Mir Qasim were followed in separating the different accounts, and in the appointment of amils and faujdars for smaller areas, though this inevitably increased the cost of collection and executive administration. While the provision for an Amil was thus made for almost every small territorial division the plan envisaged that it should be left to the Nawab to decide if the revenues of a district should be the responsibility of a zemindar or an amil.[4]

[1] Delegation's letter, 2 April. BSC, 9 April 1765.
[2] BSC, 22 April 1765; Reza Khan to Spencer, recd. 21 April 1765 (*CPC*, I, 2626).
[3] Correctly the *Khalisah Sharifah*, but Khalsa daftar was in common use.
[4] Delegation's letter, 22 March. BSC, 25 March 1765.

The Naibat Subahdari at Murshidabad, 1765

Reza Khan's duties and obligations as Naib Subah were also defined in the plan which received the approval of the Council on 26 March 1765.[1] He was to be consulted in 'adjusting the Bundobust' and in settling the collection so that, when necessary, he might make proper representation to the Nawab. As Naib Subah, he could also call on the mutasaddis for an explanation when there was any deficiency and in general his task was 'to superintend the whole that he may be able to give the Nabob a thorough insight into the affairs of the government and point out any amendment which can be made'.[2] The Nawab was still the head of the government as well as of the state. Reza Khan was his chief executive officer with his duties and functions more formally defined than were those of either Haji Ahmad in Shuja Khan and Alivardi Khan's time or of Nawazish Muhammad Khan under Alivardi. Functionally, the Khan's office included that of the Rai-Rayan, which was abolished by Mir Qasim but which Nandkumar had tried to revive in himself.

The reorganisation included a few political adjustments as well, more perhaps in the interest of Reza Khan than of the Company. The Council did not agree to all the proposals that went from the delegates. The delegates had proposed removal of Ruh uddin Husain Khan from Purnea to some other district and replacement by Jasarat Khan. Ruh uddin had a powerful influence in Purnea; his father, Saif Khan, had been posted to the district early in the century by the Emperor Aurangzeb. Jasarat Khan on the other hand had long association with Dacca as Naib of Nawazish Muhammad Khan, Rajballabh, Siraj-ud-daulah and Mir Jafar until Mir Qasim had dismissed him. The Council vetoed the proposal of the delegates 'in consideration of the circumstances they mention regarding 'Ruhud din's family, but recommended a provision for Jasarat Khan for his known 'attachment to us'.[3] The Nawab assented to the appointment of Jasarat Khan as Naib of Dacca under Reza Khan.[4] The Council did not seemingly take much interest in the delegates' proposal to replace Muzaffar Ali by Haji Mehdi, an Alivardian officer, as the Nawab's Arzbegi who as, the Nawab's private adviser helped in the formation of 'his

---

[1] Council's letter. BSC, 26 March 1765.
[2] Delegation's letter, 22 March. BSC, 25 March 1765.
[3] Delegation's letter, 22 March and Council's reply 26 March. BSC, 25, 26 March 1765.
[4] Delegation's letter, 19 April. BSC, 22 April 1765.

87

opinion of persons and things'; but they were not as unresponsive to the proposal of sending out of Mirza Daud with a ziladari to Bhagalpur.[1]

By now the delegates and the Calcutta Council were in a hurry to conclude the reorganisation of the Murshidabad government. On 22 April the Council directed the delegates to transfer immediately the allotment proposed for Rai Durlabh to such mutasaddis as enjoyed the Nawab's confidence. The Council, however, urged them to request the Nawab to allot one share to Gopal Krishna, the son of Rajballabh who died at the hands of Mir Qasim.[2] The Nawab readily consented. Reza Khan expressed himself as well satisfied with these arrangements, and happy that the mutasaddis were made powerless to be in the least dishonest.[3]

Only from one quarter did there seem any threat to the Council's plans. It was feared that the discontented people at Murshidabad were planning to create disturbances in conjunction with the soldiers of Qaim Beg, the commandant of the Nawab's troops. It was suspected that they would start the usual clamour for arrears of pay and then try to cut off Reza Khan and Rai Durlabh. The Khan, however, took the precaution of issuing the strictest orders to the mutasaddis of the armed forces to pay off the arrears.[4] Spencer also sought to minimise the danger by proposing to the Nawab a reduction of troops at Murshidabad and the placing of some of them under English command at Patna.[5] The Nawab did not readily agree. He denied having more troops at Murshidabad than were needed for the service of the various offices and a few who were necessary for the dignity of the government, and he refused to send troops to Patna on the plea that they were not disciplined enough to be of any use under English command. However, he agreed to spare a thousand horse and foot if required.[6] It was perhaps this refusal that led the Calcutta Council to order Captain Mc Pherson to remain at Murshidabad under the direction of the Resident and to 'countenance affairs there'.[7]

[1] Delegation's letter, 22 March and Council's reply, 26 March. BSC, 25, 26 March 1765.
[2] Council's letter, 22 April. BSC, 22 April 1765.
[3] *CPC*, I, 2638.
[4] Rai Durlabh to Spencer, recd. 21 March 1765. *CPC*, I, 2611.
[5] Spencer to Rai Durlabh, 24 April 1765. *CPC*, I, 2629.
[6] The Nawab to Spencer, 2 May. *CPC*, I, 2634; Reza Khan to Spencer, recd. 5 May 1765. *CPC*, I, 2638.
[7] BSC, 22 April 1765.

The Naibat Subahdari at Murshidabad, 1765

The Punyah, attended by the delegation, was held on 25 April and with it the new administration came into regular functioning even though final adjustments in administrative arrangements were still pending in some cases.[1] To the governor's letter of assurance that the Nawab would find his reposing confidence in the Khan worth while, the Nawab replied with a diplomatic assurance, seemingly not untouched by malice, that he had 'greater confidence in him than the English have'.[2] The Nawab had only to bide his time, until Clive reached Calcutta on 3 May 1765, to have the truth of his comment made manifest.

With Clive's arrival in Bengal, Reza Khan, already caught up in the group conflicts at Calcutta, found himself involved in the India House politics as extended to Fort William. The debacle in 1756 had activised politics at the India House; Clive's successes in 1757 had extended their scope. Unfortunately the early hopes of profit to the Company from the new acquisition were falsified by the costs of war and administration, while those who did gain by the revolution, individual servants of the Company, embarrassed the Company by their demands for payment in London of the bills through which they remitted their private fortunes. The embarrassment of the Company, aggravated by the general financial crisis in England, forced it to seek government aid. A second problem, allied to the first, was to maintain discipline and control over distant servants who had acquired new power, even against the Company, through their wealth and had lost any fear of the Indian ruling powers. In the defence of their Indian gains, returning Company servants struggled to control the India House, a struggle which eventually centred round Laurence Sulivan and Clive when the latter returned to England in 1760. The struggle between the two developed into an open war in 1763, Clive trying unsuccessfully to oust Sulivan from the Direction and Sulivan retaliating by ordering Vansittart and his Council in April 1763[3] to stop further payment of Clive's jagir, drawn from the revenues of twenty-four parganas. Though mauled in the first round, Clive became more determined than ever to oust his enemy from power. His opportunity came when news began trickling to London of growing trouble between Vansittart and members of his Council and

[1] Delegation's letter, 26 April. BSC, 29 April 1765.
[2] Spencer to the Nawab, 24 April and the Nawab's reply, recd. 5 May 1765. *CPC*, I, 2630, 2636.
[3] Court's letter, 27 April 1763.

89

between the English and the Nawab, and finally, in February 1764, of the outbreak of war between Mir Qasim and the English. The news alarmed the proprietors of the Company in England, who now intervened to send Clive to restore the situation in Bengal. Clive took the opportunity to dictate his own terms. He secured extraordinary powers for himself and a Select Committee consisting of W. B. Sumner and Francis Sykes, going with him, and Harry Verelst and John Carnac already in India. The powers included the right to overrule the Calcutta Council, to send Spencer back to Bombay, whence Sulivan had transferred him, and to regulate the internal trade of Bengal. Sulivan was ousted from his controlling power at the India House, though not from the Court of Directors, and Clive was granted a further period of enjoyment of his jagir. Clive's earlier services had earned him an Irish peerage and a place in the Company and national politics. He now set out for India again in high spirits and with a lively ambition to achieve further greatness in the service of the Company and the nation.

Clive had left England on 4 June 1764 but a delayed passage deprived him much of the credit which he sought for himself. Munro at Buxar had finally defeated the combination of Mir Qasim, Shuja-ud-daulah and Shah Alam on 23 October 1764, and victory had been followed by further successes against Shuja whose capital, Lucknow, was taken in the name of Shah Alam[1] who was taken under the English protection soon after Shuja's defeat at Buxar. Nevertheless, news of Mir Jafar's death received in April 1765 on his arrival at Madras still gave Clive hopes 'to become the Nawab ourselves in fact, if not in name',[2] by raising Mir Saidu, Miran's minor son, to the masnad. But on landing at Calcutta on 3 May 1765, Clive found that Spencer had already stolen a march over him by making the new settlement with Najm-ud-daulah.

Clive was a disappointed man, cheated of the opportunity to play a striking role, ready to look with displeasure upon the arrangements of his predecessor. He was critical of Spencer and his Council for 'going to the lengths they have done' in reducing the power of the Nawab—though Clive was later to go still further —and critical of the raising of Reza Khan to the heights of the Naib Subahdari. Recalling, perhaps, Vansittart's experience with

[1] Carnac's letter, 26 March. BSC, 9 April 1765.
[2] Clive to Rouse. Quoted in Forrest, *Clive*, II, 256–7.

The Naibat Subahdari at Murshidabad, 1765

the raising of Mir Qasim to a similar station, Clive wrote pungently to Carnac: 'Never trust the ambitions of any Mussulman after whatever has happened.'[1] The first meeting of the Council on 5 May turned annoyance born of frustration to anger, for Johnstone and Leycester challenged the extra-ordinary powers of the new Select Committee, granted only until tranquillity should be restored in Bengal. Clive overbore the objection, declared the Committee sole judges of their own power, and entered upon a personal vendetta. In that vendetta Reza Khan was soon involved.

In 1764 the home authorities had decided upon a form of covenant, which their servants overseas were to sign, binding themselves not to accept presents of more than a very small amount without the prior consent of the Directors. This had been resolved on by the Court of Proprietors on 2 May 1764, despatched by the Directors on 1 June and received in Calcutta in January 1765. The Council had taken no steps to ensure their execution. Instead there were rumours that the accession of Najm-ud-daulah was to be used to secure new presents for the Council, as Verelst in distant Chittagong noted in a letter of 7 March 1765.[2] To these rumours, of a 'combination between the blacks and whites, to divide all the revenues of the Company',[3] in which Reza Khan was allegedly involved, Clive turned as the means of destroying Spencer and his supporters. In their downfall Reza Khan seemed likely to be dragged down, for Clive made it clear to Carnac that he objected to his remaining Naib Subah, 'his being a Mussulman, acute and clever are reasons of themselves if there were no other, against trusting that man with too much power'.[4]

With Clive's arrival the atmosphere at Murshidabad had also become tense. Even though Nandkumar had been ousted from Murshidabad in March, the Khan was kept in constant alarm by his enemies, allies of Nandkumar, who claimed that as Mir Jafar had adopted Clive as his son they could expect great favours from him.[5] Their behaviour on Clive's arrival made it clear that they

---

[1] Forrest, *Clive*, II, 261.
[2] Verelst spoke of the current rumour in his letter to Middleton and hoped there was no truth in it, 'for it must entail, on every one concerned the world's severest censure'. Middleton in his reply of 18 March 1765 confirmed the rumour and said that 'in accepting of it; custom, the conduct of one of our worthiest men justifies it'. Verelst (*View*, 51).
[3] Clive to Carnac. Malcolm, *Clive*, II, 360–1.
[4] *Ibid.*, 359.   [5] *MN*, f. 152.

believed what they had said. Middleton, the Resident, had urged Najm-ud-daulah not to go to Calcutta 'without the approbation of the gentlemen of the Council'.[1] Nevertheless, by 8 May the Nawab had left for Calcutta for the pleasure of seeing his Lordship, whom he looked upon 'as his brother and strength of his arm'.[2] Shah Khanum, Miran's mother, who called Clive her son, sent a letter recommending Mir Saidu and Mirza Daud (Miran's son and son-in-law respectively) to Clive's favour 'as they are in a manner his own children'. She also asked for an early meeting at Murshidabad, and cautioned Clive 'not to let the Nawab Najm-ud-daulah see this letter or receive information of it'.[3] Reza Khan, protesting that his appointment as Naib was 'without my desiring', now appealed to Johnstone to preserve his honour: not only was the Nawab going to Calcutta, the Khan complained, but 'all my enemies are with him, and they will, doubtless, not be dilatory in doing me all the prejudice they can'.[4] To Motiram, Johnstone's Banian who had recently been given the title of Maharaja and the Faujdari of Hugli, the Khan observed: 'The friends of Nundcomar rejoice at Sabut Jung's [Clive's][5] arrival and say, that Mharaja will obtain Kellaat [Khilat] and return to Moorshedabad in four or five days'. Again, though the Khan was anxious himself to go to Calcutta, the Nawab had refused permission on the plea that if he went 'the business of the Nizamut would be interrupted'.[6]

Unaware of the developments in Calcutta, Reza Khan first wrote to Spencer asking for protection[7] and then to Clive. In his letter to Clive, received on 12 May, the Khan explained his appointment and the circumstances which prevented him from personally paying his respects to him in Calcutta. With his letter he sent a Nazarana or offering of eleven gold mohurs, and an agent, Mirza Muhammad Kazim Khan, 'a man of understanding, and a relation and a faithful friend', who had been known to Clive in the Deccan.[8]

[1] Reza Khan to Johnstone, May 1765. *PP*, Fourth Report, 1773, p. 542.
[2] The Nawab to Clive, recd. 12, 14 May 1765. *CPC*, I, 2643, 2646.
[3] Shah Khanum to Clive, recd. 18 May 1765. *CPC*, I, 2653.
[4] Reza Khan to Johnstone, May 1765. *PP*, Fourth Report, 1773, p. 542.
[5] Clive was always known to the Indians, except perhaps to a few, as Nawab Sabut Jang (*Seir*, II, 306, fn. 170).
[6] Reza Khan to Motiram, May 1765. *PP*, Fourth Report, 1773, p. 542.
[7] Reza Khan to Johnstone, May 1765 (*ibid.*).
[8] *Ibid.*; Reza Khan to Clive, recd. 12, 18 May 1765 *CPC*, I, 2644–5, 2650; *Seir*, III, 8. The Mirza, a Persian, was a son-in-law of Husain Reza Khan, Haji Ahmad's grandson (*ibid.*).

The Naibat Subahdari at Murshidabad, 1765

The Khan sought Clive's permission to come to Calcutta, writing five or six times. When no reply came the Khan sent another agent, Mahasingh, an old officer of Alivardi and Siraj-ud-daulah to safeguard his interest at Calcutta. After a long week of suspense the Khan at last received a call from Clive to go to Calcutta, ominously coupled with a censure for failing to accompany the Nawab. The Khan so long anxious to go to Calcutta now became apprehensive when the call came. Though on the way he met Senior at Kasimbazar on 14 or 15 May and was assured that nothing untoward would happen to him, he reached Calcutta sometime before 20 May with the 'terror and apprehension of a man going to be delivered up to his enemies'.[1]

At Calcutta the situation terrified him still further. He found that his protectors, members of the previous government, were themselves under censure. He found Nandkumar released, his trial stopped, the witnesses who had been called all the way from Patna turned back. Moreover, the Nawab had admitted Nandkumar again to the highest confidence. The Khan somehow felt that all business of the moment had been taken out of his hands.[2] Worse still, though the Khan had known that he was unwelcome to the Nawab, he now found that he had been denounced by him, jointly with Johnstone and Leycester, to the all powerful Select Committee. Najm-ud-daulah had complained that 'since the death of the late Nabob [the Khan] had distributed among certain persons nearly twenty lakhs of rupees',[3] and Reza Khan could only wait in suspense, terrified of the power of retribution of the Committee. Before the Nawab's complaint was formally presented to the Select Committee the Khan asked to be examined. He was accordingly examined and afterwards he submitted a written statement, drawn up by a 'blackman'.[4] It was probably not until the arrival of Verelst from Chittagong on 29 May that the Khan felt any relief.

The Nawab's complaint was mainly against the treatment he had received from the members of the delegation, who had forced him to sign the new treaty under threat of losing his Subahdari and had

---

[1] Reza Khan to Clive, recd. 18 May (*CPC*, I, 2651); *MN*, f. 152; Senior's evidence (*PP*, Third Report, 1773, p. 309); Barwell's letter, 15 Sept. 1765 (*BPP*, VIII, 191).
[2] *PP*, Fourth Report, 1773, pp. 536–7.
[3] For the Nawab's complaint, see BSC, 1 June 1765.
[4] *PP*, Third Report, 1773, pp. 320–1; Reza Khan's statement. BSC, 6 June 1765.

imposed Reza Khan upon him as Naib Subahdar, though he 'had long ago had evil intentions on the Nizamat' and had been regarded by Mir Jafar as an enemy, Najm-ud-daulah was intent on the restoration of his power and the re-instatement of Nand-kumar, 'my intimate well wisher'. But to Clive and the Select Committee it was the complaint that the Khan had paid twenty lakhs from the Nawab's treasury to 'such people as he thought proper'[1] which was important, for this was an instrument with which they were to beat down the members of the Council who had challenged their authority. Clive had no intention of re-instating Nandkumar. He remembered his unhappy experience of him as Company's Tahsildar in 1758, and he told Carnac plainly that 'although Nundcomar may not prove guilty of the crimes laid to his charge, yet, believe me, my dear General he will do no honour either to the Nabob or to the Company, in any great or eminent post, which he was never formed or designed for; and I can give you unanswerable reasons against his being the principal person about the Nabob...It is really shocking to see what a set of miser-able and mean wretches Nundcomar has placed about him; men that the other day were horse keepers'.[2] Clive likewise had no interest in restoring power to the Nawab—as has been seen he would have preferred to see the minor Mir Saidu on the masnad. Nor in the end was he anxious to remove Reza Khan. Najm-ud-daulah's complaint that the Khan had had claims upon the masnad made him seem politically valuable, Verelst may have spoken for him, and the Khan's timidity and intelligence, a contrast to the general haughtiness of the Muslim nobility, made him seem a useful instrument. Even more, Reza Khan's replies to the Nawab's accusations drove the allegations against the old Council further home, for the Khan in his statement laid the whole blame on Johnstone and his Banian Motiram. He declared that after Najm-ud-daulah was seated on the masnad the gentlemen of the delegation had sent a proposal to him, Reza Khan, through Motiram, later repeated by the gentlemen themselves, that the Khan should propose to the Nawab that now that they had seated him on the masnad they would expect some reward from him as on the past occasion. The Khan, in order not to offend the gentlemen, had put this to the Nawab, who readily consented. The Nawab had

---

[1] The Nawab's complaint. BSC, 1 June 1765.
[2] Clive to Carnac, 20 May 1765. Malcolm, *Clive*, II, 358–9.

asked him to prepare a list of presents which he declined to do, but subsequently a list was prepared 'before the Nabob's face and given under his hand and seal to Mr. Johnstone in the presence of all the four gentlemen'. Three or four days later, the Khan added, Johnstone had taken the list of proposed presents to the Nawab and declined to accept it if it was given unwillingly and contrary to his inclination. The Nawab assured Johnstone that the gifts were according to his 'own pleasure'. Before the payment was actually made between 12 April and 1 May, the Khan had taken the Nawab's written orders on the 'Ferd sovaul [sawal]' or office memo asking for orders. After the Nawab had given his orders in writing, the Khan paid out Rs. 8,75,000, Rs. 6,25,000 in cash from the treasury and Rs. 2,25,000 by bills on the house of the Seths.[1] The Khan thus disproved the Nawab's statement that he had disbursed money without his orders; at the same time he convicted Johnstone.

It was also revealed that presents were taken from Reza Khan himself. Johnstone, he said, sent messages through Motiram that as the Khan had been appointed His Excellency's Naib, it was proper that he too should make some presents. Ultimately a sum of Rs. 4,75,000 had been agreed upon, of which he paid Rs. 2,25,000 mostly in bills, while the remaining Rs. 2,50,000 remained outstanding. A further accusation was levelled at Johnstone by the Jagat Seth who had also come down to Calcutta on Clive's arrival. Five lakhs had been demanded from him, but the Seths agreed to pay Rs. 1,25,000.[2] (Enquiry revealed that many of the bills were still unpaid and with Motiram. There were attempts to hand them back to Reza Khan through Motiram's servant Basant Roy, but the Khan had refused to accept them.[3]) The result of the enquiry led the Select Committee to conclude that Johnstone was the principal agent and manager in obtaining and distributing the presents and that it was Motiram who had used menaces in his master's name in extorting money from both Reza Khan and the Jagat Seth. C. S. Playdell, J. Burdett, and G. Gray, they maintained, had received Rs. 50,000 each from the Nawab 'in the full persuasion that these were free gifts to the gentlemen who then composed the Board', and that J. Cartier was an absolute stranger to the arrangement and that he had not received any money. Of the delegation

---

[1] BSC, 6 June 1765.   [2] The Jagat Seth's statement. BSC, 6 June 1765.
[3] Basant Roy's statement. BSC, 7 June 1765.

only Senior, besides Johnstone, had received money from Reza Khan as well as from the Nawab and the Jagat Seth. Middleton had received presents from the Nawab and the Jagat Seth but had intended to refuse any present from Reza Khan and the same was true of Leycester.[1] (The Committee refrained from saying anything about the money which Spencer had received.[2])

The outcome of the whole enquiry was that the Select Committee declared that the Khan had 'so openly and candidly' accounted for 'every rupee disbursed from the treasury, they cannot without injury to his character and injustice to his conduct during his short administration refuse continuing him in a share of the government'. They decided, however, to retrench his authority partly, as they said, in order to 'remove the Nabob's jealousies' and partly 'to prevent the necessity of future revolutions' by removing the possibility of a great danger 'that may arise to the stability of the present establishment from suffering the whole power and absolute management of the three provinces to rest in a single person'. They, therefore, brought in Rai Durlabh again. The Nawab had prevented Spencer from imposing Rai Durlabh

---

[1] BSC, 21 June 1765.
[2] The distribution of the promised amount and amount outstanding was:

Name of the gentleman	By whom promised			Total sum promised	Amount to be paid
	The Nawab	Reza Khan	Jagat Seth		
Spencer	2,00,000	90,000		2,90,000	1,00,000
Playdell	1,00,000			1,00,000	50,000
Burdett	1,00,000			1,00,000	50,000
Gray	1,00,000			1,00,000	50,000
Johnstone	2,37,000	1,50,000		3,87,000	50,000
Senior	1,12,500	1,00,000		2,12,500	50,000
Leycester	1,12,500	1,00,000		2,12,500	50,000
Middleton	1,12,500	1,00,000		2,12,500	1,00,000
G. Johnstone younger brother of J. Johnstone	50,000	25,000	10,000	85,000	nil
Messrs. Johnstone, Senior, Leycester and Middleton			1,15,000	1,15,000	75,000
J. Cartier	1,00,000			1,00,000	1,00,000

(see BSC, 6 June 1765)

The Directors having ordered refunds of the money (not to those who paid) the Select Committee issued notice on Middleton and Playdell, who were in India, to pay the sum to the Company. Others were notified through their attorneys in India (BSC, 21 Dec. 1766). Ultimately, for political reasons the cases were withdrawn by the Company (L. S. Sutherland, *The East India Company in Eighteenth-Century Politics*, p. 171).

on him, but he could not do so against Clive. Reza Khan was advised to relinquish his title of the Naib Subah, and to accept the simpler designation of a Naib in a new administrative arrangement which was formally minuted in the proceedings of the Committee dated 21 June 1765. It stood thus:

The Nawab Najm-ud-daulah Mir Najm uddin Ali Khan Bahadur
　　　　　　　　　　　　　　　　　　　　－Nazim
The Nawab Muin-ud-daulah Saiyid Muhammad Reza Khan Bahadur
　　　　　　　　　　　　　　　　　　　　－Naib
Maharaja Durlabh ram Bahadur
　　　　　　　　　　　　　　　　　　　　－Diwan
The Jagat Seth Khushal Chand and Maharaja Udai Chand
　　　　　　　　　　　　　　　　　　　　－Chiefs of Trade

The Committee then adopted a number of regulations which further reduced the power of the Nawab, who was rendered a real cypher, besides making Reza Khan perhaps no more powerful and responsible than the other two ministers. The new regulation also laid down that the Nawab's treasury should have three keys, one with each of the three executive officers, further extending the Company's authority by arranging that a servant of the Company, of Councillor's rank, posted at Murshidabad and maintained at the expense of the Nawab's government, should keep a check on the accounts of the Nawab's government. The ministers would be required to submit their accounts to him each month.[1] These regulations were designed to be embodied in yet another treaty which was eventually executed by the Nawab in July 1765.[2]

The sum total of transactions at Calcutta during the first five or six weeks of Clive's government had a tremendous effect on the future course not only of the life of Clive and Reza Khan but also of the history of Bengal. Clive made an enemy of Johnstone, whose supporters at home had been of some help to him in defeating Sulivan at the India House. Sulivan and Johnstone later created great difficulties for Clive in the years after his return to England in 1767, and particularly in 1773 when Clive was impeached. Reza Khan, ignorant of the new developments until he arrived at Calcutta, had very soon determined the course he was to adopt for

---

[1] BSC, 21 June 1765. The proceedings of the day were not the transactions of that particular date. The decisions were taken much earlier though recorded on that day.
[2] Clive's letter, 9 July. BSC, 10 Aug. 1765.

his future conduct. He came out firmly in favour of Clive, who alone could preserve him against the combined enmity of the Nawab and Nandkumar. But in the process, Reza Khan had made a very powerful enemy in Johnstone. Reza Khan in his first statement had not given the whole story of Johnstone's transactions. When the latter challenged his facts, and declared them 'extorted' by the Committee, Reza Khan replied by coming out with the story of yet another secret transaction.[1] Over and above the Rs. 1,37,000, which Johnstone claimed from the Nawab as a joint member and senior servant on the deputation, he had further stipulated that rupees one lakh for himself and Rs. 50,000 for his brother should be paid secretly and unknown to the others.[2] Johnstone, infuriated with the Khan, described the Khan's narrative as false and forced from him 'by hope of favour or fear of disgrace',[3] but the Committee described his statement as related with great 'candor and precision'.[4] The Khan evidently become a matter of controversy.[5] Johnstone was never to forgive Reza Khan for his revelations. He maintained his grudge until as late as 1775[6] and, in his attacks in England upon the Clive faction, Reza Khan was to suffer.

In contrast to the Nawab, who evidently returned to Murshidabad dejected and in fear of Clive, to whom he had looked in vain for support, the Khan returned well satisfied. On his way back the Khan received the Dutch and the French chiefs at Hugli 'with becoming civility'[7] and on 24 June he entered Murshidabad, finally confirmed in his Naibat, though without the formal designation of Naib Subahdar. He also returned with the confi-

[1] Reza Khan to Clive, 23 June 1765. *CPC*, I, 2667.
[2] BSC, 4 July 1765.
[3] Johnstone's letter, 1 Oct. 1765. *PP*, Fourth Report, 1773, pp. 536–7.
[4] BSC, 4 July 1765.
[5] About the Nawab's complaint, Leycester first held the view that it was a 'shameful insinuation' in order to injure Reza Khan and added that 'the opinion, I entertain of Mahomed Reza Cawn's understanding and integrity inclines me to believe this a groundless assertion' (BPC, 7 June 1765). He later described Reza Khan's statement as 'mistaken in part of his detail' (BPC, 11 June 1765). Sykes, it is said, was told by Reza Khan in 1766 that the Khan made the presents to the gentlemen at his own will. (Verelst said so in his evidence in 1773. *PP*, Third Report, p. 321.) Verelst who knew the Khan very well, however, maintained the view that Reza Khan was not a man to make any present at his own will, unless it was for some service wished for (*ibid.*).
[6] Sykes to Hastings, 16 Feb. 1775. Add. MSS. 29136, f. 57.
[7] Reza Khan to Clive, recd. 19 June 1765. *CPC*, I, 2663.

dence of Clive. He had not only survived the machinations of his enemies,[1] he stood on the threshold of greatness.

Clive left Calcutta on 25 June on his way up country for a new settlement with Shuja-ud-daulah and the Emperor. When he reached Agradwip a day's journey from Murshidabad he was accorded a grand reception by Reza Khan, who looked to his comfort in the city and made all arrangement for his Lordship's further journey. He also engaged Mirza Muhammad Kazim Khan as Clive's chamberlain,[2] but more correctly as his agent in Clive's camp. These personal attentions doubtless had their effect on Clive, but there were other factors predisposing him in Reza Khan's favour. There is some evidence to suggest that the Khan helped Clive with a sum of six lakhs of rupees during his stay at Calcutta.[3] But there were public grounds, as well as possible private ones for Clive's support of the Khan. It was clear that the Khan was likely to be an admirable instrument. He had not grasped at personal power, rather Clive at this point had to prevent Rai Durlabh encroaching upon the Khan's sphere of authority. Convinced of the Khan's 'honor and moderation', Clive called Sykes to Murshidabad to support him and preserve tranquillity.[4] More, he seems to have aided Clive to improve upon what Spencer had achieved. On 9 July Clive sent the treaty, embodying the arrangements of 21 June and signed by the Nawab.[5] Only two days later, however, he was writing to the Select Committee to negotiate through Sykes an agreement on those terms, in the form of a limitation of the Nawab's expenses.[6] No such idea seems to have been conceived or broached by the English before, and it seems probable that this was Reza Khan's contribution. The genesis of the new deal is not clear, but Karam Ali tells us that it was after a secret consultation with the Khan that

[1] Nandkumar appears to have made a last effort to be reinstated in power by an offer of 25 lakhs to Sykes for the President and Council (*PP*, Third Report, 1773, p. 322).   [2] *MN*, f. 154.
[3] Reza Khan's note. *MP*, 3 Jan. 1771.
[4] 'It is with pleasure I can acquaint you that the more I see of Mohamed Reza Cawn the stronger is my conviction of his honor and moderation; ... Roy Dullub, however, has already attempted to destroy this ballance of power, and Mahomed Reza Cawn approves than resists it' (Clive to Select Committee, 3 July 1765. BSC, 7 July 1765).
[5] Clive's letter, 9 July. BSC, 10 Aug. 1765. Clive had added 'our business at the Durbar is finished'.
[6] Clive's letter, 11 July. BSC, 10 Aug. 1765.

The transition in Bengal, 1756–1775

Clive met the Nawab and told him that the Khan had complained of his lavish personal expenditure.[1] Such a complaint would have been natural, for the Khan was under constant pressure to meet the financial obligations of the Nawab's government. When the Company had demanded immediate payment of six lakhs on account of the Nawab's debts, Najm-ud-daulah denied any responsibility, saying that he was unacquainted with the collections of the country and that he did not know if there was any money in the treasury.[2] It was the Khan therefore upon whom the responsibility fell. He may have wished to curb the Nawab's personal expenditure merely to safeguard his own position—but the suggestion could not but be attractive to Clive. The Khan had put in Clive's power to perform a signal service to the Company. Before Clive left Murshidabad he had obtained Najm-ud-daukah's consent to the limitations of his expenses to some fifty lakhs of rupees a year, the balance of the revenues being appropriated to the maintenance of the army, tribute to the emperor, and payment of all outstanding debts.[3] In addition, Reza Khan 'being of a disposition extremely timorous' it was agreed that 'the payment of the cavalry and sepoys, pass through his hands, though included in the said fifty laaks'.[4]

Sykes, who was asked by Clive to come to Murshidabad to restore the balance of power between Reza Khan and Rai Durlabh, reached Kasimbazar on 22 July. His mission was meant to be temporary, but it came to be an extended one, particularly as Sykes had to negotiate a new agreement on the lines of Clive's preliminary understanding with the Nawab. The negotiation took a long time, for even though the Nawab could not resist Clive he was not as yielding to Sykes. Clive had privately advised Sykes to

[1] *MN*, f. 154.
[2] Najm-ud-daulah to Clive, recd. 9 June 1765. *CPC*, I, 2660.
[3] Even without the Diwani this arrangement would have given the control of Nawab's purse to the English. The grant of the Diwani further converted the control into a right over the Nawab's revenues. Clive felt so jubilant over this matter that he wrote to the Select Committee on 11 July saying that 'We have often lamented that the gentlemen of [Spencer's] Council, by precipitating the late treaty had lost the most glorious opportunity that could ever happen . . . which I have now the pleasure to inform you, are in a fair way of being perfectly removed' (BSC, 10 Aug. 1765). Clive had the satisfaction of having scored his first victory over Spencer.
[4] *Ibid.* Clive also safeguarded the Khan by deporting Qaim Beg to Calcutta. The Nawab was not consulted (Clive's letter, 7 July. BSC, 10 Aug. 1765).

reduce the Nawab's expenses to forty lakhs if possible,[1] but this proved impossible. On 14 August, Sykes sent to Calcutta the draft of a new agreement which was to come into force after the Diwani sanad from the Emperor Shah Alam had been received by the Company. According to the new agreement the Nawab undertook to 'accept the amount of Sicca Rupees 53,86,131-9-0 as an adequate allowance for the support of the Nizamut which is to be regularly paid as follows, viz, the sum of Sicca Rupees 17,78,854-1-0 for all my household expences, servants &c and the remaining sum of 36,07,277-8-0 for the maintenance of such horse, seapoys, peons, Bergundasses &c as may be thought necessary for my Sewarry and the support of my dignity only, should such an expence hereafter be found necessary to be kept up, but on no account ever to exceed that amount'.[2] In the same document the Nawab declared that having a perfect 'relyance' on Muin-ud-daulah [Reza Khan] the Nawab desired that 'he may have the disbursing of the above sum of Rs. 36,07,277-8-0 for the purposes before mentioned'.[3] The balance of power had again tilted in favour of Reza Khan. The new arrangement was to take effect after Clive's return from Allahabad where on 12 August 1765 the Emperor Shah Alam had granted to the Company the Diwani of the provinces of Bengal, Bihar and Orissa.[4] With Clive's return Reza Khan was to enter upon the most important phase of his career.

[1] Clive to Sykes, 3 Aug. 1765. Quoted: Forrest, *Clive*, II, 282.
[2] Draft enclosed with Sykes's letter to Select Committee. BSC, 7 Sept. 1765.
[3] *Ibid.*
[4] At Allahabad Clive acted as the representative of the Nawab of Bengal in concluding peace with Shuja-ud-daulah. The Diwani was granted to Company on condition of their guaranteeing the payment by the Nawab of Bengal of the annual tribute of twenty-six lakhs of rupees and as an altamgha (grant in perpetuity). 'Thus a business of such a magnitude' commented Ghulam Husain '. . . was done and finished in less time than would have been taken up for the sale of a jack-ass, or of a beast of burden, or of a head of cattle' (*Seir*, III, 9). But even then, it appears from Ghulan Husain's report, that as usual the formalities were all observed, 'the Company's acknowledgement and bond for the same, which are the owner's voucher, were drawn up under their seal, and entered in the Imperial registers' (*ibid.*) The grant of the Diwani and its acceptance with its formal undertaking integrated the Company within the Mughal imperial system, not merely as zemindars or jagirdars as hitherto, but as servants of the Empire. We do not know what these obligations were, but Holwell reported to the Fuller Committee in 1767 that in 1732 'the East India Company were told they forfeited their lands by the Constitution of the Empire if they raised their rents' (Add. MSS. 18469, f. 18).

CHAPTER 6

REZA KHAN AT THE ZENITH OF HIS
POWER, 1765–1767

Before the acquisition of the Diwani, Reza Khan had been merely politically useful to the Company; after it, he became the chief instrument of their administrative control of the country. Shah Alam had granted the Diwani sanad on 12 August 1765, and when, somewhat over a fortnight later, Clive returned from Allahabad to Murshidabad he had to take the practical steps needed to implement the agreement which had been concluded, in his absence, by Sykes, with the Nawab Najm-ud-daulah. The measures adopted during his brief stay served to raise Reza Khan to the zenith of his power, for, as Reza Khan put it later, 'Lord Clive found it necessary to restore the ancient form of government and set one person at the head of the administration of public affairs'[1]. That person was Muhammad Reza Khan.

To Reza Khan, who was to act for the Nawab Najm-ud-daulah and so to control the public office of the Nizamat, was transferred charge of the Nizamat finances, fixed at Sicca Rs. 36,07,277-8-0. He was also given charge of the annual pension allotted to Mir Saidu, Miran's son. Clive, while at Murshidabad, fixed the amount of the pensions and allowances to the family and dependents of Mir Jafar. These were included in the household expenses of Najm-ud-daulah, but because of his known jealousy towards Mir Saidu, nominated as his successor by Mir Jafar in 1760 in preference to Najm-ud-daulah, the pension of Mir Saidu was placed in Reza Khan's hands.[2] Since Shah Khanum, mother of Miran and half sister of Alivardi, who had been Mir Saidu's guardian, was now dead, Reza Khan was the natural guardian of the interests of Alivardi's family. Nevertheless, the charge added to his importance. As the Nawab's deputy, with authority to discharge the public functions of the Nizamat and control over the

---

[1] Reza Khan's note on the past and present state of Bengal as given to Goring in Dec. 1774. Philip Francis sent this note to Lord North on 23 March 1775 (Francis MSS. I.O. Eur. E, 28, p. 352).
[2] See Clive to Mir Saidu's mother, and to Reza Khan 11 Oct. 1765 (CPC, I, 2723-4). And Mir Saidu to Verelst, recd. 10 Feb. 1768 (CPC, II, 788).

The Khan at the zenith of his power, 1765–1767

public funds and of Mir Saidu's pension, the Khan virtually enjoyed a sovereign's dignity. When, therefore, Clive and the Select Committee told the Directors that 'the Nabob [Najm ud daulah] holds in his hands as he always did, the whole civil administration, the distribution of offices, and all those sovereign rights which constitute the essence of his dignity',[1] this was in practice untrue however constitutionally correct. Only when necessary to give extra weight to letters and parwanas to other foreign powers and settlements was it thought fit to affix the Nawab's own seal.[2]

No attempt was made to separate the Diwani administration, which continued as part of the Nawab's administration as before;[3] nor was it deemed necessary to amend formally the administrative arrangement recorded in the Select Committee's proceedings of 21 June. The formal transactions of the Nawab's government, such as the revenue settlement with the zemindars, continued to be made out in the joint names of Reza Khan, Rai Durlabh and the Jagat Seth.[4] Though even under the formal arrangement of 21 June, Reza Khan had a distinctive status as Naib, in actual practice he gradually became 'the centre of business, public and private'.[5] Only on ceremonial occasions, such as the annual Punyah, did the Nawab preside. At other times it was Reza Khan who acted as 'regent', as the Directors called him, as 'minister' or 'Prime minister',[6] as the Select Committee called him, or as Naib or Naib Nazim as he styled himself. The Khan was never formally installed as Naib Diwan, but Clive did all he could to secure for him honours and dignity befitting his real practical authority.

While Clive was securing the Diwani and other sanads for the

---

[1] Letter to Court, 24 Jan. 1767.
[2] It was a custom in dealings with all European nations in Bengal before Plassey, and with all other nations except the English after Plassey, that 'they were never allowed a personal interview with the Nabob but as a special favor nor even with his ministers, but transacted all affairs, by the Vakeels, with the mutsuddies of the Durbar' (*PCC*, Kasimbazar, 11 July 1772).
[3] The separate identity of the office of the Diwan had ceased to exist since the emergence of the 'independent' Nawabs early in the century. The office of Padshahi (imperial) Diwan existed as a matter of form and it was held formally by someone who was held next in rank to the Nawab who nominated the holder, though formally appointed by the emperor. Under Mir Jafar, the office went to Miran and after his death to his son Mir Saidu. The Company in fact, substituted Mir Saidu.
[4] Reed's letter, 17 Dec. MP, 20 Dec. 1770.   [5] *Seir*, III, 4.
[6] Court's letter, 24 Dec. 1765; Letter to Court, 24 March 1766; BSC, 31 Dec. 1766.

Company from the Emperor Shah Alam he also procured for Reza Khan the various titles, so Ghulam Husain says, of Bahadur or Valiant, Muzaffar Jang or the Victorious in War, Muin-ud-daulah or the Eminent of the State, Mubariz ul Mulk or the Foremost of the Kingdom, Khan i Khanan or the Lord of Lords. To these 'was added the privilege of riding in a Naleky...a distinction reserved to Sovereigns'.[1] Karam Ali says the titles, which Reza Khan certainly enjoyed, were conferred upon him when installed as Naib Subah in March 1765, by Najm-ud-daulah.[2] But that Clive obtained for him at least the title Khan i Khanan or Lord of Lords, and the distinction of the Sovereign's privilege to ride in a Naleky[3] and use the *Mahi Maratib* or Fish Standard is certain. Procuring titles for the Nawab, his brother Saif-ud-daulah, Reza Khan, Rai Durlabh and for the Jagat Seth and others had been a part of Clive's mission to the Emperor.[4] The Emperor might be militarily impotent and politically ineffective but Clive knew very well that he was still looked up to as the source of all honour and distinction in Indian society. Ennobled with imperial titles Reza Khan would be a more effective counterpoise to the Nawab.

The strengthening of the dignity and power of Reza Khan was very necessary, for Clive could only exploit the Diwani grant by working the established form of government. Some nineteen Company civilians[5] had been killed during the struggle with Mir Qasim, others fell victim to Clive in his ruthless war against those members of the old Council who questioned the dictatorial powers he claimed for himself and the Select Committee.[6] By January 1766 one councillor had been suspended, four had chosen to resign.[7] Clive's attempt to restore the situation by calling in men selected from the Madras establishment threatened in its turn to cause a

---

[1] *Seir*, III, 4.   [2] *MN*, f. 151.
[3] Naleky is described as 'the shell of a Palenkin' but it has neither 'the arching nor the tent' of it and is instead like 'an European chair, with two bamboos that rest upon the shoulders of eight men' (*Seir*, III, 4, fn. 5).
[4] Clive's letter 9 July. BSC, 10 Aug. 1765.
[5] They were Councillors Amyatt, Ellis and Hay; Senior Servants Chambers, Lushington and Howitt; Factors Lyon, Oakes, Smith, Amphlett, Bennet and Wollaston; and Writers Gulston, Eylon, Lake, Hutchinson, Round, Collings and Croke. In addition, two surgeons, Crooke and Ham, also lost their lives. (Letter to Court, 19 Dec. 1763).
[6] The powers were given by the Directors to meet the emergency caused by war with Mir Qasim. Clive retained the power for other purposes.
[7] Letter to Court, 31 Jan. 1766.

The Khan at the zenith of his power, 1765–1767

revolt of the Bengal servants, fearful of their prospects, and his high-handedness cracked the solidarity of the Select Committee too. Sumner who had come out with Clive as his second, with the prospect of succeeding him, refused to support Clive further, and he tendered his resignation and sailed for home at the close of 1766. So many losses left too few men even to run the commercial offices properly, especially as those remaining were often junior and in-experienced, heavily dependent on their Banians.[1] To seek to manage the revenues of the province by European agency was plainly impossible.

Maintenance of the existing administrative arrangement was also a part of the grand strategy of Clive's diplomacy in India, the corner stone of which was laid in his settlements at Allahabad. While Spencer had tried unsuccessfully to 'convince the Empire [that] we are not determined to destroy the Mussulman power' and to repudiate an established belief 'that our real views were to wrest the Empire from their hands',[2] Clive sought to achieve success by positively integrating the Company within the framework of the empire, both in the interest of the Company's security and that of his jagir, an institution of the empire.[3] With a sudden change in the subah administration, the camouflage would not have worked.

Personal considerations also drove Clive to rely upon the established Indian administration. He had returned to Bengal intending to stay only long enough to fulfil his obligations to the Proprietors by restoring order and to ensure the future security of his jagir. He had felt cheated when he found the war over and a settlement with the Murshidabad government already precipitately concluded by Spencer. But then he pulled off the coup of securing the Diwani, serving the Company's interests beyond all their expectations by securing to them the revenues of the three provinces.

Naturally, Clive expected a further reward for this extra-ordinary service. He hoped for an extension of the ten-year grant

[1] Letter to Court, 24 March 1766.
[2] Governor Spencer's letter to Directors, 14 March 1765.
[3] Mir Jafar had granted twenty-four parganas to the Company in 1757 as their zemindari and its revenues amounting to Rs. 2,22,958 per annum to Clive as jagir in 1759. When the Company stopped payment to him in 1763 he claimed his right to the payment under Mughal law. In 1764, the proprietors required him to come to India again and agreed to restore payment of jagir money to him for ten years from 5 May 1764. At Allahabad, Clive had his jagir also confirmed by Shah Alam (*FWIHC*, IV, pp. xxvi–xxviii).

of the jagir, and he soon set his agents to work—Scrafton within the Company and Walsh in political circles outside it. But if they were to win him his prize it was essential that he support their efforts by immediate material gains from the Diwani grant. Clive thus needed a spectacular and early success—such as only Reza Khan could provide. Clive himself recognised his own inadequacy in 'civil matters'; in revenue affairs he had reason to feel even more out of his depth. He could scarcely have forgotten the unhappy experience of the revenue administration of the assigned districts in 1758 and 1759. The regular armed action needed to establish the Company's authority in Burdwan and Midnapur, despite Mir Qasim's support of Vansittart and grant of a jagiri sanad, was also fresh in mind.

Only in Reza Khan's district of Chittagong had the Company's possessions been peaceful. Maintenance of the established form of government, with the Nawab nominally head of all affairs and Reza Khan as the real manager, thus seemed the best solution for the problem of making the Diwani pay. Reza Khan was therefore installed and supported, with instructions to avoid 'trouble and disturbances'[1] in matters of confirmation of jagirs and altamghas, so that no clash with their holders might foil Clive's hopes of early profits.

In pursuing this policy Clive also believed that he had chosen the most economical system. In his personal letter to the Directors justifying his use of the existing revenue administration Clive emphasised the point. 'The power of supervising the Provinces, though lodged in us, should not, however, in my opinion be exerted.' Three times the present number of civil servants, he argued, 'would be insufficient...; whereas, if we leave the management to the old officers of the Government, the Company need not be at the expense of any additional servant, yet we shall be able to detect and punish any great offenders'.[2]

Clive made one demand upon Reza Khan: that in return for power and position he should secure the largest possible net gain for the Company from the revenues of Bengal, Bihar and Orissa. Reza Khan accepted the unspoken bargain. He saw little difficulty in securing a satisfactory revenue surplus in time of peace, given sound administration. He maintained a view that 'Cossim Ally increased the Bundibust, but without judgement; Meer Jaffier

[1] Clive to Reza Khan, 10 Sept. 1765. *CPC*, I, 2700.
[2] Clive to the Directors, 30 Sept. 1765.

reduced it from indolence and mismanagement'.[1] He hoped to do better than either. Meanwhile, since Clive's stay was to be short, and his interests were in immediate action, the Khan suggested to Clive, during his short stay *en route* for Calcutta, that a new tax, to be called the Company's Nazarana, might easily be taken.[2] For such a step he had the example of Alivardi, to which he later referred as guide: 'Mahomed Ally Verdy Cawn in his time, in order to defray the expenses of the Mharattoes demanded Nuz-zeranah...and giving the expenses to the Mharattoes, the nomination of Chouth, or fourth, collected it in the Bundibust from the zemindars, which custom from that time to the present [1769] is still continued.'[3] Clive agreed, on condition that the tax might not be 'an occasion of any oppression on the country',[4] and Reza Khan accordingly prepared an estimate and sent it to Clive for approval.[5]

Reza Khan to satisfy his great supporter was ready to have recourse to such expedients, but his paramount aim was to restore the stability and moderation which he associated with Alivardi's regime. His ideas of government were based on what he had seen and learnt before disorganisation had set in after Alivardi's death in 1756, and to that golden age he wished to return. Clive, realising the importance of Reza Khan to his own plans, was ready to permit some return to the old order, and to build up the power of the Khan. But, unhappily for the Khan, Clive had come to depend much upon Sykes, his staunchest supporter in the Select Committee, and all the more valuable after Sumner's defection. It was Sykes whom Clive, despite much controversy, installed in the post of Resident at the Durbar, where he permanently replaced Middleton on 21 August 1765.[6]

Sykes was not well qualified for the post: he was ignorant of the language and perhaps also of the manners and customs of the

---

[1] Reza Khan's note (no date) handed to Goring in Feb. 1775. Francis MSS. I.O. Eur. E, 28, p. 346.

[2] Clive to Reza Khan, 10 Sept. 1765. *CPC*, I, 2700.

[3] Reza Khan's note as enclosure to Becher's letter. BSC, 25 Sept. 1769.

[4] Clive to Reza Khan, 10 Sept. 1765. *CPC*, I, 2700.

[5] Reza Khan to Clive, recd. 20 Sept. 1765; Clive's reply 22 Sept. 1765. *CPC*, I, 2705, 2707.

[6] BPC, 26 Aug. 1765. Sykes said later (BPC, 28 Dec. 1768) that the post was first offered to Sumner but he refused to accept. But after the acquisition of the Diwani Sumner asked for the post which had then grown in importance, and this time he was refused.

Court, for Karam Ali suggests he was not well received there.[1] His only diplomatic experience had been gained when he was Third at Kasimbazar factory. Hastings, the Second there, had acted as Resident, and Sykes had substituted for Hastings during his temporary absence from Murshidabad during the first phase of Mir Jafar's nizamat (1757–60). Clive's need of his support led, however, to his appointment both as Resident, and on Senior's departure for England, as chief of Kasimbazar.

Sykes was the watchdog at Murshidabad over Reza Khan's administration. He was determined to make the most of his position there, and to reap material advantage for himself under cover of active efforts to maximise the profits of the Company. Sykes was determined to win the good opinion of the Directors, and in so doing was ready to disregard both the old regime under the Khan and the ultimate good of the province. Becher in 1769 was to write 'the endeavours of all concerned [were] to gain credit by an increase of revenue during the time of their being in station without sufficiently attending to what future consequences might be expected from such a measure'.[2] Verelst, a member of Clive's Select Committee and his successor as governor, criticised even more broadly, speaking of 'immediate advantage' having been 'the object of every attention at home and here, in preference to every measure which might tend to its future prosperity'.[3] Sykes and his policies may be taken as examples of what Becher and Verelst were criticising.

Sykes's measures to cut down expenses and to push up the revenue demand could not but be distasteful, but relations got off to a bad start, thanks to an act of apparent double dealing. In July and August 1765 Sykes had negotiated with the Nawab a limitation of the latter's expenses, and had received much assistance from the Khan in this delicate task. The arrangement concluded was for the Nawab to have Sicca Rs. 17,78,854-1-0 for household expenses, to pass through the hands of the Nawab and his Nizamat Diwan. Control of the much larger public funds of the Nizamat, Sicca Rs. 36,07,277-8-0, was given, however, to Reza Khan. On 14 August Sykes reported the Nawab's agreement to these measures.[4] Five days later he sent another report to the Select

[1] *MN*, ff. 153, 156.　　[2] Becher's letter, 24 May. BSC, 8 July 1769.
[3] Verelst's minute. BSC, 11 Aug. 1769.
[4] Sykes's letter, 14 Aug. BSC, 7 Sept. 1765.

Committee, saying that the Nawab had agreed to a further reduction of eighteen lakhs 'from the 36 laaks of the Nabob's stipend that was to pass thro' M. R. Cawn's hands—and that the Nabob consents to the proposal from a conviction that it will tend to promote his ease, the peace of the country...'[1]

Sykes had used the Nawab's hatred of the Khan to obtain his consent to a proposal calculated to injure the Khan's power, patronage and influence. The Nawab thus rebelled against being treated as a cypher—indeed Karam Ali relates that, even at his last meeting with Clive at Sadiqbagh, he continued to plead for control of the people of the Nizamat[2] and readily rebelled against the increase of Reza Khan's influence. The Select Committee, in a letter of 25 August 1765 approved of the reduction Sykes had secured.[3] But it was never put into operation, probably being vetoed by Clive on his way back from Allahabad. Clive doubtless realised that the wholehearted support of Reza Khan was needed, both to make the Nawab truly innocuous and to secure the fruits of the Diwani grant. He wanted no hitch to mar his achievement. He had chartered a special ship to convey news of it to the Directors in London.

Sykes also touched very closely on Reza Khan's power when he proposed that the administration of Dacca should come under the inspection and control of Murshidabad. On Reza Khan's elevation to the Naib Subahdari after Mir Jafar's death, Spencer's government had allowed the Khan to retain direct, personal control of the Naibat of Dacca. The Company officials recognised that this government was the source of Reza Khan's private means: he drew an annual salary of Rs. 90,000 as Nawab of Dacca,[4] the same sum as he had drawn as Mir Jafar's deputy in the province.[5] Since his salary as acting Nawab was not fixed until early in 1767,[6] his Dacca income was very necessary. Moreover in Dacca, Reza Khan was able to restore and maintain the form of the old Mughal provincial administration. Immediately after his appointment at Murshidabad, in March 1765, the Khan had sent Jasarat Khan as his Naib to Dacca; and in June 1765, on confirmation in his post

[1] Sykes's letter, 19 Aug. BSC, 7 Sept. 1765.
[2] *MN*, f. 157. [3] BSC, 7 Sept. 1765.
[4] Sykes's report on Dacca. BSC, 18 April 1767.
[5] Reza Khan's salary for 21 months as Dacca Naib under Mir Jafar is shown as Rs. 1,57,000 at Rs. 7,500 per month (Dacca Factory Record. I.O. vol. 6, f. 31).
[6] Clive to Reza Khan, 25 Jan. 1767. *CPC*, I, 2811.

by Clive, the Khan promptly sent Mahasingh, a veteran of Alivardi's regime, to Dacca as Diwan, conferring on him at the same time the title of Maharaja.¹ Mahasingh replaced Ramsankar, the personal Diwan of Reza Khan, who had been acting for the Khan at Dacca.² Jasrat Khan and Mahasingh thus recreated the Mughal division of provincial authority between Subahdar and Diwan. The two officers were independent in their authority, though both were individually responsible to the Khan. They were also made to act as check upon one another: the expenses of Jasarat Khan and his department were paid by Mahasingh, those of Mahasingh by Jasarat Khan.³ Sykes's proposal would thus have imperilled both Reza Khan's personal finances and the structure he had recreated. It was turned down, however, by Clive as an 'impolitic' affront to Reza Khan 'at a time when he was of such consequence to and so principally instrumental in reducing to order and retrenching the immoderate expences of the zemindars and other officers of the Government which without his assistance would have been effected with the greatest difficulty'.⁴

Sykes also achieved only a partial success in his efforts to cut down government expenses, one of the main tasks he had set himself 'as collector of the King's revenue, under the inspection and control of the Select Committee'.⁵ By 31 October he could report considerable economies in the Patna administration's expenses. Under the Naibat of Ram Narain,⁶ and then of Mir Kazim,⁷ these had run about twenty-one and a half lakhs. With the assistance of Reza Khan, Sykes reduced this figure to some seven and a half lakhs.⁸ Even this he thought 'great and heavy', but as he reported he could not cut it further as the ministers 'declare to me that there is no superfluous expence in that sum'.⁹

¹ *MN*, f. 154; Reza Khan to Verelst, 17 March 1767. *CPC*, II, 178.
² *MN*, f. 154.　　³ Sykes's report on Dacca. BSC, 18 April 1767.
⁴ Sykes was quoting Clive in his report to Select Committee (BSC, 18 April 1767).
⁵ In these words the Select Committee described Sykes's functions as Resident at the Durbar. Letter to Court, 24 Jan. 1767.
⁶ Ram Narain, son of Rangalal, was bred in Alivardi's family, was secretary to Seraj-ud-daulah's father. He succeeded Janakiram, Rai Durlabh's father, as Naib at Patna in the time of Alivardi and continued in the post until he was dismissed by Mir Qasim in 1761. As he was killed in 1763 by Mir Qasim, Mir Jafar on his restoration appointed his brother as Diwan at Patna.
⁷ He was Mir Jafar's brother and known also as Nawab Ihteram-ud-daulah.
⁸ The sum was reduced to Rs. 750,920 from Rs. 21,53,934-2-10. Sykes's letter, 31 Oct. BSC, 5 Nov. 1765.　　⁹ *Ibid.*

The Khan at the zenith of his power, 1765–1767

One of the measures he had proposed to effect economies was the removal of Nawab Ihteram-ud-daulah, Mir Jafar's brother, and Dhiraj Narain, Ram Narain's brother, from the posts of Naib and Diwan respectively on grounds of incompetence. Reza Khan did not deny the allegations of their incompetence, but to him as well as perhaps to Rai Durlabh this was no reason to dismiss them without any alternative provision for their maintenance. The Khan did not, it appears, oppose Sykes openly in this matter. But he was about this time frequently in direct communication with Clive in Calcutta both through letters and messengers—so frequently that on one occasion, 19 November 1765, Clive wrote to the Khan acknowledging receipt of his thirteen letters.[1] By the end of September his relation and envoy, Mirza Muhammad Kazim Khan, had set out from Murshidabad to see Clive and 'to explain some affairs relative to the country, etc. to His Lordship in private'.[2] Again early in October he warned Clive that 'in answer to any letter respecting the regulations of the Subah may be deferred until the papers are perused'.[3] It may well be that as a result of this correspondence that on the 25 October the Select Committee, replying to Sykes's proposals of the 21st, laid down that Ihteram-ud-daulah and Dhiraj Narain should be continued in the dignity of their stations while the ministers selected two naibs to act for them in the actual discharge of their duties.[4] The Select Committee, ignoring Sykes's attempt to cut expenses, went on to award an annual allowance of Rs. 72,000 to Ihteram ud daulah and another Rs. 50,000 to Ruh ud din Husain Khan, the Faujdar of Purnea. The grant to Ruh ud din Husain was made 'out of regard to his family connections' rather than in recognition of ability, for in his case too the Khan had recommended arrangements to ensure 'that the revenues of Sarkar may not be lost or neglected, but be managed in the best manner'.[5]

Sykes replied on 31 October with angry complaints of 'fraud and villainy' in every department of the government and of his

---

[1] Clive to Reza Khan, 19 Nov. 1765. *CPC*, I, 2752.
[2] Reza Khan to Clive, recd. 2 Oct. 1765. *CPC*, I, 2714. Mirza Kazem, son-in-law of Husain Reza Khan, Haji Ahmad's grandson was the Khan's envoy to Clive in May and his agent in Clive's camp in mission to Allahabad.
[3] Reza Khan to Clive, recd. 4 Oct. 1765. *CPC*, I, 2717.
[4] BSC, 25 Oct. 1765.
[5] *Ibid.*; Reza Khan to Clive, 26 Sept. 1765 (*CPC*, I, 2710). Ruh ud din was a son of Saif Khan who was posted to Purnea early in the century. The family was ousted by Alivardi and restored by Mir Jafar in 1763.

'struggle with every difficulty that can be thrown in my way by the ministers, Mutseddees, Congoes [Qanungoes] and their dependents'.[1] He accepted the need to retain Ihteram-ud-daulah and Dhiraj Narain since 'our connections' with Mir Jafar and Ram Narain 'made it necessary to give them our countenance, and a proper influence in the country', and forwarded the proposal of Reza Khan and Rai Durlabh, recommending retention in office of the two incumbents, with appointment of three more officers, two on the part of the Company and one on the part of the government, 'to remain not only as checks on their actions, but to enable them to proceed in the collections with greater alacrity'.[2] Sykes had bowed to Clive's known regard for Mir Jafar and Ram Narain, and to the wish of Reza Khan to maintain the old order. But he did so reluctantly, declaring himself 'entirely for having a new class of people of less consequence to manage the affairs of that province', who he expected would be more obedient to 'any orders they might receive from hence'.[3] Though he had reluctantly given in he was as determined as ever for a 'total change' but 'by degrees' and without causing 'great disturbance and murmuring all over the country'.[4]

In the matter of Bihar jagirs and grants in altamgha, to which the Khan had taken the first opportunity to draw Clive's attention on his return to Calcutta,[5] Sykes was not so much opposed as altogether ignored by the Khan and Clive. Reza Khan persuaded Clive to restore these grants, resumed by Mir Qasim and so to restore and preserve the older aristocracy. Clive, determined to avoid 'much trouble and disturbance' at the moment, deliberately excluded Sykes from discussion of the question. Sykes complained that had it been in his power 'to enquire into that article we would find the greater part misapplied'.[6] The first reaction of the Directors was one of approval. 'Altho the Jagheer land form a considerable deduction of our revenues in Bahar', they wrote to the Select Committee on 21 November 1766, 'yet we would not have them resumed, which may have been allotted for the support or dignity of the great families or faithful servants of the Moguls or former Subah; at the same time you are not to admit any new

[1] BSC, 5 Nov. 1765.   [2] Sykes's letter, 31 Oct. BSC, 5 Nov. 1765.
[3] *Ibid.*   [4] *Ibid.*
[5] Reza Khan to Clive, recd. 9 Sept. 1765. *CPC*, I, 2697. Further correspondence on the subject, also in Sept., may be seen in *CPC*, I, 2700, 2705, 2707, 2710.
[6] Sykes's letter, 31 Oct. BSC, 5 Nov. 1765.

The Khan at the zenith of his power, 1765–1767

Jagheer either from the Mogul or the Nabob'. Within the next two years the view of the Directors had, however, changed considerably.[1]

In November the struggle between the Khan and Sykes turned from Patna to Murshidabad. Sykes began by disallowing the settlement which Reza Khan had made at the beginning of the year, at the Punyah held on 25 April 1765. He found Reza Khan's assessments often short of what they had produced in the days of Alivardi, Siraj-ud-daulah or Mir Jafar and in the interests of 'the welfare of the Nabob and our employers' he revised them, to arrive at what he considered 'the just revenues due to the government' and pushed up the demand to a gross sum of Rs. 1,60,29,016-10-2 and a net sum of Rs. 1,50,04,887-2-5. He was not satisfied even with this, and expressed the hope that further increases could be made 'without the least oppression to the farmers or tenants', though he thought 'some degree of rigour' was necessary to rouse the zemindars and collectors and stop general malpractices.[2]

Murshidabad's expenses next came under Sykes's axe, but here Reza Khan was able to save more than at Patna. While expenses at Patna had been retrenched by nearly two-thirds, those of Murshidabad were only cut by little over half, to Rs. 10,24,129-7-17. The ministers intervened to prevent any further reduction and declared what was left to be 'indispensably necessary' for the office staff, roads, charity and other contingent expenses.[3] The Murshidabad Secretariat had been reorganised by the Khan soon after his first appointment as Naib Subahdar in March, and the employees were regarded as his dependants. Rai Durlabh had likewise added to their number by appointment of his dependants. Both ministers held it to be not only uncharitable but also very undignified and dishonourable to throw such humble people out of employment or to grudge them the indulgences they enjoyed. Sykes claimed later to have had encountered difficulties in his continuous process of

[1] The Directors wrote on 11 Nov. 1768 that 'after Cossim Ally Cawn had gone through the odious task of resuming the Jaghirs, it seems to us an error to have restored them, but being restored it will appear very ungracious to resume them' and they asked to know about the 'Rank, Station and Character' of the holders. They were obviously making observation on Rumbold's report dated 6 July 1767, in BSC, 21 July 1767.
[2] Sykes's letter, 17 Nov. 1765. Quoted in Bolts, *Considerations*, App., pp. 143–4. The earlier demand is not stated, but the Select Committee in letter to Court on 8 Sept. 1766 gave Rs. 1,61,00,708, a still higher sum as net receipt.
[3] Sykes's letter. BSC, 25 Nov. 1765.

retrenchment because these people 'had long enjoyed the benefits arising from the profusion of a distracted and indolent administration and been accustomed to advantages which exceed all proportions, when compared to those under European governments', but at the same time he further claimed to have had effected it 'with all possible tenderness'.[1] In fact, however, he had not only thrown many out of employment, but had caused them further distress by not paying them their arrears of salary for over a year, and by calling upon them to render accounts for the past years, on the ground that much government money had been embezzled. The Khan's attitude is not known, but it is likely that he shared the attitude of his protégé Karam Ali who commented acidly in the *Muzaffarnamah* 'at this time the practice began in Bengal of recovering money from dismissed people and despoiling them'.[2]

That there had been irregularities was certainly true, but to dig up the past of the retrenched servants was distasteful, particularly after the recent changes, and specially after the new government of the Company had chosen to deny responsibility for most of the liabilities of the previous government. Reza Khan therefore kept out of the scrutiny of the past accounts undertaken by Sykes. He deputed Ali Ibrahim Khan to act as Amin checking the accounts with Sykes. Their strictness, the *Muzaffarnamah* declares, caused suffering to many, sufferings enhanced by the failure to pay arrears of salary for over a year and then only at a reduction of three-eighths of the sum due.[3] Where the deduction went to is not clear.

Such action contrasted strongly with the Company's attitude when others sought to secure what was owing to them. After Clive's appointment of the Seth brothers to the Murshidabad government, they sought to recover the old debts due to their house from the zemindars and taluqdars. This was resented by Sykes, the Select Committee and Clive alike. Soon after the acquisition of the Diwani, Clive, with a fine air of moral indignation, warned the Seths that 'His Lordship greatly fears that the tendency they seem to have to avarice, will not only turn greatly to their disadvantage, but will at the same time destroy that opinion he had of their inclination and disposition to promote the public good.'[4]

[1] Sykes's letter, 2 Jan. BSC, 4 Jan. 1769.
[2] *MN*, f. 156. Karam Ali wanted to write a book detailing these events, but we do not know the existence of any such work.
[3] *MN*, f. 156.
[4] Clive to the Seths, 4 Nov. 1765. *CPC*, I, 2736.

The Khan at the zenith of his power, 1765–1767

The Seths could not disregard such a warning. They had to forget about the debts due from the zemindars, or at least to abandon hope of even the long standing and customary governmental assistance[1] in their recovery. They had likewise to forget about the money they had lent to Mir Jafar's Jamadars (army leaders) during the war with Mir Qasim and Shuja-ud-daulah, at a time when the Nawab could not regularly pay them. After the Diwani grant came into operation the Seths asked Clive, Carnac and Sykes for the thirty lakhs they had lent to these Jamadars. But since the Nawab's revenues had now become the Company's, and the Nawab's income had been limited, the Company officials refused to recognise the Seths' claims. The only liability they admitted was for the twenty-one lakhs that the house of Jagat Seth had lent to Mir Jafar. This they agreed to pay by instalments over a period of ten years, half from their own revenues, half from the Nawab's.[2]

Reza Khan could have been no more than a helpless observer of the Seths' losses, for the denial of their dues came from Clive, the Select Committee, and Sykes. But in another injury to the Seths he played a more positive though very minor role. In 1773 Sykes recalled to Hastings

On my arrival at the city [Murshidabad] I found the provision of Kellauts[3] in the hands of Jagut Seat and indeed it had ever been with him, but a year after our taking the charge of the Dewanee I did propose to MRC [Muhammad Reza Cawn] the provision of the Kellauts &c on easier terms than he gave them to govt. which was accepted of, and accordingly I yearly sent money to Benarass, for the provision of such articles, as he, MRC, thought could best answer for the Pooneah &c....[4]

In abetting Sykes in this move, Reza Khan damaged the Seths more in their privilege or prestige than in their pocket. Nevertheless the expenditure on this item in 1766–7 was over two lakhs,[5]

---

[1] 'Formerly, when the zemindars and Talookdars owed money to the bankers, the government enforced the payment of it. But now in the Company's time the bankers have been plainly told that their debts could not be recovered for them'. (Reza Khan's note (no date). Add. MSS. 29136, f. 98).

[2] Fourth Report of the Committee of Secrecy, 1773, p. 102.

[3] Khilats or dresses of honour (given on ceremonial occasions. They also used to indicate an appointment or conferment of any title).

[4] Francis Sykes to Warren Hastings, 28 Jan. 1773. Add. MSS. 29133, ff. 347–54.

[5] Actually Rs. 2,16,870-10-10. BSC, 28 April 1770.

8-2

and Sykes recorded that he made '25 to 30 per cent profit' by the trade after paying commission and other expenses. The business was not conducted in Sykes's name of course, but in that of Kantu Babu[1] or some similar agent.

Reza Khan's readiness to assist Sykes in the profitable business of the Khilats was perhaps prompted by Clive's efforts to clear up the misunderstandings between the Resident and the Khan. Sykes had been to Calcutta in September and early October (1765), and Clive may have asked him to make up his quarrel with the Khan. Significantly Clive, writing on 8 October 1765, reassured the Khan that 'with Mr. Sykes' assistance the addressee will be able to carry on the business of the government in a proper manner and without interruption',[2] and the reassurance was repeated in another letter of 19 November.[3] The Khan replied, assuring Clive that he would work in concert with Sykes.[4] Undoubtedly Reza Khan never had a favourable opinion of Sykes, but thenceforth he allowed no criticism to reach either Sykes's ears or those of Clive. On the contrary, he showed extraordinary concern to enlist Sykes's approval in all matters, and to secure his goodwill by further aid in his business transactions.

In matters of internal appointments the Khan had been given absolute discretion—a liberty reiterated in writing by Clive on 19 November 1765.[5] Sykes, unacquainted until his appointment as Resident with anything but the trade possibilities of Kasimbazar, had neither authority nor competence therefore to intervene in the appointment of officials. Nevertheless the Khan was at pains to consult Sykes about his appointments—and Sykes, to return the compliment, made very little criticism of his choices. The Khan could proceed therefore, Sykes concurring, with his policy of conciliating and strengthening the old order.

He had already secured the position and honour of Ihteram-ud-daulah,[6] Dhiraj Narain and Ruh ud din Husain at Patna and

---

[1] Kantu or Krishna Kanta Nandi who made his rise as Banian of Sykes and Hastings founder of the Kasimbazar Raj family.

[2] *CPC*, I, 2722.   [3] *CPC*, I, 2752.

[4] Recd. 8 and 24 Oct. *CPC*, I, 2720, 2729.

[5] 'With regard to the different appointments the addressee [Reza Khan] has been making, he is himself the best judge of the propriety of them' (*CPC*, I, 2751).

[6] Though he retained his rank as Naib of Patna he came to live at Rajmahal. The Naib's seat, the fort at Patna, was ordered to be cleared for English use (BSC, 25 Oct. 1765).

The Khan at the zenith of his power, 1765–1767

Purnea, and he sought further to conciliate Ruh ud din after his loss of power by appointing his Pirzada (spiritual guide's son) and manager Asghar Ali as collector of Dinajpur.[1] Mirza Kazim, a fellow Persian, and a relation by marriage into Haji Ahmad's family, was rewarded with the Faujdari of Hugli, which obviously was taken away from Motiram, Johnstone's Banian. The Diwani of Purnea was given to Suchit Rai, possibly a former dependant of Shitab Rai,[2] though the latter was always a staunch supporter of Nandkumar, and therefore not much of a friend to him. In Dacca, Jasarat Khan and Mahasingh were already his Naib and Diwan; now Reza Khan made Mahasingh's son, Amrit Singh, a boy of 14, his own personal Diwan. Muhammad Aman and Mirza Amanullah, two of Siraj-ud-daulah's officers, were re-appointed to government service.[3] The Khan's keenness to make friends even with the bitterest enemies of the past is perhaps best instanced by his treatment of Ali Ibrahim Khan, at one time a great noble at the court of Mir Qasim. After Mir Qasim's defeat he had lived a wanderer's life. Now, coming to Murshidabad under Mirza Kazim's protection, he was 'received amongst the favourites and friends' of Reza Khan[4]. Reza Khan thus sought to conciliate and consolidate the leading figures of the old regime. He was careful, however, to post his own men as checks at vital points. Thus in the Khalsa Cutchery[5] where Rai Durlabh was Diwan, despite his known laxity, with his son Rajballabh in practical charge, Reza Khan put in Rai Hiralal as peshkar to Rajballabh. For further check and control the Khan put in his brother-in-law, Fath ullah Khan, as his own Naib.[6]

Sykes had raised no objections to these appointments, perhaps because of Clive's admonitions about good relations with the Khan, perhaps because the latter could now assist him in his business ventures. Reza Khan had already assisted Cartier and

[1] CPC, I, 2738; Seir, III, 11–12.
[2] One Suchit Rai is noticed as Shitab Rai's agent at Benares in 1764 (CPC, I, 2456). Shitab Rai, bred in Khan-i-Dauran's family in Delhi, was for long an intermediary between the English, the Emperor and Shuja. He played a leading role at Allahabad, and was made Dhiraj Narain's peshkar at Patna, in 1765. He was to succeed Dhiraj Narain at Patna in 1766.
[3] MN, f. 154.   [4] Seir, III, 11.
[5] The office which dealt with the revenues of the emperor was called Khalisah Sharifa, Khalsa Daftar or Khalsa Cutchery. The unassigned revenue-paying areas were called Huzury Mahls. Normally the provincial Diwan, and in Bengal, since Shuja Khan's time, the Rai-Rayan, headed the office. Mir Qasim abolished the post of Rai-Rayan and it was restored in 1772 by Hastings.
[6] MN, f. 155; Trial Papers, II, 200.

117

other gentlemen of the Dacca factory to pursue their private trade in tobacco without the Company's knowledge. The Khan now agreed to bring Sykes into the ring. Details of the transactions are scanty, but it is known that Reza Khan had agreed to distribute the tobacco to the paikars (petty wholesalers) of Dacca through his Naib and Diwan. Sykes used the system not only for himself, but for his friends and business partners, Warren Hastings being among them.[1]

Sykes also tried to break into the profitable timber trade of Purnea, which was already a monopoly of Richard Barwell, then commercial Resident at Malda. Soon after he made the proposal to Barwell, in November 1765, Sykes sent his gumashtah, Krishna Kinkar, to make purchases in Purnea. The gumashtah found that Barwell had already 'pre-arranged the proper people'.[2] Sykes thereupon reported to the Select Committee that he had received complaints from Saiyid Muhammad Khan, the Faujdar, and from Suchit Rai, the Diwan of Purnea, against Myrtle, Barwell's agent in purchasing timber. He alleged that Barwell was charging the Company more than either private merchants or the ministers would do. The case was considered by the Select Committee on 10 February 1766, and on 19 February it was decided that, since Europeans were making exorbitant profits, the trade should be entrusted to the ministers of the Murshidabad government. On the same day the Select Committee also decided to place the *chunam* or lime trade and the saltpetre trade in the hands of the ministers, to the exclusion of all Europeans and Company servants.[3]

The way was thus opened for Reza Khan to lend the cover of government to Sykes's private trade in different commodities.[4] Sykes fully utilised the opportunity, so much so that Barwell in one of his letters home, written on 28 February 1768, complained that

the exclusive right he has to the trade in Saltpetre, wood and silk is besides a fixed and certain advantage. The saltpetre gives him Rs. 50,000 and for which he does not advance one rupee; the wood in the same manner; but the silk he does advance on. The two former he

[1] Hastings to Hancock, 11 April 1770. Add. MSS. 29125, ff. 31–2.
[2] Barwell's letters 21 Jan. 1766. *BPP*, IX, 80.
[3] BSC, 10 and 19 Feb. 1766.
[4] Barwell, affected in timber trade put it thus: 'They [Sel. Com] had come to the resolution of indulging Sykes with exclusive right to trade . . . by decreeing it an exclusive right of the Nabob's' (letter 1 Sept. '66). (*BPP*, IX, 90).

The Khan at the zenith of his power, 1765–1767

deals in through the influence of the government, the last through his influence as Chief of Cossimbazar factory.[1]

Meanwhile, public expression of the new harmony between Reza Khan and Sykes was given in April 1766, when Clive, accompanied by Carnac, came to Murshidabad for the first Punyah held since the Company's accession to the Diwani. For the first time the Company, in the person of its governor Clive, took its seat at the public Durbar in the capacity of Diwan, second in rank to the Nawab, in the Mughal subah of Bengal. Clive was not ignorant of the value of such ceremonies; if he had been, Carnac with his long experience of Indian courts could have assured him that even 'the princes in the midst of distress keep up all the face of royalty'.[2] The Punyah was held with full pomp and ceremony, at a cost of Rs. 2,16,870-10-10.[3] The Khan rejoiced at the restoration of the dignity of his government, Sykes at the profit on the provision of Khilats; and Clive, Carnac and Sykes assured the Select Committee that the whole proceeding had been worth while. 'We thought it by no means advisable to deviate, upon slight occasion, from the established forms and customs of this anniversary.' In their same letter of 30 April 1766, they added, that 'the expence hath formerly been charged to the government; it must therefore, now of course, be brought to the Company's account; but the amount was so inconsiderable it was scarce worthwhile to introduce any innovation that might lessen their dignity in the eyes of the people'.[4] In fact, however, the costs of the Punyah Khilats were covered by a new tax, the Bha Khilat, but neither costs of the ceremony, nor receipts from the new tax, kept by the ministers in a separate account, were shown in the Company's books. Sykes explained the concealment to Becher in 1769 on the grounds that the Home authorities would not approve it.[5]

The visit of Clive and Carnac to Murshidabad in April and May of 1766 had more than a ceremonial importance. The end of the revenue year was the right time to review achievements and plan adjustments, for Clive would not be in Bengal at the next Punyah. He could view with satisfaction his acquisition of the Diwani— as he wrote to the Directors, 'the revenues of the three provinces

[1] *BPP*, x, 30. [2] Carnac's letter, 6 Feb. BSC, 17 Feb. 1761.
[3] BSC, 28 April 1770.
[4] Quoted in D. N. Banerji, *Early Land Revenue System in Bengal and Bihar*, p. 21, fn. Also *PP*, Third Report, 1773, p. 457.
[5] Sykes's letter to Becher, 16 Jan. 1769. BSC, 28 April 1770.

being now entirely under our direction, we no longer depend for the support of our military establishment on the bounty of the Subah'.[1] He was also very pleased with the arrangement for operating the grant. By the Select Committee's estimates the net collection for the year (1172 B.S. or 1765–6) was Rs. 1,61,00,708 from Bengal and Rs. 61,80,276 from Bihar, an increase of Rs. 11,31,978 and Rs. 5,62,261 respectively.[2] He could confidently advise his correspondents in England that the Company's net gain would be over £2,000,000 a year.[3] For this splendid result Clive and the Select Committee recognised that they were indebted to 'the diligence and abilities' of Muhammad Reza Khan.[4] They acknowledged Sykes's 'assiduity', but placed the main stress upon the Khan's 'profound knowledge in finances' for, as they said, 'without the diligence and skill in the executive officers, all the attention of the Committee to support the influence of government, to enforce the obedience of the Zemindars, and to prevent fraud, embezzlement and depredations committed on the revenue, would fail to produce the required effect'.[5]

Clive had two more major demands to make of Reza Khan before he left for England: a curtailment of the Nizamat expenses which would provide the money for an enlargement of the Company's sepoy army, and the reorganisation of the Bihar revenue administration. Both were initiated after the Punyah in 1766.

The idea of cutting the Nizamat expenditure was not new. Nine days before Shah Alam had formally granted the Diwani sanad, Clive had written to Sykes saying: 'I do not see the least necessity for the young Nabob's keeping so many seapoys and if a part of them be reduced a part of his allowances may be taken off, for so large a sum of money as 50 laaks will I fear distress the Company and if he can be brought to do this and accept 40 we can the better pay the King his 26.'[6] When he came to administer the Diwani grant, however, Clive realised that any such assault on the old order would be untimely and would antagonise Reza Khan. But by

---

[1] Select Committee to Court, 8 Sept. 1766.
[2] *Ibid.* The increase appears to have been made on the anticipated net receipts after Sykes's revision of demands in 1765, and not on the previous year's collection.
[3] Clive to Marquess of Rockingham, 6 Sept. 1766. Quoted in Sutherland, *East India Company in Eighteenth-Century Politics*, p. 138.
[4] Select Committee to Court, 8 Sept. 1766.
[5] Select Committee to Court, 9 Dec. 1766.
[6] Clive to Sykes, dated Benares, 3 Aug. 1765. Quoted in Forrest, *Clive*, II, 282.

The Khan at the zenith of his power, 1765–1767

April 1766, Clive was ready to raise the issue himself with Reza Khan—not with the Nawab, it might be noted, whom Clive ignored. In due course, on 19 April 1766, Clive reported privately to Verelst that Reza Khan had agreed to cut the public funds by twelve lakhs, so long spent on 'useless horses, elephants, buffalos, camels etc.', and that he, Clive, had resolved to raise twenty-six new battalions of sepoys.[1]

The two issues were inter-related. Clive and the Select Committee explained to the Directors that the raising of the new battalions had been made necessary by the dismissal of the Nawab's 'useless military rabble' and of the troops maintained by the various Faujdars and Rajas.[2] Nobody knew better than Reza Khan that the Nawab's troops were a useless rabble. He had constantly to ask Clive for sepoys to maintain order,[3] because the Nawab's forces were ill trained, inefficient, and indeed, at times, a source of danger to him. Clive had removed Qaim Beg in July 1765,[4] but Sher Ali, the Darogha of the Murshidabad Topkhana (or superintendent of the Artillery), had proved scarcely less of a troublemaker. Some of the officers Reza Khan managed to pacify, but others, as Karam Ali writes, 'lost their livelihood'.[5] The dismissal of many of these troops suited Reza Khan as well as Clive, while the money saved provided for the new sepoy battalions. A further advantage was also hoped for, as Clive made clear to Verelst: 'the frequent complaints made by Mahomed Reza Cawn of the power which officers assumed commanding Seapoys, and who are sent only for the purpose of collecting revenues hath made me resolve to new model the army'.[6] The complaints referred to evidently sprang from a clash of authority between the Khan and the Company's officers sent to reduce zemindars to obedience—as when Raja Damodar Singh of Pachete or Krishna Manikya of Tipperah were subdued.[7] The creation of the new sepoy force could be made an

[1] Clive to Verelst, 19 April 1766. *H.M.S.*, 739; 28.
[2] Letter to Court, 9 Dec. 1766.
[3] Reza Khan to Clive: recd. 2 Oct. 1765 (*CPC*, I, 2713, 2714), recd. 6 Nov. 1765 (*CPC*, I, 2739); Clive's replies, 8 Oct. 1765 (*CPC*, I, 2721), 19 Nov. (*CPC*, I, 2752).   [4] Clive to Najmuddaulah, 6 July 1765. *CPC*, I, 2671.
[5] *MN*, f. 155.   [6] Clive to Verelst, 19 April 1766. *H.M.S.*, 739; 29.
[7] Both the Rajas were hereditary chiefs of centuries' old ruling houses and their territories were situated on two extremities of the province, west and east. Pachete covered the area around modern Raniganj in Burdwan. They were subdued in November 1765 and in 1766 respectively (*CPC*, I, 2752 and BSC, 7 Oct. 1766).

The transition in Bengal, 1756-1775

occasion for reshaping the Company's army also. As it turned out, Clive soon became involved in reforming the Company's army in Bengal after there had been signs of indiscipline among the European officers in out-station brigades.[1]

The dissolving of a large part of the Nawab's forces might have been expected to cause discontent in one so concerned with the dignity and honour of the old order as Reza Khan. But many of the old class of army officers had been destroyed by Mir Qasim,[2] and others had disappeared during the convulsions of the late war between the English and Mir Jafar on one side, and Mir Qasim and Shuja-ud-daulah on the other. Those who survived were in the main the dependents and relations of Mir Jafar and his family and of Reza Khan and Alivardi's family. For them government service both in the Nizamat and revenue departments were still open. These were the people who now manned the higher services, and they were provided for.[3]

There remained the troopers, the Biharis, Bhojpuris and Rajputs, and the smaller number of Pathans, Rohillas and Jats, who during the troublesome days of Alivardi and the yearly Maratha incursions into Bengal, and again during Mir Jafar's wars with Shuja-ud-daulah, had flocked to Murshidabad to sell their services. The reduction of the public funds of the Nizamat to twenty-four lakhs in 1766 obviously led to many of them being discharged. But the raising of twenty-six sepoy battalions by the Company provided, far better than the Nawab had done, for the wandering class of North Indian mercenaries.

Fifteen of the new battalions were to belong exclusively to the brigades, 'not to be removed from them or employed upon any other business than fighting'. Two battalions were to go to Calcutta, commanded by Town Major and Barrack Master, and one battalion each to the 'ceded' districts of Burdwan, Midnapur and Chittagong. The other battalions were intended for Diwani duties, three to be posted at Murshidabad and three at Patna.[4] Two features about these six, later known as 'Pargana battalions',[5] were

[1] This led Clive to visit Monghyr and Patna directly from Murshidabad.
[2] Hastings to Coote, 14 May 1762. Add. MSS. 29097, f. 52.
[3] Mubarak-ud-daulah to Cartier, Reza Khan to Cartier, recd. 8 Nov. 1771. *CPC*, III, 975, 976.
[4] Clive to Verelst, 19 April 1766. *H.M.S.*, 739; 29.
[5] These Pargana battalions were later dissolved by Hastings, who created an integrated Anglo-Indian army.

important for Reza Khan. The first was the provision in the scheme that they should have 'but one commissioned officer each at their head who shall always reside at the city and whenever detachments are made no European above the rank of a Serjeant shall command [so] that there may be no disputes about receiving and obeying orders of the officers of the government'.[1] The second was that the battalions at Murshidabad were to be regarded as a 'nursary of recruiting army' from where, as Sykes had directions from the Select Committee, recruits were to be sent to the brigades on requisition, filling up the vacancies in Murshidabad battalions by new recruitment.[2] Hitherto, most of the fighting the Company had done in Bengal and Northern India had been primarily with sepoys brought from Madras and even Bombay—hence their name 'Tilangas' from the first Telegu speaking troops brought by Clive in 1756–7 from Madras.[3] The new policy, confirmed by the Directors, opened the possibility to the mercenaries in Bengal of joining the Company's sepoy army.[4] Clive's proposal that each brigade should consist of equal number of 'Gentoos and Mussalmans'[5] was certainly generous to the Muslims.

When these military changes had been set in motion, Clive turned to Reza Khan for aid in Bihar. He had been much impressed by the Khan during his stay at Murshidabad, and by September 1766[6] the Khan was committed to the delicate though not very difficult or unwelcome task of going to Patna and setting the administration in order. The Patna administration had been

[1] Clive to Verelst, 19 April 1766. *H.M.S.*, 739; 29.
[2] BSC, 3 March 1767.
[3] They were known by this name in Bengal and Oudh even after the North Indian mercenaries constituted the Company's sepoy army. Elsewhere in India they were contemporaneously known as Gardis (corrupted from Gharbis or westerners) (*Seir*, II, 334 fn. 175). In fact the name came to be applied to all troops raised and trained on the European model. Mir Qasim's army remodelled by Gregore was also known as 'Telingas' (the name was very much feared in those days). (Hastings to Vansittart, 23 May 1762. Add. MSS. 29098, p. 57.)
[4] The Directors had ordered recruitment to be restricted to the Company's territories of Bihar and Orissa (Court's letter, 11 Nov. 1768). In any case Clive had created his 'Lalpaltan' in 1757 with multi-racial mercenaries, the same class of people who composed the Nawab's army (A. Broome, *Bengal Army*, 90; Forrest, *Clive*, I, 384) and soon after he raised a battalion of Bhojpuris (A. Barat, *The Bengal Native Infantry*, p. 6).
[5] The Committee of Secrecy approved it (Barat, *op. cit.*, p. 27).
[6] Reza Khan went to Patna in September, but Clive had asked him in July (BSC, 12 Aug. 1766).

very slack. Samuel Middleton, Sykes's predecessor at Murshi-dabad, who had gone to Patna as its chief of the English factory, did not enjoy Clive's confidence. While Dhiraj Narain's incapacity was well known, disorganisation was only increased by the struggle for power between him and his more powerful Peshkar, Shitab Rai,[1] and from Murshidabad neither Sykes nor Reza Khan could exercise effective control. When Clive was at Patna in the course of his visits to army establishments, for suppressing the attempted mutiny of European officers, Shitab Rai, Ghulam Husain sug-gests, saw him to tell him of the anomalies in the Patna accounts and to ask for an enquiry by Reza Khan.[2] Clive found it useful and convenient for he certainly did not wish to appear harsh towards the brother of Ram Narain, his old protégé killed by Mir Qasim for being loyal to the English.

In September 1766, Reza Khan arrived at Patna armed with wide discretionary powers, 'the terrors of power and punishment marching before him'.[3] He examined the accounts, found them very deficient, removed Dhiraj Narain and put his officers in prison. Shitab Rai was installed as Naib of Patna in his place. Reza Khan had been under no illusions about Dhiraj Narain's abilities, nor had he failed to take due notice of Shitab Rai's appointment from Calcutta as Dhiraj Narain's peshkar. Neverthe-less Reza Khan now minimised the unpleasantness of his exit. He might well have followed the common practice, as even Mir Qasim followed with Ram Narain, of imprisoning the late Naib and enforcing payment of the deficit. Instead the Khan wrote off all outstanding balances of the pre-Diwani period,[4] and, in order to make the Raja pay for the short credits since the Company's accession to the Diwani a year earlier, the receipts from his jagir were made over to the Company. The Raja, now deprived of his jagir, was not left to starve; he was granted an allowance for his subsistence.[5]

Reza Khan next settled, as far as he could, the question of jagirs, altamghas and Madad Maash, again with much consideration for

---

[1] *Seir*, III, 17–21. Shitab Rai had accompanied Clive from Allahabad to Calcutta in 1765. Already a great favourite of Carnac, he soon rose in Clive's favour too. His appointment as Peshkar at Patna, it could be noted, was the beginning of something bigger.
[2] *Seir*, III, 21.   [3] *Seir*, III, 22.
[4] Rumbold's letter 31 Aug. BSC, 6 Oct. 1768. The writing off was perhaps of general application to landholders also.   [5] *Seir*, III, 22.

their holders. In September 1765, on Clive's return from Allahabad with the Diwani sanad, the Khan had asked Dhiraj Narain to keep all collections from the jagiri lands separate, pending final consideration about them.[1] To Clive he had proposed that Dhiraj Narain should leave the grants untouched until the holders' sanads could be examined. Where grantees had died or run away or were unable to produce sanads, the lands should revert.[2] To this Clive agreed, adding that he would not touch the jagirs of those who were alive, 'as it might be the occasion of much trouble and disturbance'.[3]

Ghulam Husain, the author of the *Seir*, spoke of this respect for grant-holders rights as 'one of the tokens of Divine goodness, and one mark of English munificence', commenting that but for this lenience 'all was over with the ancient nobility and gentry of this land'.[4] Had he been less hostile to Reza Khan he might properly have given his due appreciation to the Khan's efforts in this, for it was he who now minimised the difficulties of the older nobility by restoring many of the grants which Mir Qasim had called in, and by making new grants, particularly of Altamghas and Madad-i-Maash, which were more permanent in character.[5]

Rumbold's[6] report of 6 July 1767 makes it clear that he thought Reza Khan had been over-generous in acting 'intirely as he thought proper'. Rumbold found many of the jagirdars absentees and others incapable of producing their 'Phirmaunds' (Farman) or title deeds. He believed that if the jagirdars were asked to prove that they held imperial grants many of the estates would revert to the government. But in demanding proofs appropriate to the days of Akbar or Aurangzeb he was asking for more than the English themselves could offer: neither Clive's jagir, nor the Company's jagirs of Burdwan, Midnapur and Chittagong had been gifts from

[1] Reza Khan to Clive, recd. 9 Sept. 1765. *CPC*, I, 2697.
[2] Reza Khan to Clive, recd. 20 Sept. 1765. *CPC*, I. 2705.
[3] Clive to Reza Khan, 10 Sept. 1765. *CPC*, I, 2700.
[4] *Seir*, III, 12.
[5] List of Bihar jagirs etc. enclosed with Rumbold's report (BSC, 21 July 1767). Rumbold defined the altamghas as a gift which descended '... to the heirs of the person possessing it, whereas a Jagheer at death of the Jagheerdar returns to the King'. He, at the same time, defined the Madad-i-Maash as 'a grant of the same kind as Altamgha, but generally given in less sum to ... persons of lower rank' (Rumbold's report. BSC, 21 July 1767).
[6] Thomas Rumbold, one of Verelst's Council in Chittagong in 1761, joined as Chief of Patna and 'Collector General of Bahar' (BSC, 19 Nov. 1767) on 19 Nov. 1766, a month after Reza Khan's visit (BSC, 9 Feb. 1769).

the Emperor, and they were only confirmed in 1765. Rumbold did not press the point, however, for though anxious like Sykes to increase the Company's revenues, he was, says Ghulam Husain in 1783, 'like his other countrymen, in those beginnings of their dominion more careful and more inclined to conciliate the hearts of the natives...'.[1] He had only one proposal to canvass—that the jagir lands should be resumed, and the jagirdars paid in cash from the treasury. His plea was that the lands would 'produce a much larger yearly revenue than [they were] valued at'—implying once again that the Khan had been over-generous.[2]

Whether Reza Khan had been over-generous cannot now be ascertained. What is clear is that by the end of 1766 he had done much to restore the old institutions which he valued. At Murshidabad the Punyah had been celebrated in traditional style. At Patna he had restored many grantees to their estates, and had been given a great entertainment in his honour, and had reviewed the Company's forces on parade.[3] The army reforms instituted earlier in the year had provided for many of the soldiery of the Nawab; and in his Dacca administration, built up from the ruins, he provided for a tremendous number of people, both aristocracy and commoners. In 1775 he was to paint a picture of the ideal past when 'the ryots tho not rich, were content' and when 'the Zemindars and Talookdars were father and friend of the people'.[4] By imposing easy assessments in Dacca[5] he made possible a return to those happier times. In addition he had encouraged the main industries of Dacca, boat building[6] and the weaving of fine muslins. In November 1765 he ordered 455 pieces of cloth for the imperial wardrobe[7] and boats for the use of the Emperor,[8] appointing a special officer in the Dacca establishment to supervise their supply.[9]

---

[1] *Seir*, III, 27. [2] Rumbold's letter, 6 July. BSC, 21 July 1767.
[3] *MN*, f. 160. [4] Reza Khan's note. Francis MSS. I.O. Eur. E, 28, p. 345.
[5] See next chapter.
[6] East Bengal was long reputed for its boat-building industry. In the mid-sixteenth century, it is said, 'the Sultan of Constantinople found it cheaper to have vessels built there' (F. Bernier, *Travels in the Mogul Empire, 1656–1668*) (ed. Constable & Smith) (p. 178, fn. 2). Reza Khan's expenses under the head 'charges boats' at Dacca as found in March 1767 was Rs. 1,14,943 (Sykes's report. BSC, 18 April 1767).
[7] Reza Khan to Clive, 17 Dec. 1765, recd. 22 Dec. 1765. *CPC*, I, 2762, 2762 A.
[8] Annually three or four large boats used to be sent to the emperor (Sykes's report. BSC, 18 April 1767).
[9] The salary of the Darogha was Rs. 100 per month (Sykes's report. BSC, 18 April 1767).

The Khan at the zenith of his power, 1765-1767

The Khan had perhaps one regret, that he could not conciliate Najm-ud-daulah, though his policy of reconciliation with others had more or less succeeded. One reason for Najm-ud-daulah's continued hostility was perhaps the influence of Nandkumar, who had kept up his regular correspondence with the Nawab. The Nawab sincerely believed that Nandkumar was 'much better acquainted...with the situation and circumstances of persons in Calcutta.[1] Nabakrishna offered his help to the Nawab, but he was disregarded only because Reza Khan was friendly with him. The sudden death of Najm-ud-daulah cast a shadow of suspicion on Reza Khan at Murshidabad, as it had done on Clive in Calcutta and London.[2]

Until Najm-ud-daulah's death, on 8 May 1766, Reza Khan was just holding his own position against the Nawab's hostility; on Saif-ud-daulah's accession to the masnad on 19 May the Khan further consolidated his position. Mir Umid Ali and Lahori Beg, who had great influence with the former Nawab, were removed from their posts. Mir Abdul Ali and other trusted persons were appointed as Saif-ud-daulah's tutors. Niamat, who was Najm-ud-daulah's Darogha of the Pilkhana, was reconciled through the mediation of one Nur uz Zaman. Though Munni Begum was not Saif-ud-daulah's mother and as such could not claim the control of the Nawab's household the Khan did not, it appears, object to her continuance in her earlier status. This continued his good relation with Munni Begum.

In defending the interests of the old Alivardian order the Khan continued also to serve the interests of Clive, by furnishing him with evidence that the Diwani grant could be worked smoothly and profitably. To make sure that Clive would have a spectacular achievement to show when he returned to England to press for an extension to the period of his jagir, the Khan had pushed up the revenue demand. Yet, it appears, he had generally received the

---

[1] Najm-ud-daulah to Nandkumar, 8 April 1766. *PP*, Fifth Report, 1773, p. 555.
[2] Najm-ud-daulah accompanied by Reza Khan went to see Clive at Sadiqbagh just before his Lordship was to set out for Patna. They stayed with Clive up to 10 or 11 p.m., when the Nawab complained of indisposition. The Nawab, Sykes told a Parliamentary committee, had taken some ice water. After this the Nawab returned sick and died in 3 or 4 days. The news of the Nawab's death gave rise to a strong rumour, as Verelst informed Sykes, involving Clive (*PP*, Third Report, 1773, p. 325). The rumour was echoed in London (Court's letter, 16 March 1768). Haji Mustapha says that at Murshidabad people pointed to Reza Khan as 'the supposed author' (*Seir*, III, 13, fn. 9).

The transition in Bengal, 1756–1775

support of the zemindars and taluqdars—he had made their interests seem consonant with his own.

Two things seem to have made this possible. The increased demand possibly could be more easily met because there had been a vast immigration of agricultural labour from the west. Warren Hastings stated to the House of Commons in 1767 that the troubles of 1757–64 had driven the manufacturers from Bihar, an open country, to Bengal, 'intersected by rivers' where 'from its natural situation [they were] free from dangers of war'. 'The troubles', Hastings added, 'have caused no scarcity of food or rice.'[1] McGuire, giving evidence to the same committee of the House, argued that the movement had begun with the Maratha invasions of Alivardi's time, which had resulted in the improvement of the areas south of Calcutta.[2]

If the zemindars were thus more able to pay, they were also more willing to agree with Reza Khan's proposals because he stood between them and more direct attack from the Company. Their knowledge of the Company's earlier revenue activities were sufficient to alarm them. The Calcutta parganas had been the first to come under the Company's administration, and there, the Directors observed, 'we immediately turned out all those men who stood between the government and the cultivator' with consequent ruination of many families.[3] The Company's administration in Burdwan, Midnapur and Chittagong, though not as alarming, had scarcely been more encouraging. It was therefore in their interest to co-operate with the Khan who was unwilling to interfere in their internal administration, and had fixed notions about their rights, privileges and duties, based on Alivardian traditions. These notions which formed the basis of his policy throughout were, as reiterated in brief in 1775, that 'the land is the inherited property of the zemindar' and that 'the rent of it is the right of government'. When, therefore, the Muslim emperors, who had 'obtained possession of the country by war', the Khan added, granted 'any

[1] Hastings' evidence to the Fuller Committee of the House of Commons on 31 March 1767. Add. MSS. 18469, f. 21.
[2] W. McGuire's (Verelst's successor as chief of Lakshmipur and Ellis's predecessor as chief of Patna) evidence to Fuller Committee on 1 April 1767 (Add. MSS. 18469, f. 33). McGuire left Bengal in Oct. 1764 after 20 years' stay in the country.
[3] Court's letter, 17 May 1766. Holwell said the same thing to Fuller Committee 'What we did at Calcutta was relieving the people from their own Zemindars'. (Add. MSS. 18469, f. 19). Holwell was in Bengal from 1731 to 1760.

128

The Khan at the zenith of his power, 1765–1767

Jaghier or Altamgha (Royal immunities) they have...bestowed the rent of them'.[1] The landholders in Bengal had no better supporter against attack on their property.

The Khan had difficulties, however, in areas where the zemindars of the Bengal type did not exist, that is in much of Bihar and in Purnea. These areas had recently been battlegrounds, and both contained more jagir lands. Thus Rumbold had reported of Bihar that 'on Cossim Ally Cawn's accession to the Subahdarry he found this province of no value to him, as it then stood, distributed in Jagheers',[2] and Ducarel of Purnea that having 'no hereditarry Zemindarry was long appropriated to men of family or relations or favourites of the Nabobs of Bengall, who held it as a kind of Jagheer, paying little or no rent'.[3] Neither, therefore, had contributed much to the Nawab's treasury. On the contrary, during the whole of Shuja's nizamat (1727–39), the expenses for the province of Bihar had to be paid out of Murshidabad revenues. During Alivardi's nizamat (1740–56), Janakiram (Rai Durlabh's father), as Naib, paid three lakhs per year for three years and another nine lakhs from his own emoluments. Ram Narain paid fifteen lakhs in five years. Mir Jafar received six lakhs from Bihar during his first Nizamat (1757–60), and some twenty-five lakhs after his restoration (1763–5).[4] Purnea, brought under the Bengal Nawabs by Alivardi Khan, never yielded him more than four lakhs a year.[5] Neither area therefore had paid much, and neither had an organisation capable of absorbing the impact of sudden new demands.

Nevertheless on the Company's accession to the Diwani, under Sykes's pressure, Reza Khan agreed to a great increase in the demand. When Suchit Rai was appointed Diwan, or Amil of Purnea, he paid twenty-five lakhs to the government in two years, and in 1766–7 actually raised the demand to twenty-five lakhs for the year.[6] Suchit Ram[7] was an outsider, ignorant of the country and he was quite unable to collect the heavy revenue demanded. He borrowed from merchants to pay the government and ulti-

---

[1] Reza Khan's opinions as sent by Philip Francis to Lord North on 25 Nov. 1775. Francis MSS. I.O. Eur. E, 13, pp. 475–7.
[2] Rumbold's letter, 6 July. BSC, 21 July 1767.
[3] Ducarel's letter, 3 Dec. MP, 13 Dec. 1770.
[4] Reza Khan's note. BSC, 6 March 1769.
[5] Reza Khan's note as enclosed with Becher's letter. BSC, 25 Sept. 1769.
[6] *Ibid.* and also Ducarel's letter, 3 Dec. MP, 13 Dec. 1770.
[7] The name is variously given, and also as 'Sujaut Rai' in *MN*, f. 157.

mately found himself in prison, from which only death released him.[1] Ducarel blamed Suchit Ram's failure on the excessive expenses incurred on account of the officials, who collected the revenues at three levels, in the village, at the pargana cutcherry and at the Sadar cutcherry,[2] but that was to ignore the special nature of the area. In Bihar the outcome was similar. The heavy demand in the first year of the Diwani led to the dismissal of Dhiraj Narain from the Naibat or Diwani of Patna[3] and of Mirza Daud from the Faujdari of Bhagalpur.[4] Then the Khan himself fixed the revenue of the province for the second year at Rs. 68,53,776, inducing amils, mostly his own men, to farm the revenues.[5] This too was a very high figure, though much less than the crore of rupees which Sykes had assured Clive could be collected from Bihar. In the event, as Rumbold reported, many of the amils, particularly Muhammad Ali,[6] Mir Khalil, Mir Abdul Shukur and Sukhlal, failed to collect what the Company demanded, and became the poorer by parting with their money.[7]

Did Reza Khan make a mistake about areas with which he was not conversant? It would seem not, for Rumbold tells us that Reza Khan informed him 'he never expected the whole could be collected'.[8] It appears rather that, in areas which in effect were paying revenues for the first time, he pitched the demand experimentally high, intending to write off balances as necessary. The old practice had always been to write off legitimate outstanding balances[9]—a practice which he himself followed in adjusting the Bihar accounts in September 1766. In this way Clive would be able to impress the

[1] Reza Khan's note as enclosed with Becher's letter. BSC, 25 Sept. 1769.
[2] Ducarel's letter, 3 Dec. *MP*, 13 Dec. 1770.
[3] Shitab Rai's statement. (Trial papers relating to Shitab Rai's trial as preserved in the National Archives of India, pp. 20–1.)
[4] Mirza Daud, Miran's son-in-law, was given the Faujdari of Bhagalpur (the only Bihar district which was administered directly from Murshidabad) in April 1765 by Reza Khan. The Mirza refused 'to give a single dam more' when the demand was revised by Sykes in Nov. 1765, and left the collection without notice. The Khan then, with Sykes's concurrence, posted one Mir Waris Ali, who agreed to pay the higher demand (Reza Khan's letter, recd. 12 Nov. 1765. *CPC*, I, 2745).
[5] Rumbold's letter. BSC, 9 Feb. 1769.
[6] Perhaps he was the author of *TM*.
[7] Rumbold's letter. BSC, 9 Feb. 1769.   [8] *Ibid.*
[9] Balances, said Reza Khan in a note on the past state of Bengal in 1775, 'were formerly very uncommon; whenever they arose, inquiry was made into their causes. If they appeared reasonable the rent was lowered and the deficiency was remitted' (I.O. Eur. E, 28, p. 347).

Directors with a high estimate—and he was not going to stay to see if it was realised. So while Reza Khan was still in Bihar, Clive and the Select Committee reported to the Directors that the Khan was busy 'in regulating the collections of that province; whence we hope revenues will be reduced to more order, and raised to a greater amount'.[1] In a later despatch the Committee not only reported large increases in the current revenues, but encouraged expectations of more with statements of anticipated revenues for 1766–7.[2] What the Khan had not realised was that the Company would rigorously exact fulfilment of contracts from the unfortunate amils, without the enquiries and the abatements customary in former times.

When Reza Khan reached Calcutta in October 1766 he was accorded a vote of thanks by the Fort William Council.[3] Now that he had done what was humanly possible to fulfil Clive's expectations, it was Clive's turn to fulfil the Khan's expectations.

By March 1766 Clive had become convinced of the usefulness of Reza Khan, and had written to the Directors through the Select Committee asking them to send a present as a distinguishing mark of the Company's favour to 'spur' the Khan to further endeavours.[4] But the Directors' first comment on Reza Khan's appointment as Naib Subah, which arrived soon after the Committee's request for a present, was far from favourable to the Khan. Their letter, which was in reply to the letters from the Council and from Governor Spencer of 11 and 14 March 1765, approved the succession of Najm-ud-daulah and the appointment of a regent. But on the choice of Reza Khan for that office they commented, 'we think you passed too slightly over the charges urged against him, of being so very deficient in accounting for the revenues of the province of which he has been Governor'.[5] The Directors doubtless based their comments on the letter of Mir Jafar, received by the Calcutta Council on 30 December 1764. But it is also clear that they were unable to comprehend the political moves of Spencer's government, and that the Khan's appointment was included in the general disapproval of things done by Spencer,

---

[1] Letter to Court, 8 Sept. 1766.   [2] Letter to Court, 9 Dec. 1766.
[3] BPC, 13 Oct. 1766.
[4] They suggested that another of greater value should also be sent to the Nawab 'to prevent his regarding that useful minister with an eye of jealousy' (Letter to Court, 24 March 1766).
[5] Court's letter, 19 Feb. 1766.

the great favourite of Laurence Sulivan, which was voiced by Directors who had ousted the Sulivan party.

On 30 September 1765 Clive had written to the Directors detailing the Khan's achievements, and explaining the governmental arrangements at Murshidabad upon which the Select Committee expended so much time and energy. This letter reached London on 20 April 1766; but the Directors' reply despatched on 17 May still had no favourable comment to make on the Khan's appointment. We know in fact that in a first draft they had declared 'we differ from you in our ideas of the administration of government'. They had objected to the 21 June arrangement of four men sharing the government, a plan likely to produce discord, and had recommended the appointment of one man to conduct the affairs of the government. They had accepted Reza Khan as a proper person to take charge in that case—but had added the rider 'not that we wish to see a Musselman in the office but rather a Gentoo'.[1] Then on second thoughts they omitted all these critical comments from their letter to Bengal, conscious perhaps of their dependence on Clive's voting power. But Clive was not without a listening post in the Direction. The silence, no less than earlier criticism, must have worried Clive.

When Clive set about rehabilitating the Khan in the eyes of the Directors he did not do so by explaining the political significance of Mir Jafar's and later of Najm-ud-daulah's allegations of deficiencies in the Dacca revenues, which as Verelst said had been laid 'solely with a view to prevent him from being appointed to the management of the affairs of the government'.[2] Instead he decided to ensure the Company's protection and support of the Khan by an extraordinary measure, a vote of thanks from the Council on behalf of the Company, which should force the Directors' hands. Accordingly on 13 October 1766 Clive proposed to the Council 'that the thanks of the Board in behalf of the Honble Company be given him'. The motion was unanimously adopted following which Reza Khan was introduced and the 'acknowledgement of the Board' made to him. Reza Khan in his reply of thanks promised his utmost endeavours to continue to enjoy the 'good opinion' of the Board, and for the past success diplomatically gave the credit 'in a great measure to the assistance

[1] Despatches to Bengal, Original Draft, vol. 3, p. 375.
[2] Verelst's minute. BSC, 20 June 1769.

The Khan at the zenith of his power, 1765–1767

given him by Mr. Sykes'.[1] Clive followed this up on 16 January 1767, in his parting minute of instructions to the successor government, with a strong plea for support for the Khan and a statement of the Khan's services given in the strongest terms: 'Justice to M. R. Cawn, the Naib Dewan calls upon me to recommend him in the strongest terms, to the protection of the Committee. His diligence, disinterestedness, and abilities exceed those of any other Mussulman I have yet seen.'[2]

All that Clive could do by commendation he had done. But the Khan was not ignorant of the fact that Clive was going and Sykes remaining, and he was naturally anxious about his own security and continuance in power. He had received a pledge in the Company's name from the Council, but knowing how the decisions of the Council changed from time to time he was not fully assured. Clive had assured him of his support in England, reiterated in his parting letter to the Khan,[3] but if the Khan knew of the Directors' comments he must have felt insecure. He now raised the question of his salary. Until he had won the confidence of Clive by his work Reza Khan had not, cleverly enough, mentioned it. Now that Clive was due to leave shortly the Khan became anxious to have it settled.

He must have been made the more anxious by the actions of Sykes. During the two months that the Khan was away from Murshidabad Sykes, assisted by Ali Ibrahim Khan, had been busy making further economies. The Clive–Reza Khan understanding of April 1766, regarding the reduction of the public expenditure of the Nizamat by twelve lakhs, was incorporated in the treaty of 18 May 1766 which Saif-ud-daulah had signed before being formally installed as Nawab the next day.[4] According to this treaty the public funds at the Khan's disposal had been settled at Rs. 24,07,277-8-0, but before the treaty was signed again on behalf of the Company on 28 November 1766 by Clive and Carnac, who were

[1] BPC, 13 October 1766.   [2] Clive's minute. BSC, 16 Jan. 1767.
[3] Clive to Reza Khan, 25 Jan. 1767. *CPC*, I, 2811 (Clive left Calcutta next day).
[4] It appears that the treaty was signed twice, first on 18 May by all members of the Council except Clive, Carnac and Sykes who were absent from Calcutta, and again on 28 Nov. 1766 by the governor and Council. By this treaty the Nawab agreed that the 'king' was to be paid Rs. 2,16,666-10-9 monthly and that he would accept Rs. 41,86,131-9-0 in all per year. Out of the latter sum Rs. 17,78,854-1-0 was as before 'for my house' etc. and the rest to be spent by Reza Khan (*PP*, First Report, 1772, p. 208). Saif-ud-daulah was seated on 19 May.

The transition in Bengal, 1756–1775

absent in May, the actual amount had been further reduced, first to nineteen lakhs before November and then again to sixteen lakhs in November 1766.[1] Sykes himself seems to have felt that he had gone too far, for in March 1767 he wrote 'What advantage was lost to M. R. Cawn by this reduction I will not venture to pronounce; but am certain that the present sum cannot be lessened without lessening in a great degree the dignity and consequence of the Nabob, which we, as well as himself, do profess ourselves desirous to maintain'.[2] The Directors accepted the situation but with disapproval and sent stringent orders to Calcutta: 'We direct you never to reduce the stipend lower being desirous that he [the Nawab] should have sufficient to support his public character.'[3] Reza Khan must have been shocked by this underhand dealing, which Sykes said later was done at Clive's direction.[4] In any event the Khan became further alarmed at future prospects and became more insistent that his own salary should be fixed.

Until December 1766 Reza Khan's official sources of income had been his salary from Dacca and his jagir.[5] The only advantage he had personally derived had been, as authorised by Clive, the cost of maintenance of his bodyguard of one hundred horsemen and three hundred 'Coss-Burdar' or musketeers.[6] Whereas with Mir Jafar he had insisted that terms be settled before he took office, with Clive he left a monetary settlement to the last, though from a letter from the Khan to Verelst it seems that Clive may have promised him a salary of ten lakhs a year.[7] Now at last Clive proposed to redeem his promise and settle the question.

By November Clive had provided for the Khan's salary by making Sykes unofficially deduct eight lakhs from the Nawab's public funds. The difficulty was to make sure that the Directors would agree to the payment of a big sum despite their expressed dislike of the Khan. Once again Clive sought to tie their hands by action in India. On 31 December 1766 the Select Committee took up the question of the Ministers' salaries, as a matter arising from the

[1] Sykes's letter of 6 March. BSC, 10 March 1767.
[2] Ibid.   [3] Court's letter, 16 March 1768.
[4] Sykes's letter 6 March. BSC, 10 March 1767. The Khan, perhaps, was not aware of Clive's hand behind this deduction which made the agreement meaningless even before it was finally signed. Karam Ali puts the blame on Ali Ibrahim Khan's eagerness to court Sykes's favour (MN, f. 161).
[5] The Khan enjoyed his jagir as a Mughal mansabdar and as a gift from the emperor. His Dacca salary was Rs. 90,000 per year.
[6] By 1772 the strength had risen to 530 sepoys (TP, II, 128).   [7] CPC, II, 30.

134

repeated representation of the Khan. In a skilfully worded minute twelve lakhs was recommended for the Khan, Rai Durlabh and Shitab Rai, 'as shall be settled by the Right Hon'ble the President [Clive] their payment to commence on the last day of January next [1767]'. The distribution of the sum, which remained unspecified in the resolution of the Committee, was later communicated to the recipients as 9 lakhs for the Khan, 2 lakhs for Rai Durlabh and 1 lakh (actually 4 rupees less) for Shitab Rai.[1]

The matter was communicated to London in the last letter from the Select Committee to the Directors signed by Clive as governor, dated 24 January 1767, two days before he set sail for home. In this letter three paragraphs were devoted to the question of salary of the ministers, particularly of Reza Khan, admirably building up a case for the sanction of twelve lakhs as salary for the three— without specifying the amount fixed for each. It was observed that Reza Khan's present emoluments were eight lakhs from per-quisites; and therefore, the letter added, 'we thought it proper in the distribution of salaries, to consider Mahomed Reza Cawn in a light superior to the other ministers'. The letter continued, 'this we have recommended to the President, who will adjust, with their approbation, the several proportion to be drawn from the above appointment'. Finally, there was a strong recommendation for the sanction of that 'great and enormous' sum of twelve lakhs which had been set apart for the ministers on the ground 'that it is neces-sary and reasonable, and will appear so on consideration of the power which men employed on those important services have either to obstruct or promote the public good, unless their integrity be confirmed by ties of gratitude and interest'. The Directors were not told how the twelve lakhs were to be distributed, though Reza Khan and Rai Durlabh were told of their respective salaries by letters from Clive dated 25 January.

The slow exchange about the Khan continued with a letter from the Directors written on 21 November 1766 in reply to the Com-mittee's letter of 24 March 1766. The Directors still cautioned Calcutta against showing favour to Reza Khan and referred again to Mir Jafar's allegations. Not until 16 March 1768, after the news of the vote of thanks by the Calcutta Council and Clive's recom-mendations had been reinforced by Clive's arrival in England (in July 1767), did the Directors authorise the Fort William govern-

---

[1] Clive's letters, 25 Jan. 1767. *CPC*, I, 2811, 2813.

ment to 'assure him [the Khan] of our approbation and protection and of the sense we entertain of his services'. By the same letter the Directors accorded their sanction to the setting apart of twelve lakhs for the ministers.

When they gave their overall sanction the Directors were still unaware of the way in which the sum was allotted, and when they did finally know they could do nothing but comment that nine lakhs was too high a salary for Reza Khan.[1] Clive's manoeuvres had thus succeeded, for the Company had, in the end, to confirm what Clive left as an accomplished fact in India.

In Bengal the Khan had been definitely established in his new position by Clive. Clive's protection had saved him from all his enemies, notably from Nandkumar, whom Clive would have banished to Chittagong had not Nabakrishna's pleas on behalf of the Raja's family and caste dissuaded him.[2] Clive had also shielded Reza Khan's administration from some, though not all, of Sykes's measures of economy. The Khan had been honoured with titles from the emperor, and with the thanks of the Company delivered by the Council. He had been assured by Clive's manoeuvre of a handsome salary. The Khan had also, in his own way, helped Clive to work the Diwani and particularly to secure an extension to the terms of the grant of the Jagir by a further period of ten years beyond May 1774.[3]

To post-Clive Bengal and to the people concerned with the Company in England Reza Khan appeared, and rightly so, as the symbol of the Clive system. Reza Khan and Clive's system had become inseparable. The danger was that any reaction against Clive or against the political and administrative arrangements he had made for Bengal was likely to become a reaction against Reza Khan too.

[1] Court's letter, 17 March 1769.
[2] Barwell's note on Nandkumar (no date). *BPP*, XIII, 108.
[3] Prior to Clive's return to Bengal, the Proprietors had sanctioned Clive the enjoyment of his jagir of the revenues of twenty-four parganas amounting to Rs. 2,22,958 per year for a period of ten years from 5 May 1764. After the acquisition of the Diwani and Clive's achievement in Bengal the period was further extended by ten years at the General Court held on 23 September 1767 (Court's letter, 20 Nov. 1767).

CHAPTER 7

THE EARLY REVERSES,
1767-1768

When Clive left Bengal for the last time, on 26 January 1767, Reza Khan was at the height of his power, the essential key to the system Clive had created. The basis of Clive's system, as he explained in the minute of instructions written for his successor, was that the Company's servants should always remember 'that there is a Subah [Subahdar]...and that the revenues belong to the Company, the territorial jurisdiction must still vest in the Chief of the Country acting under him and this Presidency in conjunction'.[1]

By the phrase, 'the Chief of the Country', Clive meant Reza Khan, whom he saw as the indispensable link between the Nawab and the Company. Sykes, the co-author of the scheme and a principal executant of it, equally held Reza Khan's to be the vital role, saying two years later, 'I should be really at a loss to point out where we could find a man who would fill his station with equal dignity and propriety'.[2] The Khan and the political system were therefore inseparable. If the system failed and the Calcutta government ceased to be united behind it, Clive's towering personality being withdrawn, Reza Khan had to fall too.

Initially the system worked well; under Verelst and Cartier the Company's foreign relations, both with the Indian rulers and with the other European nations trading in Bengal, were conducted through the Khan and in the name of the Nawab. The cloak was successful in making the Indian chiefs look upon the English as the staunchest allies of the Nawab's government, thereby publicising the virtue of English friendship. So Kamdat Singh, the Raja of Morang,[3] applied to the Faujdar of Purnea and to the Nawab for assistance and support,[4] as though power still lay in his

---

[1] Clive's minute. BSC, 16 January 1767.
[2] Sykes's letter, 2 January. BSC, 4 January 1769.
[3] The name 'Morang' then applied to the areas roughly comprising the northernmost parts of Rangpur, Dinajpur and Purnea districts, and perhaps Siliguri sub-division of Jalpaiguri.
[4] Reza Khan, however, sought Verelst's advice in the matter since the Raja of that 'obscure country' had never before sought refuge in Bengal. The Khan, who had already sent some troops to the border, suggested that he

The transition in Bengal, 1756–1775

hands, and the Jat chief, Jawahir Singh, wrote to Reza Khan, when seeking friendship and alliance with the gentlemen of Calcutta.[1] Verelst played his part too by deferring the decision on Kamdat Singh's affairs until the governor had met the Khan and taken his advice.[2] In the negotiations with the Marathas, Verelst had gone even further than Clive in emphasising the independent identity of the Nawab's government.[3] The deception proved no less useful when practised upon the government of His Most Christian Majesty of France for, when the disputes which arose between the two nations in Bengal were later carried to Europe for determination, the English were able to justify their actions as allies of the Nawab, and quoted extensively from the orders of Reza Khan.[4]

Reza Khan, for his part, had reason to welcome Verelst's governorship, for, since their first meeting at Sitakund in January 1761, they had remained personal friends. It was Verelst's testimony to the Khan's abilities as an administrator and also to his integrity in financial matters which, more than anything else, had drawn Vansittart's attention to the Khan. Verelst's influence was most probably an important factor in neutralising Clive's initial prejudice against the Khan in May 1765. Indeed their long-standing personal relationship seems to have ripened into something more: when Verelst visited Murshidabad as governor he stayed at the Khan's palace, Nishat Bagh,[5] while Verelst's descendants in Ireland possessed a letter in the handwriting of Reza Khan's eldest son, which read 'Hausin Ally Khaun presents his compliments with his first essay of English writing to his good friend

should be reinstated and helped against his enemies who were assisted by the Rajas of Bhutan and Amarkot. His country was very large and it extended as far as Nepal. The Raja should be, he suggested, made to pay annual tribute and agree to allow export to timber (Reza Khan's letter, recd. 12 Feb. 1767) (*CPC*, II, 43A).

[1] Jawahir Singh's letter to Reza Khan, recd. 12 April 1767. *CPC*, II, 296.
[2] Verelst to Reza Khan, 30 March 1767. *CPC*, II, 241.
[3] Alivardi Khan had put a stop to Maratha invasions of Bengal by agreeing to pay a sum as Chauth (literally, a fourth) to the Nagpur court besides putting Orissa (minus Midnapur) under a Maratha–Nawab condominium. During the war against Mir Qasim the Calcutta government had offered to stand surety for the Bengal Chauth and urged the Marathas not to offer help to Mir Qasim. Clive had sent Mir Zain ul Abedin, a relation of Reza Khan, envoy to Nagpur. Verelst did not directly deal with the Maratha envoy, but took him to Murshidabad and there held a conference on the matter along with the Nawab, Reza Khan, and Zain ul Abidin (*CPC*, II, 77, 94, 141, 153, 381, 418).   [4] For detail, see *H.M.S.*, 102.
[5] For example, letter to Smith, 21 May. BSC, 8 June 1767.

138

The early reverses, 1767–1768

Mr. Verelst in wishing him a happy new year'.[1] Moreover, the good relations between the two men do not seem to have been based upon any corrupt bargains between them. Verelst, after he had purchased the private business of Sumner, did ask the Khan to get his officers to help him in realising the balances due at various Arangs or trade centres,[2] and on another occasion the Khan lent money to friends of Verelst, Verelst standing as surety and joint signatory to the debts.[3] The Khan also bought the Khairati Bagh in Calcutta from Verelst. But these were minor acts of friendship, not the exploitation of claims such as the Khan's dependence on Verelst might have made possible. The real value of the good relationship between them was that it prevented the growth of any mutual misunderstandings when circumstances became increasingly difficult for Reza Khan and Verelst alike.

At the bottom of many of the difficulties of both the Khan and Verelst was Francis Sykes, the man who had taken a large part in making the position of the Khan secure, and who as one of the two survivors, with himself, of Clive's Select Committee, should have provided useful support for Verelst. His pursuit of private trade and of enhanced Company revenues was to embarrass and entangle both.

The Court of Directors, it will be remembered, had on 8 February 1764 positively forbidden to their servants in Bengal all trade in salt, betel-nut and tobacco, and in June 1764 and February 1765 had reiterated the ban. However in August 1765 Clive and the Select Committee had proceeded to organise a trade society with a monopoly of these three commodities. The capital stock of the society was then divided into $56\frac{1}{2}$ shares distributed among the

---

[1] The original was in Ireland until 1908, but a transcript has been preserved in the archives of the India Office, London (*H.M.S.*, 739; 1).

[2] Verelst's agents were Huzurimul's gumashtahs, Surdas Singh at Rangpur, Maina Ram at Rajganj, Raghunath Jugal at Jagannathpur, and Sukhdev Majumdar at Handial (Verelst to Reza Khan, 27 April 1767. *CPC*, II, 364).

[3] The details of the transactions are not clear. A letter from Reza Khan to Nabakrishna (*CPC*, II, 783 B) in Jan. 1768 speaks of Verelst having asked the Khan to help M. Chevalier with a loan of Rs. 1,20,000 which Chevalier had asked from Verelst. Reza Khan found it 'impossible' to procure the sum. But Barwell, Verelst's attorney at Dacca in 1774, speaks of 'joint bond' and assures Verelst (letter of 30 Nov. 1774) that he would adjust the engagement 'between you and Mahomed Reza Khan' to the satisfaction of 'the Nabob without involving yourself' (*BPP*, XII, 190). One John Knott's letter (from London on 29 March 1774) says that the Khan had lent three lakhs of Sicca rupees to a joint concern (Ghose, *Maharaja Nubkissen Bahadur*, pp. 26–9).

sixty-one most senior members of the Calcutta government, Clive himself receiving five shares, Sumner and Carnac three, the ten Councillors and two Colonels two each.[1] Reza Khan was made to issue one hundred and six parwanas facilitating the trade. The more junior servants of the Company were excluded from membership of the society. They and the free merchants were then further provoked when, by a regulation of 5 October 1765, European servants of the Company not employed in any factory and all free merchants trading in Bengal under the Company's protection and license were called back to Calcutta. The regulation applied to the junior servants spread out in the different Arangs (trading posts) and out-stations, except such as were engaged in providing the silk investment for the Company. Moreover no one was allowed to send gumashtahs or native agents into the interior of the country without authority from the Calcutta government.

The junior Company servants and merchants were incensed, for they had been deprived of extensive means of enriching themselves. The instance of William Bolts may serve to illustrate the extent of the private trade thus forfeit. Bolts, a Dutch adventurer, who had been in the Company's service since 1760, had made £90,000 in six years[2] and in 1767 he had over eight lakhs of rupees invested in the countryside. The Company's investment in Bengal about the same time, as William McGuire told at a Parliamentary enquiry in 1767, was about forty lakhs per year at the rate of eight lakhs per ship and five ships per year.[3] It was no wonder that Bolts had found it more profitable to resign from the Company's service on 24 November 1766 to concentrate on trade as a private merchant.[4] The Company's service did not pay as well as private trade. The salary of a Councillor, Clive had observed, is 'scarcely three hundred pounds per annum: and it is well known that he cannot live in the country [of Bengal] for less than three thousand pounds. The same proportion holds among other servants'.[5]

The orders were the more galling because though issued in the name of high sounding principles, they did not stop private trade or

---

[1] Below the Council, the second category of Company servants, comprising 18 men, held 12 shares, and the third category of 28 men held the remaining shares (*Considerations*, 170–2).
[2] N. L. Hallward, *William Bolts*, p. 3.
[3] Macguire was in Bengal for 20 years until 1764 (Oct.). (Add MSS. 18469,f. 32).
[4] N. L. Hallward, *William Bolts*, p. 45.
[5] Quoted in Forrest, *Clive*, II, 300.

the monopolisation of the inland trade. The measures merely transferred the gains of trade to the senior servants of the Company, to the men in authority. Thus, while the orders of 5 October were being enforced, Clive was sending out ten European agents for the Society of Trade. Those Europeans who had influence with the members of the Council or the Select Committee were also able to secure exemptions and repeated extensions of the time allotted in which to wind up their affairs. Thus Barwell retained his station during the remainder of Clive's stay in Bengal, thanks to the influence Verelst exerted in his favour.[1] The regulations about the residence outside Calcutta and the movement of gumashtahs thus became an instrument of patronage.

Reza Khan found himself involved in the conflict between the different groups of the Company's servants over private trade. He had facilitated the operation of the Society of Trade and had provided the occasion for the regulations of 5 October 1765. This last he had done by writing at the very beginning of October, asking Clive and the Select Committee that

orders may be issued to the gentlemen of the factories of Jahangirnagar [Dacca] and Lakhipur [in Noakhali] to see that none of the dependants of the factories lend money to the zamindars, etc., without the knowledge of the *amil*, or hold any farms, or interfere in the affairs of the country, or send any people into the districts and make a disturbance. Orders may also be issued to the effect that whatsoever demands the dependants of the factories have upon the zamindars, etc., they must lay the account thereof before Jasarat Khan, the Naib at Jahangirnagar, that he may oblige the zamindars to pay whatever is just.[2]

It is clear that the Khan in so writing was seeking to strengthen the country government (and particularly his own administration in Dacca) and to make it really effective, and that he wanted restrictions to be placed upon the native agents of the factories and not upon their English masters. Indeed, though we do not know how his relations were with the English at Lakshmipur, it is certain that he was on cordial terms with those at Dacca and especially with Cartier, the chief of Dacca. His complaint, however, was made the occasion for the recall of junior servants and free merchants to Calcutta. The odium of that move was thus cast upon the Khan,

[1] Richard Barwell to his father, 1 Sept. 1766. *BPP*, IX, 89–91.
[2] Reza Khan's letter, recd. 4 Oct. 1765. The quotation is from the summary in *CPC*, I, 2715. Also BSC, 5 Oct. 1765.

the more so, as by another provision of the regulations, the Committee laid down that if any one overstayed the period of grace, allowed to 21 October, the Khan and his officers would be free to 'take what measures he thinks proper to send them down to Calcutta'.[1] The Khan was also supplied with lists of those authorised to stay in the interior of the country.[2] The Khan seems very prudently to have avoided any exercise of these powers, but he could not avoid the unpopularity of seeming to be author of the regulations.

The effect of this can be seen in the complaints which Barwell began to voice with increasing bitterness from February 1766 onwards. In a letter of 18 February, Barwell complained to the Select Committee of the 'pernicious influence tending to prejudice the Company's trade and that of their servants, [which] had been exerted by His Excellency [Reza Khan] and endangered the concerns immediately under my management'.[3] Before Barwell's complaint had reached the Select Committee, they were already seized of a complaint from Reza Khan, in terms reminiscent of those of Mir Qasim or the restored Mir Jafar,[4] of continued English interference with the free trade of the country. He wrote:

The Zamindars of the pergunnahs of Radshy [Rajshahi] Ruccunpoor, and other districts in the Subah of Bengall complain that the factories of the English gentlemen in the pergunnahs are many and their Gumastahs are in all places and in every village almost throughout the province of Bengall; that they trade in Linnen, Chunam [lime], Mustard seed, Tobacco, Turmerick, Oil, Rice, Hemp, Gunnies, Wheat &c in short in all kinds of grain, Linnen, and whatever other commodities are produced in the country; that in order to purchase these articles, they force the money on the Ryots, and having by these oppressive means bought their goods at a low price, they oblige the

[1] Clive to Reza Khan, 8 Oct. 1765. *CPC*, I, 2722.
[2] Initially the two incomplete lists contained names of the Company's servants at different factories (*CPC*, I, 2722A) and of the free merchants (*CPC*, I, 2722B).
[3] Barwell's letter, 18 Feb. BSC, 28 Feb. 1766.
[4] Vansittart, it may be recalled, had written to the Secret Committee of the Directors on 24 Dec. 1763 that '... the present system is such that it is with great difficulty a friendship can be maintained with any Nabob. Our connections in the country are so extended by the pursuit of private trade through a number of new channels in distant parts of the country ... [that] already many such [complaints] have come from Meer Jaffier in terms just the same as were ... used by Meer Cossim'.

inhabitants and shopkeepers to take them at an high price, exceeding what is paid in the market. That they do not pay the customs due to the Sircar [government] but are guilty of all manner of seditions and injurious acts, for instance, when at any time the malguzzarree [payment of revenue] is demanded of the Taalucdars, Royt &ca subjects of the Sircar, the aforesaid Gomastahs under the pretence of debts due, or accounts to be settled do not let them go, or suffer the revenue to be taken from them and upon complaints at the instance of lying informers and base men, they place their peons over the Ryots and involve them in variety of troubles; that by pressing people violently into their service and imposing many and diverse commands on the officers of the government, the inhabitants, the tradesmen and others, they ruin everybody and reduce the village Gunges [trade centres] to a state of desolation.

It is by this iniquitous practice that the people of the country, have been ruined and driven to flight and that the revenues of the Sircar have been injured; there is now scarce anything of worth left in the country.[1]

After stating the circumstances, the Khan went on to appeal:

If justice be not done in this case, how will it be possible in future to collect the duties of the government or its revenues? All the Zemindars make the above complaint and what I have herein written is only an abridgement of the accounts given in at large by them of violence and oppressions. As it is requisite for the prosperity of the country and the well-being of its inhabitants as also for the obtaining the full revenue and duties, that the poor etc. have justice done them and that disturbances be put an end to, I have therefore represented these matters to you gentlemen of the Committee.[2]

The Khan had been driven, in his defence of the old order, and of zemindars with whom he can perhaps be seen to be identifying himself, into an attack upon the gumashtahs and their interests, and more dangerously upon the English gentlemen behind them who had virtually monopolised the trade 'in grain, linnen and whatever other commodities are produced in the country'.

Once again a complaint by the Khan was used by the Select Committee as occasion for measures which, while seeming fair and harmless on paper, in practice served the interests of their own members. They placed the chunam or lime trade and the trade in timber at the disposal of the Murshidabad government while they opened the opium trade to all, 'subject to such restrictions only as

[1] Reza Khan's letter. BSC, 19 Feb. 1766.   [2] *Ibid.*

the ministers and officers of Government may think proper'.[1] The effect of this was in fact to enable Sykes at Murshidabad to establish his personal monopoly over most of these articles to the exclusion of others previously interested in them. The process can be traced in Barwell's private correspondence. A month before this regulation Richard Barwell, commercial resident at Malda, wrote to his family:[2] 'When I was at Mootajeel [Motijheel] with Mr. Sykes in November...he acquainted me of his desire to be concerned in the timber trade.'[3] Barwell had inherited a monopoly in Purnea and Dinajpur including the timber trade of Purnea, from his predecessor Gray, now promoted to Council. Barwell had found the trade profitable enough to engage European agents, a Mr Myrtle and two others,[4] to work for him at the Purnea supply point, and he was unwilling to let Sykes participate. Sykes was no less determined to secure a share, and from his vantage point at Murshidabad he proceeded to make use of the machinery of the government against Barwell. By February Barwell was already under pressure from the Calcutta government to recall his three European agents in Purnea and so to comply with the regulations of 5 October 1765. The next stage Barwell related to his father as follows:

At this time Kishen Kinker, Mr. Sykes Gomastah was in Purnea; and soon after proceeded up for the purchase of wood. Being disappointed by my having pre-engaged the proper people, he wrote, as is evident, to his master, and his master to Souchetroy the Diwan or Amil of Purnea and Souchetroy to the Resident at the Durbar, a very pretty farce, and which I confess makes my blood boil not a little...Kishen Kinker in Souchetroy's address, you will observe, is mentioned as an agent of the Nabob's though in reality Mr. Sykes Gomastah.[5]

This complaint by Sykes's gumashtah to the Nawab's officials and so to Sykes himself was followed, as has been seen, by the Select Committee, of which Sykes was a member, putting the timber trade at the disposal of the Murshidabad government. In other words, Reza Khan's name was made the cover for Sykes's neat manoeuvre to oust Barwell from the timber trade. At this date

[1] BSC, 19 Feb. 1766.
[2] Richard's father, William Barwell, was in Bengal from 1722 to 1750 and was governor of Fort William in 1748–9. (*BPP*, xvxii, 35).
[3] Barwell's letter, 21 Jan. 1766. *BPP*, ix, 80.
[4] BSC, 10 Feb. 1766.   [5] Barwell's letter, 21 Jan. 1766. *BPP*, ix, 80.

The early reverses, 1767–1768

Barwell was well aware that his opponent was Sykes, not Reza Khan, but by January 1767, when Clive's 'dual' system was fully established, Barwell had come to see the system as the enemy and to direct his attack against the existence of the 'Moorish government' under Reza Khan. In a letter to Beaumont in England he observed on 1 January 1767:

I will venture then to affirm our present government excellently calculated to fix the yoke of slavish dependence, for let me ask, who is there that will dare to breathe a wish or utter a thought that may render him obnoxious to a man or set of men who have it in their power to ruin all his future prospects...and yet this is a very natural consequence whenever this settlement shall be cursed with a villain who shall act behind or hide behind such a skreen as is this Moorish government.[1]

He added:

In such case where then is the poor sufferer to seek redress...Is he to look for it from the Board, Yes. And the Board possibly shall so far heed his representations so as to sacrifice a worthless Phousdar or a Zemindar.[2]

Barwell was voicing a personal anger, but the frustrating situation created by Clive's measures affected all the junior Company servants and free merchants. A general resentment was thus growing against the system on which Reza Khan's power and position was built.

Verelst was obliged, as a close associate of Clive, to adopt and continue the policy he had inherited, and in consequence he also inherited the hostility of Clive's critics. Barwell observed in a letter he sent home on 9 December 1767:

Since Mr. Verelst's accession to the government the system has been regarded which his Lordship thought proper to adopt, and, as the Directors themselves by their silence on some points and acquiescence on others have encouraged, if not entirely approved, the extortion of any arbitrary power the Governor, whoever he may be must prove dead indeed to ambition not to seize the opportunity that is offered him to render his will and pleasure alone the principle of governing.[3]

But Verelst had to pursue Clive's policy without Clive's strength. Clive had come armed with extraordinary emergency powers conferred on him by the Proprietors. Verelst succeeded to the

---

[1] Barwell's letter to Beaumont, 1 Jan. 1767. *BPP*, IX, 111.   [2] *Ibid.*
[3] Richard to William Barwell, 9 Dec. 1767. *BPP*, X, 9.

145

government when the emergency was over. Clive could count on unquestioned support of the Directors at home; Verelst could not. Clive had had a free hand to adopt any measure that he deemed necessary, while Verelst had a line of conduct predetermined for him without the necessary means of executing it. All that he could hope for as a Clive man was support from a pro-Clive direction which by this time was under very severe attack.

Verelst not only lacked solid support from England, his hand was also weakened in India, mainly by the changes in the power of the Select Committee. Of the original Committee of 1765, Clive, Sumner and Carnac had gone, while Sykes, more of an embarrassment than an aid, was at Murshidabad. Richard Becher, it is true, was sent out by the Directors to strengthen Verelst, and Cartier, the second in Council, generally supported Verelst, though he was no politician and so rather a lightweight. Colonel Smith, later made Brigadier-General, did not long continue a supporter,[1] while in January 1769 Sykes left for England. Moreover the Directors, by mistake or deliberate policy, further weakened the Committee by their conflicting orders about its functions. Clive had vested it with extraordinary authority and made it politically superior to the Council. But the Directors, in a letter of 12 January 1768, placed the political activities of the Committee and the expenditure of the Diwani revenues under the direction of the Council. A further letter of 16 March 1768 from the Directors confirmed the change and extinguished the extraordinary powers of the Select Committee. Thereafter the Council took charge of many of the subjects previously the Select Committee's exclusive concern, and from 22 August 1768 the Council began to sit also as a Secret Committee. Reza Khan who had so long to deal with the Select Committee alone thereafter came increasingly under the Council's control.

Verelst had had to face some interested opposition within the Select Committee, but now he had to deal with a larger Council composed of comparatively junior servants of the Company. How

---

[1] Smith had a dispute with Verelst over his designation. Clive was President and Commander-in-chief. After Clive's departure Verelst claimed the supreme command over the Company's troops as President, while Smith claimed to be recognised as the Commander-in-chief. The Colonel had ultimately to accept the position of Commander-in-chief under the Presidency (Barwell's letter of 9 Dec. 1767. *BPP*, x, 11). The Directors made an order on 30 June 1769 saying that 'our Governor is to all Intents and Purposes the Commander in Chief of our Forces', but Verelst was 'not himself to hold . . . a Warrant for appointing General Court's Martial' except in Council.

146

this reacted upon his authority can be seen in the question of a successor for Sykes at Murshidabad. Sykes had given notice of his intended resignation on 14 October 1768, and the question was raised in the Council on 18 November whether the post of Resident at the Durbar, because of its importance, should automatically go to the second in Council, in this case Cartier. No unanimity could be reached and the question was deferred while the members of the Council were circulated for their opinions as to whether the second should be stationed permanently in Calcutta or not, and whether, if the second were posted out of Calcutta, Cartier should be offered Murshidabad. The question seemed one of principle but it was evidently linked with that of the active support on which Verelst could depend in his transactions in Council. Verelst, Barwell hinted, was interested in having Cartier out of Calcutta so as to give him a sure working majority on the Select Committee,[1] and the record of voting in the question would seem to confirm Barwell. Verelst, Becher and Sykes voted for Cartier's posting to Murshidabad, Colonel Smith, Charles Floyer,[2] James Alexander, Claud Russell, Francis Charlton voted against. Cartier, though not very enthusiastic about going to Murshidabad, had asked that he should be nominated Resident, if there were no other reason than his being the Second in Council to make it inadmissible, but the Council chose Becher, thus removing another active supporter of Verelst from the Council.[3]

Reza Khan was to find that Verelst, as his governorship continued, became less and less able to support and protect him against the pressure of private interests. Immediately, however, his

---

[1] In a letter, dated 6 Sept. 1768, which he sent home, Barwell said that Verelst and Becher expected to be the majority after the departure up country of Cartier and Russell on a deputation to Shuja-ud-daulah (*BPP*, x, 34). Russell, who happened to be acting member of the Select Committee in the absence of two members, Sykes and Smith, who were permanently posted out of Calcutta, had incurred Sykes's displeasure by enquiring when he would resign the chiefship of Kasimbazar which had been ordered by the Directors. He had also offended Verelst somehow (Barwell's letter, 9 Dec. 1767. *BPP*, x, 11–12). Aldersey got the Kasimbazar post and Russell was disappointed. But in the appointments made in 1768 Verelst was beaten when he failed to get the Second's post at Kasimbazar for Maddison, and Reed, one of the sufferers under Clive, got the acting chiefship at Chittagong. As Barwell says, both Becher and Verelst had promised Chittagong to Barwell (*BPP*, x, 34). Cartier was not always helpful.
[2] Charles Floyer, a critic of Reza Khan, had been superseded by Rumbold, a friend of Verelst. It was Clive's doing (Court's letter, 16 March 1768).
[3] BPC, 28 Dec. 1768.

position was more directly threatened by his Indian rivals. Soon after Clive left repeated attempts were made against the life of Nabakrishna,[1] who had been appointed the Company's political Banian by Clive's government. The method adopted was to use English law as then administered in Calcutta by the Mayor's court, and behind the move was Nandkumar, backed by other Europeans and Indians.[2] The attempt was frustrated and Nandkumar was officially censured and threatened with withdrawal of English protection and handing over to Reza Khan.[3] But almost simultaneously with the attacks on Nabakrishna came others upon Reza Khan, first against his continuance in power and then against his life. Whether there was any connection between the conspiracies against the two very powerful native instruments of Verelst's government is anybody's guess, for no clues have been found to discover the hands which acted against Reza Khan.

In September 1767, Colonel Smith sent from Allahabad two letters bearing what were apparently Reza Khan's seals. These were found in a bamboo case near the body of a dead man, one of the two messengers said to be attacked by robbers in the province of Kora. The letters supposedly bearing Reza Khan's seals were addressed, one to Jawahir Singh, the Jat chief, and another to a Govindram, an inhabitant of Akbarabad or Agra.[4] If they had been genuine they would certainly have destroyed all trust in the Khan.

The alleged letter to Jawahir Singh, the Jat chief, began with a reference to earlier letters about the 'situation in this country, the superiority of the Nazarenes [the Christians or English], the designs laid for the expulsion of the evil minded tribe, the league formed with the Afghan raiders for the chastisement and dispersion of those who are in your quarter'.[5] It also spoke of the earlier messages sent through representatives. The preamble which followed the above introduction read:

Seeing that the ordering and regulating the affairs of the [Mughal] Empire and the extermination of the traitors of this realm are points which it becomes and behoves all the Grandees of the Throne and every noble of consequence in Hindostan to pursue as his particular cause, I

[1] Verelst, *View*, 30.   [2] N. L. Hallward, *William Bolts*, 48–9.
[3] BSC, 18 April 1767.
[4] Colonel Smith's letter, 25 Sept. 1767. BSC, 13 Oct. 1767.
[5] Alleged letter of Reza Khan to Jawahir Singh. BSC, 13 Oct. 1767.

The early reverses, 1767–1768

am well persuaded that in consequence of your well-wisher's overtures you will think seriously of this cause and the means of destroying this enormous evil.[1]

The letter went on:

Tho your well-wisher has by a course of long services made this tribe [the English] as it were his own and procured the administration of everything in these Subahs to himself; yet there is no dependence to be placed on the words and professions of these insidious word-breaking and rapacious people: In so much that I who have expended immense sums, what from my own house and patrimony and from the revenues of the country, merely for the gratification and use of their principals and agents. I who have consumed my time in attaching affections and soothing the heart of each individual, I who have labored with all my abilities and still continue to labor for them, not withstanding all that I have done I have not found one of them sincere nor have I confidence in my mind, no not the smallest for they to this hour keep up my enemy in hope among themselves.[2]

It further read:

Every year brings fresh numbers of their countrymen to the management of their affairs and just as their interest and [illegible] suggest they make changes and dispositions in their government. Hence it is, that from my attachment and devotion to them I have reduced myself to straits and now with both hands and with constant prayer I call out in the temple of God for the utter perdition of these base and evil men and in this work I am the co-adjutor and friend of you all.[3]

Explaining the opportunity then available the letter added:

Seeing that at this time several English Sardars are become without heart and discontented from the removal of Sabut Jung [Clive] (of which your excellency has probably been informed), the season is as favorable as we could wish it....[4]

The alleged letter to Govindram appears to be in reply to a petition, and states that its author had also written to Najib-ud-daulah, the Rohilla chief and an unnamed 'Mehah Rajah'. There is also an order to deliver the letter and 'on receiving the answer to commit it to the same Cossid'.[5]

[1] Alleged letter of Reza Khan to Jawahir Singh. BSC, 13 Oct. 1767.
[2] Ibid.   [3] Ibid.   [4] Ibid.
[5] Alleged letter of Reza Khan to Govindram of Akbarabad. BSC, 13 Oct. 1767.

149

The transition in Bengal, 1756–1775

As Colonel Smith observed in his forwarding letter of 25 September 1767 'the arguments made use of in his letter to the Jaut to encourage an invasion are specious and well calculated to produce effect. At Agra it would not have been known whether the letter was real or fictitious and possibly might have obtained certain degree of creditibility'.[1]

The Colonel, an irritable man and recently in dispute with Verelst over his status as Commander-in-chief, was by no means favourable to the policy of showing particular regard to Reza Khan, though his bitter criticism of the Khan was not publicly stated until October 1769. However, none of the effects expected materialised, for the Colonel at once declared the letters to be forgeries. Forwarding the letters he commented:

that if Mahomed Reza Cawn did actually write it he is deserving of the severest treatment for his perfidy. For my part I have no dependence on the gratitude of Mussulmen; but as Mahomed Reza Cawn does not want common sense, I am inclined to believe that this is rather an artifice of his enemies, to ruin him, than any ambitious project of his own: for it is by no means usual for a man of his rank to express his sentiments in writing, to a stranger with so little reserve. It is not many months since Jewhar Sing informed me 'that so far from writing to Mahomed Reza Cawn, he did not even know there was such a man in Bengal'. We may from hence suppose that Mahomed Reza Cawn would not hazard his fortune, nay his life, by a treacherous correspondence of this nature.[2]

We do not know why the Colonel so readily exonerated the Khan. It may be that he did not wish to clash again with Verelst whilst he was applying to the Directors for permission to keep two lakhs of rupees given him by the emperor.[3] But it may well be that he took the same commonsense view as the Select Committee that these were deliberate forgeries designed by an enemy of the Khan. The Select Committee, or Verelst at least, knew that the Jat Chief was acquainted with Reza Khan, but they still did not hesitate to brand the letters as 'spurious and forged' and to order Sykes 'to have the strictest enquiry made'.[4] Only a few months earlier a man

[1] Col. Smith's letter of 25 Sept. BSC, 13 Oct. 1767. [2] Ibid.
[3] The emperor had paid two lakhs to Carnac who was very respectful to him. It is doubtful if the emperor paid Smith also out of his own will despite Smith's insulting treatment with Shah Alam (see Seir, III, 10; IV, 36). Verelst did not approve of it and the Directors concurred (in letter of 11 Nov. 1768).
[4] BSC, 13 Oct. 1767.

150

had been arrested and blown from the mouth of a gun for having forged seals in his house and delivering to the Khan a forged letter purporting to have been written by Jawahir Singh.[1] There was no recorded outcome of Sykes's enquiry, and no proof of forgery nor clue as to its author. It may be pointed out, however, that in 1762 when in almost identical case Ramcharan, Vansittart's Banian, was accused of treasonable correspondence, authorship was traced by Hastings to Nandkumar.[2] In this case, too, Nandkumar must be suspect. He is known to have been in very friendly correspondence with the emperor and Shuja-ud-daulah, even when his master Mir Jafar was at war with them. Nandkumar's letter to Balwant Singh, given in chapter 5, wherein he urged the latter not 'to place any confidence in their [English] writings or agreements'[3] is paralleled in this letter to Jawahir Singh, with the phrase 'there is no dependence to be placed on the words and professions of these insidious, word-breaking and rapacious people'. The supposed letter from the Khan was evidently the work of a well informed man, and a man with wide contacts—and again Nandkumar fills the bill. After Nandkumar was convicted of forgery and executed, in Hastings' day, so Ghulam Husain tells us, 'Amongst other strange things found in his house, there came out a small casket containing the forged seals of a number of persons of distinction'.[4]

In November 1767, when it was clear that the business of letters had not shaken Reza Khan's position, there was another plot or 'dark design', this time against his life.[5] We have no details of any sort about the conspiracy so that we can neither connect nor dissociate the two attempts against him. Both, however, seem to have been externally inspired, since there was no one at Murshidabad to gain from the Khan's going, and in both cases he received staunch support from Verelst and the Select Committee.[6]

The Khan had escaped the direct attacks upon his position and life made, it would seem, by Nandkumar or other Indian rivals. He was not so fortunate in defending his own interests and those of his order from the assaults of Sykes. It will be remembered that, while Clive was still in Bengal, Sykes had proposed to carry his campaign of retrenching expenses and raising the revenue demands from

[1] *CPC*, II, 464. [2] For detail, Range 168, vol. 17.
[3] See *supra*, p. 82. [4] *Seir*, III, 79. Nandkumar was hanged on 5 Aug. 1775.
[5] Verelst to Reza Khan, 26 Nov. 1767. *CPC*, II, 679.
[6] On Clive's departure, Cartier joined the Council as Second. Cartier was an old friend of the Khan at Dacca where the Khan helped him in tobacco trade.

Patna and Murshidabad into Dacca, but that Clive had prevented any such move against Reza Khan's home ground. In his last minute instructions Clive had again warned his successor against any extension of direct English interference in the district administration: 'To appoint the Company's servants to the offices of Collectors, or indeed to do any act, by an exertion of English power, which can equally be done by the Nabob at our instance, would be throwing off the mask, would be declaring the Company Subah of the provinces.'[1] Nevertheless, within a month and a half of Clive's departure, Sykes was at Dacca. He defended this abrupt break with past policy by saying ' From a just regard to the Honor of Mahomed Reza Cawn lest it should seem strange to you, Gentlemen, that in the course of our general regulation and reduction of improper expences throughout the provinces, Dacca should have been so long neglected; I think it necessary to observe, that he never was backward or seemingly averse to this measure, that it was not carried into execution before owing to Lord Clive and other gentlemen who judged it impolitic, to aim at depriving Mahomed Reza Cawn of his private emoluments...The appointment of an allowance to him was probably reserved as the last step, and since it has been resolved on he has forwarded my enquiries with the utmost disinterestedness and shown not the least reserve.'[2]

How little truth there was in Sykes's argument that Reza Khan was not 'seemingly averse to this measure' can be seen from the apprehensive letter the Khan immediately wrote to Verelst. The letter, of which Verelst chose to take no notice in public, was an appeal to an old friend and by one who still regarded himself as principal in Dacca matters. In abstract the letter read thus:

Mr. Sykes has proceeded towards Dacca, and the writer is at present wholly engaged in the necessary business of the *Sarkar*...A statement of the annual sums received from Dacca, was some time ago transmitted to Lord Clive, and it must have been seen by Mr. Verelst. When the writer returned to Murshidabad from Calcutta [in June 1765] he invested Raja Maha Singh with authority to retrench several unnecessary expenses which were incurred at Dacca. The Raja accordingly struck off about seventy or eighty thousand rupees, by which means there will be so much saving to the *Sarkar* for the present and still further advantages will be obtained next year. The accounts are still

[1] BSC, 16 Jan. 1767.
[2] Sykes's letter, 15 April. BSC, 18 April 1767.

The early reverses, 1767–1768

unsettled and have not been examined by the writer. The Raja has been directed to furnish Mr. Sykes with a full account of these and other particulars as also of the *band-o-bast* [settlement] and after that to allow him to raise the rents in such places as admit of an increase. The expedious settlement of Dacca is highly proper and advisable. By the favour of God, all abuses will be entirely eradicated. Since the writer's allowance has finally been fixed by the Committee, he does not covet a single *kauri* [a small shell used as money] of the revenue of the country. The Raja will not fail to abolish such expenses as may be struck off with consistency. The sum of 2 *lakhs* of rupees has been set apart for some particular disbursements. These include the expenses of boats which belong to the *Subahdar*. Formerly the annual expense of boats was 3 *lakhs*, but now by these regulations, it has been reduced to one *lakh*. The writer has already represented this matter to the Governor and spoke of it to Mr. Sykes. Whatever the Governor directs will be put in force. When Mr. Sykes returns from Dacca and brings the accounts properly arranged, these will be forwarded to the Governor. The writer formerly sent Lord Clive the accounts of the balances relating to Dacca and other districts. Whatever increase has been made in the rent of Nuralipur [Nurullahpur?] has been entered in the accounts which are sent for the Governor's inspection. Mr. Sykes has already been supplied with paper of increase in the rents and nazars'.[1]

Reza Khan, it is clear, was prepared to break the isolation of Dacca and to bring it nominally into line with other districts by some increase in revenues 'in such places as admit of an increase' and by decreasing the expenses 'as may be struck off with consistency'. Under his directions the Dacca Diwan Mahasingh had already cut expenses by some seventy or eighty thousand rupees and more might be expected next year. As for himself, now that Clive had fixed his salary, he did not want a single Kauri from its revenues. But the whole letter betrays the awkwardness of a helpless man who apprehends an ugly situation and does not know how, unaided, to avoid it.

The Khan's fears were well founded, for where he had spoken of savings of Rs. 70–80,000, Sykes had proceeded to effect a 'real increase' of Rs. 8,53,709-15-17.[2] This he had achieved by reducing the expenses of Jasarat Khan and Mahasingh, between them amounting to Rs. 4,37,878 a year to a mere Rs. 65,000. He

[1] Reza Khan to Verelst, recd. 17 March 1767. *CPC*, II, 178.
[2] The statements and figures in this and the following paragraph are based on Sykes's report on Dacca, dated 15 April 1767 (BSC, 18 April 1767).

had retrenched the expenditure under the heading 'Charges Boats' by dismissing Abdullah and his men, by cutting the Khalsa secretariat establishment of 196 'Moories', Peshkars, Seristadars and Munshis to 73, and by abolishing entirely the charges for artillery 'attending the forces at different places and belonging to His Majesty'. One obvious item of saving was of course Reza Khan's salary of Rs. 90,000 a year which had been a charge on Dacca revenues since 1763. The remaining gain to the revenues of over four and a half lakhs of rupees was secured by pushing up the revenue demand from about twenty-one lakhs to a total sum of Rs. 25,81,438. Reza Khan's assessment had been lower than under Alivardi. Sykes, however, 'had recourse to the accounts made out in the time of Aliverdi Cawn and also under Meer Cossim's government' though, as he said, he did not follow them implicitly. 'In the former I found them rated at 30 laaks and in the latter at something more, but by the best lights I have been able to procure, it is evident that such sums were never collected the measures were used for that purpose most cruel and inhuman such as we should abhor the thoughts of.' It is clear that the increase must have affected the peasantry and servants and dependants of zemindars and taluqdars, while the retrenchments hit large numbers of military officers, soldiers, civil servants, boatmen, boat-makers and the thousand and one sorts of people who had found maintenance under Reza Khan's administration.

Reza Khan, and perhaps Rai Durlabh also, had exerted their utmost influence to save what they could from Sykes's 'regard for the interest of the Company'. Nevertheless, the expenditure of Rs. 3,320-13-0 on the Imambara or Husaini Dalan was swept away. The giving of Khilats at Eid was rigidly restricted to Rs. 94-7-10. The charity to beggars fixed at Rs. 4,045-8-0 was cut to Rs. 455-8-0, though a new grant for the blind and lame, amounting to Rs. 3,600, was introduced. Two other charitable items were allowed to stand: Rs. 2,823-14-0 for a Langhar Khana or soup kitchen, and Rs. 1,518-10-0 for hospital charges of 'Black doctors' and medicines for the sick poor. The one increase was under the head of Justice. Where previously there had been one Shahr Amin drawing Rs. 150 per month and a Darogha of Adalat drawing Rs. 100, there were now to be six Shahr Amins to settle disputes 'among the lower sort of inhabitants residing in the city'.[1] How-

---

[1] Sykes's report. BSC, 18 April 1767.

ever, as the new Amins only received Rs. 50 a month, the cost to the Company was not particularly great.

The other item which made up the total of Rs. 65,000 which Sykes allowed for expenses, was the Rs. 34,755 meant for the surviving dependants of ex-rulers of Bengal, the wives and children of Sarfaraz Khan, Siraj-ud-daulah and Shaukat Jang of Purnea. There was an apparent increase under this head, of Rs. 960, for the two widows of Shaukat Jang, who had not been originally included in the list of pensioners. But in fact Reza Khan had been paying this sum to them, probably from the Nizamat department of Dacca.[1] Whether the Khan could have saved all these allowances had they not formed a subject of great controversy in England between Holwell and Clive must also be doubted. Holwell, incorrectly informed as he was, had used the exaggerated reports of the Dacca murders of June 1760 at Miran's orders[2] to justify the deposition of Mir Jafar. This had angered Clive, who felt himself indebted to Mir Jafar, and on his return to Bengal in 1765 he took the earliest opportunity to look into the matter and to free the royal prisoners. They had replied with an address of thanks to Clive in which they did not fail to mention that until the coming of Reza Khan to Dacca (in 1763) they 'did not receive regularly even the slender sustenance which was allowed them'.[3] Sykes not only retained their allowances but made it a point to meet them at Dacca where 'they appeared very happy at having obtained their liberty'.[4]

Under Sykes's axe had gone not only the livelihood of thousands and the contentment of many more, but, no less tragic for the Khan, the museum piece of an old regime administration which he had gradually rebuilt from the ruins of 1763. Sykes himself made this clear. 'The province of Dacca' he reported, 'has at all times been a heavy charge to the government, by reason of many and various expences, arising not from the natural and necessary disbursements attending the collections but from articles of a very different nature kept up in conformity to the mode of government which has hitherto prevailed. In consequence of our regard for the Company,

[1] *Ibid.*
[2] Holwell's source of information was a Dacca letter which he received on 12 June 1760 (*India Tract* 378; 54). Actually Alivardi's two daughters, Ghaseti Begum and Amina Begum, were murdered by drowning.
[3] *CPC*, I, 2761; *BPP*, VII, 216–17.
[4] Sykes's report. BSC, 18 April 1767.

which must suffer greatly should the present form be continued, the ministers together with myself have thought it expedient to confine within a narrower circle and reduce to a more reasonable degree these superabundant and inconsistent expences.'[1] A few personal favours to the Khan done by Sykes were little consolation to the Khan. Indeed, the one redeeming feature of the whole episode must have been the retention in his service of the old Alivardian officials, Mahasingh and Jasarat Khan. Mahasingh, the Diwan of Dacca, was recommended to be vested wholly with the business of revenues, and Jasarat Khan to be retained as Naib Nazim. Of the latter Sykes wrote, 'Jessarat Cawn who has long acted under Mahomed Reza Cawn and has still some share in the management, is without doubt by reason of his advanced age and other infirmities, not equal to the task of a collector, nor would I recommend him to that office; yet justice to his character obliges me to declare it my wish as well as opinion, that a genteel allowance should be appointed him, and that he should remain in his present position'.[2] The foundation was thus laid of an hereditary Naib Nizamat of Dacca which was abolished after the death of Nasrat Jang in 1822, the family becoming extinct after the death of the last deputy in 1843.[3] Reza Khan thus saw his own influence in the district continued almost unabated through his old officers—an outcome not without advantage to Sykes too.

That advantage was to be found in private trade, this time in tobacco. Under Reza Khan's instructions Mahasingh and Jasarat Khan had helped with the distribution of the tobacco owned by Cartier and other gentlemen of the Dacca factory. It was probably to steal a march upon possible rivals that Sykes paid his visit to Dacca soon after Cartier's departure for Calcutta and it is possible that Mahasingh and Jasarat Khan owed their continuance in office to their usefulness in the tobacco trade. It seems certain that Sykes moved so fast so as to forestall Barwell's appointment to Dacca as chief of the factory in succession to Cartier. Just before he left for Dacca, Sykes had induced the Khan to write to Verelst protesting

[1] Sykes's report. BSC, 18 April 1767. The Khan had to agree to Sykes's plan, but at the earliest opportunity he made out a case that a number of boats 'may be built on the Company's account' (*CPC*, II, 534), proposed it to Verelst and obtained the Committee's sanction (BSC, 8 Aug. 1767).
[2] Sykes's report. BSC, 18 April 1767. Jasarat Khan's salary was not included in the sum of Rs. 65,000 allowed as Dacca expenses.
[3] W. W. Hunter, *Statistical Account of Bengal*, vol. v, *Dacca*, p. 58.

The early reverses, 1767–1768

against the prospective posting of Barwell to Dacca.[1] In his letter to Verelst, which reached the Governor on 17 March 1767, the Khan had added a postscript saying that he had been informed 'that Mr. Barwell is going to be appointed to the chiefship of Dacca. The behaviour of that gentleman to the inhabitants of Malda is as manifest as the sun. So violent were his proceedings that it was impossible to check them. The restrictions that were placed on his affairs of timber, saltpetre etc. irritated him to the most violent remonstrances. Now that he is going to Dacca he will take to his old ways again, so that much confusion and disorder will take place throughout those parts. Jasarat Khan and Raja Maha Singh, who are stationed in authority there on the writer's part, will experience the same treatment from him as the writer himself formerly did in the transactions of timber and saltpetre; and any trouble the said persons may be involved in on that account will be equally felt by the writer.'[2] He added, by way of contrast, 'Mr. Cartier, while he was Chief of Dacca, acted with so much moderation and equity towards the *amils* that the writer received constant satisfaction and the affairs of the *Sarkar* were administered with success and justice'.[3]

The Khan's letter to Verelst was supposed to be private and

[1] Barwell was to have gone to Dacca as compensation for his enforced withdrawal from Malda. Clive had allowed him to remain there to wind up his affairs. The commercial residency at Malda, being an independent outstation, and not either a factory or a residency subordinate to Kasimbazar (like Boalia or Kumarkhali), which had the primary charge of providing the Company's silk investment, became subject to the regulation of 5 October 1765 and was ordered to be closed down. (The Directors wrote on 17 March 1769 that the Fort William authorities had their permission to re-open the Malda residency if they deemed it necessary.) The closing down of Malda residency and the special recommendation of the Directors in Barwell's favour made Clive appoint him 'in the Select Committee of the 7th January' 1767 to the chiefship of Dacca. Barwell thanked Clive in his letter of 13 Jan. Verelst also had assured Barwell that he would get Dacca, and Barwell had accordingly made no application for the three important posts of resident at Midnapur, at Burdwan and Second at Dacca which on 20 Jan. 1767 all went to men junior to himself—George Vansittart, John Graham and James Harris. When the minutes of the Council proceedings of 20 January were subsequently made fair, the nomination of Barwell was found 'erased and omitted' (Barwell's letters to Anselm Beaumont, 3 April, to Hardwicke, 20 Sept. 1767. *BPP*, IX, 153; X, 3–5). The Dacca post went to Thomas Kelsall, one of those brought from Madras. It would seem that Reza Khan's letter was designed to ensure that there was no second re-arrangement in Barwell's favour of which there was some chance still (see Verelst's letter to Reza Khan, 17 March 1767. *CPC*, II, 179).

[2] Reza Khan to Verest, recd. 17 March 1767. *CPC*, II, 178.   [3] *Ibid.*

157

Verelst in fact took no public notice of it. Nevertheless by 4 April Barwell had heard from Nabakrishna about the attack upon himself. He recognised the Khan's action for what it was, however, and bore him no grudge. In a letter to Leycester written on 4 April Barwell explained : 'From my last you would suppose me by this time at Dacca; but so far am I from it that it is great favor, for as I am told, to be permitted to return to adjust my affairs at Maulda. In short I perceive I have been most ingeniously amused to my utter confusion and my friend Sykes' great satisfaction. You must understand that that genius, on his return to the city [of Murshidabad] last month prevailed on Mahomed Reza Cawn to write to Mr. Verelst...No public notice is taken of this letter, as it was wrote in a private capacity, nor should I have become acquainted with it, if it had not been for Mr. Nabookissen.'[1] Verelst's complicity in the manoeuvre he attributed to his need to keep Sykes's support for himself. In a letter to his family, dated 9 December 1767, Barwell observed 'To account for the latent cause of such behaviour from Mr. Verelst towards me I must remark that he seems long to have considered me the object of Mr. Sykes' resentment and consequently any circumstance that tends to my mortification is as a cement to his connection with that gentleman'.[2] Reza Khan's part had once again been to provide cover for Sykes's moves. But Sykes was also to make a concession to Reza Khan.

The concession was to provide for the very necessary expenses of the government for which there was no fund available after Sykes had appropriated all collection to the Company's revenues, including the customary receipts of cutcheri servants, called the resums. These resums were recognised sources of income of the cutchery servants, often in addition to their official salaries.[3] The Khan needed some such fund, not a very big amount but sufficient to meet sundry demands, such as for providing Sykes's public table, 'charges of bearers of English gentlemen and others travelling backwards and forwards on business', allowances and presents to mutasaddis and clerks and for contingency charges. Two events particularly made the creation of such a fund all the more urgent. First, the drastic cut in the Dacca expenses had rendered difficult

[1] *BPP*, IX, 155.   [2] *BPP*, X, 13.
[3] For example the Dacca accounts of 1763–4 and 1764–5 show such payments to Murshidabad staff as legitimate expenses (Dacca Factory Records. I.O., vol. 6, ff. 31–2).

the maintenance of some of the essential staff at Murshidabad, such as the sepoys guarding the treasury and the Chubdars attending the Khalsa cutcheri, whose annual salary amounting to some Rs. 2590 used for so long to be paid from Dacca. He perhaps needed to provide for some of those who were suddenly retrenched from Dacca. The second event was the severe flood causing 'great distress' to everybody. The floods, the like of which had not 'taken place within living memory'[1] had endangered the safety of the city of Murshidabad and the putting up of embankments had become urgently necessary. The Khan had proposed to Sykes that instead of providing in kind for his table, Sykes would be paid a sum of Rs. 2,000 per month. Sykes concurred and authorised the imposition of a few petty cesses, *resum Nezarat, resum 10 Annas* per cent, and *Pushtabandy* which came to be known later as *Mathote*, the accounts of which like those of the *Bha Khilat* were kept separate and unknown to the Company until Sykes's successor, Becher, made full report on them in 1770.[2] The Khan thus brought the expenses to a public account which had perhaps been so long a matter of secret and private arrangement liable to abuses. Maybe the matter was known to Verelst as well for he had attended the Punyah of 1767. In any case the creation of the fund was a minor concession compared with what Sykes was planning to do next.

Reza Khan, and indirectly Verelst too, were to suffer further from Sykes's pursuit of private trade. After Barwell's recall from Malda, Sykes as Resident at Murshidabad and chief of Kasimbazar factory was without any competitor in the districts of Purnea and Dinajpur and also in that part of Rajshahi which lay to the east of the Padma river. There was no other residency or factory in the area, and his control of the Boalia out-station for the silk investment ensured his dominance of that part of Rajshahi. However, early in 1767 orders came out from England separating the Residency at the Durbar from the chiefship of Kasimbazar.[3] Under these circumstances it was essential to Sykes's interests that his personal agents should be established in Purnea and Dinajpur. The necessary excuse for despatching them into the districts was found in their failure to answer the high demands for revenue by the end of the second year of the Diwani.

[1] Reza Khan to Verelst, recd. 22 Sept. 1767. *CPC*, II, 580, 580A.
[2] BSC, 28 April 1770. Mathote and Bha Khilat later created much uproar in England. For detail, *H.M.S.*, 68; 487–581.
[3] Court's letter, 21 Nov. 1766.

The transition in Bengal, 1756–1775

The failure was due to the mischievous attempt of Sykes and Clive to serve their immediate interest by exorbitant demands for revenue. As early as 1 January 1767 Barwell had diagnosed the trouble in a private letter: 'The enhancing the revenue of the country which appears the great aim of Lord Clive will be found, I believe, in a year more the cause of its being diminished, for the country has absolutely been plundered by those who have been appointed to make the collections. I mean particularly the provinces of Purnea and Dinagepore.'[1] Sykes, however, threw the blame on the native collectors, and on 12 March Verelst wrote to the Khan that 'It has frequently been reported to the writer that the *amils* who were sent from Murshidabad to Dinajpur, took over from the *zamindar* charge of the collections, part of which they placed to the Government's account, and put the rest in their pocket'.[2] The source of Verelst's information was obviously Sykes who returned to Murshidabad from Calcutta early in March 1767. Reza Khan indignantly denied the allegation, and he wrote to Verelst a full defence. He said:

With regard to the collections at Dinajpur, and the money said to have been embezzled there by a certain *amil* from Murshidabad, the writer [Reza Khan] says that the *amil* was sent from Murshidabad not to collect the revenues but to order the *zamindar* to deliver in the stipulated rents. The *zamindar* himself has never mentioned to the writer a syllable about his being dispossessed of his authority by the *amil* or about the embezzlement of the revenues by the latter or about the country being ruined, and by no means believe that the mischief has been done by the *amil*. Were the writer's own brother guilty, the writer would punish him. Accordingly the *zamindar* and the peshkar were summoned to Murshidabad...Mr. Sykes began an examination of them which lasted for nearly four days. The *zamindar* pleaded that he had not yet collected all the revenues, and was therefore unable to speak with certainty...At the end he applied for leave to return to his district...which was granted.[3]

There was here a complete disagreement in the views of Reza Khan and Sykes with regard to land revenue policy. Reza Khan was working to preserve the older social groups who were all dependent on income from land and its management. If the

[1] *BPP*, IX, 120.
[2] Verelst to Reza Khan, 12 March 1767. *CPC*, II, 172.
[3] Reza Khan to Verelst, recd. 21 March 1767. *CPC*, II, 186.

revenues failed this was because too much had been demanded. In 1769 he was to complain that, whereas in Alivardi Khan's day Purnea had never paid more than four lakhs, in 1766–7 the demand had been pushed up to twenty-five lakhs.[1] In the same way demand had been screwed up from twelve lakhs or less to seventeen lakhs, even in a season of widespread crop failure in Dinajpur.[2] The ministers, that is Reza Khan and Rai Durlabh, had not failed, as the Directors alleged, to make 'some severe example'[3] of the officials who had failed to keep up to the Company's expectations. Suchit Ram of Purnea had paid twenty-five lakhs to the government (though he had only done so by ruthless exactions and by borrowing from merchants and bankers). Even so he had been placed in custody from which 'he never escaped... till death released him'.[4] The same fate was likewise inflicted on Muhammad Zaman, the Amil of Dinajpur who, when the Khan was writing in September 1769, was 'yet in prison environed with misery and distress'.[5] There is no mistaking the Khan's inner emotion in the way he writes about their fate, careful though he was in his language. If in 1769 the Khan's language, despite his caution, betrayed his inner emotion, in 1767 it betrayed, as the Directors pointed out, in the case of his defence of the old class of bankers and shroffs, 'the awkwardness of a man who is maintaining an argument against the conviction of his own mind'.[6] Punishment to Suchit Ram and Muhammad Zaman were such acts of the Khan, where he had to act in the manner he did, not because they were guilty, but because punishment to them was necessary to prove Sykes's thesis, which obviously received the support not only of the Calcutta government but also of the Directors.

Sykes for his part was determined to destroy the old order, to crush out everybody between the Company on the one hand and the 'poor inhabitants' on the other. He had, in his own words,

---

[1] Reza Khan's note. BSC, 25 Sept. 1769.
[2] *Ibid.*
[3] Commenting on the outstanding balances on the expected revenues the Directors observed in a letter to Select Committee on 11 Nov. 1768 that 'we cannot suffer such a depredation of the revenues and shall not think the ministers do their duty if the Ballances ... are not all recovered, and we are astonished ... in not having made some severe examples of these great offenders'.
[4] Reza Khan's note. BSC, 25 Sept. 1769.   [5] *Ibid.*
[6] Court's letter, 11 Nov. 1768; Reza Khan to Verelst, 25 Nov. 1767. *CPC*, II, 676.

The transition in Bengal, 1756–1775

made it his 'business to see that the Company as Dewan to the
King have full and just amount of their revenues and that the poor
inhabitants in general be not exposed to suffer as they have heretofore done, by the avarice and rapacity of their governors and
collectors'.[1] With regard to what did not belong to the Company's
treasury he was guided by answer to a simple question as he
bluntly put it, 'It was this, whether it should go into a blackman's
pocket or my own'.[2] By the term 'blackman' Sykes did not mean
Kantu Babu, his Banian or others of his kind.

The deficiencies in Dinajpur and Purnea had been discussed at
the April Punyah when Verelst was at Murshidabad, and at his
suggestion the management of Dinajpur had been taken out of the
hands of the Raja, and that of Purnea from Suchit Ram, who was
dismissed and cast into prison. A nominee of Reza Khan, Saiyid
Muhammad Khan[3] was thereupon sent to Dinajpur, and without
any fixed commitment was given a free hand to collect whatever
sums were possible and credit them to the government. Sykes,
however, angrily declared that for the next five months the Saiyid
did nothing but 'write the usual and ordinary excuses and complaints with representation of the poverty of the country, distress of
the tenants and oppression of the former collector',[4] and in the
autumn of 1767 he himself went to Dinajpur. He stayed there for
five weeks, and reported the district to be 'in a plentuous [sic] and
flourishing situation'.[5] He dismissed the Raja's Nazir, Muhammad
Zaman and the Raja's Diwan, Harish Chandra, and marked them
out with all their agents and dependants for further resentment, 'as
people so long hardened in the paths of corruption'.[6] He left one
of his assistants, Redfearn, to continue his researches. He then
went to Purnea, where in the town 'the people bore evident marks
of beggary and distress', and there too he left another young
servant of the Company, Rooke, to complete enquiries. In

[1] Sykes's report on Dinajpur and Purnea. BSC, 10 Feb. 1768.
[2] Add. MSS. 29133, f. 349.
[3] He was a new immigrant from Persia and was appointed Mir Qasim's Naib at
Murshidabad. In April 1762, Hastings described him as one who 'speaks the
Indostan language but imperfectly' and was 'an elderly, plain and sensible
man and hitherto much liked at the city' (Add. MSS. 29097, p. 16). It must
have been partly due to him that the Khan could live in safety at Murshidabad
during Mir Qasim's rule. The Khan paid back the favour and kindness by
making him Faujdar of Purnea, while Suchit Ram was Diwan in 1765 (see
BSC, 10 Feb. 1766). He remained a great favourite of Reza Khan.
[4] Sykes's report. BSC, 10 Feb. 1768.   [5] *Ibid.*   [6] *Ibid.*

The early reverses, 1767–1768

February 1768 Sykes submitted a report on both districts to Calcutta.[1]

The deficiency at Dinajpur and the misery in Purnea were the results of Sykes's having overridden the moderate revenue policy of the Khan.[2] Sykes however used them as an argument for posting of English supervisors in the districts—an argument later used by the critics of the Khan and of Clive's system and by the Court of Directors. He also made them the occasion for posting his own men—his assistants at Murshidabad, in Dinajpur and Purnea, in positions which enabled him to capture the whole local private trade, Barwell being now removed and the Malda residency itself closed down. He and his assistants proceeded to exploit the situation to the full. Early in 1768 Reza Khan was forced to complain to Verelst against Sykes. On 28 February 1768 Barwell wrote to his family: 'It has been currently reported that Sykes's inordinate desire to be rich has made him transgress decency in his acquisitions. His Excellency Mahomed Reza Cawn has in private manner intimated to the Governor that from 12 to 13 lacks of rupees in Salamees [offerings as tokens of respect] and farms, have been reaped by Mr. Sykes or his banian Contoo [Kantu]. This intimation, however, was suppressed, and His Excellency discouraged from making it publick...'[3] Verelst also received denunciations of Sykes from various senior servants of the Company; Alexander, Russell, Kelsall and Aldersey, 'in consequence of repeated letters of complaint to those gentlemen from their Gomastah'.[4] Evidently there had been serious clashes of private trading interests. Indeed we know that at least once the Board had to rescind certain restrictive trade regulations which Sykes had got Reza Khan's government to issue.[5]

The complaints, however, were hushed up. Verelst already had too many critics and was too dependent on Sykes to wish to air them. Reza Khan was too busy trying to have his brother-in-law, Fath ullah Khan, the son of Ataullah Khan, installed officially as his deputy and presumptive successor to wish to antagonise Sykes. The Khan had been broken in health by the physical and mental strain of office, and on 9 February 1768 the Select Com-

[1] *Ibid.*
[2] Sykes's letter of 17 Nov. 1765. Quoted in Bolts, *Considerations*, App. pp. 143–4.
[3] Barwell's letter, 28 Feb. 1768. *BPP*, x, 30.   [4] *Ibid.*
[5] See BSC, 29 Nov. and 29 Dec. 1767.

mittee had written about a deputy for him to the Directors. 'Mahomed Reza Cawn, who frequently complained to the Presidency of the declining state of his health occasioned by the continual application to the business of the government has lately requested our permission for the nomination of some person to assist him, as he may be frequently rendered incapable of attending himself to the business of the cutcherry, or any accident should befall him; and recommended Fatey Ally Cawn,[1] who had for some time past been assisting, and whom he should as fully as in his power instruct in the business. We deemed his request but reasonable; and Mr. Sykes informing us that the person recommended was of integrity, attention and abilities, we readily consented to his appointment.'[2] Sykes, who had been asked to suggest a salary, proposed Rs. 7,000 per month for the Deputy,[3] but the Directors while regretting the ill health of the Khan and approving the appointment of the Deputy, refused to accord sanction to the Deputy's salary to be paid out of the Government's funds and suggested its payments from the Khan's salary.[4]

But though Sykes was not hostile to Reza Khan, and was prepared to give full support to such personal demands of the Khan, he refused to abandon his policies even when they necessarily undermined the Khan's authority. So he would not be satisfied with the casual visits of himself and his assistants to Purnea and Dinajpur but by July 1768 he was planning to post Rooke permanently at Dinajpur. The proposal was made to the Calcutta government jointly by Sykes and Cartier in a letter dated 1 July. Cartier had gone to Murshidabad to represent the governor Verelst at the annual Punyah. It does not appear that Cartier had any definite views about the matter. He was probably made merely to endorse the suggestion which was Sykes's and which directly concerned the latter alone, perhaps because Cartier's private trade in silk required Sykes's assistance. In August 1768, Cartier and Sykes sent Ducarel, another assistant of Sykes, to Purnea though his stay was only for a short period of five or six weeks.[5] Verelst and his government, however, refused to accept

[1] The name was Fath ullah Khan though called honorifically Fath Ali Khan.
[2] Letter to Court, 9 Feb. 1768.
[3] BSC, 6 Feb. and 23 July 1768.
[4] Court's letter, 17 March 1769.
[5] Ducarel's letter, 3 Dec. 1770. *MP*, 20 Dec. 1770.

The early reverses, 1767–1768

the suggestion or the principle underlying.[1] After he had resigned from his post of the Resident Sykes tried again, in a letter of 2 January 1769, to push his scheme for the appointment of 'gentlemen of character' in every district as checks upon the collectors. He argued that this would be of 'great benefit to the inhabitants, and future advantage to the revenues by affording a full security to the property, and consequently a further encouragement to industry'.[2] Once again, however, his proposals received no support either from Verelst or from the other senior servants of the Company in Bengal.

It may be asked how far Sykes believed that a system of English supervisorship in the district level would be of public benefit and how far he saw in it possibilities of private gain. Probably his motives were mixed, and it is now impossible to disentangle them. It is evident, however, that to his contemporaries it was clear that the holding of governmental authority in any area was the surest means of effectively monopolising the entire trade of that district.[3] Posts conferring governmental powers were therefore well worth investing in. In a letter to his sister, on 20 January 1769, Barwell had proposed: 'I can only say I would spend five thousand pounds to secure to myself the chiefship of Dacca, and to supervise the collection of the revenues of that province and which is not at present annexed to the chiefship. I would spend the same sum to procure to myself the Patna chiefship and collection of revenues.'[4] It is not the commercial appointment as chief of factory that made the posts worth investing five thousand pounds, but the supervisorship of the collection along with the chiefship that made the posts so very lucrative. On Sykes's motives and actions Barwell may be thought biased, though Verelst's steady refusal to approve his plans would suggest otherwise. But a letter which Sykes wrote in 1773, long after he had left Bengal, suggests that his appointment of assistants in the districts had not been purely disinterested. Sykes wrote to Hastings, for whom he was then acting as an attorney in England, at a time when he feared Company reform was threatening his private interests. He said, 'I beg you will immediately get

[1] Sykes's letter, 25 Aug. BSC, 31 Aug. 1768.   [2] BSC, 4 Jan. 1769.
[3] Complaining against Sykes, Barwell wrote home on 28 Feb. 1768 of the 'impossibility of purchasing one single article of merchandise in those districts over which his authority more immediately extends' (*BPP*, x, 30).
[4] For the cause 'being advanced' with a Council seat he 'would not scruple to lay out ten thousand pounds' (*BPP*, x, 233).

my stocks or cash in the Company's treasury in yours or in the name of Messrs Redfearn or Ducarel till such time as I see the storm blown over. This my friend, I expect you will comply with, as everything may be apprehended by such a sett of Directors and, therefore, I would be beforehand with them if possible'.[1] Sykes's choice of Redfearn and Ducarel as defenders of his business interests cannot but suggest that in Murshidabad an official relationship had grown into a much deeper private identity of interests. His renewed attempt in January 1769, to make the appointment of Englishmen to the districts government policy and his commendation in glowing terms of the services of his three assistants, Redfearn, Ducarel and Rooke,[2] each one of whom had been given some district experience, may thus be seen as an effort to keep his business partners in positions where their mutual private interests could be best served. His moves may even be seen as the result of pressure from his assistants, if they were as aware as Barwell of the profits to be made in district administration. Three assistants could not be provided in two districts, Purnea and Dinajpur, where only the revenue had failed, and hence possibly the recommendation to send out Englishmen to all districts, not to supplant the Khan's officers but merely to be a check upon them.

One other question arises about this episode—why were Verelst and the Council so opposed to Sykes's plea for English supervisors? Here too private and public interests may both have been at work. It was not perhaps in the interests of the senior servants to send their juniors into the districts as revenue officers. Those with interests on the commercial side may have had no wish to appoint competitors after their experience of the way in which Sykes had exploited his position to their disadvantage. The complaints of Alexander, Russell, Kelsall and Aldersey strengthened the hands of Verelst to say 'no' to Sykes's proposals. Moreover, at this time, besides their normal profits from the inland trade and the country trade, the members of the Council had established a monopoly of the supply of Bombay and Surat cotton to the Bengal weaving interest which they must have been particularly unwilling to share. A stock of Rs. 25,00,000 had been created, the shares being divided among most of the members of the Calcutta Council, and used to engross much of the west coast cotton.[3] The price of cotton

[1] Sykes to Hastings, 28 Jan. 1773. Add. MSS. 29133, p. 349.
[2] Sykes's letter, 2 Jan. BSC, 4 Jan. 1769.   [3] Bolts, *Considerations*, pp. 196–7.

had risen from Rs. 16–18 to Rs. 28–30, and when as a result a tremendous increase in the production of Kapas, a local cotton, and a large influx of supplies from northern India by the Jumna and Ganges had followed, the Council had used Reza Khan to protect their monopoly. He was induced to distribute large quantities of their Bombay and Surat cotton through the zemindars, while a prohibitive duty of 30 per cent was imposed on imports across the Bihar borders.[1] The appointment of English officials to the districts would obviously threaten the smooth working of so profitable a system.

Verelst's objections to Sykes's proposals were perhaps as much grounded on principle as on personal considerations. Verelst was an heir to Clive's policies and he, more than anyone else, was committed to uphold them. Moreover he had no authority to exceed the limitation on him by the Directors which, as Verelst later reminded the Council, was that the Company should retain the 'primitive character as merchants with the most scrupulous delicacy'.[2] For the Khan, Verelst had all sympathy, and though he could not support the Khan against the powerful interest of Sykes until there were complaints against the latter from other senior servants of the Company, when they came he firmly ignored Sykes's proposals.

Reza Khan had resisted Sykes's changes in Dacca and had voiced vigorous objection to his revenue arrangements. Nevertheless, when Sykes reacted to his loss of the Kasimbazar chiefship and to the Select Committee's loss of extraordinary powers by preparing to leave for England, the Khan betrayed some dismay at the prospect of change. He had worked with Sykes for more than three years, and at a personal level they had achieved an understanding of each other. In December 1768, therefore, the Khan did a last service to Sykes and sought the favour of the Calcutta government by writing about the impending change. The letter, accompanied by one in similar terms from Nawab Saif-ud-daulah, gave testimony to the good conduct of Sykes: 'Mr. Sykes who has resided for these three years past at Murshidabad on the part of the Company, has in every transaction conducted himself with an unblemished

[1] *Ibid.* The Directors, when they heard of this, adversely commented on the monopoly, in their letter of 11 Nov. 1768 and described it as 'so injurious to our government'.
[2] Verelst's letter. BPC, 16 Dec. 1769.

character and with the greatest equity and prudence so that both rich and poor acknowledge their obligations to him and no one has ever talked to his dispraise.'[1] More specifically the letter declared, 'no act of oppression has ever been committed and the Company's affairs have been transacted in a proper manner during his residence'.[2] One cannot but suspect that Sykes had a hand in the letter, for he was busy trying to secure the authorisation of the Calcutta authorities for his acceptance of sundry presents,[3] and was doubtless anxious to keep his official record clean in view of the changing mood of people in England. The Khan also sought to safeguard his future, by expressing the hope that the Calcutta authorities would 'appoint a gentleman to succeed him [Sykes] [who would be] possessed of his virtuous disposition and who will make it his study to promote the Company's interest and the welfare of the mankind', so that his 'mind may be at ease, the affairs of the country be properly transacted and the prosperity of the Nizamut and its subjects may be conspicuous'.[4] He ended with praise for the governor and the gentlemen of the Council 'for their judicious and upright management of the affairs of the Empire and their paying due regard to everything that concerns the welfare of its inhabitants', and no less praise for 'the wise regulations established in these soubahs' which were the effects of their just counsels.[5]

His real feelings may have been better expressed in a comment, in March, upon Sykes's self-justifying boast that Mir Jafar had seldom received more than half 'the revenues which we now get'.[6] Reza Khan's reply was that 'revenues are extorted rather than collected'.[7] He ended with the warning that the country was 'subjected to a variety of evils distructive [sic] to good order and population. The consequences which have already ensued are alarming and worse may reasonably be apprehended if a remedy be longer deferred'.[8]

---

[1] Reza Khan's letter. BPC, 27 Dec. 1768. [2] *Ibid.*
[3] The presents were, a diamond, a gold gulabpash (sprinkler of rose water) a gold betel box, a gold flower pot, the last three with appurtenances (BPC, 27 Dec. 1768).
[4] Reza Khan's letter. BPC, 27 Dec. 1768. [5] *Ibid.*
[6] Sykes's letter, 2 Jan. BSC, 4 Jan. 1769.
[7] Reza Khan's 'propositions'. BPC, 28 March 1769. [8] *Ibid.*

CHAPTER 8

CONFLICT OF INTERESTS: OPPOSITION TO TRADE MONOPOLIES AND PROPOSAL FOR SUPERVISORSHIPS, 1769

The changes which were sparked off by the replacement of Francis Sykes by Richard Becher as Resident at the Durbar ultimately made Reza Khan redundant and the system which perpetuated him obsolete, though neither Verelst nor Becher anticipated this.

When Sykes resigned his post in January 1769 Verelst had already appointed Becher to fill the vacancy. In a Council bedevilled by 'interested opposition', Becher would seem, like Verelst, to have had fewer vested interests to defend than most. And besides, being a man of moderation, Becher was also a man of vast experience. Having joined the Company's service in Bengal in 1743 he had been a witness to the rule of Alivardi. During the troubles which ended in Siraj-ud-daulah's capture of Calcutta in 1756 he was the chief of the Dacca factory. When the news of the recapture of Calcutta reached the Directors, he was chosen as one of the three to be governor of Calcutta by rotation. In the interest of the greater good of the Company and his nation, Becher gave up his rights, and jointly with Watts and Manningham offered the post to Clive.[1] Soon after, he left for home. When the news of the acquisition of the Diwani reached London, the Directors sent Becher again to Bengal with a seat on the Select Committee and in the Council, which he joined in 1767. For some eighteen months after his appointment he kept aloof from the craze for the quick acquisition of wealth. He presumably sent his gumashtahs into the countryside to conduct a private trade on his behalf[2] as did all gentlemen then resident in Calcutta.[3] But he did not use his authority to secure a lucrative upcountry post for himself, though

---

[1] BPC, 26 June 1758.
[2] One such 'man of business' employed by Becher was Charles Grant, a future Director of the East India Company. Grant had arrived in Bengal in 1769 as a cadet in the Company's service (A. T. Embree, *Charles Grant and British Rule in India*, p. 30).
[3] T. Rumbold's letter of 31 Jan. BPC, 2 Feb. 1769.

The transition in Bengal, 1756–1775

as Richard Barwell had by January 1769 noted, 'The Presidency is not a place to make a fortune at; any of the subordinate factories are to be preferred to the most lucrative employments at Calcutta.'[1] Instead he remained content with the appointment of Accountant, at an allowance of Rs. 1,000 a year only. However, as collector-general, he was responsible to the President and Council for the supervision of the revenue administration of the twenty-four parganas, Burdwan, Midnapur and Chittagong, a task previously undertaken by the Committee of Lands.[2] When, therefore, on 11 January 1769, Becher assumed charge at Murshidabad as Resident he was free from the entanglements of private trading interests and already well acquainted with the problems of revenue administration.

Between Becher and Muhammad Reza Khan there was a quick growth of understanding and an identity of views, if not of ultimate interests. Since Becher was not personally involved, Reza Khan felt free to raise the question of the manner in which the Company made its investments, the evils of trade restrictions and monopolies, and the tyranny of the gumashtahs. The Murshidabad government had complained repeatedly of the mode of investment[3] and of the distress occasioned by the gumashtahs in the countryside. But even when attention was paid to the complaints, which was rarely, and remedial regulations were promulgated, little good could follow while Sykes was both Resident and chief of Kasimbazar, for he was the author of many of the worst features of the trade restrictions and monopolies. Nor did his loss of the chiefship end the evil, for his successor, William Aldersey, upheld Sykes's system, either to satisfy private interests or to keep up the investment, and Sykes as Resident could scarcely denounce what he had established as chief of Kasimbazar. With Sykes gone, Reza Khan could make another attempt to remedy the evils of the Company's methods. Within three weeks of Becher's arrival at Murshidabad, the Khan had the satisfaction of finding himself supported in his complaints. On 30 January Becher wrote to Verelst that he was convinced that the existing mode of 'providing goods for the

---

[1] Barwell to Hardwicke, 9 Jan. 1769. *BPP*, x, 231.
[2] The actual administration of revenue collection in these four districts was undertaken by the zemindar, or English collector, of the twenty-four parganas, the residents of Burdwan and Midnapur, and the Chief and Council of Chittagong.
[3] Aldersey's letter of 5 May 1769. BPC, 19 June 1769.

170

Conflict of interests, 1769

Company at Cossimbazar and other places will prove destructive not only to the revenues but to the trade of the country'.[1] Within a fortnight he had repeated his warning.[2]

Sykes had bullied the Khan into actions he disliked, but in Becher he found an apparently sympathetic appreciation of his policies. The Khan was encouraged by the warm support he received from the new Resident to visit Calcutta in March and to make a number of representations to Verelst. He also asked Verelst to use the occasion of the approaching Punyah to come to Murshidabad for a fuller discussion.

Verelst and the Council were perhaps for the first time in a mood to listen to Reza Khan, and the Khan was encouraged to speak his mind with less reserve than before. He proceeded to submit a long memorandum upon the whole question of the trade of Bengal. He began his 'propositions' by stating, as self-evident, that 'whatever contributes to the population of the country and the general welfare of the inhabitants naturally augments the rule of government. The attention and authority of the Governor and gentlemen of the Council are necessary to establish salutary regulations for those purposes.'[3] He then entered into an account of the past affluence of Bengal and the contribution of trade to its old prosperity:

Formerly this country was the principal resort of foreign merchants who brought hither considerable sums to purchase its commodities. I am well informed that in the time of Aly Verdy Cawn the merchants of Akbarabad [Agra], Lahore, Multan, Gegerat [Gujrat], Ferkabad, Hyderabad and the port of Surat reckoning the Mabements [sic] and Hindows only, exclusive of Europeans, purchased cloth and silks to the amount of Seventy Lacks [lakhs] of rupees and from this source the Ryotts were maintained, the native merchants̄ enriched and the revenues supplied. Now every branch of foreign commerce is ruined. Men of credit and large capital are retired and the merchants who still retain a connection with these provinces scarcely purchase to the amount of Seven Lacks in the year. This sudden failure of the usual supplies of specie is already felt to such a degree that business is almost to a total stand the revenues are extorted rather than collected and the country thereby subjected to a variety of evils distructive [sic] to good order and population. The consequences which have already ensued are

[1] BPC, 19 June 1769.
[2] Becher's letter, 14 Feb. 1769. BPC, 19 June 1769.
[3] Reza Khan's 'propositions'. BPC, 28 March 1769.

alarming and worse may reasonably be apprehended if a remedy be longer deferred.[1]

Reza Khan was passing a judgement on what was supposed to be his own administration, and he accused nobody. But he made it plain that he saw the gumashtahs of the Company as mainly responsible for the decline of the trade, and for the injury to the revenues of the province. He could not repeat the language of Mir Qasim, and he was careful not to mention his political objections to the power of the gumashtahs. Nevertheless, though speaking out of regard for the Company's revenues, he asked, as Mir Qasim had done, that in disputes between the gumashtahs and the subjects of the government authority should vest first in his officers, the amils, and finally in himself. In his representation he made this clear:

The Departments of Trade and Revenue are chiefly connected. It is my duty to point out by a fair statement of facts such evils as have tended to the decay and diminution of the latter and which may by neglect be productive of more dangerous and pernicious effects. In the first place I would propose for the good order of the country that all Gomastahs who have Balances due for advances made on account of their Invest-ment make known the case to the aumil of the District where they are employed [so] that the aumil may enforce their just demands with his authority and in case of any neglect or connivance in the aumil that the complaint be referred to the Chief of Cossimbazar if the dispute arises within the district of Muxadabad [Murshidibad] and to the Chief of Dacca if within the district of Dacca; these gentlemen will communi-cate the particulars to the Resident at the Durbar to me in order to [make] the final decision.

Secondly the true spirit of trade is mutual satisfaction of the buyer and seller. There are nevertheless divers people who take upon them-selves the name of Gomastahs and under the sanction of that name carry on an illegal and oppressive trade which in its effect depopulate the country by creating general distress and dispair [sic] amongst the Ryotts and occasion considerable loss and interruptions in the depart-ment of the Revenue. Was these set of men restrained from trading on this oppressive plan the country would be preserved from these mischiefs, Balances would be never or rarely incurred and all complaints about out-standing debts [be] at an end.

Thirdly, it is an usual practice amongst the Gomastahs to grant protection to the Dellols [commission agents] Pycars [petty whole-salers] etc. who are all Ryotts and pay revenue to the Sircar and under

[1] Reza Khan's 'propositions'. BPC, 28 March 1769.

172

pretence of trade hinders the aumil from collecting the legal dues of the government. Could these Gomastahs be obliged to withdraw their protection from them and measures taken to put them on a footing with all other Ryotts [it] would be highly beneficial to the Revenue.[1]

The Khan's second suggested remedy was that the gumashtah system should be abolished, and that the Investment should be made as it had been before 1752 by contracts with independent Dadni merchants, that is with Indian merchants working on advances, Dadni, from the Company. 'To alleviate the general distress in some degree', the Khan wrote, 'your servant would recommend the re-establishment of the former mode of providing the Company's silk investment by Dadney.'[2] And still avoiding any reference to the political issues, arguing the case solely in terms of the interests of the Company's trade and revenues, he pressed the case for freeing trade as follows:

The merchants would then find an advantage as formerly, in importing specie and renewing the commerce with these provinces. The Company will receive large Investment; Multitudes whom necessity have [sic] obliged to seek for employment elsewhere will again apply themselves to the silk manufacture with cheerfulness and assiduity because with [sic] certain prospects of reaping the fruits of labor.[3]

In his next proposition Reza Khan deliberately exercised an economy of words, perhaps to avoid drawing the fire of the private trade interests of the Company's servants and their friends upon himself:

Your servant would secondly recommend that all other branches of commerce in like manner be subject to such regulations as will both secure a considerable Investment for the Company and leave an opening to the industry of the individuals. By these means manufactures of all kinds will be increased [;] cultivation become the care as it is the interest of the Ryot..[who] will be enabled to live comfortably [;] a spirit of improvement would prevail throughout the country and the revenues [would] be collected with ease and without having recourse to rigorous methods.[4]

The last point discussed by Reza Khan was linked both with the problems of declining production and commerce and with the difficulty in collecting the revenues for which he was responsible.

[1] *Ibid.* [2] *Ibid.*
[3] *Ibid.* [4] *Ibid.*

The transition in Bengal, 1756–1775

This was the difficulty caused by the shortage of precious metals particularly silver, in Bengal. Before 1757 the European companies, including the English, had paid for the goods they purchased with imported silver, which, circulating through Bengal, provided the means of paying the government's revenues. After Plassey, however, not only had great demands been made on Mir Jafar and his successors, as reward for their elevation to the masnad,[1] and the sums so exacted sent out of the country in cash or in kind, but the import of silver had declined. Further, the acquisition of the twenty-four parganas, of Burdwan, Midnapur and Chittagong and finally of the Diwani of the entire province, enabled the Company to pay for its Investment out of the revenues of Bengal, without importing money or bullion into the country. Since the Dutch and French[2] could also tap the wealth of the Company's servants by remitting their illicit fortunes against bills of exchange paid in Europe, they too ceased to import bullion into Bengal. The import of bullion into Bengal which in the ten years previous to 1767 averaged 90 to 100 lakhs a year, including 36 to 40 lakhs by the Dutch, 'the greatest importers of silver', some 12 to 14 lakhs by the English and some small amount each by the Danes, Austrians and Prussians, had practically all stopped.[3] Imports by the Asian merchants from the Red Sea and Persian Gulf ports which before Plassey amounted annually to 18 or 20 lakhs[4] had, following the establishment of the supremacy of the Company's servants in the coastal trade, also dropped considerably; though this still remained perhaps the only source of

[1] According to the calculation of a parliamentary committee (see *PP*, Third Report, 1773, pp. 311–12), the total of these exactions amounted to £5,940,498 including the amounts, received in cash by the Company, their servants, and a small amount shared by native and Armenian dependents of the latter, from the Indian chiefs, Balwant Singh, Shuja-ud-daulah and mostly from the Bengal Nawabs, from 1757 to 1765. Notable payments by the Nawabs were: To the Company by Mir Jafar £1,575,000 and by Mir Qasim £62,500. To the Company's servants and their dependents £3,588,200 (£3,248,574 by Mir Jafar, £200,269 by Mir Qasim and £139,357 by Najm-ud-daulah) (*PP*. Third Report, 1773; 311–12).
[2] The French did not trade in Bengal after 1757 until the revival of their trade in terms of the treaty of Paris (1763). The French factories were reopened in 1765. Employees of the French, M. Chevalier in particular, stayed in Bengal and acted as agents of the Company's servants in their private trade.
[3] Select Committee's letter to Court, 26 Sept. 1767.
[4] Verelst, *View*, p. 86 fn. Verelst gives the pre-Plassey annual import of bullion by Europeans as: £300,000 by Dutch (also for re-export to Batavia as *rupiah*), £250,000 by English, £200,000 by French and £30,000 by Danes (*ibid.*).

import of bullion, about five lakhs a year, or, as the Select Committee estimated in 1767, about fifteen lakhs in four years.[1] Moreover, by the treaty of 1765, the Company had agreed to remit an annual sum of 26 lakhs of rupees to the emperor. Finally, since 1757, Fort William had been sending silver needed for the English trade with China.[2] The difficulty caused by the shortage of silver was tackled, though unsuccessfully, by the introduction of gold coins, simultaneously with the currency of silver rupees. But Clive's gold rupees, first minted in 1766, which found acceptance 'rather as bullion than coin'[3] had failed to solve the problem. Only the native shroffs and bankers, if helped to re-establish their credit and business as in Alivardi's time, could be of help in the circumstances. To make things worse the shortage of silver had been accompanied by the circulation of debased coins, which, being forced by the gumashtahs on the Ryots, were paid back to the government in the form of revenue. The debased coins had only increased the problem of collecting the revenue, which was already a serious cause of worry to the government, on account of the peculiar growth of trade patterns in Bengal, which had created a traditional demand for particular types of coins in different parts of Bengal and again for transactions in different commodities,[4] while the government's demands were assessed and it was preferred to collect revenues only in Sicca rupees. The shroffs in the past coming in between the government and the revenue paying

[1] Select Committee's letter to Court, 26 Sept. 1767.
[2] *View*, p. 85. According to Verelst, the remittance to China 'continued without remission to the year 1770'.
[3] *View*, p. 101 fn.
[4] Some idea may be had from the following information extracted from a report of 1770 (*see* BPC, 12 April 1770).

Dinajpur:	Sanat (old Siccas) for rice and other grains
	English Arcot rupee for Ghee, oil
	French Arcot rupee for Ghee, oil, hemp, gunnies, etc.
	Sanat (old Siccas) for cloth (with $\frac{1}{4}$% batta for buyer)
Nadia, Hugli:	Siccas
Malda and	
Birbhum:	Murshidabad Sanat (old Sicca)
Pachet (Raniganj):	Viziry or Benares rupees
Dacca city:	Dacca Sicca
Dacca district and	
Tippera:	English and French Arcots
Purnea:	Azimabad (Patna) Sanats (old Siccas)
Rangpur:	French Arcot, Siccas, Sanat, and Naraini (for revenue)
Jessore:	Siccas, Sanats, French Arcot.

The transition in Bengal, 1756–1775

zemindars and taluqdars, received the payment in the currency of the area and paid into the government treasury in Siccas only. Trade in currency had gradually extended to recoinage of old Siccas every third year, a measure which earned profit for the shroffs and the mint besides acting as a check against debasing the metallic content of the rupee. As money lenders to zemindars and bankers to the government, and finally as suppliers of bullion, the shroffs and particularly their chief, the house of Jagat Seth, came to enjoy a very powerful position, politically as well as socially. The absolute control which the shroffs exercised over bullion prices, currency and internal credit ran counter to the interests of the English. As one of the principal importers of bullion they often resented the profits made by the shroffs merely by minting the silver they had brought in. The English tried to remedy the situation by obtaining the right to mint coins at Calcutta in their treaty with the Nawab Siraj-ud-daulah which was further confirmed by Mir Jafar after Plassey. The clash of interests further increased after Plassey when the shroffs began undervaluing the Calcutta coins and the English were equally determined to utilise their newly acquired influence in counteracting these efforts of the shroffs. The clash had further intensified with the Company becoming creditor to the Nawab, and the Company's servants and their gumashtahs becoming moneylenders to the zeminders and farmers. The most unequal fight had ruined the shroffs[1] and had affected the traditional pattern of revenue collection. Because the Company's monetary reforms were aimed partly against the entrenched position of the shroffs, Reza Khan could not be very strong in his support for them. When Verelst's government in 1767 had asked the Khan's opinion on proposed currency reforms, a feature of which was the proposal for the abolition of batta or discount on sanats (or old Siccas) and their acceptance as of the same value as Sicca rupees for the purpose of revenue, the Khan echoed the sentiment of the government at the unsatisfactory state of affairs consequent upon the 'unsteadiness of the currency in these *subahs*' as, he further declared, 'there is no fixed value of coins anywhere'. His recommendations, however, were in defence of the batta or discount and for the preservation of the 'trade of the *sarrafs*, who gain a livelihood

---

[1] See Warren Hastings to Clive, 2 August 1759 (Add. MSS. 29096, f. 160); 18 August 1759 (Add. MSS. 29096, f. 169); 9 August 1759 (Add. MSS. 29096, f. 164).

by it'.[1] The Khan's voice was almost inaudible then. With positive recommendations for the abolition of the gumashtah system and the freeing of trade, the Khan now returned to his third point with more vigour. Recommending the restoration of the old banking and shroff system as his third proposition the Khan maintained that:

It was the ancient practice for the aumils and Zemindars to negociate the gross revenues with the merchants and bankers and they paid Siccas into the treasury at a certain rate of exchange. This established the credit of the bankers and their business flourished. They imported vast quantity of specie into this country from Akbarabad [Agra], Shahjehana-bad [Delhi] and Benares to carry on their extensive concerns. From the present mode of permitting [remitting] the gross revenue into the treasury, the Government derive no considerable advantage. On the other hand the business of the bankers and merchants suffers thereby a total stagnation: the currency of the province decreases daily to the distress of all ranks and the revenues are collected with extreme difficulty. If the ancient custom of negotiating the revenues at a certain rate of exchange was revived the business of the bankers and merchants would be restored to credit, the scarcity of specie less severely felt and the revenues collected with ease.[2]

The Council proceeded to discuss the Khan's memoranda on 28 March 1769, and at last were spurred into action. They accepted the validity of his complaints, declaring, 'The Board have but too much reason to apprehend that the trade is greatly obstructed, that private merchants suffer many impediments and that an improper authority is exerted by the Residents at the out Factories'.[3] They decided as a first measure to withdraw the Residents from the out-stations of the Kasimbazar factory, and in the second place to withdraw their parwanas from the Company gumashtahs. By so doing they intended to put the gumashtahs on the same footing as other merchants, accepting the Khan's argument, that their gumashtahs, 'from these purwannahs derive an authority to the prejudice of native merchants and to the great oppression of the Pycars and Dellels [Dalals]'.[4] Further consideration of Reza Khan's memoranda, which included many other matters, they postponed until after Verelst's return from attending the Punyah ceremony at Murshidabad.

---

[1] Reza Khan to Verelst (recd. 25 Nov. 1767). *CPC*, II, 676.
[2] Reza Khan's 'proposition'. BPC, 28 March 1769.
[3] BPC, 28 March 1769.　　　　　[4] *Ibid.*

The transition in Bengal, 1756–1775

In April Verelst attended the Punyah,[1] as Reza Khan had asked him to, and for some weeks consulted with the Khan, with Becher the Resident, and with Aldersey, the chief at Kasimbazar. The latter confirmed that there had been repeated complaints by the 'country government' about the prejudice arising to the general trade of the country, 'by the mode at present adopted' for making the Company's purchases,[2] while Becher observed that the withdrawal of the parwanas of itself would achieve nothing unless followed up by further regulations.[3] By mid-May Verelst had completed his enquiries and consultations, and without waiting until his return to Calcutta he acted to re-establish control over the commercial branch of the Company. From Boalia, modern Rajshahi, on 18 May, he framed and despatched a seventeen-point set of regulations, to Aldersey at Kasimbazar. He wrote, 'having now finished my enquiries and investigated clearly the causes of the general decline of the silk trade in these districts it appears to me that under the sanction of the Company's name force has been exerted to oblige the assamies [debtors in any way or defendants] to the disposal of their Putney at an under rate and over weight [and] that [silk] winders have been compelled to work for wages inadequate to their labour a monopoly having by these methods been established which has been destructive to the trade of the foreigners and has annihilated that of the native. The authority of the government has been trampled upon; its revenue diminished and the basis of its support, its commerce, undermined.'[4] Verelst was making a very moderate statement, for the situation was really much worse than indicated. He found the situation so desperate that he urged Aldersey to promulgate the regulations immediately as an interim measure.[5]

One group of regulations was designed to re-establish the authority of the Nawab's government over the commercial agents of the Company, thus satisfying the demands made by Reza Khan in his propositions. It was declared that if any manufacturer or trader had any grievance about the price paid to him by the

---

[1] In this ceremony the Nawab Nazim presided. Since 1766 the governor and, in his absence, the Second in Council, represented the Company in its capacity as Diwan.
[2] Aldersey's letter of 5 May 1769. BPC, 19 June 1769.
[3] Becher's letter of 7 May 1769. BPC, 19 June 1769.
[4] Verelst to Aldersey, 18 May. BPC, 19 June 1769.
[5] Verelst's regulations enclosed with his letter to Aldersey. BPC, 19 June 1769.

178

Company's agents, he might appeal. All such appeals were to be accompanied by a certificate from the government officer of the market or locality, stating the market price of the commodity on the day in question. If any deduction had been made beyond 15 per cent interest a year upon any advance made to the manufacturer or trader, the payment should be held to be illegal. Again any attempt to force goods instead of cash upon a manufacturer, as his advance from the Company, was declared illegal. Goods so imposed were made liable to confiscation by the government. Another clause laid down that 'no force whatever is to be used to oblige the assamies to the disposal of their Putney to the Company or any other individuals in their service; who for the recovery of their just ballances...are to make application to the officers of the government' who would do such justice 'as the circumstances may require'. Most comprehensively, it was ordered that the 'Gunges' or markets, established near the Company's factories and out-factories were to return to the jurisdiction of the Nawab's officials. They were to judge disputes among the people, and not the Residents, who hitherto dealt with cases in their cutcheries. If a Resident were not satisfied with the official's decisions, then he must ask his superior, the chief of Kasimbazar, for further redress.[1]

Other clauses of the regulations were designed to prevent the monopoly and abusive practices carried on in the name though not always in the interests of the Company. The government officers were directed immediately to make it known throughout the districts that the seer was established at 76 Sicca weight, with an addition of half a Chhatak ($\frac{1}{32}$ of a seer) for 'turn of the scale', and that the current oppressive practice of taking 200 Sicca weight for a seer, with an additional allowance of 20 to 25 seers, was abolished. It was also ordered that all advances were to be paid in sanat or other rupees on which batta or discount was to be allowed at the bazaar rate, and that the current practice of forcing the base coins at an unjust batta was to cease. By another clause the practice of obliging private merchants to bring their goods to the local factory to verify whether they were the varieties required for the 'Company's assortment' was prohibited. This harassing practice had usually resulted in the merchant having to dispose of his goods to the factory officials, who appropriated them on the pretext that

---

[1] *Ibid.*

they were needed by the Company. It was also provided that all deliveries to the factory or receiving centres were to be sealed, and that they might not be opened except in the presence of the supplier or his agent, the weighman and at least three other witnesses. The weighman had to be acceptable to both parties. No servant of the Company or dependants were to receive Nazarana or presents from manufacturers, Pycars or others on pain of dismissal and such other punishment as the nature of the offence required. Artisans were no longer to be made, as hitherto, to pay one rupee a day on account of the peon set over them to prevent their selling contract goods to other purchasers at a better price. Sardars[1] were also prohibited from forcing winders from their houses to work at the Company's factories. If the Company's winders deserted, their names and addresses were to be given to the officers of the Nawab's government for action. The regulations ordered that 'these poor people receive the reward of their labours in proportion to their work', prohibited the infliction of corporal punishment and torture upon them, and provided that if they were proved idle, 'which can easily be ascertained by the overseer at the close of the day by bringing the work and the workmen to the Resident they may if example is necessary be punished by his direction, but by no other order whatever'.[2]

Verelst had taken note of the fact that the weavers and silk winders were rarely paid more than a third of what was due to them for their goods and their labour, and that very large sums were in dispute between such manufacturers and the Pycars, winders and Sardars. Besides legislating to prevent abuses in future, he set up two boards of arbitrators, one to deal with disputes between the manufacturers and Pycars, and the other to arbitrate between the silk winders and the Sardars.[3]

In formulating his regulations, while at Boalia and cut off from all outside influences, Verelst had been influenced both by his conferences with Reza Khan and Becher and by his experience of the realities of the situation in the districts. He was soon reminded of the opposition his reform was likely to meet from vested interests, for Aldersey objected to an immediate promulgation of

[1] Literally headman—here overseer or labour contractor.
[2] Verelst's regulations enclosed with his letter to Aldersey on 18 May. BPC, 19 June 1769.
[3] Verelst's regulations. BPC, 19 June 1769. Arbitrators chosen were Ramsundar (Pycars), Ratan (manufacturers), Ramji (winders), Ghosal (Sardars).

the regulations, suggesting that they should be deferred until the next season, and that the prior approval of the President and Council should be secured.[1] Aldersey's objections were based, officially, on the difficulties that would ensue in realising the huge amounts outstanding with the Pycars, which at Boalia alone amounted to over two lakhs, besides other big sums at Kumarkhali and Jangipur, if the Pycars lost their control over the manufacturers, to whom they in turn had made advances, by the promulgation of the new regulations. Verelst was aware, however, that these were not the only reasons for Aldersey's objections. The Resident and his staff at Boalia out-factory alone had made some Rs. 60,000 a year from Nazaranas, the Resident taking from two to six rupees from each client, the Banian and the Account Keeper considerably more.[2] Such charges upon the petty traders and manufacturers would be threatened by the regulations. Again, though Verelst put it on record that he did not regard Aldersey as author of the abuses against which he was legislating, he had taken serious notice of the malpractices of Goring and to a lesser degree of Forbes, his successor as Resident at Boalia, as well as of Kantoo Biswas.[3] The grip of the Company's servants was very strong both at Boalia and at Kasimbazar. When Verelst had sent his own men to buy silk and silk piecegoods as a test they had returned unsuccessful.[4] Even Reza Khan and the Nawab had found it necessary to seek his aid in procuring silks for their own households.[5]

Aldersey's letter was a warning of the trouble he might face over the issue, and to strengthen his position Verelst sent a detailed report to the Company from Nishat Bagh in a letter dated 5 June 1769, before his return to Calcutta. In this report many of the points made by Reza Khan and Becher, who was his warmest supporter in the matter, reappear. On the basis of his two months of enquiries in Murshidabad and Boalia he objected to the 'mistaken authority the commercial department has assumed in the country', commenting that ' . . . not content with taking villages at will for the Company's and private investment it has even gone so far as to prescribe the very districts where the little trade left to the native or foreign merchants shall be carried on'.[6] He took up

[1] Aldersey to Verelst, 30 May. BPC, 19 June 1769.
[2] Verelst's letter. BSC, 19 June 1769.
[3] *Ibid.*   [4] *Ibid.*   [5] *Ibid.*
[6] Verelst's letter of 5 June. BPC, 19 June 1769.

the Khan's complaints about the drain of silver[1] declaring that, whereas commerce had once sustained the opulence of Bengal, now under the Company it had become the cause of 'its principal loss and drain'. He illustrated the decline in silk trade from figures in the Pachetra (Murshidabad Custom House) accounts. Despite the Maratha invasions which affected the silk producing areas, the Murshidabad production of silk had never fallen below 12,000 maunds a year in Alivardi Khan's day. Between 1750 and 1757 the average exports, on which duty had been levied, had been as high as 23,000 maunds a year. From 1757, however, production had begun to fall, and since the acquisition of the Diwani in 1765 it had fallen to below 7000 maunds. Even with the addition of the silk manufactured in the Company's filatures, this represented a great falling off in production, many workers having taken to 'raising of other crops'.[2] Verelst summed up his analysis of the evils affecting Bengal thus:

An authority totally independent of and highly prejudicial to the government has been assumed....Orders have been issued to the government's officers enjoining them with severe threats not to permit any other person than those employed in the Company's name to purchase silk; These agents have exerted the most unbounded tyranny in an indiscriminating siesure of every one's property; and when by chance any of it escaped their vigilant repacity, fines, imprisonments and corporal punishments have been the lot of the distressed industrious ryots; while the intimidated landholder has silently bemoaned the fate of his oppressed tenants incapable of administering relief or of preventing the daily increasing ruin of his lands.[3]

On 19 June 1769 Verelst placed the whole issue of the Company's method of investment, together with his proposed regulations, copies of his correspondence with Becher and Aldersey and extracts from his letter to the Company, before his Council. He reported Aldersey's objections that there should be no alteration in the mode of provision of the Investment 'untill it could be changed under the sanction of the President and Council:—and concluded, 'A sanction, Gentlemen, I earnestly recommend...'[4] His request was heeded. The Council resolved to adopt the Dadni system and

[1] In his *View* (p. 81), Verelst was later to calculate the drain upon Bengal in the first five years after the acquisition of the Diwani at £4,941,611, and this on the Company's account only.
[2] Verelst's letter of 5 June. BPC, 19 June 1769. About 82 lbs make a maund.
[3] *Ibid.*   [4] BPC, 19 June 1769.

instructed the Kasimbazar factory accordingly. They also pinned responsibility for disorders in the out-stations firmly upon the factory administration itself, commenting, 'we are astonished such enormous proceedings have remained so long unnoticed'.[1] Verelst had carefully absolved Aldersey from personal responsibility for the abuses; the Council, more blunt, directed the chief and members of the Kasimbazar Council to set an 'example of integrity and assiduity' in their own conduct.[2]

On 19 June the Council adopted Verelst's regulations. On the 20th, Verelst wrote to Reza Khan that 'the scheme which the writer [Verelst] devised for the transaction of the Company's business in consultation with the Khan and Mr. Becher Bahram Jang Bahadur, has been approved by the members of the council. Accordingly the system of *Dadni* will continue...and the *gumashtahs* who were the cause of oppression will be dismissed. As the proper transaction of the Company's business depends on honest and truthful persons, it is desired [by the writer] that whenever Mr. Aldersey inquires of the Khan about the conduct of any person, the said gentleman may be informed of the fact.'[3] He concluded with the hope that this would lead to the prosperity and increase of population in the mufassil.

Over the question of gumashtahs and of abuses in the Investment, Reza Khan had apparently won his point. Many of the points in his propositions had been agreed to, and some of the authority over trade, lost after Mir Qasim's downfall, had been restored to the Nawab's government. In the larger question of revenue administration, also taken up at the time of the Punyah, he was less successful. He did persuade Verelst and Becher to agree to some reduction in the revenue demand upon the zemindars, in amounts varying from Rs. 93,602 in Rajshahi, Rs. 86,879 in Birbhum, Rs. 20,000, Rs. 12,140 and Rs. 5,000 for Edrakpur (Govindaganj in Rangpur), Rajmahal and the 4 anna zemindari of Jessore[4] respectively, to a mere Rs. 3,500 in Katwa. In Muhammadshahi and Lashkarpur, the silk-producing districts, which

[1] *Ibid.*   [2] *Ibid.*
[3] Verelst to Reza Khan, 20 June 1769. *CPC*, II, 1437.
[4] This later became the estate of Haji Muhammad Mohsin, a contemporary of Reza Khan, who constituted the property into an educational endowment known as the Mohsin Fund. See W. W. Hunter, *The Indian Musalmans*, pp. 184–6; A. R. Mallick, *The British Policy and the Muslims in Bengal*, pp. 256, 263–5.

were expected to benefit from the reforms in investment methods, nothing at all was remitted. But with Rs. 4,75,511 outstanding for the year 1768–9, the reductions could not be considered as particularly generous; they represented not so much a change in policy as a bowing to the inevitable.

The Khan, however, secured some satisfaction for his brother, Syed Muhammad Ali Khan.[1] He had been Faujdar of Hugli, and in February 1768 Reza Khan had proposed that he should receive a fixed salary of Rs. 60,000 a year, in lieu of all perquisites.[2] This had been supported by Sykes, and the Council had raised no objection.[3] However the perquisites surrendered to the Company yielded only Rs. 39,000 in 1768–9, since there was very little income from custom duties, and by March 1769 the Council was obviously repenting of its bargain.[4] When at the Punyah a deputation from Purnea asked for a good administrator to be posted to their district, the difficulty was resolved by appointing the Khan's brother, who was known for his integrity and moderation, to Purnea and by making new arrangements for Hugli.

Reza Khan was also able to secure the postponement of the farming system which both Verelst and Becher championed and Reza Khan detested, his dislike being directed more against the new class of farmers, the growing merchant and Banian class who were taking to revenue farming as an extension of commercial activity, than against the system as such.[5] It may have given him

[1] He was an elder brother of Reza Khan by a different mother. Though he is said to have been an administrator of Chittagong (*Seir*, III, 87) the district did never have any Faujdar or Thanadar of his name. Perhaps he was an officer at Chittagong during Reza Khan's Faujdari (1760–1) as he became Faujdar of Sylhet when Reza Khan held the Naibat of Dacca which controlled also the administration of Sylhet. Muhammad Ali held the Faujdari of Sylhet at least from 1765 (*CPC*, I, 2738) if not from 1763 and until 1767 when he was posted to Hugli after the dismissal of Mirza Kazim. After serving at Purnea from 1769 to 1771 he was reposted to Hugli in 1771. In 1772 he was dismissed by Hastings when Reza Khan was arrested. Muhammad Ali retired to Purnea where he lived until his death, his family perhaps finally settling there. Reza Khan had married his widow (*Seir*, III, 87).
[2] BSC, 16 Feb. 1768.
[3] Sykes's letter, 15 May. BSC, 23 July 1768.
[4] Joint letter of Verelst and Becher, 30 June. BSC, 8 July 1769. Reza Khan's reminder. BPC, 28 March 1769.
[5] Reza Khan very seldom gave vent to his inner feelings. In Dec. 1774 he gave a note on his observation on the past and present state of Bengal to Goring who had contacted him for and on behalf of Philip Francis. In this note (see I.O. MSS. Eur. E, 28) he not only described the zemindars and taluqdars as 'father and friend of the people' (p. 345) he strongly com-

some satisfaction to find that Pran Bose and 'Buji' Mohan Mitra, probably nominees of Sykes, were discredited and removed from Rajshahi and Dinajpur respectively and that Rani Bhawani was restored to the administration of her zemindari.[1] Buji Mohan was replaced in Dinajpur by Ram Chandra Sen,[2] Becher's nominee, who had been recommended by the Resident's Banian.[3] The gain in Rajshahi by restoring authority of the zemindar was lost in Nadia, its zemindar, Maharaja Krishna Chandra, having 'unjustly' defaulted in paying Rs. 1,17,000 on an annual settlement of Rs. 7,75,000 for 1768–9. Either because of the almost continuous black record of the Raja so far as payment of the stipulated revenues was concerned,[4] or on account of the Raja's relationship with Nandkumar, the Khan did not apparently defend the continuance of the Raja's administration in the district and readily gave in to Verelst and Becher's plan of farming of revenues. The farming of the district went to the Company's political Banian, Maharaja Nabakrishna and to fourteen others, Calcutta merchants and creatures of the new power.[5] The Nadia arrangement, however, did not have his hearty approval and at the earliest opportunity he was to work for its annulment.

One other issue, in which Reza Khan was much interested as an upholder of the old order,[6] was the provision made for the members of the old ruling family of Sarfaraz Khan (1739–40).

mented on the farming system which had become universal by then. He said: 'The whole country is now farmed to the best bidders. The effect will best shew what advantage is to be expected from establishing this practice. But the Company must never hope to derive any increase of revenue from it. The Renter has neither knowledge of the country nor interest in the improvement' (p. 346).

[1] Buji Mohan's name was perhaps Braja Mohan. He had been put in Dinajpur by replacing the old officials who had incurred Sykes's displeasure. Becher found both Bose and Mitra undesirable; Bose had collected more than he was entitled to while Mitra had failed to produce satisfactory accounts (Joint letter of Becher and Verelst 30 June. BSC, 8 July 1769).

[2] Barwell's note on Ram Chandra Sen (no date). *BPP*, XIII, 99–100.

[3] *Ibid.*

[4] The Maharaja of Nadia has been a source of trouble at least since the beginning of Mir Jafar's rule. Mir Jafar had assigned the revenue of the district to the Company to clear his debts but Scrafton, the Resident, was so exasperated that he suggested that the Calcutta Council should threaten him 'with the loss of his cast [sic] . . .' (BPC, 8 July 1758).

[5] Reza Khan's parwana. *CPC*, II, 1475. For names, *see* page 234, fn. 2.

[6] Reza Khan had also appealed for a suitable pension for Maharaja Dhiraj Narain in his 'proposition' (BPC, 28 March 1769) and this was answered by sanctioning a monthly allowance of Rs. 1,200 (*ibid.*).

The transition in Bengal, 1756–1775

Murshid Quli (1700–27) had bought and set aside the Khas Taluq of Assadnagar for his daughter, the mother of Sarfaraz Khan, and wife of Shuja-ud-din (1727–39). When Alivardi Khan became Nawab after the defeat and death of Sarfaraz Khan, he continued to appropriate the income from the Taluq to the maintenance of Sarfaraz Khan's family, held prisoner at Dacca. Siraj-ud-daulah, on his accession, appropriated the estate but sanctioned a monthly allowance of Rs. 5,000 for the prisoners, now joined by the dependants of his defeated cousin, Shaukat Jang of Purnea. Mir Jafar added the dependants of Alivardi and Siraj-ud-daulah to the group, but reduced the allowance to Rs. 2,500 which too was not paid regularly. In March 1769 Reza Khan had raised the question of a more generous provision in his propositions. He pointed out that the Khas Taluq was yielding Rs. 62,000 a year and appealed to the Council's benevolence, 'for the relief of such as labour under misfortune and are deprived of their just rights'. He had suggested either an increase of the allowance or a reversion of the Taluq to the family, 'whom the reverses of fortune have humbled and reduced from a situation of affluence to misery and dejection'. Relief to the family in either way, he maintained, would result in 'universal praise' for English liberality.[1] On 30 June, Becher and Verelst, in their joint letter, supported the Khan's plea[2] and on 11 August, Verelst again urged on the Select Committee a reversion of the Taluq to the family. He commented ' . . . we have laid before you the nature of the claims together with the miserable indigence of Serfraz Cawn's family and surviving dependants. I must beg leave to add that their claims to the lands in question, are allowed by the greatest enemies of the family and their condition commiserated by all who are acquainted with it. To behold the undoubted heir to this Subah confined to so small a pittance, as is insufficient even to support nature, is in the highest degree unworthy of their high rank and give me leave to observe unworthy also the reputation which the English government has acquired for acts of generosity to the unfortunate. It has shown acts of generosity to many; let it not now refuse an act of justice to those who demand it so particularly at our hands.'[3] However, the appeals of Becher, Verelst and

[1] Reza Khan's 'propositions'. BPC, 28 March 1769.
[2] This joint letter was presented to the Select Committee on 8 July 1769. (BSC, 8 July 1769).
[3] Verelst's minute. BSC, 11 Aug. 1769.

Conflict of interests, 1769

Reza Khan were virtually turned down by the Committee. They voted on 11 August for the continued retention of the Taluq by the Company, merely adding a further Rs. 1,000 to the existing monthly allowance of Rs. 2,500 from which one hundred and fifty members of the ruling families of Bengal had to be supported.

The Committee's action was indeed disappointing to Reza Khan but it should also be seen as a sign that Verelst was losing control not only of the larger body of the Council but also the smaller body of the Select Committee. Reza Khan's propositions of 28 March had been in part accepted, and Verelst's Regulations of 18 May had been adopted by the Council on 19 June, but the interested opposition which had built up against Vansittart in Mir Qasim's day was ready to make itself felt once more against Verelst and Reza Khan. The weakness of Verelst's grip over the Council had been shown as early as September 1768 when he failed to get Maddison appointed as Second at the Kasimbazar factory,[1] and when the post of acting chief of Chittagong, virtually promised to Barwell by Verelst and Becher, had been taken by Reed.[2] He had suffered another defeat at the Council when Becher and not Cartier had been nominated to succeed Sykes as Resident at Murshidabad.[3] Becher's posting to Murshidabad was a serious loss to Verelst. Sykes's resignation in January followed by Francis Charlton's resignation in March [4] had further weakened him. Rumbold's posting to Patna in 1766 became a cause of further weakness to Verelst in 1769 and when Rumbold resigned late in 1769 his vacancy was filled by James Alexander whose departure for Patna meant a further weakening of Verelst's hold over the Council and the Committee. Cartier was not an ambitious man, nor was he a dependable party man. Claud Russell was certainly offended when Aldersey, and not he, succeeded Sykes at Kasimbazar;[5] while with Brigadier-General Smith early differences had developed into ugly hostility. Moreover Verelst, as inheritor of Clive's regime, was exposed to the hostility of those

[1] Having failed to get Robert Maddison the Second's post Verelst had sought to favour him by other means as well. Robert's brother John was recommended for a writer's post (letter to Court, 25 Sept. 1768) and later Robert was recommended for a new post of Deputy Resident (*ibid.* 2 Feb. 1769).
[2] Barwell's letter, 6 Sept. 1768. *BPP*, x, 33.
[3] BPC, 18 Nov. and 28 Dec. 1768.
[4] Letter to Court, 2 March 1769.
[5] Barwell's letter, 9 Dec. 1767. *BPP*, x, 11–12.

187

servants of the Company whose immediate prospects Clive had injured by importation from Madras, and by the end of 1769 those men, John Reed, Francis Hare, Joseph Jekyll and Thomas Lane had all become members of the Council. If Verelst could have helped it he would never have wished to see them in the Council. The governor had deferred filling the vacancies caused by the departure of Sykes and Charlton by about eight to ten months because of his serious difference of opinion with the majority over the question of the method of selection; Verelst was for selecting and others for seniority. Verelst's failure to induce the Council to approve his suggestion was in itself a signal of his weakness, which became further confirmed when Reed and Hare were elected to the Council on 17 October[1] on the basis of seniority, to be followed soon by Jekyll and Lane on the resignation of Smith and Rumbold.

Verelst's situation was further complicated by the steady influx of junior servants from England. The Bengal establishment had seen twenty-six new-comers, in addition to four from Madras, added in 1765, another sixteen in 1766, four more in 1767 and thirty-four in 1768,[2] the last batch arriving in Bengal about June 1769.[3] Few of these gentlemen had come out prepared to live within the nominal salaries and allowances sanctioned by the Company. Sons and nephews of the Directors and their friends, as they were, they had come with hopes of quick fortunes such as the post-Plassey 'Nabobs' had acquired. Like many already in Bengal they were restive under a system where most of the advantages had become the special privileges of the seniors, and were therefore anxious for wider openings in the revenue administration than those offered by Burdwan, Midnapur and Chittagong.

But perhaps the greatest blow to Verelst, and so to Becher and to Reza Khan was the changed mood and tone of the Directors. By

---

[1] Verelst's argument in favour of selecting members for the Council was based on the Company's letter of 17 May 1766 (para. 33) asking the Governor and Council not to admit anyone in the Council unless they were satisfied in every way, including character. With a divided Council Verelst could not use this power. See BPC, 25 Aug. and 17 Oct. 1769. Barwell had observed in a private letter on 25 Dec. 1769 that 'The majority being for succession by seniority, the governor's system of advancing by selection has been overruled; this has mortified him not a little'. *BPP*, x, 244.

[2] The figures are from I.O. Personal Records, vol. 14, pp. 468–70.

[3] One of them was John Shore, the future Lord Teignmouth, whose first appointment on 1 June was in the secretariat of the Select Committee.

Conflict of interests, 1769

1767 the Directors, under pressure from the enemies of the Company's monopoly, had been forced to compromise with the government in England and agree to pay £400,000 a year to the government.[1] Political pressure had likewise made it impossible for the Company to press home its legal proceedings against Johnstone and others who had shared in the presents exacted from Najm-ud-daulah, Reza Khan and the Jagat Seth in 1765.[2] The proprietors for their part were clamouring for higher dividends. These pressures had broken the cohesion among the Directors themselves, who had become involved in national politics, just as the politicians became involved, through Clive's struggle to retain his jagir,[3] in the Company's affairs. The Directors, already soured by domestic conflict, became bitter when they found that the acquisition of the Diwani had only added to their problems, extending the financial commitments while diminishing the Company's internal autonomy. They were not tolerant or objective, therefore, when they heard from Sykes of failure in the revenues of Dinajpur and Purnea, or of the Faujdar of Hugli, Mirza Kazem Khan's failure to pay that district's collection in full. Their anger found an echo in their letters, from that of 11 November 1768 onwards, to the governor and Council and to the Select Committee. Without the patience to seek out the true causes of the deficiencies, they condemned the amil system, charged the ministers with negligence, and reflected adversely on Reza Khan for aiding the private trade of the governor and members of his Council in Bombay and Surat cotton. There was even a renewed demand that the Calcutta government was to report on the very old allegation against Reza Khan made by Mir Jafar and Najm-ud-daulah regarding the Dacca revenues. The Directors had not even spared their governor in Bengal from their bitter comments. By the end of 1768 the opposition led by Lawrence Sulivan, now joined by Vansittart and Johnstone, had gathered great strength, and in April 1769 Sulivan swept back into power. The opponents and critics of Verelst in

[1] See Court's letter of 20 Nov. 1767. In addition the Company was to pay about £200,000 a year for compensating the government's loss of revenue 'for lowering the Duties and allowing a drawback upon the exportation of Teas to Ireland and the British Colonies in America' (ibid.).
[2] Court's letters, 21 Nov. 1766, 4 March 1767 and 16 Mar. 1768.
[3] Clive's jagir of Sicca Rs. 2,22,958 was extended on 23 Sept. 1767 for a further term of ten years from 5 May 1774 or date of decease if earlier (Court's letter, 20 Nov. 1767).

The transition in Bengal, 1756–1775

Bengal, in direct contact with developments in London and in many cases with the Sulivan group, were strengthened by the developments at home.

Circumstanced as he was, Verelst had attempted an almost impossible task by his regulations of 18 May. As the First servant of the Company in Bengal he was evidently conscious of the paradoxical situation which he described later in these words: 'Experience must convince the most prejudiced that to hold vast possessions, and yet to act on the level of mere merchants making immediate gain our first principle; to receive immense revenue, without possessing any adequate protective power over the people who pay it; to be really interested in the grand and generous object, the good of the whole, and yet to pursue a narrow and partial end; are paradoxes not to be reconciled, highly injurious to our national character, dangerous to the best defended establishment, and almost bordering on inhumanity.'[1] Verelst had lent his weight in favour of the 'good of the whole' in preference to the 'narrow and partial end' which was the making of 'immediate gain'. The Clive system was already under a severe strain and the mounting opposition to the system now became focussed on a definite point of counter-attack. Reza Khan was the eventual sufferer. To effect reforms Verelst had to point out then current irregularities and abuses, but Barwell's comment in a private letter is sufficiently indicative of the origin of the counterblast that engulfed Reza Khan. He wrote: 'The Cossimbazar investment has afforded Verelst an opportunity to expatiate on the rapacity of the Company's servants of the lower class. I wish for the sake of the service that the frauds pointed out at Bauleah had not been noticed, but measures taken to prevent such mismanagement in future.'[2] The service had taken the challenge which found expression first in the protests of Aldersey, and then in the measures of the Select Committee. The service again, it should be remembered, was primarily commercial in motive if not always in actual assignment of duties, and Verelst's dream of a Company's administration 'totally free from commercial views and connections'[3] was yet too premature. While Verelst was still making his enquiries and the Council had not gone beyond the decision to withdraw their

[1] Verelst's letter. BPC, 16 Dec. 1769.
[2] Barwell to R. Leycester, 24 Dec. 1769. BPP, x, 239.
[3] Verelst's letter. BPC, 16 Dec. 1769.

parwanas from the gumastas, Aldersey had, on 5 May, addressed a
long letter to the governor observing that 'However justly the
Company's agents and the Gomastahs of private merchants may
be accused of having [made] a bad use of their authority in the
country the divesting them only will not give the due relief to the
farmer unless precaution can be effectively taken at the same time
to remedy the abuses so universally complained of having been
committed by $\frac{7}{8}$ collectors of revenues dispersed all over the
country, for where is the encouragement if after receiving 6,
instead of 5 rupees a seer for his silk he is liable to be deprived of the
whole by such unlimited exactions.'[1] This was not so much an
attack upon freeing of trade which he declared '...is most certainly
to be wished for...', or a defence of the gumashtahs as such, as it
was a tactical and diversionary move by opening a new offensive,
this time against the instruments of government. Aldersey's
immediate objective was apparently to retain the control of the
commercial branch over the territory if only by sharing in the
authority of the Resident. He was persuaded 'no attention will be
wanting on the part of the gentlemen now residing at the Durbar
that may induce the ministers of the country government to take
every necessary measure...but these abuses are so grafted in the
very frame of the government that to eradicate them effectually
must probably be a work of time'.[2] He had duly taken note of the
current thinking of the authorities which was to make success of
the investment depend on officers of the government 'in whose
hands the power will then wholly rest'; but he was of the opinion
that 'the person superintending the silk Investment be vested
with such a share of authority as may be requisite for its support
without injury to the farmer or the private merchant'.[3] Aldersey's
concrete proposal was that since the revenues and the investment
were so closely connected, 'they ought to be under the direction
of one power', but was prepared as an alternative to agree to
'participate in the Resident's authority', though in the event of
investment and revenues remaining in separate hands 'each might
be naturally inclined to the support of his own particular department without sufficiently attending to the consequences that might
ensue to the prejudice of the other...'.[4] Aldersey's complaint was
an echo of the old conflict between the Nawab's government and

---

[1] Aldersey's letter to Verelst, 5 May 1769. BPC, 19 June 1769.
[2] *Ibid.*   [3] *Ibid.*   [4] *Ibid.*

the Company's servants which in a later period took serious dimensions between the two wings of the Company's administration, English revenue officials and the commercial officers of the Company.[1] Verelst's reply on 19 June was a refusal of the authority which 'Mr. Aldersey as chief of Cossimbazar is desirous of sharing with the Resident at the Durbar'. Instead, he suggested reliance on the Nawab's officials: 'every purpose would be fully answered by the attendance of an officer of the government on the Chief of Cossimbazar in his circuit to the Aurungs, who might immediately redress any grievances pointed out and might assist him in any enquiry necessary for his information and the Resident would, I imagine, be glad of being acquainted with whatever might tend to the ease and encouragement of the Ryots'.[2] The rebuff was followed by the passing of his Regulations by the Council the same day.

Aldersey did not gain his point but he had raised a cry against the instruments of government. This came in handy for Becher and perhaps to a lesser extent also for Verelst, who now planned and set up a parallel executive machinery for the districts and an administrative organisation for Murshidabad, working directly under the Resident, and independent of Reza Khan's control, but acting as a watch-dog on his administration. The Calcutta government had, as early as March 1766, sought the Company's permission to hold the Punyah at Calcutta, ostensibly to boost the sales of woollen imports, but the Directors had been very emphatic in refusing the 'innovation' which would mean 'in a manner removing the capital of the province from Muxadabad to Calcutta'.[3] Short of transferring the revenue capital from Murshidabad to Calcutta, expansion of the Resident's establishment was the only alternative. Again Clive had been emphatically against using Englishmen in the districts without being countermanded by the Directors; the alternative being the extensive use of a new class of native agents.[4] Just as Aldersey had also spoken 'of the undue influence exerted

---

[1] See below pp. 283–5 and also A. T. Embree, *Charles Grant and British Rule in India*, pp. 87–90.   [2] BPC, 19 June 1769.

[3] See Court's letter of 4 March 1767 (para. 19).

[4] Banian (meaning the new class of people dependent on the English) influence had steadily increased at Murshidabad since 1765. Motiram was introduced by Johnstone, Nabakrishna by Clive, Kantu by Sykes and Gokul Ghosal by Verelst. The number of such men who received Khilat at 1769 Punyah was larger than ever before (Khilat account. BSC, 28 April 1770).

by the Gomastahs and Pycars' as responsible for introducing 'a complicated scene of oppression which aggravated the distress of the country' in order to argue his case for a share in the Resident's authority,[1] so also Becher echoed Aldersey's attacks on revenue collection in order to push forward his plans to establish more direct control over the revenue administration. On 24 May, nearly a week after Verelst had already come to a firm decision on the line of his reforms,[2] Becher introduced his case in an often quoted letter:

When the English first received the grant of the Dewannee their first consideration seems to have been the raising of as large sums from the country as could be collected...The Zemindars not being willing or able to pay the sums required, Aumils have been sent into most of the districts. These Aumils on their appointment agree with the ministers to pay a fixed sum for the districts they are to go to and the man that has offered the most has generally been preferr'd. What a destructive system is this for the poor inhabitants.[3]

Becher added:

The Aumils have no connection or natural interest in the welfare of the country where they make the collections, nor have they any certainty of holding their places beyond the year; the best recommendation they can have is to pay up their Kistbundee punctually, to which purpose they fail not to rack the country...Uncertain of their office, and without opportunity of acquiring money after their dismission can it be doubted that the future welfare of the country is not an object with them? Nor is it to be expected in human nature. These Aumils also have had no check on them during the time of their employment; they appoint those that act under them; so that during the time of the year's collection their power is absolute.[4]

Becher, less crudely and openly than Sykes, had nevertheless been seeking to curb the Khan's power in some degree;[5] and hence his solution was not to be found either in a more reasonable fixation of revenue or in an attempt to remove the deficiencies of the current system by granting real responsibilities to the zemindars and security of employment to the amils, though his own

---

[1] Aldersey's letter to Verelst of 5 May 1769. BPC, 19 June 1769.
[2] See Verelst's Regulations of 18 May. *Ibid.*
[3] Becher's letter of 24 May 1769. *Ibid.*   [4] *Ibid.*
[5] 'I have since my residence at the Durbar [since Jan. 1769] induced the Nabob to concur in measures that tended to lessen his authority' (Becher's letter, 10 Oct. BSC, 12 Oct. 1769).

letter tended to suggest this. Instead, his remedy was to post a
Naib selected by the Resident alongside every amil appointed by
the Khan. Another new group of officials, these Naibs, who were
in all probability nominees and dependants of Banians and
gumashtahs, were thus added to the existing set of officials. These
Naibs were 'designed as checks on the Aumils, who were directed
not to do anything but with their knowledge'.[1] They were to
keep copies of all accounts and to correspond directly with the
Resident.[2] This move in the field was paralleled by another at the
headquarters, where the Resident duplicated the work of the
Khalsa cutcheri by appointing his own staff 'to take copies of all
papers relative to revenues'.[3] Reza Khan had welcomed this
enlargement of staff, and, with an eye to finding alternative employment for mutasaddis and clerks retrenched by Sykes, had offered
to help select the new men. The governor and the Resident,
however, refused his offer, apprehending that such men, being
the Khan's nominees, would prevent the accomplishment of 'our
plan'.[4] Becher and Verelst had set up the nucleus of a native but
non-Mughal administration[5] under direct English control before
the governor returned to Calcutta to get his Regulations of 18
May approved by the Council on 19 June.[6] They possibly hoped
that by these measures they would be able to meet Aldersey's
objections to the native government before the Regulations conferring wide powers to the government's officers were enforced.

The Council's decision on 19 June had been taken when there
were only three other members, Cartier, Alexander and Floyer,
besides Verelst present.[7] A major decision on policy relating to a
very controversial matter taken by such a depleted Council,
though legally binding, was not likely to have hearty response.
The arrival, in May,[8] of the news of the development at the India

[1] Joint letter of Becher and Verelst, 30 June 1769. BSC, 8 July 1769.
[2] Joint letter of Verelst and Becher, 30 June. BSC, 8 July 1769.
[3] *Ibid.*   [4] *Ibid.*
[5] One point which Becher sought to emphasise in his letter of 24 May was the
foreignness or Persian origin of the Mughal officials, and his new measures
sought to remedy this, by putting in 'natives'. These 'natives' were obviously
Calcutta-based Banians and their dependants, all Hindus.
[6] The joint letter of Verelst and Becher dated 30 June 1769 was a report on the
Punyah and other transactions at Murshidabad in which both had participated.
Verelst had returned to Calcutta long before 30 June.
[7] Russell was absent due to illness. Other members were spread outside Calcutta,
as chiefs of factories and as Resident at Murshidabad.
[8] The General letter was received, in Verelst's absence (BPC, 29 May 1769.)

Conflict of interests, 1769

House and particularly of the Directors' letters of 11 November 1768 containing censures for Reza Khan and Verelst's government further weakened the authority behind the Regulations. It seems very probable that Aldersey and others continued to resist Verelst's move in the hope of a change, for after 19 June complaints of the inability of the Company's agents to procure the Company's Investment became much more frequent. It was alleged that with the transfer of power to the government's officers, the Pycars and Dalals had been prevented from clearing their debts to the Company, as they themselves were said to be unable to recover advances from the manufacturers. The merchants dealing with the Kasimbazar factory regretted their inability to comply with the new terms of business. The price of silk goods was reported to have gone up from Rs. 5-10-0 to Rs. 7-2-2 per piece for the cheapest variety and from Rs. 16-8-0 to Rs. 21-1-6 for the most costly. Increases in the prices of raw silk were likewise reported from all the centres under Kasimbazar, by over 25 per cent at Kasimbazar, rather more at Paddapar across the Padma, and by over eighty per cent at Kumarkhali.[1]

Two days after these difficulties had been considered at Calcutta, on 16 August, the Select Committee resolved to put English supervisors and English assistants in the districts. In proposing this the Committee accorded their endorsement to the earlier condemnation of the abuses committed by the gumashtahs but took note also of 'the numerous train of dependants and underlings whom the Collectors entertain, whose demands as well as the avarices of their principals are to be satisfied from the spoils of the industrious ryotts who thus lose all confidence in the government and seek protection in other places'.[2] They also attacked the zemindars, another group of miscreants, whom they described as tools or screens or as associates of the collectors in their illegalities.[3]

---

[1] BPC, 14 Aug. 1769. The actual price increases for raw silk, as reported by Kasimbazar, were per seer of 72 Sicca weight, from Rs. 7-9-6 to Rs. 9-14-3 at Kasimbazar, from Rs. 7-3-6 to Rs. 9-14-3 at Paddapar, and from Rs. 5-5-3 to Rs. 9-9-3 at Kumarkhali (ibid.). Aldersey had first opposed Verelst on the plea that the manufacturers 'actually refuse to deliver silk...and offer to return their advances' despite higher prices being offered (see letter of 26 May. BPC, 19 June 1769), four days later his plea was that the advances were irrecoverable (letter of 30 May. BPC, 19 June 1769). It is not perhaps an accidental coincidence that the Kasimbazar merchants also offered to work the new system from the next year (BPC, 14 Aug. 1769).

[2] BSC, 16 Aug. 1769.   [3] Ibid.

They went further and attacked the morals of the people, the 'venality which forms part of the genius of the people and which is known or tacitly allowed by Government without drawing any shame or discredit on the guilty or being thought any peculiar hardship on the injured'.[1] From the people they proceeded to an attack upon the Mughal aristocracy, who generally manned a good number of the higher offices in the province, attributing the distress in the country to the want of sufficient checks on the 'Instruments of Government who are generally adventurers from Persia educated in the manner and principles of a government whose tyranny, corruption and anarchy are predominant, who are strangers to the customs and indifferent to the welfare of this country and who cannot by any vigilance be restrained or by any severity be deterred from practising their native oppressions over a timid, servile and defenceless people'.[2] They also found 'want of persons of integrity and reputation among the natives [Bengali Hindus] to supply their places'.[3] Finally they expressed their lack of confidence, however mild the wording, in Reza Khan himself. They declared that '. . .the degree of power, without controul, of knowledge without participation and of influence without any effective counter-action is too important and replete in consequences to be vested in any three ministers, or rather one single man, who allowing him the clearest preference for integrity, ability and attachment amongst his country-men, cannot be supposed superior to temptation and at least ought not in good policy to be trusted so extensively and independently, as has been necessarily the consequences of the present system'.[4] The answer then must lie in an extension of European control, by posting of Englishmen in every district: 'While the Company are in reality the principals in the revenue of this country and the most interested in the good conduct of its government every bar should be removed that tends to preclude them from a knowlege of its real state.'[5] Here was the direct answer to the restraints imposed on the activities of the Company's servants by Verelst's regulations and to his renewal of the authority of the Nawab's government. As Barwell reported, all that Verelst could do was to acknowledge the Committee's resolutions 'with the best grace possible'.[6]

[1] BSC, 16 Aug. 1769   [2] *Ibid*   [3] *Ibid.*
[4] *Ibid.*   [5] *Ibid.*
[6] Barwell to Leycester, 4 Oct. 1769. *BPP*, x, 236.

Conflict of interests, 1769

Verelst certainly could do no better than he did. Ever since the Directors had placed the Diwani expenditure and political activities of the Select Committee under the direction of the Council in 1768,[1] the Select Committee and the Governor had lost much of their independence of action and the influence of the commercial branch which dominated the Council became increasingly dominant. The chiefs of factories immediately seized the opportunity in obtaining for themselves, and in violation of the positive orders of the Company, a share of the commission of two and half per cent upon net collections of revenues which the Company had set apart for its civil and military servants when the Society of Trade was abolished. Originally the percentage had been divided into a hundred shares, from which the factory chiefs of Kasimbazar, Patna, Dacca and Chittagong were specifically excluded by the Directors.[2] But Rumbold, who held the double office of the chief of Patna factory and collector-general of Bihar, had argued on behalf of the chiefs that since the Company had limited the private trade of all its servants to the export and import trades only, the chiefs should be compensated for this.[3] Though the restrictions were never in practice heeded, the commercial branch got its share in the commission on land revenues.[4] Verelst did not oppose the measure which directly contradicted the positive orders of the Company in the hope, perhaps, of winning the support of the senior servants of the Company. But whatever gain he might have had in this respect was lost after he had got the Regulations of 18 May through the Council on 19 June, though with only a third of the Council members present on the occasion. The Regulation had affected not only the chief of Kasimbazar but also other senior Company servants including Cartier, who shared in the silk trade of Boalia through the

[1] Court's letters, 12 Jan. and 16 March 1768. Secret Cons. 22 Aug. 1768.
[2] Court's letter, 20 Nov. 1767. These 100 shares were ordered to be distributed among the senior servants, some principal sharers being as follows: the Governor 31 shares; the Second in Council 4½ shares; the Commander-in-chief (not to share as a member of Council or Committee) 7½ shares; the Resident at Durbar (not to share as a member of Council or Committee) 4½ shares; Member of Select Committee 3½ shares (if not a factory chief); Member of the Council (but not a factory chief) 1½ shares; Col. 2½ shares; Lt.-Col. 1½ shares; Major ¾ share, etc. (ibid.).
[3] Rumbold's letter, 31 Jan. BPC, 2 Feb. 1769. He also complained of the decline in private trade of factory chiefs on grounds of the large increase of Company's investment and competition from Calcutta gentlemen (ibid.).
[4] The factory chiefs were to get 1½ shares each (BPC, 2 Feb. 1769).

197

The transition in Bengal, 1756–1775

Resident.[1] The Regulation had affected the private trade of all in that it had put an end to the usurped territorial jurisdiction and judicial powers of the Company's servants and their gumashtahs, exercise of which alone ensured a high margin of profit, higher than that of others who did not enjoy those powers. The demand was for restoring the powers and that through its normal channel namely the revenue administration. In the face of a determination to make good the declining profits from private trade and the curtailed chances of easy money in the commercial branch by a wider English participation in revenue management Verelst was helpless. With Becher and Rumbold stationed up-country and the commercial branch antagonised, Verelst could no longer hope to carry the Council with him. Even the grip over the Committee was in doubt, for Verelst could count on the support of only one man, Alexander; and he was faced with Cartier, whose stand was indefinite, and with Russell, who was disgruntled. Floyer, who very often acted for an absent member, was apparently no dependable supporter of the governor. To make matters worse for Verelst, Richard Smith had returned to Calcutta early in August to increase Verelst's embarrassments both in the Council and at the Committee.[2] Instead, therefore, of persisting in his old stand in opposition to what appeared to be popular demands, Verelst revised his own position and sought to retain the initiative in the new measures in his own hands.[3] Five days before the Committee adopted the scheme of supervisorship for the Diwani districts, on 11 August, Verelst submitted a lengthy minute to the Committee dilating on the oppressive and overgrown powers of the Company's commercial agents, particularly that '...undue influence which has been in general exerted by the agents of the Europeans; who joining the power which they borrowed from their masters names and ascendancy

---

[1] In May 1769 Verelst had allowed one Mr Pattle to stay at Boalia for four to six weeks for 'collecting in of the outstanding advances on account of Mr. Cartier, Mr. Barwell and other persons' (Verelst to Aldersey, 18 May. BPC, 19 June 1769).

[2] Smith, on his return from Allahabad, attended the Select Committee on 11 August when it met after a long interval since 8 July 1769. Verelst's opposition to his acceptance of a money present of two lakhs of rupees, which was confirmed by the Directors, had obliged him to refund the sum to the emperor. (The emperor's receipt dated 3 July. BPC, 7 Sept. 1769.)

[3] Another issue on which he gave in about the same time was the method of filling Council vacancies. He was obliged to adopt the principle of seniority, but sought to make a virtue of it (BPC, 25 Aug. and 17 Oct. 1769).

to their native proneness to oppress, became tyrants instead of merchants...'. In the same minute he also joined the chorus of condemnation of the Mughal officials, though in this he tended to be moderate and discriminating. He had observed: 'There cannot be more fatal misfortune befall any country, than the destruction of the confidence between the government and the subject, nor can any power have a more pernicious tendency than that which is delegated for an occasional service, to one who is an alien to the country by birth, and who besides his indifference or total disaffection to it has these additional motives, to a rapacious conduct, an insecure appointment, a variety of temptation and the greatest opportunity to concealment and elusion. The Aumils are cankers to the industry of the Ryott; necessity alone has hitherto obliged us to employ them. The transactions of each day are so many instances of infidelity and unfitness for such trusts; and supposing that a few of them should possess some claims to favour and commendation, the extent of the provinces under their charge, is so considerable to expect or even hope for any great services from the best endeavours.'[1]

Verelst was to regain the initiative, if only to determine the course of events, which were moving very fast, and to endeavour to preserve as much unimpaired as possible the system which he, jointly with Becher, had sought to strengthen so very recently. He could perhaps hold out against the pressure for a wider English participation in revenue management, but not when the Directors had, perhaps unwittingly, lent support to that demand. In their letters of 11 November 1768, the Directors, besides commenting adversely on the Amils,[2] had spoken with considerable praise of the administration in Burdwan[3] and approvingly of the direct

[1] Verelst's minute. BSC, 11 Aug. 1769.
[2] The comment was in the letter to the Select Committee. Reza Khan vigorously protested against this comment (see his note annexed to Becher's letter. BSC, 25 Sept. 1769).
[3] Burdwan was granted by Mir Qasim to the Company as a jagir in 1760. In 1762 farming for 3 years was introduced in the district, the bidders being 'men without fortune or character' as Verelst describes them. In 1765 Verelst was appointed supervisor of Burdwan. The Raja's Khas (or directly administered) lands were farmed out to 'new farmers', with 'assurance of not being dispossessed' (*View*, p. 71). The Directors had observed 'that we are perfectly satisfied with the administration ... in which there seems nothing capable of further improvement, but an attention to the Chakeran lands and the letting the lands out in long leases; which will have a happy effect ... by attaching the [new] landholders more strongly to our interest'. (Court's letter, 11 Nov. 1768).

The transition in Bengal, 1756–1775

English management of the Calcutta lands.[1] 'Their last letter', the Select Committee observed on 16 August, 'has now afforded us the sanction that was so essentially necessary, for the welfare and improvement of these provinces as well as for our own vindication in the pursuit of such plans as we may judge advisable to adopt. By that letter the Directors seem to approve of the distribution and allotment of the country into Farms and of the appointment of European gentlemen to supervise the different provinces and to controul the conduct of the agents of the country government. From this permission we have well grounded expectation of success to our design of introducing new Regulations.'[2] The truth was, as Verelst later said, the Committee took 'advantage of an equivocal permission'.[3]

Verelst sponsored the scheme under pressure, but he also sought, as appears from the instructions drafted by him, to restrict the scope of the supervisors' activity, at least for the time being, to research. The supervisor would be primarily responsible for collecting information about the district to which he was posted. He was to prepare a summary history, not going back further than Shuja Khan's day (1727–39), of the district's rulers and possessors, their order of succession, revolutions in their families, their connections and other relevant matters. More widely he was to record local customs and the privileges enjoyed by different classes; the state, produce and capacity of the lands; the revenues paid by the Ryots, and the methods of collection; the regulation and pattern of commerce; the administration of justice. Such information, he maintained, was necessary and would take some time. He therefore wished to see the young gentlemen devote themselves to research, initially taking no part in the work of administration. To soften the blow to their ambition he authorised their indulgence in private trade, adding the pious wish that it should not be immoderate.[4] Verelst's initiative prevented an immediate dislocation in Reza Khan's administration.

The resolution of the Committee taken on 16 August was only too welcome to the Council when it was communicated to them on 4 September.[5] They lost no time in approving the scheme, or in appointing the persons who were to be sent out into the various

---

[1] Court's letter, 11 Nov. 1768.   [2] BSC, 16 Aug. 1769.
[3] *View*, p. 75.   [4] BSC, 16 Aug. 1769.
[5] Secret Cons., 4 Sept. 1769.

Conflict of interests, 1769

districts as supervisors and assistants. Accordingly Kelsall, the chief of the Dacca factory, was made supervisor of that district, with J. Sumner, W. Holland and A. Staples as his assistants. George Vansittart was chosen for Dinajpur with John G. Haliberton and W. Pye as assistants. Ducarel in Purnea was given one assistant, David Anderson. For Rajshahi, to the east of the Padma, the supervisor was W. B. Rous, accompanied by Francis Gladwin, while the lands northwest of Murshidabad and west of the Padma, including Rajmahal and Bhagalpur, went to William Hardwood, with William Rooke as assistant. Hugli was earmarked for John Graham who was to have Thomas Graham as assistant. For Rangpur and Nadia the supervisors designated were John Grose and Jacob Rider, with Robertson and John Hogarth as their respective assistants. The combined charge of Birbhum and Pachet went to the Honourable Charles Stuart, with Matthew Dawson as his assistant. The first result of the scheme formulated by the Committee and approved by the Council was thus to introduce twenty Europeans into the revenue administration.[1] Later, on Becher's recommendation, Walter Wilkins was chosen for the Tipperah supervisorship, which he was to hold in addition to his chiefship of Chittagong which Verelst had secured for him, and Robert Wilmot was chosen for the new district of Jessore.[2]

On 8 September, Verelst undertook the difficult task of announcing the proposed changes to Reza Khan. He did so with all the delicacy possible, making it clear that it was the subordinate staff whose failings required this English intervention, not the Khan, zemindars or amils. Verelst began 'The Khan perhaps remembers how often he and the writer have discussed face to face the question of dishonesty and incompetence of the amlah [subordinate officials] of the zamindars and tahsildars [collectors], who in spite of the repeated warnings that have been issued by the Nizamat, have not yet reformed themselves'.[3] The letter went on to refer to the Khan's expressed wish to see the ryots of the whole province made 'happier and richer than those of Burdwan'. Reform on the

---

[1] Appointees totalled 21 but of them Ducarel was already at Purnea. The Directors had asked the Select Committee (see letter of 11 Nov. 1768) to appoint one or more 'of our most experienced servants' for investigation in Purnea, 'such as has been made in Burdwan'.
[2] Becher's letter of 26 Nov. and Select Committee's reply. BSC, 10 Dec. 1769.
[3] Verelst to Reza Khan, 8 Sept. 1769. *CPC*, II, 1580.

lines adopted in Burdwan[1] was not difficult, but in the past this could not be effected for 'dearth of capable men'. Now, however, that difficulty had ended, for this year the Directors had sent out a large number of men. Verelst then outlined the plan. The English amins were to correspond with the Resident not the Khan, but, Verelst explained, they were not to interfere with the revenue administration. Their function would be 'to gather accurate information regarding the state of the Sarkars and Parganahs [revenue divisions and subdivisions] in Bengal, the resources of the land, the present revenue, the increase and decrease of the same, the good and bad qualities of cloth and other goods, the number of Tantis [weavers], in fact all matters, a full knowledge of which is essential to the English[2] who are anxious to promote the prosperity of the country'.[3] (Verelst concealed from Reza Khan that the non-intervention in administration would end as soon as the necessary information had been secured.) If the amils, 'high and low', created difficulties for the supervisors, as was likely, the Khan was asked to inflict heavy punishment on them. The letter concluded with an appreciation of the Khan's past services, and with the hope that 'in the present instance also he will exert himself in a way that may gain him good opinion of both the English Sardars [chiefs] and the people of this country'.[4]

Reza Khan was no fool, and doubtless he realised how much the posting of supervisors would undermine his authority, but he was helpless. All he could do was to fight a delaying action. The Khan therefore hastened to write back to the governor welcoming the decision of the Council as necessary for the complete eradication of the 'abuses which will remain', for safeguarding the rights and

[1] Long-term farming without auction which had benefited the Company had earned the praise of the Directors though it was equally ruinous for the old privileged classes. Burdwan, Verelst claimed, 'exhibits the face of a garden' and was proof 'of the propriety of the plan I introduced' in 1765 (Verelst's minute. BSC, 11 Aug. 1769). See also *View*, pp. 70–1 and M. Huq, *East India Company's Land Policy and Commerce in Bengal, 1698–1784*, pp. 54–67.

[2] Verelst had great interest in past history, even if it was for administrative reasons. Only five days before the Committee adopted the scheme, on 11 August he was dilating on its importance. During his stay at Murshidabad he was himself making enquiries. He had arranged to take copies of records and had hoped some young gentlemen would learn Persian and in 4 or 5 years would produce a 'perfect English copy' (BSC, 11 Aug. 1769). The Khan must have been aware of this craze of Verelst's.

[3] Verelst to Reza Khan, 8 Sept. 1769. *CPC*, II, 1580.   [4] *Ibid.*

Conflict of interests, 1769

improving the conditions of the ryots and for the prosperity of the country. But as 'a sincere well-wisher of the Company' he ventured to suggest 'that the scheme might be deferred until next April, as half the revenue year was already over'.[1] The Khan's letter which had reached Verelst on 18 September also mentioned that 'although the English gentlemen may not interfere with the collections, yet the Zamindars and Amils will plead dryness of the season on one hand, and the appointment of the English gentlemen on the other, as an excuse for holding back large balances, the recovery of which will be difficult if not impossible to effect.'[2] He thus shrewdly struck at the Company's weak point, its want of money and dread of any interruption in the flow of revenues. This was the most effective argument[3] for counteracting the pressure on Verelst, if the move were the Council's rather than the governor's own. Three days later, Reza Khan returned to the point, expressing his regret that Verelst had given him no warning of the Council's plans for sending supervisors into the districts. Had he been advised beforehand he would certainly have asked for enforcing the scheme at the commencement of the year or after the closing of the accounts. He urged again to defer the matter till then in 1770 so that 'the designs of artful people may be defeated, and things proceed in a proper manner'.[4]

The Khan might also hope for the support of Becher, who too had been caught unawares. The information of the proposed changes reached him in a communication from the Select Committee as an accomplished fact, though he had been asked to give his sentiments 'at large on the several points we have already discussed'.[5] The measures had been decided upon without even consulting him, despite Verelst's urgings on 11 August that 'no measure should be taken without his privacy and no resolution formed without consulting his opinion'.[6] The committee's delibeate act of ignoring him, besides some indirect references to him in

[1] Reza Khan to Verelst, recd. 18 Sept. 1769. *CPC*, II, 1596.
[2] *Ibid.*
[3] The almost bankrupt state of the Company's treasury in Bengal had induced the Council to withhold the remittance of Rs. 24 lakhs to China and to curtail the Company's investment from Bengal to Rs. 45 lakhs for the next 2 to 3 years (Secret Cons., 7 Aug. 1769).
[4] Reza Khan to Verelst, recd. 21 Sept. 1769. *CPC*, II, 1610.
[5] Select Committee to Becher, 16 Aug. BSC, 16 Aug. 1769. A copy of the entire proceedings was enclosed.
[6] Verelst's minute. BSC, 11 Aug. 1769.

the deliberations,[1] was offensive enough to make the Resident view the decision with disfavour. As Resident it was in Becher's interest to defend the Khan and maintain the *status quo*. With Verelst's support he had already resisted Aldersey's demand for a share in the powers he enjoyed as Resident. Now having just devised the means of extending his influence throughout the Diwani areas of Bengal and Bhagalpur,[2] by appointing his own native agents as Naibs to the Amils, he was unlikely to welcome the appointment of European supervisors to those same districts, directly subordinate to the Resident though these supervisors were. His opposition to the Committee's plan was the more probable because he had decided to stay in Bengal for one year more, and, though on Verelst's departure he would become Second in Council, he hoped to be allowed to stay at Murshidabad as Resident. Under such circumstances he too had an interest in deferring the posting of the supervisors to the districts. When therefore the Council wrote to him again, confirming the Committee's decision and to have the plan 'immediately adopted' and worked,[3] Becher also welcomed the decision but declared it immediately unworkable 'without imminent risk to the present year's collections'.[4] He requested permission to visit Calcutta in order to comprehend the plan better and to explain his views, and by the end of September he came down to Calcutta together with Reza Khan to whom Verelst had promised 'the secrets of his heart'[5] when they would meet shortly in Calcutta.

Before he came to Calcutta, Reza Khan had already written at length about various recent measures of the Calcutta government and about the series of comments which the Directors had made in their letter of 11 November 1768, extracts from which were

---

[1] The argument that 'the delegation of authority to one or to a few which require the abilities and activity of many to execute' was an indirect reflection on the Resident himself. See BSC, 16 Aug. 1769.

[2] Bhagalpur was the only Bihar district which was administered directly from Murshidabad. Reza Khan in keeping up with his usual policy of giving up the least important to save the rest had offered to work the new plan in Bhagalpur (see his letter to Verelst, recd. 18 Sept. 1769. *CPC*, II, 1596). Extension of Becher's influence to Bhagalpur brought about a clash between Becher and Patna factory over the saltpetre trade of the area and Verelst supported the Faujdar who was under Becher's influence (BPC, 3 July 1769).

[3] Council's letter to Becher. Secret Cons., 4 Sept. 1769.

[4] Becher's reply to Council, 14 Sept. Secret Cons., 5 Oct. 1769.

[5] Verelst to Reza Khan, 19 Sept. 1769. *CPC*, II, 1600.

made available to the Khan in June.[1] He welcomed the Council's and Directors' decision to make it illegal for Europeans to trade in salt, betel-nut and tobacco,[2] but he criticised the raising of the duties on these articles, especially on the last two. About the duty on salt which 'was formerly fixed at $2\frac{1}{2}$ per cent from the Mussel-mans and 5 per cent from the Gentoos [and which] is now generally established at 30 Rs. per 100 Mds[maunds]' he was doubtful of its wisdom. Unaware, perhaps, of the Directors' orders to raise between £100,000 and £120,000 as salt-duty and of the eagerness of the Calcutta authorities to be on the safe side to assure this amount without any adequate knowledge of the amount of salt produced in the country,[3] he gave his opinion as mouthpiece of the Company's revenue interest. Native traders, he reminded the Calcutta government, were men of small capital and it might prove that they could not bear such high duties, and that the revenues might ultimately suffer.[4] The Khan showed his dislike of the new farming system which had been hailed by the English and which was introducing a new class of rich, Calcutta-based Banians as controllers of land, by opposing the pressure of London and Calcutta for the full establishment of the system. He briefly remarked that 'as the districts in Bengal are many, it is impossible to farm them out at once, without foreseeing the disorder it would occasion'.[5] The Khan, however, promised to execute the decision

---

[1] See BSC, 20 June 1769 and Becher's letter of 26 June (BSC, 8 July 1769).
[2] Reza Khan's note enclosed with Becher's letter. BSC, 25 Sept. 1769.
[3] From the knowledge they could gather locally in England the Directors estimated that a salt duty of £100,000 to £120,000 could be collected, but having had no definite information 'from any of your Registers' they advised the Calcutta authorities 'to settle how many Sicca Rupees p. 100, Buzar Maunds it will amount to'. (Court's letter, 20 Nov. 1767). Fort William authorities fixed Rs. 30 per 100 maunds, but without any knowledge of the salt produced. Absence of any information in Calcutta records induced the Directors to send a reminder again in 1771 (General letter of 28 Aug).
[4] Reza Khan's note enclosed with Becher's letter (BSC, 25 Sept. 1769. See also M. Huq, *East India Company's Land Policy and Commerce in Bengal*, pp. 240–41). Reza Khan had withheld his judgement until after two years when the effects of this high rate of duties would appear. The Company's income from salt revenue did in fact fall for more reasons than one, but the Directors held Reza Khan as responsible for this loss of revenue which formed one of the charges against the Khan in 1771 (Court's letter of 28 Aug. 1771).
[5] Reza Khan's note enclosed with Becher's letter (BSC, 25 Sept. 1769). The initial effect of the new farming system in Burdwan has been as noticed by Verelst (BSC, 14 Sept. 1765), that 'the old farmers who had posses-sion perhaps from father to son for many years past, continued to rise in their offers, and probably exceeded the real value of the lands,

of the Company gradually, a beginning having been made already in Nadia and Rajshahi. The Khan then turned to the accusations of the Directors,[1] which he vigorously rejected. He disagreed with the Directors' reasoning about the shortfall in revenue from Purnea and Dinajpur and denied his over-leniency to Souchet Ram, Muhammad Zaman and Mirza Kazim. Souchet Ram was in prison 'till death released him', while Muhammad Zaman, who was put in custody in 1767, was 'yet in prison environed with misery and distress'. To please the English he had been very severe even with the Mirza, a fellow Persian, a friend and by marriage into Alivardi's family a close relation. Neither he nor they were blameworthy—it was the excessive demands which had caused the shortfalls in Purnea and Dinajpur and the Mirza had held back a sum of Rs. 1,30,000 which he claimed as his emoluments as Faujdar of Hugli for two years.[2] The failure in the revenues of the frontier districts of Tipperah and Pachet had their obvious explanation in the revolts of their Rajas.

Reza Khan also protested strongly against the aspersions cast on the Mughal judicial system:

The exacting of fines has heretofore never been a means of exempting the guilty from punishment; on the contrary every degree of severity and torture has been and is still inflicted on them as enjoined by the Laws of God. Had a thirst for fines caused any deviation in this point, the bad consequences to which it would have tended in the regulations and institutions of this Empire would have sufficiently appeared before this juncture.[3]

rather than be turned out of what they had esteemed as their estate and habitation and insulted by the newcomers'. Ultimately they failed to pay and surrendered.

[1] The Directors' comments were based on Sykes's report on Purnea and Dinajpur (BSC, 10 Feb. 1768) which is already noticed in the previous chapter.

[2] As Verelst reported to the Select Committee, on 20 June 1769, Mirza Kazim had already paid the money due from him. The Khan had put the Mirza also into confinement (BSC, 20 June 1769).

[3] Reza Khan's note enclosed with Becher's letter (BSC, 25 Sept. 1769). There was as yet no direct attack from the Directors on the judicial system, but an indirect one, made in paragraph 11 of their letter to the Select Committee on 11 Nov. 1768. Observing that they were happy that the shortfall in Dinajpur 'has not arisen from depopulated or oppressed state of the country, but solely from the villainy profusion and folly of the Rajah and his ministers', the Directors had added that 'We cannot suffer such a depredation of the revenues, and shall not think the ministers do their duty if the ballances . . . are not all recovered, and we are astonished at the lenity of the Nabob and

Conflict of interests, 1769

He was equally bold in defending the amil system, pointing out that it was not, and had not been, the practice to appoint them for just a year or two.

These Soubahs consist of thousands of districts, and every district contains hundreds of Pergunnahs, Talooks, and villages, and the Aumils who manage their collections do not receive their appointments on condition of one year only: whoever for years together gives proof of his diligence in the cultivation of the country, the Ryotts are satisfied with his conduct and no complaints made against him, is never dismissed.[1]

He added:

We look out for men of capacity, principle and religion, but from amongst thousands we pick out one for his appearance and good character, it is only a course of business, and they seeing him vested with power, that will convince us of his good or bad disposition, and in whomsoever this latter appears, and the Ryotts complain of his oppressions, he is of course necessarily dismissed.[2]

Then from this outspoken defence of the quality and efficiency of Mughal system, the Khan turned to a bitter rejection of the accusations made by the Directors against him personally. He emphatically asserted that he had paid into the treasury whatever he had collected, 'to the last trifle'. He then recalled that it was Mir Jafar who, after his restoration, had insisted on the Khan's acceptance of the office of Naib Nazim as the Khan enjoyed the confidence of the English. Knowing the distracted state of the district he had been unwilling to go to Dacca, and had only gone on being absolved from any set contract. In the second year he had been detained for five months at Murshidabad and had then had a contract forced upon him by the Nawab at the instigation of the mutasaddis—meaning Nandkumar. These troubles of 1764 in

Mahmud Reza Cawn in not having made some severe examples of these great offenders. There has always been a most dishonourable practice of fining for crimes which is unbecoming all well administered governments . . .'
[1] Reza Khan's note enclosed with Becher's letter (BSC, 25 Sept. 1769). Reza Khan appears to have had reacted sharply to the remarks like 'an almost annual change' and 'a succession of rapacious governors' which were made in the Directors' letter of 11 Nov. to the Select Committee. Amils, it appears, formed a cadre of service and were posted to different districts as and when deemed necessary.
[2] Reza Khan's note enclosed with Becher's letter. BSC, 25 Sept. 1769.

which Samuel Middleton had also been involved should have been well known and it must have appeared strange to the Khan that they should be raked up now. The Khan made no complaint against any individual, not even Nandkumar, but he turned bitterly upon the Company: 'If with all my attention to the Company's affairs and attachment to their interest, they inspect an agreement which mere force compelled me to accept, and bring the balance thereof into question, it is widely distant from either friendship or equity'.[1] He concluded with a challenge to his accusers: 'The accounts of my collections are ready, the Country is ready and I am ready; make your enquiries'.[2]

On arrival in Calcutta Becher asked the Governor and Council to advise the Court of Directors that he would be available for the position of Second in Council but that he would like to return to England late in 1770 or early in 1771. The Council noted and approved his request.[3] Then, on 10 October, before he had said anything about continuing as Resident, he wrote to the Select Committee to urge the deferment of the posting of supervisors until the ministers had been induced to work the scheme wholeheartedly. He was sure he could win Reza Khan's co-operation, given time to convince him of the propriety of the plan, and without his agreement his subordinates would try every art to frustrate it. He also observed, 'I think the interest of the Company materially concerned and that it is political to shew Mahomed Reza Cawn every mark of respect we can, without deviating from our plan of reformation and I think he has a claim to this, from the indefatigable pains he takes and the service he has rendered the Company'.[4]

Only after making this point did Becher, on 23 October seek the Council's permission to continue as Resident at Murshidabad, arguing that the station was 'next in importance to that of the Governor', and that he thought himself by now 'at least as qualified to conduct that branch, as any member of the Board that can be sent'.[5] Becher's request to stay as Resident caused no lengthy debate, perhaps because he had already canvassed his case

---

[1] Reza Khan's note enclosed with Becher's letter. BSC, 25 Sept. 1769.
[2] *Ibid.* The challenge was accepted by the Company though for other reasons. A lengthy trial in 1772–4 could not disprove the Khan's case.
[3] BPC, 3 Oct. 1769.
[4] Becher's letter, 10 Oct. BSC, 12 Oct. 1769.
[5] BPC, 23 Oct. 1769.

very thoroughly. Nevertheless, he did not retain the post without
what Barwell reported as 'a pretty hard struggle',[1] which showed
in the minutes as a proposal by Floyer that Becher must comply
with the rule of 28 December 1768 that the Second in Council
must always stay in Calcutta, ready to take over the governorship
in emergency. Brigadier Smith naturally supported Floyer and
Rumbold, Becher. Rumbold argued that as Becher was only
staying in Bengal for another year he could not be regarded as the
eventual successor to the governorship, and that the rule might
therefore be waived in this exceptional case.[2]

On the proposal to defer the posting out of supervisors, however,
opposition was more open and prolonged.[3] Though the Council
did eventually recommend a postponement of the scheme until
after February 1770, except in Nadia, Rajshahi, Purnea and
Rajmahal, and in any other district which the Resident might
suggest, Floyer and Smith entered long dissents against delay.
They opposed Becher's plea for time to win over Reza Khan, and
they objected to the 'idea of appointing persons on behalf of the
[Nawab's] Government to accompany our Supravisors'. Smith
maintained that the Khan had sense enough to understand that
it was his duty 'fully to conform to whatever is directed by this
Board' and that to send persons on behalf of the Country government would be 'to send so many spies of the ministers' into the
districts. To wait for the ministers' approval was useless, he
argued, for it never could be their wish or interest to 'enable us in
some future time not only to bring in a large surplus of revenue to
the Company's treasury but to have ministers as we have the
Nabobs merely nominal'.[4]

Smith then proceeded to attack Reza Khan directly, declaring,
'I never did subscribe to the very high encomiums which from
time to time have been bestowed upon Mahomed Reza Cawn; for
whether I survey his conduct in general or a particular view, I
think there is more cause for censure than for applause'. 'In a
general point of view', Smith observed, 'I presume it will not be
contested with me, that this country is by no means so flourishing
a state at this period, as when he was first invested with almost

[1] Barwell to his father, 25 Dec. 1769. *BPP*, x, 244.
[2] BPC, 23 Oct. 1769.
[3] This subject was taken up by the Council in its secret session. Secret Cons.,
26 Oct. 1769.
[4] Smith's minute of dissent. Secret Cons., 26 Oct. 1769.

supreme power. It has been urged in his behalf, that the country was originally over-rated: supposing that to be the case whom are we to blame for such an injudicious measure; a measure which has been productive of such very unfavourable consequences to the Company's affairs, as well in India as in England?' For a particular example of the mismanagement he censured, Smith then turned to Purnea, commenting that 'in the course of three years a fine fertile and extensive province is reduced one fourth part from the value it was estimated at when Mahomed Reza Cawn came into power and this too during a time of the most profound tranquility'. Smith held that these were 'surely no proofs of our minister's extraordinary abilities'. He ended with another sinister attack, claiming that when the ministers were making huge reductions in the demand on Purnea 'Aqa Razy who was the humble dependant of the ministers, and invested with immediate authority over this unhappy province did accumulate such a fortune as in so short a space of time could only be accumulated by rapine and extortion'.[1] In similar vein, though Verelst had already given his findings, on local enquiry, that Mir Jafar's accusations about Reza Khan's Dacca collections were politically motivated,[2] Smith declared the Khan's statement to be a lame excuse, and went on to question the size of the salary of the Khan, whose 'most superlative degree of merit' had been 'most superlatively rewarded'.[3]

Smith thus proceeded from the implication that Reza Khan was to blame for over-rating the country, for employing the severe hand of oppression to enforce those demands and for introducing the practice of anticipating next year's revenues to cover deficits in the current collections to the direct imputation of corruption practised through his dependant. The Council may have given little weight to the charges of one who was the least informed amongst them about the actual working of the administration, but Smith's arguments were very useful to those in England who wished to condemn the Clivite regime in Bengal, and were seeking a scapegoat. Smith either did not know, or he had deliberately ignored the fact that Sykes had revised Reza Khan's assessments for 1765–6 sharply upwards, soon after the Company's acquisition

[1] Smith's minute of dissent. Secret Cons., 26 Oct. 1769.
[2] Verelst's report to Select Committee. BSC, 20 June 1769.
[3] Smith's minute of dissent. Secret Cons., 26 Oct. 1769.

of the Diwani, and that it was Souchet Ram not Aqa Razy who had been in charge of the Purnea revenues. He seemed well informed about Purnea only because Ducarel's report of 17 August was before the Select Committee on 12 October, but ignored the reporter's observation that 'the fault is not wholly to be laid upon the people of this country'.[1] But for the opposition in London who had re-entered the Directorate in April 1769, Smith's strictures were valuable ammunition, whether well founded or not. Significantly every word of censure of Reza Khan in Smith's minute of 26 October 1769, and of Floyer's very similar attack on 29 March 1770 was underlined in red ink at Leadenhall Street.

Smith and Floyer were not of course alone in objecting to the postponement of the supervisor scheme. There were others no less keen in championing the junior servants of the Company and no less convinced of the need to send 'our own countrymen' into the districts. Barwell was one of these, and his writings to England also served to excite opinion against the Khan and his administration. As early as 10 September, before the Council's decision, he had written to Vansittart, already appointed one of the three Commissioners to come to India with exceptional powers,[2] saying 'The present mode of collecting the revenue calls loudly for a reform, and unless abilities to plan and a spirit to execute be equally exerted the golden prospect of the nation will assuredly vanish'.[3] After the Khan's request for deferment became known, he wrote to his father still more decidedly and alarmingly:

A system has been proposed for collecting the revenues of these provinces and universally approved when proposed. Since that the gentlemen of the Council seem very indifferent to the carrying of it into execution. His Excellency the Nabob [Reza Khan] has wrote publickly to have the scheme postponed, and God knows whether private considerations may not supersede the public good. The Company's possessions whilst the present mode of collecting the revenue is continued, appears to me precarious; all the revenue is anticipated for the payment of the army and for the provision of the Company's investment. Should then an enemy invade the country the Zemindars will naturally withhold the rents, and if Mahomed Reza Cawn on whom the officers of the government are entirely dependant carries on any private

---

[1] Ducarel's report to the Resident, dated 17 Aug. BSC, 12 Oct. 1769.
[2] The three commissioners appointed were Vansittart (representing Sulivan's party), Scrafton (Clive's party), and Forde.
[3] Barwell to H. Vansittart, 10 Sept. 1769. *BPP*, x, 31–2.

14-2

intrigues, how easily can he influence a total stop to the collections. What then is to support their army? In such exigency the sending up Europeans will be of little consequence.[1]

To sum up the developments of 1769, Reza Khan, feeling a little more free after Sykes's departure from Murshidabad, came out with his suggestions for a remedy of the situation in which the country had been left by Sykes's administration both as Resident and chief of Kasimbazar. This was possible because of the sympathetic response he received from the new Resident Becher and also from Verelst, who were roused from their complacency by the decline in revenues and trade. The reforms suggested met opposition from the deep rooted vested interests of the commercial branch of the Company's service as well as from servants of the Company in general. Verelst, acting on the propositions, then carried through his reforms, designed to reassert the control of the Nawab's government and its officers, with just one-third of the Council's members present. He acted courageously but perhaps unwisely. As a result the opposition to Clive's system, already growing in strength because of events in London as well as in Bengal, was led to a decisive counteraction. Verelst's Regulations of 18 May were answered by the scheme of supervisorship which transferred superior power in the districts to the European servants of the Company. This rendered Reza Khan and his instruments potentially redundant.

Reza Khan could only fight a rearguard action: as Barwell put it, the Khan 'not liking the new system, has put off the evil day'.[2] That he was able to achieve even this much was perhaps due to the Company's need to maintain the farce of the Country government so as to resist the British government's claims to the territorial revenues of Bengal and the demand of the rival merchant groups within the City of London for a free trade to India and the ending of the Company's monopoly. He had also been able to use the conflict of interest between the dwindling number of senior servants and the ever increasing number of junior servants of the Company in Bengal. Finally, until December 1769, the Khan

[1] Barwell to his father William Barwell, 4 Oct. 1769 (*BPP*, x, 235). William Barwell had great influence in the Company's affairs in London. An ex-servant of the Bengal establishment (1722–50), ex-governor of Calcutta (1748–9), he was a proprietor and also a Director on many occasions (1753–7, 1758–65, 1766–7)(*BPP*, VIII, p. 188 n. *BPP*, XXVII, 35).
[2] Barwell to Leycester, 4 Oct. 1769. *BPP*, x, 236.

could rely upon the support of Verelst who saw, more clearly perhaps than any one else, how near the appointment of supervisors brought the Company to a decisive break with all its past in Bengal.

Verelst, who had sponsored the scheme under pressure, supported the Khan's plea that the posting of supervisors to the districts should be deferred. Not only that, he also sought, as appears from the instructions drafted by him, to restrict the scope of the supervisors' activity to research, conceding officially, at the same time, their right to private trade. Verelst had also taken his vengeance on the commercial branch by creating a rival private trade interest to break the hitherto monopoly of the commercial branch. Senior servants of the Company, who were in the Council and the Committee and who had earlier forced Verelst to adopt the scheme, becoming perhaps suddenly alive to the threat had, as Barwell reported, 'grown cool'[1] and lent their support to Verelst. With Smith's departure for England in November, Verelst was relieved of his most vocal critic, though the gain was neutralised by the departure also of Rumbold in the same month. The changed situation enabled Verelst not only to confirm the deferment of the scheme but also to vest the Resident with extended powers. On 10 December the Select Committee had conferred on Becher the powers of recalling any supervisor from his station—only Kelsall of Dacca being excepted—and of making any additions which he and the ministers thought necessary to the Letter of Instructions which was to be regarded as indicative of general directions.[2] The scheme in August was seen as a common threat to the Khan as well as to Becher and the interests of the two had coalesced as never before; and with Becher's position thus reinforced on 10 December, Becher also sought almost immediately to stabilise the Khan's position as near as possible to *status quo ante*. On 20 December, Becher had instructed one of the earliest supervisors to be sent out saying 'that it is not the intention of the President and Council to alter the present form of government, but that the

[1] Barwell's complaint on this score is made in a letter to Leycester on 4 Oct. 1769. He wrote: 'A plan has been laid down by V – – and approved by the Board . . . The Council are grown cool, and when it will be executed is to me a secret. I hope, however, private considerations will not explode a measure absolutely necessary for the welfare of the country and the Company' (*BPP*, x, 236). Barwell who was to enter Council on Verelst's departure (and he was called to Council on 2 Jan. 1770) had not yet developed the interest of the Councillors which, as later events proved, came into violent collision with the private trade interest of supervisors.   [2] BSC, 10 Dec. 1769.

gentlemen employed by them as Supravisors are to support the authority of the government's officers...and proper respect to be paid to them—at the same time the Supravisors are to recommend such regulations as appear necessary for the welfare of the country and the benefit of our Employers—advising me whenever the officers of the government refuse to acquiesce in what you propose that I may if I find it expedient apply to the ministers to issue their orders for enforcing the measure'.[1] The limited controlling power over the district administration which found a place in Becher's instruction was again a decision of the Committee in order that the supervisors might not be 'incumbered in their important researches', though this, it was declared, should not be 'an immediate active power'.[2] The disclaimer, however, did not deceive Verelst. On 16 December 1769, when Verelst joined the Council and presented his farewell message for the instruction of his successor Cartier and of the Directors, he drew upon his twenty years of experience in India—and three as governor—to emphasise the revolutionary nature of the plan to appoint supervisors. He commended the scheme as a nursery of able and vigorous administrators for the future. But he warned that

there is a rock, and a dangerous one which requires the greatest circumspection to avoid. We have stepped forth beyond all former precedent or example. We have the best and most laudable arguments to justify our conduct. But it should be remembered, that we have reached the supreme line, which to pass would be an open avowal of sovereignty. It should be remembered that we cannot be more, without being greater than sound policy allows; the interests of our employers at home, no less than our national connections abroad, forbid it.[3]

For that reason, he urged:

If we were, before the change, cautious of interfering with the native government...we ought now to redouble our prudence. The change itself, supposing the greatest forbearance on our part, has an unavoidable tendency to destroy the name of the Nizamut...[4]

Such a destruction of the name of the Nizamat and the consequent open avowal of the Company's authority must injure the Company

[1] Becher's letter to Jacob Ryder (Nadia), 20 Dec. 1769. Quoted in D. N. Banerji, *Early Land Revenue System in Bengal and Bihar*, I, 80–1.
[2] BSC, 15 Dec. 1769.
[3] BPC, 16 Dec. 1769.   [4] *Ibid.*

by becoming the source, as already had happened in England, 'of perplexities and jealousies'.

In history there is no going back, and Verelst knew that he could not return to the old ordering of things. But he could and did advise a balanced compromise between the two systems, the old and the new, a 'middle way' where 'moderation must guide and continue us; where we may walk with safety, advantage and consistence without danger of too much confinement, or too much liberty'.[1] As Clive before him, so Verelst now urged his successors, 'Exteriors should be regarded as essentials. Every order should scrupulously wear the sanction of the native government'.[2] There must of necessity be a show of dependence, wherein delicacy to the ministers 'should appear most conspicuous in all transactions, either of business or ceremony'.[3] Such a policy of restraint and regard for ministerial feeling had never been easy and, as Verelst foresaw, it was likely to be 'more difficult to produce a proper conformity in the supravisors'.[4]

Verelst did not fail to record his sense of the difficulties facing his successor Cartier. 'I am not ignorant', he wrote, 'how difficult it is always to preserve and affect that temperate rule of conduct which I mention, when the power and direction of all departments so entirely concentrate in your Board.'[5] But he also allowed himself to express some doubt about how far the scheme of supervisors would be beneficial to the country. He saw that it was not possible as yet 'to form an administration totally free from commercial views', since every Englishman in the Company's service in Bengal derived his 'sole advantage from commerce, carried on through black agents, who again employ a numerous band of retainers'.[6] There was a danger therefore that these 'Banians and agents by the spirit with which they act and the force of their example' would obstruct the good effects of the administration of the European gentlemen.[7] The remedy Verelst proposed was again the same—'that the whole weight and vigilance of the Board should be exerted to check the most trifling variation from the line, and to preserve the idea of native government, its dignity and superiority over all, as entire and unimpaired as possible'.[8] Verelst had rendered the last service which he could to the system he had inherited and within which Reza Khan worked.

[1] Verelst's letter to Cartier and Council. BPC, 16 Dec. 1769. [2] *Ibid.*
[3] *Ibid.* [4] *Ibid.* [5] *Ibid.* [6] *Ibid.* [7] *Ibid.* [8] *Ibid.*

CHAPTER 9

THE CONFLICT DEEPENS, 1769–1770

With Verelst's departure from Bengal in December 1769, Reza Khan had entered a long and bitter struggle for survival. In this he had received much assistance from Richard Becher, whose interest as Resident until the close of 1770 had become linked with his. The difficulties had been made easier to bear by the warmth and sympathy of John Cartier, an old friend of the Dacca days,[1] who had succeeded Verelst as governor. But the times were difficult even for Cartier. Verelst's parting letter of advice, submitted to the Council on 16 December 1769, was a catalogue of problems bequeathed to his successor. These problems did not diminish in 1770, but grew in number and complexity. Bengal was in the grip of a still mounting famine and of an epidemic of smallpox which was soon to claim the Nawab Nazim as one of its many victims. The difficult task of introducing the scheme of supervisorships, put off by Verelst, had soon to be tackled. In London events were moving towards a revolution in the Directorate and a crisis in the Company's relations with the state. Already three Commissioners for India had been appointed to come out with extraordinary powers, and the news of their appointment weakened Cartier's authority. In Bengal the group conflicts within and without the Council were still unresolved and still acrimonious. They were soon to develop into an open battle between the Committee and the Council for control over the revenue administration. And for dealing with these problems Cartier was personally ill prepared, for unlike Verelst he had no political and administrative experience, his whole career until his elevation to the governorship having been in the commercial line. In most difficult circumstances all that he could do was to stick to the course charted for him by his predecessors until he was forced by circumstances to change

[1] Both Reza Khan and Cartier were posted to Dacca in 1763, the Khan as Naib Nazim and Cartier as chief of English Factory. They had co-operated in war efforts against Mir Qasim and remained friends ever since.

direction. His loyalty to the system he had inherited and inability to manoeuvre proved costly to him.[1]

The most pressing problem which faced Cartier when he assumed office in December 1769 was still that of the great famine sweeping Bihar[2] and western Bengal. Reza Khan had officially advised Calcutta of the 'dryness of the season' as early as September 1769.[3] Since then the drought had continued, destroying the autumn harvest and ruining the prospects of the winter one. On 23 October Rumbold told the Council that famine conditions had forced him to abolish the duty on food grains coming into Patna, where rice was already selling at ten seers per rupee, while Becher reported 'great dearth and scarcity' at Murshidabad.[4] The Council ordered 1,20,000 maunds of rice to be laid in for the Company's army, 80,000 maunds from Dacca and Bakarganj, and 40,000 by Reza Khan from Purnea and Dinajpur, supposedly less affected districts. A supply of rice, promised earlier to Madras, was suspended. Directions were given to build storehouses at Patna and Murshidabad, whose Supervisor and Resident were told to exert themselves to prevent monopolisation of food grains and to encourage cultivation of 'pulse, gram, barley and every sort of grain that can be raised in the dry season'.[5] Nevertheless, when Cartier assumed office Barwell was writing to England, 'all the western districts of Bengall and Bahar are in a terrible condition, and in most places rice sells at eight and twelve seers per rupee'.[6]

Before 1769 was out, Reza Khan and Shitab Rai had sent a joint

[1] Cartier and Becher were dismissed by the Directors in 1771 for their opposition to the junior members of the Council. The Directors disapproved 'the opposition given by our Select Committee', and ordered Russell and Floyer, the other two members, to Madras wherefrom they had been brought (Court's letter, 25 April 1771). See next chapter.
[2] Since Rumbold's appointment in Nov. 1766 at Patna the administration of Bihar was made independent of Murshidabad's control, though Patna accounts used to be sent to Murshidabad for incorporation in the Diwani accounts. Though Shitab Rai worked directly under Rumbold, he sometimes channelled his representations to Fort William also through Reza Khan who besides being the acting Nawab for the three subahs was frequently consulted by Verelst also about Bihar problems.
    Excessive rains in August 1768 had destroyed crops in Bihar and this was followed by drought. Reza Khan supported Shitab Rai's argument for an abatement in demand (BSC, 6 March 1769).
[3] Reza Khan to Verelst, recd. 18 Sept. 1769. *CPC*, II, 1596.
[4] BPC, 23 Oct. 1769.
[5] *Ibid.*　　　　[6] To Leycester, 24 Dec. 1769. *BPP*, X, 238.

representation to the Calcutta government suggesting measures in which heavy collections would not fall indiscriminately on all ryots who would only be obliged to pay 'according to the success they have had during the season in the cultivation of their lands'. The measures were particularly intended for Bihar, which was going through a successive second year of crop failure, because of rains and floods in 1768–9 and excessive drought in 1769–70. Observing that any pressing and rigorous demands 'at this season of distress' would only tend to impoverish the country without any corresponding gains to the treasury, they represented that

The ryots, both of Bengal and Behar, when much reduced or harassed by Government, sell their children to raise money, much less do they spare their effects and cattle. The plough consequently stands still, and numbers of them desert their homes; and supposing something [is] collected in this manner this present year, where will be a fund for the next? It will become difficult, if not impossible, to retrieve the country after such a drain. Considering these and all other circumstances, the following seems to be the most expedient and reasonable plan. Let the third part of the present year's crops of grain, and the fourth part of other productions, such as sugar, poppies, &c., be given to the ryot for his stock and subsistence, and let the remainder be received by Government in payment and sold by Commissioners. The produce will be considerable, and the ryots being, on the other hand, enabled to support themselves, will apply themselves to labour.[1]

The suggestion sought at least to ensure physical survival of the vast agricultural population of the famine stricken area from the produce of their own land and labour, for the Bengal peasants did not keep on hand a large enough reserve of food grains to provide for even one crop failure.[2] There was as well a possibility of creating a large stock of food grains in the hands of the government for meeting the needs of those who lived in towns and cities and generally purchased their own requirements. With the spread of death and destruction[3] the Khan had been roused, not only by the

[1] Proposal by Reza Khan and Shitab Rai. BSC, 7 Dec. 1769. The Council took no action but left the matter with Alexander.
[2] Embree, *Charles Grant and British Rule in India*, p. 35.
[3] Charles Grant, Becher's agent in 1769–70 and future Director of the Company, who was a witness to the scene, observed, 'The famine was felt in all the northern districts of Bengal as early as November, 1769 and before the end of April following had spread death and destruction through the three provinces. Rice rose gradually to four, and at length to ten, times its usual price . . .' Quoted by Embree.

218

sense of charity which his religious traditions enjoined on him,[1] but also by the need to preserve his public image. To the people he was now known as Khan-i-Khanan, lord of lords, and to him they naturally turned for help and relief. When the Council still failed to plan relief, the Khan together with Becher put forward, in February 1770, a scheme to open six centres in the city of Murshidabad for the free distribution of half a seer of rice a day per head. This was well received, and the Council authorised an expenditure of Rs. 87,250 for this purpose, Rs. 40,000 by the Company and the rest by the Nawab and his ministers.[2] The Nawab was to provide Rs. 21,000, Reza Khan Rs. 15,250, Rai Durlabh Rs. 6,000 and the Jagat Seth Rs. 5,000.[3] In the event the sum sanctioned was much exceeded, for as month followed month in 1770 without the hoped-for rain, the destructiveness of the famine steadily increased. In May 1770 Reza Khan drew attention to the universal agony in a report which in summary read as follows:

Up to the present hour the writer has managed the collection of the revenue and every other business of the Nizamat most diligently and as far as he could help it he has not been guilty of any fault. But there is no remedy against the decrees of Providence. How can he describe the misery of the people from the severe droughts and the dearness of grain. Hitherto it was scarce, but this year it cannot be found at all. The tanks and springs are dried up and it is daily growing difficult to procure water. In addition to these calamities, dreadful fires have occurred throughout the country, impoverishing whole families and destroying thousands of lives. The small stores of grain which yet remained at Rajganj, Diwanganj and other places in the districts of Dinajpur and Purnea, have been consumed by fire. Hitherto each day furnished accounts of the death of thousands, but now lakhs of people are dying daily. It was hoped that there would be some rain during the months of

---

[1] An instance of his private charity was the establishment of a market with sheds on his private lands at Chitpur in Calcutta, outside the area of his own administrative responsibility, 'the profits of which he constantly applied to the assistance of wearied and unfortunate travellers'. In 1781 the Board of Revenue exempted the Khan from paying any government dues on the income of the market. In 1790 the usual income of Rs. 100 per month was stopped when Mr. Colebrooke forbade any more collection of dues and customs from buyers and sellers in the market. The Company's government was to have reimbursed the Khan. As late as 1796 the Khan and after him his son continued to pay 'those pensions to the poor people' which used to be defrayed from the income of the market (*BRP*, Range 89, vol. 22, 1 July 1796). See also p. 277.
[2] BPC, 13 Feb. 1770.
[3] Reza Khan's account of the expenses for famine relief (*MP*, 3 Jan. 1771).

April and May, and that the poor ryots would be enabled thereby to till their lands, but up to this hour not a drop of rain has fallen. The coarse crop which is gathered in this season is entirely ruined, and though the seed for the August crop is sown during the months of April and May, nothing has been done in that direction for want of rain. Even now it is not too late and if there are a few showers of rain, something may be done. If the scarcity of grain and want of rain were confined to one part of the country, some remedy for the alleviation of the distress could be found. But when the whole country is in the grip of famine, the only remedy lies in the mercy of God. The Almighty alone can deliver the people from such distress.[1]

On 2 June Becher gave his estimate of the deaths 'as six is to sixteen of the whole inhabitants', adding that 'certain it is that in several parts, the living have fed on the dead'.[2] On 12 July he reported that five hundred persons were perishing daily in Murshidabad city alone, while 'in the villages and country adjacent the numbers said to perish exceed belief'.[3]

To meet this distress the expenditure at Murshidabad was increased, from the sanctioned Rs. 87,250 to a total of Rs.1,52,443-4 annas while a further sum of Rs. 30,839-5 annas was spent in the charitable distribution of rice at Purnea, Bhagalpur, Birbhum, Hugli and Yusufpur or Jessore.[4] In addition, the Khan made further charitable grants from his own resources. Karam Ali, the author of the *Muzaffar-namah*, gave Rs. 70,000 as Reza Khan's contribution to the public fund—the same as the Company provided—and Mubarak ud daulah's as Rs. 50,000. The difference between these figures and those listed in the Company's records

[1] Reza Khan to Cartier, recd. 15 May 1770. *CPC*, III, 209.
[2] Becher's letter, 2 June. BSC, 9 June 1770. Grant gave a more horrid account when he wrote, 'There were persons who fed on the forbidden and abhorred animals, nay, the child on its dead parents, the mother on her child'. Quoted by Embree, *Charles Grant and British Rule in India*, p. 36.
[3] Becher's letter, 12 July. BSC, 19 July 1770. Distressing reports were coming from the districts, notably from Nabkishore, Ajagarmal, Mirza Muhammad Husain and Sadr ul Haq Khan, Amils of Bishnupur, Jessore, Rangpur and Bhagalpur; from Rajas Asaduzzaman Khan and Shib Nath of Birbhum and Edrakpur, Faujdar Pratit Rai of Rajmahal and from supervisors Ducarel, Hardwood, and Ryder in Purnea, Bhagalpur and Nadia. These reports were before the Committee in April (BSC, 28 April 1770).
[4] Reza Khan's account (*MP*, 3 Jan. 1771). Grant said, 'In Murshidabad, seventy-seven thousand were daily fed for several months . . .' (see Embree, *op. cit.*, p. 35). Murshidabad's example was later adopted to feed about 3000 men daily at Calcutta and Burdwan, for which a daily expenditure of Rs. 50 and Rs. 20-25 was sanctioned (BPC, 3 April 1770).

The conflict deepens, 1769–1770

can perhaps be accounted for by supposing them to include their private charity. Both Becher and Karam Ali agree that men of property gave very generously towards the relief of the poor, others mentioned being Munshi Sharafat Muhammad Khan and Haji Muhammad Mohsin, the future founder of the Mohsin Fund.[1] On 1 February 1771 the Calcutta Council gave the Company's contributions from the general revenues as Rs. 56,911 and those of the Nawab and his ministers as Rs. 58,776, adding that 'exclusive of this they have severally expended considerable sums in distribution of rice to the poor'.[2] This last remark may include the Khan's provision of rice at cheap rates. Becher had supplied rice from Barisal to the Company's dependants at fifteen seers per rupee,[3] and the Khan was led to make similar provision for the employees of the Nizamat, servants of the Nawab and in fact for everyone who cared to come to the cheap grain centre that was opened at his palace, the Nishat Bagh.[4] There was, however, a big difference between the two operations. Whereas Becher's supply of 55,449 maunds of rice, 30,476 to troops at Monghyr, Berhampore and Muradbagh, and 24,973 maunds to other immediate dependants at Kasimbazar and Murshidabad, even at the rate of fifteen seers per rupee, had earned a net profit of Rs. 67,595 for the Company,[5] Reza Khan's purchases for the public charity centres and so possibly also for private distribution, made from Becher's Diwan and Ganga Govind Singh

[1] *MN*, f. 184.   [2] Secret Cons., 1 Feb. 1771.
[3] Becher's letter. *MP*, 24 Dec. 1770; *MN*, f. 185. Becher sold 55,449 Mds 35 srs 2 Chhataks of Rice for a total sum of Rs. 1,56,764-8-7-2. After sundry charges amounting to Rs. 4,481-14 annas, the net price collected was Rs. 1,52,282-10-7-2. In the accounts given, no retail rate is given for 16,622 Mds 14 srs 2 ch. sold at Murshidabad or 9,302-1-6 ch. sold at Monghyr, for total sums of Rs. 46,246-0-17-2 and Rs. 32,013-12 but 8351-1-12 ch. sold to the dependants at Kasimbazar and 21,184-18-12 ch. sold to sepoys and Brigade at Muradbagh and Berhampore were at 15 seers of 82 Sicca weight per rupee (*Famine Papers*, vol. 1, p. 35). 16 ch. made a sr. and 40 srs a Md.
[4] *MN*, f. 185.
[5] This amount was ultimately adjusted towards the cost of additional expenses incurred for charitable distribution of rice from 1 Mar. to 4 Sept. 1770. During the period a total sum of Rs. 1,83,282 was spent, Rs. 1,52,443 at Murshidabad, Rs. 17,294 at Purnea, Rs. 5,067 at Bhagalpur, Rs. 4,476 at Hugli, Rs. 2,940 at Birbhum and Rs. 1,062 at Yusufpur (Jessore) (see Secret Cons., 1 Feb. 1771 and *Famine Papers*, vol. 1, p. 35). The total cost was met jointly, the Company paying Rs. 56,911 from general revenue, Rs. 67,595 by transferring the profit (or Rs. 1,24,507 in all) and the rest being paid by the Nawab (Rs. 26,893), Reza Khan (Rs. 19,507), Rai Durlabh (Rs. 6000) and Jagat Seth (Rs. 6,375), the last three paying from their own resources (see Secret

of the Qanungo's office,[1] were at a much higher price—less than 'six or seven seers per rupee of the coarsest rice'[2] at the height of the famine. The Khan also arranged to pay workmen employed on construction of three buildings of the Nishat Bagh in rice instead of in cash.[3]

As has been seen, the Council early issued orders to its servants at Patna and Murshidabad—and also in Calcutta—to prevent hoarding of food grains and profiteering. Reza Khan had soon to complain, however, of such malpractices. On 13 February 1770 the Council thus had before them a letter, forwarded by Becher, 'complaining that the English Gomastahs monopolize the rice'.[4] Both Reza Khan and Becher had issued orders to the Amils to prevent this monopolisation and the use of violence in purchasing grains, for they feared that if these remained unchecked, the peasants 'will not have sufficient seed for the next harvest'.[5] Neither Reza Khan nor Becher mentioned any particular incident, nor did they point out to any individual offender perhaps because, as the Directors later suspected, 'they could be no other than persons of some rank in our service'.[6] Becher, however, proposed in his forwarding note that 'there ought to be a prohibition of Europeans or their Gomastahs purchasing rice till after the next August harvest'.[7] The Council did not, as the Directors later pointed out, either order an enquiry into the allegations of Reza Khan or adopt 'the only particular remedy'.[8] Karam Ali comments that Reza Khan failed to hold grain prices down because he lacked power to punish 'mischievous people and trouble mongers'.[9] The 'Bengali[10] grain dealers, finding the English unconcerned, opened

Cons., 1 Feb. 1771 and *Famine Papers*, vol. 1, p. 36). The Council, however, noted that 'the first subscription of the Nabob and the ministers exceeded ours and their addition to it still makes the amount superior' (Secret Cons., 1 Feb. 1771). They had ignored the amount of profit which they transferred to charity.   [1] *MN*, f. 185.   [2] Reza Khan's account. *MP*, 3 Jan. 1771.
[3] *MN*, f. 185. Floyer's attempt to pay the workmen employed on the construction of Fort William similarly in rice proved 'ineffectual'. 33,913 Mds of rice had thus to be auctioned, and diverted possibly to black market. From January to March the number of workmen had risen from 3165 to 7418 (BPC 25 Jan., 6 March, 3 April 1770).   [4] BPC, 13 Feb. 1770.   [5] *Ibid.*
[6] Court's letter, 28 Aug. 1771.   [7] BPC, 13 Feb. 1770.
[8] Court's letter, 28 Aug. 1771.   [9] *MN*, f. 184.
[10] By the term 'Bengali' Karam Ali meant Bengali Hindu. The terms 'Bengali' and 'Bengali Hindu' have been synonymous in West Bengal and Calcutta where even today Muslim and Hindu localities within the same village or town are known locally as Musalman Para (locality) and Bangali Para.

the path of cruelty',[1] so that the situation went from bad to worse. Reza Khan certainly seems to have done his best to keep prices down at Murshidabad, and the distribution of charity rice and the supply of subsidised rice by Becher and the Khan together with payment of wages in rice must have had a useful effect. A black market nevertheless flourished, and the Khan may well have been correct when he pointed out the gumashtahs of the English as the principal offenders. A curious case recorded by Karam Ali may turn upon this point. He relates that the boats of Khairati Ram, Darogha of Bahramganj in Murshidabad city, who was under the protection of Maharaja Amrit Singh, the Khan's Diwan, were found involved in an illegal trade in grain. The boats were seized at Bhagwangola, but the Darogha's guilt could not be proved. The Khan's agents who had taken the initiative in detecting the crime consequently 'felt ashamed'.[2] Karam Ali was a protégé of the Khan, and it seems strange that he should relate the story involving Amrit Singh, the Khan's Diwan. However, one reason why the Diwan's protégé escaped punishment may perhaps be found in the fact that the young Maharaja was no longer solely dependent on the Khan's favour. Already as a man with considerable independence, the Maharaja was on excellent terms with the English. He had built a palace, the Ayash Bagh, in the English style, and many European servants of the Company 'used to have gay time' there, enjoying the Maharaja's hospitality.[3] It is perhaps also significant that when in February Becher asked for a ban on English trade in rice, the Council refused to issue any such general prohibition. All that they would do was to prohibit exports of rice from Dinajpur and Purnea except to Murshidabad, and to empower Becher, but not the Khan, to enquire into any clamour which the gumashtahs might make against this partial restriction.[4] The Khan's repeated complaints against these men could only deepen his conflict with the monopolist interests.

Famine was very soon accompanied by pestilence, particularly smallpox, which added to the heavy mortality in Bengal.[5] Among the thousands who died of smallpox were the Nawab Nazim

[1] *MN*, f. 184.   [2] *MN*, f. 185.
[3] *MN*, f. 189. It was built originally for Mubarak-ud-daulah at Reza Khan's direction and was a two-storeyed building.
[4] BPC, 13 Feb. 1770.
[5] Estimates vary between three and ten million (Embree, *Charles Grant and British Rule in India*, p. 36).

The transition in Bengal, 1756-1775

Saif-ud-daulah, his brother Ashraf Ali Khan, nicknamed Mir Jan, and Reza Khan's relations Fath ullah Khan and Haji Ismail Khan.[1] One of the Khan's sons was also smitten, but recovered. As if famine and pestilence were not enough the drought had caused big fires throughout the country to add to the destruction of life and particularly of property, houses and food stores. In Murshidabad city alone a big fire caused heavy destruction with only a few houses escaping its ravages.[2]

The sudden death of Saif-ud-daulah on 10 March 1770 opened the succession to Mir Jafar's fifth son Mubarak-ud-daulah, then aged eleven or twelve.[3] Becher, reporting the Nawab's death, asked the Council if the new Nawab's stipend was to be reduced, but the Council at Cartier's suggestion refused to cut down the Nawab's allowances.[4] Though for this Cartier was later to receive strongly worded censure from London,[5] he was guided by the positive orders of the Directors to the Select Committee 'never to reduce the stipend lower'.[6] By a new agreement entered into between the Company and Mubarak-ud-daulah, the latter was recognised as Nawab Nazim and was formally installed on the masnad by Becher and Aldersey on 21 March. The administrative arrangement continued as under Najm-ud-daulah and Saif-ud-daulah, but because the new Nawab was a minor Reza Khan was appointed his guardian.

This change further strengthened the Khan's position at Murshidabad. Najm-ud-daulah had never reconciled himself to the Khan's appointment as Naib and Saif-ud-daulah also disliked his authority. Munni Begum, widow of Mir Jafar and domineering mother of the two Nawabs, had fomented their ill-will towards the Khan, despite his efforts to maintain good relations with her. Now, however, her position as head of the Nawab's household ended, for Mubarak's own mother Babbu Begum was alive and she did, as by custom she could, claim that position.[7] Reza Khan sought to please both, Babbu Begum by supporting her right and Munni Begum for her old and established status. When therefore Cartier asked for the Khan's opinion in the matter, he maintained

---

[1] *Seir*, III, 25-6.   [2] *MN*, f. 185.
[3] Karam Ali puts him at 11, Becher 'not above 12 years' (see *MN*, f. 182; Becher's letter, 10 March. BPC, 13 March 1770).
[4] BPC, 13 March 1770.
[5] Court's letter, 10 April 1771.   [6] Letter of 16 March 1768.
[7] See Cartier's reply to Babbu Begum, 26 May 1770. *CPC*, III, 231.

that by custom 'the place of honour rightfully belongs to his [Mubarak-ud-daulah's] mother, but it would be better if the two begams were given equal rank and authority'.[1] It was Cartier who decided that since Mubarak-ud-daulah was now the Nazim his mother should be vested with the real authority while 'as a matter of form and etiquette, she should treat the mother of the late Nawab Najm-ud-daulah as her superior'.[2] Cartier's fears that the Khan's proposal to confer equal rank and authority to both would not prevent dispute— 'for God has not endowed women with prudence and they are naturally quarrelsome'[3]—unhappily proved correct, despite Cartier's acting contrary to the Khan's advice. Munni Begum could not tolerate the change, more because she could not possibly forget that from the position of a dependant of Babbu Begum and a slave girl of Babbu's mother[4] she had risen, since the death of Miran and consequent dislodgement of Shah Khanum, to the position of the head of Nawab's household in Mir Jafar's day with authority and power even over Babbu Begum. Finally it became necessary to separate the establishment of Munni Begum from that of the Nawab. Munni Begum held Reza Khan responsible for her dislodgement and became a willing tool in the hands of Reed later in the year, and of Hastings in 1772, to work against the Khan. Immediately, however, the long-standing tension in the relations between Reza Khan and the Nawab had ended. In order to improve upon them still further, the young Nawab with Babbu Begum's consent was betrothed to the daughter of the Khan's sister-in-law, the grand-daughter of Rabia Begum and Ataullah Khan.[5]

Reza Khan, as official guardian of the young Nawab, further strengthened his hold upon the household by a series of appointments. Ali Ibrahim Khan became Diwan-i-Sarkar with complete control of expenditure, Nasr ullah Khan and Saiyid Ahsan ud din Khan became Mir Samani, controllers of the household and Muhammad Niamat was appointed Darogha-i-Fil, superintendent of the elephant stables. Mir Nannu who had been out of favour under the previous Nawabs became Mir Emarat, superintendent of buildings. Four tutors were appointed, Ali Naqi Khan, Amir

---

[1] Reza Khan to Cartier, recd. 22 May 1770. *CPC*, III, 224.
[2] Cartier to Reza Khan, 24 May 1770. *CPC*, III, 226.   [3] *Ibid.*
[4] *Seir*, III, 147, and Reza Khan's letter of May 1770. *CPC*, III, 224.
[5] *MN*, f. 183, and Mubarak-ud-daulah's letter. *H.M.S.*, 202; 109.

The transition in Bengal, 1756–1775

Beg Khan, Khwaja Abdullah and Muhammad Naqi, and a solemn promise was taken from the young Nawab that, contrary to the practice of his predecessors, he would learn Persian and keep his beard.[1] The Khan, it would seem, was determined that his charge should grow up a good Muslim ruler. The most notable of all these changes was the appointment of Ali Ibrahim Khan as Diwan, for he replaced Rajballabh who had been appointed Saif-ud-daulah's household Diwan on Clive's instruction in 1767.[2] For some unknown reason relations between Reza Khan and Rajballabh and Rai Durlabh, his father, had cooled. The replacement of Rajballabh, followed in May 1770 by the death of Rai Durlabh[3] (whom Karam Ali called Nimakharam,[4] traitor to his salt), left Reza Khan without a rival in Murshidabad government.[5]

While accident thus strengthened his hand in the Durbar, and his charitable efforts to relieve famine in the city won him popular regard, the Khan did not neglect to do all that he could to safeguard his position with the English. This, as he knew, could best be done by maintaining the level of revenue collection. His brother, Saiyid Muhammad Ali Khan, Faujdar of Purnea, showed what was required. Writing to Becher he observed,

I have so often expatiated to you on the distressful condition of this district, that I am ashamed to repeat my representations; nor can the full extent of our misery possibly gain credit with you untill someone in whom you can confide is sent from the city to be an eye witness of it.

The distress of the poor is now beyond description—hardly a day passes over without 30 or 40 people dying. From the drought of the season such a misery is occasioned that multitudes already have and continue to perish of hunger. Intent on the prosperity of the country I have not been wanting in my endeavours to preserve the necessary grain for seed. But the ryotts of many villages, for want of rain, have been reduced to the necessity of selling their grain for seed, and then cattle and utensils in order to support themselves; in so much that they even offer their children for sale, but none can be found to buy them.

Such is the distressful state of the ryotts and inhabitants of this place,

---

[1] *MN*, f. 182 and *Seir*, III, 26.
[2] See Rajballabh's arzi (petition). *MP*, 20 Dec. 1770.
[3] Rai Durlabh died on 31 May 1770. Becher's letter 1 June. BSC, 21 June 1770.
[4] *MN*, f. 186.
[5] Reza Khan continued to maintain some grip upon Dacca affairs. In 1769, when his Diwan, Maha Singh, retired to Murshidabad, he was replaced at Dacca by his brother Himmat Singh, who was equally a favourite of the Khan (*MN*, f. 183).

that impoverish'd by former years calamities, and now reduced to extremities by the failure of their crops, setting aside the payments of their rents, they are perishing for want of grain. Never was there in any place before so melancholy a scene. Often when I contemplate the prevailing misery my compassion and pity are excited. Nevertheless, overruled by my regard for the welfare of the government, appearing blind to their distress and deaf to their lamentations I neglect not the interest of the Sircar.[1]

Reza Khan wrote in similar vein about his own role to Cartier,

Your servant with a view to Company's prosperity, your excellency's good name, and his own honour, notwithstanding the draughts [sic] which have prevailed has by exerting his utmost abilities collected the revenue of 1176 [Bengali year of 1769–70] as closely as so dreadfull a season would admit. The remainder cannot be collected without evident ruin of the ryotts, desolation of the country and a heavy loss to ensuing year.[2]

At the end of 1770, in a letter to the Controlling Council of Revenue at Murshidabad, Becher summed up the efforts he and the Khan had made, under 'unfavourable circumstances', to keep up the collections. During 1769 and 1770, he said,

the provinces labored under the most severe calamity, that any country was ever afflicted with, a continued drought for many months when rain was most wanted which occasion'd such a failure in the crops and produced such famine and mortality among inhabitants as I believe history does not furnish us with an instance of, but will I hope evince that no endeavours were wanting on my part, nor as far as I am able to judge on the part of the Nabob M. R. Cawn, to realize as large a revenue as under such circumstances, and in the mode till then adopted and approved for conducting that branch could be effected, with due consideration to the preservation and relief of the inhabitants to which essential objects I gave constant and assiduous attention, and large as the ballance is of the calculated revenue of the last year, am persuaded that had there been the least relaxation either on my part or that of M. R. Cawn, the Company would have been much more considerable sufferers.[3]

If by 1770 Reza Khan lost ground in his efforts to keep the confidence and support of the Company it was not from want of trying. The extraordinary situation created in the countryside by the

---

[1] BSC, 28 April 1770.
[2] Reza Khan to Cartier, recd. 2 June 1770. *H.M.S.*, 202; 65.
[3] Becher's letter. *MP*, 24 Dec. 1770.

The transition in Bengal, 1756–1775

famine was not the only problem affecting Cartier. He had also to suffer a tremendous accession in the power and influence of the anti-Clive party within his own government. By December 1769, Reed, Hare, Jekyll, Lane and Barwell had all been appointed to the Council, though two of them did not join immediately. Barwell, the juniormost member was only called to Council on 2 January 1770 while Reed delayed still longer at Chittagong, as Barwell commented in a private letter of 8 February 1770, to 'do his utmost to enrich himself during the short period he has to stay there'.[1] Since the old Clivites, Alexander, Becher, Aldersey, and Kelsall were permanently out of Calcutta in their stations at Patna, Murshidabad, Kasimbazar and Dacca respectively, the new men enjoyed a working majority in the Council at Calcutta.

Had Cartier been certain of support from home, as Vansittart had been from 1760 to 1764, the hostile majority might still have been controlled. But in the elections to the Directorate in April 1769, Laurence Sulivan 'had returned from his years in the wilderness',[2] bringing with him Henry Vansittart whom Clive had first antagonised and then ineffectually sought to detach from Sulivan's party. The old power block at the Direction was not overthrown but it was seriously weakened. Within two months of the elections the Company had decided to send out three Commissioners with the widest possible powers for reform in India, 'as if we the Court of Directors were ourselves present upon the spot'.[3] The decision had been in part induced by rumours of Haidar Ali's movements against Madras and apprehensions of renewed French designs against the Company. These, however, also caused a crash in Company stock which involved Sulivan, Vansittart and their supporters in near ruin. There were therefore prolonged negotiations between the power groups in the Company about the personnel of the Commission, so that it was not until 30 September that Vansittart of Sulivan's party, Scrafton of Clive's, and Francis Forde, a supposed neutral,[4] sailed from Spit-

[1] To Rumbold. *BPP*, xi, p. 35.
[2] Sutherland, *The East India Company in Eighteenth-Century Politics*, p. 190.
[3] Court's letter, 30 June 1769. In a subsequent letter they added that Vansittart on account of his past rank in Bengal was to be treated as 'first Commissioner' and he was to be paid military honour' in the same manner as is done to the Governor, whose Honours we do not mean should be suspended in any degree . . .' (Court's letter, 15 Sept. 1769).
[4] For his biography see L. Forde, *Lord Clive's Right Hand Man*.

The conflict deepens, 1769–1770

head in H.M.S. *Aurora*. The decision to send out the Commission had been communicated to Calcutta in a general letter of 30 June 1769 which was sent off from Falmouth in the *Lapwing* on 5 July 1769. This letter reached Calcutta at the commencement of Cartier's administration, and Barwell reported that, as was natural, 'Mr. Cartier is not very well pleased at the news of a commission that supersedes his authority and in fact annuls his power'.[1]

The only consolation to Cartier was that the Commission seemed likely to affect the interests of all—'the powers of the Governor and Council cannot be said to exist whilst a controuling authority is vested in others', as Barwell put it[2]—so that in the first half of 1770 there was a drawing together against the common danger. Cartier also conciliated the opposition in the Council by agreeing to backdate the allowances as Councillors of Reed and Hare to the dates at which Sykes and Charlton resigned,[3] though this ran contrary to the deliberate act of Verelst in this regard.

The latent conflicts within the Council, and within the Select Committee whose working members at Calcutta were reduced to Cartier, Russell and Floyer by the absence up-country of Alexander and Becher, could not for very long be repressed, however. The occasion for their breaking out was inevitably the reopening of the question of supervisors. In this Reza Khan was very soon involved.

It will be remembered that Reza Khan's first public reaction to the scheme of supervisorships had been to welcome it. The welcome had been backed by an offer to surrender Bhagalpur immediately for the experiment. The aim was to save Bengal by surrendering the only Bihar district still directly administered from Murshidabad. (During Rumbold's supervisorship of Bihar, from 1766 to 1769 the administrative autonomy of Bihar had been almost complete, though accounts and other routine reports came to Murshidabad for incorporation in the Diwani papers.) Bhagalpur was thus no great loss, especially as the district was very much in ruins on account of the movement of English troops to and from Patna.[4] That the Faujdar of the district, Sadr ul Haq Khan,[5] was

---

[1] Barwell to Thomas Rumbold, 8 Feb. 1770. *BPP*, XI, 35.
[2] Richard Barwell to his father, 8 Feb. 1770. *BPP*, XI, 35.
[3] BPC, 12 April 1770.   [4] Becher's letter, 30 March 1770. BSC, 28 April 1770.
[5] Sadr ul Haq, whom Hastings was later to raise as Reza Khan's substitute for administering justice, was born in Gujrat. When he came to Bengal in Alivardi's day, the Nawab made him the Darogha of Adalat and once his

The transition in Bengal, 1756–1775

in no great favour with the Khan may also have had some importance. Moreover, since the Khan had made the surrender on the grounds that the revenue year in the Bihar districts commenced later in the calendar year (in Kartick or mid-October) the postponement of the experiment in Bengal districts, where the revenue year had already commenced in Baisakh or mid-April, was made more plausible. As a result the Council had deferred the execution of the scheme until the end of February 1770, except in such districts where the Resident felt he could send supervisors 'without any detriment to the collections'.[1] The Khan thus gained a breathing space.

Reza Khan had urged 'the dryness of the season' as another reason for postponing the innovation. The growing seriousness of the famine towards the close of 1769, with increasing threat to the collection of estimated revenue, had been in fact the main reason for delay. Another was the gigantic administrative problem of demarcating the territorial jurisdiction of the supervisorships. Since in 1770–1 revenue was settled at Murshidabad city with 257 separate units, 65 zemindaris and faujdaris paying from Rs. 10,569 to Rs. 26,40,138, and 192 petty mahals ranging from non-territorial items like Nazr Hollandazi, or customary presents made by the Dutch, to territorial revenues of as little as one village in extent,[2] the problem was clearly no light one. Finally there was also to be settled the question of the status of the different supervisors *vis-à-vis* the Resident at Murshidabad. Verelst, in his draft instructions approved by the Committee on 16 August 1769, had placed them all under the Resident, and neither the Committee nor the Council had noticed the implications of the arrangement. The delay in implementing the scheme enabled members to reflect,

envoy to the Marathas (*Seir*, III, 102–3). Nothing is known of him during the Nizamat of Siraj-ud-daulah and Mir Jafar (1757–60). In 1764 he was Faujdar of Dinajpur (*CPC*, I, 2507), where he was posted perhaps by Mir Qasim. (At Dinajpur, the zemindar was politically more important, since Mir Qasim had dismissed Baidyanath and appointed his step-brother Kantunath, son of Ramnath. Kantu, having sided with Mir Qasim in the war, was replaced by Baidyanath by Mir Jafar on his restoration (see George Vansittart's letter of 22 Dec. *MP*, 31 Dec. 1770). Sadr ul Haq, who possibly replaced Mir Waris Ali at Bhagalpur, had become a great favourite of Nawab Saif-ud-daulah (see Punyah account of 1766–7. BSC, 28 April 1770), and was consequently no favourite of Reza Khan.
[1] Secret Cons., 26 Oct. 1769.
[2] BSC, 15 Sept. 1770. A few other non-territorial items were professional taxes on brokers and silk winders, and other taxes like those on silk bales, receipts from the English Company. The smallest amount was Rs. 45.

230

however, and the Select Committee, on 10 December 1769 declared that the power of control and suspension of the supervisors which had been vested in the Resident should not apply to Kelsall, the chief of Dacca, who was a member of the Council. Behind this move was a covert attack on the influence of Reza Khan, exercised through Becher. This Becher spotted and, in a letter of 22 December 1769, he pointed out that, if the new scheme was to succeed without subverting the form of government established since Clive's day, it was necessary that the supervisor of Dacca should not be independent either of the ministers or of the Resident.[1] The issue was not then pressed, but when the time came for posting the supervisors after February 1770 it was revived. At the same time discussion broke out afresh about the role of the supervisors. Verelst had sought to soften the impact of the scheme by making their first duty that of research into the history, customs and resources of the districts. Those who sought to extend the power and opportunities of the English in Bengal were not content with so limited a position. This issue, too, grew sharper as the time for implementing the scheme approached.

These differences first found expression within the Select Committee in their deliberations of 29 March 1770. The Committee had to consider a letter of 1 March from Kelsall in Dacca, asking that the Committee should draw 'a precise line' of jurisdiction between the Resident and himself as supervisor of Dacca. They had already decided that Kelsall as a member of Council should have a special status, and had had Becher's letter urging subordination of all supervisors to the ministers and Resident. Now the Committee decided that Kelsall should normally go by the advice of Murshidabad,[2] and if he disagreed with Becher on any issue he should refer this to Calcutta for decision. The resolution was passed by Cartier and Russell, Floyer dissenting.

Floyer started with his own interpretation of the function of the supervisors, whom he wished to see replacing, not working with, the Nawab's officials. 'I must confess', he minuted, 'I wish not to have any person appointed on behalf of the Country government to cooperate with the Supravisors; the nature of their commission being to investigate the great abuses which have been committed by the officers of that government.'[3] If the supervisors were to be

[1] Quoted in Banerji, *Early Land Revenue System in Bengal and Bihar*, p. 78.
[2] BSC, 29 March 1770. [3] *Ibid.*

inquisitors then Reza Khan must have no authority over them, for, though the Khan had shown ability and indefatigable attention to business and had won high honours from the English government, he could not be expected to 'engage heartily in an investigation of the many abuses committed by those very persons whom he has placed in the administration of publick affairs'.[1] This remained true, Floyer argued, even though the existing ties between Reza Khan and the Company might 'possibly engage him to show outward signs of approbation'.[2]

If this shrewd estimate of the Khan's attitude was accepted then the supervisor of Dacca should not be placed under the Resident, for the latter was bound to seek Reza Khan's advice about Dacca matters, particularly as Dacca had been Reza Khan's own charge and subsequently under his agents Jasarat Khan and Himmat Singh. This comment was already a departure from the spirit of Verelst's parting instructions, but Floyer then launched into a personal attack upon the Khan. He alleged that Reza Khan had for years deprived the Company of its legitimate revenues from Dacca. He claimed, 'Whatever increase of revenue may arise from the proposed investigation within the district of Dacca [after the introduction of the supervisorship] should be deem'd so much loss to our employers from the year they were in possession of the Dewannee'.[3] Reza Khan's answer to Mir Jafar, that he had not agreed to any fixed revenue settlement in view of the disorder in the district was no answer: 'for altho' it may be said that Mahomed Reza Cawn was ignorant of their produce when he first took them at an annual rent (an argument which I think he cannot well maintain when reminded of having collected their revenue, ruled that country and resided on that spot for sometime before that period [1765]) it might surely have been expected that after the first year's experience he would have pointed out the advantage which that country was capable of yielding to the Company under proper management'.[4] Reza Khan had been guilty in not increasing the Dacca revenues until Sykes did so in 1767 and again in not going beyond the figure set by Sykes. 'For his silence on the subject I must infer, either that those districts are not capable of improvement, or that Mohamed Reza Khan was desirous of reaping every advantage which could be derived therefrom.'[5]

[1] Floyer's minute. BSC, 29 March 1770.   [2] *Ibid.*
[3] *Ibid.*   [4] *Ibid.*   [5] *Ibid.*

The conflict deepens, 1769–1770

Since the extent, fertility and situation of the Dacca districts all suggested that the revenues could have been increased, Floyer pressed home the charge against Reza Khan: 'I must frankly own that the latter is the inference I draw without the least hesitation.'[1]

Floyer was voted down in the Select Committee,[2] which maintained the old line, restated on 16 December 1769 by Verelst, of support for the ministers. But he had voiced a challenge to that attitude with his demand that the old officials be replaced by the English supervisors—and their Banians and dependants—and his indictment of Reza Khan's administration roused the suspicions and hopes of the Court of Directors. These last, desperately in need of money, underlined every word of Floyer's minute when it reached London.

The next stage in the conflict between the Khan and the old officialdom and the supervisors and their dependants came when the English officials actually went out into their districts. By March 1770 four had been posted out into their districts, and to three of these—Rider in Nadia, Hardwood in Rajmahal and Bhagalpur, and Stuart[3] in Birbhum and Bishnupur—Becher had issued definite instructions that it was 'not the intention of the President and Council to alter the present form of Government'.[4] Their activities were not without some advantage to the Khan. Both Hardwood and Stuart for example were soon sending in reports on 'the general declining state of trade'[5] and 'the miserable state' of their districts, and their testimony was worth any number of reports from the Faujdar of Rajmahal or the Amil of Birbhum in convincing Becher and the Calcutta authorities of the real distress. Their reports substantiated the Khan's explanation of the causes of decline in revenue and provided support for his efforts, earlier unsuccessful, to secure abatements in demand and the grant of Taqavi loans to the peasants. The Council had on 13 February refused any abatement, but on 28 April, on the basis of the supervisors' testimony, the Committee agreed to a reduction of

[1] Floyer's minute. BSC, 29 March 1770.
[2] Kelsall also was not satisfied with the Committee's decision and on 15 May asked for autonomy for Dacca administration in the same way as Patna enjoyed it (Kelsall's letter, 15 May 1770. LCB, p. 59).
[3] The name is given both as Stewart and Stuart. The fourth was Rous at Nator (Rajshahi). Rider is also spelt as Ryder.
[4] Becher to Rider, 20 Dec. 1769 (BSC, 28 Jan. 1770): to Hardwood, 20 Jan. (LCB, p. 40).
[5] Hardwood to Becher, 31 Jan. 1770. (LCB, pp. 49–50).

Rs. 3,37,621 in the demand, as well as to a further temporary remission of Rs. 2,66,948. They were also readier to take heed when Becher reported that the ministers were asking for more money to be advanced as Taqavi or agricultural loan to the peasants for purchases of bullocks, ploughs and other 'utensils of husbandry'.[1] This loan, Becher assured, was repayable with twelve and half per cent interest per annum.

Reza Khan may also have felt some secret satisfaction from the way in which events moved in Nadia. This had been yielded to Verelst at the 1176 Punyah in April 1769 and had been taken out of the Raja's hands and given on a three year farming system to Nabakrishna and certain other leading Calcutta merchants.[2] The farmers had soon demanded powers that would have deprived the Raja of his 'just rights',[3] they acted oppressively, and more important, they failed to pay the revenues according to their agreement. The farming system was thus discredited, and the support of Reza Khan was won for Raja Krishna Chandra who had pressed his claim to take over the district again, on the same terms as the farmers had offered.[4]

With the arrival of Rider in Nadia as supervisor events took a more threatening turn, however, for Rider was soon in violent conflict with the Raja. Becher, as has been seen, had instructed Rider that the present form of government was not to be altered. But by 30 March Becher himself had shifted ground. In a letter to the Committee he stated that he saw no need to retain the Amils who had been a 'severe scourge' to the people and no need to make the annual settlement at Murshidabad, since the supervisors could make settlements locally. Thereafter, he said, 'Either the Zemindar or an officer of the government will be necessary, nominally to conduct affairs, but the English gentlemen should ...be spring of every action'.[5] He proposed, as a corollary that 'the allowances of these [government] officers may be certainly greatly reduced' while from the sum thus gained the supervisors

[1] Becher's letter, 30 March 1770. BSC, 28 April 1770.
[2] The Calcutta merchants were Jay Narayan Sharma, Ram Lochan Palit, Ram Tanu Datta, Balaram Biswas, Ram Sundar Bharat, Gayaram Ghose, Manohar Sharma, Sukhdev Mallik, Bhawananda Roy, Raghunath Mitter, Durga Charan Mitter, Hara Narayan Roy, Ganga Narayan Chatterji, and Harikrishna Bose (see Reza Khan's parwana. *CPC*, II, 1475).
[3] Becher's letter, 30 March 1770. BSC, 28 April 1770.
[4] *Ibid.*   [5] *Ibid.*

could be paid an annual allowance of Rs. 12,000 each and their assistants Rs. 2400 each, though these sums would 'appear high in Leadenhall Street'.[1] With Rider at Nadia and Rous at Nator already at odds with the old officials, and Becher moving away from Verelst's position, Reza Khan seemed as threatened in the countryside as in Calcutta.

With the arrival in their districts of the other supervisors at the end of April the conflict with the older system came fully and violently into the open. Rider in Nadia had already been denouncing the 'infamous character of the Raja'[2] and the Raja complaining that 'Mr. Rider is the ruler here'.[3] Now, within four days of his arrival in Rangpur, Grose was reporting on the abuses of the large number of paiks or foot soldiers entertained by the government and of the wastage of Rs. 50,000 on men 'employ'd on the part of the government', and demanding 'disbanding the whole tribe',[4] together with the recall of every sepoy not in the Company's pay or under the charge of Captain Mackenzie.[5] Complaints also poured in of oppressions by the amils and zemindars,[6] collusive efforts to conceal information,[7] forcible seizure of property in one case,[8] murder in another,[9] and these were directed not only against the amils, but against the Diwans and Qanungoes also. Of particular importance were the complaints which really flowed from the supervisors' attempts to establish themselves as masters. One letter to Becher revealed the mortification of a supervisor that an amil and a zemindar had gone to Murshidabad without the supervisor's consent or knowledge.[10] In another case it was resentfully explained that had not Becher absolutely required the amil's presence at Murshidabad, the supervisor 'cou'd not have suffered him to have gone, not only on account of the confusion of the publick accounts but [also of the] great demands of individuals upon him'.[11] Another telling instance was that of the agent of a jagirdar who twice refused to take notice of a summons by the supervisor and his assistant saying, it was indignantly reported, that 'he was answerable to none but Mahomed Reza Cawn'. This case touched the Khan very closely for the jagirdar in question was

[1] Becher's letter, 30 March 1770. BSC, 28 April 1770.
[2] *LCB*, p. 115. [3] *LCB*, p. 178.
[4] *LCB*, p. 1. [5] *LCB*, p. 2.
[6] *LCB*, p. 21. [7] *LCB*, p. 28.
[8] *LCB*, pp. 26-27, 33. [9] *LCB*, p. 163.
[10] *LCB*, p. 3. [11] *LCB*, p. 3.

The transition in Bengal, 1756–1775

Husain Reza Khan, a grandson of Haji Ahmad, a near relation of the Khan and of the old royal family of Bengal. It seems that Grose, the supervisor of Rangpur and Robertson, Grose's assistant at Govindaganj, had heard that Husain Reza Khan was holding a jagir at Salbari (Selbarsha in Bogra) in lieu of a pension of Rs. 3,300, and that the jagir was yielding more income than this. Robertson, supposing Husain Reza Khan to be resident at Salbari, summoned him to meet him with all the jagir papers. The agent, who did reside there, disregarded Robertson's message and another from Grose to whom his assistant had complained. The matter had now become an issue of prestige, and Grose had the agent forcibly secured and brought to Rangpur. Grose found that the agent had no papers, and being told that these had been taken to Murshidabad he wrote, in very peremptory style, to Becher, asking that Husain Reza Khan be ordered to report to him at Rangpur immediately, with the original sanad and other documents of the jagir.[1]

To this rather abrupt letter from Grose, Becher replied that he had been misinformed about the jagir, which was a royal grant, and also about the papers having been carried to Murshidabad, and that enquiry showed that the complaints against Husain Reza Khan were 'unjust and groundless'. He further emphasised that Husain Reza Khan's character was much respected in the country and that the family was of high birth and importance.[2] Experience of the actions of the supervisors, and the complaints about them coming in through Reza Khan from the local authorities of the old system, as well as from older aristocracy of the land, were driving Becher back to Verelst's original position, and he soon showed himself dissatisfied with many of his young subordinates. In a letter to Stuart on 23 May 1770 he sharply observed, 'If the Nabob's [that is Reza Khan's] and my orders are in this manner slighted there is an end of Government' and he added the warning, 'If I hear more complaints of this sort I shall give such directions as will effectively put a stop to them, being determined to support the Government here in its proper authority'.[3] A month later he had to write to Stuart again, about the complaint of Nabakishore, the

---

[1] *LCB*, pp. 34–5. Firminger appears to have misread Salbari as Lalbari. Salbari was possibly the simplified English rendering of the Persianised name of Selbarsha in modern Bogra, which was Silberis.

[2] *LCB*, p. 132.   [3] Becher to Stuart, 23 May 1770. *LCB*, p. 139.

The conflict deepens, 1769–1770

Amil of Bishnupur, that he had been put in confinement by one of Stuart's gumashtahs. Becher took the occasion to voice his dislike of all such Banians and gumashtahs, creatures and agents of the new ruling power: 'Experience having convinced me that there is scarce an instance of an English Gomastah or servant when out of his master's sight, but has used his influence in acts of oppression and violence so that I cannot help having my apprehension that the same consequences may ensue from the employment of such under English Supravisors, notwithstanding all the care and precaution which may be taken by their masters, and which it is their duty to do to the utmost of their power and I strongly recommend to you.'[1]

By June Becher, by his warnings and advice, had come out again as the champion of the old order against the supervisors and their Banians. The supervisors for their part had hardened in their hostility to the old officialdom. Grose, for example, on 14 July, replied to Becher: 'You mention that Bengal of late years has suffer'd much by the oppressive measures of English Gomastahs. It is true there has been too great cause of complaint against them; however Sir, that is not what has hurt the country so much, as the oppressions committed by the several persons employed in the collections'.[2] Even though the supervisors were not yet officially intended to assume any active power, they were already in conflict with those instruments of government whom it was their duty to support and maintain. This must have been quite clear to both Becher and Reza Khan, who had to deal with the complaints from both sides.

The problem took a more serious turn when the settlement for 1177 (or 1770–1) became due. The punyah had been unusually delayed. Cartier refused to travel to Murshidabad because of the intense heat.[3] Because of the poor collections for 1176 all parties wished to extend the period of collections so as to reduce the outstanding balances which had risen to Rs. 17,91,103[4] and in view of the continuing drought could not possibly be reduced before July. Most important of all, however, the whole issue of the controlling powers of the supervisors had been re-opened by letters from Reza Khan and Becher.

[1] Becher to Stuart, 22 June 1770. *LCB*, p. 148.
[2] Grose to Becher, 14 July 1770. *LCB*, p. 36.
[3] Cartier to Reza Khan. *CPC*, III, 207 (in reply to Reza's invitation).
[4] Becher's letter, 2 June 1770. BSC, 9 June 1770.

The transition in Bengal, 1756–1775

Cartier received a letter from Reza Khan on 2 June 1770 saying that 'the business for the year 1177 should be settled at this time but when I speak to zemindars about the terms of the business they flatly answer "we have no footing in the district, how can we charge ourselves with the bundibust of the present year". Accordingly every person has delivered written representation to Mr. Becher who will transmit translation thereof to your excellency.'[1] The Khan added that apart from one or two persons long attached to him, no one would even come to Murshidabad for the settlement. A week later another letter was received, addressed by Reza Khan to Becher, relating that the zemindars had pleaded, 'when we are governed by two magistrates in what manner are we to provide for the revenues. From two orders being circulated business will be delayed and thrown into confusion'.[2] This was a more open threat that the zemindars and amils would not enter into agreements before being certain that the controlling power of the supervisors would not be confirmed. In an accompanying letter Becher confirmed Reza Khan's report of the general unwillingness to agree to any settlement for the new revenue year.

In his letter Becher also reported the many complaints he had received from the ministers that their orders were not properly respected in the districts. For this he blamed the inexperience of the 'young gentlemen' who had been posted to the countryside and more especially the supervisors' dependence on 'Black dependants and Banians chiefly from Calcutta', who were themselves unacquainted with revenue matters.[3] He therefore recommended that the controlling power which had been given to the supervisors in December 1769 should not generally be confirmed. 'It has ever been my opinion that innovations and changes in the mode of conducting the revenues should be gradual and tried in a few districts before it [sic] is undertaken in general.'[4] He proposed that full powers could be given only to a few, such as Graham, George Vansittart, Stuart and Ducarel. 'I am well aware, Gentlemen,' Becher concluded, 'that it will be urged that the objections raised by the Zemindars are in consequence of the art and intrigues of the people at the city, who are unwilling to lose their influence

[1] Reza Khan to Cartier, recd. 2 June 1770. *H.M.S.*, 202; 65.
[2] Reza Khan to Becher. BSC, 9 June 1770.
[3] Becher's letter, 2 June. BSC, 9 June 1770.
[4] *Ibid.*

238

which must be the effect of power being lodged in the supervisors hands'.[1] He refused, nonetheless, to modify a demand which he knew must be most unpopular in Calcutta.

The demand certainly was unpopular. Floyer's opinion was already on record with the Select Committee and it reflected the opinion of many of the Company's servants, and particularly of those who stood to benefit. Even though Cartier might be willing to support Becher, and Russell might be very moderate in his views and ready to back Cartier, it was extremely difficult for them to agree to the requests of Reza Khan and Becher. The Committee proved unwilling to budge an inch from the position they had taken with 'so much circumspection and such flattering hopes of success' in order only to satisfy 'the pretences and evasion of Aumils, Zemindars and collectors'.[2] They pointed out that the demand was contrary to Becher's own plan of 30 March.[3] They concluded by telling Becher that the difficulties created by the 'desperate men who had long feasted on the spoils of the poor native' could be overcome with the assistance of Reza Khan.[4]

The Committee had put Becher in an awkward situation, for he had anticipated the Committee's approval of his recommendations and had already given the zemindars and amils the assurance they required, presumably at the Punyah ceremony on 24 May 1770.[5] His difficulties were increased by the demand for a written confirmation, made by the amils and zemindars, that 'in case the supravisors disregarding the orders of the government interfere in the matters of revenue they are not to be accountable for the ballances'.[6] Becher, in order to induce the amils and zemindars to settle for 1177, had earlier given a verbal assurance that 'the supravisors shall not interfere in any matters of revenue and collection' and that 'if any of the supravisors should interfere a prohibition would be immediately issued by the government'.[7] As Reza Khan wrote to Cartier, the zemindars and amils, not content merely with verbal assurances, required written statements from both Reza Khan and Becher. With his letter the Khan also forwarded a draft of the undertaking which the zemindars and amils were said to want.

[1] *Ibid.*
[2] BSC, 9 June 1770.
[3] *Ibid.*
[4] BSC, 9 June 1770.
[5] Reza Khan's letter, recd. 12 June 1770. *H.M.S.*, 202; 72; *CPC*, III, 251.
[6] Reza Khan's letter to Cartier, recd. 12 June 1770. *H.M.S.*, 202; 72.
[7] *Ibid.*

The transition in Bengal, 1756–1775

The zemindars and amils would declare as follows: 'Your servant in compliance with your orders accepts the terms of the bandobast of the parganah...for the year 1177 on condition that he shall possess full authority in revenue matters and in all other matters appertaining thereto. He will not be remiss in the performance of his duty, in the improvement of the lands or in the collection and remittance of the stipulated sums. Should a supervisor or any other person interfere in those matters or molest the gumashtahs of the amils, your servant will duly report the matter to the Presence in the hope that his grievances will promptly be redressed. But if this is not done he will not be answerable for the revenues.'[1] In return they would be given the assurance, 'Apply yourself with confidence and contentment to the business of collecting the revenues. Should a supervisor or any other person interfere with you, prompt measures will be taken to redress your grievances. But if this is not done, you will not be held responsible for the balances.'[2] Who had drawn up the draft is unknown, but in the absence of any other recognised leader, we might suspect that it was the work of Reza Khan himself. With splendid tact the Khan added, 'I am from my heart and soul ready in the performance of your order and those of the Committee but I do not think myself empowered without your sanction to subscribe to the propositions since they are unprecedented and were never yet granted to any Aumil or Zemindar. However should they renew their demand which probably they will at the close of the year when the accounts are to be settled, it may terminate in my bad name.'[3]

Reza Khan was naturally very anxious to protect himself from the consequences of the fall in revenue which he saw must follow from the failure of Becher's recommendation to the Committee. He had asked Cartier to be present at the Punyah and had been told that it was not necessary as 'Izzat ud daulah Mr. Becher Bahadur Bahram Jang' would be there to represent him.[4] He had then sought 'agreeably to Mr. Becher's directions' to bring the amils, zemindars and farmers 'to temper' and to a settlement. Then he had joined with Becher in giving a public assurance about the supervisors. But Becher would have left Bengal before the revenue year ended, and the Committee had refused to confirm the verbal assur-

---

[1] *CPC*, III, 252; *H.M.S.*, 202; 73.   [2] *CPC*, III, 253.
[3] *H.M.S.*, 202; 72–3.
[4] Cartier to Reza Khan, 10 May 1770. *CPC*, III, 207.

ance given by him and Becher. He now sought to make sure that all the responsibility should not be left upon him. He therefore wrote his absolution into these words: 'You Sir and gentlemen of the Committee are masters. Be pleased to signify what you deem most expedient for the happy administration of the Company's affairs and I shall act accordingly. But let not your servant hereafter be called upon to be made answerable for the Bundibust.'[1]

Despite a very reasonable and strong suspicion that Reza Khan was behind the whole move, it was impossible to establish his personal involvement. He had not associated himself with the amils and zemindars in the public records. Cartier in his reply also kept him dissociated from his officials, the amils. In order perhaps to break the combination, the governor also carefully avoided the zemindars, and turned his entire bitter attack against the old official aristocracy who also constituted the social aristocracy of Bengal. Cartier replied:

As the Khan has an unrivalled knowledge of the manners and habits of the people of this country, the writer hopes that he will use his best endeavours to expose the villainies of this wicked set. To tolerate them would be to lend them the sanction of the government. Let it not be said that during the writer's government and the Khan's ministry the welfare of the mankind and the existence of the Company were sacrificed to the interests of a few blackguards.[2]

For the Khan too there was a veiled warning from a 'sincere friend':

The Khan has in the past rendered valuable services to the Company. The English sardars are fully aware of it and will always have his interests at heart. But now yet a greater service is required of him. It is to cooperate with the English sardars in making the above scheme [of supervisorship] a success. If he acquits himself well in this task, he will have his reputation increased tenfold; but if, which God forbid, he disappoints the English sardars in this affair, the writer is afraid that the Khan will lose the reputation he has already gained.[3]

The Committee's refusal to support Becher's recommendations did not end the matter. Becher was not only committed with the Amils and zemindars, he was committed with the supervisors

---

[1] *H.M.S.*, 202; 73.
[2] Cartier to Reza Khan, 16 June 1770. *CPC*, III, 257.
[3] Cartier to Reza Khan, 16 June 1770. *CPC*, III, 257.

also: he could not draw back without a struggle. On 25 May 1770, the day after the Punyah was held at Murshidabad, Becher had written to Grose at Rangpur pointing out that the great problem, in view of the famine and very unfavourable prospect of the approaching harvest, was to secure revenues sufficient to meet the very large demands of the troops and other Company expenses. It was his duty to suffer nothing to come into competition with the collection, and he therefore instructed Grose, for this reason, 'to interfere as little as possible in the collections, and in the course of the enquiries and regulations, to take no measure that can possibly affect the revenues'.[1] A similar letter was sent to Stuart, supervisor of Birbhum, Bishnupur and Pachet,[2] and also perhaps to other supervisors. Becher in issuing such instructions to these junior servants of the Company had risked his whole prestige.

On 18 June, therefore, Becher again addressed the Select Committee, pointing out the difficulties which would follow the grant of controlling power to the supervisors, especially by providing an excuse to the revenue collectors for running up balances. He was also again emphatic about the villainies of the 'black' dependents of the English. He made the further point that the bankers who, as usual, had helped the zemindars to pay their revenues for 1769–70 were unwilling to advance money in future unless the authority of the zemindars was guaranteed.[3] Thus pressed, the Committee on 21 June agreed to accept Becher's recommendation for the curtailment of the power of all but a few selected supervisors, in the hope that by doing so 'all further difficulties will be obviated and the currency of business and public credit renewed'.[4] The letter from the Committee went out on 28 June, and on 30 June Becher was writing to the supervisors of the decision. He thus informed Grose that controlling power would be granted for the present season only over districts worth seventy lakhs. 'Selection has been made for this purpose of these provinces which are under the inspection of Gentlemen that have had opportunities of acquiring knowledge in that branch of business which appears to me absolutely necessary for conducting it properly, and in other districts I have judged it requisite for the

[1] Becher to Grose, 25 May 1770. *LCB*, pp. 127–8.
[2] Becher to Stuart. *LCB*, pp. 141–2.
[3] Becher's letter, 18 June 1770. BSC, 21 June 1770.
[4] BSC, 21 June 1770.

present season to restrain the authority of the English supravisors, and leave the management of the collections in the hands of those appointed by the Government, here, to superintend them.[1]' Grose was informed that he was not one of those selected.

Reza Khan had scored a triumph. Becher, who in March was thinking of transferring the settlement of revenues to the supervisors, to which plan the Committee also had given its concurrence,[2] had been made not only to reverse his plan but also to fight for and win back the independence of the zemindars and amils. It is true that part of the province had to be made over to supervisors, but the loss was slight when compared with the gain. Moreover, of the four supervisors to whom controlling power had been confirmed three, Graham, Ducarel and George Vansittart, were by no means undesirable from the Khan's point of view. Graham at Hugli had had considerable revenue experience in Midnapur and Burdwan and he had deep sympathy for the old regime.[3] He was later to become one of the greatest supporters of the Khan in his dark days. Ducarel at Purnea had been on good terms with Reza Khan at Murshidabad and with the Khan's brother enjoyed the best relations. He was also a favourite with Becher. George Vansittart was another man with long experience, and as brother of Henry Vansittart, to whom the Khan owed so much, could not but be welcome. With Henry Vansittart due to arrive in Bengal as first in rank of the Company's three Commissioners, his brother was obviously worth conciliating. This left only Stuart as an uncertain element. His jurisdiction was to have been over three districts, but eventually his control was limited to Birbhum[4] while Ghulam Mustafa took over Bishnupur. Stuart had been polite in his dealings with Becher, but his words had often in them the ring of opposition.[5] On balance, the four fully empowered supervisors were very acceptable to Reza Khan.

The victory, however temporary it soon turned out to be, was a real and significant one. Reza Khan had shown skilled leadership

---

[1] Becher to Grose, 30 June 1770. *LCB*, p. 129.
[2] See Letter No. 98 and its enclosure. *LCB*, pp. 126–7.
[3] See Graham's letter to Clive, 24 Dec. 1765. *BPP*, v, 82. Graham was known as Nawab Babar Jang (see *CPC*, III, 372).
[4] The revenue of the district was, however, settled with its Raja, Asad uz zaman Khan, whose territory was not finally subordinated to the Murshidabad government until the time of Mir Qasim.
[5] For example, Stuart's letter of 26 June 1770. *LCB*, pp. 148–50.

16-2

in organising a joint front of zemindars, amils and bankers, frustrating the efforts of the Calcutta government to divide them. Theirs had been the first organised public protest against the superior power of the English and against the imposition of direct Company rule. It was also the last successful attempt to prevent the new Banian element from extending its sphere of activity to land management and land control.

The triumph, like that of 1769, was a short-lived one and productive of an equally violent counter-measure. Two days before the Select Committee accepted Becher's renewed plea for the maintenance of the *status quo* in 1770–1, and for restricting the controlling power to only four supervisors with limited territorial jurisdiction, a break in the truce between the two groups in the Calcutta Council occurred. The Council met on 19 June 1770 in a session of their Secret Department, with Cartier, Russell, Reed, Hare, Jekyll, Lane and Barwell present, and Floyer away ill. Certain of the members proceeded to raise a question about the authority of the Select Committee in matters relating to the Diwani administration. They maintained that the Company's letter of 30 June 1769, containing instructions about the diwani matters, was addressed to the Council and not to the Select Committee. The instructions had been laid aside pending the arrival of the Commissioners from England, but as they now seemed unlikely ever to arrive, the opposition urged that the Council, to whom the letter was addressed, should take it into consideration. Before that was done, however, the question of the jurisdiction of the Committee and Council in revenue matters should be determined. No other powers of the Select Committee were questioned.

Why was the attack upon the Select Committee's authority in revenue matters launched at this time? Briefly, one may answer, because the question of supervisors' powers involved powerful interests, both of the Company's servants and their Calcutta Banians; because the caution imposed by the Commissioners' arrival had ended with their presumed death; and because the changes in the Directorate seemed to assure those opposed to the Clivites in Bengal of support from home. Once Becher had committed himself to upholding the old system, the only way to counteract his influence as Resident was to take authority over the Diwani administration out of the hands of the Select Committee and to secure it to the majority in the Council who did not belong

244

to the Committee. So long as the Committee refused to endorse Becher's recommendations all was well. But after 9 June it had become apparent to all that the Select Committee would not long withstand the pressure exerted by Becher and Reza Khan: the Council majority was thus forced to act.

The issues in the conflict over the supervisors' powers were not merely administrative and political. For many of the junior servants of the Company, attracted to India by the prospect of early fortunes, but denied them since the Regulations of 1769, however ill enforced, in the commercial line, great material interests were at stake. It was only out of Calcutta, in the districts, that the prospects of gain were still fair, and the numbers pressing for opportunities were rapidly growing: in the 1769 season, after Sulivan's group had returned to power, forty-seven new civil servants were sent out to Bengal as well as two dismissed servants who had been reinstated.[1] Moreover, behind these English aspirants for office was ranged a Banian interest no less greedy, it is reasonable to presume, and no less bold.

How powerful the Banian influence had by this time grown may perhaps best be illustrated by a letter of 8 February 1770 from Richard Barwell, a member of Council, to Thomas Rumbold: 'Gocul delivered me a letter from Knott, and I expected, from what Wilkins said, it was from you; but whether from you or from Knott, Gocul's connections certainly entitle him to any assistance I can afford; but faith I believe he is much more capable to assist me than I him.'[2] The reference was to Gokul Ghosal, the founder of the Bhukailash Raj family. When Verelst's Banian in Chittagong he had become the sole owner of the Noabad or newly planted lands in Chittagong,[3] besides extending his control over Sandwip Island. Abu Torab Choudhury of Sandwip who opposed him was branded a rebel and killed in action, and his military commander Mulkan was publicly hanged at Verelst's instance.[4] In 1765 when

---

[1] I.O. Personal Records, vol. 14, pp. 471–2. One of the dismissed servants who was reinstated was Samuel Middleton. While coming to India Henry Vansittart was bringing his son Arthur who, having perished like the rest on the H.M.S. *Aurora*, was replaced by Henry junior in 1771 (Court's letter, 10 April 1771).
[2] Barwell to Rumbold, 8 Feb. 1770. *BPP*, XI, 35.
[3] For detail, see H. J. S. Cotton, *Memorandum on the Revenue History of Chittagong*.
[4] For details see Jonathan Duncan's report on the Sundeep Insurrection, 1766–1767 (*BRP*, 1 Aug. 1780), together with *CPC*, II, 305, 332, 336.

The transition in Bengal, 1756–1775

Verelst became supervisor of Burdwan and a third of the district was given out in farm to new men, Gokul had a big share.[1] Perhaps almost naturally he was involved also in the Nimak or salt Mahals of Midnapur.[2] In December 1768 Gokul applied for a monopoly farm of the entire waste lands in the twenty-four parganas, despite Becher's known wish as collector-general that the quantity of land given to any one individual should be restricted.[3] In December 1769 Verelst had his esteem for Gokul Ghosal's 'thorough knowledge of the business of the revenue' written into the public record.[4] By 1770–1 he was farmer of Gaya pargana in Bihar[5] and of Muhabbatpur in Bengal,[6] acquisitions probably made while Rumbold was supervisor at Patna and Verelst was governor. Such men were the natural allies of the supervisors and their assistants, while the latter were still allowed the right of private trade, and were their undercover agents when that right was withdrawn. Becher's success in withdrawing controlling power from most of the supervisors hit the Banians at least as hard as it did their masters.[7] Would it be too much to suggest that the Banians were also much involved in the struggle to reverse the victory of Becher and Reza Khan?

By June 1770, nine months after H.M.S. *Aurora* had sailed with the three Commissioners from England, it was clear that some accident had befallen them. The opposition to the Clivites in Bengal need no longer consider action to be expected from the Commissioners, and could therefore turn to the instructions sent out by the Court of Directors on 30 June 1769. After April elections of 1769 they knew that they could expect support from within the Direction. They might also have had known that the Directors' letter of 30 June 1769 was addressed to the Council as a deliberate act,[8] as they were also possibly aware of the messages it contained. The Company was known to be in great need of money—there was £400,000 a year to pay to government as its

[1] M. Huq, *East India Company's Land Policy and Commerce in Bengal*, p. 64.
[2] *MP*, 26 Nov. 1770. [3] Quoted in *LCB*, pp. 122–26.
[4] Verelst's letter, 16 Dec. BPC, 16 Dec. 1769.
[5] Secret Cons., 11 Oct. 1770. [6] BSC, 15 Sept. 1770.
[7] In fact, Banians had a more permanent interest than their masters, who stayed only for a short period. One of the results of direct Company rule through supervisors as Hastings observed in 1773 was that the ancient families had been pulled down 'to make way for the upstarts' (Letter to Aldersey, 1 July 1773. Add. MSS. 29125, f. 225).
[8] The first draft was addressed to the Select Committee.

246

agreed share out of Company's territorial revenue receipts in India and another £200,000 as the agreed indemnity on tea.[1] Already by 1767 the Company came under an obligation to pay an additional sum of £128,000 by increasing the rate of dividend from six to ten percent per annum, and the proprietors were in a lively expectation of a still higher dividend.[2] The Company was also finding it increasingly difficult to make good the payments in England of the bills of exchange drawn on them against cash payments in Company's treasuries in Bengal. They had been obliged also to restrict such remittance even at the known risk of diverting money into the treasuries of their rivals, the French and the Dutch. They had been compelled to permit export of gold and silver to England and to buy pounds sterling in London at a higher price against payment in rupees in Bengal.[3] Moreover the return of Sulivan and his allies to the Direction meant that there would be new friends and dependants to be satisfied by the exercise of patronage,[4] and there were many fortunes, ruined by speculation in the Company's stock which had preceded the election, to repair,[5] though the full extent of this need may not have been realised in Bengal. The bulk of all these expectations, public and private, had to be satisfied from the produce of Bengal and Bihar.

The opposition in the Calcutta Council were also aware that in the discussion about how Bengal and Bihar could be made to yield the necessary resources, home opinion had been moving their way. For example, at the 1767 enquiry held by a Parliamentary Committee presided over by Fuller, Holwell from his twenty-eight years of experience in Bengal had testified that Bengal could produce nine and a half crores of rupees and that the real revenue

---

[1] By an agreement confirmed by an Act in 1767 the Company was to pay an indemnity for lowering the duties on tea consumed in Great Britain by one shilling per pound in weight and for allowing a drawback on export of tea to Ireland and British colonies in America. The Company had hoped for an advantage even after paying this sum, but friction with the Colonies ruined the hope (Court's letter, 20 Nov. 1767; Sutherland, *The East India Company in Eighteenth-Century Politics*, p. 227).

[2] Court's letter, 20 Nov. 1767. Even though the expectations had risen to 14 per cent and 16 per cent it was raised to 12½ per cent in 1771 (Sutherland, *op. cit.*, pp. 166–8, 227).

[3] Court's letters, 16 March 1768, 11 Nov. 1768 and 30 June 1769.

[4] The largest number of servants, 47, was sent out in the 1769 season.

[5] Even Henry Vansittart was one of them, and he was so much reduced to ruin that 'nothing but an immediate return to India could save him'. (Sutherland, *op. cit.*, p. 192).

yield was three or four times as great as that which the Company actually received.[1] This picture of a vast real produce being concealed by an interested native regime had been widely accepted. It was made all the more plausible by the success of English administration in the jagiri districts.[2] The Directors ignored the fact that the encouraging results in the Company's lands were secured in part by seducing peasants from the adjoining diwani lands to new areas, brought under cultivation by farmers who enjoyed much more favourable terms than those prevalent in the diwani areas,[3] or even in the older settled lands of the Company.[4] They ignored also the effect upon the older classes of officials, nobles and the gentry of the pressure of English administration. While the Directors were full of praise for the improvements in Burdwan, the Sradh or funeral ceremonies of its Raja, Tilokchand, could only be met by melting the household plate.[5] Ignoring the disruption of Bengali society, the new Direction in their letter of 30 June had expressed their great satisfaction at their servants' administration of Burdwan, Midnapur, Chittagong and the Calcutta Parganas and had condemned the administration of the diwani areas 'where the numerous tribes of Fougedars, Aumils, Sikdars etc. practice all the various modes of oppression'.[6] Their aim, the Directors said, was not to injure the zemindars, 'much less to add anything to the rents to be collected from the tenants', but rather to reduce 'that immense number of idle sycophants who for their own emolument and that of their principals are placed between the tenants and the public treasury and of which every one must get his share of plunder, the whole mass of which must amount to a most enormous sum'.[7] The members of the Calcutta Council, the supervisors and their assistants, their Banians and gumashtahs could not but welcome such views, since they aimed at placing themselves in the very advantageous position from which the older agencies of administration were to be ousted.

---

[1] Holwell was in Bengal from 1731 to 1750 and again from 1751 to 1760. For his evidence on the above see R. Gregory's copy of the Proceedings (Add. MSS. 18469, ff. 12–13).
[2] Twenty-four parganas granted as jagir to Clive by Mir Jafər, Burdwan Midnapur and Chittagong to the Company by Mir Qasim.
[3] See Gokul Ghosal's letter quoted in *LCB*, pp. 125–6.
[4] See Graham's report. BPC, 20 Nov. 1769.
[5] BPC, 31 May 1770.
[6] Court's letter, 30 June 1769.   [7] Court's letter, 30 June 1769.

The conflict deepens, 1769–1770

With Becher's renewed plea for the curtailment of the super-visors' powers already before the Committee, the opposition in the Council moved the question of the Select Committee's authority. This was on 19 June 1770. On 21 June the Committee conceded what Becher had demanded, induced to do so, it would appear, by the Council's questioning of their authority. But publication of this decision was withheld until after the next meeting of the Council, which took place on 27 June. If Cartier was hoping for some accommodation with the opposition he was to be disap-pointed, for at the Council meeting the question of jurisdiction was again raised. Russell, backed by Floyer, who sank all his earlier differences with Becher in a common defence of the Committee's authority, argued that the management of the Diwani administration was 'foreign' to the Council's rights, as the Company's letter of 12 January 1768, confirming authority to the Select Committee, was still unrevoked. Cartier moved that there should be no debate on the issue. Reed, however, while declining any wish to 'intrude on the powers of the Select Committee', asked for a debate. Barwell, the most junior member of the Council, then pressed the issue, and supported by Lane, Jekyll and Hare, carried the motion by a majority vote.[1]

The Select Committee met on the following day, 28 June, and wrote to Becher communicating their decision of 21 June to restrict the supervisors' powers, denouncing the Council's motion of 19 June and proceedings of 27 June as 'highly unconstitutional and tending to the subversion of good order in Government', and asking Becher and Alexander to obey the Select Committee as before.[2]

On 3 July, however, the opposition completed their rout of the Select Committee. The Court of Directors' letter had indicated their resolve to establish a committee of some of their ablest servants for the management of the diwani revenues at Murshida-bad for the province of Bengal and at Patna for that of Bihar; these Councils 'to have the controul of all the business relating to the revenue, but Mahmud Reza Cawn or some other principal person of the country must be appointed Naib Duan (that is the Company's Deputy) and all business must be carried on thro' the Naib and under his seal and signing. And in the like manner

[1] Secret Cons., 19 June and 27 June 1770, and BSC, 21 June 1770.
[2] BSC, 28 June 1770.

Shitabroy or some other principal person at Patna for the Bahar province.'[1] The Directors had further ordered the employment of as many junior covenanted servants for assistants as might be required 'to be sent into the several provinces to correct abuses and maintain the intended reformation'.[2] The majority in the Council now voted that these orders be implemented.[3] On 6 July they proceeded to nominate two of the Calcutta Council, Becher and Reed, two Senior servants, Lawrell and Graham, to constitute the Murshidabad Council, and again one from the Calcutta Council, Alexander, and two Senior servants, Vansittart and Palk, to consti-tute the Patna Council.[4] On 13 July they wrote informing Becher and Alexander of the formation of the two Councils and laid down that they should start functioning from 1 September 1770.[5] On 19 July the Select Committee made a last bid to recover control, writing to Becher and Alexander that the new Councils must obey the Committee.[6] On 24 July, however, Barwell proposed and carried a resolution that Becher, who now became chief of the Murshida-bad Council, might neither pay nor receive any official visit unless accompanied by at least one other member of his Council.[7] By 16 August the Calcutta Council had drafted its instructions to the new Councils.[8] On 17 September Lawrell and Graham reached Murshidabad ready to take up their new duties, and soon after Reed also arrived.[9] The new Council met for the first time on 27 September 1770, with Reed in the chair. Becher had left the city some three weeks earlier on grounds of ill health.[10]

When on 28 June the Select Committee agreed to his requests to withhold controlling power from the supervisors, Becher hastened, within twenty-four hours, to issue confirmation of his Punyah promise to allow 'the Aumils to carry on the collections without interruption'.[11]He had at least technically redeemed his assurance to the amils and zemindars. On 8 and 12 July respec-

---

[1] Court's letter, 30 June 1769. Only after implementation of this order could Reza Khan be said to be holding a formal appointment as Naib Diwan.
[2] Court's letter, 30 June 1769.
[3] Secret Cons., 3 July 1770.   [4] Secret Cons., 6 July 1770.
[5] Secret Cons., 13 July 1770.   [6] BSC, 19 July 1770.
[7] Secret Cons., 24 July 1770.   [8] Secret Cons., 16 Aug. 1770.
[9] Lawrell and Graham's letter of 22 Sept. and their letter of 27 Sept. jointly with Reed (Secret Cons., 11 Oct. 1770).
[10] It seems that Becher had left Murshidabad on 5 Sept. or soon after. By 9 Sept. Cartier had received Reza Khan's letter advising Becher's departure (*H.M.S.*, 202; 110).   [11] *LCB*, p. 47.

tively, Alexander and Becher wrote to the Select Committee approving of their stand against the Council.[1] But by 28 July, Becher had acknowledged defeat, saying that he would obey the Committee, unless 'controuled by a superior power'.[2] By that date the Council had established itself as the superior power, and the Committee could do no more than appeal, in vain as it turned out, to the final authority of the Directors.[3] Two days later, on 30 July, Becher advised the Council of his determination to leave for Europe by the end of 1770 or beginning of 1771,[4] and before the new Council could reach Murshidabad had, with Cartier's permission, left the city on the plea of ill health.

On 11 September the majority in the Calcutta Council in a letter to the Murshidabad Council of Revenue informed them of the policy decisions they had taken on 16 August. The heart of the letter was the confirmation of the controlling power of the supervisors and the promise of further powers if they should prove necessary. One of the functions of the supervisors, according to the new instructions, was to 'inquire into the characters and conduct of the officers of government from the highest to the lowest'.[5]

On 21 October 1770, in a letter tendering his resignation of the chiefship of Murshidabad Council and asking for the appointment of a successor by the close of December at the latest, Becher made his formal protest against the Council's actions.[6] He registered his personal regret that after long service of the Company there should be such a lack of confidence in him. He protested particularly at the requirement, inserted at Barwell's instance, that he must be accompanied by some other member of the Council whenever he met officials of the government. Had he been inclined to retain the office to which he had been nominated, he said, he 'could not have done so with that degree of dignity or authority necessary in my opinion, for the advantage of our employers, or for my own credit under the restrictions' which the Council had laid upon him. He then turned to the Council's confirmation of the controlling power of the supervisors. This too he held to be very derogatory to his station, but he attacked it on wider grounds, protesting for Reza Khan as well as for himself. 'You cannot be unacquainted,

[1] BSC, 19 July 1770. [2] BSC, 9 Aug. 1770.
[3] BSC, 9 and 11 Sept. 1770. The result was the dismissal of Cartier and Becher and the transfer of Russell and Floyer to Madras.
[4] Secret Cons., 2 Aug. 1770.
[5] Secret Cons., 16 Aug. 1770. [6] Secret Cons., 30 Nov. 1770.

The transition in Bengal, 1756–1775

Gentlemen,' he said, 'that at the season for the settling for the present years revenue great difficulties occurred in consequence of the controuling power with every supravisor, and that I as Resident at the Durbar and Mahomed Reza Cawn as the acting minister was so fully persuaded of the necessity of restraining some of the supravisors, that we made strong representations to the Select Committee and obtained their approbation for taking such measures as we judged absolutely necessary for securing the present year's revenues. In consequence of this, agreements were entered into on Mahomed Reza Cawn's and my part stipulating that the supravisors in particular districts should not have the controuling power till after the close of the present year's collections...I shall here touch on the slight put on your Resident at the Durbar and the minister appointed by the Court of Directors for managing the revenue branch, by sending an order which cancell [sic] the obligations they have entered into without even consulting or asking them a question; Obligations, also give me leave to say, entered into with proper authority, as they had the sanction of the Select Committee to which the Court to Directors had thought proper to entrust that important branch, the Dewannee revenues; nor am I acquainted that to this hour [21 October 1770] the Court of Directors have withdrawn that power from their Select Committee.'[1] Being thus authorised, he had with confidence, 'jointly with Mahomed Reza Cawn pursued such measures as were judged most conducive to obtain the end desired. People had no doubts of the validity of our agreements, they entered on business, credit was restored and money begun [sic] to flow into our treasury.'[2] He asked the Calcutta Council to consider, 'what ideas will they form when they find these agreements broke, and in what light they will in future esteem M. R. Cawn and myself'.[3] He found it impossible to continue as chief of Murshidabad Council 'after being reduced so low in the eyes of the natives and even in those of young servants who are supravisors'.[4]

Becher, so circumstanced, could resign his office in protest and prepare to go home to a peaceful retirement. But Reza Khan's position was far harder. Admittedly he had been confirmed by the Company and the Calcutta Council as Naib Diwan, but he could not but see that the Mughal society, to which he belonged and of

---

[1] Becher's letter, 21 Oct. Secret Cons., 30 Nov. 1770.
[2] *Ibid.*   [3] *Ibid.*   [4] *Ibid.*

252

which he was necessarily the protector, was now gravely threatened. He had acted as soon as he heard of the conflict in Calcutta between the Committee and the Council, sending his vakil, Raja Kashi Nath, with a personal communication to Cartier,[1] which has purposely been kept off the record. What is on record is a very polite reply, received by Cartier on 12 July, to his letter of 16 June to Reza Khan, in which the governor had described the entire class of old officials as a 'wicked set' of 'a few blackguards'. Welcoming Cartier's letter, particularly 'that plainness [which] best suits your excellency's disposition' and the 'regard as calculated for my interest and advantage', the Khan observed that 'as the natives of this country look to no further than the present, they comprehend not the intrinsic advantage which must arise from establishing English forms and regulations, and ignorant [as they are] of the happy consequences to themselves attending the complete introduction of the plan, the Aumils and Zemindars merely because it was new to them entered into imaginary apprehensions, and with one voice started all these objections which I have already represented'. After pleading for the 'ignorant' natives, to protect the amils and zemindars from any counter-action, the Khan deemed it necessary to explain his own conduct: 'I as your servant as ready in obedience and the vassall [sic] of the Committee fearing lest my concealing the objections of the Zemindars and Aumils might afterwards be wrong[ly] interpreted, and convinced within myself that such concealments would be prejudicial to me, laid before you a minute account of all the particulars.' The Khan concluded after a reiteration of 'my labors for the due establishment of the Company's affairs' that 'I now likewise pledge that you shall behold [me] not less earnest in me [sic, possibly my] endeavours to establish the supravisors and effect the object of your grand design', and expressed a wish: 'Your well wisher offers up this prayer continually that you may long and happily govern and protect the people.'[2]

It was the more painful thereafter for Cartier to have to write on 18 September 1770, informing the Khan of the change in his powers and the replacement of the Resident by a Council of Revenue. Cartier glossed over the change by saying that the Council had been appointed because the work of Resident had

---

[1] See Reza Khan's letter, recd. 8 July 1770. *CPC*, III, 293.
[2] Reza Khan to Cartier, recd. 12 July 1770. *H.M.S.*, 202; 90–2.

impaired the health of all who had single-handed held the office. He explained that the Council's task would be to look into the revenues, ascertaining what the ryots paid and had paid, and to manage the affairs of the Diwani, but that all orders were to be signed and sealed by the Khan, who would be consulted in all things by the Council. The Khan was told that as Naib Diwan of the Company he should not sign any orders touching the Company's interests without the approval of the Murshidabad Council. Not a single word was said, however, about the revesting of controlling authority in the supervisors to which the Calcutta Council had compelled Cartier to agree.[1]

Cartier's letter was softly worded, but there was little softness in Reed's proceedings. Cartier had advised Reza Khan to meet Reed at Daudpur,[2] a distinction hitherto reserved for the governor, though Reed was officially only Second in the Murshidabad Council. Reed did not reciprocate the courtesy, for the Khan was not invited to the first Council meeting, on 27 September 1770. At the second meeting, on 1 October, the Khan was given a Persian translation of eight of the sixteen paragraphs of the Calcutta Council's letter of 11 September and was thus informed of the decision to give controlling powers to all supervisors. He was directed to prepare parwanas reporting this to the zemindars and amils and to give his opinion as to how far this might affect the engagements they had entered into.[3]

Reza Khan replied that in districts where the zemindars and amils were jointly responsible for the revenue, the zemindar 'alone might sufficiently answer the purpose...provided the Zemindars did not urge the Aumil's continuation as a plea for adhering to their engagements', and that in districts where amils only were in charge, they might be continued if they were prepared to act under the supervisor's authority, and if not then they should balance their accounts and leave.[4] Reza Khan had been assured by the Calcutta Council that the zemindars 'who hold certain districts by inheritance' were secure in their positions unless they died without heirs. His reply to Reed and his Council was therefore directed to safeguarding his officers, the amils. His readiness to see them settle their balances and leave the districts was doubtless based upon the certainty that after two years of famine the revenues

[1] Cartier to Reza Khan, 18 Sept. 1770. *CPC*, III, 372.　　[2] *Ibid.*
[3] *MP*, 1 October 1770.　　[4] *Ibid.*

were going to fall short of the estimates. Bumper crops were in prospect in some areas, but there had also been disastrous floods in eastern Bengal:[1] the amils would do well in such a situation to end their commitments, especially now that the supervisors' powers had been restored. Dual authority, Reza Khan was convinced, must breed confusion and discord. His own treatment by the Murshidabad Council showed only too clearly what his officials must expect when the supervisors came to undertake 'the examination of accounts and the unravelling exploring of all transactions in the different districts'. He had been ordered, on 1 October, to prepare twelve varied sets of statements, had been told to sign nothing without Council approval, had had his power of receiving and disbursing money from the treasury taken from him, though he was still allowed to keep an agent there,[2] and in general had been treated as a subordinate, with none of the respect extended by Clive, Verelst and even Vansittart.

On 29 October the question of the amils was brought up again by a letter from the supervisor of Jessore complaining of the amil's misuse of funds and collection of salamies—'a fresh and convincing proof', the Council declared, 'of the defective conduct, and unprofitable services of government Aumils'.[3] The Murshidabad Council now asked Reza Khan whether the amils were bound to make good any revenue deficiencies in their districts. Reza Khan replied that if an amil embezzled or misapplied money passing through his hands he could be called to account, but that 'if the revenue of the district or rather the collections made by him, allowing for his reasonable expences, prove insufficient to fulfill the Khalsa Bundibust, the Aumil is not bound to make good the deficiency'. The Khan maintained that the amils had taken office 'for the sake of subsistence' and that none of them had either the intention or the ability to make themselves answerable for deficiencies. The Council thereupon concluded that the welfare of the country and the interests of the Company would be better promoted without them, 'men of needy fortune'.[4]

Any decision about the amils had, however, to be deferred, for

[1] In order to meet the rice shortage Madras was requested to permit rice cargo to Bengal (Fort William's letter. BPC, 24 July 1770).
[2] *MP*, 1 Oct. 1770.
[3] The supervisor of Jessore in his letter of 22 Oct. alleged that the amil had applied Rs. 9,999-15-9 in private investment (*MP*, 29 Oct. 1770).
[4] *MP*, 29 Oct. 1770.

early in November a letter from the Directors restored control to Cartier and the Clivites. This letter, of 23 March 1770, restored Samuel Middleton, who had lost his service on account of Clive's hostility, to the service and to a post in the Calcutta Council next in seniority to Alexander. But the Clivites still gained in that it also reduced the Council's membership from twelve to nine, inclusive of the governor, but exclusive of the Commander-in-chief. Further it was laid down that no Councillor might be stationed outside Calcutta except for the Resident at the Durbar and the Commander-in-chief.[1] On 3 November Cartier moved immediate compliance with these orders of the Directors. Floyer, Kelsall and Russell spoke in favour of their immediate execution, Hare, Jekyll and Lane meekly followed suit, while Barwell also agreed, at the same time offering his help to the Council if required. Barwell had encouraged Lane, Jekyll and Hare also to make the same offer of their services but all four were rebuffed and so quit the Council. Middleton made a feeble attempt to keep the four in Council until the packet lying at Madras for the Commissioners had been seen, but Becher silenced him with the argument, used by the opposition in June, that the Commissioners must be presumed lost.[2] The Council now consisted of Cartier, Becher, Alexander, Aldersey, Kelsall, Floyer, and Russell, generally Clivite in sentiment with only Middleton and Reed, recalled from Murshidabad, to represent the opposition. Cartier could have kept the four in office, acting for Alexander, Aldersey and Kelsall while they were up-country winding up their private affairs, but instead he hastened to oust them.[3] Becher, though he did not withdraw his resignation or change his determination to leave for England, decided now to return to his post at Murshidabad.

Reed had continued in his hostility to the old system to the last, reversing Becher's policy, and also taking deliberate moves to injure Reza Khan. Thus he entertained complaints by Munni Begum, who had been encouraged by his attitude, that Reza Khan had deprived her both of money and estates.[4] She explained that

---

[1] Court's letter, 23 March 1770.   [2] BPC, 3 Nov. 1770.

[3] *Ibid.* Cartier, while not allowing them to participate in the Council, asked Russell and Floyer to continue in the Committee until the return of its new members from up-country. Russell and Floyer had also lost their seats in the Committee after the recall of all senior servants to Calcutta and Middleton's reinstatement as Fourth in the Council (BSC, 7 Nov. 1770. See also BPC, 8 Dec. 1770).

[4] Munni Begum's Arzi (*MP*, 20 Dec. 1770).

she had not spoken earlier because whenever Becher visited her
he was accompanied by the Khan. It was her 'good fortune', she
said, that Reed, Lawrell and Graham had come to Murshidabad,
enabling her to lay the complaint before them and to petition the
Council.[1] Nothing came of the allegations since by early January,
after both Becher and Reed had left Murshidabad, the Council
found Reza Khan's decision equitable.[2] Reed likewise received and
forwarded a petition from Rajballabh for his continuation in his
father's jagir, stopped by the Calcutta authorities on Rai Durlabh's
death, and with it the complaint, covertly hitting at Reza Khan,
that he had been 'without any manner of cause displaced' from his
office of Diwan.[3] To both these complaints Reed drew the particular attention of the Murshidabad Council in a letter of 17 December
in which he expressed his own hostility to Reza Khan. He expressly
opposed the Khan's independent authority as Naib Nazim, declaring that this 'would be placing too much power in the hands of
any one man, and especially an Asiatick and one under whose
management there is too much reason to apprehend that great
abuses have been committed'.[4]

Becher's return to Murshidabad, in the second week of November,[5] halted the attacks of Munni Begum, Rajballabh and Nandkumar who had been busy procuring letters, authentic and forged,
which might injure the Khan.[6] Becher also proceeded to undo the
damage inflicted by Reed on Reza Khan's authority and prestige.
On 19 November, at his second Council meeting, he pointed out
that the collections for Kartik, October–November, had fallen

[1] *Ibid.* [2] *MP*, 3 Jan. 1771.
[3] Rajballabh had lost his post of nizamat Diwan or Diwan-i-Sarkar in the
changes following the Nawab Saif-ud-daulah's death in March, and he complained in December. He claimed that the diwani was his as much by right, as
the masnad belonged to Mir Jafar's sons (*MP*, 20 Dec. 1770).
[4] Reed's letter, 17 Dec. *MP*, 20 Dec. 1770.
[5] Becher had returned to Murshidabad after about two months. Before he had
left the city, he left a note dated 5 Sept. for his colleagues (see *MP*, 27 Sept.
1770). He attended the Select Committee on 2 Nov. and the Council on 3
Nov. at Calcutta (BSC, 2 Nov. and BPC, 3 Nov. 1770) and then attended his
first Council meeting at Murshidabad on 15 Nov. 1770.
[6] Among letters found in Purnea in the possessions of Nobit Roy and Rahmat
Khan, who were employees of Golab Roy, Nandkumar's vakil to Shuja-ud-
daulah of Oudh and the Rohilla Chief, Dundi Khan, there was one addressed
by Dundi Khan to Reza Khan commending Golab Roy for a suitable job.
The curious thing is that Golab Roy was said to have had instructed his
agents to deliver the letter for Reza Khan to Nandkumar. In the packet there
were found a few forged letters too (BSC, 7 Nov. 1770).

heavily into arrears in Bhaturia, Birbhum, Bishnupur, Rangpur, Dinajpur, Jessore and Nadia and that if collections did not improve in the next two months, when collections were at their momentum, the balances must prove irrecoverable. He proceeded to ask his junior colleagues for their suggestions for a remedy, indicating his own disapproval of the measures already taken. The security of the current year's revenue, he pointed out, was of far greater consequence than the pressing forward of the supervisors' investigations. He was prepared to concede that his colleagues had acted in conformity with the instructions of the Calcutta Council, but had he been present he would have delayed execution of them until the grounds for altering the revenue system were presented. The earnest representations of Reza Khan against a restoration of the supervisor's controlling powers at the most critical period of collections ought to have been urged upon the Calcutta Council. As it was the attention and energy of all connected with collections had been diverted to the preparation of papers and statements and to explaining them to the supervisors, matters which could easily have been deferred until the months of March and August, when collections were less important.[1] Becher did not bother to remind them of his letter of 5 September, in which he warned them against any change in system and reminded them of the confidence so long reposed in Reza Khan,[2] for his minute was in itself sufficient to throw them fully on the defensive. Reed, Lawrell and Graham were all anxious to absolve themselves of responsibility for the threatened deficiency in the year's collections, and in a joint minute of 20 November they virtually surrendered, promising to review their decision regarding the amils and to unite with the President in framing new regulations. They also suggested that, if Becher thought proper, they might order the supervisors to confine their researches to the records available in the Sadar cutcherries until the period of heavy collections was over.[3]

Becher had regained his position and it was open to Reza Khan to continue his amils in office. But the Khan had no wish to push a purely temporary advantage. Even if there had been no possibility of an early change in the Calcutta Council, Becher was known to be leaving shortly. So when Becher asked for a restatement of his opinion about the recall of amils, he emphatically pressed for their

---

[1] Becher's minute. *MP*, 19 Nov. 1770.   [2] See *MP*, 27 Sept. 1770.
[3] Joint minute of Reed, Lawrell and Graham. *MP*, 20 Nov. 1770.

The conflict deepens, 1769–1770

recall, stressing that with divided authority in the districts their stay would 'be attended with a degree of disadvantage'.[1] Becher could do no more than confirm the Murshidabad Council's earlier decision. The Select Committee thereupon authorised the Council to recall the amils and Faujdars from all districts except Hugli. The Naibat of Dacca was also to be retained, for the Committee explained that it was their wish to 'have the appearance of the Country Government preserv'd where it may have any connection with the other European powers'.[2] Currently, in fact, Cartier had been using Reza Khan's agents to check European ships, especially French ships, entering the Hugli, by establishing a Chauki, an outpost, at Kalpi, south of Calcutta.[3] Accordingly the Murshidabad Council nominated Saiyid Muhammad Ali, Reza Khan's brother, as Faujdar of Hugli and decided to continue Jasarat Khan, the Khan's old protégé, as Naib of Dacca.[4] On 13 December orders were issued to the supervisors, accompanied by parwanas from Reza Khan, for the withdrawal of all other amils and Faujdars. The Khan's officers were directed to make over charge to the supervisors and come to Murshidabad for the final adjustment of their accounts.[5] By the beginning of 1771 the administration of the districts had passed completely out of Reza Khan's control.

The dispute over the powers to be given to the supervisors had ceased to be any more important. But the heat it had generated was not immediately dissipated, as became apparent when on 23 November Becher drafted a circular letter to supervisors restricting their enquiries to Sadar cutcherries and forbidding them to call people from the interior of the districts. This was in accord with the earlier suggestion of Reed, Lawrell and Graham, but Reed now came up with an amendment to the effect that this prohibition should not prevent supervisors going into the districts to make personal enquiries there.[6]

The issue was by itself insignificant and Lawrell and Graham, anxious about their position, for Becher had now been confirmed in the eventual succession to the governorship, voted with Becher

[1] Reza Khan's note. *MP*, 20 Nov. 1770.
[2] Select Committee's letter of 3 Dec. *MP*, 10 Dec. 1770.
[3] For the Anglo-French dispute and Reza Khan's involvement in it as Naib Nazim, see *CPC*, III, 87, 105, 156, 206, 213, 214, 242, 261, 477, 493, 513, 527, 628, 629, 634.   [4] *MP*, 10 Dec., 13 Dec. 1770.
[5] *MP*, 13 Dec. 1770. Himmat Singh, the Dacca Diwan, another protégé of Reza Khan, was also made an exception (*MP*, 4 Feb. 1771).
[6] *MP*, 23 Nov. 1770.

259   17-2

to throw out the amendment [1] But Reed's decision to return to the role of champion of the junior servants and particularly of the supervisors against Becher and other senior servants re-opened the old conflict.

On 23 November Becher set out his views on the Company's directions contained in their letter of 30 June 1769, and on the Calcutta Council's orders in their letter of 11 September. In his long minute he also sought to show how a new policy might be formulated without either contradicting the Company's wishes or worsening the state of the country, which he saw heading to ruin. He argued that it was not impossible to meet the Company's wishes and yet preserve the older social classes. But to do this required a change of direction: 'Every Zemindar, Talokdar, Landholder or Farmer as well as the Aumils and others employed in the collections by the Government', he maintained, 'are alarmed by having their Acc[oun]ts called for and seem apprehensive [that] they shall be deprived of all advantages they derive from holding lands under any denomination.'[2] There were many examples to which he could refer. Thus Higginson, the supervisor of Birbhum, by 10 October 1770 had retrenched expenses and increased the Company's income by cutting down by a third the number of persons in the Raja's employ from 12,853 to 8,832, resuming in the process 61,434 bighas out of 150,237 bighas of land enjoyed by them revenue free.[3] In like manner in Dinajpur, George Vansittart had not only resumed much uncultivated land but had cut the pay of the amil's servants from Rs. 3289 a month to Rs. 1000, of the zemindar's servants from Rs. 6,749 to Rs. 4,695, and of the horsemen and matchlockmen sanctioned by Reza Khan for keeping law and order, from Rs. 20,000 to Rs. 10,000 a year, had resumed 64,473 bighas of revenue free land out of 156,673 bighas so long enjoyed by the paiks, horsemen, matchlockmen and peons, and had dismissed 3,940 out of 7,560 such men in employ.[4] Similar reductions in numbers, in pay and in the amount of service

---

[1] *MP*, 23 Nov. 1770.
[2] Becher's minute. *MP*, 23 Nov. 1770.
[3] Birbhum report. *MP*, 23 Oct. 1770.
[4] George Vansittart's letter, 16 Oct. *MP*, 31 Dec. 1770. Reza Khan had sanctioned Rs. 24,000, though expenditure for horsemen and matchlockmen before Vansittart's reduction was Rs. 20,000 a year. The number of horsemen was reduced from 77 to 10, and of matchlockmen from 464 to 222. Their reduced pay was Rs. 20 and Rs. 3 respectively.

lands had taken place in almost every district. Against such action by the supervisors Becher now protested.

He also protested against the enlargement of the revenue demand, and here he blamed all including Reza Khan for the first time. He asked the Council to compare the money which had gone into the Company's treasury with the amount collected by the Nawabs in the same period of years before the grant of the diwani. He admitted that the miseries of the country had been increased by the oppressive measures of the amils,[1] but, as a later minute makes clear, his real criticism was of the general demand for increases of revenue 'from the Court of Directors to everyone employed in that branch'. This had been 'the occasion of measures that have not tended to the general welfare of this country and its inhabitants'.[2]

Finally, Becher expressed his indignation at 'the want of a free trade', the root cause of all other evils. The increased activity of the English and their banians and gumashtahs in the countryside made him very apprehensive that the native merchants would be still further impoverished. He concluded with a powerful plea for reform in all these matters:

Increase of revenue to the Company should in my opinion arise chiefly from increased cultivation and manufactures: these advantages tho' slow will be permanent and promote the real benefit of the Company, and I further think that justice to [the] principal natives require it, and that we shall never see this country in the flourishing state we wish it nor the future interest of the Company properly pursued, 'till Dadney merchants are again established for the provision of their investment, and natives of family and character are allowed to reap reasonable advantages in the collecting branch between the treasury and the ryott or tenant, and surely such men have an equitable claim to a proportion of the good things of their country as well as the English East India Company, and I must here beg leave to express my disapprobation [of] all measures that tend to reduce the Zemindars and other natives of family to a lower state than they are in at present, and sincerely wish the reverse could be effected.[3]

Lawrell and Graham, though they chose to regard Becher's minute as more a matter 'for the observation of his superiors and

[1] Becher's minute, *MP*, 23 Nov. 1770.
[2] Becher's minute, *MP*, 3 Dec. 1770.
[3] Becher's minute, *MP*, 23 Nov. 1770.

261

employers' than for a debate in the Council, did not fail to answer Becher.[1] They would not accept that the revenue demands since 1765 had increased unduly. Even if it had, they believed, 'the only purposes thereby answered have been the promoting and gratifying every species of corruption avarice, embezzlement thro all the classes of native officers'.[2] Similarly the fall in trade could not be, they said, attributed to any improper use of influence in the provision of goods, but rather to the political disturbances in the markets of North India, Arabia and Iran. They were silent about the preservation of natives of family and character urged by Becher, but stated that it was the Company's intention to encourage 'Farmers and every other useful subject'.[3] While deferring to the expressed wishes of the Company that the zemindars should not be deprived of 'their ancient profits and emoluments' they insisted that their gross income must be ascertained so as to stop 'feeding the insatiable thirst of avarice' with the 'secretions or alienation of the revenues'.[4] Since the zemindars had been born and bred under despotic government, and so 'familiarized to almost continual breaches of public engagements, arbitrary seizures of their property and every act of tyrannical oppression', it was not by mere assurances alone, they maintained, but by certain and proved experience of 'the lenity, mildness and justice of the authority' which then ruled over them that the English could expect to ensure the confidence of the zemindars and 'ingratiate their affections'.[5] This must wait until 'a more distant' date, and meanwhile increases of revenue must properly accrue to the Company, from the resumption of 'illicit emoluments' and retrenchment of charges.[6]

The conflict between the two systems of thought was thus once more clearly and forcibly expressed. Reza Khan saw that such divergent views could not be reconciled within a government. He was later to express again the view, which he shared with Becher, that 'every European has his Banyan, who let his master's integrity be ever so great, will avail himself of the influence of his name, and share in the plunder'[7] and his consequent opposition to the con-

---

[1] Lawrell and Graham's minute. *MP*, 26 Nov. 1770.
[2] Lawrell and Graham's minute. *MP*, 26 Nov. 1770.
[3] *Ibid.*   [4] *Ibid.*   [5] *Ibid.*   [6] *Ibid.*
[7] See Francis MSS. I.O.Eur. E, 28, p. 347. Hastings was also to say the same thing when he wrote to Dupre on 6 Jan. 1773, 'They [the supervisors] are most of them agents of their own Banyans and they are devils' (Gleig, *Hasting,*

trolling power of the supervisors over the districts. But he could now see that the battle was lost, and that it was useless and dangerous 'to join natives and Europeans in the management of the collection'.[1] It was this realisation which made him determined to withdraw his officers, the amils.

1, 269). He spoke from experience when he warned Impey on 24 Oct. 1774 that though he might consider a Banian 'such a servant only as a steward, or one...providing common necessaries' he was in fact a 'minister'. (Add. MSS. 29125 f.365). 'These are the people', he added, 'through whom every concern of whatever nature passes to their masters and are often the cause of infinite mischief by the ill use they make of their influence, which often is greater than that from which it is derived, and by their artful suggestion. Most instances of public misconduct and many of the private dissention flowed from this source (*ibid.*). Consequently, to him 'of all the natives of Bengal men of Calcutta, though there are exceptions, are the most dangerous to be trusted and most hateful to the rest of the people' (*ibid.*).

[1] Reza Khan, as quoted by Francis in a letter to Clive, dated 21 May 1775. Francis MSS. I.O. Eur. E, 13, p. 241.

CHAPTER 10

THE REARGUARD ACTION
AND REZA KHAN'S ARREST,
1770–1772

Despite the temporary restoration to full authority of Becher, Cartier and others of the Clive school in the autumn of 1770, Reza Khan made no attempt to restore the old Mughal revenue structure. He could no longer hope to exclude the supervisors and their attendant Banians and gumashtahs from the districts, and rather than suffer a dual authority in the countryside he recalled his amils and abandoned the field.

But though he had yielded ground in the diwani he was still firmly resolved to defend those other areas of Mughal authority in the Nizamat. This he made clear when on 1 October 1770, at his first meeting of the Murshidabad Controlling Council of Revenue, he asked how he was to conduct himself 'in the administration of justice in general and relative to criminal cases in particular'.[1] The question was not just an administrative point: Reza Khan was reminding Reed and his Council that their legitimate power did not extend beyond the diwani, and that the Khan, Naib Nazim, though formally designated now as Naib Diwan,[2] could not be treated merely as a servant of the Company.

Murshidabad referred the question to the Calcutta Council. However on 22 October they proceeded to prejudge the issue by laying down that all criminal cases should be tried in the existing faujdari Adalat, but that sentences before execution should have the approval of the Council. It was further decided that causes relating to property in land and to revenue should be referred to the Khalsa cutcheri, and causes for debt to a different Adalat, these two courts to be constituted of all the members of the

[1] *MP*, 1 October 1770.
[2] Until the Court of Directors had asked in their letter of 30 June 1769 to appoint someone at Murshidabad and another at Patna as Naib Diwan there was no separation of Diwani administration from the general administration of the province. The new order became effective on 1 Oct. 1770.

Murshidabad Council. Reed and his Council further ordered Reza Khan to say whether any parwana was necessary for the arrest of persons accused of robbery and murder, and he was directed to give them copies of all parwanas then in force or issued in future. Reed had thus taken away the whole judicial authority of the Nazim as exercised by the Khan.[1]

The Calcutta Council's reply when it came was a non-committal, 'the administration of justice should remain as usual'; but with the addition that all transactions 'relative to government' should ultimately come before the Murshidabad Council.[2] Becher, however, opposed Reed's claims and supported the Khan's independence in nizamat matters. In a minute of 23 November he argued that the Council might properly control every action of the Naib Diwan and the district officials engaged in diwani matters, but that in criminal cases, causes of property, quarrels and complaints under nizamat jurisdiction, the English should avoid appearing as principals. He stressed that the destruction or denial of that independence would harmfully affect the Company's relations with the French and other European powers and doubtless earn the disapprobation of Parliament.[3] Lawrell and Graham, who had earlier concurred with Reed in usurping the nizamat powers, now revised their stand and maintained that, in the absence of any clear direction on the matter from the Company, there was scope for more definite direction from Calcutta.[4]

On 3 December 1770, Reza Khan indicated where he thought a proper line of authority should be drawn between his two offices of Naib Diwan and Naib Nazim:

It formerly was the practice when the Nazim and Duan were appointed by the King, for the former to transact whatever related to His Majesty, and the latter whatever related to the Vizier, yet nothing was executed by the Duan without orders and approbation of the Nazim. Accordingly all these forms of conducting business are now before the Mutsudees of the Dewannee and are still observed in regard to Sunnuds &cta. but whatever mode you gentlemen please to adopt shall be complied with—

[1] *MP*, 22 Oct. 1770.
[2] Fort William Secret letter of 11 Oct. *MP*, 22 Oct. 1770. In October the opposition dominated the decisions of the Calcutta Council.
[3] *MP*, 23 November 1770. Becher, while upholding the independence of the Nizamat in diwani areas, wished to act as a check on the Adalat to prevent injustice.
[4] *MP*, 26 November 1770.

The transition in Bengal, 1756–1775

Account of what belongs to the Duanny [Diwani]

The appointing of Aumils into Muffussul;
The Collections and whatever belongs thereto;
The settling a Bundibust of the Pergunnahs;
The examining of Dewanny Sunnuds [which were issued] under the signature of the Nazim for Taloks, charity lands and religious donations of Berhameter [Brahmottar] and Deoter [Devottar].
The investigating the districts and forming a Hustabood;
The uniting and separating one district from another.
The placing and displacing the Zemindars with consent of the Nazim;
The cultivation of the Country and whatever tends to increase its revenue.
The examining [of] complaints against Aumils and Zemindars [about their] making illegal demands.
The limiting the boundaries of a Zemindary and adjusting complaints not deserving of capital punishment.
The examining of Taloks, and adjusting the rights of Talokdars;
The writing of Perwanas to inforce payment of revenue and the recalling of Aumils from the Muffussul on any complaint.

Account of what falls under the Nizamut

Household affairs of the Nazim, Mirsummany [Mir-i-Samani] Bhela and Sepoys;
The placing and displacing of Naibs and Cazees Ytisabs [ihtisabs], and Naib of Adawlut and Fougedars.
The sentencing and inflicting of capital punishment.[1]
The calling of robbers &ca. out of the Moffussul [meaning perhaps the rooting out of robbers from the countryside];
The protecting of Talokdars from the oppression of individuals.[2]

The Khan made it clear that he intended to act according to this rule, ignoring the claims Reed and the Council had advanced in October. He memorialised the Council accordingly:

The Council at Calcutta having determin'd and express'd it in their instructions, that the Naib Duan shall make no appointments, nor issue any order under his seal without first obtaining the approbation of you gentlemen. I am in that case subject to your commands and will never carry anything of importance into execution that appertains to the

---

[1] At Dacca, however, Jasarat Khan, the Naib, 'exercised a power of life and death in capital offences, without reference . . . to Muxadabad' (*vide* Kelsall's letter, 15 Nov. 1770. *MP*, 27 Dec. 1770).
[2] Reza Khan's statement. *MP*, 3 Dec. 1770.

266

The rearguard action, 1770–1772

Dewannee without your consent and advice. But there are several matters of less consequence, which if not immediately settled will excite complaints from the poor, and create confusion. These...if you approve of it I will perform the writing part and immediately acquaint the Chief; after which the particulars shall be laid before the Council. All affairs relating to the Nizamut, I will as usual carry into execution under my own seal.[1]

For functioning in his newly formalised office as Naib Diwan of the Company he had also had a new seal prepared.[2]

The Murshidabad Council forwarded Reza Khan's memorial with a further request for guidance from the Calcutta Council about the distinction between the diwani and nizamat in the administration of justice. They pointed out that the practice had been for justice to be administered in the districts by an officer of the Nazim, or more correctly a deputy of the Sadar Adalat of Murshidabad, acting under the orders of the Faujdar or amil. Since the Mughal officials had now been withdrawn from the districts and replaced by English supervisors, it would be necessary, were the administration of justice allocated to the nizamat, to say what establishment should be set up in the district.[3] The posting of supervisors also raised two further problems: the Murshidabad Council was directed to obtain Reza Khan's advice on district matters and all orders were to be issued under the Khan's seal and signature. To obey the first injunction required that all accounts and statements from the supervisors should be intelligible to the Khan, they therefore suggested that they should be accompanied 'by an exact Persian translation';[4] to obey the second required some Mughal official to whom the Khan could direct his corres-

[1] Reza Khan's memorial (*MP*, 3 Dec. 1770).
[2] *MP*, 23 Nov. and 3 Dec. 1770. The inscription of the new seal as approved by the Murshidabad Council declared the Mughal emperor as sovereign, the Company as Diwan and 'Rulers of Affairs' and the Khan as Naib. As apparently incorrectly rendered in English, it read: 'A loyal subject of the Victorious Emperor Shaw Allum (King of the World). The English Company, Ruler of Affairs Dewan of Soubah Bengall, Bahar and Orissa, Naib, the Champion of the Empire, the Ally of Fortune, Cawn Syed Mahomed Reza Cawn Behader, Victorious in War.'
[3] *MP*, 3 Dec. 1770.
[4] Accounts in districts were kept in Bengali and these used to be translated in Persian and sent to Murshidabad. With the posting of Englishmen as supervisors there was a further translation in English. Thus three languages were used until the transfer of Khalsa to Calcutta in 1772 when there was no more need of using Persian in revenue matters.

267

pondence in every district cutcherry. The Murshidabad Council suggested both measures for adoption[1] which ensured continuance of some of the old officials in service, though on lower salary, but at the same time undoing all that Reed had done in October as chief of that Council.

Reed had ceased to attend the Murshidabad Council after 23 November, though he did not leave the city until 18 December.[2] However, he had kept himself informed of the Council's proceedings[3] and on 17 December he sent a long letter to the Council laboriously refuting and opposing Becher's views and denouncing the Khan. He argued that since the country was in English hands, it was a duty incumbent upon them to save the inhabitants from flagrant injustice: only the English could protect them from the enormities 'rooted as it were in the constitution of the Moorish government'. To avoid an overt interference which would lead to complications with other European powers, however, he urged that cases should be decided 'in our houses and not in publick courts'.[4]

Though Reed maintained this attitude when the Fort William Council took up the matter on 17 January 1771,[5] the Council agreed that the Khan's parwanas should be addressed to the principal zemindars and that his judicial orders should be sent to the Maulvis of the Sadar cutcherries. They thus accepted Reza Khan's and Murshidabad Council's main recommendations, though they still sought clarification about whether the Diwan could take cognisance of misdemeanours, riots and matters of property, and of the apparent contradiction between the nizamat power of protecting the taluqdars from oppression and the Diwani power of examining and adjusting the rights of taluqdars.[6] However, before Reza Khan could clear up these points,[7] the

[1] *MP*, 23 Nov. 1770. [2] See letter to Fort William. *MP*, 20 Dec. 1770.
[3] As evidenced by his reference to Ducarel's letter of 3 Dec. and Hardwood's letter of 29 Nov. 1770 (*MP*, 13 Dec. 1770) in his letter of 17 Dec. 1770.
[4] Reed's letter of 17 Dec. *MP*, 20 Dec. 1770.
[5] Secret Cons., 17 Jan. 1771.
[6] Fort William letter. *MP*, 4 Feb. 1771.
[7] Reza Khan clarified the apparent contradiction between the diwani and nizamat powers regarding taluqdars by asserting the superior power of the Nazim. According to him, the disputes regarding boundaries, settlement of inheritance, complaints of illegal demands and oppressions on ryots, debts to merchants were matters of the Diwan to settle 'with the consent and approbation of the Nazim'. Referring as proof to the old sanads, the Khan

268

The rearguard action, 1770–1772

Murshidabad Council had been driven by the actions of Grose to a full-blooded enunciation of the principle that all districts under the Nawab's government were 'subject to the Moorish jurisdiction and usages'.[1] Supervisor Grose had allowed himself to be driven by the French into the position of judicial authority in his district, accepting letters from the French chief at Chandernagore and requests from the local French agent at Kurigram to send a merchant Brindaban to Chandernagore for examination. Murshidabad therefore overruled him, ordering him to leave the matter to the local Adalat and 'not to interfere therein', and issued their statement about 'Moorish jurisdiction' over the districts.[2] Their action was approved by the Calcutta Council which wrote from its Committee of Revenue on 21 May 1771: 'Although we wish to interfere as little as possible with the business as appertains to the Nizamut, and established by long usage of the country, yet as we are desirous of checking the arbitrary proceedings of the Moorish court of justice from a duty we owe to the happiness and security of the inhabitants, we must therefore desire that you [Murshidabad Council] will give the strictest attention to prevent injustice as much as possible by your representations to government, as occasions offer'.[3]

The position of the Calcutta Council was thus one of overt acceptance of the jurisdiction of the nizamat, that is of Reza Khan, but also of covert interference. This was a far cry from the orders of the Directors, given on 16 March 1768 that 'the English are never to appear as Principals, nor even to pretend to an influence, but leave all such disputes as may arise in the lands of the Dewanny to the Durbar at Moorshedabad',[4] but it proved to be in line with

further maintained that 'in all Dewanny sunnuds whether for Zemindaries or Talookdaries or the like, it is expressed that they have been granted agreeably to the terms sign'd by the Nazim' (*vide* Reza Khan's note. *MP*, 11 Feb. 1771). [1] Letter to Grose. *MP*, 4 Feb. 1771.
[2] For letter from Grose and letter to Grose. *MP*, 4 Feb. 1771.
[3] Fort William letter. *MP*, 10 June 1771.
[4] Court's letter, 16 March 1768. The Directors had further directed that even in case of disputes in Burdwan these were to be left 'to the Rajah and his ministers, and to answer directly to no disputes, but such as may happen in the Company's lands'. This technically restricted the judicial authority of the English to Calcutta and twenty-four parganas for the other two districts, Midnapur and Chittagong, were, like Burdwan, jagiri districts. But legal disabilities did not prevent the English from exercising active power in these districts. The faujdari power, for example in Chittagong, was on a reference from Reed, ordered to be exercised by the chief and Council (BPC, 27 June 1769). Already in 1760 Verelst had been so authorised (see p. 37 n).

269

the latest thinking of the Directors. On 20 December 1771 the Calcutta government informed Murshidabad that the Directors had ordered that all sanads appointing judges for Muslims and Brahmins for the Hindus were to be registered, and that the judges' power of imposing 'arbitrary fines' and other taxes or duties upon plaintiff and defendant, and of exacting security for the payment of Chouth (fees) in arbitration cases was to be abolished.[1]

Reza Khan reacted very firmly to these proposals. He pointed out that fees and Chouth had 'been before prohibited', and urged only that the prohibition be more strictly enforced.[2] But he refused to accept the orders touching the power of judges to impose fines and the appointment of Brahmins. These touched the legal and constitutional sovereignty of the empire and consequently the supremacy of the laws of Islam, and would mean 'an innovation in Mahommedan laws and religion'. 'The case is this', he elaborated, 'that from the first propagation of the faith [that is the establish-ment of Muslim political power in India] the power of deciding all disputes and controversies has been vested in the Mussulmen, Brahmins never having been appointed for the tryal of Indoos many of whose disputes are settled agreeable to the Mahommedan laws and others such as relate to the customs of the cast, their rules of society and the like after being referred to the arbitration of Brahmins and people of their own cast are ultimately decided by Mussulmen.'[3]

Warren Hastings and his Council, replying on 13 April 1772, concurred with the Khan, stating that they had never proposed 'any alteration in the established Courts or forms of justice or to adjudge crimes or misdemeanors by arbitration'. They denied any intention to 'subvert any of the established laws, but to facilitate the course of justice'. They seemed to agree 'that all cases of inheritance, marriage or other matters for which Mahomedan law has made a provision should be decided by the established magis-trate with the assistance of the expounders of the law', and in the like manner, 'that all matters respecting inheritance and the particular laws and usages of the casts of Gentoos should be

---

[1] *MP*, 4 Jan. 1772.
[2] Reza Khan's note. *MP*, 26 March 1772. The delay was due to the month of Ramadhan which intervened and kept the Khan virtually off from much work.
[3] Reza Khan's note. *MP*, 26 March 1772.

decided by the established magistrate assisted by Bramins and the heads of Casts according to Gentoo law'. This they professed to be their understanding of 'the invariable practice of all Mahomedan Governments in Indostan'. Arbitration they had suggested only for civil cases regarding debts and disputed accounts.[1]

This gloss upon their orders was far from satisfying Reza Khan, who set out his objections in a statement to the Murshidabad Council:

I must remark that ever since the Mahomedan religion has been established in Hindostan it never has been customary to decide matters regarding the participation of the estate of the deceased persons, inheritance or other disputes with the assistance of the Bramins or the heads of several sects in any Mussulman government or jurisdiction.[2]

This could not be, for the Hindus as a subject people were subject to the laws of 'true faith'. Hence

to order a magistrate of the faith to decide in conjunction with a Bramin would be repugnant to the rules of the faith, and in a country under the dominion of a Mussulman Emperor it is improper that any order should be issued inconsistent with the rules of his faith, [and] that innovations should be introduced in the administration of justice.[3]

Hindus were not obliged to bring their disputes to court if they could settle them amongst themselves. But if they failed to decide the dispute and came to the court they must accept the court's decision as binding. There were two good reasons why they should. The magistrate, by his training, was fitted to decide causes with greater accuracy 'than what could be effected by the degree of penetration and discernment possessed by Bramins and heads of Gentoo tribes'.[4] And, 'was the magistrate to disregard the rules and usages of his jurisdiction and conform in his decree with the determinations of a Bramin, the foundation of the system of justice, which has for long series of time been binding on the whole body of the people whether Mussulmen or Jentoos, must undergo a subversion'.[5] This constitutional and religious point was the heart of Reza Khan's objection, but he also pointed out the conflict and difficulty which would follow from any attempt to apply Hindu law when the Hindus had such a multiplicity of laws,

---

[1] Fort William letter of 13 April 1772. *MP*, 20 April 1772.
[2] Reza Khan's statement. *MP*, 4 May 1772.
[3] *Ibid.*   [4] *Ibid.*   [5] *Ibid.*

The transition in Bengal, 1756–1775

varying according to their castes and place of origin. This alone
was sufficient reason why 'none of the former emperors down to
the present ever appointed a Bramin to assist a magistrate'.[1]

Reza Khan, upholding Mughal sovereignty and the existing
legal system based on the supremacy of Islamic laws, also reacted
sharply to the accusations of defects in the existing system expressed
in official communications, and to the prevalent English attitude
of contempt for Muslim or Mughal institutions. He refused to
admit any fault in the system: if the instruments were at fault then
the remedy lay in the punishment of the guilty. He claimed that
there could be 'no defect or abuse in the administration of justice
without treachery and malversation'.[2] Therefore, 'let repeated
orders be sent on this subject into every Zellah, and let the
Supravisors be written to, that whenever any of the officers of
justice are detected of committing any abuse or oppression to send
them immediately to Moorshedabad, in order that they may
receive the reward of their deeds—By these means no defect or
abuse will take place'.[3] Reza Khan's defiant defence was silenced
by his arrest on 27 April 1772, and it was only after his removal
from Murshidabad that the two Sadar Adalats were transferred
from that city to Calcutta. Hastings justified the transfer on the
grounds that criminal jurisdiction was 'so connected with the
revenue and the Mahometan courts are [so] abominally venal, that
it was necessary',[4] but he admitted also that the change was
'almost an act of injustice, the criminal judicature being a branch
of the Nizamut'.[5] Reza Khan would have agreed with the latter
judgement—except for the word 'almost'.

The conflict over the courts, begun in 1770, was but one of a
series of rearguard actions which Reza Khan fought between 1770
and 1772 in defence of the Mughal system. One minor skirmish
which he won was over the rate of duties payable by Muslim and
non-Muslim merchants. Hardwood, the supervisor of Rajmahal,
complained that at Akbarnagar (Rajmahal) the Hindus paid double
the Muslim rate. The Murshidabad Council, desirous of remedy-

[1] Reza Khan's statement. *MP*, 4 May 1772. Before this statement was considered
by the Murshidabad Council on 4 May Reza Khan had been arrested on 27
April 1772. Islamic laws, unlike laws of modern national states, were meant only
for the Muslim community and conferred absolute autonomy to non-Muslim
communities in Muslim states. This led to the enjoyment of extra-territorial
rights by the European colonists in the Mughal empire.
[2] Reza Khan's statement. *MP*, 26 March 1772.   [3] *Ibid.*
[4] W. Hastings to DuPre, 8 Oct. 1772. Add. MSS. 29125, ff. 156–7.   [5] *Ibid.*

272

ing the 'evil' by fixing one rate for all, asked for Reza Khan's opinion. He opposed the 'innovation' and the Council was obliged to fix the rate at three per cent for Muslim and five per cent for non-Muslim merchants.[1]

The Khan fought with no less success to preserve the dignity of the Nizamat when Becher, in his last letter to the Murshidabad Council, on 24 December 1770, suggested that from the next revenue year, 1771–2 one or two supervisorships might be created for the area around Murshidabad for which he as Resident had been responsible.[2] When asked his opinion about such a change in the Huzury Zila, Reza Khan vehemently opposed any such insult to the dignity of the Nazim. It had been proper, he declared, 'when Mr. Becher applied for their being left under him', so as to maintain 'a proper dignity over the inhabitants without which both himself and the Nazim would appear light in the eyes of the people'.[3] But, he added pungently, 'it gives me surprize that that gentleman should afterwards [write] to the Committee and Council to have these districts [made in] to Zelahs because in his own time he endeavour'd to preserve his own dignity, but after his departure took no care for his successors'.[4] The appeal to *amour-propre* of the Murshidabad Council worked, and they endorsed his plea. So, by a letter of 7 May 1771, did the Fort William authorities, though not without comment upon Reza Khan's boldness of speech—'a reflection thrown on our late Resident Mr. Beecher, which we deem very improper to come from the Naib Duan and desire you will acquaint him that it meets with our disapprobation'.[5] Their displeasure was given tangible form when at the close of the year 1770–1 they recovered Rs. 45,000 from Reza Khan's salary when Ram Chandra Sen, farmer of Lashkarpur, a part of the Huzury Zila, fell into arrear.[6]

[1] The supervisor had complained that the rate of duty applicable to 'Moors' which was 2½ per cent had by additional exactions gone up to 3½ per cent. The Council's decision did not restore the old basis, but it did retain the distinction (*MP*, 27 Dec. 1770).
[2] Becher's letter. *MP*, 24 Dec. 1770. The Huzury Zila included part of the Rajshahi zemindari south-west of the Padma, Malda, Lashkarpur and their adjoining Taluqs.
[3] Reza Khan's statement. *MP*, 4 March and 11 March 1771.
[4] Reza Khan's statement. *MP*, 11 March 1771.
[5] Fort William letter of 7 May 1771. *MP*, 23 May 1771.
[6] Ram Chandra Sen who was a nominee of Becher's Diwan had defaulted a sum Rs. 46,552 on account of Lashkarpur and another sum of Rs. 72,873 on

Another question touching the dignity of the nizamat which Reza Khan took up was that of Khilats for the Punyah ceremony. By a letter of 18 March 1771 Fort William had laid down that the only Europeans to receive Khilats should be the Governor, and the Chief and members of the Murshidabad Council, and then of not higher value than Rs. 5,000, Rs. 2,000, and Rs. 500 respectively. A Khilat of the usual value should be continued for the Nawab Mubarak-ud-daulah, one of not more than Rs. 4,000 for Reza Khan, and for all others the order was to retrench expenditure as much as possible.[1] Reza Khan knew that the orders stemmed from the Court of Directors, who were involved in a financial crisis, but he, nevertheless, opposed them. The Khilats given to the governor and members of the Council were meant to augment their dignity—those proposed would 'only tend to render them inconsiderable'.[2] Khilats to the zemindars and taluqdars were tokens of confirmation of their appointments and to deny them would be tantamount to dismissal. The same was true of the Khilats given to the officers of the Nizamat: were they not granted it would 'spread through the whole world that the Nizamut is abolish'd', while to offer them Khilats of inferior value would reflect discredit on all who received them.[3] The Khan offered his own share of the Khilat: 'it is no matter; because nobody shall know it'. But he urged 'if my officers do not receive them the name of the Neabut Dewanny will also be abolish'd'.[4]

Reza Khan also raised the further argument that if the Company discontinued or curtailed expenditure on Khilats then the Rs. 2,25,000 retrenched from the Nizamat allowance to cover this item should be restored. The grant of dresses of honour was an essential ceremony: 'it had long been customary for the Nazim of the province in behalf of His Majesty to invest the Dewan and his officers with this honour, and for the Dewan to replace the expence of it to the Nazim from the Khalsah'.[5] Clive and Sykes had recognised this in the financial arrangements of 1766, and if the Company wished to renounce responsibility then it was necessary that 'the sum of 2,25,000 Rs. be restored to answer this addition of expence to the Nizamut; and that the Nazim of the country

account of Saiyidpur. Out of these two sums Rs. 45,000 was recovered from the Khan and the fugitive farmer still owed Rs. 74,425 (*BPP*, XIII, 100).
[1] *MP*, 8 April 1771.
[2] Reza Khan's note. *MP*, 15 April 1771.
[3] *Ibid.*   [4] *Ibid.*   [5] *Ibid.*

274

The rearguard action, 1770–1772

agreeable to the ancient custom in behalf of His Majesty yearly invest the several officers & ca with Khelauts according to their respective stations'.[1]

The Murshidabad Council supported Reza Khan and they reacted sharply to Calcutta's reluctance to revise their original stand. They re-emphasised the need of observing the ceremony in its 'full force and influence' and suggested that total abolition would be better than parsimony.[2] However, the Calcutta government would agree to the expenditure of no more than Rs. 60,000—[3] a tremendous reduction from the Rs. 2,16,870 spent on Khilats in 1766.[4] They naturally ignored the suggestion of a restoration of the cut in the nizamat allowance.

Reza Khan had been defending the dignity and power of the nizamat, reminding the Company and its servants that Bengal was still a part of the Mughal empire, and that the Company was no more than the Diwan of the province. He also continued to defend the old order on the diwani side against Englishmen who more and more acted as though the country was theirs by right of conquest. Since the Khan had withdrawn his officials, the amils, from the districts it was upon the zemindars and taluqdars that the hand of the supervisors fell—those 'sovereigns of the country...heavy rulers of the people'[5] as Hastings called them. In Burdwan, the Raja's private estate, his 'Dewry' lands had been left for his maintenance.[6] In the Diwani districts, such as Nadia or Rajshahi, these were handed over with the rest of the zemindari to the farmers installed by the Company. Reza Khan had therefore to intervene in support of such zemindars' claims to a maintenance allowance suitable to their ancient status. Thus, in July 1771, he

[1] *Ibid.*
[2] Fort William letter of 24 April and Murshidabad Council's reply of 9 May 1771. *MP,* 9 May 1771.
[3] Fort William letter of 20 May. *MP,* 27 May 1771. Calcutta had sanctioned Rs. 60,000 against Murshidabad's minimum estimate of Rs. 70,000.
[4] Out of Rs. 2,16,870 spent on Khilats in 1766 (the amount was still lesser than what was deducted from the Nawab's allowance) a sum of Rs. 76,605 was spent for zemindars and Faujdars, Rs. 46,750 for English gentlemen, Rs. 38,800 for the Nawab, his family and ministers, Rs. 22,634 for Cutcherry servants, Rs. 22,525 for nizamat servants, and Rs. 4,357 for the people belonging to Clive, Carnac and Sykes (BSC, 28 April 1770).
[5] W. Hastings to Jonas Du Pre, 26 March 1772. Add. MSS. 29126, f. 138.
[6] Lawrell and Graham's minute. *MP,* 26 Nov. 1770. As late as 1770 the Burdwan Raja used to be treated with due respect. In that year the governor presented the Raja and his Diwan with elephants (see *CPC,* III, 278).

275 18-2

pleaded for the Nadia Raja who had asked for Rs. 3,00,000, saying 'his request is reasonable, because his Zemindarry is hereditary and in case the collections of the district are made . . . on an accurate investigation he can have neither advantage [n]or influence remaining. He has a numerous family, and many dependants. His ancestors lived with affluence and respect.'[1] In view of the eminence of the Raja, the number of his dependants and the fact that his income from the zemindari had been as much as Rs. 3,50,000, the Khan considered Rs. 3,00,000 a reasonable demand. However, since the district was much exhausted the Khan did not press for more than Rs. 2,00,000 as the Raja's allowance.[2] In like manner he supported the claim of Rani Bhawani of Rajshahi to an allowance of Rs. 3,50,000, her usual income, but suggested that Rs. 2,50,000 might do.[3] His recommendations in both cases were accepted by the Council, who hoped to gain more from the lands than they paid out in allowances to the zemindars. The actions of the Company's servants put the profits—and more important still—power and influence of the zemindars in jeopardy. Reza Khan secured the recognition of the old principle that if the zemindar was ousted from management he was entitled to provision appropriate to his status.[4]

In the case of the Yusufpur zemindari, in Jessore, he secured recognition of a further principle—that the state had positive as well as negative responsibilities to the zemindars. The case there was of an estate involved by its Diwans in debt while the zemindar was a minor.[5] Reza Khan here supported a claim to a maintenance allowance of Rs. 2,000 a month during the minority, with such addition as was possible after further enquiry and settlement of debts.[6] In other words the state assumed responsibility for the minor.

Reza Khan also sought to establish the exclusive right of zemindars to create independent taluqs, and their right to create

---

[1] MP, 25 July 1771.   [2] *Ibid.*   [3] *MP*, 8 Aug. 1771.
[4] By December 1771, two other zemindars (Dinajpur and Birbhum) had applied for increase of allowances. *MP*, 27 Sept. and 12 Dec. 1771.
[5] The mother of the minor zemindar Srikanta had of her own accord applied for the zemindari administration to be taken over by the supervisor and to be relieved of persecution on account of debts. She had asked for an allowance of Rs. 5,000 a month, though the family's income from all sources was shown as Rs. 90,000, or Rs. 30,000 more per year (*MP*, 10 Dec. 1770).
[6] Reza Khan recommended Rs. 2,000 a month 'for her own expences' (*MP*, 7 Jan. 1771).

revenue-free charitable grants within their estates. The first issue was raised when Lokenath Nandi bought land in various zemindaries and sought confirmation of his purchases from government. Reza Khan laid down the principle involved as follows:

It has been the established usage of the country, that when Zemindars dispose of Talooks of their own free will and accord, they first grant Cubaulas [Kabala or deed of sale] under their own signature, and afterwards conformably to them, Sunnuds are issued from the Nizamut and Dewanny. For this reason if any one, without having previously procured Cabaulas and Sunnuds from the Zemindars, should obtain Sunnuds from the government, it would be deemed oppressive, illegal, and unusual, unless in such cases where in consequence of misbehaviour on the part of the Zemindar, the government think proper to bestow his Zemindarry on another.[1]

The second issue concerned Ratan Chand Gossain, who held the village of Rahimpur as a revenue-free grant from the zemindar. On this the Khan, himself creator of many charities,[2] declared

it has long been the nature of institution of Bharjahy (sequestration of land for religious uses) that when particular villages or lands are allotted to this purpose by the Zemindars, or established from the presence [meaning the Nawab or Government], the Zemindar in lieu of the revenue thus alienated levies a proportionable encrease from the several Talooks under his jurisdiction and makes good the amount to the government, and the villages or lands so sequester'd are appropriated solely to the purposes of Bermooter, Dewuttur, the entertainment of travellers and the like. None of the officers under former Nazims were opposed [to it] or discountenanced this usage; as it had therefore been a practice of long duration I granted Sunnuds to the Gossein. The Bharjahy is a charitable institution, and in consideration of its being an ancient usage it ought to be preserved.[3]

In both these cases Reza Khan was defending decisions he had earlier made, but which had come under scrutiny by the supervisors.

At much the same period the Khan was also busy defending the old official classes of Qanungoes, Muhtasibs, Waqainigar, Sawaninigar and Akhbarnavis from the same hostile supervisors. Thus

[1] *MP*, 14 March and 30 May 1771.
[2] See Kelsall's letter from Dacca, dated 24 Feb. 1771. *MP*, 4 March 1771.
[3] Reza Khan's note. *MP*, 11 April 1771.

The transition in Bengal, 1756–1775

Rous, Lushington, Rooke, Kelsall, Wilkins, Higginson and Rider[1] all reported that the Qanungoes were useless. Reza Khan agreed that in the districts with big zemindaries, whose records were kept at Murshidabad, the Qanungoes were not vital to administration, but he pointed out that in faujdari districts, with large numbers of small estates, they were still useful, as the favourable reports from Hardwood in Rajmahal and Grose in Rangpur indicated.[2] They were needed also at Dacca and Hugli where they alone could furnish authentic information. Were the district Qanungoes to be abolished, he argued, 'the original revenue, the state of the Talooks and the tenure by which they were held which are now known at the Suddur must in future be obscured'.[3] To accusations that they misled the zemindars, he replied with the denial of the Sadar Qanungoes and their promise of severe punishment for any who could be proved guilty. He concluded his defence of the Qanungoes by an appeal to the constitution of the Empire: 'as this office has been instituted ever since the first dominion of the emperors, as Lutchmynairrain and Mehindernairrain [Lakshmi Narayan and Mahendra Narayan] hold their appointments by right of inheritance, and as the procuring of all papers depends on their Duftur...and in consideration of the long time this office has descended in the families of the said Canoongoes, the continuance of it is necessary'.[4] The Council decided to continue the Sadar and Mufassil Qanungoes and ordered the supervisors to pay their usual salaries, making full use of them.[5]

The Khan felt that the case for retaining the office of Muhtasib, censor or superintendent of morals, was much weaker, since it had little utility by this date. He made the case, however, that Muhtasibs and Qazis had been appointed ever since the Muslims reached India, according to the laws of religion. He admitted that 'in the process of time as the Hindoos became entrusted with important offices in the finance, and invested with power and authority over the districts' the administration of Ihtesab had grown relaxed and irregular, while the authority of the Muhtasib had dwindled in some districts to the regulation of weights and measures. But the Muhtasibs were often still engaged, as far as lay within their

---

[1] These gentlemen were supervisors respectively of Nator, Hugli, Jessore, Dacca, Tipperah, Birbhum-Bankura and Nadia.
[2] *MP*, 2 July 1771.
[3] *Ibid.*   [4] *MP*, 2 July 1771.   [5] *Ibid.*

278

power, in preventing forbidden and unlawful actions and in guiding and correcting the morals of the people. Apprehension of complaint by the 'numerous tribe of Hindoos' had limited the efficiency of the institution, but its purpose was still the improvement of mankind. He also pointed out that except in Rangpur the dues of the Muhtasibs did not come from the government revenues. He then summed up the reasons against abolition as follows: 'In the first place such a measure will be repugnant to the revealed laws and the dictates of the Prophet: and in the second it will be promulgated throughout the four quarters of the world that the foundation of religion in Bengal is shaken.'[1] The Council, deeming it 'too delicate a point to think of subverting it', continued the Muhtasib's office as a religious establishment.[2]

Reza Khan did not seriously try to defend the mufassil staff of Waqainigar, Sawaninigar and Akhbarnavis, the various grades of official news reporters. This was perhaps in accordance with his usual strategy of sacrificing the inconsequential in order the better to defend what was important. He explained their original functions:

It was established in ancient times that wherever there were Nazims, Naib Nazims, Fougedars, or other rulers there should also be stationed Gomastahs from these offices who had free admission to their presence. Many papers regarding important disputes in the districts were rendered authentick, by their seals, and they are now amongst the attendants necessary for the support of the dignity of the Nizaumut: their rissooms [meaning customary allowances] are extremely small, and [are] not imposed on the revenue collections, or the produce of the lands .... The persons in whom the offices...are vested hold them hereditarily.[3]

He then suggested that the mufassil offices might be abolished, but that those at Murshidabad should be retained, so that their holders might 'attend in the Presence, and that the names of these offices which are of ancient institution may not be entirely extinguished'.[4] The Council agreed with the Khan's recommendations and the three officers at Murshidabad were allowed to continue on fixed monthly allowances.[5]

[1] *MP*, 2 July 1771. [2] *Ibid.*
[3] Reza Khan's note. *MP*, 2 July 1771. [4] *Ibid.*
[5] The three officers confirmed were Subhan Ali Khan (Sawaninigar), Ainuddin Ali Khan (Waqainigar) and Akram Ali Khan (Akhbarnavis) on salaries of Rs. 200 ,Rs. 100, and Rs. 50 per mensem respectively (*MP*, 2 July 1771).

The transition in Bengal, 1756–1775

Reza Khan can also be observed busily defending the interests of the old community of bankers against the reforming hand of the Company, in an old controversy over coinage which dragged on with greater intensity from 1768 until the end of 1771. Rupees coined in the Mughal mints bore the regnal year of the Emperor in which they were struck. The *Sicca* rupees with the issue of new coins of the following year became known as Sanats and with the elapse of each successive year they declined in value. Bankers accepting Sanats in payment therefore charged a batta or discount upon them. On 11 November 1768 the Court of Directors had given positive orders to abolish the batta system, commenting,

the only objection that occurs to us...is how to get the better of the combination that will certainly be among the bankers, but we suppose if the ministry will zealously adopt it an absolute government can never be defeated in a measure so calculated for the public good and as you have by perseverence broken the combination there was against the currency of the Calcutta Siccas, so we presume you must finally in this in which no doubt but you will be supported by all the foreign nations. The abolition of the batta on Sonnauts must therefore be carried into execution.

Despite these positive orders, Verelst's government was induced to support the native bankers and leave the system unchanged.[1] Apart from other reasons, the payment of batta could not be entirely abolished so long as many types of rupee circulated in Bengal—Arcot, Viziery, Benares, Naraini as well as Dacca, Murshidabad, Patna and Calcutta Siccas—whose use entailed money-changers' operation.[2] But Cartier's government decided at least to prevent the charging of batta upon Sanat rupees (that is old Siccas of Bengal and Bihar mints). In 1770 they suggested that Sanats and Siccas should be accepted at the same rate in payment of revenue. Reza Khan further advised that to obliterate the dis-

---

[1] Reza Khan was primarily responsible for the decision of Verelst's government in 1769. Besides supporting the case of the native bankers in his joint letter with Becher dated 30 June 1769 (BSC, 8 July 1769) Verelst said on 11 Aug. (*see* BSC, 11 Aug. 1769) that 'when Mahomed Reza Cawn was in Calcutta [in March] and during my stay at the city he represented that the numbers of shroffs and merchants—a set of men who were wont to serve the government on emergency have been reduced to beggary or forced to relinquish their business since the revenues have been received according to the specie in which they are collected'. A large number of bankers had already left Bengal (also Reza Khan's note, BPC, 28 March 1769).

[2] For specific uses of these coins, BPC, 12 April 1770. See also p. 175 n.

The rearguard action, 1770–1772

tinction, all rupees coined in future at the Murshidabad, Patna, Dacca and Calcutta mints should be of one weight and fineness and dated 11 Sun, that is the eleventh regnal year of the emperor.[1] But when the Calcutta Council agreed to this, the Khan had second thoughts. The change he saw would injure the shroffs and bankers, the only wealthy native class remaining in the country— 'if the Siccas of the former years pass for the same value as new Siccas from where is the advantage of the shroffs and merchants to arise...?'. The shroffs, he added 'seek up Sunnauts at different places to carry to the mint in order to have such as are short weight recoined...[and] pay a duty to government....'[2] As the Council was currently employing Reza Khan's influence with the shroffs to secure urgent remittances of money to Bombay and Surat by Hundi or banker's draft,[3] they abandoned the proposed change to conciliate the native bankers.

In September 1770 Reza Khan proceeded to strike Siccas of 12 Sun at the Murshidabad mint and sent the usual Nazarana with specimens of the new Sicca to His Majesty Shah Alam and to Cartier. There was no response from Cartier, so in May 1771 Reza Khan wrote privately to Cartier,[4] and by way of the Murshidabad Council, pointing out that it was getting late for the new coins to be circulated.[5] The Council replied by reviving the reform proposals of 1770 and, calling the Khan's attention to his plan for perpetual circulation of 11 Sun rupees, asked why he had struck 12 Sun coins.[6] The Khan, in evident difficulty, could only say that he had deduced from the Council's long silence that reform had been abandoned: without positive orders he could not make such a break with custom. He pointed out, however, that with the mint idle revenue was being lost and a quick decision was needed. 'Besides it is necessary if they establish the 11 Sun Siccas forever', the Khan added, 'that they give intelligence thereof to His Majesty ...If now the new Siccas be struck, a Nazzer be sent to the Presence, and they afterwards not be circulated, it will be an impropriety towards the King and a slight to the Throne.'[7] The Murshidabad Council supported the Khan and provided the additional argument that unless the regulation could be enforced

---

[1] BPC, 12 April 1770.   [2] BPC, 8 May 1770.
[3] See Reza Khan's note, *MP*, 23 Dec. 1771.
[4] Reza Khan to Cartier, recd. 20 May 1771. *CPC*, III, 753.
[5] *MP*, 16 May 1771.
[6] Fort William letter, 23 May. *MP*, 30 May 1771.   [7] *MP*, 24 June 1771.

281

in adjoining kingdoms Calcutta's ends would never be achieved. They also agreed with the Khan that there would be a flight of bullion to Allahabad, Benares and other mints where Siccas enjoyed a premium, thus decreasing bullion supplies and mint revenues and throwing on the Company the expense of recoining the old Sanats remaining in Bengal.[1]

The Fort William government decided that 'the annual coinage of Siccas shall hereafter continue to be marked as usual with the current year of the King's reign' and also that all coins beginning from 11 Sun coins 'shall not fall in their value' nor pass into 'the state of Sonauts'.[2] On 2 September 1771 Reza Khan therefore proceeded to issue coins for the 13th Julus or regnal year,[3] his last issue as Naib Nazim and Naib Diwan. He had contrived to assist the old Indian bankers to survive against the determined hostility of the Directors, and to maintain in Bengal the continuity of Mughal mint traditions, though very much in a mutilated form.[4]

In the great issue vexing the Calcutta authorities, that of English private trade, Reza Khan took no part. He had spoken out in December 1770 against monopolies in the rice trade, representing to the Murshidabad Council that 'notwithstan[ding] this is the time of harvest, the price of rice instead of falling rises daily in and about the city, he there[fore] requests [that] orders may be sent to the different Supravisors, to enforce an entire freedom of purchase and sale of this article in the districts, to take every measure in their power to prevent monopolies and to remove every obstacle to the transportation of grain from place to place'.[5] He did not name the culprits, for he was too cautious—more cautious than before—to press complaints against the servants of the Company. That he left to the Calcutta Council, whose members, confined to Calcutta by the Directors' orders of 23 March 1770, found themselves at a disadvantage in their pursuit of private trade. The Company had granted them freedom of private trade so long as this did not conflict with the Company's own interest,[6] but as Middleton, Aldersey, Floyer and Reed jointly complained, 'it is

[1] *MP*, 24 June 1771.   [2] *MP*, 20 Aug. 1771.
[3] Reza Khan to Cartier, recd. 9 Sept. 1771. *CPC*, III, 901.
[4] Not until 1773, when Hastings started his new banking scheme, was there any further attempt to dislodge the old banker class from their control of the internal money-market.
[5] *MP*, 6 Dec. 1770. Becher was still at Murshidabad.
[6] Court's letter of 23 March 1770 and Fort William letter of 14 March 1771 (see *MP*, 21 March 1771).

evident, that the share which the members of the Council are to enjoy in such trade, is subject, as the matter now stands, to the determination of the gentlemen employed in the different parts where it is carried on, who it is natural to conclude will give preference to their own interests'.[1] Cartier, Jekyll, Lane and Dacres complained of 'a secret influence which operates in every district of the country'.[2] The gumashtahs of the Council members were helpless, for no one would dare accept their advances 'without an order for so doing from the Resident of the district'.[3] The private trade interests of the junior servants which Reza Khan, Becher and Verelst had fought in 1769 with temporary success, had now triumphed.

The renewed power of the supervisors in the districts also caused another round of conflict with the Company's servants in the commercial branch, and with their gumashtahs and agents. The opposition to the latter, which had been headed by Reza Khan and Becher in 1769, was now led by the supervisors. The supervisor of Jessore, Rooke, informed the Murshidabad Council that he daily received complaints of 'every specie of oppression towards the inhabitants' committed by the Company's gumashtahs despite his repeated orders to them 'to desist from the unwarrantable proceedings they have too long practised...'.[4] Hardwood in Rajmahal complained that the gumashtahs used Company sepoys to oppress the ryots.[5] The supervisor of Dacca had to use force to prevent the gross frauds on the revenues by misuse of Company dastaks (passes) in the tobacco trade.[6] The commercials countered with complaints against the supervisors and their agents. The gumashtahs of Jangipur thus complained against Hardwood,[7] the Kasimbazar factory renewed Aldersey's demand for a share in the authority of the government, while the commercial Resident at Malda declared that the Directors' demands for an increased and improved investment could not be met unless 'the share of credit and authority necessary for the well conducting the investments entrusted to

---

[1] BPC, 27 Dec. 1771. These four had even formed a joint stock venture to trade in salt, betelnut and tobacco. Kelsall disapproved the idea, while Russell and Hare joined for a time.
[2] BPC, 27 Dec. 1771.   [3] *Ibid.*
[4] Rooke's letter, 9 May. *MP*, 20 May 1771.
[5] Hardwood's letter, 21 April. *MP*, 25 April 1771.
[6] *MP*, 18 Nov. 1771.
[7] Kasimbazar letter, 23 April. *MP*, 25 April 1771.

their management' were restored to the gumashtahs.[1] The clear orders of the Directors, issued in March 1770, that the Investment must be sustained, since it was the only means of transferring funds from Bengal to England to answer the demands on them, led the Council at Fort William to consider granting more authority to the commercial branch. Before acting, however, they decided to ask Reza Khan and the Murshidabad Council.[2] The Khan thus found himself involved once more in the clash of interests between the various branches of the Company's service. He refused to comment on Kasimbazar's demand for a share in the governmental authority, but he made it clear that he believed that any deficiency in the silk Investment could only be met by restoration of absolute freedom of trade. It was the oppressions of the Pycars and Dalals in their purchases,[3] coupled with the famine mortality which had caused a decline.[4] If the government placed its authority behind the gumashtahs, the artisans would 'be disprited and abandon that branch of culture', even if higher prices were offered. Similarly he opposed Calcutta's suggestion that mulberry cultivators and silkworm rearers might be induced to 'pay such a proportion of their rents in kind' as would provide for the Investment.[5] He commented, 'it does not occur to my weak judgement, that this measure would remove the obstacle in the purchase of silk, but that it would rather increase them', since the peasants, once they had to pay their rents in kind, would look upon that article as 'seized upon by government' and 'entirely fling up the business'. Freedom of trade, strict protection from arbitrary proceedings and oppressions by Pycars and Dalals, and positive encouragement for mulberry cultivators and silkworm rearers— grant these the Khan argued, and the 'produce of silk would be

[1] Kasimbazar letter, 23 April, and Bathoe's letter, 23 Feb. *MP*, 25 April, 7 March 1771. (Bathoe was commercial Resident at Malda, after the residency was re-opened under orders of the Court of Directors).

[2] Court's letter, 23 March 1770, and Fort William letter, 28 Oct. *MP*, 2 Nov. 1771.

[3] The Murshidabad Council maintained that the artisans and peasants had been reduced 'to a state [of] actual slavery', the process being that 'the original advances having been studiously made, so as to leave a ballance at the close of the year ... this ballance becomes immediately burthened with an exorbitant rate of interest, which continues to accumulate in such a proportion so as to leave the poor labourer totally incapable of ever satisfying [his] merciless creditor'. Any attempt to 'break the chain' ends in 'immediate beggary and total ruin' (*MP*, 11 Nov. 1771).

[4] *MP*, 11 Nov. 1771.   [5] *Ibid.*

increased and become plentiful and cheap'. He ended, however, on a note of resignation: 'As to the rest, you gentlemen are [the] judges, and may do what is best.'[1] The Khan was putting up a lone fight for almost a lost cause, for monopoly continued. The dispute was over who should have the monopoly, the commercial or the revenue branch. The Khan could have felt some technical satisfaction when the Fort William Council, acting on the latest orders from London, had on 18 December 1771 resolved to re-introduce the Dadni system.[2]

But already by March 1771 the Khan had quickly reacted to the new threats to peace and prosperity, as he saw them in Murshida-bad Council's proposal for its members to go on circuit to settle the revenues of 1178 or 1771–2.[3] The Khan opposed the proposal, as advisor to the Council; his advice fell on deaf ears. As the Khan may have anticipated, Lawrell's circuit of the districts of Dinajpur and Rangpur, which was not free from subsequent allegations of making of private profits by him,[4] resulted in further 'dismission of Chowdries and inferior collectors'[5] and their replacement by an additional set of Calcutta based farmers and revenue agents. The Khan was emphatic that the promotion of agriculture and popula-tion and increase of Company's revenues and reputation could not be possible 'till the affairs of the country were committed to the natives...' for they alone, and not outsiders, had 'a thousand ways of intercourse one with another'.[6]

By October 1771 Reza Khan was faced with yet another on-slaught on the old Mughal order. This was Cartier's request to the Nawab Mubarak-ud-daulah and Reza Khan to disband the Nawab's troops—described as disorderly rabble—and to replace them with four battalions of English troops, to be paid for from the Nizamat allowance of sixteen lakhs of rupees.[7] As guardian of the minor Nawab the difficult task of resisting the English demand fell upon Reza Khan. The Nawab's reply,[8] doubtless drafted by Reza

---

[1] *Ibid.*   [2] BPC, 18 Dec. 1771.
[3] *MP*, 11 March 1771. By then banditry had grown into a serious problem, even peaceful rural people being driven to it 'to procure themselves a sub-sistence' (Rous's letter, *MP*, 15 April 1771), and certainly joined in by dis-banded soldiers, and others.   [4] *MP*, 23 March 1772.
[5] *MP*, 16 Sept. 1771.   [6] *MP*, 11 March 1771.
[7] Reza Khan's acknowledgement was received by Cartier on 29 Oct. 1771. H.M.S., 203; 137 (also *CPC*, III, 972). In this Reza Khan promised a reply.
[8] Mubarak-ud-daulah to Cartier, recd. 8 Nov. 1771. H.M.S., 203; 138–40; *CPC*, III, 975.

Khan, expressed appreciation of Cartier's concern for the 'increase of honor and dignity' of the Nawab, but denied that the Nizamat troops 'pay an improper attendance'. That allegation he was sure was based upon unfounded reports. The Nawab then reminded Cartier of the great reductions since Najm-ud-daulah's day in the nizamat allowances, from which 'the relations, domesticks and the chiefs of the city who have a right upon me...and are [so] to say inseparable from the nizamat, all receive their wages...'. He pointed out that except for certain matchlockmen employed on faujdari and cutcheri duties, the horse and foot of the Sawary were old servants 'fixed upon the door of the Mahal'. He pleaded that 'if my relations, connections, and principals of the city who after repeated curtailments have only their mere livelyhood...are to be turned from the service it will be considered as the greatest reflection [upon my honour and dignity]'. Stressing that the 'allowances cannot be further curtailed' the Nawab's letter rang with an emotional note: 'Whilst they receive not the means of livelyhood, without regarding my honor and dignity, even my own subsisting is not proper...' Moreover, though he was ready to maintain the proposed English force, he was at a loss to understand how he could pay them. He concluded with a reminder to the Company's treaty obligations: 'If therefore the Company's Seapoys are to be considered out of the 16 lacks of rupees there is not only an impediment in the honor and reputation which I receive from the gentlemen but even the greatest bad name and a weakness [sic] in former promises and engagements.'

Reza Khan also sent a letter of his own.[1] Giving a resumé of how, in the Company's interest, he had gradually reduced Nizamat expenses by some twenty lakhs of rupees, he repeated the facts in the Nawab's letter. He maintained that the governor's wishes could not be fulfilled unless all the men maintained by the nizamat were dismissed. This could not be done. These people were connections and relations of both the present and former Nawabs and so inseparable from the nizamat. To refuse to recognise their claims would be the greatest indignity for the Nazim and the nizamat. Among the servants of the household, the Khan maintained, he had left no superfluous persons for further retrenchment. Nor would it answer to dismiss the matchlockmen employed in the faujdaries and cutcherries and for night patrol and attendance upon

---

[1] Reza Khan to Cartier, recd. 8 Nov. 1771. *H.M.S.*, 203; 140–3; *CPC*, III, 976.

the Nazim. This would involve great loss of dignity to the nizamat while the savings which would accrue would not suffice to maintain even one Company battalion. It was not worth while, he declared, 'for such a trifle as this to make the noise of dismission of the servants of the Nizamut'.[1] It does not appear that Cartier pressed the matter any further.

On 6 December 1771, however, the Calcutta government received a letter from the Court of Directors, written on 10 April 1771, which increased the pressure on Cartier to seek some relief for the distressed state of the Company's finances. Among other reflections on Cartier, the Directors included an undeservedly harsh comment on the financial terms of the treaty made with Mubarak-ud-daulah at his accession. Cartier had obeyed earlier orders of the Directors by continuing to the Nawab the nizamat allowances paid to his predecessor Saif-ud-daulah. For this the Directors now attacked him:

When we advert to the encomiums you have passed on your abilities and prudence, and your attention to the Company's interest...we cannot but observe with astonishment that an event of so much importance as the death of the Nabob Syful- Dowla and the establishment of a successor in so great a degree of non-age should not have been attended with those advantages for the Company which such a circumstance offered to you in view.[2]

Their criticism was not of the recognition of a minor, but of Fort William's folly in continuing to him 'the stipend alloted to his adult predecessor'.[3]

Necessity knew no law, and in violation of the publicly pledged treaty with Mubarak-ud-daulah concluded in their name, the Directors now ordered Cartier to reduce the Nawab's allowance during his minority by nearly half, to sixteen lakhs of rupees. They added sententiously that they would consider 'every addition thereto as so much to be wasted on a herd of parasites and syco- phants who will continually surround him'.[4]

Though the Calcutta Council had asked Cartier to inform the Nawab of the reduction (on 9 December), he was in no hurry to do so, for his letter to Mubarak-ud-daulah was only despatched on 11

---

[1] Reza Khan to Cartier, recd. 8 Nov. 1771. *H.M.S.*, 203; 240–3.
[2] Court's letter, 10 April 1771.
[3] *Ibid.*   [4] Court's letter, 10 April 1771.

January 1772.[1] He could afford to take his time, for since 26 February 1770 his Council had directed the Resident to keep stipends as much in arrear as he could.[2] By 1772 the arrears to the emperor, the Nawab and Reza Khan amounted to £60,406, £125,085 and £26,373 respectively.[3] The Khan was doubly affected by this underhand manoeuvre for most of the arrears to the Nawab were in respect of the nizamat administration which was his responsibility. He found himself powerless, however, either to help the Nawab or himself. On 8 August 1771, despite his usual delicacy, he was compelled to complain to the Murshidabad Council:

The amount of my expences and the demands of my servants who receive from me monthly allowances are so obvious that it is unnecessary to enlarge on the subject. The stipend appointed me by the Company comprehends the whole of my income. This also is manifest to all the gentlemen. Was my stipulated allowance to be paid me regularly every month it would not suffice to discharge my expences. Nevertheless, there is a ballance due on account of last year and 4 months are now elapsed of the present, and how shall I describe to you my exegencies [sic] and urgent demands of my servants who compose a numerous body and are reduced to a state of distress.[4]

When this had no effect he made a further representation to Murshidabad Council explaining that had be been an isolated individual he would have somehow continued to support himself, but that his servants and other dependants were very numerous.[5]

The Khan's petition was sent to Calcutta, but the authorities there, by a letter dated 20 August, refused to pay the arrears as they felt it would distress the Company to pay so large a sum, and would open the door to other claims upon them.[6] The Khan received the disagreeable news with as much grace as was possible. 'If putting myself to an inconvenience by delaying the receipt of my allowance will prevent the embarrassment of the Company', the Khan observed, 'no doubt my satisfaction and interest consist in doing it.'[7] The Khan could secure justice neither for himself nor for the Nawab.

[1] BPC, 9 Dec. 1771 and *CPC*, III, 1016.
[2] BPC, 26 February 1770.
[3] *PP*, Fourth Report of the Committee of Secrecy, 1773, p. 102.
[4] *MP*, 8 Aug. 1771.   [5] *Ibid.*
[6] Fort William letter, 20 Aug. *MP*, 2 Sept. 1771.
[7] Reza Khan's note. *MP*, 5 Sept. 177.

The rearguard action, 1770–1772

Cartier had only postponed payment of Reza Khan's arrears of salary. The Directors, however, by April 1771 had decided that the continuance of his salary of nine lakhs was unnecessary. As early as 15 September 1769 in their instructions to the three Commissioners they had drawn attention to 'the immense salaries and allowances...paid to Mahomed Reza Cawn' and urged their reduction to 'moderate bounds'.[1] Now they ordered a general onslaught on the ministers' salaries, writing to Cartier that 'At a time when every justifiable measure should be adopted for availing the publick and the Company of all the advantages we had in prospect from our possession of the Dewanny—we cannot but reflect on the dissipation of a considerable part thereof by the allowances to the Nabob's ministers'.[2] Having thus declared their breach with Clive's policy of uniting the leading natives to the Company by ties of gratitude and interest, they ordered that the annual allowance to Jagat Seth as assistant to Reza Khan be stopped: they were well assured that he had never afforded them 'a single instance of service', and that his salary (of one lakh of rupees per year) was a drain on the revenues.[3] They agreed to continue Rai Durlabh's[4] salary (of two lakhs of rupees per year) in view of his age and past services, but ordered that on his death it should not be given to any other person whatever. Finally, they ordered Reza Khan's salary to be reduced to five lakhs, observing in an echo of the words used by Smith[5] in October 1769 that 'how great soever the application of Mahomet Reza Cawn and his adherence to the Company's interest, may have been, his rewards have been more than adequate thereto'.[6] The Directors had never reconciled themselves to the commitment forced on them by Clive. The introduction of the supervisorships had now given them an excuse for going back upon it. They explained to Calcutta that, the supervisors having mastered 'the business of the collections', there would be need of 'little or no assistance from the minister', and no reason, therefore, for continuing his then salary. That would be a waste of the resources essential for the security of the

[1] Sinha, *FWIHC*, v, 242.   [2] Court's letter, 10 April 1771.
[3] Perhaps they paid no salary but made annual repayments for government's debts agreed to by Clive. See p. 115.
[4] They were ignorant of Rai Durlabh's death in 1770.
[5] Smith's minute in the Secret Consultations of 26 October 1769 appears underlined in red in the India Office copy.
[6] Court's letter, 10 April 1771.

Company's possessions and the extension of the investment in Bengal. It was only because of the need to appoint someone of experience to be guardian to the young Nawab that they recommended the salary of five lakhs of rupees now granted to Reza Khan.[1] Cartier was in no hurry to communicate the Company's orders to the Khan. He wrote to the Khan on 11 January 1772,[2] the same day as he wrote to the Nawab about the reduction of the Nizamat allowances.

The delay was partly due to the upsetting news brought by the *Lord Holland* from England which reached Calcutta by 6 December 1771. It carried a copy of the Company's orders dated 10 April and their subsequent orders dated 25 April 1771.[3] The letter of 10 April notified the appointment of Warren Hastings, then second at Madras, to be second at Calcutta and that of 25 April notified the dismissal of Cartier and his Clivite colleagues. Hastings's appointment was due in part to the canvassing of his friends in England, men such as Sykes who soon became his attorney there,[4] in part to the general awareness of the fast deteriorating conditions in Bengal. The outgoing Court of Directors of 1770–1 in their final General letter to Bengal, dated 10 April 1771, intimated their appointment of Hastings 'Second of Council at Fort William and to succeed Mr. Cartier, as President and Governor of Bengal and we have accordingly directed Mr. Hastings to proceed to Fort William as expediously as possible'. There was no word of dismissal of Cartier though his actions and policy had been commented upon very unfavourably.

On 10 April 1771 again a new Court of Directors was elected which included Laurence Sulivan, Clive's bitterest enemy and Robert Gregory, Nandkumar's attorney in England. On 17 April the various committees were formed, including the Committee of Secrecy. On 25 April the new Direction, dominated by Sulivan even though he had not secured the chair, struck down their opponents. Orders were sent that 'Mr. Cartier do resign the

---

[1] Court's letter, 10 April 1771.
[2] Cartier to Reza Khan, 11 Jan. 1772. *CPC*, III, 1015.
[3] The *Lord Holland* sailing from England on 14 May reached Calcutta apparently earlier than the ship *Colebrooke* which had sailed on 30 April 1771. Even before the official intimations had reached, rumours of changes in England were known in Calcutta (BPC, 2 Dec. and 6 Dec. 1771).
[4] Hastings to Sykes, 2 Feb. 1771. Add. MSS. 29126, f. 55, Add. MSS. 29134, ff. 228, 234.

government to Mr. Hastings', 'Mr. Becher be dismissed from our Council in Bengal' and that 'Mr. Claude Russell and Mr. Charles Floyer be immediately removed from our service in Bengal and that they return to Madras with all convenient dispatch'.[1] The justification of the move was the alarming disunion among the Company's servants in Bengal, for which Cartier, Becher, Russell and Floyer were held guilty, and the attempt by the Select Committee to prevent the positive orders sent out by the *Lapwing*[2] from being put into execution.

In their rush to oust the known Clivites in the Calcutta Council the new Directors apparently forgot that their orders about Becher were pointless, since he was already on the way home. They showed themselves blind to administrative needs by originally ordering that Cartier be sent home by the first ship of the season, though on second thoughts they did extend the period of his handover to Hastings by allowing him to sail on the last ship of the season. In dismissing Floyer they took no note of the fact that except for one occasion when he supported the Select Committee's claim to authority in revenue matters, he had uniformly supported the junior members of Council in denouncing Reza Khan and in upholding the cause of supervisors. Finally, they took no note of the Select Committee's reasons for opposing the Council in June 1770, of the fact that the junior members of the Council had been as remiss as the senior in not putting their orders by the *Lapwing* into immediate execution, and that in any case those orders were for the Commissioners whose appointment they had reported less than a week before the *Lapwing* sailed.[3] The truth was that their arguments had but one end in view, to provide the occasion for clearing of the Clivites out of the Bengal government.

The Directors having swept Cartier, Becher, Russell and Floyer away, sought to reward those who had rebelled against the old guard by nominating them to the Calcutta Council, whose

[1] Court's letter, 25 April 1771.
[2] The letter of 30 June 1769 was despatched by the Directors by the *Lapwing*. The first draft of the letter was addressed correctly to the Select Committee, but on second thoughts the Directors had addressed the Council. Nowhere in the letter did they say anything about the change in the powers of the Committee or of the Council.
[3] The appointment of the Commissioners was announced in the Court's letter of 30 June 1769 and the *Lapwing* carried the letter, sailing from Falmouth on 5 July 1769.

19-2

number went up from nine to fourteen again.[1] Moreover, by assigning a specific place to each, they rendered impossible any such exclusion as Cartier had practised when the Court's letter of 23 March 1770 arrived. To the heroes of the fight against Cartier they added only two names, those of Dacres and Rumbold, fifth and twelfth, with Lane thirteenth and Barwell 'fourteenth and last of Council'.

Reza Khan could not but be alarmed at the news of the revolution in Calcutta. His main support, the Clivites, were under orders of dismissal. In addition, the various measures ordered by the Directors in their letter of 10 April 1771, which arrived by the same ship that carried the orders about Cartier and other Clivites, were all ominous for Reza Khan, since they constituted a direct attack upon the whole scheme of government provided by Clive. But for the Khan personally even more ominous was their revival of old doubts about his handling of Dacca revenues and the voicing of new ones about his management of nizamat expenditure. Paragraphs 66 and 67 in the Company's letter implied that the Directors had information suggesting that there was something wrong with the post-1765 Murshidabad accounts, as also with the Dacca revenue accounts prior to Reza Khan's transfer to Murshidabad as Naib. The Directors having mentioned a sum of forty lakhs on the Dacca account observed, 'Although it cannot be supposed that the materials from whence the... statement is collected are so explicit, or that they are an authority sufficient to warrant a positive determination of any specifick sum being due from Mahomed Reza Cawn to the Circar they are nevertheless an undoubted proof that he has not fully accounted for the very considerable sums above mentioned'.[2] An accompanying letter from the Company's secretary related to the checking of accounts of the receipts and disbursements of the nizamat which suggests that in this field too, the Company now entertained doubts about Reza Khan's integrity.[3] The Directors did not disclose the sources upon which they based their accusations against the Khan. It was

[1] Court's letter, 25 April 1771. Before, however, this letter arrived on 6 Dec. 1771, Lane and Barwell had been called to the Council (on 2 Dec.) vice Russell and Kelsall, who had left for home in November (BPC, 2 Dec. 1771).
[2] Court's letter, 10 April 1771.
[3] Two letters from the Company's secretary dated 8 May 1771 were received on 6 December and acted upon (BPC, 6 and 9 Dec. 1771. *MP*, 30 Dec. 1771; 23 Jan. 1772).

probably soon an open secret, however, that Nandkumar was their origin. Having repeatedly failed to dislodge the Khan, he had now successfully played upon the Company's hope of relief to their finances. The Company had already ignored their treaty obligations to the Nawab and his ministers; they were now to be persuaded that further relief could be secured by outright overthrow of Reza Khan.

The Company's orders regarding investigation into the nizamat accounts did not come up before the Murshidabad Council before 30 December 1771 but already the changes in Calcutta government and the news of the appointment of Warren Hastings must have made Reza Khan very much uncertain. It was certainly much more embarrassing for Reza Khan than the coming of Middleton and Barwell as chief and Second of the Murshidabad Council in January 1771. It was the Khan's statement in 1765 which was used by Clive to secure Middleton's dismissal from Company's service and again it was his recorded statements which helped the Calcutta government in preventing Barwell's posting to Dacca in 1767. When Middleton was posted as chief of the Murshidabad Council, the Khan was assured by Cartier that 'the gentleman has forgotten and effaced from his mind the feeling of irritation that formerly existed between him and the addressee' Reza Khan.[1] Cartier's assurance ultimately proved true,[2] but the Khan had reasons to be uncertain of Hastings's attitude towards him. Ever since Hastings's return to India with a posting to Fort St George, Reza Khan had sought to establish friendly contacts with him. One such attempt, it seems, was made before 11 April 1770 and another a little later when some presents also were sent to Madras.[3] On both occasions Hastings had replied, but had taken care that his letters were seen on their way by Cartier. Such overcautiousness must have been noted by the Khan, perhaps as a veiled rebuff. He may well have recalled Hastings's friendliness to Mir Qasim, the Khan's bitterest enemy, and the fact that it was while Hastings was with Mir

[1] Cartier to Reza Khan, 16 Jan. 1771. *CPC*, III, 557.
[2] Middleton during his visit to Dacca recommended confirmation of Himmat Singh as Diwan for the Huzury Mahal (estates which formerly and until Mir Qasim's day paid directly at Murshidabad) and maintenance of separate identity of the Nizamat Mahal as a concession to Jasarat Khan and to 'the small remains of his authority and consequence'. (*MP*, 25 April, 14 May 1771). Both Himmat Singh and Jasarat Khan were Reza Khan's men.
[3] Hastings to Hancock, 11 April 1770. Add. MSS. 29125, f. 32, also ff. 71–2. T. S. Hancock acted as Hastings's private trade agent in Bengal.

The transition in Bengal, 1756–1775

Qasim that his application for the Faujdari of Hugli had been rejected, despite Vansittart supporting him. When Hastings reached Calcutta on 17 February 1772, Reza Khan sought to establish friendly relations with him and sent Ali Ibrahim Khan, an old favourite of Mir Qasim and a friend of Hastings in the old days, to Calcutta to prepare the grounds. When Hastings assumed his new office as governor, the Khan was anxious to meet him. But his request for an interview was politely turned down, saying that meeting the Khan's envoy Ali Ibrahim, 'whose excellent qualities have long been known' to him was 'really like having half an interview with the Nawab himself'.[1] The coolness of Hastings together with his disagreement with the Khan's assertion of Mughal sovereignty and supremacy of Muslim law, on the very first day of Hastings's governorship,[2] were indications enough of the shape of things to come. The augury was not good.

Within a fortnight of Hastings's assumption of office as governor Reza Khan had been placed under arrest and was on his way from Murshidabad to Calcutta as a prisoner.

In the evening of 23 April 1772 the ship *Lapwing* reached Calcutta with a letter from the Committee of Secrecy addressed to Hastings personally. On 24 April Hastings wrote to Middleton, chief of the Murshidabad Council, that he had the previous evening received a letter from the Secret Committee of the Court of Directors in which they 'direct and enjoin me immediately... to issue my private orders for securing the person of Mahomed Reza Cawn, and to bring him to Calcutta'.[3] He could have asked the commanding officer of Berhampur brigade to carry out these orders, but fearing this would be 'productive of much disturbances', he entrusted the task to Middleton. He was told that the orders were peremptory and required immediate compliance and all secrecy. The only delay allowed was such time as the Khan might require for 'furnishing himself with such conveniences as he may want on his way'. The Khan was to be treated with 'every mark of tenderness and respect' consistent with the execution of the order. Hastings suggested, however, that it would be best for Middleton to avoid any personal meeting with the Khan, though this was left to his discretion. After Reza Khan and Amrit Singh

[1] Warren Hastings to Reza Khan, 17 April 1772. *CPC*, IV, 2.
[2] Fort William letter, 13 April 1772. *MP*, 20 April 1772.
[3] Hastings to S. Middleton, 24 April. Secret Cons., 28 April 1772.

294

had been despatched to Calcutta, guards should be placed on Reza Khan's house so that nothing might be removed until further instructions from Calcutta.[1] No explanation of the reason for this arrest of the Khan were given.

Middleton received these orders on 26 April. Quite early in the morning of 27 April, eight companies of sepoys from the Berhampur brigade took control of Murshidabad city to prevent 'any evil consequences'.[2] Then while Anderson, an assistant of the Murshidabad Council, went to Reza Khan's palace to communicate the disagreeable orders received from Hastings, Middleton himself, with a part of the Berhampur force and some companies of Pargana sepoys, hastened 'to the Killah with a view to explain the matter to the young Nabob and to obviate any consternation or surprise which might have seized him from an event thus sudden and unexpected, and at the same time to prevent any irregularities which at this critical juncture the Nizamut sepoys or the Nabob's own servants might have been tempted to commit'.[3]

The precautions proved unnecessary. Reza Khan showed no wish to oppose or impede the execution of the order, but as Middleton reported, 'made a voluntary resignation of himself and effects to the officer who was deputed to take him into custody'. Middleton added,

I should not do justice to the calm submission with which he [Reza Khan] met his unhappy fate was I not to notice the readiness he manifested to comply with your orders in the fullest extent and so far from wishing to protract the period of his departure from hence, I can venture to assure you, you cannot be more anxious for his arrival in Calcutta than he appears to be.[4]

The Khan's palaces, Nishat Bagh and Nau-Sakht were quietly taken over and his force of 100 horse and 530 sepoys was replaced by the Company's troops. Before day broke on 28 April Reza Khan who, in Hastings's language, 'was in every thing but the name the Nazim of the provinces and in real authority more than the Nazim',[5] was on his way down the river Hugli as a prisoner, escorted by two companies of English troops, under the command of Lieutenant Lucas.[6] Accompanying him, also as prisoner, was his

---

[1] Hastings to Middleton, 24 April 1772. Secret Cons., 28 April 1772.
[2] Middleton's letter to Hastings. Secret Cons., 28 April 1772.
[3] *Ibid.*   [4] *Ibid.*
[5] Hastings to Secret Committee, 1 Sept. 1772. Add. MSS. 29125, f. 134.
[6] Letter to Fort William. *MP*, 28 April 1772.

The transition in Bengal, 1756–1775

Diwan, Maharaja Amrit Singh and their dependants; the party required a convoy of three budgerows and fifteen baggage boats, besides boats for the service of the escorting troops.[1] Thus was completed the fourth and last of the 'revolutions' to have occurred within fifteen years in the city of Murshidabad, and the least violent of them all.

If there was no violence, there was a demonstration of a new and impressive kind. Ghulam Husain, that critic of the Khan, had to note that 'a vast concourse of people' followed the Khan in their own fashion down to Plassey and some even to Calcutta.[2] This silent demonstration was not lost upon Hastings either. Four months after the Khan's arrest he reported to the Committee of Secrecy that 'Mahmud R. Cawn's influence still prevailed generally throughout the country. In the Nabob's household and at the capital it was scarce affected by his present disgrace. His favour was still courted and his anger dreaded'.[3] Still later he wrote to Dupre that he was informed that it had at one time been resolved in the Nawab's private circle that the Nawab 'should solemnly protest against them, claim the administration of his own affairs, or declare his resolution to abdicate and retire to Calcutta'.[4] Even Munni Begum, 'who had her mind so obscured by the dust of boldness and discontent as to wish for Mahmed-rezaqhan's disgrace' also forgot her enmity.[5] The Khan's personal tragedy had evidently been taken by the principal persons in Murshidabad as their common calamity.

This identification was to cause further personal miseries to Reza Khan, for not only the Company's interest required 'extirpation'[6] of the Khan's influence, but execution of Hastings's projects also required the destruction of his public image. The consequence, naturally, was the commencement of what Barwell later described as 'our inquisition business'.[7]

[1] Letter to Fort William, *MP*, 28 April 1772.   [2] *Seir*, III, 39–42.
[3] Hastings to Committee of Secrecy, 1 Sept. 1772. Add. MSS. 29125, f. 136.
[4] Hastings to DuPre, governor of Madras, 8 Oct. 1772. Add. MSS. 29125, f. 156.
[5] *Seir*, III, 40.
[6] Committee of Secrecy to Hastings, 16 April 1773. Add. MSS. 29133, p. 518.
[7] Barwell to Becher, 30 Nov. 1774. *BPP*, XII, 90.

CHAPTER II

'THE INQUISITION',
1772-1775

On 27 April 1772, Reza Khan was arrested and Murshidabad went through a revolution. But it seemed nobody exactly knew why it was necessary and who had it set in motion. The Nawab was possibly the first to ask the question. In a letter to Hastings he asked to know what grave offences the Khan had committed and to stress that Reza Khan had both served him faithfully and had the Company's interest at heart.[1]
It was not surprising that the Nawab should ask why Reza Khan had been arrested, for the whole affair had been shrouded in secrecy. Middleton knew nothing beyond what Hastings had said in his letter of 24 April, and to the Khan himself Hastings had written only to say that he was sorry that in view of the latest orders of the Directors he could not continue the cordial relations which his predecessors had maintained with him.[2] The Khan was also asked to refer to Middleton for further details[3] while Middleton was asked to avoid personal meeting with the Khan.[4] Reza Khan then wrote to Hastings through Ali Ibrahim Khan asking for a translation of the Company's orders, but Hastings in his replies of 13 May did no more than assure the Khan and the Nawab that the particulars would be sent soon.[5] Even the Calcutta Council were left in ignorance until 28 April, when they were told that the Khan was under arrest and on his way to Calcutta. He explained that he had been given sufficient authority to act alone,

---

[1] See Hastings's acknowledgement of the Nawab's letter. *CPC*, IV, 25.
[2] Hastings to Reza Khan, 30 April 1772. *CPC*, IV, 13. (This letter is dated three days after the Khan's arrest and removal from Murshidabad.)
[3] *Ibid.*
[4] Hastings to Middleton, 24 April. Secret Cons., 28 April 1772.
[5] The Khan had first been told of the Company's intentions verbally through Graham who was deputed by the Council to receive the Khan on his arrival in Calcutta. The Khan had first asked for the charges against him, by a letter through Graham and was told in reply that the particulars would be sent soon. Failing to get the particulars the Khan again asked for the charges through Ali Ibrahim Khan, and received the same reply (see Hastings's letters to Reza Khan, 5 May, 6 May and 13 May 1772. *CPC*, IV, 18, 20, 26.)

and had done so 'to avoid the risk of an opposition to put the matter beyond dispute'.[1] He had obviously feared opposition to the Company's orders, for he commented 'I could not suppose him [Reza Khan] so inattentive to his security, nor ill versed in the maxims of eastern policy as to have neglected the due means of establishing an interest with such of the Company's agents as by actual authority or by representation to the Hon'ble Company might be able to promote or obstruct his views'.[2] Even when Hastings reported his actions to the Council he did not explain the purpose behind the arrest, quoting only so much of the letter from the Committee of Secrecy as established his right to arrest the Khan.[3]

It would also appear that the orders of the Committee of Secrecy had been concealed from the Court of Directors in London. Sykes for example, despite his close contacts with Verelst, elected a director in 1771, knew nothing of them. It is true that the Directors' general letter required, in paragraph 22, a strict enquiry into the allegations against the Khan, and ended, 'we have directed our President to order him to repair to Calcutta, there to answer to the facts which shall be alleged against him'.[4] But the allegations, most of them, were not new—they had been voiced in the letter of 10 April 1771—and the summons to Calcutta was merely a repetition of that of 1765 when the Khan was called to explain his expenditure from the Nawab's treasury before the Select Committee. It seems very probable that the nature of the revolution intended by the Committee of Secrecy was unknown to the Court of Directors as a whole.

The Committee of Secrecy's orders for Reza Khan's arrest were not the only secret instructions from the Directorate meant for Warren Hastings alone. The Company's secret letter of 18 December 1771 to Hastings was to 'be delivered to him only and in case of the decease [of] the same to be returned' unopened, to the Directors.[5] But the letter of 18 December had been signed by the Directors as a body, just as was a later letter of 16 April 1773

---

[1] Hastings to Committee of Secrecy, 1 Sept. 1772. Add. MSS. 29125, f. 134.
[2] *Ibid.*
[3] Hastings quoted paragraph 2 of the secret letter (see Secret Cons., 28 April 1772). Significantly there is no copy of this secret letter bound up in the regular volume of the official despatches to Bengal.
[4] See Court's general letter of the same date, 28 Aug. 1771.
[5] This direction was given in the general letter of 18 Dec. 1771.

to which the Directors added that 'notwithstanding this letter is
signed by us, the Court of Directors we mean it as secret, and
transmit it confidentially to you [Hastings] only; and we leave to
your discretion to lay the contents or any part thereof before the
Council, if circumstances should in your opinion render it necessary or if you should judge it for our interest so to do and not
otherwise'.[1] The orders for the arrest of Reza Khan were therefore
quite exceptional in that they had been signed by the Committee
of Secrecy alone. The propriety of their action is doubtful. The
function of the Committee of Secrecy, as set out after almost every
election of Directors, was 'to take such precautions as they shall
judge necessary for the safety of the Company's outward and
homeward bound shipping'.[2] Their orders 'for this purpose'
were binding, provided they were signed by at least three members.
But the order to arrest Reza Khan was not a shipping matter, and
it is probable that the order was itself illegal and that Hastings in
carrying it out incurred a personal liability for the damage done
to the Khan. Sykes told Hastings on 16 December 1775 that the
Company's counsel told him that 'you are responsible in your own
fortune for the injury done M R C by obeying, an order from the
Select Committee consisting of five[3] when the Company's bylaws
expressly say that no governor is to obey any order but from a
majority of the Court of Directors'.[4]

Why was this probably illegal method adopted? It would seem
that those who took it believed that they might not carry a majority
if they put it before the full Court, but that the deed once done
they might secure retrospective approval—as indeed they did. As
Dr Lucy Sutherland has shown, the 1771 election was in effect a
truce between the Clive group and Sulivan, backed by Lord
North's ministry, and the whole issue of Reza Khan's position
may have been thought too closely tied to the old quarrels to be
safely aired. If this be the case, it must still be asked who had
initiated the move against the Khan. Sulivan would seem the most
obvious candidate for the role. He had been the arch enemy of
Clive in past years, and he was certainly a vigorous exponent of the
policy of raising Nandkumar's consequence at the expense of

[1] Court's letter, 16 April 1773.
[2] For example, Court's letter, 26 April 1765.
[3] The Committee of Secrecy, again, had eight members, not five.
[4] Sykes to Hastings, 16 Dec. 1775. Add. MSS. 29136, f. 431.

The transition in Bengal, 1756–1775

Reza Khan's. In 1772–3 when he shared the chair with Sir George Colebrooke he strongly supported that policy as he explained in a letter to Hastings on 16 April 1773 after he and Colebrooke lost their position:

Upon mature considerations it has been thought right to detain these ships to give a short letter approving your measures for an entire silence added to the late revolution [in the Direction] depriving you of Colebrooke and me, it was thought might allarm you. I told the Director who asked my opinion, that I considered the appointment of Nuncomar's son as a great political manoeuvre and in the present hour perfectly right to raise Nuncomar's consequences at the expence of Mamud Reza Caun, nor is the Direction so much altered as to check your persevering boldly. I think you have powers sufficient to lay the axe to the root. I wish you would not stop, for perhaps no extraordinary commission will go from hence; if there should, the measure is at a distance. Mamud Reza Caun amuses himself in vain when he thinks there will be a change in his favour. Those times are forever at an end.[1]

But if Sulivan heartily approved of the downfall of Reza Khan, and he was a member of the Committee of Secrecy which ordered it on 28 August 1771,[2] he nevertheless disclaimed leadership in the move. Sulivan was later to say to Hastings, on reading a letter to him from Reza Khan, that it was clear that the Khan had 'been taught to consider me as the leader in this prosecution, when the chap who set the wheel in motion hugs himself in the deceit'.[3] And in the same letter he says, 'As the materials against this man [Reza Khan] were handed to us by a snake, who was one of our body, I knew what use would have been made of a refusal'.[4]

Who then was 'the chap who set the wheel in motion', and who was a member of the Direction at this time? Almost certainly Robert Gregory,[5] one would think, possibly abetted from outside the Court by Carnac. These two had been insistent with Clive in 1765 that Nandkumar be reinstated in the Murshidabad government. They were the London correspondents of Nandkumar— Sykes reported to Hastings '... I dined yesterday with Gregory

[1] L. Sulivan to Hastings, 16 April 1773. Add. MSS. 29133, f. 515.
[2] Other members of the Committee then were Chairman John Purling, Deputy Chairman George Dudley, and Harrison, Manship, Pigou, Rous, Savage (see Court's Minute, 17 April 1771).
[3] Sulivan to Hastings, 20 Dec. 1774. Add. MSS. 19135, f. 407.   [4] *Ibid.*
[5] Gregory had been for twenty years a private trader in Bengal (see his evidence before a Parliamentary Committee, 1 April 1767. Add. MSS. 18469, f. 38).

when Carnac and others [were present] and find Nundcomar writes them everything which happens and something more, by every ship. This is a fact for I found they had everything from him.'[1] From Sulivan we also find that Gregory acted as Nandkumar's attorney in England.[2] It was Gregory again who presented to the Directors Huzurimul's accusation that Reza Khan had participated as a monopolist in the rice trade during the famine—and it does not seem at all impossible that Huzurimul's accusations were in fact furnished by Nandkumar.[3] When Hastings in Bengal asked Huzurimul for information about Reza Khan's monopolising grain, he declared he could give none.[4] In just the same way Hastings received a letter supposedly from Munni Begum, before he left Madras, denouncing the tyranny of Reza Khan and referring Hastings for further information to Maharaja Nandkumar—and when in Bengal she was asked for details the Begum 'solemnly disowned her having ever written such letters, or authorised such a commission'.[5]

It does not appear that Gregory had any reason to be vindictive against Reza Khan in particular. Rather he distrusted all Indians, and particularly those leading men 'who has ever had any office or connexion with political affairs'.[6] Gregory would therefore merely

[1] Sykes to Hastings, 6 Feb. 1774. Add. MSS. 29134, f. 298.
[2] Sulivan wrote to Hastings on 20 Dec. 1774 (see Add. MSS. 29135, f. 402) that 'Nuncomar by Mr. Gregory his attorney' sued Burdett (of Spencer's Council in Bengal in 1765) for a principal sum of £5,200 and obtained a decree for £11,200 including ten per cent interest.
[3] The Committee of Secrecy's letter of 28 Aug. 1771 to Hastings said that they received the 'information of Mohammed Reza Cawn's having increased the calamities of the poor, during the height of famine by a monopoly of rice and other necessaries of life' from Huzurimul's letter to Gregory. They had also sent an extract from that letter to Hastings (Francis MSS. I.O., Eur. E, 28, pp. 99–100).
  It may be noted that the Punjabi merchant Huzurimul, brother-in-law of Umichand of the 1757 conspiracy notoriety, was an influential merchant of Calcutta. Clive used to be his tenant in Calcutta from 1 Feb. 1757 to 31 Jan. 1760, the monthly rental of the house being Rs. 125 (BPC, 4 Feb. 1760). He was associated with Hastings's private trade as late as 1770 (*vide* Add. MSS. 29125, f. 356). During Nandkumar's administration of Nadia as the Company's Tahsildar, Umichand, and after Umichand's death in Nov. 1758, Huzurimul participated in it as security (BPC, 26 Oct., 13 Nov. 1758, 1 Sept. 1760).
[4] Hastings to Sulivan, 20 March 1774 (see G. R. Gleig, *Memoirs of the Right Hon. Warren Hastings*, I, 391).
[5] Hastings to Committee of Secrecy, 24 March 1774 (see M. E. Monckton-Jones, *Warren Hastings in Bengal, 1772–74*, 197).
[6] Hints from Mr Gregory to P. Francis (Francis MSS, I.O., Eur. E, 12, p. 169).

The transition in Bengal, 1756–1775

have been the channel through which Nandkumar sought to influence the Directors against Reza Khan. The material on which the Court had earlier based their estimate that some forty lakhs of rupees were due from Reza Khan on account of the Dacca revenues was certainly supplied by Nandkumar, for this was one of the allegations made by Najm-ud-daulah against the Khan, at Nandkumar's instigation, when the attempt was made in 1765 to prevent his appointment as Naib at Murshidabad. The material on which the Court were now acting seem scarcely less certainly to have been supplied by Nandkumar. The instructions sent to Hastings by the Committee of Secrecy on 28 August 1771 can only lead to this conclusion. The Committee wrote:

In this research your own judgement will direct you to such means of information as may be likely to bring to light the most secret of his transactions. We however cannot forbear recommending to you to avail yourself of the intelligence which Nundcomar may be able to give respecting the Naib's administration; and while the envy, which Nundcomar is supposed to bear this minister may prompt him to a ready communication of all proceedings which have come to his knowledge, we are persauded that no scrupulous part of the Naib's conduct can have escaped the watchful eye of his jealous and penetrating rival. Hence we cannot doubt that the abilities and dispositions of Nundcomar may be successfully employed in the investigation of Mahommed Reza Cawn's administration and bring to light any embezzlement, fraud or malversation, which he may have committed in the office of the Naib Duan, or in the station he has held under the several successive Subahs.[1]

They added:

And while we assure ourselves that you will make the necessary use of Nundcomar's intelligence, we have such confidence in your wisdom, that we have nothing to fear from any secret motives or designs which may induce him to detect the maladministration of one, whose power has been the object of his envy, whose office the aim of his ambition; for we have the satisfaction to reflect that you are too well apprized of the subtilty and dispositions of Nundcomar, to yield him any trust or authority which may be turned to his own advantage, and prove detrimental to the interest of the Company.

Though we have thought it necessary to intimate to you how little we are disposed to delegate any power or interest to Nundcomar, yet should his information or assistance be servicable to you in your in-

[1] The Committee of Secrecy to Hastings, 28 Aug. 1771 (Francis MSS, I.O., Eur. E, 28, pp. 99–101).

302

vestigating the conduct of Mohammed Reza Cawn, you will yield him such encouragement and reward as his troubles and the extent of his services deserve.[1]

One further question remains to be answered: why did the Directors, or part of their number, choose to take such drastic action against Reza Khan at this particular time? That Reza Khan had no further usefulness on the revenue side had long been clear, and he himself had opposed any attempt to continue the dual system when the supervisorships were revived in October 1770. Lawrell and Graham in the Murshidabad Council on 26 November 1770 had recorded their opinions that the Naib was no longer necessary.[2] The Directors had also come to this view when in their letter of 10 April 1771 they ordered the continuance of Reza Khan as Naib Nazim only, during the Nawab's minority, at a reduced salary of five lakhs. Now these were still their orders as late as 14 May when the *Lord Holland* sailed for Calcutta with their orders and instructions of 10 April and 25 April. What then led them to decide sometime before 28 August upon Reza Khan's arrest?

Part of the explanation must be in the steady worsening of the Company's domestic situation. The high hopes excited by Clive's despatch from Bengal in September 1765 had led the British government to demand a large share in the expected territorial revenues. The share-holders clamoured for higher dividends, while the free-traders demanded that all should have a place at the trough. Thanks to the clash between Clive and Sulivan the affairs of the Company had become party political issues, while the return of the new class of get-rich-quick 'Indians' or 'Nabobs' roused the jealous alarm of the old ruling classes, both in the Directorate and in Parliament. The repeated attempts by the Company to obtain greater control over their servants through Parliamentary intervention had failed, and the hopes pinned to the despatch of the three Commissioners Vansittart, Scrafton and Forde had foundered with their ship. By the end of 1770 the accounts of the Bengal famine had started arriving in England, and by August 1771 Clive had already guessed that the Company must be in serious difficulties,[3] though this remained a closely guarded secret. The Direc-

---

[1] *Ibid.*   [2] *MP*, 26 Nov. 1770.
[3] Lord Clive to Hastings, 1 Aug. 1772. Add. MSS. 29132, f. 434. In this letter Clive had hinted that his suggestions were not being listened to by the Directors and that the latter might put all blame on their servants.

The transition in Bengal, 1756–1775

tors were also only too well aware of the conflicts within the Calcutta government, for so many people had an interest in the India trade and everyone of them had his correspondents in India to send reports coloured by their own prejudices and interests about the failings of men and institutions there. Reza Khan as a key figure in the Bengal administration could not but be involved in these reports, true or false.

That another financial and administrative storm was brewing for the Company there could be little doubt. The Directors required some scapegoat, without partner or patron among their members or servants, upon whom blame could be safely pinned. Reza Khan was just the figure they required.

The charge which they levied against him, of monopolist activities during the famine, was particularly apt to their purposes. They had failed to take any serious note of the official information of the outbreak of famine which they received from the records of the Bengal government for 1769. Even when they received a full picture of its virulence in 1770, they had not thought it necessary to devote more than one of the 162 paragraphs of their general letter of 10 April 1771 to the subject. And in that one paragraph their concern had been limited to the comment 'The repeated accounts we have received of the excessive draught which is so long continued throughout the provinces affect us with the utmost concern for the consequences which are to be feared from it—for while we lament the distresses to which the inhabitants may be reduced thereby, we cannot divest ourselves of the anxious apprehensions concerning the effects which a continuance of the draught may have on the collections of our revenues. However, we are willing to hope that this calamity will not extend to any great degree. It affords us some consolation to find that your collection had not at the time of your advices suffered any considerable diminution.'[1] They said nothing about relief, rehabilitation or the behaviour of their servants, and in their subsequent letter of 25 April were completely silent about the famine. By 28 August 1771 however the new Direction felt obliged to take note of the subject, for the famine had caused not merely alarm about its effects upon the Company's finances, but much humanitarian concern especially as ugly stories became increasingly current in England about the way in which the servants of the Company and

[1] Paragraph 69 of Court's letter of 10 April 1771.

304

their native agents had exploited the situation to their own ends.[1] In their general letter of 28 August 1771 they answered public criticism. They expressed their approval of 'every well meant and generous effort to relieve the miseries of the poor inhabitants', and commended those servants who had sought to alleviate distress. Then they expressed their indignant horror at finding charges of monopolising grain levied even at Englishmen and their agents, by Becher and Reza Khan. They had expected to hear of strict enquiry and exemplary punishment in Bengal for those who had dared 'to counteract the benevolence of the Company', and to 'entertain a thought of profiting by the universal distress of the miserable natives whose dying cries, it is said, were too affecting to admit of an adequate description'—instead they found no culprit specifically named by Becher and the Khan, and the remedy suggested from Murshidabad, 'of totally prohibiting all Europeans in their private capacity or their Gomastahs from dealing in rice', ignored. This could only suggest that the guilty were persons of some rank in the service with influence sufficient to prevent an enquiry into their proceedings. The Directors ordered that any Englishman found guilty should be dismissed and shipped home as a warning example.[2] The Court of Directors thus cleared its public conscience, threw the burden of enquiry on Calcutta, and answered its critics in England.

But while Calcutta was left to enquire into the faults of Englishmen, the Directors proceeded to announce in London the guilt of Reza Khan. In the same letter of 28 August 1771, they declared 'Notwithstanding we observe that Mahomed Reza Cawn has

[1] As Sutherland (*The East India Company in Eighteenth-Century Politics*, p. 222) quoted from Palk's letter to Goodlad, 'at an unlucky time, mankind in general being willing to suspect that so many great fortunes cannot be fairly acquired'.
[2] Court's letter, 28 Aug. 1771. Hastings was further empowered personally (see letter of 18 Dec. 1771) to make strict enquiry against all civil and military servants involved without any 'biass of friendship'. Enquiry was made and no Englishman was found involved (*see* an article on the subject by Nanigopal Choudhury in *The Indian Historical Quarterly, 1945*). The secret was that Hastings was unwilling to antagonise anyone. In a letter to Dupre he wrote on 8 Oct. 1772: 'I should have added to the list of things to be done, an enquiry into the trade in salt, betelnutt, tobacco and rice, carried on by the principal persons of this government—which their commands have directed me to prosecute, a mark of distinction on which my friends in England congratulate me—Such partial power tends to destroy every other that I am possessed of, by arming my hand against every man, and every man's of course against me' (Add. MSS. 29125, f. 157).

complained of a monopoly of rice being carried on by other persons: we have received information that he himself in the very height of the famine has been guilty of great oppressions—that he has been guilty of stopping merchants' boats, loaded with rice and other provisions intended for the supply of Muxadabad [Murshidabad] and has forcibly compelled the owners to sell their rice to him at a price so cheap as from 25 to 30 seers p[er] rupee and resold it afterward at the rate of 3 or 4 seers p. rupee and all other eatables in proportion' and that this conduct of Reza Khan, which was 'so inhuman and so very unworthy the station' he held, had 'operated in the destruction of many thousands of people'.[1] In denouncing the Khan the Directors contrived to end the last remnant of the Clivite regime and to satisfy their critics, all at no cost to themselves.[2]

One other reason for the Company's attack upon the Khan was their wish to clear themselves of any claims on account of 'such injuries, as individuals may have sustained by the exercise of his power or the effects of his avarice'.[3] They had recently been much harassed by two Armenians who had arrived in England along with Bolts from Bengal in 1769 in order to claim damages on account of loss of personal liberty and freedom of trade with the dominion of the Nawab Wazir of Oudh. They were prevented by Verelst's government and Reza Khan from violating Clive's agreement with Shuja-ud-daulah to exclude the servants and dependants of the English from his dominion, since they were regarded no more than agents of Bolts, an ex-servant of the Company who after resigning his service had taken to an extensive private trade employing in most cases Armenian agents. The Armenians were imprisoned by Reza Khan while Bolts was confined in Calcutta and shipped to Europe in 1768. In England the Armenians were backed by Bolts

---

[1] Court's general letter, 28 Aug. 1771 (para. 18).
[2] There is an interesting parallel in the Director's technique here and in 1768–9 when they heard of the monopolising of Bombay cotton by a ring of senior servants. Then they had ordered the Commissioners (see Court's letter of 15 Sept. 1769) to 'pay a strict regard and attention to prevent monopolies of any kind ... in which the influence and authority of Mahomed Reza Cawn has been improperly exerted over the zemindars, to oblige them to buy it' (Sinha, *FWIHC*, v, 244). Now in 1771 they found it once again much easier to attack the Khan than their own men. For the last Clivite administration in Bengal, which already stood dismissed (see Court's letter, 25 April 1771), there was however an implied censure that the Khan's conduct had been 'overlooked by those in power' (para. 18 of Court's letter, 28 Aug. 1771). [3] Para. 22 of Court's letter, 28 Aug. 1771.

and Johnstone's party and in 1775 were awarded £8,000 damages against Verelst, whom the Company refused to indemnify.[1] In 1771 the Directors were wishing to keep themselves clear of any further liability by throwing the burden of responsibility upon Reza Khan, though certainly he acted in accordance with the instructions of the Company's government in Bengal.

Indeed the Directors must have hoped to make a profit from their manoeuvre. They had cut Reza Khan's salary from nine to five lakhs of rupees a year, keeping even that in arrears, now that sum too could be saved. And from their other charges against him, of misappropriation of part of the Dacca revenues and embezzlement of nizamat allowances, they might expect a further windfall, most welcome in their current financial distress. Their orders of 28 August were clear on this point, 'while we enjoin you to pursue your researches with unremitting care and attention we expect you to obtain not only a just and adequate restitution of all sums which may have been withheld from the Sircar or the Company either by embezzlement or collusion'.[2]

Whether the Company had any competence to enquire into these matters is not clear.[3] The Company in cutting the nizamat allowances from 32 to 16 lakhs had argued that this was necessary as a temporary measure, also to liquidate certain pre-diwani debts.[4]

[1] The Armenians Gregore Cojamaul and Johannes Padre Rafael had unsuccessfully applied to the Company for redress on 12 Sept. 1769 and later applied to Parliament on 18 May 1772 (*PP*, Second Report, 1772, pp. 265–6, 281–2). Approving Calcutta's suggestion regarding Bolts, the Directors ordered them on 11 Nov. 1768 of oblige 'him to repair to Europe by the first opportunity which if not already done must be carried into execution by the first ship'. Before the order had reached Calcutta Bolts was sent to Europe (*see* letter to Court dated 24 Sept. 1768). In the circumstances, on his return Verelst was never given rest by them (Sykes to Hastings, 20 Dec. 1774 and 16 Dec. 1775. Add. MSS. 29135, ff. 394–5; 29136, f. 431).

[2] Para. 22 of Court's letter, 28 Aug. 1771.

[3] This is perhaps the first time that the Company openly interfered in what it so long recognised as the internal affair of the Nawab. In 1765 Nandkumar was brought down to Calcutta for an enquiry, but then the Nawab, though compelled to agree to the enquiry, did not permit the English to bring him to Calcutta under escort of their own troops. The Raja was sent under escort of Nizamat troops, who were later joined on the way by the English troops.

[4] The pre-diwani debts listed (in Court's letter, 10 April 1771) were: Mir Jafar's promised donation to the army; balance on account of restitution which Mir Jafar was made to agree to pay in respect of illegal trade of the Company servants and their dependents which had suffered because of Mir Qasim and war with him; Col. Munro's two lakhs which was said to have been promised by Mir Jafar; money advanced to government by Bolaqidas; and an annual sum of one lakh to Jagat Seth, according to Clive's arrangement.

But if pre-diwani debts were the Nawab's responsibility, then the Dacca affair was the Nawab's business too. The nizamat disbursements were of course by treaty the Nawab's affair and nothing to do with the Company. It may also be doubted whether the Company had any intention of parting with such restitution as it might secure. In 1765 Sykes had despoiled the servants of the Nawab's government whom he dismissed, arguing that they had been guilty of fraud in the past, and put the proceeds to the Company's account. In like manner when the Company had declared the cash presents received by their servants from Najm-ud-daulah to be illegal and contrary to their engagements, the intention was not to restore the sums to the Nawab but to confiscate them to the Company. The Directors' eagerness to ensure restitution from Reza Khan seems, therefore, to have been prompted less by concern for the Nawab's finances than for those of a Company, which being forced by various considerations early in 1771 to raise the dividend to the maximum of 12½ per cent,[1] was soon to find itself obliged to stop all payments for want of cash in 1772.[2] It was probably in order to give the Company a *locus standi* in the matter of the jurisdiction to put the Khan on trial and to impose restitution from him that the Directors included a number of allegations of injury to the Company's interests and disobedience to the Company's orders as Naib Diwan, in their letter of 28 August 1771.

These charges of injury to the Company's interest, later to be virtually ignored by Hastings and his Council in their conduct of the trial, were four in number. First, there was a general allegation that 'large sums have by violent and oppressive means been collected by Mohammed Reza Cawn on account of the Dewanny revenues, great part of which he has appropriated to his own use, or distributed among creatures of his power and instruments of his oppression'.[3] No specific evidence was adduced for this charge which was possibly based on Smith's minute in the secret proceedings of the Calcutta Council dated 26 October 1769.[4]

---

[1] Sutherland, *The East India Company in Eighteenth-Century Politics*, p. 227.
[2] Sykes in a letter to Hastings on 28 Jan. 1773 described the reaction, that the Directors 'have been treated in a very free manner by the proprietors and their character struck at' (Add. MSS. 29133, f. 347).
[3] Para. 21 of Court's letter, 28 Aug. 1771.
[4] Hastings described the charges as 'general without any specificates of time, places or persons' (*see* Secret Cons., 24 March 1774).

The 'Inquisition', 1772–1775

Secondly, Reza Khan was charged with assisting the monopoly trade in salt, 'in direct contradiction of the Company's orders'. This was based on a single act of the Khan's granting a parwana to the zemindars of Jessore and Nadia permitting a native merchant, Tiloke Ram, to produce salt in their lands for three years.[1] The Calcutta merchants and possibly certain Company servants raised a clamour against the grant, and when Cartier was made aware of the grant he stiffly ordered Reza Khan to withdraw the parwana. Such was the pressure on him that Cartier himself also wrote to the zemindars cancelling it. The Khan, in complying with Cartier's orders, said that he had granted the parwana on a representation that salt manufactories were unoccupied and the merchants discontented.[2] The Directors disapproved of Cartier's lenience, disbelieved the Khan's explanation and suggested that the merchants' discontent was probably caused by the Khan's exercise of undue influence.[3]

From this second charge against the Khan, the Directors developed their third—that the grant to Tiloke Ram had been indicative of the cause of a decline in the revenue from salt duties.[4] The Khan had forewarned the decline in 1769 when the Calcutta government arbitrarily fixed an exorbitant duty of Rs. 30 per 100 maunds[5] and by 1770 the decline had been apparent. Becher then had explained it in a letter to the Select Committee as the result of a large amount of salt 'passed up the country' duty free 'with Dustucks from the Committee of Trade'.[6] The implied accusation of misuse of passes by the gentlemen in Calcutta and their gumashtahs was promptly repudiated by the Select Committee. They prefered to cast suspicion on the Faujdar of Hugli as either 'extremely negligent in his duty or dishonest in the management' of his charge.[7] The Directors now went one better, blaming both Reza Khan and Cartier's government. How could the Fort William authorities 'advert to the fact of salt being monopolized under the express authority of Mahomet Reza Cawn', they asked, 'and not be aware of the consequences, namely, that he having presumed to trans-

---

[1] The date of the parwana is not known, but it could not be too long before 20 April 1770 when Cartier wrote to the Khan and to the zemindars (*CPC*, III, 175, 176, 177 and *H.M.S.*, 201, 29–30).
[2] Reza Khan to Cartier, 15 May 1770. *CPC*, III, 210.
[3] Para. 13 of Court's letter, 28 Aug. 1771.
[4] Paras. 14 and 15, *ibid*.   [5] See above, pp. 204–5.
[6] Becher's letter. BSC 15 Sept. 1770.   [7] BSC, 15 Sept. 1770.

gress the Company's commands would also avail himself of his station and screen his agents from paying duties or compel them to compound with him for the same to the damage of the Company'.[1] The charge was absolutely hollow, for the grant to Tiloke Ram of the right to manufacture salt had not exempted him from payment of duty, and it had in any case been promptly cancelled. To accuse Reza Khan served however to divert attention from Becher's authoritative complaint against the Committee of Trade and from the creation in February 1771 of a salt combine among certain members of the Calcutta Council.[2]

The fourth and last charge of the Company against Reza Khan was that 'the diminution of the Dewanny revenues have been owing to the misconduct or malversation of those who have had the superintendency of the collection', namely Reza Khan and his officers who had disappointed them in their expectations of 'a considerable increase in the revenues'.[3] Even if the Directors were once again firmly prejudging the outcome of the enquiry, they were not, it seems, too far away from Floyer's accusations against Reza Khan made at the Select Committee on 29 March 1770.[4] They concluded, therefore, by saying

we should not think ourselves justified to the Company or to the publick were we to leave to him in future, the management of the Dewanny collection and as the transferring the like trust to any other minister would yield us little prospect of reaping any benefit from the change, we are necessitated to seek by other means the full advantage we have to expect from the grant of the Dewanny.[5]

The decision was against not Reza Khan alone, but against all native instruments. Their usefulness was over. Consequently, the Directors were now determined 'to stand forth as Dewan; and by the agency of the Company's servants to take upon themselves the entire care and management of the Revenue'.[6]

---

[1] Par. 15 of Court's letter, 28 Aug. 1771.
[2] Joint letter of Middleton, Aldersey, Floyer and Reed. BPC, 27 Dec. 1771. These four had formed a combine in which Russell and Hare also joined for a time. Russell later withdrew and Hare died. They were to trade in salt, betelnut and tobacco.
[3] Para. 20 of Court's letter, 28 Aug. 1771.
[4] See above, chapter 9.   [5] Para. 21 of Court's letter, 28 Aug. 1771.
[6] *Ibid.* The Directors blandly ignored the fact that revenue management had passed from Reza Khan and his officials to the supervisors and Council at Murshidabad in October 1770, Reza Khan retaining only an advisory role.

The 'Inquisition', 1772–1775

One final aspect of the situation existing in the autumn of 1771, which led to the Directors orders for the arrest of Reza Khan, requires some comment: the renewal of the attacks upon Clive and those associated with him. Sykes puts the point in a letter written after the event to Warren Hastings:

The Directors came to a resolution of telling the public that their distress was owing to the rapacity and bad management of their servants abroad, and in order to support their argument employed one Wilks at £600 p. annum to examine the Company's records from 1756 to this present time for every circumstances of a civil or military nature.... This work they certainly had in view, at the time they ordered M R C to be confined, in order, if possible to find matter to support their argument and draw all attention of the public upon the conduct of their servants.[1]

Dr Lucy Sutherland has shown how the case brought by Bolts and his two Armenians against Verelst was taken up by the Johnstone party.[2] They extended the attack to Clive, against whom John Petrie, one of the officers cashiered by Clive, now laid charges before the Directors. From the Court of Directors the conflict was then extended to the Press, by Bolts in his *Considerations on Indian Affairs*, and then by Dow, in a third volume to his *History of Hindostan*. Finally, upon the Company's failure to pay their dividend in 1772, the attack upon Clive, his associates and Verelst was carried to the House of Commons. A Select Committee of the Commons under Burgoyne was set up to investigate 'the most atrocious abuses that ever stained the name of civil government'.

This succession of events had a double effect upon Reza Khan's case. It meant, in the first place, that when news of the orders to arrest the Khan became known in England 'many months after'[3] the sailing of the *Lapwing* his friends there were unable to assist him since by then they themselves were subjects of enquiry and attack. In the second, it meant that Reza Khan was himself made a subject of the Press attack unleashed by Bolts and Dow. The latter in particular ensured that the Directors' attack upon the Khan within the Company was reinforced by the creation of a violent prejudice against him, his officials, and the bankers and zemindars of Bengal, among the public at large.

[1] Sykes to Hastings, 8 Nov. 1773. Add. MSS. 29134, ff. 118–19. See p. 303, n. 3.
[2] Sutherland, *The East India Company in Eighteenth-Century Politics*, pp. 219–21.
[3] Sykes in a letter to Hastings on 28 Jan. 1773, said that 'the orders sent on this occasion [to arrest the Khan] was in the most secret manner by the Committee, unknown for many months after, even to the Directors' (Add.MSS.29133, p.348).

The transition in Bengal, 1756–1775

In the year 1765, upon the demise of Jaffier [Mir Jafar] whom we had, for the first time, raised in 1757 to the government for his convenient treachery to his master, Nijim-ul-Dowla, his son by a common prostitute was, in his eighteenth year of age, placed upon the throne, in the capital of Murshedabad...The wretched Nijim-ul-Dowla was a mere name; a figure of state more despicable if possible than the meanness of his family. The whole executive government turned upon Mahommed Riza. A resident was sent from Calcutta to check the accounts of the nominal government; as if one man who knew very little of the language, manners and opinions of the people, could prevent the fraud of an artful minister, and ten thousand of his dependents, versed in the management of finance. The consequence might be foreseen with little penetration. Unable, and perhaps unwilling to oppose the current, the resident fell down with the stream, and became so far a check upon Mahommed, that he appropriated to himself a part of what the minister might otherwise have thrown into his own treasure.[1]

The gratuitous comments did not end here. Dow continued:

Mahommed Riza, as a small salary of office, received annually, one hundred twelve thousand and five hundred Pounds with three hundred and seventyfive thousand a year to be distributed among his friends. The minister, with his other good qualities, had no other local attachment to friends. They were of various complexions and religions; fair faced Europeans, as well as swarthy Indians; and, though professing Mahommedanism himself, he was so far from being an enemy of the uncircumcised, that it is said the most of his pensions and gratuities were bestowed on good Christians born in Great Britain and Ireland. Mahommed, however, did not take up his whole time with acts of benevolence to our nation. He applied himself to business and he was more rigid in executing the government which the revolted Nabobs had established in Bengal, than fond of introducing innovations more favourable to the prosperity of the country.[2]

At a time when public concern was mounting in England at the Company's increasing difficulties in meeting its financial commitments at home, Dow did not miss the opportunity to indicate where the money was being spent. For example, comments Dow, the Khan squandered $27\frac{1}{2}$ per cent of the country's revenues, locally at Murshidabad, upon the annual Punyah ceremony, an amount shared 'between Mahommed Riza, his friends and the bankers of Murshedabad', obliquely pointing out at the same time

[1] A. Dow, *History of Hindostan*, vol. III, xc–xci.
[2] *Ibid.*, xci–xcii.

that 'The place of the Company's resident at the Durbar...was honestly worth one hundred and fifty thousand Pounds a year'.[1]

Realising perhaps that he had been too abusive about his fellow countrymen, Dow then hastens to add that

Mahommed Riza made it his invariable policy to keep the servants of the Company in ignorance of the true state of affairs; and when one deception was practised another was formed to conceal it from view. He entered into collusion with many of the farmers. Occasional accounts were framed and the usual accounts were studiously involved in inextricable confusion. Men, averse to trouble, throw them aside; and neglect their duty in their indolence. The servants of Mahommed Riza not only escape censure but retain their places; and this iniquity furnishes to itself a new field, for a repitition of its execrable talents.[2]

It will be remembered that Dow was no ordinary pamphleteer.[3] His two earlier volumes based on Firishta's works had established his reputation as an historian, his third volume was a respectable work designed for the King's perusal. Upon an ill informed public its effect was therefore more complete. Whatever punishment the Directors might wish to impose upon Reza Khan, it could not but be regarded by the British public as well deserved. And in any case, in public eye in England, the enquiry against Clive and his associates in England had become linked with that against Reza Khan in Bengal. Anxiously, therefore, Sykes wrote to Hastings in January 1773.

Situated as the House of Commons, now are, their minds inflamed, the diabolical disposition of the present Directors, makes many of us, gentlemen anxious to have the result of M. Reza Cawn's conduct being enquired into...whatever consequences this may have affecting dispositions, characters at home and abroad, I cannot tell, but I fear it will in a greater or less degree, the whole will depend on the mode of enquiry and the line of conduct given M. Reza Cawn.[4]

Something has been seen of the mixed motives which led the critics and enemies of Reza Khan in England to approve and order

[1] *Ibid.*, p. xciv.　　　　　　[2] *Ibid.*, p. xxviii.
[3] Horace Walpole noted in his Journals, 'Some books had been published, particularly by one Bolts and Mr. Dow, the first a man of bad character, the latter of a very fair one ...'. Quoted by Sutherland, *op. cit.*, p. 221. Caillaud, an ex-military servant of the Company in Bengal, however, commented to Hastings on 27 March 1772 (Add. MSS. 29133, f. 90): 'If Mr. Bolts has bruised where he has intended to strike, Mr. Dow cutts with fine edge'.
[4] Sykes to Hastings, 28 Jan. 1773. Add. MSS. 29133, f. 348.

his arrest. It is now time to consider the attitudes displayed towards the Khan by the Company's servants in India, and in particular by Hastings, who was charged with the duty of arresting the Khan and bringing him to trial.

Hastings had no personal grudge against Reza Khan. Indeed the Khan, involved in Hastings's private trade in Dacca tobacco, had won Hastings's esteem by his just dealing.[1] The coolness which Hastings at Madras had displayed towards the Khan's overtures, and the coldness towards the Khan's appeals shown by Hastings when governor of Bengal had their origin in the wider political plans and ambitions of Hastings. He wished to utilise the fall of the Khan, like the Directors' orders to stand forth as Diwan, to effect changes in the structure of the Company's power in Bengal which he had long seen to be necessary.

One major problem, to which as early as March 1767 he had traced the insubordination of the Company's servants in India, was the complete dependence of the annually elected Directors upon the unstable court of proprietors. This prevented the formulation of long term policies for India, left the Company's servants there without reliable guidance and emboldened them to defy the orders of the Company in the hope that their defiance would be condoned by whatever new Directorate was in power when news of their insubordination at last reached England.[2] This problem was not in Hastings's power to solve, but he could feel some assurance of stable support from the fact that he had been nominated governor before Sulivan returned to power, and approved after that event.[3] As Lucy Sutherland puts it, 'he seems to have owed his nomination to a widespread appreciation of his high qualities as an administrator rather than to party manoeuvres. The reconciliation of parties...gave a good augury for the support he might expect from home....'[4]

The second problem facing Hastings was the absolute helplessness of the governor against his subordinates, both within the Council and without. In a letter to Sykes, from Madras, on 2 Feb-

[1] Hastings to Hancock, 11 April 1770. Add. MSS. 29125, ff. 31–2.
[2] Evidence of Hastings on 31 March 1767 (Add. MSS. 18469, f. 20).
[3] Hastings's appointment was ordered on 10 April 1771 by the outgoing Direction. The new Direction which was voted to office on 10 April 1771 hastened Hastings's succession by ordering Cartier's dismissal (see Court's letters of 10 and 25 April 1771).
[4] Sutherland, *The East India Company in Eighteenth-Century Politics*, p. 205.

The 'Inquisition', 1772–1775

ruary 1771 he laid down that whoever governed Bengal 'must have great authority'.[1] Within a week of his arrival in Calcutta in 1772 Hastings made this point again in a letter of thanks to John Purling, chairman of the Court of Directors, declaring

...that the powers of this government are more ostensible than real. If the several districts are subject to the jursidiction of the inferior servants of the Company, if the business of the revenue is entrusted to the chiefs and Councils of Murshedabad and Patna, though subject to the Presidency which can only judge of the propriety of their trans-actions from their own materials—I will take upon me to affirm that ye [the] authority of the Presidency is in these points merely nominal nor ought it to be charged with the consequences of any mismanage-ment, if any may have been committed in the country.[2]

A month later he was harping upon the same theme in a letter to Colebrooke: 'The government of this country consists of three distinct powers, the Supravisors, the Boards of Revenue at Murshedabad and Patna, and the Governor and Council at Cal-cutta.' He added wryly, that the order in which he named them was 'not accidental but consonant to the degree of trust, power and emolument'.[3] (By 'emolument' Hastings clearly did not mean official salary only, but also the profits of private trade, perquisites and positive corruption.)[4] To Dupre, governor of Madras, Hastings wrote, 'This is the system which it seems my predecessor was turned out for opposing and I will be turned out too, rather than suffer it to continue as it is'.[5]

Finally, Hastings also saw the need to finish the process of making the Company supreme in Bengal. The order to stand forth as Diwan gave him the opportunity to complete the change already initiated by the grant of effective power to the supervisors. The order to arrest the Khan opened the way to a thoroughgoing invasion of the Nizamat authority.

To Hastings, determined to undo the existing system in Bengal, the Company's orders of 28 August 1771 came as a godsend. He

[1] Hastings to Sykes, 2 Feb. 1771. Add. MSS. 29126, f. 55.
[2] Hastings to Purling, 22 Feb. 1772. Add. MSS. 29126, f. 126.
[3] Hastings to G. Colebrooke, 26 March 1772. Add. MSS. 29127, f. 15.
[4] By January 1774 Hastings had increased his fortune. Appointing Sykes as his attorney in England, in addition to J. Woodman and W. Waller, Hastings explained, in a letter to Woodman on 2 Jan. 1774 (Add. MSS. 29134, f. 234), that it was 'necessary . . . as my remittances are likely to become considerable'.
[5] Hastings to DuPre, 26 March 1772. Add. MSS. 29126, f. 138.

was already fortunate in that the rapid changes in the Council, begun in November 1771 (with the departure of Russell and Kelsall for home) and speeded up by the Directors' orders for the dismissal of Cartier, transfer of Floyer and enlargement of Council membership from nine to fourteen and temporarily obliterated party groupings. Before party lines could be redrawn Hastings was armed with authority to relax promotion by seniority, and then, on receipt of secret orders dated 18 December 1771, with personal power of enquiring into the past conduct of all servants, civil and military. He was thus very much more strongly armed than Cartier had been, as well as being—perhaps because of his long years as a Resident[1]—more determined to exercise active power and to intervene in the internal politics of the Indian princes.

Nevertheless, Hastings felt obliged at first to move with caution. He was not sure yet how much support he could depend on within the Direction, and dared not go too far on the strength of instructions from the Secret Committee alone. It was no secret that the Directors had a plan to send out further commissioners, and though the threat was thwarted by Parliamentary action in December 1772, it was not until he received positive orders from the Directors, in their secret letter of 16 March 1773, that he was entirely reassured. Meanwhile until he had won support within the Council, Hastings was not ready to act boldly.

These doubts dictated the course of action Hastings pursued towards Reza Khan. He was vaguely apprehensive lest the Khan should prove to have some influence in the Company at home, and even more afraid that if he proceeded at once against the Khan there would be strong opposition within the Council. To delay the trial of the Khan, therefore, became a part of his political stategy.

That such a policy was wise was demonstrated by the reactions of the Council on 28 April 1772 to the news which Hastings gave them of the arrest of Reza Khan. The arrest was not opposed, but there was a dispute about what the next step should be, and in particular about how the Khan should be received in Calcutta. It was agreed that consistently with the Company's orders he could not be shown the honours 'paid him on the occasion of his

---

[1] He assisted Scrafton at Murshidabad from 1757 and then held independent charge from 1758 to 1760. It was he who introduced Mir Qasim to the English and was Resident at his court in 1762. At Madras he dealt with Arcot affairs.

The 'Inquisition', 1772–1775

former visits to Calcutta'.[1] But here the agreement ended. A majority of the Council, Dacres, Lane, Barwell, Lawrell and Graham, voted that 'considering the rank of His Excellency Mahomed Rezza Cawn, the station he has filled, the character and consequence he has held in the empire of Hindustan by the honours and dignity conferred on him by the King at the particular instigation of Lord Clive and his Council on the part of the Honorable Company, [the Council] judge it proper that one of its members be sent to intimate to him the cause of his seizure, and to inform His Excellency on the points on which the Hon'ble Company express their displeasure, and that they look to us to obtain satisfaction from him for the injuries which they conceive their affairs have sustained by his mismanagement and corrupt administration'.[2] They resolved in consequence that 'Mr. Graham be appointed to wait upon His Excellency on his arrival', with a letter from Hastings, and with offer of option to the Khan either to stay at Chitpur or to proceed to his own house in Calcutta. Graham, while telling him in general terms what were the main heads of accusations levied against him, was also to reassure him about his personal safety by making clear that the arrest was designed 'merely to make him amenable to a due course of justice'.[3]

Hastings, with Aldersey, Harris and Goodwin entered a dissent to this majority resolution. Goodwin while expressing the hope that Reza Khan would ultimately 'prove himself innocent of the crimes the Company suspect him guilty of', pointed out that the Company would scarcely have gone to the 'expence of sending out a packet on purpose' if they had not got substantial grounds for their proceedings. To act in the manner proposed was contrary to the Company's evident intentions and would discourage the natives from voicing complaints against the Khan.[4]

Harris could not agree to the proposal of the majority as a member of that tribunal before which the Khan was 'to prove his innocence or stand condemned' for he maintained that Reza Khan 'must be considered as a culprit till he has vindicated his conduct'. He argued that though the majority, doubtless, acted from a 'most humane sentiment', their proposed marks of favour and distinction to the Khan must 'bias the weak minds of the natives in general and of those whose evidence may be necessary

[1] Secret Cons., 28 April 1772.
[3] Ibid.
[2] Ibid.
[4] Ibid.

317

in particular'. The President's assurance of a candid and fair trial, and his own 'conscious innocence' should be a sufficient consolation to the Khan.[1]

Aldersey took a moderate line. Every appearance of compliment to the Khan should be avoided as 'inconsistent with the intentions of our employers both as to the mode they have prescribed for making a scrutiny' and to the 'express commands' they had received from them. He held that a communication from the Council through the hands of the Secretary or the Persian Translator should be sufficient.[2]

Hastings opposed the majority motion no less temperately, evidently weighing the reactions of his Council without committing himself too deeply. Thus he agreed that it was proper 'to shew Mahommed Rezza Cawn every mark of attention and even of respect due to the station which he has so lately filled in the administration of these provinces, and still proper, while his conduct is only a subject of enquiry'. He went further, recording his opinion that it was only 'becoming the dignity and justice of the government to give him such assurances as a man in his situation may stand in need of, whose ideas of the consequences of ministerial disgrace have been originally formed on the despotism and violence of Asiatic manners; that however rigidly prosecute the enquiries which the Company have ordered to be made into his conduct, no personal ill will shall be allowed to take place against him, and that equal and strict justice shall be done him'.[3] He showed that in his private letter to Reza Khan he had assured him that the Khan might count upon him in his private capacity for every testimony of goodwill and attachment. But then, having disarmed criticism, Hastings went on to declare that it would be 'very unbecoming the character and dignity of a member of this administration to be employed on a public deputation to a man who stands accused by the Court of Director themselves of the most criminal conduct'. Here was a clear, if veiled warning to any who might be tempted to support the Khan, that to do so would be to associate themselves in the eyes of the Directors with the Khan's criminal conduct. Hastings then went on to stress once again that for Graham to visit the Khan in his official capacity would lead to the creation in the public mind of the idea that the Khan's power 'is but suspended'.[4] Hastings was determined that

[1] Secret Cons., 28 April 1772. [2] *Ibid.* [3] *Ibid.* [4] *Ibid.*

Reza Khan should never be restored to his old position as Naib Nazim, whatever the outcome of the trial.

Hastings's determination to bring the Nizamat under the Company's control must have been strengthened when he found time to read Reza Khan's comments upon his judicial proposals, and in particular the stiff declaration that 'in a country under the dominion of a Mussulman Emperor it is improper that any order should be issued inconsistent with the rules of his faith, and that innovations should be introduced in the administration of justice'.[1] To a man who five years earlier had asserted that there was no real king in India, and that the English 'must be considered as the master and governing power',[2] such a defence of the rights of the Nizamat could scarcely have been pleasing. Hastings's reaction was to defer Reza Khan's trial for as long as possible while he won the support of his Council for an extension of the English control over the Nizamat, and ensured that he was supported by the Directorate.

For Reza Khan an early trial was essential if he was to retain his influence and save himself from financial ruin. On 4 May, the day he reached Calcutta, he expressed his hope to Graham that he would soon be furnished with an exact copy of the charges against him, so that he might confront those who had complained to the Company, 'to the prejudice of his honour and good name'. Graham reported to the Council on 5 May that the Khan had 'insisted a good deal more on the subject of the enquiry which all tended to express his anxiety for an opportunity being afforded him of justifying his character from the present heavy reproaches'.[3] Hastings acknowledged the receipt of Reza Khan's request for a copy of the charges, but it was not until 13 May, after a further request had been made by the Khan through Ali Ibrahim Khan, that Hastings promised that a copy would be sent to him soon.[4] On 16 May the charges were set out in five 'Articles of Impeachment' by the Council, and it was resolved that a day should be fixed for the trial as soon as the Khan's reply had been received.[5] On 22 May a Persian translation of the charges was formally sent

---

[1] See above, chapter 10, p. 271.
[2] Hastings's evidence before Fuller Committee, 1767. Add. MSS. 18469, f. 25.
[3] Graham's Report to Council, 5 May 1772. Secret Cons., 7 May 1772.
[4] Hastings to Reza Khan, 6 May, 13 May, 1772. *CPC*, IV, 20, 26.
[5] Secret Cons., 16 May 1772.

to the Khan.[1] To these the Khan had replied by 18 June, with a request that he might have an early opportunity to confront those who had lodged accusations against him with the Company.[2] Hastings then arranged that the matter be postponed until the return of the newly formed Committee of Circuit, then just about to set out for Kasimbazar. It was presumably in reply to a reminder that the Khan's case was still unattended to that Hastings wrote to Aldersey from Kasimbazar on 24 June saying 'I thought it had been formally resolved that as so great a part of the Board would be absent the enquiry into the conduct of M.R.C. and R.S.R. [Raja Shitab Rai] should be postponed. I remember a minute was formed to that effect and I think I recollect that it was agreed to let it rest till M.R.C.'s answer was received. Something should be said: if more than this, nobody can better express it than you.'[3] Hastings evidently wished Aldersey to fob Reza Khan off once more, and perhaps write something into the record to soothe the Directors. What Aldersey told Reza Khan is not known, but by September the Khan was certainly pressing Hastings again for an early enquiry, in letters sent through Ali Ibrahim Khan, for on 29 September Hastings replied to him. He was sorry to hear that the Khan was suffering, repeated his promise to institute the enquiry soon, but explained that as a servant of the Company he could not ignore their orders.[4] In the event Hastings chose to take up the trial of Shitab Rai first,[5] and it was not until 22 January 1773 that he asked Reza Khan to produce his accounts, and not till 12 February 1773, after nine and a half months of confinement and suspense, that the trial of Reza Khan was formally opened.

It is evident that in the early months of his governorship, charged with a complete reformation in the administration of Bengal, Hastings was a much preoccupied man. Moreover, as he hinted to Dupre on 8 October 1772 and was to state again more fully to the Committee of Secrecy on 24 March 1774, the Directors' charges against the Khan were 'general, without any specificates

---

[1] Governor to Reza Khan, 22 May 1772. *CPC*, IV, 33.
[2] The reply must have been sent sometime before the Council took it up on 18 June 1772. The Khan was evidently very quick in replying.
[3] Hastings to Aldersey, 24 June 1772. Add. MSS. 29125, f. 100.
[4] Hastings to Reza Khan, 29 Sept. 1772. *CPC*, IV, 82. It is not clear what Hastings wanted to convey by referring to the Company's orders. It was never ordered by the Company to delay the trial.
Shitab Rai's arrest and trial were ordered by the Council, and not by the Directors. Secret Cons., 28 April 1772.

of time, places or persons', so that he had 'neither witnesses, nor vouchers nor materials of any sort to begin with'.[1] It was necessary, therefore, to call publicly for information about any misdemeanour of the Khan, though this was only done in August 1772.[2] Perhaps the gigantic nature of the enquiry, requiring 'some months' to conduct it, also made him, as he told Sykes in December 1772, afraid of 'entering upon it'.[3] It may be also that he was not anxious to proceed with so important a measure as the trial until he was sure again of the backing of the Directors. His secret letter to the Directors on 1 September 1772, reporting that Reza Khan and Shitab Rai 'had conceived hopes of a relaxation of the Company's orders. Mahmud R. Cawn had even buoyed himself with the hopes of a restoration to his former authority by the interest of his friends and a change in the Direction',[4] may have been designed to sound out the situation, while proclaiming himself in effect a party man of Sulivan and Colebrooke. (If so, his letter was successful, for it drew a secret reply, signed by all the Directors on 16 April 1773, assuring Hastings that 'although sundry changes have lately taken place in the Direction...those changes will not in the least affect the measures in which you are engaged').[5] But even after giving the fullest weight to these considerations, it seems impossible to acquit Hastings of the charge of having deliberately denied justice to the Khan until all the measures necessary to ensure the destruction of the Khan and of his office of Naib Nazim had been pushed through. While in September 1772 Hastings was assuring the Directors that though 'It may at first sight appear extraordinary that Mahmud Rizza Cawn and Rajah Shitab Roy have been so long detained in confinement without any proofs having been obtained of their guilt or measures taken to bring them to a trial' the delay had valid reasons and that 'neither...complained of the delay as a hardship',[6] he was about the same time explaining the delay, as seen already, in a letter to the Khan, as due to the orders of the Company. To Graham, Hastings wrote on 24 October 1772 saying that 'Mahmud Rizza

---

[1] 'Here now I am ... with the trials ... to bring on without materials, and without much hope of assistance' (Hastings to DuPre, 8 Oct. 1772. Add. MSS. 29125, f. 157). See also Monckton-Jones, *Warren Hastings in Bengal*, p. 195.
[2] Proclamation issued by the Governor and Council. *CPC*, IV, 63.
[3] Hastings to Sykes, 10 Dec. 1772. Add. MSS. 29125, f. 183.
[4] Hastings's secret letter to Court, 1 Sept. 1772. Add. MSS. 29125, f. 137.
[5] Court's letter (secret to Hastings), 16 April 1773.
[6] Add. MSS. 29125, ff. 135-7.

The transition in Bengal, 1756–1775

Cawn is desirous of being brought to a hearing. Had it been possible his desire should have been fulfilled e'er this—A[li] Ibraheem C[awn] wanted no encourag[ement], but both chose to throw the choice on me'.[1] Hastings perhaps was conscious that he was being cruel to the Khan just because he had become the symbol of the nizamat powers, but it could not be avoided. He wrote, therefore, to Sykes in March 1773, when the trial also had formally commenced, saying that 'in one point only I am against him. I will never suffer him, if I can help it, to regain his power. The Directors are mad if they do; for the government of the province is now entirely at their disposal, without a competitor for the smallest share of their authority'.[2]

This then was the good use to which Hastings put the delay in bringing Reza Khan to trial. He had begun by ignoring the Directors' instructions to appoint a new Naib Nazim,[3] hoping perhaps to see the office lapse by default. On 21 May, however, the issue was raised by a letter from Murshidabad Council stressing 'the necessity there is for speedily appointing a Naib to the Nizamut as the business of that department particularly the course of justice here as in the Mufussul is suspended for want of a person properly authorized to confirm the decrees of the several courts of justice and to pass sentence on criminals; besides various other matters of business wherein the interposition of the Soubah is immediately necessary'.[4] Murshidabad went on to suggest Ihteram-ud-daulah (Mir Kazim), Mir Jafar's brother, the eldest male survivor of the Nawab's family and thus the natural guardian of the young Nawab, as a suitable candidate. They also forwarded a letter from him stating that he had been invited by Munni Begum to accept the post of guardian.[5] Hastings, having quite other plans for the nizamat, persuaded his Council to recommend to Murshidabad that they should ask the Nawab to authorise the Adalat officers to use the nizamat seal for the time being, until the matter could be finally determined.

A minority of members of the Calcutta Council including Graham continued, as Hastings told Aldersey, to 'adhere to the

[1] Add. MSS. 29125, f. 165.
[2] Gleig, *Memoirs of the Right Honourable Warren Hastings*, I, 283.
[3] In paras. 24, 25, 26 of Court's letter (general) of 28 Aug. 1771, the Directors had ordered appointing a substitute on a salary of three lakhs a year.
[4] *MP*, 18 May 1772 and Secret Cons., 21 May 1772.
[5] *MP*, 18 May 1772.

letter of the Company's orders which authorise the appointment of a Naib Subah'.[1] Nevertheless, on 11 July 1772 at a meeting of the Committee of Circuit at Kasimbazar, present Hastings, Middleton, Dacres, Lawrell and Graham, it was decided that a new Naib Nazim was not necessary. The Committee agreed that since the only purpose in having a Naib Nazim was for 'holding out the authority of the Country Government to European powers, in all cases wherein their interests may interfere with those of the Company', there was no need to grant 'an extra-ordinary permanent authority to any single minister of the Nabob'.[2] Any Nawabi officer, of whatever rank, might be appointed to act for the Nawab when occasion arose to deal with other European nations. To install a regular Naib Subahdar, at three lakhs a year, 'merely for the sake of giving eclat to the negociations or authenticating the priviledges of their rivals in trade' was folly, when the purpose could be achieved by other means. Having thus appealed to the Company's cupidity, the Committee proceeded to argue on political grounds against the retention of the post of Naib Nazim, whereby 'the rights and prerogatives of the ancient government will still be preserved and the minds of the people, instead of being familiarized to the authority of the Company will be taught to look forward to the time when the Nabob shall resume the sovereignty...'. They held that 'whatever faith may be due to treaties subsisting' a dividend or dual government could not last, but must end in conflict and bloodshed. It was essential, therefore, to seize the invaluable opportunity of the Nawab's minority 'to retain openly and in our own hands the whole conduct of the government for the present, to accustom the people to the sovereignty of the British people and to divide the officers of the Nizamaut and to suffer no person to share in the management of the domestick affairs [of the Nawab] who from birth, rank, personal consideration or from actual trust may have it in his power to assist his master with means or ever to inspire him with hopes of future independence'.[3]

Hastings from the start had been determined not to allow the restoration of Reza Khan or the appointment of anyone else as

[1] Hastings to Aldersey, 8 July 1772. Add. MSS. 29125, f. 102.
[2] *The Proceedings of the Committee of Circuit* (or *PCC*), Kasimbazar, 11 July 1772.
[3] *PCC*, Kasimbazar, 11 July 1772 (also Secret Cons., 6 Aug. 1772).

21-2

The transition in Bengal, 1756–1775

Naib Nazim, who 'would of course become the principal as Mahomed Rizza Cawn did'.[1] He intended to bring all authority down to Calcutta and to grasp it himself. But how had he won over his Council, of whom in April a majority had shown themselves unwilling to break with Reza Khan, and a minority until July still anxious to see the office of Naib Nazim upheld? Mainly, it would seem, by his manipulation of the instructions he had received from the Committee of Secrecy, the full tenor of which he carefully concealed from both colleagues and friends.[2] The fact that he had been armed with the power to enquire into 'the trade in salt, betel nutt, tobacco and rice carried on by the principal persons of this government' was doubtless a useful instrument of persuasion, though as he pointed out to Dupre he had no intention of using a power which 'by arming my hand against every man', necessarily armed every man's against him.[3] More useful, however, was the opportunity his secret instructions provided for spreading the notion that he had been instructed to destroy 'the ancient system of government'. So on 8 July 1772 he wrote to Aldersey 'The Company have ordered a new system to take place, which totally subverts the ancient system of government—they express their apprehensions of the influence and power of Mahomed Reza Cawn and order us to use every means to destroy it'.[4] The Company had been nothing like so decisive and clear sighted, but when Hastings presented such a measure as was designed apparently to establish the sovereignty of the Company, it was unlikely that the members of the Council would oppose it. The chances of opposition had been to a great extent reduced by splitting the Council, some members constituting the Committee of Circuit and going upcountry for settling the revenues while another group remained stationed at Calcutta. Hastings had indeed won over most of his Council colleagues also by the use he sought to make of the Company's orders of 28 August 1771, to stand forth as Diwan. He was to use it for transferring the executive authority in revenue matters from the subordinate agencies in the districts to the members of the Calcutta Council. The Directors, by their orders of August 1771, had meant 'by the agency of the Company's

[1] Hastings to Dupre, 8 Oct. 1772. Add. MSS. 29125, f. 156.
[2] Hastings to Secret Committee, 1 Sept. 1772. Add. MSS. 29125, f. 139.
[3] Hastings to Dupre, 8 Oct. 1772. Add. MSS. 29125, f. 157.
[4] Hastings to Aldersey, 8 July 1772. Add MSS. 29125, f. 102.

servants to take upon themselves the entire care and management
of the revenue',[1] but, as Hastings had observed in a letter to Dupre
in January 1773, 'the change had taken place [in 1770] two years
before I arrived' in Bengal.[2] Having therefore nothing further to
do in the matter of Europeanisation of revenue administration,
Hastings had deemed it necessary 'to undeceive the Company' by
redesignating the supervisors as what they really were, collectors,
and also to transfer full authority in revenue matters to the
Calcutta Council. 'The collectorships are more lucrative than any
post in the service (the government itself not excepted...)'
Hastings had used the Company's new orders to attempt a
reversal of the situation 'for who would rest satisfied with a
handsome salary of three or four thousand rupees a year to maintain him in Calcutta who could get a lac or three lacs,...and live at
no expense in the districts?'[3] After Hastings had taken the move
that was to benefit the councillors, opposition was most likely to
weaken, though Graham in the Committee of Circuit and Barwell
stationed at Calcutta continued to offer opposition to Hastings for
sometime more. By December 1772 Hastings had decided to use
Graham's abilities in revenue administration and they were 'on
friendly terms'.[4] Barwell's posting to Dacca in 1773 reduced the
chance of open clash in Council until Sulivan intervened to patch
up the differences between Hastings and Barwell.[5] Having in this
way secured his Council's approval for measures presented to them
as required by the Directors, Hastings was then able to write with
confidence to the Court of Directors urging the advantages of
abolishing the Naib nizamat and 'the necessity of prefacing the
enquiry by breaking his [Reza Khan's] influence'.[6]

Having made sure that no new Naib Nazim was created as an
obstacle to his plans, Hastings could turn to the task of destroying
the old incumbent of the office. It is clear that Reza Khan was
regarded by Hastings as the one effective defender of the old

[1] Para. 21 of Court's letter, 28 Aug. 1771.
[2] Hastings to Dupre, 6 Jan. 1773. Gleig, *Memoirs of the Right Hon. Warren
Hastings*, pp. 268–9.
[3] *Ibid.*
[4] Hastings to Sykes, 10 Dec. 1772. Add. MSS. 29125, f. 183.
[5] Sulivan to Barwell, 20 May 1773 (Add. MSS. 29133, f. 561); Letter to Court,
16 Aug. 1773. Barwell opposed the transfer of the Khalsa to Calcutta and
suggested that 13 members of the Council should be responsible for different
zones (Secret Cons., 3 Aug. 1772).
[6] Hastings to Secret Committee, 1 Sept. 1772. Add. MSS. 29125, f. 137.

order. This appears also from the very different treatment given to Shitab Rai, whose arrest together with Basant Rai, his Diwan, and Sundar Singh, his peshkar, had been ordered by the Council on 28 April 1772 as soon as it came to know of Reza Khan's arrest. According to Kalyan Singh's history, troops were sent to Barh a few days before his arrest so that he could join them as if proceeding to Calcutta, as formerly he did, accompanied by a military escort.[1] His departure from Patna was 'saluted with a discharge of cannon by the Chief of Patna',[2] his son, Kalyan Singh, was continued in the management of his private and public affairs,[3] and his request that the sepoy guard over his house at Patna should be withdrawn was attended to.[4] Finally he was brought to trial before Reza Khan. While the injury to Shitab Rai's dignity and importance was thus minimised, that to Reza Khan's influence and standing was not.

Reza Khan had applied, as Shitab Rai had done, that the guards posted on his house be removed. He sought an interview with the President and Council writing:

I flatter myself that I may be honored with an interview with you and the gentlemen of the Council that you will issue your directions for withdrawing the guards of the Sircar, for they being stationed over me, is the occasion for many evils. In the first place my helpless children both here [Calcutta] and Moorshedabad are terrified: in the second place being dismissed from my station it is requisite, that I should consider my expences, and plan for the payment of the loans of the merchants which are very great; and the writers [meaning private clerical staff] on account of the centries [sic] cannot have access to me with their papers and accounts. And it is not probable that without understanding the accounts of the merchants and [of] my servants, that I can plan for lightening my expences. I have particularly represented my circumstances; whatever your understanding the repository of justice point out, [you may] direct [so] that I may not be sunk under the weight of my expences, and that I may no longer be ruined in the eyes of the public.[5]

[1] *Khulasat ut Tawarikh* (English translation in the *Journal of the Bihar and Orissa Research Society* or *JBORS*, VI, 430).
[2] Ironside to Caillaud, 23 Dec. 1773. Orme MSS. OV 41–3, f. 140.
[3] Kalyan Singh in his *Khulasat*, *JBORS*, VI, 427–30.
[4] Hastings wrote privately to Vansittart on 12 June 1772 'requesting that you may grant him on the subject . . . all relief which depends on you and which you deem within your power consistent with orders . . . from the Board' (Add. MSS. 29125, f. 92).
[5] Reza Khan's letter. Secret Cons., 16 June 1772.

The 'Inquisition', 1772–1775

While Hastings responded to Shitab Rai's plea, writing privately to George Vansittart about the matter,[1] Reza Khan's request does not appear to have been considered at all.

Similarly, whereas Kalyan Singh was allowed to act for his father at Patna, Hastings, with the concurrence of a majority of his Council, chose to appoint an old opponent of the Khan, Munni Begum, as guardian of the Nawab, and Raja Gurudas, son of another avowed enemy, Nandkumar, as the Nawab's Diwan. In appointing Munni Begum Hastings had ensured the destruction of Reza Khan's influence within the Nawab's household. And in appointing Gurudas he had carried the Secret Committee's orders to make full use of Nandkumar against the Khan, without permitting Nandkumar to secure any share in the management of the Nawab's household. This had been a difficult manoeuvre. By Hastings's own admission Nandkumar had been his personal enemy from 1759 'to the time I left Bengal in 1764',[2] and a majority in the Council had also been opposed to any appointment which gave power, even indirectly, to Nandkumar. Opposition to Raja Gurudas had also come from Munni Begum, who referred to the 'villainies of his father', and Raja Rajballabh,[3] Rai Durlabh's son who was soon to become Rai-Rayan heading the Khalsa on its transfer to Calcutta. However the appointment served Hastings well, both by inciting Nandkumar to provide material against Reza Khan, and by fomenting palace intrigues at Murshidabad which he could manipulate, through Samuel Middleton, who after the abolition of the Council at Murshidabad again became Resident at the Durbar in September 1772.

The changes at the court of the Nawab yielded further dividends. Hastings was able, while executing the Directors' orders of 10 April 1771, to reduce the Nizamat expenses from thirty-two to sixteen lakhs of rupees a year, to lessen further the influence of Reza Khan. The effecting of so vast an economy was largely Hastings's work, and he reported his achievements to the Directors in a general letter of 10 November 1772 which read:

---

[1] We do not know officially the action that followed, but Vansittart's attitude in the matter is known from his official communication speaking of the 'uneasiness which such an act of violence [as the arrest and placing of guards] may occasion among men of credit' (Secret Cons., 16 May 1772).

[2] Hastings to Secret Committee, 1 Sept. 1772. Add. MSS. 29125, f. 139.

[3] Nandkumar to Hastings, 18 June 1772 (Add. MSS. 29133, f. 160) and Hastings to S. Middleton, 9 July 1773 (Add. MSS. 29125, f. 218).

The transition in Bengal, 1756–1775

To bring the whole expenses of the Nizamut within the pale of 16 lacks it was necessary to begin with reforming the useless servants of the court and retrenching the idle parade of elephants, menageries etc., which loaded the civil list. This cost little regret in performing, but the President [Hastings]...suffered considerably in his feelings when he came to touch upon the Pension list. Some hundred of persons of the ancient nobility of the country, excluded under our government from almost all employments civil or military, had ever since the revolution depended on the bounty of the Nabob and near 10 lacks were bestowed that way. It is not that the distribution was always made with judgement and impartiality, and much room was left for a reform, but when the question was to cut off the greatest part, it could not fail to be accompanied with circumstances of real distress. The President declares that even with some of the highest rank he could not avoid discovering under all pride of eastern manners, the manifest marks of penury and want. There was however no room left for hesitation.[1]

But however much Hastings suffered while cutting the pension list, he had at least one consolation, that nearly all those who were removed were appointees of Reza Khan. According to a report from Middleton those who had previously been maintained from the Nizamat public funds could be categorised as follows:[2]

Appointed by	Men	Women	Horses	Amount involved per month in rupees	Number of 'Dustakut' or signatures or orders
Mir Jafar, 1763–5	386	11	46	7602–8 annas.	425
Mirza Muhammad Erich Khan, Naib Nazim, 1763–5	276	10	33	3287–8 annas.	323
Najm ud daulah 1765–6	8	6	—	2338–8 annas.	19
Saif-ud-daulah 1766–70	10	—	1	358–8 annas.	15
Mubarak-ud-daulah during 1770–2	3	—	—	725–0 annas.	4
Reza Khan, Naib Nazim, 1765–72	1437	90	181	41,488–13 annas.	686

That the numerous body of servants and pensioners taken on by Reza Khan should be the most hit by Hastings's economy measures was understandable, but the severity they felt could only appear as

[1] Quoted in Monckton Jones, *Warren Hastings in Bengal*, p. 192.   [2] *TP*, II, 195.

328

the result of a policy. Notice was being publicly served that to be connected with Reza Khan would henceforth be a disadvantage.[1]

Hastings can be seen in 1772 systematically preparing the destruction of Reza Khan's influence and the transfer of the Nizamat functions into English hands. He was careful to disguise the full extent of what he was doing from those in England who might have opposed him, writing to Clive for example that he would abide by his Lordship's 'good advice', and that it would be his study 'to confirm without extending the power of the Company in this country....'[2] But his skill in making change profitable to the Company and in presenting his actions as the general policy of his Council ensured that he would receive the Directors' support. His reward came in the secret letter of 16 April 1773, signed by the whole Court of Directors, which gave their general blessing to his measures. The letter categorically stated that

the extirpation of Mahmud Reza Khan's influence was absolutely necessary, and the apprehending of Shitabroy equally so: as the latter had been too long connected with Mahmud Reza Khan to be independent of him...and as to any hopes Mahmud Reza Khan may entertain of profiting by changes in the Court of Directors those hopes must steadily vanish; for however different their sentiments may be in some particulars, they heartily concur in the propriety and necessity of setting him aside and of putting administration of the Company's affairs in the hands of persons who may be rendered responsible in England for their conduct in India.[3]

The Directors also expressed their approval of Munni Begum's appointment as guardian to the Nawab, and of Raja Gurudas as Diwan. They added

the use you intend making of Nundcomar is very proper; and it affords us great satisfaction to find that you could at once determine to suppress all personal resentment, when publick affairs seemed to clash with your personal sentiment relative to Nundcomar.[4]

The Directors may not have been aware of all that Hastings intended, but they gave him all the support for his attack upon the nizamat which he could have wished for.

---

[1] Hastings carried on discrimination against known dependants of Reza Khan even privately. For example, he told Harris on 31 July 1772, 'I shall never consent to anyone of the dependants of Himmat Sing' for appointment as Diwan of Jessore (Add. MSS. 29125, f. 123b). Himmat Singh was the Khan's protégé.   [2] Quoted in Monckton Jones, *op. cit.*, p. 182.
[3] Add. MSS. 29133, f. 518.   [4] *Ibid.*

The transition in Bengal, 1756–1775

The trial of Reza Khan formally began on 12 February 1773, with a special session of the Council attended by Hastings, the Commander-in-Chief Sir Robert Barker, Aldersey, Reed and Goodwin. At this session the Company's letter of 28 August 1771 was re-read, together with the five charges framed on the basis of that letter by the Council on 16 May 1772. The charges then framed had been:

1. That Reza Khan had withheld the payment of a large balance due from him on account of Dacca revenues;

2. 'That of his own authority and knowing the same to be contrary to the express order of the Company and the regulations of the Select Committee, he did grant perwannah to certain merchants for a monopoly of the trade in salt for 3 years and thereby occasioned a loss of the Company's duties on that article';

3. That besides being guilty of many acts of violence and injustice towards the natives and subjects of the province of Bengal by various means he had contributed 'to the destruction of many thousands of the people';

4. That by abusing the trust reposed in him as Naib Diwan the Khan had caused by his misconduct and malversation the diminution of the Diwani revenues and had appropriated to his own use the large sums of money that were collected by violent and oppressive means; and

5. That the Khan had misappropriated to his own use sums that were placed at his disposal on account of the stipend of Najm-ud-daulah and Saif-ud-daulah.[1]

The Council, which had before it the Khan's denial of these charges, given in June 1772,[2] proceeded to reframe them, omitting the second, relating to salt, though this was the only one in which the Company's interest had been directly engaged. The remaining charges were reduced to four main topics:

1. The monopolising of grain during famine,
2. The embezzlement of or neglect in accounting for the Dacca revenues,
3. Mismanagement of the revenues as Naib Diwan, and
4. Mismanagement of the Nawab's stipend.[3]

---

[1] Secret Cons., 16 May 1772.   [2] Secret Cons., 18 June 1772.

[3] Proceedings of the special sessions of the Council held for the trial of Reza Khan. *TP*, I, 12 Feb. 1773.

330

Hastings recommended that the four items should be taken in the above order, 'beginning with the first as the most flagrant'.[1] However, before the day's proceedings concluded he had added a new charge, of treacherous correspondence with the Emperor and the Marathas, based on Barker's letter of 18 June 1772 wherein the general had spoken of 'some secret business carrying on between His Majesty [Shah Alam] and Muhummud Rezza Cawn'.[2]

To support the first charge of profiteering during the famine, Hastings publicly advertised for complaints, had given a free hand to Nandkumar to procure evidence and witnesses against the Khan, and had allowed a free use of his own and the Company's name. He now told the Council that he had obtained the depositions of several witnesses (eleven in number) and asked that as it would take some time to go through their depositions, 'and in the mean time the witnesses will be exposed to be tampered with', that the witnesses should be called in 'and sworn to the information now produced'.[3] Hastings's anxiety to bind the deponents whom he had with such effort procured is understandable. It is no less understandable why he should have arranged that they should submit prepared written statements (to him personally), to which they swore (in the absence of the Khan who was already a prisoner for ten months in Calcutta), rather than make their deposition in person before the Council. For, in May (1773) much of what they had deposed was exposed as contradictory and fictitious when Reza Khan cross-examined them, and submitted his written statement in reply.[4] Despite Hastings's efforts to establish the trustworthiness of his witnesses not a single member of the Council in the end proved ready to accept their word in order to convict the Khan of monopolizing grain during the famine. The furthest that George Vansittart would go was to say that

My opinion coincides in general with the President both as to the creditability or rather plausibility of the evidences and the frivolousness of many of the objections made by MRC in his defence. I say plausibility because there are some considerations which render me suspicious of them all.[5]

He then proceeded from his own experience, supported by extracts from official records, to show that while it was true that Reza Khan had procured grain from various places, this had been done on the

---

[1] *TP*, I, 12 Feb. 1773.   [2] *Ibid.*   [3] *Ibid.*
[4] *TP*, I, 14 May 1773.   [5] *TP*, II, 3 March 1774.

orders of the Fort William authorities to supply the Berhampur garrison. He concluded unambiguously, 'I do not think these evidences sufficient to prove that Mahomed R C had himself a property in the grains'.[1] Graham, who likewise quoted from personal experience as well as official documents, was even more scathing in his criticism of Hastings as well as his witnesses. He summed up:

The President has gone through the evidence with great minuteness and attention. He has pointed out the consistency and connection of the depositions, and with a few exceptions he has allowed their credibility. The witnesses in general do not appear to be either faithful or uniform in their deposition but as even the whole sum of evidence does not in my opinion, if admitted collectively, amount to a proof of the charge....[2]

It had not helped Hastings's case, of course, that one of the eleven deponents had to be imprisoned by the Council, during the course of the trial, on a charge of perjury. Hastings wrote to Aldersey on 1 July 1773 reporting that 'Sevooram, one of the grain dealers who complained against M.R.C. is in confinement for false evidence—I leave him to the justice of the Board, yet I could wish they would let him go'.[3] Hastings's hopes were not fulfilled, and although the Council's formal verdict on the first charge was not given until March 1774, they had virtually acquitted the Khan on this point by August 1773. In their general letter of 16 August in the Secret Department they informed the Court of Directors,

we have only yet been able to go through the 1st article of impeachment viz. the charge of monopolizing the grain during the famine. We have examined a number of evidences in support of this charge, but we must acknowledge that they do not establish any clear or conclusive proof of the Naib's guilt; on the contrary the belief which prevailed in the country of his being concerned in that trade seems in great degree to have taken its rise from the notions of the people, who not having access to better intelligence blended and mistook the duties of Mohammed Reza Cawn's public station in the measures which he pursued for the relief of the city during the height of the famine for the exertion of sordid views to gratify and promote his private interest.[4]

[1] *TP*, II, f. 210 (3 March 1774).
[2] Graham's minute, 3 March 1774. *TP*, II, 213.
[3] Add. MSS. 29125, f. 228.
[4] See Monckton Jones, *Warren Hastings in Bengal*, p. 193. The letter appears more as a justification of the Khan's accusers and was possibly a compromise. Hastings took particular pains to defend Huzurimul in his letter of 20 March 1774 to Sulivan (Gleig, *Memoirs of the Right Hon. Warren Hastings*, I, 391).

The 'Inquisition', 1772–1775

Hastings had not relied solely on the eleven witnesses who submitted depositions, or wholly on the abilities, observation and active malignity of Nandkumar. He had taken 'such other precautions as were most likely to produce information' against Reza Khan.[1] He also secured an attestation, signed by seventy persons, containing various allegations about the Khan's grain purchases and activities during the famine. This was procured by Shaikh Muhammad Naseem, 'servant of Mharajah Nundcomar', and besides attacks upon Reza Khan also included encomiums on the Maharaja's great concern for the sufferings of the natives.[2]

Shaikh Naseem's memorial was a reply to an earlier one procured by Mir Sadr-ud-din on behalf of his client Reza Khan. Sadr-ud-din had appealed to the 'knowledge of men of station, rank and family and all others the inhabitants of Moorshedabad etc', upon the conduct of the Khan during the whole period of his Naibat.[3] He asked them in particular to testify on two points:

(a) Had not the Khan 'continually exerted himself to promote the happiness and security of the people and demonstrate his attachment to the Company', particularly during the famine;

(b) 'Whether he did not to the extent of his abilities expend large sums of money in the charitable donation of grain and refrain from all trade in this article which both the sacred law [of religion] and general opinion deem illicit, and in a time when scarcity prevails is the very worst of actions'.

Sadr-ud-din then set out four charges of making private profits by abuse of official position during famine made against the Khan, calumnies 'brought by the corrupt seduction, support and instigation of malicious persons who entertain inveterate hatred and envy' against his client, and asked for testimony 'without variance and exaggeration' to refute them. To his memorial Sadr-ud-din secured two hundred and eighty-seven signature or attesting seals. Some gave particular answer to the questions and charges, others merely appended their seal or signature testifying in general to the Khan's innocence. Among these signatories were Shaikh Faiz ullah, the Sadr of Bengal, Muhammad Mohtadi, the Mufti of Bengal, Muhammad Ufa, the Chief Qazi, Jagat Seth Khoshal Chand and Maharaja Udai Chand, the Seth brothers, Aqa Ali and

---

[1] *See* Monckton Jones, *op cit.*, p. 195. [2] *TP*, II, 73–84 (26 Nov. 1773).
[3] *TP*, II, 17–72 (26 Nov. 1773).

333

The transition in Bengal, 1756–1775

Aqa Muhammad, merchants, the market superintendents of Jafarganj and Bahramganj, Rai Gulab Singh, superintendent of the mint, twelve grain merchants of Mansurganj, and three grain merchants of Shahmatganj and Makbaraganj. The high standing of many of the signatories is evident (there being none higher in Murshidabad left out except the Nawab himself), but even more telling was the evidence they offered of the quality of the contrary evidence procured by Nandkumar for Hastings. They reported that Nandkumar had been trying to secure depositions against Reza Khan by offers of service or of payments up to Rs. 100 a month, while his son Gurudas had been using his official position to put pressure on individuals, even by posting guards and peons upon them. One signatory enclosed a note in Nandkumar's hand offering a remission of arrears due to the government and his service into the bargain in return for evidence against the Khan.[1]

Hastings's own comment on the two memorials, in a private letter of 20 March 1772 to Sulivan was

Mahommed Reza Cawn has produced the attestation of above 200 persons, mostly of credit, in vindication of his conduct during the famine. His adversary [Nandkumar] has produced a similar paper of attestation against him signed indeed by fewer names and those little known. Neither merit the smallest consideration. No honest man in this country would have set his hand to the latter, though he believed it to be true. Few would have heart to refuse signing the former, although he believed it to be false.[2]

It was convenient to discredit all native testimony when the great weight of it was cast so clearly against his charge.[3]

By February 1773 again Hastings was privately engaged in procuring materials that 'may indeed corroborate the information or accounts which I expect from Nundcomar' regarding the second charge against the Khan, relating to the Dacca revenues,[4] though the Council formally took up the case on 5 August 1773. Reza Khan admitted that the first contract for these which he had signed was for an amount considerably greater than any he had subsequently collected. But he was able to show that the original contract had been forced on him by the Nawab Mir Jafar under pressure

[1] The attestation procured by Mir Sadr-ud-din. *TP*, II, 17–72 (26 Nov. 1773).
[2] Gleig, *Memoirs of the Right Hon. Warren Hastings*, I, 391.
[3] Reza Khan's activities during the famine have been detailed in chapter 9.
[4] Hastings to Middleton, 24 Feb. 1773. Add. MSS. 29125, ff. 199–200.

334

from Nandkumar and that he had later secured an undertaking from the Nawab that he would be held to account only for what he actually collected from that very distracted district. This undertaking, in Mir Jafar's writing, the Khan submitted in evidence to the Council.[1] A letter from Middleton enclosing extracts from contemporary correspondence provided additional support for Reza Khan's argument.[2] Having made the point, the Khan went to show that his accounts of collection tallied with those locally collected.

Nandkumar, however, produced his accounts to show that for the period 1169 to 1171 that is from 1762–3 to 1764–5 (which included a year before Reza Khan's appointment at Dacca) there was an outstanding balance of over twenty seven lakhs due from the Khan. The Council requested Hastings to ask Nandkumar to furnish proof of these allegations to Barwell and the Dacca Council who were conducting the local enquiry. From 20 December 1773 to 6 January 1774, the Dacca Council devoted six sittings to an open enquiry in this matter, examining the office staff and almost all the Naibs of those zemindars who paid over Rs. 1,000 in revenue. Everyone of them declared under oath that they had paid no more than was shown in the account. What was more, the Dacca Council found that every item of receipt and disbursement tallied with the Khan's accounts. Then, just as the enquiry was closing, one Mir Ismail handed another paper to Barwell, who was then on a visit to Calcutta, wherein the outstanding balance was shown as 57 lakhs. This paper was handed to Barwell at Nandkumar's instigation and when Nandkumar was asked to produce the man, so that he could prove his allegations, the Maharaja reported that the Mir had gone to Hugli where he had sickened and died. Hastings was careful that the paper had been submitted apparently without his knowledge or permission. It is clear that Nandkumar was ready to submit a fresh charge whenever the enquiry seemed about to conclude, and a further set of accounts was submitted, it is said by Hastings, in which the outstanding balance was set over 98 lakhs of rupees. However, despite every attempt to secure some flaw in Reza Khan's accounts, none was found. The only possible further

---

[1] Reza Khan had submitted a memorial to the Council. *TP*, I, 190–201 (9 June 1773).

[2] *TP*, 5 Aug. 1773. In a letter to Middleton on 24 Feb. 1773 while asking for proof to corroborate Nandkumar's account against the Khan, Hastings commented: 'I can learn nothing from your book of correspondence that can serve as a proof' (Add. MSS. 29125, f. 200).

check would have involved a verification of all the papers in the zemindars's cutcherries to see whether there were any payments additional to those sworn to by the zemindars and their Naibs. The task would have been inordinately lengthy and costly, and even then could not have established the guilt of the Khan, who could not be held liable for excess payments taken by his subordinates. By the Khan's own account there was a balance due from him, but only of Rs. 1,812-14-8-3, a slip in accounting rather than a deliberate malversation. The verdict of the Council could not but be 'not guilty' and so it was.

Reza Khan was found not guilty on the third count of mismanagement of the diwani revenues. Here the Council proceeded to verify the amount credited to the Company and the disbursements from that sum. They found that during the Khan's five year administration, from 1765–6 to 1770–1 the revenue account stood as follows:[1]

Demand	Rs. 9,35,84,745- 6- 3-2.
Collected	Rs. 8,59,94,232-13- 6-1.
Balance	Rs. 84,67,983- 3- 8-0.

Of this balance an abatement had been authorised in the

Sum of	Rs. 81,97,692-11- 7-2, leaving a
Final balance of	Rs. 2,70,290- 8- 0-2.

The Khan accounted for the whole of this final balance and the charge on this head was therefore dismissed.

For his management of the Khalsa and Household expenditure Reza Khan submitted full accounts of receipts and disbursements; every item of which was proved correct by Middleton by reference to the records, vouchers and statements of individuals at Murshidabad.[2] Gurudas, however, spotted that the Khan had not accounted for the special fund arising from batta on the cash disbursements,[3] but as soon as the omission was pointed out the Khan produced full accounts of the amount so received and of its expenditure upon the maintenance of traditional expenses. The Khan held a balance of Rs. 1,215-15-19. Once again the charge

---

[1] *TP*, II, 86–7.   [2] *TP*, II, 124–9 and 204–6.

[3] *TP*, II, 202–3. The Khan, it would appear, was forced to the creation of this fund only to maintain certain public servants and to continue to pay certain traditional expenses such as gratuities to amils and others during certain festivals, in order to preserve the traditional image of the government after he had been deprived of all other means to do so.

against the Khan proved untenable. Hastings in disappointment complained to Sulivan:

I have taken every measure, by proclamation, protection and personal access, to encourage evidences against him [Reza Khan], and have given many valuable hours, the whole days, of my time to the multiplied and indefinite accounts and suggestions of Nundcomar. I presided in every examination, one day excepted, and was myself the examiner and interpreter in each. The proceedings will show with what wretched materials I was furnished.[1]

The last charge, of treacherous correspondence with his sovereign, was also dropped as it was found that the Khan was in no way personally involved. In 1772 Zain ul Abedin, a relative of the Khan, had gone to Delhi to escort his sister to Bengal, but hearing of the situation in Bengal (created by the Khan's arrest), had decided to seek employment in Delhi. To this end he had posed as a representative of the Khan and had caused the Khan's seal to be forged for this purpose. Hastings did not attempt to press the charge against Reza Khan, who was declared innocent.

On 15 March 1774 the Council declared Reza Khan innocent of all the charges and recommended his release from confinement. The Khan was asked, however, to give an undertaking not to leave Bengal until the pleasure of the Court of Directors was known. The approval of the Khan's acquittal was given on 3 March 1775 and reached Calcutta in October.

By the time the trial closed with an acquittal Reza Khan had been in a state of arrest for twenty-three months, fourteen of them under very close arrest with guards over his houses, making it impossible, as the Khan had complained, even for his personal staff to come in or go out and causing terror to his children. The Council had recommended the withdrawal of guards on 16 June 1773, as might otherwise 'appear to the world an act of wanton severity'.[2] The Khan's movement ever since was restricted to Calcutta, which now after his acquittal was still confined to Bengal.

---

[1] Hastings to Sulivan, 20 March 1774 (Gleig, *Memoirs of the Right Hon. Warren Hastings*, I, 391). This letter was written five days after the Khan had been acquitted by the Council of all charges.

[2] *TP*, I, 273. By 16 June 1773 the Council had had all evidences against the Khan before them. Time had come for 'receiving his defence and passing judgement upon them'. They felt that 'other charges which remain to be enquired into relate solely to the matters of accounts for investigating which information already received and the public records . . . are the only materials wanted'.

The transition in Bengal, 1756–1775

The delay in starting proceedings, the slowness with which they were conducted, had both been deliberate. Hastings was determined to establish a new system, in which 'there can be but one government and one power in this province',[1] and for this it was essential that the Khan should be rendered powerless for as long as possible. On 8 October 1772 Hastings explained his plan to DuPre:

For the better management of the Dewannee it was proposed and agreed to, to bring the collection to Calcutta. Hither too we have brought the superior courts of justice. We have established two at the Presidency for appeals of civil causes, and for the inspection and confirmation in capital cases; and two inferior courts of like kind in each district. By this arrangement, and the government of the provinces will center in Calcutta, which may now be called the capital of Bengal. The establishment of the courts of justices in Calcutta was almost an act of injustice, the criminal judicature being a branch of the Nizamut... It met with no opposition and it is now a point determined, although neither of these courts have yet begun to exercise their functions for want of proper places to sit in.[2]

He might have added that this act of injustice had met with no opposition because the one man who might have raised it, Reza Khan, was confined under guard. He continued to be held without trial for nearly ten months, while Hastings used all the means open to him to spread the belief that when the trial did come it would end in the Khan's conviction. Thus when Cartier expressed a wish to call on the Khan before sailing for England, Hastings first delayed a reply and then vetoed the proposal. On 4 January 1773, Hastings wrote to Cartier

My opinion is that your visiting Mahmud Riza Cawn will furnish occassion for false surmises and conjectures with respect to the issue of his present disgrace. However he may have been injured by the original authors of it, untill he is brought to a formal trial it will be impossible... to counter the opinion that he has such protectors as may effect the restoration of his former authority and consequence, as the same impression will prove of detriment also to the system newly adopted untill it shall be well established... but I shall be perfectly satisfied with any determination which you may form upon it... according to your own discretion.[3]

[1] Hastings to Committee of Secrecy, 24 March 1774 (Monckton Jones, *Warren Hastings in Bengal*, p. 198).
[2] Hastings to DuPre, 8 Oct. 1772 (Add. MSS. 29125, ff. 156–7).
[3] Hastings to Cartier, 4 Jan. 1773 (Add. MSS. 19125, f. 191). The Khan was by then held without trial for eight months.

338

Hastings was determined that the great opportunity opened before him of establishing the 'sovereignty of the British people' over Bengal, and of himself within it should not be lost. He explained to Dupre that he needed the period of the Nawab's minority 'to establish and confirm the Company's authority in the country', though he had hopes that the young Nawab would be entangled thereafter in enmity with Munni Begum 'because she now rules him'.[1] At the same time he was writing to Colebrooke asking for additional powers for himself. 'A system of affairs so new', he wrote, 'requires a new system of government to conduct.' He explained that this meant that the governor must have 'such a degree of actual control as may enable him to support with credit the character of the ostensible head of Government to give vigour to its decrees and preserve them from inconsistencies'.[2] And later in the same year (1773), he was dropping broad hints to Sulivan that he ought to be confirmed for some considerable period in his governorship, with comments upon the 'well known infirmities of our constitution according to which the governor is changed frequently'.[3] With the power of the diwani and nizamat brought down to Calcutta, and with himself installed as governor with enhanced power for a term of years, he could hope to satisfy his desire to direct affairs in India and also secure for himself and his Council those possibilities of profit which Cartier had allowed to fall into the hands of the supervisors and members of the Murshidabad and Patna Councils. By September 1772 the Council at Murshidabad was abolished, Middleton reverting to the post of the Resident at the Durbar; and by January 1773 Hastings was reporting to Dupre that he had allowed the supervisors to continue under a new title of collectors 'but their power is retrenched; and the way is paved for their gradual removal'. This cautious move was necessary, Hastings explained, because 'it appeared that there were amongst them, so many sons, cousins, or *élèves* of directors, and intimates of the members of the Council, that it was better to let them remain than provoke an army of opponents against every act of administration by depriving them of their emoluments'.[4] He had so built up the case against the supervisors that the

---

[1] Hastings to DuPre, 6 Jan. 1773 (Gleig, *Memoirs of the Right Hon. Warren Hastings*, pp. 269–70).
[2] Hastings to Colebrooke, 7 March 1773 (*ibid.* pp. 290–1).
[3] Hastings to Sulivan, 11 Nov. 1773 (*ibid.* p. 369).
[4] Hastings to DuPre, 6 Jan. 1773 (*ibid.* p. 269).

22-2

The transition in Bengal, 1756–1775

Directors felt obliged to order their recall in their letter of 7 April 1773. By 2 January 1774 Hastings was appointing a third attorney in England, this addition being 'necessary as a guard against what may happen, as my remittances are likely to become considerable from some engagements into which I have lately entered'.[1] All these plans hinged, as would appear, on rendering the Khan politically impotent.

However, as has been seen Hastings continued to do all he could to destroy the Khan's authority by appointing his enemies and critics to posts of confidence in the Durbar and by dismissing his pensioners and protégés who formed a great part of the ancient nobility of Murshidabad. He also turned down the Khan's pleas, of June 1773, for relief from the financial distress into which his arrest had plunged him. The Company owed a great deal to the Khan on account of his salary as Naib Diwan, as he pointed out, and even before he was brought down to Calcutta he had incurred debts to the extent of five or six lakhs of rupees to the Murshidabad bankers; from whom he had borrowed to tide over the irregular payment of his salary.[2] Reza Khan did not raise the question of his arrears of salary until after his release in 1774,[3] but in June 1773 he did ask Hastings to buy his house for the Company—it stood near the Government House in Calcutta—so that he could meet the demands of his creditors. The Khan had been obliged to offer his house for sale for he found no other alternative. He had repeatedly asked the governor for a loan but Hastings did not bother even to reply. The Khan could not agree to sell the effects in his house for that was humiliating. His pride prevented him from selling the house to a new rich Banian. He therefore offered it to the Company and suggested that if the Company could not pay him in cash they might give a bond which he could endorse in favour of his creditors.[4] The proposal was turned down[5] but the Council intervened and agreed to take the house on lease at a monthly rental of Rs. 1,000 from July 1773.[6]

By 15 March 1774, when the Council declared that Reza Khan was innocent of the charges against him Hastings had so firmly established his new system, and so weakened the Khan's influence

---

[1] Hastings to Woodman, 2 Jan. 1774. Add. MSS. 29134, f. 234.
[2] Reza Khan to Hastings, recd. 24 May 1774. *CPC*, IV, 1045.   [3] *Ibid.*
[4] Reza Khan to Hastings, recd. 9 June 1773. *CPC*, IV, 354.
[5] Hastings to Reza Khan, 20 (14?) June 1773. *CPC*, IV, 377.
[6] Hastings to Reza Khan, 24 (14?) June 1773. *CPC*, IV, 394.

340

and authority that he was willing to propose the Khan's release from arrest (which however was no longer tenable after his innocence had been established). Hastings made it clear that he did so because he believed that he had broken the Khan:

I have said I have no political motive to desire his continuance in arrest. The influence which his long established authority gave him in these provinces, might have been a powerful and dangerous impediment to the introduction of the authority which the Company themselves have thought proper to exercise without a foreign intervention, in the character of Dewan of these provinces, had he remained free and at large when their orders to this effect were required to be carried into execution. The system which they have dictated has since been completely and radically established nor have a shadow of apprehension left for any efforts which he might make, supposing him so inclined, to subvert or obstruct it.[1]

However, Hastings was not one to leave anything to chance, and while he was explaining to the Council that the Khan's sufferings had been a temporary necessity, he was writing to the Committee of Secrecy of the Court of Directors pleading with them not to restore the Khan to his former office or authority. In his letter of 24 March 1774 he said,

Whatever your resolution may be concerning the future fate of Mohammed Reza Cawn, it is my duty, although I believe it unnecessary, to represent that whatever reparation you may think due for his past sufferings, the restoration of any part of the power which he before possessed will inevitably tend to the injury of the Company's affairs, and the diminution of your influence.[2]

The strident assertion that there was no 'shadow of apprehension left' that Reza Khan once acquitted could undo the new order in Bengal, coupled with the private plea to the Secret Committee that the Khan should not be restored to any 'part of the power which he before possessed' suggest that in reality Hastings was still anxious about outcome of events. He had cause for anxiety. The Company's financial distress had led to the intervention of Parliament and to the impeachment of Clive, his associates and Reza Khan. Sykes on 28 January 1773 reported to Hastings

---

[1] Hastings minute, dated 14 March 1774. *TP*, II, 242–3.
[2] Hastings to Committee of Secrecy, 24 March 1774 (Monckton Jones, *Warren Hastings in Bengal*, pp. 197–8).

The transition in Bengal, 1756–1775

The Court of Directors ushered into the House of Commons a kind of complaint against MRC, Becher and myself for instituting an arbitrary tax in Bengall...never heard of before, unauthorised, unsanctified, drawn from the bowells of the inhabitants, and a variety of languages of this nature.[1]

But by 21 May 1773 the attack upon Clive had ended with praise for his achievements,[2] three days earlier the Bill for the Regulating Act was introduced, and by 13 October Sulivan was writing to Hastings to hurry through his revenue and military reforms before General Clavering, Colonel Monson and Philip Francis could reach Calcutta as members of the new five-man government set up under the Regulating Act, with Hastings as Governor-General and Barwell as another representative of the Company's interest in the new set up. Sulivan had added,

I could also wish you to have the whole credit in Mahomed Rezah Cawn's business, for it is my opinion that these matters are intended to be probed to the bottom.[3]

Uncertainty about developments in England may well be at the back of Hastings's attempt late in 1773 to ease his personal relationship with Reza Khan. There seems no other explanation for his sudden invitation to the Khan's two sons, Nawab Saiyid Husain Ali Khan Bahram Jang and Nawab Saiyid Muhammad Taqi Khan Dilawar Jang to attend a theatrical performance in December 1773, which was followed by others in January, May and July 1774, together with one to the Khan himself immediately after his acquittal in March.[4] Hastings's proposal in that same month for the Khan's release from arrest seems to be another move to guard himself against a reversal in English attitude towards the Khan. Shitab Rai, it should be noted, had been tried before Reza Khan, quickly acquitted, and in 1773 re-appointed Naib Nazim and Rai-Rayan for Bihar, though on half his previous salary and with his income from Patna customs duties stopped. But he was an aged man, brought up in the highest circles in Delhi, and could not survive the humiliation inflicted on him. He died soon after his

---

[1] Sykes to Hastings, 28 Jan. 1773. Add. MSS. 29133, f. 350.
[2] Clive wrote in October 1773 to report this triumph over his enemies to Hastings (Forrest, *Clive*, II, 410).
[3] Sulivan to Hastings, 13 Oct. 1773. Add. MSS. 29134, f. 70.
[4] Hastings to Reza Khan, 22 Dec. 1773, 15 Jan. 1774, 23 May, 26 July, 27 July 1774 (*CPC*, IV, 713, 764, 1042, 1182, 1185). Ali Ibrahim Khan was also an invitee.

The 'Inquisition', 1772–1775

return to Patna.[1] It was against this background that, on 14 March 1774, Hastings urged the Khan's release:

Allow me, gentlemen, to add my feelings both for myself as an individual and for the reputation of the Hon'ble Company with which, no less than their interests, I am materially charged as their first representative in this administration, when I reflect on the consequences which may happen from an extension of the disgrace and confinement under which Mahmud Rezza Cawn has long laboured. Few are the instances of such a reverse of fortune befalling a man of his important station which has not hastened the period of his death, and the world is ever prone to attribute an event of this kind to the causes of the most criminal reproach, equally affecting the personal character of the immediate agents of Government, and the justice and honour of the supreme power in whose name and for whose behalf the original act of authority first issued wch [which] may have been followed by such a catastrophe.[2]

At the same time, in a letter to the Committee of Secrecy, he made the nature of his fear still clearer:

I am aware of the violent prejudices which were taken up at once against Mohamad Reza Cawn by all ranks of people both here and at home. I am also aware that in England, where the very name of enquiry into the management of past affairs in India flatters the passion of the times, and raises expectations of great and important detections, the result may balk those expectations and turn the torrent of public clamour another way.[3]

Letters from Becher and Verelst to Barwell were to indicate that Reza Khan's old friends were still concerned about his fate.[4] (Verelst, of course, was still in debt to Reza Khan.)[5] But Sykes, Hastings's confidant and agent, made it still clearer that sympathy for the Khan was live and growing. He asked anxiously about the Khan, who had assisted him to fortune and political influence. On 30 March 1774 Sykes wrote to Hastings expressing his hope that 'MRC has come off with honour' and asking Hastings to convey his respects to the Khan, 'for whom I have a great regard'.[6]

[1] Monckton Jones, *Warren Hastings in Bengal*, pp. 198–9. See also *Khulasat* (*JBORS*, VI, 436).   [2] Hastings's minute, 14 March 1774. *TP*, II, 243.
[3] Monckton Jones, *op. cit.* p. 196.
[4] Barwell, reporting the outcome of the trial proceedings to Becher, said (on 30 Nov. 1774), 'I think they cannot fail to give you satisfaction' (see *BPP*, XII, 90).   [5] See above, chapter 7.
[6] Sykes to Hastings, 30 March 1774. Add. MSS. 29134, ff. 362–3.

343

The transition in Bengal, 1756–1775

Before the year was out he was writing more openly, to tell Hastings

> The people here are much shocked at the treatment to MRC. The Directors, I mean those who signed the letter for his being seized, deserve to be hanged. I was with some of them today and told them so. They seem determined to do something for him wch, I think they ought to do, or I would prosecute them for false imprisonment.[1]

Such sentiments can scarcely have been palatable to a man who had taken upon himself the task of destroying the Khan in every possible way.

Hastings, however, had problems nearer at hand than public sentiment in London. He had brought the nizamat authority to Calcutta, and had himself undertaken the supervision of criminal justice conducted through Sadr ul Haq Khan, who had been the chief of the Sadar Nizamat Adalat: the author of the Seir observed, the post was 'by all means above the old man's capacity and strength'.[2] The burden therefore fell the more heavily upon Hastings who wrote in July 1774 to George Vansittart complaining 'I am fatigued and plagued to death by the Fowjdaries and Adawluts'.[3] Hastings needed someone of authority to whom he could transfer his burden, and he needed a Muslim to administer criminal justice for and on behalf of the Nawab.[4]

Unfortunately, therefore, the party he had chosen to elevate against the Khan was quite unfit to be entrusted with the task. Munni Begum was a woman; Nandkumar and Gurudas, however high they might be placed, were unacceptable. Nandkumar was quite ready to help deprive Reza Khan of the Nizamat powers, but he was no more ready than the Khan to see the Mughal sovereignty pass to the Company. As Hastings reported to the Secret Committee in March 1774, Nandkumar, soon after the appointment of his son Gurudas as Nizamat Diwan, was sending drafts of letters by way of him to Munni Begum 'which he recommended her to write to me, enumerating the many encroachments which had been made by the English government on the rights of the Nizamut, and reclaiming them' for and on behalf of the minor Nawab.[5] Again

---

[1] Sykes to Hastings, 20 Dec. 1774. Add. MSS. 29135, f. 393.   [2] Seir, III, 91.
[3] Hastings to G. Vansittart, 30 July 1774. Add. MSS. 29125, f. 339.
[4] Muslim law continued to be the criminal law of the country until the end of the Company's rule in India. Till then Muslim law officers were essential for administration of criminal justice.
[5] Monckton Jones, *Warren Hastings in Bengal*, p. 197.

344

The 'Inquisition', 1772–1775

in the attestation against Reza Khan procured by Nandkumar through Shaikh Muhammad Naseem, the claim had been made that 'the [Mughal] King had committed this country to the Company's management, to the end that the people being maintained in security and happiness might pray for the King's and the Company's prosperity'.[1] When Hastings failed to convict Reza Khan, and was trying to ease his personal relationship with the Khan, the disappointed Nandkumar was quite ready to turn against him. It may also have been that Nandkumar, judging from his own failure to produce convicting evidence against Khan, had foreseen the ultimate victory of Reza Khan and had, therefore, become beforehand with new rumours not merely to explain what must have become apparent as the likely result of the case, but also to prevent Reza Khan's restoration to favour, this time involving his two enemies, Reza Khan and Hastings. By 13 January 1774, over two months before the Khan was acquitted in India, Sykes was warning Hastings from London that a rumour had been spread by his enemies that he was about to return to England having made 'a fortune by MRC'.[2] It was believed that Nandkumar through his correspondents in England had helped float the rumour. Hastings for his part was soon revealing to the Directors his fear of

the dark and deceitful character of Nundcomar, whose gratitude no kindness can bind, nor even his own interest disengage him from the crooked politics which have been the study of his whole life.[3]

For a variety of reasons Hastings was thus driven to seek a reconciliation with Reza Khan, the natural enemy of Nandkumar.[4] After the arrival of Clavering, Monson and Francis, who sought to use the Maharaja against Hastings, the advantage of winning over Reza Khan became even more obvious. Ghulam Husain records that Ali Ibrahim Khan was used by Hastings as a go-between in an effort to win over Reza Khan by harping on Hastings's role in saving Reza Khan's life and honour.[5]

[1] Shaikh Muhammad Naseem's attestation, TP, II, 73.
[2] Sykes to Hastings, 13 Jan. 1774. Add. MSS. 29134, f. 260.
[3] Monckton Jones, op. cit., pp. 196–7.
[4] When proposing the release of the Khan from the state of arrest, Hastings observed on 14 March 1774 that the Khan 'cannot quit the country without sacrificing all his interests in it, and his hopes of future fortune and protection' (TP, II, 242). It is not clear if he was also offering 'hopes of future fortune and protection', though indirectly.
[5] Seir, III, 80. Ghulam Husain appears to be combining a fact, that of Ali Ibrahim's acting as a go-between with a very common belief which grew after

345

The transition in Bengal, 1756–1775

Reza Khan was a ruined man and he knew the situation he was placed in, but he did not respond to such a belated offer of friendship. Nor, however, did he participate in any way in the Hastings–Nandkumar tussle that ultimately ended in Nandkumar's conviction in the Supreme Court on charges of forgery and execution by hanging on 5 August 1775. For one with less strong traditional sense of dignity it would have been perhaps difficult, if not impossible, to resist the temptation of joining hands with the enemies of Nandkumar.[1] Neither was he enthusiastic when Philip Francis made approaches to him though Goring. The latter wrote:

The Nabob [Reza Khan] complains loudly of the indignity and want of respect shown him at the time of his confinement by Mr. Hastings and that the proceedings against him were carried on more on the stile of a felon than of the first Black Man in the country.

Goring further reported that the Khan

is unwilling to say anything at present respecting what has passed between him and several gentlemen here as he esteems it beneath his dignity to inform against anyone and imagines his character would suffer by it but is ready at all times to give the best advice in his power for the future management and welfare of the country and longs exceedingly for a personal interview with the General and Colonel. [The Khan] is perfectly sensible of the high commission the gentlemen newly arriv'd bear and sincerely wishes to hear of some salutary measure pursued by them by wch [which] the whole country may know that they are come out to protect and save it from destruction, for till such measure is put in execution all men of consequence will keep aloof.[2]

Goring's report of December 1774 thus gives a glimpse of the Khan's feelings about Hastings, the man who had dragged him through mud and mire and had done his best to destroy the old Mughal authority in Bengal. He was indeed bitter about Hastings's treatment with him, but 'he esteems it beneath his dignity to inform against anyone'. All that he wished was that something should be done positively to save the country 'from destruction'. Unless measures were taken in that direction, he declared, no

Nandkumar's execution for forgery, which could never be taken as a capital offence in India. It was commonly believed that Nandkumar paid with his life because of enmity with Hastings.

[1] By 1773 even Jagat Chand had become hostile to his father-in-law Nandkumar, who then began accusing him of having joined Reza Khan's party. (Add. MSS. 29125, f. 202).
[2] Goring to P. Francis, Dec. 1774 (Francis MSS. I.O., Eur. C, 7, pp. 7–8).

The '*Inquisition*', *1772–1775*

Indian 'of consequence' would come forward and co-operate with the English rulers. As for himself he was prepared to give 'the best advice in his power'. Since Goring was on a mission to sound out the possibility of the Khan's joining the Clavering–Monson–Francis party he was induced to hint his willingness to do so, 'provided he found protection and favour'. Until that assurance was forthcoming 'he would peacably remain where he was, at the same time acknowledging his obligation for the kindness shew'd him [by Francis] in sending a gentleman to enquire after him'. The Khan might have been waiting also to hear the Directors' decision on Calcutta's recommendations for his acquittal.

It was not until 3 March 1775 that the Court of Directors signified their formal agreement; but on 16 February 1775 Sykes had reported to Hastings that the Directors, despite the opposition of the Johnstone group, had assured him that they would endeavour to get for the Khan the best office they had yet at their disposal.[1] The Directors' orders of 3 March 1775, declaring their repugnance to the continuance in office of Raja Gurudas, in view of the 'inconsistent and unworthy' conduct of his father Nandkumar, and their desire to see the re-appointment of Reza Khan without any 'improper degree of power' being given to him led eventually to a dispute over interpretations, between Hastings and Barwell on the one hand and Clavering, Monson and Francis on the other. On 18 October 1775, however, the majority prevailed and ordered

that the Secretary acquaint Mahomed Reza Cawn that the Hon'ble the Court of Directors have been pleased to approve of the proceedings of the late Board on the investigation of his conduct...and that he be further acquainted that the Hon'ble the Governor and Council have therefore, been pleased to recommend him to the Nabob Mobarek O'Dowla to be Naib Soubah or minister of the Sircar and guardian of his minority with authority to transact the political affairs of the Sircar, to superintend the Faujdari Courts, and the administration of criminal justice throughout the country and to enforce the operation of the same on the present establishment or to new-model or correct it. As the Board wish that he shall have full control of the criminal courts in the character of Naib Soubah, they propose to remove the Nizamat Adalat, now in Calcutta to be held in future at Moorshedabad.

The Khan thus returned to power, but he was already involved in the controversy over the restoration of Mughal authority in Bengal.

[1] Sykes to Hastings, 16 Feb. 1775. Add. MSS. 29136, f. 57.

The transition in Bengal, 1756–1775

He had found in Philip Francis a staunch supporter for his ideas,[1] while Hastings was seeking to maintain the new order created by him. He was necessarily involved thereafter in the fluctuating fortunes of the struggle between Francis and Hastings.

It is not intended here to trace the further career of Reza Khan in any detail. It should be noted that Reza Khan had sought to come to terms with Hastings when the latter was first appointed Governor of Bengal. His approaches had been rejected and he was thereafter subjected to personal humiliation and financial ruin[2] of a deliberately prolonged trial while Hastings encouraged Nandkumar to a campaign of malicious accusations. Even after the trial was over, when Hastings found himself thrown on the defensive, outvoted in his own Council, the Khan was reluctant to join the triumphant majority against him just for personal reasons. Francis, who came out from England with the blessings of Clive, the Khan's original patron, tempted the Khan with proposals for a reversal of Hastings's administrative measures, but the Khan refused the offer. Francis reported to Clive in a letter of 21 May 1775, which Clive did not live to receive,

[1] In Feb. 1775 Francis gave his views to Lord North saying, 'We coin money in the name of Shah Allum. We collect and appropriate the revenue by virtue of his grant: and if there be any such thing as justice in the country, it must be administered in his name, or that of his representative the Subah of Bengal. It has been the policy of Mr Hastings to abolish the sovereignty of the Mogul in fact, and to deny it in argument, without however attempting to substitute any other but his own' (see J. Parkes and H. Merivale, *Memoirs of Sir Philip Francis*, II, 27). With such a view the Khan was more likely to agree. The actual state of criminal justice in the country seemed to be in utter confusion. While the rest of the country came under the jurisdiction of Sadr ul Haq Khan, the creature of Hastings, Murshidabad was excluded (Add. MSS. 29134, f. 175). In July 1774 Hastings was complaining 'I can confine neither to method nor the observance of the orders' (Add. MSS. 29125, f. 339). In the confusion, as Hastings himself observed, 'a Hindoo has presumed and allowed to officiate as Daroga' of the faujdari adalat at Birbhum (*ibid.* 304) supposedly administering Muslim law.

[2] The Khan, who was heavily indebted to bankers at the time of his arrest, was never in a position to repay his debts. He was indebted to the Jagat Seth to the extent of three lakhs of rupees, and as the *Calcutta Gazette* editorially noticed on 10 July 1788: 'Juggat Sett, when visited in his last sickness by Mahommed Reza Khan, tore the latter's bond for three lakhs of rupees, as a return for the kindness and protection he had received from him, as well as from personal regard' (C. S. Seton-Karr, *Selections from Calcutta Gazette*, I, 259). Yet he was obliged to mortgage his Calcutta house, which later became known as the Old Government House, to Captain Thomas Burgess in 1788 for a sum of Rs. 1,07,733 (*BPP*, XIV, 176–7).

348

The 'Inquisition', 1772–1775

Mahomed Reza is almost the only man of any credit and consequence left in the country. My good opinion of him was very much confirmed by his declining the offers I made him. They were such as hardly any other black man would have refused. His objections were in general to the inutility or danger of any system that was to join natives and Europeans in the management of the collection. Yet he confessed that, in our situation, and with the executive magistrate against us a total change in the mode of collecting would be too hazardous a measure...liable to fail of success—and as to himself, he should be disgraced and rendered incapable of serving us hereafter. I acquiesced in reasons which I could not answer....[1]

Hastings showed no such forbearance towards the Khan when, by the death first of Monson and then of Clavering he was restored to power. In March 1778 on an engineered complaint from the Nawab, Hastings removed the Khan from office.[2] It was necessary for the Directors to overrule and censure Hastings, and order Reza Khan's reinstatement in their letter of 4 February 1779, before Hastings's vindictiveness was finally rendered ineffective against him. Reza Khan was restored to the post of Naib Nazim in 1780 and continued to hold the office with decreasing power until the office itself was abolished by Cornwallis on 1 January 1791. On 1 October of that same year Reza Khan died. He was buried in the Nishat Bagh, beside the grave of his brother Muhammad Husain Khan, the Nawab Mubarak-ud-daulah, the Nawab Nazim of Bengal, Bihar and Orissa assisting at the funeral ceremonies.[3]

[1] Philip Francis to Lord Clive, 21 May 1775 (Francis MSS., I.O., Eur. E, 13, f. 241). Lord Clive died in England on 22 Nov. 1774 (Forrest, *Clive*, II, 411).
[2] Hastings made another attempt to win over Reza Khan through Anderson, but on the Khan's refusal declared him as his enemy (Hastings to Sykes, 23 April 1778; Gleig, *Memoirs of Right Hon. Warren Hastings*, II, 189–92). Hastings's treatment of Reza Khan was to have been one of the twenty-two charges against Warren Hastings in 1786, but this was eventually dropped in the final drafting of the 'Articles of Impeachment' in 1787 (P.J. Marshall, *The Impeachment of Warren Hastings*, pp. xiv–xv). One wonders if James Grant's *Analysis* in 1786 played any role, however minimal.
[3] *TM*, f. 476. Reza Khan had five children, three sons, two daughters. His eldest son Husain Ali (Bahram Jang) had predeceased him. His second son, Dilawar Jang, who was earlier recommended by the Khan to succeed him, became the founder of the Chitpur Nawab family.

A SELECT BIBLIOGRAPHY

This has been compiled under two major heads, 'Primary and Contemporary Sources' and 'Secondary and Later Sources'. Of these the first group has five sections: 1, Original Official Records in manuscript; 2, Published Official Records; 3, Contemporary Private Papers in English (unpublished); 4, Contemporary Published works in English; and 5, Contemporary Persian works. The second group has four sections: '1, Works in English'; 2, Unpublished theses (London University); 3, Works in Bengali; and 4, Articles in Bulletins, Periodicals and Journals in English.

PRIMARY AND CONTEMPORARY SOURCES

1. Original Official Records in manuscript (In the British Museum)

Parliamentary papers in manuscript being Robert Gregory's copy of the 'Evidence taken before an open Committee [chairman, Mr. Fuller] of the House of Commons on the state of Bengal in 1767' (in March and April). The British Museum Add. MSS. 18469.

In the India Office Records (Commonwealth Relations Office)

A. Abstracts of Despatches to Bengal, vol. 1 (24 Jan. 1753–27 Jan. 1785).
B. Abstracts of Letters received from 'Coast' and 'Bay', vols. 5 and 6 (5 Sept. 1744–3 March 1760).
C. Bengal Board of Revenue Miscellaneous Proceedings—Committee of Lands. Range 98, vols. 10–12 (1759 to 3 Sept. 1762).
D. Bengal Public Consultations (or BPC).
Range 1, vols. 14–51 (4 Jan. 1740–28 April 1772);
Range 2, vols. 1–13 (4 May 1772–11 March 1776).
E. Bengal Secret Consultations (or Secret Cons.), being minutes of proceedings of the Council at Fort William (commencing 22 Aug. 1768).
Range A, vols. 16–34 (22 Aug. 1768–29 Feb. 1776);
Range 68, vols. 52–53 (10 Jan. 1772–30 Dec. 1773).
F. Bengal Secret and Military Consultations (or BSC), being minutes of proceedings of the Fort William Council in the Secret Department (since 1756) and of the Select Committee (from May 1765). Range A vols. 1–15 (22 Aug. 1756–19 March 1774).
G. Board of Revenue proceedings (Sayer).
Range 89, vol. 43 (1796).
H. Court Minutes (Minutes of Proceedings of the Court of Directors). Vols. 79 and 80 (11 April 1770–10 April 1771; 10 April 1771–7 April 1772).
I. Despatches to Bengal (original drafts).
Vols. 1–7 (28 Nov. 1753–15 Dec. 1775);
Vol. 10 (20 Jan. 1779–27 Oct. 1779).

Select bibliography

J. Factory Records:

(a) Dacca, vols. 2–12.
Vols. 2–5 in Range 68;
No. 47 (Nov. 1736–Dec. 1748),
No. 48 (Jan. 1757–Dec. 1757),
No. 49 (Jan. 1762–Dec. 1762),
No. 50 (Jan. 1763–Dec. 1763).
Vol. 6 (in Range 69, 69. 1) being proceedings of inquiry into Reza Khan's accounts (29 Dec. 1773–6 Jan. 1774).
Vols. 7–12 (in Range 69, Nos. 2–7) being consultations of the Provincial Council of Revenue (from 9 Dec. 1773–27 May 1776).

(b) Kasimbazar, Range 70, Nos. 7–14 (4 Dec. 1740–28 Feb. 1759).

(c) Murshidabad:
(i) Letter Copy-Book of the Resident at the Durbar.
Range 70, No. 4 (Sept.–Oct. 1770)
Range 69, Nos. 54–6 (14 Dec. 1773–28 Dec. 1775);
(ii) Proceedings of the Controlling Council of Revenue.
Range 69, Nos. 47–53 (27 Sept. 1770–8 Sept. 1772).

K. Home Miscellaneous Series (see 'Catalogue of the *H.M.S.* in the India Office Records' by S. C. Hill, London, 1927) or *H.M.S.*
Volumes with direct relevance to Reza Khan are 68, 102, 115, 122, 201, 202, 203, 584 and 739 while those having relevance to this study are 24, 36, 47, 78, 92, 94–5, 98, 100–1, 106, 119–21, 123–5, 191–3, 196, 198–200, 204, 212, 217, 228, 230, 260, 262, 369, 381, 424, 455, 455D, 456F, 521, 629, 634, 765–6, 768–9, 773, 804–6, 808–10 and 814.

L. Index to Despatches to Bengal, vols. 1 and 2 (1753–86).

M. Letters received from Bengal (or Letter to Court), vols. 1–14 (3 Jan. 1709–20 Jan. 1776) and vol. 30 (4 Aug. 1791–11 May 1792).

N. Miscellaneous Proceedings. Vols. 39A and 39B being defective typed copy of special proceedings of the Calcutta Council relating to Reza Khan's trial (1772–4) from the only original document now in the National Archives of India, New Delhi.

O. Nizamat Accounts of the Nawab Mubarak-ud-daulah, Range 154, No. 38.

P. Personal Records, vol. 14.

Q. Proceedings of the Calcutta Committee of Revenue (consisting of the entire Council), Range 67, Nos. 53–60 (1 April 1772–28 Dec. 1775).

R. Proceedings of the Committee of Circuit.
Range 69, No. 17 (June–Sept. 1772) at Nadia and Krishnagar,
Range 70, No. 15 (Oct.–Nov. 1772) at Dacca,
Range 68, No. 54 (Dec. 1772) at Rangpur,
Range 68, No. 55 (Jan. 1773) at Dinajpur.

S. Report on the Sundeep (Sandwip) Insurrection (of 1766–7) by Jonathan Duncan (see Bengal Revenue Proceedings of 1 Aug. 1780). Range 50, vol. 27.

Select bibliography

T. Special proceedings of the Fort William Council on the trial of Nandkumar.
Range 68, vol. 16 (13 Jan.–19 Feb. 1761),
Range 68, vol. 17 (31 July–4 Oct. 1762).

In the National Archives of India, New Delhi
Special Proceedings of the Fort William Council relating to the trial of Maharaja Shitab Rai and Muhammad Reza Khan. (A microfilm copy was obtained but references are to the typed copy in I.O.)

2. Published Official Records

A. *Assam District Records: Sylhet*, vol. 1 (1770–1785). Shillong, 1913.

B. *Bengal Government Records* (*Bibliography of Bengal Records 1632–1858* by C. W. Gurner, Calcutta, 1925 may be seen).

1. District Records.
   (a) *Chittagong District Records*, vol. 1 (1760–1773). Calcutta, 1923.
   (b) *Midnapur District Records*, vols. 1–IV (1763–1774). Calcutta, 1914–26.
   (c) *Rangpur District Records*, vols. 1–VI (1770–87). Calcutta, 1914–28.
   (d) *Supplement to Bengal District Records*, vol. 1, *Rangpur*, (*1770–1779*). Calcutta, 1923.

2. *Letter Copy-Book of the Resident at the Durbar at Murshidabad* (or *LCB*).
   (a) Two vols. (1769–70) in one. Calcutta, 1919.
   (b) Letters (28 Sept. 1772 to 2 March 1774) published along with vol. XII of the *Proceedings of the Controlling Council of Revenue* (2 July–8 Sept. 1772). Calcutta, 1924.

3. *Letter Copy-Book of the Supervisor of Rajshahi at Nator* (Letters issued 30 Dec. 1769–15 Sept. 1772). Calcutta 1925.

4. *Proceedings of the Committee of Circuit* (or *PCC*).
   (a) Krishnagar and Kasimbazar, vols. 1–3 (10 June–17 Sept. 1772).
   (b) Dacca, vol. 4 (3 Oct.–28 Nov. 1772),
   (c) Rangpur, Dinajpur, Purnea and Rajmahal, vols. 5–8 (16 Dec. 1772–28 Feb. 1773). Calcutta 1926–7.

5. *Proceedings of the Controlling Council of Revenue at Murshidabad* (or *MP*).
   Vol. I (Sept.–Nov. 1770). Calcutta, 1919.
   Vol. II (3 Dec.–31 Dec. 1770). Calcutta, 1920.
   Vol. III (3 Jan.–14 Feb. 1771). Calcutta, 1920.
   Vol. IV (18 Feb.–28 March 1771). Calcutta, 1921.
   Vol. V (1 April–15 July 1771). Calcutta, 1922.
   Vol. VI (18 July–26 Aug. 1771). Calcutta, 1922.*
   Vol. VII (2 Sept.–28 Nov. 1771). Calcutta, 1922.*
   Vol. VII A (2 Sept.–21 Oct. 1771). Calcutta, 1923.
   Vol. VIII (5 Dec.–30 Dec. 1771). Calcutta, 1922.*
   Vol. IX (4 Jan.–28 Feb. 1772). Calcutta, 1923.
   Vol. X (2 March–4 May 1772). Calcutta, 1923.

Select bibliography

Vol. xi   (7 May–25 June 1772). Calcutta, 1924.
Vol. xii   (2 July–8 Sept. 1772). Calcutta, 1924.**
N.B.   * Vols. vi–viii published in one.
      ** Vol. xii published with Letter Copy-Book of the
      Resident (28 Sept. 1772–2 March 1774).
6. *Proceedings of the Select Committee (1758).* Edited W. K. Firminger.

C.   *Government of India Publications*
(*a*) *Calendar of Persian Correspondence*–or *CPC* (11 vols.), particularly vols. i–iv (1759–75). Calcutta, 1911–25.
(*b*) *Selections from Records of Bengal Government, 1748–67.* Edited J. Long. Calcutta, 1869.

D.   *India Office Records, Parliamentary Branch,* or *PP.*
(*a*) No. 6. *Reports 1–5 of the Select Committee of the House of Commons (Chairman, Col. Burgoyne, 26 May 1772–18 June 1773)*
(*b*) No. 7. *Reports 1–9 of the Committee of Secrecy appointed by the House of Commons (7 Dec. 1772–30 June 1773).*

E.   *The National Archives of India,* New Delhi.
Fort William India House Correspondence (or *FWIHC*). 9 vols., but particularly vol. v (Public Series letters of 1767–9), edited by N. K. Sinha. Delhi, 1949.
Also vol. iv (Public letters 1764–1766). Edited by C. S. Srinivasacheri. Delhi, 1962.

F.   Published by order of the Honourable the Court of Directors for the Affairs of the East India Company.
A Bengal Atlas containing maps of the theatre of war and commerce on that side of Hindoostan, compiled from the original surveys. . . . By J. Rennell. London, 1781.
Note: Other records are noticed under the names of their editors in a subsequent section.

3. Contemporary Private Papers in English (unpublished)
In the British Museum

Warren Hastings's papers (consist of 264 vols.). Those consulted are:
Add. MSS. 29096. Letters written by Warren Hastings during his residence at Murshidabad (Nov. 1757–July 1760).
Add. MSS. 29097. Letters written by Hastings during his residence at Mir Qasim's Durbar (in Bihar) in 1762 and also those written at Calcutta in 1763 and 1764.
Add. MSS. 29098. Copies of Hastings's correspondence with Fort William (March–July 1762).
Add. MSS. 29099. Memoranda on relations with Mir Qasim (1760–3).
Add. MSS. 29122–3. Letters from natives of India (translations).
Add. MSS. 29125–7. Hastings's correspondence (Sept. 1769–Sept. 1776).
Add. MSS. 29131. Clive to Hastings, original letters (Feb. 1758–Oct. 1773).

Select bibliography

Add. MSS. 29132–6. (5 vols.) Correspondence (1758–75).
Add. MSS. 29209–10. (2 vols.) Hastings's notes on various subjects.
In the India Office Library (see 'India Office Library Catalogue of manuscripts in European Languages', vol. II, Part 1 by S. C. Hill, London, 1916 and vol. II, Part 2 by G. R. Kaye and E. H. Johnstone, London, 1937).

(a) Charles Grant's 'Observation on the State of Society Among the Asiatic Subjects of Great Britain, particularly with respect to morals, and on the means of improving it', 1797. Eur. E, 93.

(b) Orme MSS. (collections of Robert Orme–O.V. and India volumes), particularly vols. IX, XVII, and J.

(c) Philip Francis's Papers (I.O. has its own numbering but the volume numbers given below are those given in Kaye and Johnstone catalogue).
Vols. 47–8, 50–53, 57, 60, 64–5, 73–6, 78–80, 82, 85 and 102.

4. Contemporary Published works in English

Anonymous. *A State of British Authority in Bengal under the Government of Mr. Hastings in his conduct in the case of Mahomed Reza Khan with a debate upon a letter from Mobareck ul Dowlah, Nabob of Bengal.* London, 1780.

Barwell, Richard. *Letters (1765–1780).* Published *BPP*, VIII–XVIII, Calcutta.

Bolts, William. *Considerations on Indian Affairs.* London 1772.

Boughton-Rous, C. W. *Dissertation concerning the landed property in Bengal.* London, 1791.

Caillaud, J. *A Narrative of what happened in Bengal in 1760.* London, 1764.

Clive, Robert. *A Letter to the Proprietors of East India Stock.* London, 1764.

Debrit, J. *Transactions in India from 1756 to 1783.* London, 1786.

Dow, Alexander. *History of Hindostan,* translated from the Persian of Firishtah, vols. I, II, London, 1770, vol. III. London, 1772.

Francklin, W. *History of the Reign of Shah Aulum the Present Emperor of Hindustan* (1798). Allahabad, 1915.

Gladwin, F. '*Transactions in Bengal*' from the Persian *Tawarikh-i-Bangala.* Calcutta, 1788.

Grand, G. F. *The Narrative of a Gentleman long resident in India* (Cape of Good Hope, 1814). Calcutta, 1910.

Grant, James. *Historical and Comparative Account of the Finances of Bengal* (first published, 1786). See *Fifth Report,* vol. II, Calcutta, 1917.

Hastings, Warren. *Memoirs Relative to State of India* (containing also English translation of Mirza Jawan Bakht's account). London, 1786.

Holwell, J. Z. *An Address to Luke Scrafton in reply to his Observation on Vansittart's Narrative* (see India Office Tract No. 378).

Holwell, J. Z. *Interesting Historical Events Relative to Bengal and the Empire of Indostan* (in two parts). London, 1765 and 1767.

Select bibliography

Ives, E. *A Voyage from England to India in the year MDCCLIV.* London, 1773.

Nota Manus *alias* Raymond *alias* Haji Mustapha. Translation of *Seir Mutaqherin* as '*View of Modern Times Being an History of India*'. Published 1789. Reprinted, Calcutta, 1902.

Orme, Robert. *Historical Fragments of the Mogul Empire* (published London, 1782). London 1803.

Orme, Robert. *A History of the Military Transactions of the British Nation in Indostan from the year 1745 to which is prefixed a Dissertation on the Establishment made by the Mahomedan conquerors.* London, 1803.

Pattullo. *An Essay upon the cultivation of Lands and Improvement of the Revenues of Bengal.* London, 1772.

Pearse, Col. T. D. *A Memoir* (1768–1789). See *BPP*, vols. II–VI. Calcutta.

Scott, Major J. *A Narrative of the Transactions in Bengal during the administration of Mr. Hastings.* London, 1788.

Scrafton, Luke. *Reflections on the Government of Indostan.* London, 1770.

Scrafton, Luke. *Observation on Vansittart's Narrative* (*see* India Office Tract No. 378).

Stavorinus, J. S. *Voyages to the East Indies* (translated from Dutch by S. H. Wilcocke). London, 1798.

Steuart, James. *Principles of Money applied to the Present State of Coin in Bengal.* London, 1772.

Stewart, C. *The History of Bengal.* London, 1813.

Vansittart, Henry. *A Narrative of the Transactions in Bengal from 1760 to 1764* (Warren Hastings had a hand in its draft). London, 1766.

Verelst, H. *A View of the Rise, Progress and Present State of the English Government in Bengal.* London, 1772.

Watts, William. *Memoirs of the Revolution in Bengal.* London, 1764.

5. *Contemporary Persian works*

(In this connection, two works, namely, 'The History of India as told by its own Historians' by H. M. Elliot and edited and continued by J. Dowson, vol. VIII, London, 1877; and 'Persian Literature, a Bio-Bibliographical Survey' by C. A. Storey, London, 1939 may also be seen.)

Ahwal-i-Alivardi Khan. By Yusuf Ali (see extracts and translation in J. N. Sarkar *Bengal Nawabs*, Calcutta, 1952).

An Account of the death of Nawab Muzaffar Jang (no Persian title found). Anonymous (copy obtained from the Tubingen Staatsbibliothek through the kindness of the German Consulate at Dacca).

Chahar Gulzar Shuja'i. Hari Charan Das (*see* extracts and translation published in Elliot and Dowson's *History of India*, vol. VIII).

Jami ut Tawarikh. Fakir Muhammad (*see* extracts and translation in Elliot and Dowson's *History of India*, VIII).

Khulasat ut Tawarikh. Kalyan Singh, Maharaja Intizam ul Mulk Mumtaz-ud-daulah Bahadur. English translation by S. H. Khan in *JBORS*, vols. V and VI (1919, 1920).

Select bibliography

Muzaffarnamah. Karam Ali of Alivardi's family. (A part in extracts and translation in J. N. Sarkar, *Bengal Nawabs,* Calcutta, 1952.) I.O. Persian MSS. no. 4075.

Naubahar i Murshid Quli Khan. Azad al Husaini (*see* extracts and translation in J. N. Sarkar, *Bengal Nawabs,* Calcutta, 1952).

Riyaz us Salatin. Ghulam Husain Salim. (Text published, Calcutta, 1890–1. English translation by A. Salam, published, Calcutta, 1902–4.)

Seir Mutaqherin. Saiyid Ghulam Husain Khan Tabatabai 'an actor and spectator', written 1780–1. (English translation by Haji Mustapha or Nota-Manus. First published 1789. Reprinted, Calcutta, 1 March 1902.)

Tawarikh i Bangala. Munshi Salimullah. (English translation by F. Gladwin, published in Calcutta in 1788 under the title of *A Narrative of the Transactions in Bengal during the Soobahdaries of Azeem us Shan, Jaffer Khan, Shuja Khan, Sirafraz Khan and Alyvirdy Khan.*)

Tarikh-i-Mansuri. Extracts translated by H. F. Blochman in the *JASB,* Calcutta, 1867, Part I, no. 2 (a mid nineteenth century Persian work).

Tarikh-i-Muzaffari. Muhammad Ali Khan (a part in extract and translation in Elliot and Dowson's *History of India,* vol. VIII). References are to the British Museum MSS.

Tarikh-i-Nasrat Jangi. History of East Bengal and Dacca from Akbar's time to 1785–86. Text Published by Harinath De as a Memoir of the Asiatic Society of Bengal, Calcutta, in 1908. The work took its name from that of Nasrat Jang a descendant of Jasarat Khan who succeeded the latter as Naib Nazim of Dacca.

SECONDARY AND LATER SOURCES

1. Works in English

Ascoli, F. D. *Early Revenue History of Bengal and the Fifth Report, 1812.* Oxford, 1917.

Aspinall, A. *Cornwallis in Bengal.* Manchester, 1931.

Auber, P. *Rise and Progress of the British Power in India.* London, 1837.

Aziz, Abdul. *The Mnasabdari System and the Mughal Army.* Lahore, 1945.

Baden-Powell, B. H. *The Land System of British India.* Oxford, 1892.

Balkrishna. *Commercial Relations between India and England, 1601–1757.* London, 1924.

Banerji, B. N. *Begams of Bengal.* Calcutta, 1942.

Banerji, D. N. *Early Land Revenue System in Bengal and Bihar.* Calcutta, 1936.

Banerji, D. N. *Early Administrative System of the East India Company in Bengal,* vol. I. (Printed in India but published London, 1943.)

Banerji, P. N. *Indian Finance in the days of the Company.* London, 1928.

Barat, A. *The Bengal Native Infantry—its organisation and discipline, 1796–1852.* Calcutta, 1962.

Basu, B. D. *Rise of Christian Power in India.* Calcutta, 1931.

Beale, T. W. *The Oriental Biographical Dictionary.* London, 1894.

356

Select bibliography

Bell, Major E. *The Bengal Reversion*. London, 1872.
Bernier, Francois. *Travels in the Mogul Empire, 1656–1668*. Oxford, 1934. Translated Archibald Constable and edited V. A. Smith.
Beveridge, H. *A Comprehensive History of India*. London, 1862.
Beveridge, H. *The District of Bakarganj, its history and statistics*. London, 1876.
Beveridge, H. *The Trial of Maharaja Nandkumar*. Calcutta, 1886.
Bhattacharya, S. *The East India Company and the Economy of Bengal*. London, 1954.
Boulger, D. C. *Maharaja Deby Singh* (Nashipur Raj family). Calcutta, 1914.
Broome, A. *History of the Rise and Progress of the Bengal Army*. Calcutta, 1850.
Bruce, J. *Annals of the Hon'ble East India Company*. London, 1810.
Buckland, C. E. *Dictionary of Indian Biography*. London, 1906.
Busteed, H. E. *Echoes from Old Calcutta*. Calcutta, 1897.
Carey, W. H. *The Good Old Days of the Honorable John Company*. Calcutta, 1907.
Chakrabarty, R. M. *A summary of the changes in jurisdiction of districts in Bengal, 1757–1916*. Calcutta, 1918.
Chandra, Satish. *Parties and Politics at the Mughal Court, 1707–1740*. Aligarh, 1959.
Chatterji, Nandalal. *Mir Qasim*. Allahabad, 1935.
Chatterji, Nandalal. *Verelst's Rule in India*. Allahabad, 1939.
Chatterji, Nandalal. *Bengal under the Diwani Administration*. Allahabad, 1956.
Chaudhuri, S. B. *Civil Disturbances during the British Rule in India (1765–1857)*. Calcutta, 1955.
Cotton, H. E. A. *Calcutta, Old and New*. Calcutta, 1907.
Cotton, H. E. A. *The Journal of Archibald Swinton*. Calcutta, 1926.
Cotton, H. J. S *Memorandum on the Revenue History of Chittagong*. Calcutta, 1880.
Crawford, D. G. *A Brief History of the Hughli District*. Calcutta, 1902.
Dacca University. *History of Bengal*, vol. II. (General Editor J. N. Sarkar.) Dacca, 1948.
Dasgupta, A. P. *Studies in the History of the British in India*. Calcutta, 1942.
Datta, Kalikinkar. *Studies in History of the Bengal Subah*, vol. I. Calcutta, 1936.
Datta, Kalikinkar. *Alivardi and His Times*. Calcutta, 1939.
Datta, Kalikinkar. *The Dutch in Bengal and Bihar (1740–1825)*, Patna, 1948.
Davies, A. M. *Strange Destiny—A Biography of Warren Hastings*. New York, 1935.
Davies, A. M. *Clive of Plassey*. London, 1939.
Davies, C. C. *Warren Hastings and Oudh*. London, 1939.
Dodwell, H. H. *Dupleix and Clive*. London, 1920.
Dodwell, H. H. [Ed.] *The Cambridge History of India*, vol. V, 1497–1858. Cambridge, 1929.

Select bibliography

Dunbar, G. D. S. *Clive.* London, 1936.

Dutt, R. C. *Economic History of India under Early British Rule (1757–1837).* London, 1950.

Elphinstone, M. *The Rise of British Power in the East.* (Edited E. Colebrooke.) London, 1887.

Embree, A. T. *Charles Grant and British Rule in India.* London, 1962.

Feiling, K. *Warren Hastings.* London, 1955.

Firminger, W. K. [Ed.] *The Fifth Report* (with lengthy introduction). Calcutta, 1917. (He had also edited a number of Bengal Records for detail of which *Bibliography of Bengal Records, 1632–1858*, Calcutta, 1925 may be seen.)

Forde, L. *Lord Clive's Right Hand Man—A Memoir of Colonel Francis Forde.* London, 1910.

Forrest, G. W. *Life of Lord Clive.* London, 1918.

Foster, W. *John Company.* London, 1926.

Francis, Beata and Eliza Keary. *The Francis Letters.* London, 1900.

Furber, H. *John Company at work.* Cambridge, 1948.

Ghosa, K. C. *Famines in Bengal (1770–1943).* Calcutta, 1944.

Ghose, N. N. *Memoirs of Maharaja Nubkissen Bahadur* (Sovabazar Raj family). Calcutta, 1901.

Ghosh, J. M. *Sanyasi and Fakir Raiders in Bengal.* Calcutta, 1930.

Glazier, E. G. *A Report on the District of Rungpore.* Calcutta, 1873.

Glazier, E. G. *Further Notes on Rungpore Records.* Calcutta, 1876.

Gleig, G. R. *The History of the British Empire.* London, 1830–5.

Gleig, G. R. *Memoirs of the Right Hon. Warren Hastings.* London, 1841.

Gleig, G. R. *Life of Robert, First Lord Clive.* London, 1848.

Goetz, H. *The Crisis of Indian Civilization in the Eighteenth and Early Nineteenth Century.* Calcutta, 1938.

Gopal, Ram. *How the British occupied Bengal. A connected Account of the 1756–1765 Event* (printed in India). London, 1963.

Gopal, S. *The Permanent Settlement in Bengal and its results.* London, 1949.

Griffiths, P. J. *The British in India.* London, 1946.

The British Impact on India. London, 1952.

Guha, Ranajit. *A Rule of Property For Bengal.* Paris, 1963.

Gupta, Brijen K. *Siraj-ud-daulah and the East India Company 1756–1757. Background to the Foundation of British Power in India.* Leiden, 1962.

Hallward, N. L. *William Bolts.* Cambridge, 1920.

Hamilton, C. J. *The Trade Relations Between England and India (1600–1896).* Calcutta, 1919.

Hill, S. C. *Bengal in 1756–1757* (collection of records with a lengthy introduction). London, 1905.

Hill, S. C. *Yusuf Khan, the Rebel Commandant.* London, 1914.

Holzman, J. M. *The Nabobs in England. A study of the Returned Anglo Indians (1760–1785).* New York, 1926.

Hunter, W. W. *The Annals of Rural Bengal.* London, 1868.

Hunter, W. W. *Remarks on the Great Famine of Bengal, 1769–70,* appended to the *Famine Papers.* Calcutta, 1868.

Hunter, W. W. *Famine Papers* (compiled by G. Campbell). Calcutta, 1868.

Select bibliography

Hunter, W. W. *The Indian Musalmans*. London, 1871.
Hunter, W. W. *A Statistical Account of Bengal* (20 volumes edited). London, 1875–1877.
Hunter, W. W. *The Indian Empire*. London, 1886.
Hunter, W. W. *Bengal Manuscript Records (1782–1807)*. (Four volumes of records with an introduction.) London, 1894.
Hunter, W. W. *A History of British India*. London, 1899–1900.
Huq, M. *East India Company's Land Policy and Commerce in Bengal, 1698–1784*. Dacca, 1964.
Hutchinson, L. *The Empire of the Nabobs*. London, 1937.
Hyde, H. B. *The Parish in Bengal (1678–1788)*. Calcutta, 1899.
Ibn i Hasan. *The Central Structure of the Mughal Empire and its practical working up to the year 1657*. London, 1936.
Imperial Gazetteer of vol. II and vol. IV. Oxford, 1908, 1907. India.
Indian Records. With a commercial view of the Relations between the British Government and Nawab Nazims of Bengal, Bihar and Orissa. London, 1870.
Irvine, William. *Army of the Indian Mughals*. London, 1903.
Irvine, William. *Later Mughals* (edited J. N. Sarkar). London, 1922.
Jain, M. P. *Outlines of Indian Legal History*. Delhi, 1952.
Karim, Abdul. *Murshid Quli Khan and His Times*. Dacca, 1963.
Karim, Abdul. *Dacca, the Mughal capital*. Dacca, 1964.
Keene, H. G. *The Fall of the Mughal Empire of Hindustan*. London, 1887.
Keith, A. B. *A Constitutional History of India, 1600–1935*. London, 1936.
Kincaid, Dennis. *British Social Life in India, 1608–1937*. London, 1938.
Lockhart, L. *Nadir Shah*. London, 1938.
Lockhart, L. *The Fall of the Safavi Dynasty and the Afghan Occupation of Persia*. Cambridge, 1958.
Low, C. R. *History of the Indian Navy, 1613–1863*. London, 1877.
Majumdar, N. *Justice and Police in Bengal 1765–1793—A study of the Nizamat in decline*. Calcutta, 1960.
Majumdar, P. C. *Musnud of Murshidabad*. Murshidabad, 1905.
Majumdar, R. C. *Maharaja Rajballabh*. Calcutta, 1947.
Malcolm, J. *The Life of Robert, Lord Clive*. London, 1836.
Malleson, Col. G. B. *Lord Clive*. London, 1882.
Malleson, Col. G. B. *The Decisive Battles of India*. London, 1883.
Mallick, A. R. *British Policy and the Muslims in Bengal*. Dacca, 1961.
Mansur Ali, Sayyad, Nawab Nazim of Bengal Bihar and Orissa. *Correspondence regarding the conduct of His Highness the Nawab Nazim of Bengal, Bihar and Orissa and the petition of His Highness to Her Majesty's Secretary of State for India in Council against the proceedings of the Governments of India and Bengal*. Calcutta, 1864.
Marshall, Peter James. *Impeachment of Warren Hastings*. London, 1965.
Marshman, J. C. *The History of India from the Earliest period to the close of Lord Dalhousie's administration*. London, 1867.
Misra, B. B. *The Central Administration of the East India Company, 1773–1834*. Manchester, 1959.

Select bibliography

Misra, B. B. *The Judicial Administration of East India Company in Bengal, 1765–1782*. Delhi, 1961.

Misra, B. B. *The Indian Middle Classes; their growth in modern times.* London, 1961.

Monckton-Jones, M. E. *Warren Hastings in Bengal, 1772–1774.* Oxford, 1918.

Moreland, W. H. *From Akbar to Aurangzeb*. London, 1923.

Moreland, W. H. *Agrarian System of Moslem India*. Cambridge, 1929.

Moon, E. P. *Warren Hastings and British India*. London, 1947.

Muir, R. *Making of British India, 1756–1856*. Manchester, 1915.

Namier, L. B. *The Structure of Politics at the Accession of George III.* London, 1929.

Owen, S. J. *The Fall of the Mogul Empire*. London, 1912.

Panikkar, K. M. *India and the Indian Ocean*. London, 1945.

Panikkar, K. M. *Asia and Western Dominance*. London, 1953.

Pant, D. *The Commercial Policy of the Moguls*. Bombay, 1930.

Parkes, Joseph and Merivale, Herman. *Memoirs of Sir Philip Francis.* London, 1867.

Philips, C. H. *East India Company, 1784–1834*. Manchester, 1940.

Philips, C. H. *India*. London, 1948.

Philips, C. H. *Handbook of Oriental History*. London, 1951.

Prasad, I. Durga. *Some Aspects of Indian Foreign Trade, 1757–1893.* London, 1932.

Price, J. C. *Notes on the History of Midnapore*. Calcutta, 1876.

Ramsbotham, R. B. *Studies in the Land Revenue History of Bengal.* Oxford, 1926.

Roberts, P. E. *History of British India*. Oxford, 1933.

Robinson, F. P. *The Trade of the East India Company, 1709–1813.* Cambridge, 1912.

Roy, Atul Chandra. *The Career of Mir Jafar Khan, 1757–1765* A.D. Calcutta, 1953.

Saran, P. *Provincial Government of the Moghuls, 1526–1658*. Allahabad, 1941.

Sarkar, J. N. *Mughal Administration*. Patna, 1920.

Sarkar, J. N. *A Short History of Aurangzeb*. London, 1930.

Sarkar, J. N. *Fall of the Mughal Empire*. Calcutta, 1932–5.

Sen, S. N. *Off the Main Track*. Calcutta, 1944.

Seton Karr, C. S. *Selections from Calcutta Gazette*. Calcutta, 1864.

Seth, M. J. *Armenians in India from the earliest times to the present day.* Calcutta, 1937.

Sinha, J. C. *Economic Annals of Bengal*. London, 1927.

Sinha, Maharaja R. *Official Records of Maharaja Devi Singh of Nashipur.* Calcutta, 1914.

Sinha, N. K. *Economic History of Bengal. (From Plassey to Permanent Settlement.)* Calcutta, 1956, 1962.

Spear, T. G. P. *The Nabobs. A study of the social life of the English in Eighteenth Century India*. London, 1932.

Spear, T. G. P. *India Pakistan and the West*. London, 1949.

Select bibliography

Spear, T. G. P. *Twilight of the Mughals. Studies in late Mughal Delhi.* Cambridge, 1951.

Srivastava, A. *Shujauddaulah.* Calcutta, 1933.

Srivastava, A. *The First two Nawabs of Oudh.* Agra, 1954.

Stokes, Eric. *The English Utilitarians and India.* Oxford, 1959.

Sutherland, Lucy S. *The East India Company in Eighteenth-Century Politics.* Oxford, 1952.

Teignmouth, Second Baron (Charles John Shore). *Memoirs of the Life and Correspondence of John, Lord Teignmouth.* London, 1843.

Thurston, E. *History of Coinage of the Territories of the East India Company and Catalogue of Coins in the Madras Museum.* Madras, 1890.

Wahed Husain. *Administration of Justice during the Muslim Rule in India.* Calcutta, 1934.

Wali, Abdul. *Life and Work of Jawad Sabat.* Calcutta, 1925.

Walsh, Maj. J. H. T. *A History of Murshidabad District.* London, 1902.

Weitzman, S. *Warren Hastings and Philip Francis.* Manchester, 1929.

Westland, J. *A Report on the District of Jessore, its antiquities, its history and its commerce.* Calcutta, 1874.

Wheeler, T. *Early Record of British India.* Calcutta, 1878.

Wilson, C. R. *Early Annals of the English in Bengal.* Calcutta, 1895–1917.

Wilson, H. H. *A Glossary of Judicial and Revenue Terms.* London, 1855.

2. Unpublished theses (London University)

Banerji, R. N. *The Commercial Progress and Administrative Development of the East India Company on the Coromandel Coast during the First Half of the Eighteenth Century.* Ph.D., Arts, 1965.

Chattopadhyaya, A. K. *Slavery in the Bengal Presidency under East India Company rule, 1772–1843.* Ph.D., 1963.

Narain, V. A. *The Life and Career of Jonathan Duncan, 1765–95.* Ph.D., 1958.

Serajuddin, A. M. *The Revenue Administration of Chittagong, 1761–1785.* Ph.D., 1964.

3. Works in Bengali

Bandopadhyaya, Kaliprasanna. *Bangalar Itihasa: Nababi Amal* (History of Bengal; the Nawabi period). Calcutta.

Bandopadhyaya, Brajendranath. *Bangalar Begum.* (An account of six Begums of Bengal: LuftunNessa, Amina, Ghaseti, Munni, Zinnat un Nessa (mother of Sarfaraz Khan) and the Begum of Alivardi Khan.) Calcutta.

Chattopadhyaya, Bankim Chandra. *Ananda Math.* (An historical novel dealing with Bengal under Reza Khan's administration, which gave the Hindu nationalists their song 'Bande Mataram' to be taken up later as the anthem of Indian National Congress.) Calcutta.

Datta, Amar Chandra. *Haji Muhammad Mohsin.* Dacca.

Deva, Binay Krishna. *Kalikatar Itihasa* (History of Calcutta). Calcutta.

Devabarman, Probodh Chandra Sena. *Bagurar Itihasa* (History of Bogra). Calcutta.

Devaroy, Munindra. *Hugli Kahini* (An account of Hugli). Bansbaria.

Select bibliography

Gupta, Jogendra Nath. *Vikrampurer Itihasa* (History of Vikrampur in Dacca). Calcutta.

Gupta, Rashiklal. *Maharaja Rajballabh Sen O Tatkalin Bangalar Itihasher Sthul Sthul Vivaran.* (Maharaja Rajballabh and m⊔in events of history of Bengal of that time.) Calcutta.

Lahiri, Durgadas. *Rani Bhawani.* Calcutta.

Maitra, Akshay Kumar. *Mir Qasim.* Calcutta.

Maitra, Akshay Kumar. *Siraj-ud-daulah.* Calcutta.

Mallick, Kumud Nath. *Nadia Kahini* (An Account of Nadia). Calcutta.

Marshman, J. C. *Bangalar Itihasa* (translated from Marshman's *History of Bengal*). Calcutta, 1848.

Rakshita, Haran Chandra. *Rani Bhawani.* Calcutta.

Roy, Jatindra Mohan. *Dhakar Itihasa* (History of Dacca). Calcutta.

Roy, Nikhil Nath. *Murshidabader Itihasa* (History of Murshidabad). Calcutta.

Sen, Chandi Charan. *Diwan Ganga Govind Sinha.* Calcutta.

Sen, Chandi Charan. *Maharaja Nandkumar.* Calcutta.

Shastri, Satya Charan. *Maharaja Nanda Kumar Charita* (A life of Maharaja Nandkumar). Calcutta.

Vidyasagar, Iswar Chandra. *Bangalar Itihasa* (History of Bengal). 6th edition. Calcutta, 1858.

4. Articles in Bulletins, Periodicals and Journals in English

Relevant articles in

1. *Bengal Past and Present.* Calcutta.
2. The *Bulletin of the School of Oriental Studies of the University of London.* London.
3. The *Calcutta Review.* Published by the University of Calcutta.
4. The *Indian Historical Quarterly*, Calcutta.
5. The *Journal of the Asiatic Society of Bengal*, Calcutta.
6. The *Journal of the Asiatic Society of Pakistan*, Dacca.
7. The *Journal of Economic and Social History of the Orient.* Leiden.
8. The *Muslim Review.* Journal of the Muslim Institute, Calcutta.
9. *Proceedings of the Indian History Congress.*
10. *Proceedings of the Indian Historical Records Commission.*
11. *Proceedings of the Oriental (All India) Conference.*
12. *Proceedings of All Pakistan History Conference.*

INDEX

Abdali (Ahmad Shah), 2, 7
Abdul Wahab Khan, 32
Abid Ali Khan, 54
Abu Torab Choudhury, 245
Adams, Major Thomas, 50–1, 55
Adawlut Alia, *see* Sadar Adalat
Afghans, 17, 27n
Agha Baqar (Bakar), 32n
Agha Nizam (or Nazim), 34, 53
Agha Sadiq, 32
Agha Saleh, 53–4, 65n
Agradwip, 99
Ahsan ullah Khan, 55n, 64, 73n
Ainuddin Ali Khan, 279n
Ajagarmal, 220n
Akbar, Emperor, 13, 125
Akbarabad (Agra), 148, 171, 177
Akbarnagar (Rajmahal), 272
Akhbarnavis, 277, 279
Akram Ali Khan, 279n
Alamgir II, Emperor, 28
Alavi Khan, 17
Aldersey, William: on Council, 256, 282–3; and Hastings, 317–24; at Kasimbazar, 147n, 170, 178, 180–3, 187, 191–3, 204, 228; Reza Khan's trial, 330, 332; and salt combine, 283n, 310n; and Sykes, 163, 166
Alexander, James, 147, 163, 166; on Council, 194, 249–51, 256; at Patna, 187, 198, 228–9
Ali Gauhar, Prince, 28, 29; *see also* Shah Alam
Ali Ibrahim Khan, 114, 117, 133, 134n, 225–6, 294, 297, 319–20, 345
Alinagar (Calcutta), treaty of, 7
Ali Naqi Khan, 225
Alivardi Khan, Nawab of Bengal, 21n, 22, 28n, 32, 35, 45n, 61n, 87, 93, 107, 110n, 111n, 113, 122, 128–9, 138n, 154, 161, 169, 175, 186, 206, 229n; death, 20; policy, 2, 7–9, 13–14, 17–19
Alivardi's Begum: imprisoned at Dacca, 26–7
Allahabad, 101, 105, 109, 111n, 117n, 124n, 198n, 282
Altamgha, 112, 124–5, 128–9
Amani Khan, son of Sarfaraz Khan, 53

Amarkot, 138n
Ameer Ali Midhut Jung, vii
America, British colonies in, 189n, 247n
Amina Begum, mother of Siraj-ud-daulah, daughter of Alivardi, 20, 27, 155n
Amir Beg Khan, Mir Jafar's faujdar, 24, 27; retires to Basra, 30n
Amir Beg Khan, Nawab Mubarak-ud-daulah's tutor, 225–6
Amphlett, death, 104n
Amrit Singh, 117, 223, 296
Amyatt, P., 10, 37n, 42–3, 50, 84n; death, 49n, 104n
Anderson, David, 201, 295, 349n
Aqa Ali, 333
Aqa Muhammad, 334
Aqa Razy, 210–11
Arcot, 4–5, 11, 175n, 280, 316n
Armenians, 3, 44, 306–7, 311; *see also* Khojah
Asad ullah Khan, physician, 38n
Asad uz Zaman Khan, Raja of Bir-bhum, 11n, 30, 47, 77, 220n, 234n
Asghar Ali, 117
Ashraf Ali Khan, *see* Mir Jan
Ashrafi (gold mohur), 29n, 92
Assam, 4
Ataullah Khan, Sabut Jang, 9, 19, 28n, 163, 225
Attock (Indus), 17n
Aurangzeb, Emperor, 87, 125
Aurora, H.M.S., 229; lost at sea, 246
Austrians, 174
Azimabad, *see* Patna
Azim us Shan, 3, 4n

Babbu Begum, 224–5
Babupur, 54, 66
Bahadur Ali Khan, 7
Bahram Jang, *see* Saiyid Muhammad Husain Ali Khan
Bahramganj, 19n, 334
Baidyanath, Raja of Dinajpur, 230n
Bakarganj (Barisal), 32n, 217, 221
Ballia, 60
Balwant Singh, Raja of Benares, 54n, 59n, 81–3, 151, 174n

Index

Bandel, 3

Bankura, 278n

Barh, 326

Barisal, see Bakarganj

Barker, Sir Robert, 330–1

Barwell, Richard, ix, 75n, 118n, 119n, 139n, 142n, 144n, 145n, 147n, 156n–8n, 188n, 198n; on Council, 228, 244–5, 249–51, 256, 292–3, 342; Dacca, 163–4, 325, 335; letters quoted, 165, 170, 209, 211–13, 217, 229, 296; and Reza Khan, 317, 343, 347

Barwell, William, 144n, 212n

Basant Rai, Shitab Rai's diwan, 326

Basant Roy, Motiram's employee, 95

Basra, 30n

Batavia, 174n

Bathoe, 284n

Batson, S., 42, 47, 60, 81, 82n

Beaumont, Anselm, 145, 157n

Becher, Richard, 10, 108, 119, 218n, 224n; account of, 169–71; dismissed, 217n, 291; famine, 291; at Murshidabad, 147, 159, 178, 213–14; and Reza Khan, 184–8, 192–204, 212–13, 225–83, 305, 310, 343; and Verelst, 180–1, 209, 283

Benares, 15, 175n, 280, 282

Bengal, 1–3; Diwani, 12, 101; see also under separate Nazims, i.e. Mir Jafar, Mir Qasim, Mubarak-ud-daulah, Najm-ud-daulah, Saif-ud-daulah, and the Naib Reza Khan

Bennet, 104n

Belghaur Khana, 66

Berhampur, 22, 221, 294, 332

betel-nut, 4, 139, 283n

Bhagalpur, 15, 19, 88, 201, 204, 221n, 229, 230n, 233; famine, 220

Bhagirathi, 52

Bharat, Ram Sundar, 234n

Bhaturia, 258

Bhojpuris, 122, 123n

Bhukailash Raj family, 245

Bhutan, 138n

Bibi Raushan, 83

Bihar, 46, 49, 59, 106, 112, 120, 123, 230–1, 246–7, 248, 342, 349; Company's Diwani, 101; famine, 218; Nandkumar and, 79–81; Reza Khan and, 110–12, 124–6, 129–30; Rumbold and, 229

Billers, W., 81n, 82n

Birbhum, 8, 30, 47, 175n, 183, 221n, 233, 242–3, 258, 276n, 278n; famine, 220

Bishnupur, 220n, 237, 242–3, 258

Biswas, Balaram, 234n

Biswas, Kantoo, 181

Boalia (Rajshahi), 157n, 159, 178, 181, 185, 190, 197, 198n, 201, 206, 209, 276

Bogra, 236n

Bolts, William, 2, 140, 306, 307n, 311, 313n

Bombay, 11, 123, 306n

Bose, Hari Krishna, 234n

Bose, Pran, 185

Brahmins, 270–2

Brindaban, son of Janakiram, 22, 85

Brindaban, Kurigram merchant, 269

British Museum, ix, x

Buji (Braja) Mohan Mitra, 185

Bulaqidas, 47, 57n, 307n

bullion, import of, 174

Burdett, John, 71–2, 77, 85, 95, 96n, 301n

Burdwan, 6n, 23, 35–6, 80n, 121n, 157n, 201n, 204n, 220n, 269n; Johnstone at, 70–1, 106, 122, 125, 128, 170, 188, 199, 202, 243, 248, 275; Nandkumar and, 28

Burgess, Capt. Thomas, 349n

Burgoyne, 311

Buxar, battle of, 57, 90

Bysack, Radamohon, 301n

Caillaud, Col. John, viii, 29, 31, 33, 35, 313n

Calcutta, 11, and passim; capture of, 3, 20; famine measures at, 220n, 222n; merchants at, 234n; recapture, 4, 7; see also Fort William Council

Carnac, J. R., 43, 48n, 57, 73, 84n, 115, 150n, 275n; and Nandkumar, 59, 60, 81, 82n, 83n, 94, 300–1; Select Committee, 90–1,119,133,140

Cartier, John, 96n, 151n, 250n, 251n, 314n; at Dacca, 55,95,117,141,157; dismissed, 217n, 290; Governor, 216–17, 224–41, 244, 249, 253–6, 259, 264, 280–1, 285–6, 289, 309, 316; and Hastings, 290, 338–9; Second in Council, 137, 147, 156, 164, 187, 194, 198, 214–15

Index

Chambers (Senior Servant), 104n
Chandernagore, 269
Charlton, Francis, 147, 187, 229
Chatterji, Ganga Narayan, 234n
Chattopadhyaya, Bankim Chandra, ix n
Chevalier, M., 139n, 174n
Chikan, 45
China, 175, 203n
Chitpur, 219n, 317, 349
Chittagong (Islamabad), 3, 4, 57, 91, 93, 106, 122, 125, 128, 136, 147n, 170, 174, 184n, 187-8, 201, 228, 245, 248, 269n; Company and, 34-8, 39n, 53; Reza Khan and, 32-42
Choudhury, Nani Gopal, viii n, 305n
Chouth, 138n
Clavering, John, 342, 345, 347-8
Clive, Robert (baron), viii, 135, 137, 148, 160, 167, 169, 175, 215, 226, 231, 255, 303, 311, 317, 329; army reform, 122-3, 126; in Bengal (1757-60), 5, 8, 21, 23-30; return to Bengal (1765-7), 64, 74, 89; Calcutta retaken, 4; enquiry against, 313, 341-2; jagir, 105n, 106, 127, 136, 189, 248n; and Mir Jafar, 10-12, 155; the policy and system adopted, 91-136, 187, 190, 192, 212, 274, 289; private trade, 138-45; and Reza Khan, 136, 151-2, 163; and Siraj-ud-daulah, 4-6
Clivites, the, 210, 228, 246, 256, 264, 290-2, 299, 306
Colebrooke, 290n
Colebrooke, Calcutta Collector, 219n
Colebrooke, Sir George, 300, 321; and Hastings, 315, 339
Collings, 104n
Comilla, 40, 54
Committee of Circuit, 320, 323-5
Constantinople, 19n, 126n
Coote, Sir Eyre, 43, 48n, 84n
Cornwallis, Charles (marquis), viii, 1, 349
cotton trade, 142, 166-7, 180
Croke, 104n
Crooke, surgeon, 104n
currency, 175, 179, 280-2

Dacca (Jahangirnagar), 15, *and passim*; hereditary Naib Nazims of, 156; Reza Khan at, 27-8, 49-68, 74, 76-8
Dacres, 283, 292, 317, 323

Damodar Singh, 121
Danes, 174
Darul Harb, 13n
Darul Islam, 13n
Darul Shafa, 66
Datta, Ram Tanu, 234n
Daudpur, 254
Dawson, Matthew, 201
Deccan, 32, 92
Deendyaul Missir, 82
Delhi, 2, 17, 18, 117n, 337
Dhiraj Narain, 80, 111-12, 117n, 185n; removed from Patna, 124, 130
Dilawar Jang, Rheza Khan's son, *see* Saiyid Muhammad Taqi Khan
Dinajpur, 117, 137n, 144, 175n, 185, 189, 201, 206n, 223, 258, 260, 276n, 285; deficiency at, 159-66
Diwanganj, 219
Diwani of Bengal, Bihar and Orissa, 101, 106, 119, 129
Dow, Alexander, viii, 311-13
Drake, Roger, 3, 5, 6, 10, 22
Droze, S., 69
Ducarel, G. G.: at Purnea, 129-30, 164, 166, 201, 211, 220n, 243, 268n
Duncan, Jonathan, viii, 245n
Dundi Khan, Rohilla chief, 257n
Dupre, Jonas, of Madras, 296, 305n, 315, 320, 324, 339
Dutch, 2, 174, 230, 247

East India Company, 89-90; Court of Directors of, 189, 246-7; instructions to Calcutta, 91, 132, 146, 197n, 199, 200, 205n, 246-50, 255-6, 269-70, 274, 282, 285, 287, 289-90; Clive to Bengal, 90-1; Commission appointed, 211n, 228-9; Committee of Secrecy, 294-302, 316, 320, 343-4; and Reza Khan, 135-6, 189, 195, 204-8, 249, 289-90, 292, 294-303; and Verelst, 145-6, 188-9, 195, 306-7; *see also* Fort William Council
Edrakpur, 183, 220n
Ellis, W., 41, 45, 84n, 104n, 128n
Ektay Sharifa, 86
Eylon, 104n

Faizullah, Shaikh, 333
Fakhrut-tujar, *see* Khwaja Wajid
Falmouth, 229

365

Index

Index

Haliberton, J. G., 201
Ham, surgeon, 104n
Hancock, T. S., 293n
Handial, 139n
Hardwicke, 157n
Hardwood, William: at Bhagalpur and Rajmahal, 201, 220n, 233, 272, 278, 283
Hare, Francis, 188, 228–9, 244, 249, 256, 283n, 310n
Harish Chandra, 162
Harris, G., 317, 329n
Harris, James, 157n
Harun Khan, 25
Hastings, Warren: viii, 128, 275; Governor, 117n, 122n, 229n, 282n, 290–4, 314n, 315n; Kasimbazar, 108; and Mir Qasim, 34–7, 44–7; and Nandkumar, 48n, 49, 72, 151, 327, 345, 346n; private trade, 44–5, 118; as Resident, 10, 11, 23n, 24n, 30n, 32n, 44n, 45n, 108, 316n; and Reza Khan, ix, 2, 19n, 47, 69, 225, 270–2, 293 ff; Sykes's correspondence 115, 165, 299, 311–47; see also Fort St George (Madras)
Hay, 37n, 84n, 104n
Heath, 34n
Higginson, N., 260, 278
Hijli, 23
Himmat Singh, Dacca Diwan, 226n, 232, 259n, 293n, 329n
Hindus, 3, 22, 270–2, 278–9
Hogarth, John, 201
Holwell, J. Z., 11, 21, 30, 33, 44, 48n, 101n, 128n, 155, 247, 248n
Homnabad, 54
Howitt, 28n, 104n
Hugli, 4, 15, 23–4, 27, 44n, 46–7, 92, 117, 175n, 184n, 221n, 259, 278n, 295, 309, 335; famine, 220, 221n; Graham at, 201, 243
Husain Ali Khan, 66
Husain Ali Khan, Bahram Jang, see Saiyid Muhammad Husain Ali Khan
Husain Quli Khan, 32n
Husain Reza Khan, 92n, 111n, 236
Husain uddin Khan, 32n
Husaini Dalan (Imambara at Dacca), 66, 154
Hutchinson, 104n
Huzurimul, 139n, 301, 332n
Hyderabad, 171

Ihteram-ud-daulah (Mir Kazem Khan), Mir Jafar's brother, 110–12, 116, 322
Ikram-ud-daulah, see Mirza Mahdi
Imtiaz Muhammad Khan, vii
industries: at Dacca, 66, 126, 156; silk in Bengal, 178–82, 284
Iran (Persia), 1, 17, 162n, 262
Irani, 12
Ireland, 138, 139n, 189n, 247n, 312
Islamabad, see Chittagong
Ismail Ali Khan, 77
Ismail Khan, see Muhammad Ismail Khan, Saiyid

Jafarganj, 334
Jagat Chand, Raja, son-in-law of Nandkumar, 56, 61, 74, 346n
Jagat Seth, 4, 13n, 28, 47, 69, 103–4, 176, 219, 221n, 289, 307n; and Clive, 4, 97, 114–15; presents given, 95–6, 189; and Reza Khan, 115, 175–7, 340, 348n
Jagannathpur, 139n
Jagir, 13n, 125n, 128–9; in Bihar, 112, 113n; of Clive, 39n, 89–90, 105–6, 125–7, 136n; of the Company, 36, 39, 73, 101n, 125–6; of Dhiraj Narain, 124; of Husain Reza Khan, 236; of Muhammad Husain Khan, 18n; of Rai Durlabh, 257; Reza Khan and, 124–6, 134
Jahangirnagar, see Dacca
Janakiram, Raja, Rai Durlabh's father, 9, 110n, 129
Jangipur, 181, 283
Jasarat Khan, at Dacca, 34n, 52–3, 87, 109–10, 117, 153, 156–7, 232, 259, 266n, 293n
Jats, 122
Jawahir Singh, Jat chief, 138, 148, 151
Jawan Ali Khan, Dacca official, 66
Jawan Mard Ali Khan, 40
Jekyll, Joseph, 188, 228, 244, 249, 256, 283
Jessore, 46n, 55n, 64, 175n, 183, 220, 221n, 255, 258, 276, 278n, 309, 329n; famine, 220; Rooke at, 283; Wilmot at, 201
Johannes Padre Raphael, Bolts's Armenian Agent, 307n, 311; see also Armenians

367

Index

Index

Lawrell, J.; on circuit, 323; at Murshidabad, 250, 257–62, 265, 303; and Reza Khan, 285, 317

Leycester, Ralph, 158, 213n; in council, 75, 83n, 86, 91, 93; at Dacca, 55; Delegation to Murshidabad, 75–86; presents to, 96; and Reza Khan, 96, 98n

lime trade, 118, 142–3

Lokenath Nandi, 277

London, 127n, 139n, 205, 211, 233

Lord Holland, 290, 303

Lucas, Lt, 295

Lucknow, 90

Lushington, death, 104n

Lushington, Henry, 278

Lutfunnessa Begum, wife of Siraj-ud-daulah, 27, 29, 155

Lyon, 104n

MacDowall, Ensign, 25

McGuire, W., 128, 140

Mackenzie, Capt., 235

McPherson, Capt., 88

Madad-i-Maash, 124–5

Maddison, John, 187n

Maddison, Robert, 147n, 187

Madras, 217n, 251n, 255n, 316n; *see also* Fort St George

Mahabat Jang, 9

Mahasingh, Maharaja, Diwan, 93, 226n; at Chittagong, 34; at Dacca, 110, 152–3, 156–7, 226n

Mahi Maratib, 104

Mahtab Chand, Jagat Seth, 47n, 69n; *see also* Jagat Seth

Maina Ram, 139n

Majumdar, N., vii

Malbous Khas, 66

Malda: Barwell at, 144, 157, 163; English commercial residency at, 75, 144, 157n, 283, 284n; Gray at, 75, 144

Mallik, Sukhdev, 234n

Manickchand, Raja, 6

Mankura, 62

Manningham, Charles, 10, 169

Manohar Sharma, 234n

Mansurganj, 334

Marathas, 5, 8, 107, 128, 138, 230n, 331

Marriot, Randolph: at Benares, 82; at Chittagong, 36; in Tipperah, 38, 40

Masulipatam, 78n

Mathews, Lt, 39

Mathote, 159

Middleton, Samuel: in council, 245n, 256; on Delegation, 75–88; at Lakshmipur, 34; Murshidabad Council, 293–5, 297, 323, 327, 339; at Patna, 124; presents to, 91n, 96; private trade, 282, 283n, 310n; Resident at Murshidabad, 67, 69–70, 72, 92, 107, 124, 327, 328, 335–6, 339; and Reza Khan, 67, 96n, 293–5, 335–6

Midnapur, 36, 38, 80n, 106, 122, 125, 128, 157n, 170, 188, 243, 246, 269n; Company's jagir of, 125, 269n; Graham at, 243; Johnstone at, 36n, 80n; Misri Khan (last Faujdar) at, 36n; Nimak (salt) Mahals of, 246; G. Vansittart at, 157n

Mir Abdul Ali, Saif-ud-daulah's tutor, 127

Mir Abdul Shukur, 130

Mir Ali, 25

Miran (Nawab Mir Sadiq Ali Khan, Shahmat Jang), Mir Jafar's son, 21–2, 25, 27, 29, 32–3, 35, 70n, 71, 92, 102, 103n, 130n, 155, 225; death, 33, 35

Mir Ashraf, English protégé in Bihar, 59, 60n, 81–2

Mir Falouri, *see* Najm-ud-daulah

Mir Habib, 4n

Mir Hadi, 39n

Mir Ismail, 335

Mir Jafar, Nawab Nazim of Bengal, Bihar and Orissa, vii, 6–12, 20, 47n, 57n, 77n, 87, 102, 103n, 106–8, 111, 122, 131, 134–5, 174n, 176, 185n, 224–5; abdication, 36; and Clive, 8–12, 20–1, 23–7, 29–30, 36n, 46n, 91–2, 105n, 248n; death 68–70, 90, 109; and Hastings, 10, 21, 25, 31n, 33–5, 44n, 108; and Holwell, 30–1, 48n, 155; and Nandkumar, 26–30, 49–52, 56–68, 81; and Rai Durlabh, 7, 9, 20–3, 50, 58–9, 85; restoration, 48–64, 142, 207; and Reza Khan, 28–30, 32–4, 50–2, 56–7, 60–2, 64–8, 94, 106–7, 109, 131, 134–5, 189, 210, 232, 334–5; and Scrafton, 23–6; and Spencer, 64; succession to, 70–8; and Vansittart, 34n, 35–6, 42–3, 49, 55n, 56, 58–64, 73, 83, 142n

369

Index

Mir Jan, son of Mir Jafar (Ashraf Ali Khan) 77n, 224
Mir Jumla, 3, 4n
Mir Kazem, An Alivardian officer, 25–7
Mir Kazem Khan, Mir Jafar's brother, see Ihteram-ud-daulah
Mir Khalil, 130
Mir Nannu, 225
Mir Qasim, Nawab Nazim, viii, 19n, 34n, 36, 61n, 64, 69n, 76, 84n, 86–7, 106, 110n, 112, 113n, 117, 123n, 124–5, 142, 172, 174n, 183, 187, 199n; and Hastings, 33–5, 44, 47n, 293–4, 316n; and Reza Khan, 29–30, 32–48, 106, 162n, 216n; war, 37n, 45n, 49–60, 80–1, 90–1, 104, 115, 122, 138n, 307n
Mir Sadr-ud-din, 333, 334n
Mir Saidu, Miran's son, Diwan of Bengal, 33, 35, 70n, 71, 90, 92, 94, 102, 103n
Mir Umid Ali, 127
Mir Waris Ali, 130n, 230n
Mir Zain ul Abedin, 138n, 337
Mirza Amanullah, 117
Mirza Daud, Safavid prince, Miran's son-in-law, 33, 34n, 47, 88, 92, 130
Mirza Eraj (Erich) Khan, Mir Jafar's deputy at Murshidabad, 77, 328
Mirza Kazem, 26–7
Mirza Mahdi (Ikram-ud-daulah), Siraj-ud-daulah's brother, 19, 21
Mirza Muhammad Ali, at Hugli, 30
Mirza Muhammad Husain, at Rangpur, 220n
Mirza Muhammad Kazim Khan, Reza Khan's officer, 92, 99, 111, 117, 184n, 189, 206
Mirza Saleh, of Hugli, 46–7
Mirzai, son of Agha Baqar, 32n
Misra, B. B., vii–viii
Misri, Khan, last Faujdar of Midnapur, 36n
Mitter, Durga Charan, 234n
Mitter, Raghunath, 234n
Mohanlal, Rai, Siraj-ud-daulah's officer, 9n
Mohsin Fund, 183n
Mohsin, K. M., 19n
Monghyr, 70, 122n, 221
Monson, Col., 342, 345, 347

Moors or Moorish (Muslim), 3n, 4n, 46n, 80n, 145, 269, 273n; see also Muslim
Morang, 137
Motijhil, 78
Motiram, Raja, 92, 94–5, 117
Mubarak-ud-daulah, son of Mir Jafar, 71n, 223n; Nawab Nazim, 220, 224–6, 285–8, 295–7, 322–3, 327, 349; nominal Naib Nazim of Orissa, 70n; and Reza Khan, 223n, 224–6, 285–6, 296–7, 349
Mughals, 1, 7n, 12–16, 17n, 112–13, 196, 199, 252, 264–5, 267; system defended by Nandkumar, 344–5, and by Reza Khan, 1, 14–16, 206–7, 252, 270–9, 281, 285–7, 344, 346
Muhabbatpur, 246
Muhammad Ali Beg, Mir Qasim's deputy at Dacca, 51, 53–4, 64
Muhammad Ali Khan, Saiyid, Reza Khan's brother, 17, 184, 259
Muhammad Aman, 117
Muhammad Husain Khan, Saiyid, Reza Khan's brother, 17, 18, 28, 38n, 66, 349
Muhammad Ismail Khan, Saiyid, Reza Khan's brother, 17, 63
Muhammad Mohtadi, Mufti of Bengal, 333
Muhammad Naqi, Mubarak-ud-daulah's tutor, 226
Muhammad Naseem, Shaikh, Nandkumar's agent, 333, 345
Muhammad Niamat, of Murshidabad Pilkhana, 19n, 127, 225
Muhammad Shah, Emperor, 2, 17
Muhammad Taqi Khan, Mir Qasim's officer, 49n
Muhammad Ufa, Chief Qazi of Bengal, 333
Muhammad Zaman, Dinajpur official, 161–2, 206
Muhammadshahi, 183
Mukarram Ali, 38n
Mulkan, 245
Multan, 171
Munilal, Murshidabad Mutasaddi, 33, 45
Munni Begum, Najm-ud-daulah's mother, 71n, 322, 327, 329, 344; and Reza Khan, 127, 224–5, 256–7, 296, 301

Index

Munro, Sir Hector, 12, 71, 73, 77, 81, 90, 307n
Munshi Sharafat Muhammad Khan, 221
Muradbagh, 67, 221
Murshidabad, 6 and passim; Council at, see Revenue, Council of
Murshid Quli Khan, Nawab Nazim, 3, 186
Muslim or Musalman, 12, 13n, 26, 35, 91, 94, 105, 132, 150, 270–3, 278–9; see also Moors
Muxadabad, see Murshidabad
Muzaffar Ali Khan, 65, 83n, 87
Muzaffar Jang, see Reza Khan
Muzaffarnamah, x, 20n, 114, 220
Myrtle, Barwell's agent in Purnea, 144

Nabakishore, at Bishnupur, 220n, 236
Nabakrishna, Maharaja, of Sobha-bazar, 50, 63, 136, 139n, 148, 158, 185, 192n, 234; and Reza Khan, 127
Nadia, 23, 28, 35, 73n, 185, 201, 206, 209, 220n, 258, 276, 278n, 301n, 309; Calcutta farmers in, 234n; Howitt in, 28n; Rider in, 201, 220n, 233–5
Nadir Shah, 2, 17
Nagpur, 138n
Najabat Ali Khan, see Saif-ud-daulah
Najib-ud-daulah, Rohilla chief, 149
Najm-ud-daulah (Mir Falouri), Nawab Nazim, son of Mir Jafar, 35; death, 127; installation, 69–79; new treaties, 70–9, 91–7, 100–1; presents from, 91–6, 189, 308; and Reza Khan, 76–80, 87–9, 91–7, 99–100, 104, 109, 127, 131n, 224–5
Naleky, 104
Nandkumar, Maharaja, 26, 28, 44n, 48n, 49–50, 59n, 60n, 61n, 63n, 69–84, 87, 90–4, 99n, 257n, 300, 301n; Carnac, 48n, 59–60, 81n, 82n, 94, 300; Clive, 24–8, 77, 84, 94, 99n, 136, 290, 300; the Company, 72, 290, 292–3, 299–303, 327, 329, 347; the Council, 48n, 49–50, 58–60, 63, 69, 71–5, 77, 81–2, 99n; execution, 151, 346; Hastings, 48n, 49, 72, 151, 327, 331, 333–5, 344–6; Mir Jafar, 26–8, 30, 49–50, 53, 58, 60–5, 67; the Mughal, 58, 78, 81, 344–5; Nabakrishna, 50, 136, 148;

Najm-ud-daulah, 70, 77, 82–6, 92–4, 127; Rai Durlabh, 26–7, 29–30, 58, 64, 71–2, 80–1; Reza Khan, 50–2, 56–68, 72–84, 91–4, 99n, 127, 136, 151, 257, 292–3, 299–303, 327, 329, 331, 333–5, 344–6; Vansittart brothers, 48n, 49, 56, 81–2
Naqi Ali Khan (Hakim-i-Mamalik of Delhi), Reza Khan's uncle, 17
Naraini (Coochbehar coin), 175n, 280
Narhat-Samai, 11n, 30
Nasr ullah Khan (Mir Samani at Murshidabad), 225
Nator, 233n, 235, 278n
Nau-Sakht (Reza Khan's palace), 295
Nawara, 66
Nawazish Muhammad Khan, Diwan of Bengal, Naib of Alivardi, Naib Nazim of Dacca, 13, 19, 22, 32n, 87
Nepal, 138n
Nishat Bagh (Reza Khan's palace), 138, 222, 295, 349
Nobit Roy, Golab Roy's employee, 257n
Nobit Roy, Mir Qasim's Patna official, 43n
North, Lord, x, 102n, 299
Nota Manus, 19n; see also Haji Mustafa
Nunagarh, 39
Nur uz Zaman, 127

Oakes, 104n
Omar Quli Khan, Mir Jafar's vakil in Oudh, 7n
opium (and poppy), 4, 143, 218
Orissa, 101, 106, 349; Maratha-Nawab condominium, 138n; Mid-napur separated from, 138n; Mirza Saleh in, 46n; Rai Durlabh in, 9

Pachete, 121, 175n, 242
Paddapar, 195
Padma, 195, 273n
Palit, Ram Lochan, 234n
Palk (Patna Council), 250
Pargana battalion (or sepoys), 122, 295
Paris, the Treaty of (1763), 78n, 174n
Parliamentary enquiry, 247–8, 311, 313, 341–2; see also Fuller Committee

371

Index

Pathans, 122

Patna (Azimabad), 19, 33, 43, 44n, 45, 50, 59, 62, 88, 93, 110–13, 116, 117n, 122–5, 127n, 130, 152, 165, 175, 197, 217n, 229, 233n, 246, 249–50, 264n, 280–1, 326–7, 342–3; Alexander at, 187, 198, 228–9; Amyatt at, 42–3; Carnac at, 59; Clive visits, 122n, 127n; Dhiraj-narain at, 11–12, 130; famine, 217; Ihteram-ud-daulah, Naib at,111–12; McGuire at, 128n; Middleton at, 124; Ramnarain at, 33, 45, 50, 110; Reza Khan and, 110, 123–5; Rumbold at, 125n, 130, 187, 197, 217, 229, 245–6; Shitab Rai at, 117n, 124, 217–18, 249–50, 326, 342–3; G. Vansittart at, 327

Pattle, at Boalia, 198n

Persia, see Iran

Persian (native of Iran), 194n; (language), 202n, 267n

Persian Gulf, 174

Petrie, John, 311

Pilkhana (and Darogha-i-Fil): at Dacca 66; at Murshidabad, 19n, 127, 225

Pitt, William, 12

Plassey, 67, 174, 296; battle of (1757), viii, 2, 7n, 8, 12, 22, 34n, 44, 174n, 182

Playdell, C. S., 95, 96n

Portuguese, 2, 3

Pratit Rai, 220n

presents to Company's servants, 91, 95–6, 98

private trading concerns: cotton monopoly, 166–7, 189; salt-combine, 283n, 310n; see also Society of Trade

Prussians, 174

Punyah, 66, 89, 113, 119, 164, 177–8, 183, 192n, 230n, 237, 239–40, 242, 250

Purling, John, 315

Purnea, 6, 9, 15, 19, 60, 87, 111, 117, 137, 155, 160–4, 175n, 184, 189, 201, 210–11, 220, 221n, 223, 226–7, 243, 257n; Aqa Razi in, 210–11; Diwani of Suchet Ram in, 117–18, 129–30, 162n; Ducarel in (first visit, 1768) 164, (as supervisor) 129–30, 201, 211, 220n, 243; famine, 220, 221n,

223, 226–7; Reza Khan and, 60, 87, 111, 116–17, 129, 160–1, 162n, 163, 184, 189, 206, 210; Rooke at (1767), 162; Saiyid Muhammad Khan at, 118, 162n; Saiyid Muhammad Ali Khan, Faujdar of, 184, 226, retires to, 184n

Pushtabandy, 159

Pye, W., 201

Qaim Beg, Commandant at Murshidabad, 65, 83, 88, 100n, 121

Qamar Ali, 53

Rabia Begum, daughter of Haja Ahmad, mother-in-law of Rezi Khan, 19, 27–9, 225

Rahim Khan, 7

Rahimpur, 277

Rahmat Khan, 257n

Rai Durlabh (Maharaja Durlabhram Bahadur), son of Janakiram, 9, 22, 48n, 110n, 111–13, 257, 289, 327; death, 226, 257; famine, 219, 221n; Mir Jafar, 7, 9, 20–31, 50, 58–9, 64, 85; Najm-ud-daulah, 71, 85–6, 96–7, 103; Nandkumar, 24, 26–7, 29–30, 48n, 58, 71–2, 80–1; Reza Khan, 72, 86, 96–9, 103, 111–13, 117, 135, 154, 161, 226; Scrafton, 22–6

Rai Gulab Singh, 334

Rai Hiralal, 117

Rai Rayan, 3, 13n, 35, 75, 86, 117n, 327

Rai Umid Ram, see Umid Rai

Rajaram, 27, 30, 36n

Rajballabh, Raja, son of Krishnadev of Dacca, 21n, 87, 88; conspiracy, 21; death, 45n, 50; diwan of Miran and Mir Saidu, 33, 35; opposes Mir Qasim, 35; succeeds Ramnarain, 43; Nobit Roy succeeds, 43n

Rajballabh, Raja, son of Rai Durlabh, 22, 327; and Reza Khan, 117, 226, 257

Rajmahal, 15, 183, 209; Ataullah Khan, Faujdar of, 19; Hardwood at, 201, 220n, 233, 272, 278, 283; Ihteram-ud-daulah settles at, 116n

Rajshahi, see Boalia

Ram Chandra Sen, 185, 273

Ram Mohan, Reza Khan's diwan, 37

372

Index

Ram Sankar Roy, Reza Khan's diwan, 63, 110
Ram Sundar, 180n
Ramcharan, Vansittart's Banian, 151
Ramji, 180n
Ram Narain, Raja, Alivardi, Siraj-ud-daulah and Mir Jafar's naib at Patna, 33, 45, 110–11, 124, 129; death, 45n, 50; dismissed, 43, 110n
Ramnarain Mustaufi, head of Ektay Sharifah, 86
Ramnath, Raja, of Dinajpur, 230n
Rangamati, 4, 53, 66
Rangpur, 15, 60, 139n, 175n, 183, 258, 285; Abid Ali Khan at, 54; Grose at, 201, 235–7, 242–3, 269, 278; Hogarth in, 201; Mirza Muhammad Husain at, 220n; Robertson in, 201, 236
Rangalal, father of Ram Narain and Dhiraj Narain, 110n
Rani Bhawani, of Rajshahi Zemindari, 276
Raniganj, 121n, 175n
Rasbehari, son of Janakiram, 22
Ratan, 180n
Ratan Chand Gossain, 277
Raymond, M., see Haji Mustafa
Razi Khan, Saiyid, 21n
Redfearn, W.: in Dinajpur (1767), 162; and Sykes, 166
Reed, John: at Chittagong, 147n, 187–8, 228; in Council, 188, 244, 249, 250, 268; in Murshidabad Council, 250, 254, 257–8, 260, 264–5, 268; private trade, 228, 282, 283n, 310n; and Reza Khan, 225, 254, 256–7, 260, 264–5, 268
Revenue, Council of (Murshidabad), 246, 249–50, 253–5, 257–60, 264–8, 272–85, 288, 293–5, 297, 315, 322–3, 327; abolished, 339
Reza Khan, Saiyid Muhammad, Muzaffar Jang: account (briefly), 17, 20, 30–1, 34, 41, 49, 60, 67, 69, 79, 87, 97, 102–3, 219n, 264–5, 267, 272, 277, 330, 337, 347, 349; acquittal, 337, 347; administrative ideal, 13–16; alleged letters, 148–51; arrest, 272, 294–305, 311–13, 316–18; attempt on life, 151; and Barwell, 142, 144–5, 156–8, 163, 293, 317, 335, 343; and Becher (as Resident, 1769–70), 169–265, 273;

and Bihar (1765–69), 110–13, 123–31, 217–18; and Cartier (Governor, 1769–72), 216–94; charges against, viii–ix, 93–8, 131–2, 135, 189, 207–10, 231–3, 261, 292, 300–2, 304–13, 319–20, 330–1; and Clive, 13n, 29, 79n, 90–104, 106–7, 109–12, 116, 119–25, 127, 131–7, 151–2, 163, 311, 313, 341–2, 348; contemporary opinions, viii–ix, 1, 19, 41, 91, 98n, 99n, 133, 312–13, 343, 349; Dacca (including Naibat at, 1763–5), 18n, 27–9, 34n, 49, 64, 65n, 66–8, 74, 76–9, 87, 109–10, 117, 126, 132, 134, 141, 151–9, 167, 207, 226n, 232, 293n, 334–6; death, 1, 349; defends: the old order amils, 13, 160–1, 207, 252–3, 255, 258–9, aristocracy and officials, 87–8, 111–14, 116–17, 120–7, 143, 153–6, 158–9, 167, 185–7, 285–7, 328, institutions, 119, 159, 272–82, law and justice, 14, 206, 265–72, native bankers, 14, 115n, 143, 161, 173–7, 280–2, zemindars, 15, 127–9, 160, 184–5, 233–4, 238–41, 276; demonstration in support, 296; early life, 17–31, 34n; famine, 217–23, 233, 305, 333, 334n; Faujdari of Islamabad (1760–1), 32–42; Faujdari of Katwa (1756), 20; and Hastings, ix, 2, 19n, 47, 69, 225, 270–1, 293 ff.; imprisoned, 64–5, 67; memorial in favour, 333; the Naibat, 79, 87, 96–7, 102–3, 113, 168, 192–3, 200–1, 233–5, 264–7, 295–6, 347; and Nandkumar, 50–2, 56–68, 72–84, 91–4, 99n, 127, 136, 151, 257, 292–3, 299–303, 327, 329, 331, 333–5, 344–6; opposes trade monopolies, 141–3, 163, 171–3, 183, 222–3, 282, 284–5, 305; opposition to, 75, 80, 142, 145, 192–4, 196, 209–11, 231–9; reinstated, 347; revenue administration, 13–14, 39n, 106–7, 113, 124, 126–31, 152–4, 160–3, 168, 183, 184n, 185, 205; salary and emoluments, 109n, 134–6, 154; and Sykes (as Resident, 1765–8), 99–101, 107–20, 129, 132–4, 139, 144–5, 151, 163, 167–8, 171; titles, 79, 104; trial, 330 ff.; and Verelst (Governor, 1767–9), 137–216, 232, 236, 255, 306

373

Index

rice, 142, 255n, 282; during famine, 217–23

Rider, Jacob: at Krishnanagar, 201, 220n, 233–5

Riza Quli Khan, Reza Khan's vakil, 61–2, 65

Robertson, J.: at Govindaganj, 201, 236

Rohillas, 27n, 32, 122

Rooke, William, 201; at Jessore, 279, 283; at Muradbagh, 166; at Purnea, 162

Round, 104n

Rous, W. B., 201; at Nator, 233n, 235, 278, 285n

Roy, Bhawananda, 234n

Roy, Hara Narayan, 234n

Ruh uddin Husain Khan, of Purnea, 87, 111, 116–17

Rumbold, Thomas, 147n, 245, 292; in Bihar, 113n, 125n, 187, 197n, 217n, 229; Chittagong, 36; Council, 188, 197–8, 209, 217; leaves, 187–8, 213; and Reza Khan, 125–6, 129–30, 217n

rupiah, 174n

Russell, Claud: Council and Select Committee, 147, 187, 194n, 198, 229, 231, 239, 244, 256; leaves, 213, 292n; ordered to Madras, 217n, 251n, 291; private trade, 163, 166, 283n, 310n; and Sykes, 147n

Sadaqat Muhammad Khan, see Agha Sadiq

Sadar Adalat (Adawlut Alia), 14, 267–8

Sadiqbagh, 109, 127n

Sadr ul Haq Khan: at Bhagalpur, 220n, 229; Darogha of Sadar Adalat, 344; early account, 229n

Safavids, 1, 17

Saif Khan, of Purnea, 87, 111n

Saif-ud-daulah (Najabat Ali Khan), Nawab Nazim, son of Mir Jafar, 70n, 104, 127, 226; death, 216, 223–4, 157n; and Reza Khan, 127, 224; treaty with, 133–4

Saiyid Ahmad Khan (Saulat Jang), father of Shaukat Jang, son of Haji Ahmad, 19

Saiyid Ahsan ud din Khan (Mir Samani), 225

Saiyid Badal Khan, Mir Quasim's officer, 53

Saiyid Hadi Ali Khan, see Hadi Ali Khan

Saiyid Muhammad Ali, author of TM, x, 29, 130

Saiyid Muhammad Husain Ali Khan, Bahram Jang, Reza Khan's son, 138, 342, 349n

Saiyid Muhammad Khan, 118, 162

Saiyid Muhammad Taqi Khan, Dilawar Jang, Reza Khan's son, 342, 349n

Saiyidpur, 274n

Salar Jang, 47n

Salbari, 236

salt, 4, 44n, 139, 205, 246, 283n, 309, 310n

salt duty: the Company's demand, 205n; Reza Khan's reply, 205

saltpetre, 4, 118, 204n

Sandwip Island, 54, 245

Sarfaraz Khan, Nawab of Bengal, 5n, 7, 21n, 47, 53, 185–6

Sarkar Saran, 60

Saulat Jang, father of Shaukat Jang, of Purnea, see Saiyid Ahmad Khan

Sawaninigar, 277, 279

Scrafton, Luke, 9n, 23n, 106, 211n, 228; Hastings succeeds, 24, 316n; letters quoted, 21, 22n, 26, 34; lost at sea, 303; and Mir Jafar, 22–3, 26; and Rai Durlabh, 21–6; revenue farming, 23, 45n

Selbarsha, 236

Select Committee: secret department of the Council during 1756–7 troubles, 8, 9n; a new one after May 1765: Clive and, 90–1, 93–8, 104, 145–6, members of, 90, 105, 107, 139, 146, 147n, 187, 198, 229, 249, 256n, powers and functions, 90, 145–6, 197, 200, 206n, 244, and Reza Khan, 131, 133–5, 146, 195–7, at variance with Council, 216, 244–5, 249–52

Senior, A. W.: at Dacca, 54; on deputation, 75, 77; leaves, 108; and Reza Khan, 68n, 93, 96

Seth brothers, 114–15, 333; see also Jagat Seth

Shah Abdul Wahab, see Abdul Wahab Khan

374

Index

Shah Alam, Emperor, 2, 28–31, 57–8, 70–1, 77–8, 90, 110, 120, 125–6, 150, 154, 162, 345, 348n; Carnac and, 78, 150n; Clive's mission to, 99–104, 105n, 125–6; grants Diwani, 101, 120; grants Northern Sarkars, 78n; pledged tribute to, 101n, 133n, 175, 288; Reza Khan and, 104, 136, 271, 274–5, 281–2, 331, 337; Smith and, 150n, 198n

Shah Khanum, Miran's mother, 8, 20, 92, 102, 225

Shahmatganj, 334

Shahmat Jang: title of Miran, 22; title of Nawazish Muhammad Khan, 19, 21n

Shahr Amin, city official at Dacca, 53, 55, 154

Shaista Khan, Aurangzeb's viceroy in Bengal, 4n

Shamshir, Faujdar of Tipperah, 38n

shares: commission on revenue, 197n; cotton monopoly, 166; Society of Trade, 139–40

Sharma, Jay Narain, 234n

Sharma, Manohar, 234n

Shaukat Jang, of Purnea, 6, 7, 155, 186

Sher Ali, 121

Shitab Rai, Maharaja, 117, 124n, 249–50; arrest, 320n, 321, 326–7, 329; death, 342–3; early account, 78, 117n, 124; famine, 217–18; and Reza Khan, 117, 124, 217n, 326, 329; salary and emoluments, 135, 342; trial, 320, 342–3

Shore, John (later Lord Teignmouth), viii, 188n

Shuja Khan, see Shuja uddin

Shuja-ud-daulah, of Oudh, 71, 73, 85n, 90, 117n, 122, 147n, 174n; and Clive, 99, 101n, 306; and Mir Qasim, 47n, 57–9, 60n, 81, 90, 115; and Nandkumar, 58, 59n, 81–2, 151, 257n

Shuja uddin, Nawab of Bengal, 8 13, 21n 45, 129, 186, 200; model of administration, 13n

Shukrullah Khan, son of Sarfaraz Khan, 47n

silk trade, 118, 140, 159, 183, 191, 284–5; see also industries

silver, 174–5, 182n, 203n, 282; export to England, 247

Siraj-ud-daulah, Nawab of Bengal, viii, 3, 20n, 21n, 27, 29, 30, 32n, 44, 50n, 77, 87, 93, 110n, 113, 117, 186, 230n; and Clive, 4–6, 20; murder of, 21; regret at overthrow of, 30; and Reza Khan, 19–20, 30; treaty with, 7, 176

Sitakund, 37, 138

Sitaram, Raja, Mir Qasim's diwan, 45

Smith, 104n

Smith, Col. Richard, 146–8, 150, 187, 198, 209, 213, 289n; and Reza Khan, 150, 209–11, 289, 308

Soane, R., 57

Society of Trade, 139–41

Sombre, 60

Sooty, 51, 52n

Souchetroy (Souchet Ram), see Suchit Rai

Spencer, John: and Clive, 90–1, 96, 100n, 105; Council, 63–4, 69–88; and Reza Khan, 55n, 65, 67–8, 72–7, 79, 87–9, 92, 96; and Nandkumar, 69, 72–6, 82–4

Srikanta, of Jessore Zemindari, 276n

Stables, Captain, 69, 81

Stuart, Honourable Charles, 201, 233, 236–7, 242–3

Subhan Ali Khan, 279n

Suchit Rai (also Souchet Ram, Souchetroy, Suchit Ram or Sujaut Rai), 117–18, 129–30, 144, 161–2, 206, 211

Sukhdev Majumdar, 139n

Sukhlal, 130

Sulaiman Beg, Faujdar of Hugli, 30n, 46

Sulivan, Lawrence: and Clive, 89–90, 97, 132, 189–90, 211n, 228, 245, 247, 290, 299, 303, 321, 337, 339, 342; and Hastings, 298–301, 314, 321, 325; and Reza Khan, 299–300

Sumner, J., 201

Sumner, W. B.· in Council (1760); 31, 41; at Dacca, 21; Second in Council (1765–6), 90, 105, 107, 140, 146

Sundar Singh, Shitab Rai's peshkar, 326

Surat, 167, 171

Surdas Singh, 139n

Suri, 34n

Sutanuti, 3

Sutherland, L., 299, 305n, 311, 314

Lightning Source UK Ltd.
Milton Keynes UK
UKOW02f1506210816

281122UK00001B/19/P